PUBLICATIONS OF THE
NATIONAL BUREAU OF ECONOMIC RESEARCH, INC.

NUMBER 31

PRICES IN RECESSION
AND RECOVERY

Officers

JOSEPH H. WILLITS, Chairman
GEORGE SOULE, President
DAVID FRIDAY, Vice-President
SHEPARD MORGAN, Treasurer
JOSEPH H. WILLITS, Executive Director
CHARLES A. BLISS, Executive Secretary
MARTHA ANDERSON, Editor

Directors at Large

HENRY A. DENNISON, *Dennison Manufacturing Company*
GEORGE M. HARRISON, *President, Brotherhood of Railway and Steamship Clerks*
OSWALD W. KNAUTH, *President, Associated Dry Goods Corporation*
HARRY W. LAIDLER, *Executive Director, The League for Industrial Democracy*
L. C. MARSHALL, *Department of Commerce*
GEORGE O. MAY, *Price, Waterhouse and Company*
SHEPARD MORGAN, *Vice-President, Chase National Bank*
BEARDSLEY RUML, *Treasurer, R. H. Macy and Company*
GEORGE SOULE, *Director, The Labor Bureau, Inc.*
N. I. STONE, *Industrial and Financial Consultant*

Directors by University Appointment

WILLIAM L. CRUM, *Harvard*
WALTON H. HAMILTON, *Yale*
HARRY JEROME, *Wisconsin*
HARRY ALVIN MILLIS, *Chicago*
WESLEY C. MITCHELL, *Columbia*
JOSEPH H. WILLITS, *Pennsylvania*

Directors Appointed by Other Organizations

FREDERICK M. FEIKER, *American Engineering Council*
DAVID FRIDAY, *American Economic Association*
LEE GALLOWAY, *American Management Association*
WINFIELD W. RIEFLER, *American Statistical Association*
GEORGE E. ROBERTS, *American Bankers Association*
ARCH W. SHAW, *National Publishers Association*
MATTHEW WOLL, *American Federation of Labor*

Research Staff

WESLEY C. MITCHELL, Director

ARTHUR F. BURNS   FREDERICK R. MACAULAY
SOLOMON FABRICANT   FREDERICK C. MILLS
SIMON KUZNETS   LEO WOLMAN

EUGEN ALTSCHUL, DAVID L. WICKENS, Associates

PRICES

IN RECESSION AND RECOVERY

A Survey of Recent Changes

FREDERICK C. MILLS

A Publication of

THE NATIONAL BUREAU OF ECONOMIC RESEARCH, INC.

in Cooperation with

THE COMMITTEE ON RECENT ECONOMIC CHANGES

New York · 1936

COPYRIGHT, 1936, BY NATIONAL BUREAU OF ECONOMIC RESEARCH, INC.

1819 BROADWAY, NEW YORK, N. Y. ALL RIGHTS RESERVED

LIBRARY
FLORIDA STATE UNIVERSITY
TALLAHASSEE, FLORIDA

DESIGNER: ERNST REICHL

PRINTED AND BOUND IN THE UNITED STATES OF AMERICA

BY H. WOLFF, NEW YORK

INTRODUCTION

BY THE COMMITTEE ON RECENT ECONOMIC CHANGES

Prices and price relationships almost completely dominate the economic life of the nation. Fundamental to human welfare as are the activities of production, distribution and consumption of goods, it is prices as a medium of control which, in their ceaseless changes and readjustments, stimulate or retard the very processes by which our industrial and commercial life is carried on, and govern the direction of human effort.

Yet not until recent years have economists and the business community fully realized the basic importance of the role played by prices, or clearly sensed the necessity of studying their behavior and influence in the cyclical course of our economic progress.

In 1927 Dr. Frederick C. Mills made an important contribution toward an understanding of the nature and function of prices in a volume entitled *The Behavior of Prices*, published by the National Bureau of Economic Research. In 1932 he made a further contribution in a second work entitled *Recent Economic Tendencies*, published in cooperation with the Committee on Recent Economic Changes. In the present volume, also sponsored by this Committee, Dr. Mills has rounded out this study of prices by carrying it through the recent period of recession and revival.

These three works, covering the relationship and movement of prices since the beginning of the century, represent a monumental undertaking in economic research in which the Committee has been happy to participate. They form an objective exploration into the realm of prices and their nature and influence, by an economist aloof from the pressure and the prejudices of business or politics; and they comprise a record that doubtless will serve as source material for generations.

The present volume is of particular significance because it is an authentic record of price movements made concurrently during the course of a serious depression and the following period of revival. It is a revealing picture of the price mechanism as it has been affected by, and in turn has affected, the pattern of our economic life during a time of great stress.

For the scientific competency of the study and the character of the material presented, together with the interpretation placed upon it and the conclusions drawn, the National Bureau of Economic Research is solely responsible; but it is with genuine satisfaction that the Committee on Recent Economic Changes joins in presenting so carefully prepared and comprehensive a record as this volume represents. Herein will be found the complete 'working papers' on which the author's inferences and deductions have been based, together with an explanation of the statistical method used. These afford the reader an opportunity to check or challenge for himself the soundness of the interpretations, as well as the adequacy and acceptability of the data from which they have been made.

The great value of the work is that it makes available to the producer, the fabricator, the distributor, the consumer, the economist, the leaders of labor, and the agencies of government, a factual basis for a more intelligent attack on the fundamental problem of economic stability.

It is this aim that has motivated the Committee on Recent

INTRODUCTION

Economic Changes in all the studies it has sponsored or in which it has participated, as represented by the two-volume *Recent Economic Changes* (1929); *Planning and Control of Public Works* (1930); *Economic Tendencies in the United States* (1932); *Strategic Factors in Business Cycles* (1934), and the present volume, *Prices in Recession and Recovery*.

In this enterprise of observing and recording recent economic experience the Committee has had the generous support and encouragement of the Rockefeller Foundation, the Carnegie Corporation, the Economic Club of Chicago, and various socially-minded groups and individuals, which support is here gratefully acknowledged.

ARCH W. SHAW, *Chairman*   LEWIS E. PIERSON
RENICK W. DUNLAP   JOHN J. RASKOB
WILLIAM GREEN   SAMUEL W. REYBURN
JULIUS KLEIN   LOUIS J. TABER
JOHN S. LAWRENCE   DANIEL WILLARD
MAX MASON   CLARENCE M. WOOLLEY
ADOLPH C. MILLER   OWEN D. YOUNG
EDWARD E. HUNT, *Secretary*

October, 1936

RELATION OF THE DIRECTORS TO THE WORK OF THE NATIONAL BUREAU OF ECONOMIC RESEARCH

1. The object of the National Bureau of Economic Research is to ascertain and to present to the public important economic facts and their interpretation in a scientific and impartial manner. The Board of Directors is charged with the responsibility of ensuring that the work of the Bureau is carried on in strict conformity with this object.

2. To this end the Board of Directors shall appoint one or more Directors of Research.

3. The Director or Directors of Research shall submit to the members of the Board, or to its Executive Committee, for their formal adoption, all specific proposals concerning researches to be instituted.

4. No study shall be published until the Director or Directors of Research shall have submitted to the Board a summary report drawing attention to the character of the data and their utilization in the study, the nature and treatment of the problems involved, the main conclusions and such other information as in their opinion will serve to determine the suitability of the study for publication in accordance with the principles of the Bureau.

5. A copy of any manuscript proposed for publication shall also be submitted to each member of the Board. If publication is approved each member is entitled to have published also a memorandum of any dissent or reservation he may express, together with a brief statement of his reasons. The publication of a volume does not, however, imply that each member of the Board of Directors has read the manuscript and passed upon its validity in every detail.

6. The results of an inquiry shall not be published except with the approval of at least a majority of the entire Board and a two-thirds majority of all those members of the Board who shall have voted on the proposal within the time fixed for the receipt of votes on the publication proposed. The limit shall be forty-five days from the date of the submission of the synopsis and manuscript of the proposed publication unless the Board extends the limit; upon the request of any member the limit may be extended for not more than thirty days.

7. A copy of this resolution shall, unless otherwise determined by the Board, be printed in each copy of every Bureau publication.

(*Resolution of October 25, 1926, revised February 6, 1933*)

FOREWORD

RECESSION, depression and recovery in the United States over the years 1929–1936 were marked by elements as diverse and complicated as any this generation has known. To the economic forces operative in the business cycles of less troubled eras were added various residual influences of the World War, including a notable breakdown of the basis of international financial and commercial dealings and accentuation of economic ills by nationalistic political developments. Finally, the application of a far reaching program of governmental action designed to aid economic recovery introduced still other factors. A cyclical pattern loose and irregular at best was modified in important respects by these novel influences.

In seeking to follow some of the strands that run through this complex web, no attempt is made at definitive appraisal of the forces at work. This report presents a monographic treatment of certain aspects of recession and recovery in the United States during the last seven years. Various measurements constructed by the National Bureau in connection with its continuing work are of some current interest to economists and others who follow economic movements. Discussion of these and related materials falls easily into half a dozen divisions, dealing with the background of the price recession of 1929, its world setting, and the fortunes of primary producers, fabricators and consumers during the disturbed years from 1929 to 1936. Although no rounded survey of the situation as a whole is made, something of unity in the price history of these various groups is found in tracing the incidence of productivity changes in manufacturing industries and their relation to changing costs and prices. This topic is developed in the final chapter.

Members of the research staff and of the Board of Directors of the National Bureau of Economic Research have aided in the preparation of this report with suggestive comments and helpful advice. I am happy to express my thanks. To my associates Charles A. Bliss and Solomon Fabricant I am particularly indebted for counsel and criticism. And with deep appreciation I acknowledge the continuing assistance given me by Miss Maude Remey and Miss Mildred Uhrbrock in the many tasks connected with the preparation of this monograph.

F. C. M.

CONTENTS

I GENERAL ASPECTS OF RECENT PRICE
    MOVEMENTS   3
  Some Factors in the Price Recession of 1929   6
  Price Recession and Recovery: Comparative Measurements   9
  International Aspects of Price Recession and Price Recovery   19
  Price Relations and Some Current Issues   25
    Changes in commodity prices and in the purchasing power of given groups of producers   28
    On price disparities   33

II THE PRE-RECESSION SITUATION   39
  Factors Affecting the Price Structure of 1929   39
  Prices of Raw and Processed Goods; Price Position of the Farmer   43
  Margin between the Prices of Raw and Processed Goods, 1929   46
    Wholesale prices   46
    Fabrication costs   53
  Prices of Capital Equipment and Consumption Goods   57
  Post-War Price Schism   61
  Purchasing Power of Major Producing Groups, 1929   70
  World Price Structure in 1929   75
    Economic non-intercourse and the world price structure   76
    Disparities in production costs   79

Disparities between prices of raw materials and manufactured goods	82
Disparities in Post-War Price Relations	89

III PRICE MOVEMENTS AND RELATED ECONOMIC CHANGES DURING RECESSION AND DEPRESSION — 95

Primary Products in the Price Recession	95
Prices and purchasing power of farm products	100
Prices at the farm and prices paid by farmers	103
Aggregate purchasing power of primary producers	105
Price Changes and Fabricational Margins during Recession	109
Price movements among raw and processed goods	110
Movements of manufacturers' margins, as shown by changes in the prices of similar commodities at different productive stages	116
Manufacturing costs, 1929–1933	117
On the incidence of recession among manufacturing industries	132
Aggregate purchasing power of manufacturing producers	135
Summary: Changes in fabricational margins during recession	137
Prices and Volume of Production of Capital Equipment and Building Materials during Recession	140
Construction costs	144
Price Changes among Consumers' Goods during Recession	146
Variation in living costs and retail prices	149
Prices of consumers' goods and consumer purchasing power	151
Price Relations and Problems of Recovery	156

IV THE WORLD PRICE STRUCTURE IN RECESSION AND RECOVERY — 162

Recession and Recovery in World Prices: A General View	163

CONTENTS

World Price Relations in 1933	170
Disparities of price levels	171
Disparities of production costs	174
Disparities of commodity prices	179
Prices of agricultural and non-agricultural products	180
Prices of raw and processed goods	181
Prices of investment equipment and of goods for human consumption	184
Some consequences of dislocations in the world price structure during the depression	186
Problems of readjustment and recovery	191
World Price Movements in Recovery	194
The Structure of World Prices in 1936	197
Disparities of price levels	197
Disparities of production costs	204
Disparities of commodity prices	210

V PRICE CHANGES AND THE FORTUNES OF PRIMARY PRODUCERS IN RECOVERY — 222

Raw Materials in Price Recovery	223
Farm Products in Wholesale Markets	231
Prices Received by Farmers and Prices Paid by Farmers	234
Agricultural Processing Taxes and Price Changes	239
Recession and recovery in the prices of important raw materials	243
Timing of Price Changes during Recovery: A Monthly Record	243
Changes in the Aggregate Purchasing Power of Primary Producers during Recovery	253
Farm Prices, Farmers' Incomes and the Burden of Farmers' Debts	265
Recent Changes in the Prices of Agricultural Products, in Relation to their Pre-War Purchasing Power	268
Summary	277

VI MANUFACTURING INDUSTRIES IN RECOVERY — 285

Problems of Recovery in Manufacturing Industries	290

CONTENTS

Price Changes among Manufactured Goods and Raw Materials ... 295
On Recent Changes in Production, Prices, Employment and Wages in Manufacturing Industries ... 307
    The data, and some limiting conditions ... 312
    The recovery of 1933–1936 ... 318
        Manufacturing gross income and component elements ... 320
        Total manufacturing employment and component elements ... 321
        Physical volume of manufacturing production and component elements ... 322
        Total wage disbursements of manufacturing industries, and elements of the total ... 324
        Summary of the changes of recovery in manufacturing industries ... 327
        Recovery movements in relation to a pre-recession standard ... 328
    Economic changes in manufacturing industries during five periods of business expansion, approximately equal in respect of degree of recovery ... 331
Summary: Industrial Productivity, Manufacturing Margins and Selling Prices ... 342

VII CAPITAL EQUIPMENT AND CONSTRUCTION IN RECOVERY ... 354
Problems of Recovery in Capital Goods Industries ... 355
    Some conditions in the markets for capital goods ... 355
    Capital goods industries in periods of revival; problems of recovery, 1933–1936 ... 358
Prices and Cost Changes in Capital Goods Industries ... 363
Availability and Cost of Capital Funds ... 375
    Production of capital goods ... 378
        Comparison of production and price movements, durable and non-durable goods ... 381
Factors Affecting the Revival of Capital Goods Industries, 1933–1936 ... 384

CONTENTS

VIII CONSUMERS' GOODS IN RECOVERY	393
Price Changes among Consumers' Goods	400
Living Costs and Retail Prices	405
Purchasing Power of Consuming Groups	409
Output of Consumption Goods	417
The Consumer in Recovery	419
IX THE PRICE SYSTEM, INCREASING PRODUCTIVITY AND RECENT ECONOMIC CHANGES	430
Expansion of Fabricational Margins, 1913–1936	431
On the Incidence and Effects of Gains in Industrial Productivity	435
Division of the Gains in Industrial Productivity: The Historical Record, 1899–1933	441
Shares of producers	442
Shares of consumers	445
Industrial Productivity and Economic Frictions	456
Appendices	469
List of Tables	565
List of Charts	570
Index	573

PRICES IN RECESSION

AND RECOVERY

CHAPTER I

GENERAL ASPECTS OF RECENT PRICE

MOVEMENTS

THE phases of business cycles to which we apply the terms crisis and recession are marked, characteristically, by a general reduction of prices, a shifting of relative values and a downward readjustment of a great mass of creditor claims. The severity of these deflationary processes varies, of course, from cycle to cycle, being affected by all the forces at play in the cyclical fluctuations of business. Their character and consequences vary, also, with changes in economic organization. With a heavier burden of fixed expenses, with a more extensive debt structure, with a money economy that penetrates more deeply into the everyday activities of men, a general deflation and the readjustments it entails may be expected to place greater strains upon the economic system. This is not to say that the causal forces, if we could locate them, necessarily differ from time to time. Different reactions to these forces may be expected because the organization and operating characteristics of the system at large have been modified with the passage of time.

For this reason a survey of certain aspects of the most recent recession is of special interest. Here we may follow the process of deflation in a modern industrial economy and the movement towards readjustment on a new operating basis. With the single exception of the 1920–21 recession, which was so closely tied to the aftermath of war as to lose somewhat in broader economic significance, the latest recession provides our only example of a major crisis in the working of the highly integrated, industrialized economies, with their complex price and financial systems, that have reached maturity in the last quarter century. In this study, it is true, we shall be dealing only with certain aspects of recession and recovery, but to view these movements in proper perspective some account should be taken of the changes that the twentieth century has brought in the economic systems of western nations.

The present investigation centers in the behavior of prices, in relation to the general operations of the economic system, during a period preceding and including the recession and recovery of 1929–36. Price movements played a dominant role in the recession of general business that began in the United States in the summer of 1929, and in the ensuing phases of this business cycle. There have been longer price declines in American economic history, but if we take account of the combined factors of scope, duration and intensity, it is improbable that our price system has ever been exposed to destructive forces more devastating than those of 1929–33. For no less than forty-three months prices declined and the price structure crumbled. The economic ills engendered by the general decline were intensified by the extreme inequalities of the changes occurring in different parts of the price system. A score of major disparities developed, and these continued to increase as the price decline persisted.

The pains of this severe recession have emphasized the role of prices in a modern industrial economy. The exchange mechanism that intervenes between the processes of production and consumption, in an economy marked by great division of labor, is ordinarily an unobtrusive element in our economic environment. When it functions smoothly and well we give little heed to it. But when matters do not go smoothly we are acutely aware of our dependence upon an elaborate system of exchange relationships, a system that has been growing more complex and delicate with the passage of time.

This dependence of physical economic processes upon a pricing system is well recognized, but it is perhaps not as clearly realized that the character and degree of dependence vary from time to time, and that the instruments of exchange take on new attributes as they develop. Indeed, the severity of the most recent depression may be attributed in considerable part to the characteristics of the exchange mechanism and to its failure to meet the requirements placed upon it by an industrial system that has itself been profoundly modified during recent decades. Changing industrial processes on the one hand, changing attributes of the pricing and exchange system on the other—these are two of the major dynamic elements of economic life today. In combination, they have played a leading part in accentuating the severity of the second great post-War depression.

In this study no attempt is made to deal exhaustively with all the many-sided monetary and price problems that this depression has generated. Since we are interested in the general efficiency of our present price system as an instrument facilitating the physical processes of economic life, we shall seek to define the broad characteristics of the price recession and the subsequent recovery in relation to earlier experience. But our major concern is with the changing positions of certain important producing groups, and with the varying fortunes of consumers, under the impact of changes in industrial productivity and shifts in the distribution of purchasing power. The economic movements of the fifteen years preceding the recession of 1929 and the wide fluctuations of the last seven years have brought important alterations in the status of different producing groups. A knowledge of these shifts and of the forces that lie behind them is essential to an understanding of the economic changes of recent years.[1]

Some Factors in the Price Recession of 1929

The causes of a general price decline are seldom open to precise definition. A general break in prices may be initiated by minor and obscure factors, when the structure of prices is weak. Certain factors contributing to the recent collapse of world prices may be defined in general terms, but no attempt is made to indicate their relative importance, or to set forth the exact combination of circumstances that precipitated the decline. In this account we deal in the main with world conditions, for the price recession in the United States was but a phase of a world-wide decline.

During the first post-War decade facilities for the production of foodstuffs and major raw materials were over-developed, relatively to the opportunities for sale through existing markets at the prices necessary to cover costs and yield satisfactory profits. Resulting price weakness was in part concealed, because of the influence of ample credit (which facilitated the application of valorization schemes) and of heavy foreign lending to raw material producing countries. The maintenance of consumer demand in the United States through the development of new credit instruments and the presence of non-recurring elements of income (notably speculative profits) served also to support expenditures and

[1] It is impossible, of course, to define with precision changes in the relative status of different economic groups when prices alone are compared. Concurrent changes in costs and in volume of output bear directly upon the analysis of price movements. In the present study use is made of supplementary cost and production records, where available, in interpreting price changes. But our chief concern is with the inter-relations of prices. Though the price record alone is inadequate, it is more comprehensive and more accurate than any other general record of economic changes.

prices prior to 1929. Heavy international lending, at rates that declined up to 1928, helped to maintain buying power and stimulated the shouldering of excessively heavy financial obligations by raw material producing countries. The check to lending to debtor countries, which was first felt in 1928, and the increased difficulty of securing credit, placed such countries in serious straits. Domestic expenditures were reduced, many valorization schemes had to be abandoned, and the service of foreign debts became difficult. The forced selling in foreign markets of the major products of these debtor countries (raw materials, primarily) weakened the markets, and prices of important staples fell.

The usual instruments for the correction of such a situation (a correction made in pre-War years through the gold standard and international credit mechanisms working under conditions of relatively free trade) were ineffective, partly because of the lack of highly developed financial institutions in most debtor countries, partly because of the faulty working of the post-War gold standard when creditor countries were unwilling to receive goods, partly because of the very magnitude of the difficulties involved.

Reduced buying by debtor countries contributed to a drop in production and employment in industrial countries. This situation was aggravated by the reduction of domestic purchasing in the United States as speculative profits turned to losses with the ending of the boom in securities.

The resulting curtailment of expenditures for both capital equipment and consumption goods led to further declines in prices and production, further unemployment, and further reductions of income disbursements. The necessity of reducing costs, which was faced by manufacturing establishments as a result of declining sales and the pressure of declining prices among important commodity groups, entailed serious and cumulative deflation in industrial areas. The vicious spiral thus started was made worse by the spread of uncertainties and fears, which still further reduced expenditures for new equipment and, to some extent, for consumption goods. This curtailment of general business activity was reflected in a marked decline in the velocity of circulation of money and credit.

The gold situation intensified the movements due to these conditions. The general resumption of the gold standard in the middle years of the post-War decade led to an increased demand for the existing stocks of gold. The resulting demands upon the gold supply were accentuated by a world distribution of gold that was disproportionate to the world's commercial and financial needs. There is no clear evidence of pressure upon prices from the monetary side prior to 1929, but there appears to have been no great margin of gold supply above the world's needs, under the existing banking conditions. Causal relations between the movements of prices and gold reserves during the recession are difficult to establish. It is probable, however, that a deficiency of gold and credit contraction in certain areas combined with other economic conditions to push the world price level constantly lower. But causal relations almost certainly ran in the other direction also. It is not necessary to assume a one-way relationship between monetary conditions and prices. Unequal price declines, reflecting variations in the incidence of world recession, contributed to the disparate movements of national gold reserves which were so conspicuous a feature of this period.[2]

[2] Evidence of a relationship in time between declining gold reserves and price movements from 1929 on is given by Layton and Crowther, *An Introduction to the Study of Prices* (London, Macmillan, 1935), p. 189, citing Kitchen's data. In 1929 the gold reserves of five strong 'creditor' countries (United States, France, Switzerland, Holland and Belgium) began to rise sharply, while the gold reserves of the rest of the world fell off rapidly. The

The price recession thus initiated reached a bottom, in the United States, in February 1933. Within five months of that date the level of wholesale prices in the United States had advanced 15 per cent; within twenty-four months, 33 per cent. The upward turn was sharper and more pronounced than in the usual cyclical advance. Rates of gain varied, but the stimulus of recovery was felt on a broad front. For many reasons this price advance is of peculiar interest, and the immediate problems raised by it are of exceptional urgency.

Price Recession and Recovery: Comparative Measurements

The distinctive characteristics of the price decline of 1929–33 may be best appreciated when it is contrasted with similar movements of the past. The declines closest to it in severity are those that occurred during the business recessions of 1873 and 1920.[3] The fall of prices in 1920–22 was the most

movements of world prices paralleléd the general decline of gold reserves in the majority of countries.

If this relationship is taken to be causal, the argument assumes that the increasing gold reserves of the five creditor countries did not furnish offsetting stimulation towards higher prices. It is true that domestic conditions in these countries were not conducive to the use of new reserves in credit expansion. In considerable degree, then, gold surpluses were inactive while gold deficiencies were active factors, during this period. But these very deficiencies, as we have noted, were probably related to disparate world price movements. Unequal price movements, reflecting the play of a variety of specific forces, helped to create disparities in gold reserves; where such reserves were forced lower, credit was contracted and downward pressure exerted on prices. Where such reserves were augmented, surpluses were in good part sterilized; they did not exert an upward pressure on domestic and international prices. Just such a mixture of circular relations in a disorganized world economy characterized the chaotic price situation of 1929–1933.

[3] Records of changes in wholesale prices during the three recessions are shown below. In interpreting these movements we must note that the index numbers for recent years are more comprehensive, and that greater weight is given to manufactured goods. Since these conditions would be expected to

severe of the three declines (wholesale prices fell 45 per cent), but the briefest. The storm had passed within twenty months. Most prolonged was that which began in 1873. A net decline of 39 per cent in the level of wholesale prices was stretched over more than six years. Practically the same net fall, 38 per cent, occurred from 1929 to 1933, but it extended over forty-three months only. In rapidity of price decline, per month, the last recession was between the two earlier ones.

These changes are plotted in Figure 1, which reveals clearly certain marked differences between these periods, with respect to the behavior of general prices. Prior to the beginning of the price decline of 1873 the price level moved upwards slowly. (There were, in fact, twenty preceding months of irregular price advance, following seven years of irregular decline.) Before the recession of 1920–21 the price level rose sharply. (This rise had continued, with minor interruptions, more than five years.) Before the current recession the price level sagged slightly. (A slight declining tendency had prevailed since 1925.) More striking are the differences prevailing forty-three months after the initiation of the several recessions. This stage finds the decline of the '70's still in progress. Prices had fallen 20 per cent, but an equal fall, extending over two and one-half years, lay ahead.

make the later indexes more sluggish, the amplitude and intensity of the recent decline are the more significant.

The index covering the first period is that of Warren and Pearson, *Prices* (Wiley, 1933), pp. 10–14. The index of the Bureau of Labor Statistics was used in tracing price movements during the other periods.

	DATE OF HIGH	DATE OF LOW BEFORE ADVANCE	DURATION OF DECLINE (*months*)	DEGREE OF DECLINE (*per cent*)	RAPIDITY OF DECLINE (*per cent per month*)
1873–79	April 1873	June 1879	74	39	0.7
1920–22	May 1920	Jan. 1922	20	45	3.0
1929–33	July 1929	Feb. 1933	43	38	1.1

FIGURE 1
WHOLESALE PRICES IN THE UNITED STATES DURING THREE PERIODS OF RECESSION AND SUBSEQUENT CHANGE

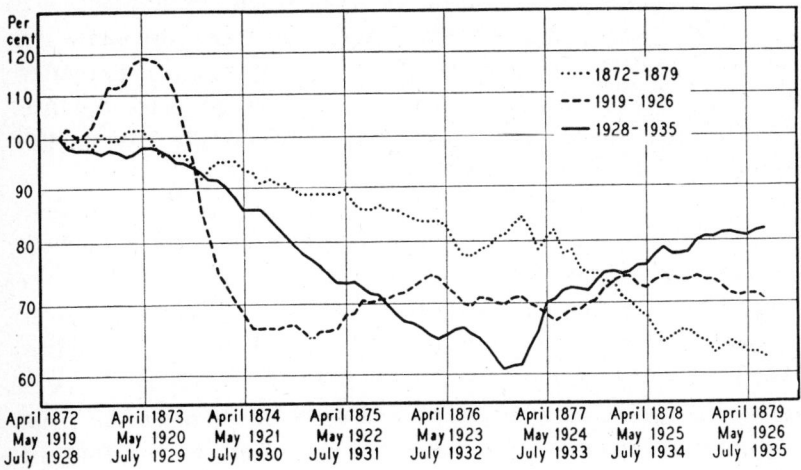

Ratio scale

The drop of 1920–22 had reached its bottom and a steady price recovery was in progress. Already prices had advanced 7 per cent above their low point. Forty-three months after the beginning of the decline of 1929–33 a bottom had apparently been reached. The months that followed were to witness a sharp upturn, the nature of which will concern us in subsequent sections.

These three price drops—the slow, persistent decline of the '70's, the violent but relatively brief collapse of 1920–22, and the steady cumulative pressure of the drop that began in 1929—illustrate diverse types of price behavior during severe economic recessions. The distinctive features of the most recent decline reflect, in part, the novel characteristics of the preceding expansion. Some of these are discussed in the next chapter.

A quick view of the course of recovery during the first nine, twelve and twenty-one months of advance after the depression low in each of these phases of recovery will provide perspective in judging recent events. Price changes during these periods are shown graphically in Figure 2.[4] The rise that began in 1879 was the most rapid of the three over the first nine months of recovery. A gain of 25 per cent was registered, as against 19 per cent between February and November 1933, and 9 per cent in the first nine months of 1922. The advance of 1879–81 was sharply curtailed, however. During the first twelve months of recovery the most recent period has the highest record, with that of 1879–81 next. If we extend the record to cover twenty-one months (up to November 1934, for the last period) the advance of 1933–34 still has a striking lead. A decline, associated with the next cyclical recession, had already terminated the price recovery of 1922–23.

The rapidity of the latest advance is the more striking because of the greater scope and sluggishness of the index numbers for recent years. When we follow the movements of fully comparable measurements, Warren and Pearson's index numbers of the prices of thirty basic commodities,[5] the contrast is enhanced. In nine months of 1933–34 these prices rose 44 per cent, as against advances of 27 and 37 per cent in

[4] Following are the corresponding measurements:

	DATE OF LOW BEFORE ADVANCE	DEGREE OF ADVANCE IN FIRST 9 MONTHS (*per cent*)	DEGREE OF ADVANCE IN FIRST 12 MONTHS (*per cent*)	DEGREE OF ADVANCE IN FIRST 21 MONTHS (*per cent*)
1879–81	June 1879	25	14	18
1922–23	Jan. 1922	9	12	9
1933–34	Feb. 1933	19	28	23

[5] Constructed by George F. Warren and Frank A. Pearson, New York State College of Agriculture, Cornell University.

FIGURE 2

WHOLESALE PRICES IN THE UNITED STATES DURING THREE PERIODS OF RECOVERY

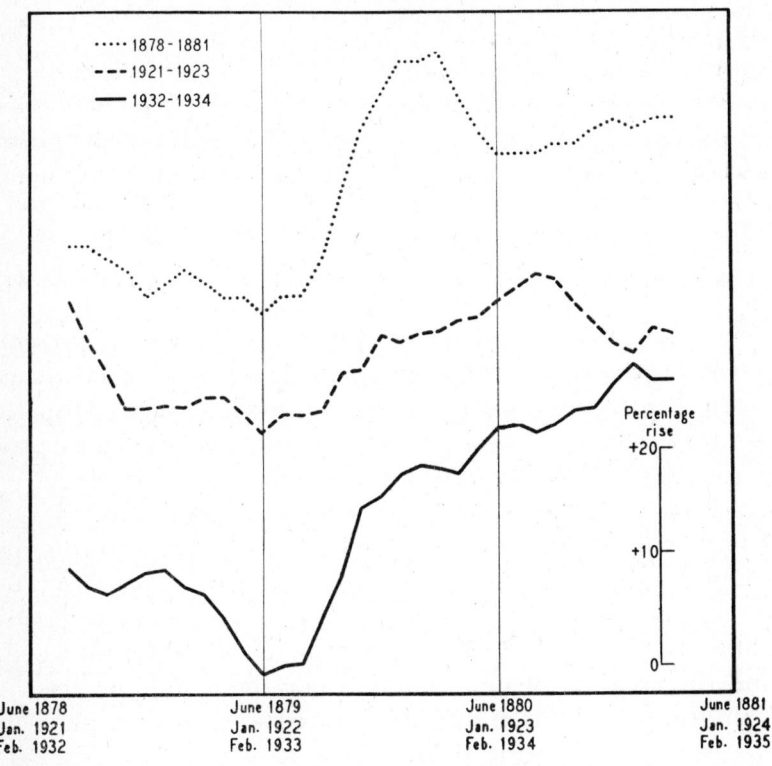

Ratio scale

periods of equal length in 1879–81 and 1922, respectively.

But it was not only the general fall in prices that subjected the American economy to great stress, during the recent decline. The marked inequalities of the changes in various parts of the price structure added a further burden. The character and magnitude of these inequalities are indicated by the accompanying measurements.[6] (The index numbers

	July 1929	Feb. 1933	Feb. 1934	Feb. 1935	Feb. 1936	June 1936
RECESSION AND RECOVERY						
Wholesale prices	100	62	76	82	84	82
Cost of living of industrial workers	100	74	78	81	81	82
Prices received by farmers	100	37	56	76	74	73
Hourly earnings, employed manufacturing labor	100	77	96	103	104	104
RECOVERY						
Wholesale prices		100	123	133	135	132
Cost of living of industrial workers		100	106	109	110	112
Prices received by farmers		100	151	202	198	194
Hourly earnings, employed manufacturing labor		100	125	134	135	136

shown are not comparable in detail; they serve the present purpose, however, in defining major changes among elements of the price system during recession and recovery.) Disparities resulting from these and similar movements reflect pronounced shifts in the relative incomes and buying power of different groups. Under contemporary conditions, in an economy marked by important frictions that prevent prompt adaptation to changed relations, these shifts may lead to severe and persistent disturbances. The movement of goods along previously existing channels of exchange is impeded, and the creation of new channels may be a slow process. A significant diminution of the indicated schisms took place in the recovery following February 1933.

Recession and revival, as their cumulative effects are felt throughout the price system, tend to follow certain fairly

---

[6] The index number of wholesale prices is that of the U. S. Bureau of Labor Statistics; the cost of living index is that of the Bureau of Labor Statistics with interpolations based on the index of the National Industrial Conference Board; the index of hourly earnings was secured by splicing an index of the Bureau of Labor Statistics for 1932–36 to an index of the National Industrial Conference Board for 1929–32. The index of prices received by farmers is constructed by the U. S. Bureau of Agricultural Economics.

uniform patterns. The typical recession is marked by a few initial declines in the prices of the most sensitive commodities, followed closely by a more general and more precipitous drop. The entire movement is a relatively concentrated, unified downturn, as the price structure reacts to the impact of recession. Price revival is a different process, slower in its cumulative spread and more extended in time. The generation of recovery has not the swiftness of movement that marks the destructive phase of the cycle. These two phases are represented by the upper diagrams in Figure 3 which show the timing of price recession and revival in wholesale markets during the business cycle that ran its course in the United States between 1919 and 1923. These furnish standards with which we may compare more recent price fluctuations.[7]

The movements during the recession of 1929–33 and the subsequent revival, which are represented by two of the distributions shown graphically in Figure 3, constitute a striking reversal of customary experience during price recessions and revivals. In place of the usual concentrated, compact downturn of prices during recession, such as occurred in somewhat exceptional degree in 1920, we have a far more protracted change centering about the July 1929 turning point. Recessions of individual commodity prices extended over many months, instead of being concentrated within a few months.[8]

The reasons for this marked difference in behavior are found, in part, in the economic details of the two recessions —in the price and quantity relations among the hundreds of individual commodities entering into trade. Perhaps more

[7] The corresponding measurements are given in Appendix I.
[8] Comparable measurements of the degree of 'scatter' in the timing of price declines in the recession of 1920–21 and in that of 1929–33 are, respectively, 5.4 and 14.2. (These are the standard deviations of the two distributions plotted. The standard deviation of the distribution of average figures representing ten phases of recession occurring between 1892 and 1924 is 8.4.)

FIGURE 3
SHOWING THE DISTRIBUTION OF PRICE CHANGES OVER TIME, IN PERIODS OF RECESSION AND REVIVAL

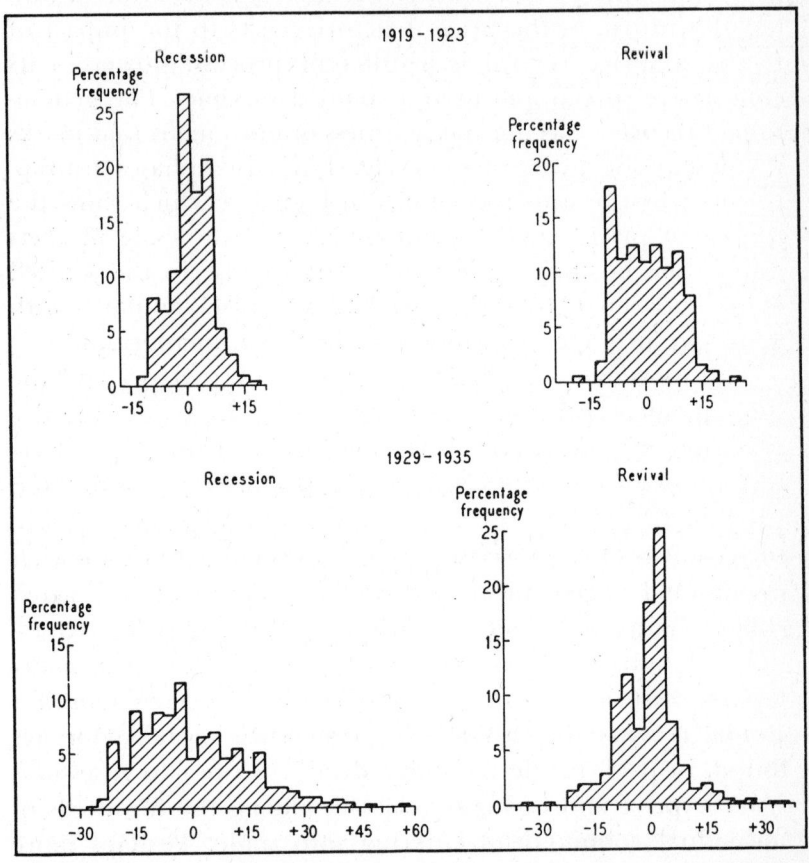

The figures on the horizontal scales measure deviations in months from the dates of turns in the wholesale price index.

important, however, were the differences in the immediate backgrounds of the recessions, and their effects upon the pricing policies of business men. The 1920 recession followed the sharp War-time price rise, a rise that bore none of the aspects of permanence. Values had not become entrenched at the high levels of 1919 and early 1920, nor did heavy capital investments at those levels serve to maintain existing values. There was little basis, then, for resistance to liquidation, once the forces of recession were felt. A concentrated, fairly brief period of fall was the result.

The decline in commodity prices that began in 1929 occurred at the end of a quite different period, marked by fairly stable prices and by heavy investment at existing levels. Here we had strongly entrenched values and a corresponding reluctance to reduce prices. The more protracted and more painful character of the decline that began in 1929 is partly attributable to this condition.

The differences between the two periods of revival are not so pronounced. Both depart somewhat from experience in that price recovery was relatively compact and unified, with the price movements of individual commodities closely concentrated in time. This was particularly marked in the most recent recovery. Up to and including a date four months after the low point in the general index (that is, up to June 1933) approximately 80 per cent of a list of 538 commodities had advanced in price. Over similar periods in ten business revivals between 1892 and 1922 about 61 per cent of the groups of commodities studied rose in price, on the average. In 1933, in place of the slow cumulative recovery of the usual cyclical revival, we had the concentrated reversal in the direction of price movements and the swift transmission of the stimulus to change that usually characterize price recessions. This particular recovery of prices was not the usual slowly-germinating movement, but a speedy reaction to a changed economic outlook.

In other respects, too, recent price movements were marked by distinctive features. Study of the sequence of change in the prices of individual commodities during a number of cyclical revivals reveals evidence of a general pattern to which price movements during particular cycles conform in greater or less degree.[9] Moreover, the pattern of price revival is not unrelated to the pattern of the preceding recession. There is not complete uniformity, of course, but the tendency towards a common sequence of price movements is clearly apparent in the records of the last forty years.

When the sequence of price recovery in 1933 is compared with the standard pattern of revival, a degree of conformity less than that usually prevailing is found.[10] So, also, the relationship between the sequence of recession in the prices of individual commodities in 1929 (and the years following) and the sequence of recovery in 1933 is distinctly less marked than that usually prevailing between recession and succeeding revival.[11] The movements of 1933 show few of those regularities usually found in the cyclical behavior of commodity prices (regularities seldom of a very high order, it is true). It was a price rise stimulated by novel forces and, in

---

[9] Cf. *The Behavior of Prices* (National Bureau of Economic Research, 1927), p. 135.

[10] The coefficient of correlation between measurements defining the sequence of price movements in the recovery of 1933–36 and similar measurements defining the average sequence of recovery during eleven revivals between 1892 and 1924 is +.28. For earlier revivals the coefficient averages about +.50. (The fact that the data of earlier revivals enter into the averages that define the standard pattern would tend to make the second of these coefficients higher than the first, but not by the amount of the difference here existing.)

[11] The coefficient of correlation between the timing of price changes during the recession of 1929 and the recovery in 1933 is +.21, for records extending to November 1932, for recession, and to June 1936 for revival (the number of commodities included is 515). The addition of later observations for both recession and revival would raise this coefficient to a value approximating +.30. The coefficient of correlation between the average timing of price changes during revival and recession for ten complete cycles between 1892 and 1924 is +.72.

GENERAL ASPECTS

its detailed manifestations, differing significantly from the run of cyclical revivals.

International Aspects of Price Recession and Price Recovery

To secure a just conception of the price movements in the United States during the last seven years they must be seen as phases of a world-wide change. The severity of the second post-War depression and the difficulty of breaking it have been due in considerable part to the universality of the crisis. No nation, except Soviet Russia, escaped. Industrial centers and colonial areas alike felt the impact of the general decline. Here, again, we find differences in the degree, duration and intensity of the decline and in the degree of recovery to date. The record of changes in wholesale prices in thirty-two countries is summarized in Table 1.[12] Price movements in twelve countries (in terms of the various national currencies) are portrayed graphically in Figure 4.

The record of drastic and universal price decline revealed by this survey of the changes in different parts of the world has no counterpart in recent economic history. Between March 1928, marking the high point of prices in Latvia prior to the recession proper, and September 1929, when New Zealand prices reached their peak before recession, thirty-two countries felt the crumbling of their price foundations.[13] The median decline in wholesale prices among the countries

[12] The index numbers from which the measurements in this and the following table are derived are not comparable in the details of their composition. Significance should not be attached, therefore, to small differences between the figures given.

[13] It is not easy to set the precise date at which price recession began in each country, because price levels were declining throughout the world prior to the beginning of this recession. But variations in the timing of the recession are probably fairly well indicated by the entries in Table 1.

FIGURE 4

INDEX NUMBERS OF WHOLESALE PRICES IN TERMS OF NATIONAL CURRENCIES, 1929–1936, TWELVE COUNTRIES

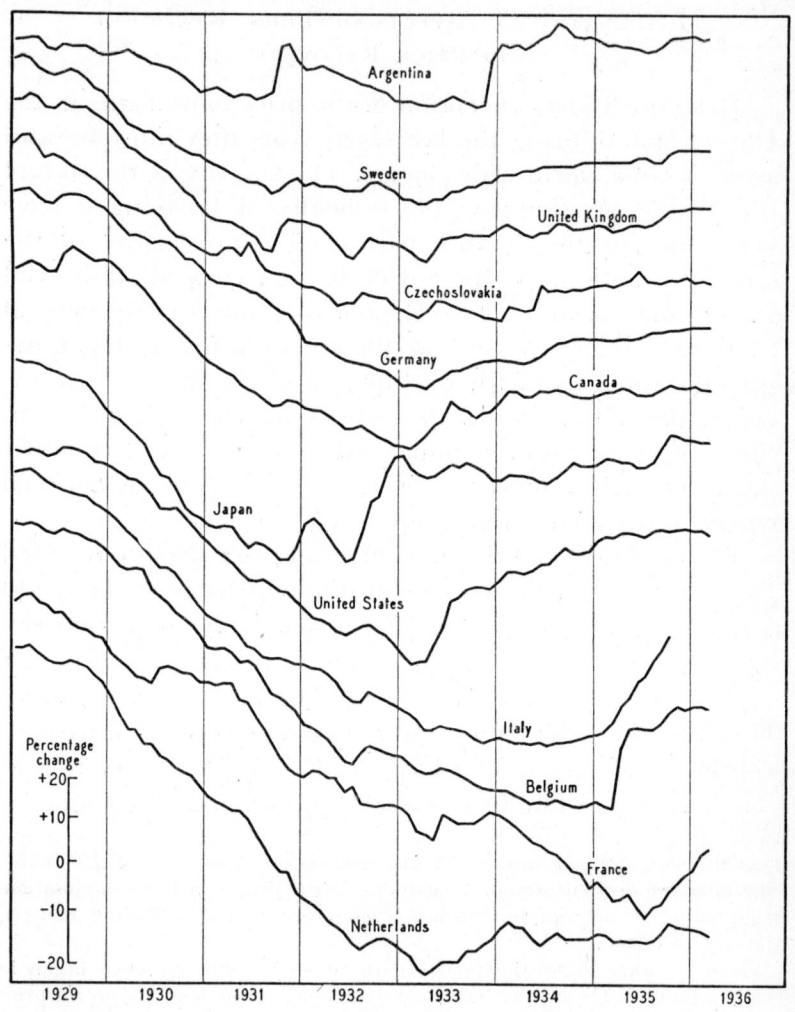

Ratio scale

GENERAL ASPECTS

here represented was 36 per cent, the median duration 54 months. The price drop of 1920–21, which started from a highly inflated level, was somewhat more severe in amplitude, but in duration was far short of the recent drop.

TABLE 1

PRICE RECESSION IN THIRTY-TWO COUNTRIES, 1928–1936

A Summary of Changes in Index Numbers of Wholesale Prices

(Price movements are here measured in terms of the various national currencies.)

	DATE OF HIGH BEFORE RECESSION 1928	DATE OF LOW	RECESSION DURATION (months)	DEGREE (per cent)	INTENSITY (per cent per month)
Latvia	March	June	1934[1] 75	−38	−0.6
Argentina	May	October	1933 65	−15	−0.2
Sweden	May	April	1933 59	−31	−0.6
Jugoslavia	May	September	1933 64	−44	−0.9
Germany	July	April	1933 57	−36	−0.8
Norway	August	January	1934[1] 65	−24	−0.4
Finland	August	September	1931 37	−23	−0.7
Union of South Africa	October	October	1932 48	−28	−0.7
Spain	November	May	1933 54	−9	−0.2
Egypt (Cairo)	November	May	1933 54	−50	−1.3
Japan	December	June	1932 42	−36	−1.1
	1929				
Czechoslovakia	February	January	1934 59	−33	−0.7
Denmark	February	September	1931 31	−31	−1.2
France	March	July	1935 76	−51	−0.9
Belgium	March	March	1935 72	−47	−0.9
Chile	March	October	1931 31	−29	−1.1
Estonia	March	June	1933 51	−36	−0.9
United Kingdom	March	April	1933 49	−31	−0.7
Hungary	March	November	1933 56	−49	−1.2
Italy	March	July	1934 64	−46	−1.0

SOURCE: The original index numbers underlying the present measurements have been collected by the League of Nations, Geneva, and published in the *Monthly Bulletin of Statistics*.

[1] The low dates here recorded for Latvia, Norway and Austria are those

TABLE 1 *(cont.)*

PRICE RECESSION IN THIRTY-TWO COUNTRIES, 1928–1936

	DATE OF HIGH BEFORE RECESSION 1928	DATE OF LOW	RECESSION DURATION (months)	DEGREE (per cent)	INTENSITY (per cent per month)
Netherlands	March	April 1933	49	−52	−1.5
Peru	March	April 1932	37	−14	−0.4
Poland	March	March 1936[2]	84	−48	−0.8
Bulgaria	April	January 1934	57	−53	−1.3
Austria	May	February 1933[1]	45	−22	−0.5
Dutch East Indies	May	March 1936[2]	82	−57	−1.0
United States	July	February 1933	43	−38	−1.1
Switzerland	July	March 1935	68	−40	−0.7
Canada	August	February 1933	42	−35	−1.0
Australia	September	February 1933	41	−28	−0.8
India (Calcutta)	September	March 1933	42	−43	−1.3
New Zealand	September	January 1933	40	−16	−0.4

preceding actual price recovery. Slightly lower points were reached earlier. If recession be measured with reference to these earlier low points, we have the following records for these three countries.

	DATE OF HIGH BEFORE RECESSION	DATE OF LOW	RECESSION DURATION (months)	DEGREE (per cent)	INTENSITY (per cent per month)
Latvia	March 1928	December 1931	45	−39	−1.1
Norway	August 1928	September 1931	37	−26	−0.8
Austria	May 1929	January 1931	20	−22	−1.3

[2] The low dates recorded for Poland and the Dutch East Indies are the latest for which index numbers are available.

Early price weakness in raw materials is reflected in some degree in the timing of price recession, by countries, but the international pattern is not a simple one. Between the autumn of 1928 and the autumn of 1929 the gradual subsidence of prices that had been in progress throughout the world since 1924–25 was converted into a general retreat. The Orient, the Near East, the Argentine and Western Europe felt the force of the decline before the spring of 1929

GENERAL ASPECTS

was over. Summer and autumn carried the storm of price recession throughout Europe and into North America and the British dominions. Unlike the break of prices in 1920, the course of which could be charted as it swept eastward from Japan, across the Americas, and thence to Europe, the decline of 1928–29 followed no consistent geographical path. Price weakness, penetrating the structure of world prices, was apparent in widely scattered areas before the general flood was released.

The record of recovery summarized in Table 2 shows equally diverse beginnings. In only two of the thirty-two countries here represented did wholesale prices fail to advance, in some degree. In three countries price lows were reached in 1931, and in three countries in 1932. In sixteen countries wholesale price levels touched their depression lows in 1933. That year, and notably the quarter extending from February to April, was marked by a general upward

TABLE 2

PRICE RECOVERY IN THIRTY-TWO COUNTRIES, 1931–1936

A Summary of Changes in Index Numbers of Wholesale Prices Since Dates of Depression Lows

(Price movements are here measured in terms of the various national currencies.)

	DATE OF DEPRESSION LOW	REVIVAL FROM LOW TO MARCH 1936		
		DURATION (months)	DEGREE (per cent)	INTENSITY (per cent per month)
	1931			
Denmark	September	54	27.5	0.5
Finland	September	54	15.3	0.3
Chile	October	53	155.3	1.8
	1932			
Peru	April	47	17.5	0.3
Japan	June	45	30.3	0.6
Union of South Africa	October	42[4]	14.8	0.3

TABLE 2 *(cont.)*

PRICE RECOVERY IN THIRTY-TWO COUNTRIES, 1931–1936

	DATE OF DEPRESSION LOW	REVIVAL FROM LOW TO MARCH 1936		
		DURATION (months)	DEGREE (per cent)	INTENSITY (per cent per month)
	1933			
New Zealand	January	38	9.4	0.2
Australia	February	37	11.7	0.3
Austria	February [1]	37	1.2	.0
Canada	February	37	13.8	0.4
United States	February	37	33.1	0.8
India (Calcutta)	March	36	10.8	0.3
Germany	April	35	14.2	0.4
Netherlands	April	35	9.9	0.3
Sweden	April	35	12.4	0.3
United Kingdom	April	35	12.8	0.3
Egypt (Cairo)	May	34	35.5	0.9
Spain	May	34	7.2	0.2
Estonia	June	33	13.9	0.4
Jugoslavia	September	30	16.1	0.5
Argentina	October	29	16.2	0.5
Hungary	November	28	29.9	0.9
	1934			
Bulgaria	January	26	9.7	0.4
Czechoslovakia	January	26	9.1	0.3
Norway	January [2]	26	10.1	0.4
Latvia	June [3]	21	6.1	0.3
Italy	July	15 [5]	27.5	1.6
	1935			
Belgium	March	12	24.6	1.8
Switzerland	March	12	5.2	0.4
France	July	8	16.7	1.9
	1936			
Dutch East Indies	March [6]			
Poland	March [6]			

[1] Slightly lower point reached in January 1931.
[2] Slightly lower point reached in September 1931.
[3] Slightly lower point reached in December 1931.
[4] October 1932 to April 1936.   [5] July 1934 to October 1935.
[6] The last figure available is the lowest to date.

GENERAL ASPECTS 25

surge in prices, world-wide in scope. Low points were reached by five countries in 1934, and by three in 1935.

We have given above a general picture, in terms of broad averages, of the recession of wholesale prices in the United States and of the course of price recovery through the early months of 1936, the whole reviewed against the background of similar movements at other periods and in other areas. Forty-three months of demoralizing decline, five months of sharp rise and thirty-five months of irregular advance left a price level in the United States, in June 1936, 32 per cent above the February 1933 low, 18 per cent below the 1929 peak, and 14 per cent above the 1913 average. This series of changes was not unprecedented in our history, but it is improbable that any previous movements imposed strains of comparable severity upon the economic system of the United States.

Price Relations and Some Current Issues

In following the course of recession and recovery no attempt is made to cover all aspects of the economic scene, or to deal with all the monetary and price problems that have arisen. Attention will be concentrated on selected issues and relations of major importance among elements of the price system. Four matters are of particular interest:

1. The margins, or differentials, between the prices of goods of the same type at successive stages of the route from primary producer to ultimate consumer are a factor of major importance in the movement of goods into use. In a sense, goods move uphill from primary markets to final consumers. Labor must be expended upon them at each stage of their progress. The immediate stimulus to the activities of fabrication and transportation necessary to transform raw materials into ultimate finished goods is provided by a series of price differentials, which are appraised

by the business man with reference to the number of units of goods that may be moved.[14]

In measuring changes in the fabricational-distributional margin we shall not deal with the innumerable price differentials affecting the movements of individual commodities, but with certain broad averages. For the present purposes chief interest attaches not to such items as the spread between the price of wheat and the price of bread, but to the major or general differential between the average prices received by primary producers for raw materials and the average prices paid by final consumers for the wide variety of finished goods into which these materials enter. The margin between average prices at these primary and terminal stages represents the cost of the services of the middlemen who fabricate, transport and distribute the goods by which we live. This is the central margin upon which all productive and distributive activity, other than that of primary production, depends. In tracing variations in this margin and in the elements of cost and of selling price that define it we shall be dealing with a magnitude of central importance in the working of the economic system. Movements persisting over extended periods are reflected in long-term variations in this margin. The first impact of a change in industrial productivity falls upon the costs of fabrication that are covered by this margin. The incidence and economic consequences of inflation and deflation may be most readily traced through the effects of such movements upon this same major differential. And the study of recent changes in this margin is of special interest because of critical movements that occurred prior to and during the recession of 1929.

---

[14] Because of changes in overhead costs, per unit of product, with variations in quantities handled, a price differential offering attractive profits under certain conditions may involve operating losses, with a reduced volume of production and trade, under other conditions.

Over a long period the incentive to business activity is provided, of course, not by profit per unit of goods handled but by rate of return on invested capital and, for the small entrepreneur, by rewards secured for time and effort expended. But the factors that enter into these appraisals are not ignored in applying the more immediate test of per unit profit.

Changes from 1933 to 1936 in this differential reflected the influence of the National Industrial Recovery Act and the Agricultural Adjustment Act, as well as of elements customarily present in recovery. The effects of the new factors upon the immediate groups concerned, upon the margin between material costs and selling prices to consumers and upon the working of the price system as a regulatory mechanism have been of particular significance during certain stages of recovery.

2. Notable among the elements of the price structure are those defining the economic position of primary producers. Among these, farmers stand in a distinctive position in the American economy, which combines the features of an industrial and an agricultural country. In spite of protective tariff walls farm products are peculiarly exposed to the forces of world competition and to changes in world economic conditions. New elements were introduced into the farm situation by the enforcement of the Agricultural Adjustment Act and the Soil Conservation Act. Special problems of other types center about the work of other primary producers.

3. Capital goods industries play a crucial part in a modern industrial economy. As they lead in expansion, so do they play a dominant role in economic recession and depression. We must trace price changes in these industries and the relations of these changes to economic processes at large.

4. Finally, and perhaps most urgently, we are concerned with changes in the prices of goods ready for sale to final consumers. Prices prevailing at the terminus of the productive-distributive process stand in a position of high strategic importance in the working of the economic system. Prices to consumers condition the movement of goods at all earlier stages and help to determine the volume of finished goods that may be marketed. Faulty relationships among these prices and the prices of unfinished goods may seriously impede productive activities.

These four points noted for special attention are by no means unrelated. The costs of fabrication and distribution that are represented by the margin between the prices of raw and processed goods have an obvious relation to the selling prices of finished goods, whether intended for capital equipment or human consumption. And the real rewards of primary producers are conditioned, in part, by the costs of fabrication and the prices of finished goods. The economic developments of the stormy years from 1914 to 1936 wrought great changes in the fortunes of primary producers, fabricators and buyers of finished goods. The succeeding chapters trace some details of these developments.

Changes in Commodity Prices and in the Purchasing Power of Given Groups of Producers

The relation between changes in prices and in the broad streams of goods moving from producers to consumers calls for special attention. For time differentials in the responses of prices to the forces of recession and of revival may appear, at a given instant, as disparities—discrepancies that may substantially alter the volume of goods produced and sold, or their distribution among consuming groups, or both. This relation is worthy of brief demonstration.

The per unit price of a given commodity multiplied by the number of units produced during a stated period yields, of course, its total money value. Or, if we are dealing with *changes* in these factors, rather than with absolute magnitudes, a relative number (p), defining the change in per unit price over a period, multiplied by a relative number (q), defining the change in number of units produced, yields a measure (pq) of the change in aggregate value of product over this period. This measure defines changes in monetary values. If interest attaches to changes in the aggregate purchasing power of the producers in question this measure of relative value must be divided by a measure (P) of the average change, over the same period, in the per unit price of the goods to be purchased by these producers. Thus, using the symbols suggested, pq/P (the measures all being in relative form) defines the change, with reference to any given

GENERAL ASPECTS

base, in the aggregate purchasing power of the producers of a given commodity. The ratio of this quantity to q, the relative defining degree of change in the amount produced, is $\frac{pq/P}{q}$ which reduces to p/P, the ratio of the price of the product to the average price of goods to be purchased (both in relative form). This simple ratio, then, may be taken to define the relation between changes in two important physical aggregates—the aggregate physical rewards (or purchasing power) of a given group and its aggregate physical production or contribution. If we have knowledge concerning changes in these factors we may trace the major shifts in the economic status of various groups of producers and consumers.

We should note that shifts in the ratio of the physical production, or the physical rewards, of a given group, to the total physical output of the economy are not defined by the above measurements. To measure such changes of *relative* status we should have an index of Q, the total physical output.

Other issues with which we shall be concerned in the following pages relate to more general aspects of the working of the price system. One of the important external connections of the network of interrelated values that constitute the price structure is that defining the value of the monetary unit in terms of gold. (This external bond may, of course, run to some commodity or commodities other than gold.) The stimulus to change may come to the price system through this connection, as well as from any of the elements bound together in its internal structure.

Changes in the system of prices arising from the play of internal forces may be far reaching. Changed conditions of production of a raw material that affect its price will be reflected, in a free price system, at all stages of the productive-distributive routes along which that material moves to ultimate users. These same changes will be reflected in the prices of competitive materials and of all their products, and thus will spread, as do ripples in a pond, to all parts of the price structure. If the internal force is of major proportions, arising from the changed status of a whole group of producers, the repercussions upon other parts of the price system will be more violent, and the period of readjustment will be longer.

The character of this readjustment and the period necessary for its attainment will depend upon the closeness of the ties that bind the element in which the disturbance originates to other parts of the price structure, as well as upon the violence of the initial disturbance. In a perfectly free and fluid system, in which all parts were free to adjust themselves promptly to changed relations (and in an economic system in which corresponding physical adjustments could be as readily made), these two factors would be, presumably, the only ones conditioning the reaction of the system to an internal change and affecting the ultimate readjustment. Prices, as passive, sensitive indexes of changed economic conditions, would transmit the necessary intelligence and would promptly readjust themselves to the new physical relations resulting from the change. If, however, prices were not free, the degree of price inflexibility (or the degree of tardiness of prices in their response to changes in physical conditions, or in other prices) would enter as a third factor affecting the duration and the character of the economic readjustment. Under these conditions prices would cease to serve as effective instruments for the transmission of economic intelligence. As soon as restraints upon the free movement of prices are introduced (restraints arising from monopoly power, price-fixing through formal or informal agreements or public regulation, the inertia of custom, the rigidity of debt and other fixed charges, or the like), prices reflect these restraints rather than the quantitative conditions of

GENERAL ASPECTS 31

market supply and demand. Inflexible prices, the market representations of these restraints, may thus become active, positive factors in economic change, influencing the physical processes which in an ideally free system they would merely mirror.

The same general considerations apply to a stimulus to change developing on the monetary side, a stimulus transmitted through the bond that ties the price system to a gold (or other) standard. A change originating here, arising from an alteration in the value of the monetary unit, would, under conditions of perfect freedom, be communicated directly to all parts of the price system. (It is assumed that a free gold, or other, standard prevails, with full convertibility.) All prices would change in equal degree, and the relationships established on the basis of the new real value of the monetary unit would be the same as those prevailing under earlier conditions. Prices would, again, be passive instruments, merely recording the monetary change, exerting no direct influence upon economic processes proper. But if the price system were not free in all its parts, if business conventions, monopolistic powers, legal restrictions, contractual obligations, overhead charges and the physical conditions of production imposed varying time differentials upon prices during the process of readjustment to changed monetary values, the primary reactions to such a change would be irregular and incomplete. Here, again, prices would cease to play a passive role. Instead of merely transmitting intelligence concerning economic changes on the physical side, prices would actively affect economic processes. New price relationships created by the lagging adjustment to altered monetary values would necessarily be reflected in changed relations among physical forces.

This argument may be put in slightly different form: under the conditions noted the prices of individual commodities respond to the influence of forces other than those competitive elements of supply and demand that are assumed to be the active factors in price changes in a free price system. It is true, of course, that other (non-price) elements always lie behind the behavior of prices. Prices themselves cannot be in any sense final causes. Prices are the focusing points of a complex of market forces and reactions, and price movements and relations are the net resultants of these forces and reactions. Prices may, however, be important intermediate factors in a circular relationship. This point has a bearing on the preceding reference to free prices. The concept of a completely 'free' price system is highly abstract and unreal. The condition is one that could never be realized under contemporary conditions. Time differentials in price readjustments to changing conditions are inherent in any system of which we may conceive. Technical conditions of production, habits, debts and other contractual obligations, institutional factors of many sorts are bound to create such time-lags in the responses of prices to forces making for change.

What is perhaps of chief importance here is that it is precisely during a period of rapid and extreme change that such normally passive technical and institutional elements become active factors in the economic situation. For when wide fluctuations occur in the average level of prices, rigidity in some parts of the price structure tends to prevent prompt adaptation of all its elements to the new situation. The resulting changes in price relations condition the process of physical readjustment. And since the readjustment of physical conditions (of consumption, production, trade) to sharply modified price relations is likely to be an extended and economically painful process, price disparities may constitute real barriers, in a positive sense, to a prompt restoration of full economic activity.

GENERAL ASPECTS

On Price Disparities

In the preceding section, and in various other parts of this study, reference is made to 'price disparities', and to some of their implications and consequences. The meaning that is here given to this term should be explained.

The use of the term 'price disparities' rests upon an implicit assumption that the activities of a modern economy may be viewed as the working of a closely-knit system of interdependent parts. The price system, a coherent body of related price quotations on commodities, services and disposable values of all sorts, is one element of this general structure. The operations of the economic system, in the allocation of productive factors, in the production and distribution of goods and services, in the apportionment of income, are conditioned by the relations among the working parts of the system as a whole and, more particularly, by the relations among quoted prices of the factors of production and of other commodities.

The economic system at large and the price system (which permeates the general system as the nervous system permeates the human body) are subject to the play of forces that alter the relations among their constituent elements. If we assume a state of equilibrium prior to one of these changes, compensating movements must occur after the initial change in a given relation. In a highly integrated industrial economy such as ours today these compensating movements may extend over a wide area and may require considerable time, before balance is again achieved. The extent of the compensation necessary and the time required for compensation to be effected will depend upon the magnitude of the original change, upon its economic incidence (if it originates outside the economic system) and upon the nature and closeness of the relations that bind the elements first affected to the system at large.

Our immediate concern is with certain aspects of the changes that are manifest in the system of prices, changes that may originate anywhere, within or without the economic system proper.

We define as a price disparity the condition prevailing after a shift in price relations to which there has not been complete adaptation among elements of the economic system at large. We take the term adaptation, in the above definition, to mean such adjustment in respect of the volume or character of production, allocation of man-power, investment of capital, distribution of income, or disposition of other elements of economic life as may be necessary to a working balance of economic elements, with effective utilization of available productive resources.

This general definition of price disparity and of economic maladjustment suffers because definite criteria of disparity and of maladjustment are not available. The definition goes back to a rather vague conception of a state of balance, or equilibrium, or mutual adjustment among the working parts of an abstract entity called the economic system. In the present state of our economic knowledge, when the conditions of balance, or even of operating efficiency, in the economic system at large may not be precisely defined, this weakness in the definition is hard to correct. We shall shortly suggest certain more concrete types of evidence, bearing upon the presence or absence of what we have called price disparities. These are more specific than the general condition noted in the definition, but the precise circumstances of disparity remain elusive.

With reference to the general definition given above, disparities are, of course, always present. They are, indeed, a customary condition of economic life, since changes in market conditions and price relations are continually occurring, with favorable consequences in some directions, unfavorable consequences in others. In respect of price disparities, as in so many other economic problems, it is the time factor, in relation to the experience upon which economic behavior is based, that is of central importance. Serious difficulties develop only when a state of non-adaptation persists beyond the period within which adjustment is to be expected, on the basis of experience. If, in the market for a perishable product, current marketings are not promptly adapted to changed price and buying conditions, producers may suffer serious loss. Here a real disparity may develop over a very short period. Similarly, a disparity involving harmful consequences may develop in the field of agricultural prices if adaptation to changed conditions is not effected within a single planting, growing and harvesting season. In such a market as that for capital goods the duration of a business cycle may be the period within which experience leads us to expect mutual adjustment of prices and physical conditions to a changed set of relations.

It is, then, only when a price disparity continues beyond the expected period of adjustment that we may think of it as *persistent*. True, reduced production and reduced real incomes may result from (or accompany) disparities that are not persistent, in this sense. Non-persistent disparities, equally with persistent disparities, may be manifestations of economic pathology. For the disparities developing and being corrected over the course of a single business cycle may entail serious losses. The term disparity may properly be used for both types of maladjustment, although persistent disparities are of special interest because of their probable connection with enduring changes in the economic structure.

A fair question arises as to the circumstances that may be responsible for the prolongation of the period of adjustment beyond normal expectancy. In general, perhaps, an extension of the time required for adaptation to changed economic relations of any sort may be attributed either to exceptional severity or persistence of the force creating disparity, or to change in the operating characteristics of the system affected. By the latter is meant a change that alters the reaction of the system to given influences. Thus a loss of flexibility by important elements of the economic system might seriously reduce the adaptive powers of the system as a whole. Persistent post-War price disparities might be attributed to the excessive severity of the forces affecting the price system and the economic system at large, or to changes in these systems that caused them to react, in post-War years, in a manner different from that prevailing in earlier times.

Circumstances of both types probably played a part in the observed changes.

Specific manifestations of price disparity are difficult to define. Innumerable price changes occur from day to day and from month to month, and it is impossible to draw a sharp line between those that constitute disparities, representing definite economic faults, those to which adjustment has been readily effected and those that actually stimulate activity through the opening of new profit opportunities. As a working basis for a review of price movements, we may say that *prima facie* evidence of price disparity in a competitive economy is provided by the following conditions:

> Rapid and violent alteration of a set of established price relations.
>
> Price changes of considerable magnitude not accompanied by corresponding changes in production costs.
>
> Important changes in productivity, not accompanied by corresponding changes in selling prices.
>
> A sharp reduction in the volume of production and trade.
>
> Unemployment of productive factors.
>
> A considerable variation over a relatively short period in the relations among the incomes of producing groups.

Whether the presence of one or more of these conditions, in a given situation, is in fact evidence of price disparity must be determined, as well as may be, in the light of all the known circumstances.

We may not here explore the implications and consequences of price disparities. These will concern us in the course of the detailed discussion in later sections. Shifts of economic advantage and of purchasing power from group to group, changes in the volume and character of commodities produced, in the amount and form of savings and in the direction of investment —these may result from, or accompany, inequalities in the changes occurring among different elements of the price system to which adaptation of their economic elements has not been effected.[15]

In following the course of events between 1929 and 1936 we shall be concerned with some general problems suggested by the preceding discussion. A price system operating under conditions of partial freedom and partial rigidity, composed of elements marked by diverse modes of behavior and bound together by ties of varying degrees of intimacy, was exposed first to a violent recession and then to the forces of a recovery marked by highly novel elements. How did it respond? Was its role in the recession that of transmitting intelligence of changes on the physical side, or did it play an active, positive part in determining the character of the recession and the course of the depression? How did the system as a whole, and its chief elements, respond to the stimulus of recovery? Did prices furnish clear guides to the economic activity required under the conditions of depression and recovery? These questions suggest some of the general problems faced in a survey of recent price changes.

Other issues arise more directly from the program of recovery initiated in the United States early in 1933. Reference has already been made to the potential influence upon prices of the National Industrial Recovery Act and of the various industrial codes based on it. The suspension of provisions of the anti-trust acts, the permission, in some cases, of price-fixing agreements, the recognition of open-price agreements, the setting of minimum wage rates and the writing into many codes of provisions that selling prices should not be lower than costs of production, brought important changes in the structure and working of the price system, during the

---

[15] I have discussed some implications of price changes in a non-flexible economic system in a paper in the volume, *Economic Essays in Honor of Wesley Clair Mitchell* (Columbia University Press, 1935), pp. 377–81.

period of code enforcement. Again, the setting by law of a precise standard to which the average purchasing power of farm products should be restored, if possible, introduced another and entirely novel factor into the economic situation. Of a different order were the monetary measures adopted by the Administration in the effort to check deflation, to bring about a general price advance, and to lighten the burden of debts carried over from an era of higher prices. Here were forces impinging upon the price system from without, modifying its structure and conditioning its working. These also belong in the picture of price changes in the recent past.

This introduction is intended to provide the setting of the present inquiry. General aspects of the decline and of the recovery to date have been dealt with. An attempt has been made to provide perspective by setting recent movements in the United States against movements at other times and in other regions. Finally, reference has been made to certain features of the price structure, and various questions have been raised that will require consideration in later sections. We pass now to a brief consideration of the situation prevailing when the storm of 1929 was loosed.

CHAPTER II

THE PRE-RECESSION SITUATION

A SUMMARY view of the economic situation prevailing in 1929 is essential to an understanding of the changes that followed so quickly. The shift in the direction and velocity of movement was so pronounced, in that year, that it is well to survey the course of pre-recession movements and the character of the pre-recession situation before proceeding to the events of the recession itself.[1]

Factors Affecting the Price Structure of 1929

Conceiving of the price structure as a set of relations prevailing among the prices of all the commodities and services that enter into economic activity, it is useful to consider the system existing in 1929 as the resultant of the following general conditions and forces:

1. As a foundation, providing the general framework of the 1929 structure, we must note the relations that had been built up over a considerable period of gradual change before the War. The chief influences bearing upon the price system during this period, which we may say extended from 1896 to 1914, may be summarized in these terms:

a. A slow, secular rise in the price level caused aggregate commodity values to increase more rapidly than the volume of physical production, tended to keep labor and overhead costs down,

[1] A more detailed account of certain tendencies prevailing in the United States prior to the recession of 1929 is given in *Economic Tendencies in the United States* (National Bureau of Economic Research, 1932).

relatively, and contributed to certain of the changes in price relations noted below.

b. Raw materials rose more rapidly in price than manufactured goods. The price differential representing fabricational costs was steadily narrowed.

c. The real per unit value of products of American farms, in raw state, was steadily enhanced. The average real value (i.e., per unit purchasing power) of other commodities declined.

d. Consumers' goods (goods in shape for use by final consumers) and producers' goods (articles of capital equipment and goods intended for consumption, after further fabrication) advanced in price at substantially equal rates.

e. After increasing in price during the expansion that culminated in 1906 and 1907, commodities intended for use in the construction of capital equipment fell appreciably in relative value.

f. Productivity in manufacturing industries advanced notably. Labor costs in manufacturing were reduced, relatively to general prices. The real wages of manufacturing labor were barely maintained during this period of industrial expansion.

2. Superimposed upon the foundation provided by these movements were the shifts arising from the revolutionary economic changes of 1914–22, a period covering the War and the first great post-War recession. Changes in price relations during this period were in part of internal origin, reflecting the play of non-monetary forces. Perhaps more important, however, were alterations due to drastic changes in monetary values. These were transmitted with varying degrees of lag and in varying intensities to the different elements of the price system.

In summary, we note these movements:

a. The rapid price advance of 1916–20 and the recession of 1920–21 brought a sharp reversal of earlier relations between the prices of raw materials, particularly industrial raw materials,

THE PRE-RECESSION SITUATION 41

and manufactured products. War demands, the exploitation of new territory, and the stimulation of a rapidly rising price level had caused a rapid expansion in the output of raw materials. The checking of War-time demand, the inability of raw material producers to adapt themselves promptly to the new situation, and the greater promptness of manufacturing producers in adapting production schedules to changed conditions were factors in this reversal. In 1921 raw material producers throughout the world were in a position of extreme price weakness, and manufacturers in a relatively strong price position.

b. The steady pre-War improvement of the average status of farmers was followed by War-time affluence. Then came abrupt decline in 1920–21 to a position lower than any that farmers had known in a quarter of a century.

c. Producers' goods in general were materially cheapened as a result of the price shifts of 1914–21, while the real per unit value of consumers' goods was greatly enhanced. Buying and selling prices were alike favorable to the reaping of profits in the operation of business enterprises, when the advance of 1922 started.

d. In contrast to this favorable price situation on the operating side the costs of capital equipment in general and construction costs in particular were high in 1922.

e. Although employment fell sharply in the recession of 1920–21, real wage rates were substantially advanced as a result of the War and immediate post-War shifts. Labor costs, as a consequence, were relatively high at the opening of the industrial expansion of the nineteen twenties.

3. The price structure that existed in 1922 was subject, during eight years, to a new set of influences. In brief summary:

a. The physical volume of production increased between 1922 and 1929 at a rate in excess of that which prevailed during the decade preceding the World War.

b. The productivity of manufacturing labor increased more

rapidly than during any other period for which records are available. (Acceptable records go back to 1899.)

c. In the expansion of this period an increasing proportion of the nation's productive resources was devoted to the output of durable goods and of luxury goods, both being types marked by high elasticity of demand.

d. Articles of capital equipment were being produced at a rate materially greater than that prevailing for physical goods in general.

e. Heavy foreign lending and rapid growth of the volume of export trade characterized this period. The dominant export groups consisted of goods of elastic demand.

f. The aggregate amount of capital funds available to American industry increased at a notable rate. This helped to maintain an upward swing in security prices for an exceptionally long period. It facilitated the improvement of mechanical equipment, and was thus a major factor in enhancing the productivity of labor and in contributing to technological unemployment.

g. The period as a whole was marked by an apparent loss of flexibility in certain important elements of the price structure. This loss of flexibility—a loss due in part to the steady advance of overhead costs, price regulation, trade agreements, valorization efforts—paralleled movements that tied together even more closely the various elements of the industrial structure, and made a continuing and flexible adjustment of working parts more essential to economic stability.

h. Commodity prices were marked by a slightly declining trend during the first post-War decade. A declining trend intensifies the difficulties of readjustment after a cyclical recession, and compels more thoroughgoing liquidation than is necessary when the secular push of prices is upward.

In passing now to a brief account of 1929 price relations in the United States, we deal again only with certain salient aspects of the general situation.

PRICES OF RAW AND PROCESSED GOODS; PRICE POSITION OF THE FARMER

Raw materials as a class rose in price in the United States between 1922 and 1929; processed goods declined. Although these movements tended to correct the extreme disparities created during the 1920–21 recession, they left raw materials in an unfavorable position in 1929, in terms of pre-War relations. This is clearly shown by an examination of relevant index numbers of wholesale prices.[2] These measurements

	1922	1929	1913	1922	1929
Raw materials	100	106	100	133	141
Manufactured goods	100	98	100	155	152

indicate that in average per unit worth, in terms of commodities in general at wholesale, raw materials were in 1929 some 5 per cent lower than in 1913, manufactured goods 2 per cent higher. (In deriving these measurements the index numbers of wholesale prices given in the table have been divided by the corresponding index of general commodity prices, at wholesale.) In default of accurate and comprehensive records of changes in production costs we may not appraise this shift with precision. It is known that production costs of many raw materials were reduced during the decade and a half following the beginning of the War.[3] Some of the technical gains that manufacturing industries

[2] Unless otherwise noted, the index numbers presented in this monograph have been computed by the National Bureau of Economic Research from quotations compiled by the U. S. Bureau of Labor Statistics. The detailed measurements, with notations concerning the number of commodities represented, are given in Appendices III and IV.

[3] Important technical improvements occurred in the copper, lead, zinc, silver and petroleum industries, and the production of tin and wheat was marked by increasing mechanization. Cf. *Raw Material Prices and Business Conditions*, Melvin T. Copeland (Publications of the Graduate School of Business Administration, Harvard University, Vol. XX, No. 3, May 1933).

had enjoyed earlier were now realized in extractive industries. But it is doubtful that such cost reduction equaled the very substantial declines in production costs in manufacturing industries during the decade prior to 1929. The advantage brought by relative price movements to manufacturing industries during these years was probably real.

The loss that the American farmer suffered in price position in 1920–21, a loss which wiped out the gains of many years, was in part made up during the succeeding eight years. Dealing first with the situation in wholesale markets, we have the following record of changes in the wholesale

	1922	1929	1913	1922	1929
All products of American farms, raw	100	110	100	137	150
All other commodities	100	98	100	151	148

prices of raw farm products and all other commodities (including processed farm products and raw and processed non-farm products). Between 1922 and 1929 the prices of raw farm products gained distinctly on other commodities. As is shown by the entries on the 1913 base, this gain more than corrected the 1922 disparity, putting farm products slightly above the general average in 1929.[4]

Wholesale prices, although useful as a common denominator in the comparison of changes affecting different groups of producers, do not necessarily indicate the true buying and selling position of the farmer. To define this position we compare the course of prices actually received at the farm

---

[4] In this, as in all other comparisons of index numbers, we must note the limitations attaching to measurements of price changes over time. Only for staples of relatively unvarying quality are these measurements accurate. Changes in quality and in design, among fabricated goods, may not be adequately translated into terms of price and are, indeed, usually ignored in the construction of index numbers. Errors due to such changes are usually slight over short periods, more serious in comparisons covering a number of years (see footnote 6, p. 45).

THE PRE-RECESSION SITUATION 45

with changes in the prices of goods bought by farmers. The

	1922	1929	1913	1922	1929
Prices received by farmers	100	111	100	131	145
Prices paid by farmers for production and family maintenance	100	103	100	148	151

index of farm prices relates to thirty major agricultural products; the index of prices paid is based on payments by farmers, at retail, for articles used for productive purposes and for direct consumption and use.[5] Here, again, a substantial gain is shown for the years between 1922 and 1929, but the advance started from a lower relative position in 1922 than is indicated by the wholesale price quotations. In 1929 the per unit purchasing power of farm products, measured with reference to the prices paid by farmers, was lower than in 1913.

This record leaves out of consideration possible changes in production costs of farm products and changes in the quality of some articles bought by farmers. It is certain that changes of these types occurred between 1913 and 1929. While the resulting gains may not have been sufficient to offset the price disadvantage revealed by the above index numbers, there is no doubt that by 1929 farmers, as a class, had made great strides towards recovering their pre-War economic status.[6]

---

[5] Index numbers computed by the U. S. Bureau of Agricultural Economics. The index numbers on the pre-War base are only slightly modified if the standard of reference be the five years, August 1909 to July 1914, instead of the single year 1913.

	August 1909–July 1914	1922	1929
Prices received by farmers	100	132	146
Prices paid by farmers	100	149	153

[6] The measurements of changes in the purchasing power of farm products, cited in the text, are derived from the comparison of price changes among two groups of commodities—farm products, and commodities bought by

MARGIN BETWEEN THE PRICES OF RAW AND PROCESSED GOODS, 1929

We have stressed in an earlier section the economic importance of the differential between the prices received for materials by primary producers and prices prevailing for finished goods at the other end of the productive-distributive process. This differential measures the cost of those activities, so characteristic of modern economic life, that intervene between the extractive processes and the final consumption of physical goods. Available data do not span the entire range of this differential, but it is possible to measure the changes over substantial portions of this important margin.

WHOLESALE PRICES

The customary comparison, in tracing changes in the manufacturing margin, is between the prices of all raw materials and all manufactured goods. This is significant, but it is not entirely appropriate to the purpose; for a considerable group of raw materials consists of products such as

farmers for use in production and in family maintenance. The first is composed of standard raw materials (wheat, cotton, hogs, cattle, etc.) subject to only minor variations in quality. The second includes diverse materials, such as farm machinery, automobiles, tractors, many of which have been marked by steady improvement in quality with the passing years. It is estimated, for example, that the quality—the productive efficiency—of farm machinery increased 70 per cent between pre-War years and 1932 (estimate cited in *Index Numbers of Prices Paid by Farmers for Commodities Bought, 1910–1934*, U. S. Department of Agriculture, September 1934). Automobiles have been marked by similar improvements in quality, over the period of their general use. It is obviously erroneous, if long periods are involved, to set against the prices of goods of unvarying quality prices of equipment that has improved so substantially in quality, without taking account of quality changes. The above measurements, therefore, certainly overstate somewhat the degree of loss in the purchasing power of farm products between 1913 and post-War years.

THE PRE-RECESSION SITUATION 47

vegetables, eggs and milk, which are purchased in their raw form by ultimate consumers. Such raw consumers' goods are, in general, subject to price-making forces quite different from those that operate among raw materials subject to more or less complex processes of fabrication before being ready for use, either for purposes of consumption or as instruments of further production. It is the latter group of raw producers' goods that should properly be compared with manufactured commodities, if interest attaches to changes in the manufacturer's price margin.

Price tendencies prevailing among these two classes of goods during the years preceding the 1929 recession are shown by the accompanying index numbers, which define

	1922	1929	1913	1922	1929
Producers' goods, raw	100	103	100	127	131
All processed goods	100	98	100	155	152

changes in the average wholesale prices of broad classes of goods at successive stages of production.[7] (They do not relate, we should note, to precisely the same commodities at these stages.) The net effect of the eight years of expansion that began in the United States after the depression of 1921 and continued without grave interruption until 1929 was to reduce the relative margin between the prices paid by manufacturers for their raw materials and the prices, at wholesale, at which processed goods were sold. Raw producers' goods rose slightly in price, manufactured goods declined slightly on the average. If we neglect questions relating to costs, productivity and changes in degree of fabrication and in volume of output, questions that naturally affect the interpretation of the changed differential, we find an apparent tendency

---

[7] See Appendices II–IV for index numbers by years, with an explanation of their derivation.

towards a reduction of fabricational charges between 1922 and 1929.

But a longer view is needed if the situation in 1929 is to be properly understood. The preceding measurements indicate that in 1929, as well as in 1922, the margin was exceptionally wide, that the costs of the services of the manufacturers (and, in some degree, distributors) to which this margin relates remained high, relatively to pre-War standards, during the whole post-War period. In 1929, at the peak of the expansion of this period, the average per unit price of raw producers' goods was 31 per cent above the 1913 average; the average per unit price of manufactured goods was 52 per cent higher. In comparison with these wide differences the slight narrowing of the margin between 1922 and 1929 is not impressive. The post-War decade, it appears from this evidence, was marked by high prices for the services covered by this basic differential.[8] It is to be expected that such a change would be paralleled by notable shifts in the real incomes and in the relative economic status of different economic groups.

Measurements based upon a threefold division of commodities, which includes a representative group of semi-finished goods as well as raw materials and finished commodities, suggest that this widening of the manufacturing differential was not universal, in fabricational processes. Thus, while raw producers' goods rose 33 per cent between 1913 and 1929, and all finished goods rose 54 per cent, the group of semi-finished goods advanced only 28 per cent in

---

[8] The general relations between the price index numbers for raw producers' goods and manufactured goods are not altered when a broader pre-War base is used:

	1909–1913	1922	1929
Producers' goods, raw	100	127	132
All processed goods	100	158	155

THE PRE-RECESSION SITUATION

price.[9] These measurements indicate that the costs that had risen, and that dominate the general index numbers previously cited, were those relating to the later stages of the manufacturing process, rather than to the simpler manufacturing processes that intervene between raw and semi-finished stages.

Further aspects of the change prior to 1929 in the major differential between prices of raw and processed goods must be studied, and possible reasons for it sought, in a more detailed examination of price differences and manufacturing costs. In the following summary we distinguish three groups of producers' raw materials and corresponding classes of manufactured goods.

	1922	1929	1913	1922	1929
Crops, raw, producers'	100	107	100	127	136
Crops, processed	100	97	100	146	142
Animal products, raw, producers'	100	108	100	130	140
Animal products, processed	100	110	100	150	165
Minerals, raw, producers'	100	97	100	140	135
Minerals, processed	100	95	100	159	151
Metals, raw, producers'	100	106	100	121	128
Metals, processed	100	108	100	151	164

The manufacturer's margin in the fabrication of farm crops appears to have been reduced rather substantially be-

---

[9] Following are the index numbers of wholesale prices for these three commodity groups. The entries in this table, it should be noted, do not relate to identical commodities at three different productive stages. Indeed, many classes of goods included in the 'raw' and 'finished' groups are not included in the 'semi-finished' group. But the three sets of index numbers may be taken to be generally representative of three successive stages of production.

	NO. OF COMMODITIES	1913	1922	1929
Producers' goods, raw	90	100	129	133
Producers' goods, semi-finished	47	100	134	128
All finished goods	319	100	156	154

tween 1922 and 1929. No significant change occurred in the other two main groups. The measurements on the pre-War base give a different picture. The manufacturing differential was distinctly wider in 1929 than in 1913 for animal products, appreciably greater among mineral products, and slightly greater for farm crops. In the subgroup metals a rise of but 28 per cent in the prices of raw materials subject to processing was accompanied by an advance of 64 per cent in the prices of manufactured goods. Our search for groups exercising preponderant influence upon the major differential leads us, then, to two important commodity groups—animal products and metals. In the fabrication of these goods, apparently, the advance in costs between 1913 and 1929 was greater than the rise in prices of raw materials, and of commodities in general.

The part played by fabrication costs in the price changes of the pre-recession period is strikingly revealed by a series of index numbers of price changes among manufactured

GROUP	NO. OF COMMODITIES	1922	1929	1913	1922	1929
A	99	100	108	100	129	140
B	157	100	96	100	156	149
C	87	100	95	100	185	175

goods, classified according to the degree of fabrication through which they have passed.[10] Group A is made up of

[10] Total costs of fabrication, including profits, are defined by the figures on 'value added by manufacture' in Census compilations. The percentage relations of fabrication costs to total value of product, upon which the present classification rests, are based upon figures for 1925. This is true also of the figures relating to wages and total value of product, upon which the classification in the next table is based. Some changes occur, of course, from year to year but these changes are not such as materially to affect the present classifications.

The price quotations used in constructing these index numbers are those compiled by the U. S. Bureau of Labor Statistics. The data used in the classification of commodities are drawn from the Census of Manufactures.

THE PRE-RECESSION SITUATION 51

commodities for which fabrication costs constitute less than 25 per cent of the total value of product, group B those for which fabrication costs constitute from 25 to 50 per cent of total value of product, and group C those for which fabrication costs are 50 per cent or more of total value of product. From 1922 to 1929 slightly fabricated materials (group A) increased in price, more heavily fabricated goods declined. But this movement must be interpreted with reference to the situation in 1922. Here we find a definite relationship, slightly fabricated goods being lowest in price, relatively to 1913, more highly fabricated goods standing next in order, with most heavily fabricated goods far above the other two classes. These differences had been reduced by 1929, but the same general relations persisted. As against a relative of 140 (1913 base) for slightly fabricated goods, we have 175 for the highly fabricated articles in group C. These clear progressions, prevailing in 1929 as well as in 1922, give unmistakable evidence of the part played by manufacturing costs (including profits) in shaping post-War price differences.[11]

If we base our classification upon wages expended in the manufacturing process, instead of upon all fabrication costs, similar conclusions emerge. Below are given index numbers of wholesale prices for three groups of commodities, those for which manufacturing wages constitute less than 10 per cent of the total value of product (group D), those for which they make up from 10 to 25 per cent of total value of prod-

---

[11] We should avoid the implication that the chain of causal relations necessarily runs from higher fabricational costs to higher selling prices. In general, when the level of prices is rising, it is probably true that conditions in the markets for finished products allow higher fabricational costs to be incurred and higher profits to be paid. (Even at such a time, of course, the force of competition may prevent a rise in the fabricational margin.) When the level of prices is falling, the active factor in expanding the fabricational margin (relatively to general prices) is more likely to be found on the cost side. Overhead and labor costs are less flexible than material costs when business conditions necessitate a downward adjustment of prices and costs.

uct (group E), and those for which they make up 25 per cent or more of the total value of product (group F). In 1922

GROUP	NO. OF COMMODITIES	1922	1929	1913	1922	1929
D	123	100	106	100	131	138
E	139	100	94	100	161	152
F	81	100	96	100	187	180

goods in group D stood only 31 per cent higher in price than in 1913; goods in group F stood 87 per cent higher. Here is a striking difference. By 1929 the discrepancy had been reduced, but we still find a definite progression; those goods for which wages were a relatively small item in total value were lowest in relative price, while goods with relatively high labor costs were highest.

We have noted, in using index numbers relating to the prices of specific classes of goods at different stages of the productive-distributive process, that precisely the same commodities are not necessarily represented at these different stages. More exact (though more limited) comparisons are possible if we deal with the prices of identical commodities at different productive stages. Index numbers derived from such prices, which are given in Appendix V, show conflicting movements between 1922 and 1929, in respect of the fabricational margin. More significant for the immediate purpose are index numbers on the 1913 base. With only three exceptions in the entire list of eighteen groups of related commodities, the relative margins between the prices of primary products and of more highly processed goods were distinctly wider in 1929 than in 1913. The long-standing pre-War tendency towards a narrowing of this differential was clearly reversed, if we take account of the net change over this sixteen-year period.

FABRICATION COSTS

Some limitations attach to a study of price differentials through the comparison of price movements at different manufacturing or distributive stages. Production costs may vary with changing industrial productivity; the degree of fabrication may vary; the share of overhead costs allocated to each unit of manufactured output may vary markedly with changes in the volume of production. We may approach the same subject from a different direction, and avoid certain of the more important of these sources of possible error, by tracing changes in the costs and selling prices of American manufacturing industries.[12] As in the earlier account we devote our attention to the situation in 1929 and to the changes occurring during the years of post-War expansion and the longer period dating from 1914.

INDEX NUMBERS MEASURING CHANGES IN MATERIAL COSTS, SELLING PRICE AND FABRICATION COSTS, MANUFACTURING INDUSTRIES OF THE UNITED STATES

(All measurements relate to average price and cost changes per unit of manufactured product.)

	1923	1929	1914	1923	1929
Selling price	100	91	100	159	145
Cost of materials	100	89	100	153	136
Fabrication costs, plus profits	100	95	100	174	166
Labor costs	100	86	100	182	157
Overhead, plus profits	100	102	100	168	172

These records reflect changes of the same general character as those defined by the measurements already reviewed. Between 1923 and 1929 material costs (which here include

[12] The technical methods employed in deriving these measurements are described in *Economic Tendencies in the United States*. The measurements are derived from compilations of the Census of Manufactures, and are thus available only for Census years.

the costs of semi-manufactured goods) dropped, the selling prices of manufactured goods declined, and fabrication costs declined, though by a smaller amount. In the present analysis we may distinguish two elements of fabrication costs, labor costs and a composite of overhead costs plus profits. The decline in fabrication costs during the period of post-War expansion appears to have been the resultant of two conflicting movements—a substantial drop (14 per cent) in labor costs, a small advance (2 per cent) in overhead costs plus profits. In interpreting these movements we should recall that these years were marked by the steadily increasing mechanization of industry, and that this process tended to lower labor costs and to increase overhead costs. The capital funds at the disposal of manufacturing corporations were increasing rapidly, and if mechanization had proceeded at an equal rate the addition to current overhead charges would have been substantial. A definite tendency in this direction undoubtedly prevailed.

For a true conception of the 1929 situation a longer perspective is required. If we look back to 1914 we find that the present evidence clearly substantiates that of the earlier sections. Over the fifteen years 1914–29 the cost of materials (including semi-finished goods), per unit of manufactured product, increased 36 per cent; the selling prices of finished products advanced 45 per cent; fabrication costs, plus profits, increased no less than 66 per cent. The services of fabrication agents were definitely more expensive in 1929, by an amount materially exceeding the rise in the general price level. The two constituent items of fabrication costs both advanced more than the average selling price of manufactured products. The rise in overhead costs plus profits was the greater.[13]

---

[13] These index numbers, based upon a larger group of industries, differ somewhat from those cited in *Economic Tendencies*.

THE PRE-RECESSION SITUATION

FIGURE 5

CHANGES IN AVERAGE SELLING PRICE, COST OF MATERIALS AND ELEMENTS OF FABRICATION COSTS PLUS PROFITS, PER UNIT OF PRODUCT, 1914–1929

MANUFACTURING INDUSTRIES OF THE UNITED STATES

(Percentage deviations from 1914 level, in dollars of constant purchasing power at wholesale)

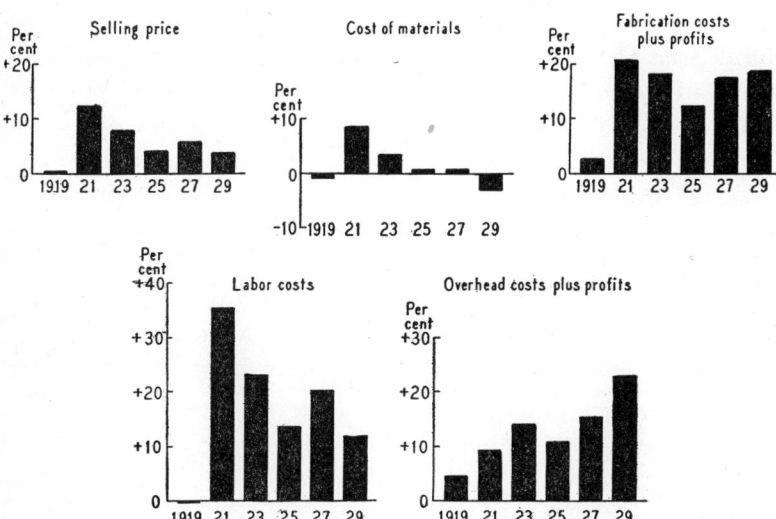

These general movements are shown graphically, in dollars of constant purchasing power at wholesale, in Figure 5. Supporting data appear in Appendix VI. Here, again, qualitative factors cloud the interpretation of these results. The particular 'price' that is defined by fabrication costs, per unit of product, does not relate to a standard and unchanging economic good, especially over periods a decade or more in length. As for the changes from 1914 to 1929, a detailed study of the record suggests that several important factors contributed to the notable widening of the fabricational margin we have observed. Real advances in fabricational costs, in excess of the concurrent increases in selling prices, occurred among numerous industries turning out standardized products. There is good evidence (other than the statistical data here cited) that manufacturing labor and ownership were in positions of strategic advantage, after the World War, in their relations with producers of raw materials, and that their rewards increased correspondingly. But it is also true that the degree of fabrication to which materials of manufacture were subjected was increasing. In 1929 the actual physical contribution of fabricators to the average product of manufacture was greater than in 1914. Refinement and improvement of fabrication in the making of machine products, elaboration of fabrication in the production of food products and in their preparation for the market, were characteristic of this period. This qualitative change was unquestionably a factor in the widening of the fabricational margin that was so distinctive a feature of the years between 1914 and 1929, intensifying the influence of a substantial real rise in the price paid for the services of fabricators.[14]

The fifteen years prior to the recession of 1929 were marked by an exceptionally rapid advance in the output of durable goods, both capital equipment and durable consumers' goods. The production of durable goods increased 112 per cent, as compared with increases of 63 per cent for semi-durable goods and 71 per cent for perishable commodities. (Each reference applies to the output of manufactured goods. The measurements given are based upon index numbers constructed by the National Bureau of Economic Research.) Examination of index numbers relating to the va-

---

[14] In certain cases in which the degree of monopolistic or semi-monopolistic control was increased during this period the widening of the differential between material costs and final selling price may be attributed to this control, rather than to an increase in fabricational costs proper.

rious elements of production cost, for these three groups of manufactured goods, reveals substantial equality in respect of changes in material costs, between 1914 and 1929. The chief differences appear in the movements of labor costs (up 69 per cent for semi-durable goods, 54 per cent for perishable goods and 49 per cent for durable goods) and overhead costs plus profits (up 76 per cent for semi-durable goods, 75 per cent for durable goods and 66 per cent for perishable goods). The very considerable rise in overhead costs plus profits for durable and semi-durable goods is notable, the more so because of the great increase over this period in the volume of durable goods produced. Indeed, such charges for durable goods had increased no less than 13 per cent per unit of output during the period of rapid industrial expansion between 1923 and 1929. Heavier overhead charges, in the broad sense in which that term is here used, were an important element in the maintenance of a high fabricational margin during the post-War period.

Prices of Capital Equipment and Consumption Goods

In distinguishing between the prices of goods for capital equipment and of articles intended for direct human consumption or use we are setting off two major fields of economic activity. Processes of investment and of consumption, processes relating to the building up of the instruments of production and processes directed towards the satisfaction of immediate human wants, are conditioned by these prices. Proper coordination of these two central types of activity is essential to the maintenance of order in our economic life.

In a comparison of price changes among these classes of commodities we should use the prices of finished goods only. For our interest lies now not in the margin representing fabricational or distributional costs, but in the relative costs of capital goods, finished and ready to perform their instrumental role in production, and of commodities ready for direct and final consumption. It is these prices of final products that are significant in shaping the courses of investment [15] and of consumption. But we are faced here by deficiencies of data. Available quotations on the finished instruments of production—machinery and equipment of all sorts—are few. As the best approximation to changes in such prices we shall follow changes in the prices of processed goods intended for use as capital equipment or in the construction of such equipment. Since we are interested not in absolute prices but in price changes, the approximation will be reasonably accurate. Price changes among these goods are compared, in the accompanying summary table, with changes in the prices of goods ready for use by final consumers and in the general level of wholesale prices.

	1922	1929	1913	1922	1929
Producers' goods for capital equipment, processed	100	97	100	165	160
Consumers' goods, all	100	104	100	155	160
All commodities	100	100	100	148	148

Between 1922 and 1929 prices of these two types of goods, both representing terminal stages of the productive-distributive process, diverged somewhat; goods for capital equipment fell slightly in price, consumers' goods rose. But over the longer stretch of years between 1913 and 1929 the two groups moved upward by the same relative amount—60 per cent, as compared with an advance of 48 per cent in the general price level. The high 1929 prices of both these classes stand in marked contrast to the very low prices of

---

[15] High prices of capital goods may, of course, be counter-balanced by low interest rates. Moreover, high prospective returns may outweigh high current costs of construction. These factors in the problem of investment and of capital goods creation are not discussed at this point.

those producers' goods which are intended for human consumption, after fabrication. (The average price of such goods, in 1929, was only 29 per cent above the 1913 average.) The wide margin between these unfinished goods and goods ready for consumption has been discussed in an earlier section.[16] Equally striking is the contrast between the low prices paid by producers for goods to be fabricated and the high prices paid for goods entering into capital equipment. On the operating side price relations were very favorable indeed to manufacturing profits. But on the investment side the situation was less pleasing. Manufacturers reached the end of the prosperous period of the 1920's with a large volume of new capital equipment, much of it constructed under conditions of exceptionally high cost. The full weight of this burden was not felt while activity remained at high levels, but after 1929 these capitalized costs became a major factor in the problem of readjustment.[17]

[16] The group of consumers' goods, the prices of which are given here, includes both raw and processed goods, although it is more heavily weighted with the latter. These two subdivisions followed different courses between 1922 and 1929. The one group of raw materials that remained relatively high in price during this post-War period, and ended the period in a position of marked price advantage, was composed of goods ready for final consumption in a raw state.

	1913	*1922*	*1929*
Consumers' goods, raw	100	154	175
Consumers' goods, processed	100	155	157

[17] Construction costs enter into the production of both capital equipment and durable consumers' goods (residences). In the following table the *Engineering News-Record's* index of construction costs, which includes wage rates of labor engaged in the building industries as well as prices of building materials, is contrasted with general wholesale prices. Costs of construction were high in 1922, some 18 per cent above wholesale prices (on the 1913 base). During the seven years following wholesale prices showed no net change, but construction costs rose to a level 40 per cent above that of

In the existence of a plateau of high prices for goods ready for use, whether by final consumers or in an instrumental way by producers, we have a very significant feature of the post-War decade. Such a condition places obvious difficulties in the way of continued movement of goods, in customary volume and in customary channels. It involves a transference of purchasing power to fabricators, a reduction in the purchasing power of primary producers and of those ultimate users (consumers and industrial users of equipment) who do not profit from the enlarged fabricational margin. Deficiencies in the aggregate purchasing power of these groups may, of course, be temporarily filled if new sources of credit (such as consumer credit) are being tapped, or if other elements of income (such as speculative profits) are swelled. It is possible, too, that equilibrium within the industrial structure may be re-attained, in the face of such a price situation, after changes in the division of national income and in the make-up of the aggregate volume of goods marketed. But a condition of the first sort (a filling of the voids in the purchasing power of adversely affected groups) would seem to be necessarily temporary, while a change of the second type (a permanent alteration in the division of aggregate purchasing power) would involve very considerable economic and social changes, if substantial price shifts were to persist. These considerations will concern us when we trace the developments of the recession that began in 1929, and of the succeeding period of recovery.

wholesale prices. Here was an important additional factor contributing to high capital costs and to high costs of consumers' goods.

	1922	1929	1913	1922	1929
Construction costs	100	119	100	174	207
Wholesale prices	100	100	100	148	148

THE PRE-RECESSION SITUATION

Post-War Price Schism

There is an obvious relation between the various price phenomena described in the preceding pages. Relatively low prices of primary products and high prices of manufactured goods intended for human consumption and for use in capital equipment are concomitants of a wide fabricational margin. The evidence reviewed indicates that in the United States, prior to the recession of 1929, the margin between the prices of raw industrial materials and of manufactured goods was distinctly wider than in pre-War years. The statistical data show that this condition became pronounced, for the first time, between 1919 and 1922, although some relative weakness in raw materials developed between 1917 and 1919.[18] The gap then opened between the prices of finished goods and of raw materials intended for fabrication persisted, in the main, during the entire decade of the 'twenties. In certain industrial fields the gap was narrowed, and, indeed, in some fields no such gap existed, but for manufacturing industries in general the fabricational margin that prevailed in 1929 was significantly wider than before the War.

[18] The major shift between 1917 and 1922 may be traced in the following index numbers of wholesale prices:

	1913	1917	1918	1919	1920	1921	1922
Producers' goods, raw	100	180	194	195	201	118	127
All processed goods	100	169	198	206	240	163	155

Pertinent, also, are data showing the relations between changes in the cost of materials and in fabrication costs, per unit of product, in manufacturing industries:

	1914	1919	1921	1923
Cost of materials	100	202	156	153
Fabrication costs	100	209	173	174

(Costs of materials, as reported in the Census of Manufactures, include some fabrication costs, since semi-finished goods constitute 'materials' for many producers.)

The persistence of this margin constitutes one of the most striking features of the post-War economic situation. It is notable, for one thing, because its existence represents a reversal of tendencies that had prevailed in this country for many years prior to the War. The history of the quarter century prior to the War is a history of a steady cheapening of fabricated products in terms of raw materials, a steady reduction in the cost of the services of manufacturing industries. The margin is notable, again, because it was not solely a domestic phenomenon. The post-War world was marked by a wide disparity, relatively to pre-War standards, between the prices of raw materials and of manufactured goods. The terms of exchange between raw material producing areas (with certain exceptions) and manufacturing areas were altered, by the events of 1914–22, to the marked disadvantage of the former. There developed, to a degree not equaled in modern times, a price schism between raw material producing areas and manufacturing areas that materially impeded the ordinary processes of trade. Some of the economic consequences and accompaniments of this schism—depleted purchasing power and a forced draught to production in raw material producing areas, reduced volume of trade and consequent unemployment in industrial areas, uneconomic movements of short- and long-term loans—have been outstanding features of the post-War world situation.

It is desirable that we briefly summarize the factors that appear to have contributed to the development of this margin and to its persistence during the post-War decade, in direct reversal of earlier tendencies. In doing so we shall be speaking primarily of the domestic situation in the United States although certain world conditions bear upon it.

The sharp widening of the fabricational margin occurred in the price recession of 1920–21. As factors affecting this movement we may note the following:

THE PRE-RECESSION SITUATION

a. The usual sensitiveness of raw material prices to the forces of economic recession, and the greater stability of the prices of finished goods. The reasons for this difference are many, including the inelasticity of demand for many primary products, the inability of primary producers to limit supply in the face of falling demand (contrasted with the high degree of control exerted over the output of most fabricated products) and the greater importance of relatively fixed costs in the production of manufactured goods.

b. The accentuation of this sensitiveness of raw material prices by an exceptionally weak position at the end of the War. A forced draught had been applied during the War to the production of raw materials throughout the world. Indeed, as we have already noted, the peak of raw material prices in the United States in relation to general prices occurred in 1917. Thereafter the prices of manufactured goods rose more sharply. This relative weakness, appearing prior to the peak of the War-time boom, is highly significant. The ending of the War left large stocks on hand, and the expansion of production by the warring countries, with the end of the fighting, intensified these difficulties.

c. The customary lag of wage rates and overhead charges, at a time of price recession. Here, again, the usual tendency towards a relative increase in fabricational costs, as a result of this lag, was accentuated by the magnitude and intensity of the general price decline. During the preceding advance of prices, from 1914 to 1920, labor shortage and War-time demands had stimulated a sharp rise in wage rates. Much of this gain was held during the sharp break of prices in 1920 and 1921.

d. The violence of the first post-War price recession and its brief duration, relatively to the magnitude of the change in the price level. In 1920–21 the average level of wholesale prices dropped 45 per cent in twenty months. This was almost three times the intensity (in rate of decline per month) of the 1929–33 decline and four times the intensity of the 1873–79 price drop. Under these conditions a rapid widening of the margin between flexible and inflexible prices was inevitable. Time was not given for adaptation and adjustment. Subsequent readjustment was, of course, to be expected, barring the presence of factors tending to perpetuate the conditions that developed during the recession.

World conditions of supply and demand, the customary behavior of the prices of different classes of goods, the relatively strong position of agents of fabrication in 1920–21 and the intensity of the drop in general prices all contributed to the initial widening of the fabricational margin, and to the consequent depressing of raw material prices and the elevation (relatively) of the prices of finished goods. But the emergence of the margin, as a cyclical phenomenon, was in accord with experience. What was altogether exceptional was the persistence of these conditions during the succeeding eight years of economic expansion and of rapidly rising productivity in manufacturing industries. We list below certain factors that appear to have played important roles in these years:

a. The continued weak position of primary producers. The effects of the War-time stimulus to the output of raw materials did not pass over night. Large supplies from new sources, combined with the re-entry of producers in the former combatant countries, maintained price weakness among raw materials.[19]

Actual cost reductions in the production of certain raw materials, as a result of gains in productivity, served also to lower prices. This was a factor of considerable importance in the output of certain minerals and of some farm products. The post-War years witnessed considerable improvement in technical methods of mineral extraction and of agricultural production. Price declines reflecting cost reductions do not necessarily involve reduc-

---

[19] We should note, however, that for raw materials in general "the effects of war stocks and war expansion . . . had worn off before 1929" (Copeland, *loc. cit.*, p. 44). We must look, in the main, to other conditions for an explanation of the persistent post-War margin.

tion of incomes. However, such cost reductions are never effected uniformly, by all producers. Lowered costs by some, particularly by large producers, may change the location of the margin of production, forcing to the margin, or beyond it, producers formerly comfortably within it. In such an industry as farming, where complete retirement from production is difficult, this condition may cause real and persistent distress.

b. The persistence of a price level some 35 per cent below that of 1920. Had prices moved upwards again, to the approximate pre-recession level, wage costs and overhead costs in manufacturing industries would probably have been reduced, relatively, and earlier relationships with prices in general approximated. The customary lag of such costs would have contributed to this readjustment. But the gains scored by the agents of fabrication during recession were consolidated, in large part, because of the succeeding stability of prices at a level close to that reached in the 1921 depression.

c. The economic strength of industrial labor. The prolonged expansion that followed the first post-War depression began just when immigration restriction was curtailing the supply of industrial labor, particularly unskilled labor. Thus the bargaining position of labor was strong in these early years of expansion, and this circumstance contributed to the maintenance of the earlier gains in real wage rates. Related to this, but arising from other conditions as well, were the high living costs and high living standards of industrial labor after the War. There are, of course, circular relations here. Living standards were high, in part, because a wide manufacturing differential made it possible for high wages to be paid. But there is something more to it than this. The high standards gained during the War tended to perpetuate themselves. Wage earners, and all other consuming groups, cling tenaciously to gains in standards of living. This became a positive factor, tending to maintain the wide differential of the early post-War years.

d. The possible increase in distributional costs. During the decade of the 'twenties national advertising increased rapidly and other forms of selling pressure received new emphasis. These costs were reflected in the prices paid by final consumers. We cannot say whether or no this selling pressure actually increased volume of sales sufficiently to reduce distributional costs per unit of product. They may well have done so in some industries. Where advertising is largely competitive, drawing business from other producers instead of promoting an increase in aggregate sales, increased advertising would add to the average per unit cost of goods sold. Some such addition was probably made during the expansion of the 1920's. Certainly the persistence of a high level of prices to consumers does not indicate that the great expansion of advertising in these years served to lower the living costs of the population at large.

e. Quality changes, representing actual increases in the degree of fabrication to which the materials of manufacture were subject. In 1929 (and in 1933) the actual physical services of fabricators constituted a larger proportion of the bundle of materials and services bought by the final consumer than in 1914. Improvements in the quality of mechanical goods and the grading and packaging of food products are obvious examples of changes of this type. Perhaps some of this extra service, as in the making of ornate containers, was not a real gain to the consumer. Nevertheless, the service was rendered and a higher fabricational margin was required to pay for it. This emphasis on quality changes, real or apparent, and the desire to give specific products special appeal through refinements of fabrication, were probably more characteristic of the years since 1914 than of the period before. If so, they help to explain the curious reversal in the relative trends of prices of raw materials and of manufactured goods that occurred after 1914.

f. Fortuitous additions to the purchasing power of consumers. It was not enough to ensure the persistence of relatively high rewards to fabricators that their bargaining position should be strong, or that the position of primary producers should be weak. It was necessary that the buyers of finished products be able to purchase, in quantity, at the relatively high price level prevailing for such goods. Low returns to primary producers, who constitute an important element of the total body of consumers, would tend to lower the aggregate income and purchasing power of consumers. High returns to fabricators would tend, of course, to maintain such purchasing power, but fabricators constitute only one restricted part of the total consuming group. Something more than the boot straps of fabricators was needed to maintain the buying power of consumers at large at levels necessary to ensure the marketing of an expanding volume of consumers' goods at post-War prices. Three circumstances contributed to the enhancement of consumer purchasing power during the period of expansion that began in 1921–22. Some of the proceeds of heavy foreign loans served, directly or indirectly, to finance the purchase of consumers' goods in the United States. Many of the profits realized from speculative operations in real estate and securities found the same outlet. Not least important was the swelling of consumer purchasing power by the tapping of the new reservoirs of credit—consumer credit—through which installment selling was financed. During the expansion of such credit the additions to the total volume outstanding represented net increases in the current buying power of consumers.[20] All these

[20] These sums, while not of great magnitude in any one year, relatively to total national income, constituted a steady addition to the current income of consumers during the decade preceding the recession. The following table (based upon estimates given in Lough and Gainsbrugh, *High-Level Consumption*, McGraw-Hill, 1935, p. 312) indicates the magnitude of the annual additions to consumer income between 1919 and 1929. The debts of which account has been taken in preparing this table include those arising from purchases and from personal loans. All sums are in millions of dollars.

	TOTAL SHORT-TERM CONSUMER DEBTS	ANNUAL CHANGE IN TOTAL CONSUMER DEBTS	CHANGE IN CARRYING CHARGES	NET CHANGE IN CONSUMER PURCHASING POWER FROM PRECEDING YEAR
1919	5443			
1920	6006	+563	+ 1	+562
1921	6118	+112	+78	+ 34
1922	6053	− 65	−31	− 34
1923	6829	+776	+47	+729
1924	7190	+361	+14	+347
1925	7675	+485	+54	+431

(Note 20 concluded on p. 68)

elements were essentially non-recurring. They bolstered the demand for goods during the major expansion of the 'twenties, and supported the price relations we have described. There was no promise in this situation, however, that these price relations would be stable when consumer buying power was again confined to disbursements arising from the normal productive operations of the economy.

g. Favorable conditions for sellers in the markets for capital equipment. Sellers of finished goods for use in capital equipment

(*Note* 20 *concluded*)

	TOTAL SHORT-TERM CONSUMER DEBTS	ANNUAL CHANGE IN TOTAL CONSUMER DEBTS	CHANGE IN CARRYING CHARGES	NET CHANGE IN CONSUMER PURCHASING POWER FROM PRECEDING YEAR
1926	7914	+239	+47	+192
1927	8177	+263	+53	+210
1928	8786	+609	+55	+554
1929	9477	+691	+58	+633

The derivation of the final entries may need a word of explanation. The increment of 563 million dollars from 1919 to 1920 represents new purchasing power placed in the hands of consumers in 1920. However, carrying charges on short-term consumer debts, which had amounted to 384 million dollars in 1919, came to 385 millions in 1920. Thus the net increase in consumer purchasing power from 1919 to 1920 was 563 millions less one million, or 562 million dollars. The figures for other years were similarly derived.

With but one exception, each of these ten years was marked by a net addition (over the preceding year) to consumer buying power, as a result of increasing loans to consumers. In four of the ten years the increase exceeded 500 million dollars. These figures are the more significant if we recall that they represent increases on a continually expanding base.

The above interpretation of the consumer debt figures differs from that given by Lough and Gainsbrugh. These authors deduct the total carrying charges each year from the figures representing annual changes in total short-term consumers' debts. If the changes from one year to the next in the actual sums available to consumers for the purchase of goods are being computed, the Lough-Gainsbrugh procedure involves the assumption that no payments on account of carrying charges were made during the first year. This is obviously faulty. If the amount of consumer debts and annual carrying charges were constant from year to year, there would clearly be no change, from one year to the next, in the sums available to consumers for purchasing goods.

were favored by similar fortunate circumstances during the expansion of the 'twenties. Low rates for capital funds, high profits, which facilitated the growth of corporate surpluses, and a spirit of optimism, which inspired business men to expand their plants and add to equipment without severe scrutiny of costs, stimulated heavy sales of capital equipment. Under the circumstances, relatively high prices for such equipment did not dampen sales.

These, then, were important factors contributing to the creation and persistence of the exceptionally wide post-War margin between the prices of raw materials and manufactured goods and to the high price level of finished goods. It may, indeed, be argued that the persistence of these conditions was due to the incompleteness of the liquidation and readjustment effected between 1920 and 1922. That violent world-wide price recession would be considered a first stage in a necessary process of readjustment; thereafter fortuitous conditions made possible a recovery in the United States before readjustment was completed. But we do not know enough about the conditions essential to economic stability to be sure that this was the case. The relations revealed by a study of post-War prices and their comparison with pre-War relations would not be inconsistent with such an hypothesis, however.

We have noted certain conditions on the operating side which bear upon this post-War price differential. Quality changes, reflecting more intensive fabrication, occurred in many manufacturing industries. Where the finished product thus represented a greater relative contribution on the part of fabricators and increased utility to consumers, some expansion in the manufacturing differential and some rise in the price of the finished goods were to be expected. Yet this cannot be looked upon as the sole or indeed as the chief factor in the widening of the differential. A detailed study, by industries, reveals increased costs of fabrication as a typical post-War condition, prevailing where quality changes are known not to have occurred, as well as where they did occur.

On the other hand, as against increased contributions of fabricators, industrial productivity increased notably during the decade 1919–29. Output per wage earner employed in manufacturing industries increased 15 per cent from 1921 to 1923. This followed a gain of 1 per cent, from 1919 to 1921, and was followed by a gain of 8 per cent, from 1923 to 1925. In part, these gains in productivity were due to heavier capital investment, and the installation of better equipment. But the actual reduction of production costs, it is fair to assume, more than offset the average gain in quality, among manufactured products. That the increase of productivity occurred concurrently with a widening, instead of a contracting, fabricational margin is noteworthy. We shall be concerned at a later point with some economic consequences of enhanced industrial productivity accompanied by a wide fabricational margin.

Purchasing Power of Major Producing Groups, 1929

The significance of changes among the various elements of the price structure is not always readily apparent to the economic agents involved. Of immediate concern to these agents are the shifts in actual command over goods that follow directly upon changes in the relations among prices. We turn now to a brief survey of the changes in the relative status of different economic groups, in respect of aggregate purchasing power prior to 1929. We deal here only with general movements, for the available data do not make possible a high degree of accuracy in the measurement of purchasing power changes.

Three factors affect the direction and degree of change in

the aggregate purchasing power of a given economic group over a stated period: changes in the average per unit price of its products (or services), changes in the quantity produced and sold, and changes in the average price of the commodities and services for which its money income is expended. Obviously, records of these changes are not to be had for all important economic groups. Indeed, they are not available, in detail and with a high degree of accuracy, for any economic group. For a few major groups, however, we may approximate the changes in these factors with sufficient accuracy to obtain fairly reliable indications of the changes in their aggregate purchasing power. In picturing the general situation prevailing in 1929 we take 1914 as a standard of reference.

In 1929 the aggregate physical volume of production in the United States (excluding construction) was approximately 64 per cent greater than in 1914. If the net gains of these fifteen years had been divided equally among all producing groups an increase of this amount would have been recorded in the total volume of goods commanded by each group, that is, in its aggregate purchasing power, as that term is here used. Actually, of course, no such equality is found. Following is a summary of the changes among certain important producing groups:

PRODUCERS OF RAW MATERIALS

Farmers

Aggregate purchasing power in 1929 some 20 per cent greater than in 1914, in wholesale markets, 10 per cent greater in the markets in which farmers actually spent their money. The advance in farmers' purchasing power was due primarily to increased farm output, which was 11 per cent greater in 1929 than in 1914. The per unit purchasing power of farm products advanced in wholesale markets, declined somewhat in the markets in which farmers buy.

72   PRICES IN RECESSION AND RECOVERY

Producers of raw mineral products

Aggregate purchasing power in wholesale markets in 1929 approximately twice that of 1914. This gain was the net resultant of an increase of about 70 per cent in volume of production and of about 20 per cent in the purchasing power of each unit produced.

Producers of raw forest products

Aggregate purchasing power in wholesale markets in 1929 about 18 per cent greater than in 1914. This gain was the net resultant of a drop of some 6 per cent in number of units produced, an advance of about 25 per cent in average purchasing power per unit.

AGENTS OF FABRICATION

All agents

Aggregate purchasing power of all agents of fabrication (i.e., those whose rewards are secured from the differential between costs of materials to manufacturers and the selling price of manufactured goods) in 1929 in wholesale markets approximately 120 per cent greater than in 1914. This gain resulted from an increase in output of some 84 per cent and in per unit purchasing power of about 20 per cent.

Manufacturing labor

Aggregate purchasing power in 1929 about 71 per cent greater than in 1914, owing chiefly to an increase of 77 per cent in the physical output of manufacturing labor. The actual purchasing power of the pay received for each unit of goods produced declined about 8 per cent, with reference to the items included in the budget of the average industrial worker. (If purchasing power changes in wholesale markets be measured, for comparison with similar measurements for other groups, we have advances of 100 per cent in aggregate purchasing power, 12 per cent in per unit purchasing power.) The change in rewards per unit of goods produced is to be interpreted with reference to a gain of approximately 49 per cent in output

THE PRE-RECESSION SITUATION

per wage earner in manufacturing industries between 1914 and 1929.

Ownership and management in manufacturing industries
Aggregate purchasing power in wholesale markets in 1929 approximately 135 per cent greater than in 1914. The gain was due to an increase in output of about 90 per cent, in per unit purchasing power of approximately 23 per cent.[21]

These several estimates of changes in the aggregate purchasing power of important producing groups are not perfectly comparable, and indeed, in default of accurate index numbers of the prices prevailing in the markets in which these groups spend their money incomes, it is impossible to secure comparable measurements. With this important qualification, we may use these measurements as indications of certain major changes in the distribution of purchasing power between 1914 and 1929. We should note, in so using them, that we do not have here measurements of net income distribution, either personal or by functional groups. No account is taken of the deductions from gross returns necessary for the determination of net incomes, nor is attention given to changes in amount of investment or in the numbers of income recipients in the several groups named. But as indexes of movements over a fifteen-year period in certain broad divisions of gross income, in physical terms, the measurements throw light on important phases of economic change.

Among the three major groups, farmers, mineral extractors and those engaged in manufacture, the last-mentioned

---

[21] See *Economic Tendencies in the United States*, pp. 505–13, for an explanation of the procedure employed in deriving these measurements, and for a fuller explanation of their significance. Because of revisions in the original sources the present measurements differ in some respects from those in *Economic Tendencies*.

scored the major gain. With a total output some 80 per cent greater than in 1914, their aggregate physical rewards more than doubled. Mineral producers gained only slightly less, while the aggregate gains of farmers approximated 10 per cent. Among manufacturing producers labor gained about 70 per cent, in aggregate purchasing power; the residual share going to ownership and management advanced about 135 per cent.

These figures represent the resultants of mixed forces, indistinguishably blended. In part they reflect cyclical changes in the real incomes of farmers, mineral producers, manufacturing labor, and owners and investors in manufacturing enterprises. In part they define deep-seated and enduring shifts in the relative importance of these elements of the national economy. The expansion of manufacturing plant with the growing industrialization of the country would of itself lead to permanent alterations in the division of aggregate physical output among producing groups. Similar fundamental changes affected other groups.

We should note the particularly striking gains of those engaged in manufacturing, which accompanied a notable increase in industrial productivity. The advance in output per worker between 1914 and 1929 was about 49 per cent; in the ten years 1919–29 it exceeded 40 per cent. Over the manufacturing field as a whole this striking increase in efficiency was not reflected in lower selling prices. The immediate benefits accrued to agents of fabrication—labor, management, ownership, and the service agencies whose compensation is included in the 'value added' by manufacture. Some of the economic consequences of the increase in productivity and the division of the resulting gains during the post-War decade will concern us at a later point, after the record of the recession and the recovery has been surveyed.

The World Price Structure in 1929

The function performed within national boundaries by a domestic price structure is performed for the world economy by a world-wide system of related prices. The flow of raw materials from colonial to industrial areas, the reverse movement of manufactured goods, the interchange of manufactured goods among industrial nations are all directed with reference to price relations. More broadly, the productive activities of different economies are coordinated and capital movements and short-term lending are directed in terms of these same relations. Through this mechanism the elements of production costs are in some degree controlled and the various parts of the world economy are held in some sort of equilibrium.

But the system of world prices is not a perfect agency for the coordination of international economic processes. In even greater degree than the domestic structure it is subject to the play of disturbing forces, which prevent the proper performance of the functions suggested. These disturbing forces were especially strong between 1914 and 1929; as a result the world price system of 1929 differed from that of 1914 not only in internal structure but, as well, in its efficiency as a coordinating agent.

The price structure of 1914 constituted a fairly satisfactory instrument for the regulation of international economic activities. The gold standard extended over the industrial world, and its operation held international price movements in reasonable balance. The general price advance of the twenty years preceding had affected different domestic price structures in much the same way. Differences in standards of living and in production costs prevailed, of course, and tariff barriers existed. In part, these differences were compensated by corresponding differences in industrial productivity; to the degree that this was not true there had been adaptation to them over the several decades of fairly undisturbed relations that had previously prevailed. After 1914, however, a number of forces were at work, tending to alter price relations and to affect the efficiency of the world price system. The factors and conditions of major importance to an understanding of the 1929 structure of world prices may be discussed under three general headings.

ECONOMIC NON-INTERCOURSE AND THE WORLD PRICE STRUCTURE

From 1914 to 1918 the War set barriers to free economic intercourse between important elements of the world economy. Even where no definite barriers were set up, the channels and the character of trade were so fundamentally altered by the exigencies of war as substantially to modify the economic relations of certain countries and, in effect, to isolate important elements of their economic life, so far as international competition was concerned. Severe currency disturbances, some of which persisted for seven or eight years after the Armistice, combined with the general disruption of the gold standard to prolong this period of non-intercourse, so that in all over a decade passed before the way was open to the resumption of earlier relations among important trading countries. During this period the usual checks to the continuance of divergent tendencies among different elements of the world economy were inoperative. The continual adjustments customarily made among economies closely bound by trade and financial ties were prevented, and extreme divergencies persisted. The full force of these accumulated results of non-intercourse was felt when trading relations were again established. The different elements of the world economy were no longer in gear, as parts of a working

THE PRE-RECESSION SITUATION 77

world order. Economic disharmonies and inconsistencies abounded.

It would be far from accurate to say that all these disharmonies originated in disparate price changes. For the origins of the unbalanced and discrepant conditions that appeared during the era of non-intercourse were to be found, in the main, in the general economic systems of the various nations. Trade was over-developed in one region, in relation to the needs of a reconstructed world order; population was excessive in another, in relation to the world situation that existed when trading relations were generally re-established; production costs in given industries might be entirely out of line with those of competitors, once the period of non-intercourse was terminated. Yet, whether the price structure occupied a primary or secondary place with respect to the origins of these economic discrepancies, it is true that the inequalities, as direct obstacles to the resumption of trade relations, found expression most directly through the price system.

Evidence of such faulty adjustments is especially difficult to obtain. Trade between countries is not conducted on the basis of relations between price levels, as measured by the familiar index numbers of prices. Trade proceeds on the basis of innumerable specific relations among prices, wages and costs of production; these specific relations were broken or distorted during the disturbed years following 1914. Information on these numerous individual relations is not generally available, and we are forced to lean heavily on the less pertinent index numbers. Some conclusions of value may be drawn from their study. Gold prices are used, since international relations are in question.

In measuring the divergence of price levels in different countries between 1913 and 1929 we suffer from lack of perfect comparability of the available measurements. Index numbers differ in respect of content and technical methods of construction. It is probable, however, that the general picture would not be materially changed if fully comparable index numbers were available.

WHOLESALE PRICES IN GOLD, THIRTY COUNTRIES

	INDEX NUMBERS	
	1913	*1929*
Australia	100	166
India (Calcutta)	100[1]	158
Peru	100	156
Japan	100	155
Denmark	100	150
Canada	100	149
Norway	100	149
Dutch East Indies	100	148
New Zealand	100	147
Bulgaria	100[1]	145
Netherlands	100	142
Switzerland	100	141
Sweden	100	140
Indo-China	100	139
Germany	100	137
United States	100	137
Spain	100	136
United Kingdom	100	136
Italy	100	131
France	100	127
Argentina	100	125
Belgium	100[1]	124
Greece	100	121
Latvia	100	120
Chile	100	118
Estonia	100	117
Union of South Africa	100	116
Egypt (Cairo)	100[1]	116
Hungary	100[1]	104
Austria	100[1]	93

SOURCES: League of Nations, *Statistical Year-Book, 1934–1935*, pp. 227–29; Handbook of Foreign Currency and Exchange, U. S. Department of Commerce, Bureau of Foreign and Domestic Commerce, Trade Promotion Series No. 102, Washington, D. C., 1930

[1] 1914=100.

THE PRE-RECESSION SITUATION 79

The differences among wholesale price levels, ranging from a fall of 7 per cent for Austria to a rise of 66 per cent for Australia, are fairly wide, though not excessive in terms of pre-War experience. The single averages do not, of course, convey any accurate picture of the status of the various national price structures. It was within and among the elements of these price structures—among production costs, wages, costs of capital equipment, and all the prices of individual commodities and services entering into international trade— that faulty adjustments prevailed, serving as barriers to free economic intercourse.

DISPARITIES IN PRODUCTION COSTS

In periods not marked by extreme disturbances in international economic relations production costs in different trading countries stand in certain rather definite relationships. Through the play of competition import and export trade is adapted, in respect of content and price, to differing production costs in different countries. The elements of fabrication cost (i.e., wages, interest charges and other overhead expenses, and the related factor of industrial productivity) do not ordinarily suffer violent change, so that trading relations based upon established conditions of cost are not subject to sudden alteration. In the post-War price structure, however, elements of cost, in different producing countries, were widely diverse and their relations were quite different from those existing before the War.

Differences in price levels would be expected to lead to differences of this sort, but many of the inequalities of cost actually prevailing could not be thus explained. For two countries may have identical gold price levels, with reference to a given base, but the internal relations among elements of their domestic price structure may be quite different, as a result of recent inflationary or deflationary movements. Deflation, with the characteristic lagging of wages and of all fixed charges, leaves production costs high, relatively to other elements in the price structure, while inflation, accompanied by the same lags, creates a price structure in which production costs are relatively low. Such cost differences were of particular importance after the stabilization efforts of the middle 'twenties, for the restoration of the gold standard offered wide opportunities for variation in the relation of old and new parities, and such variations were reflected in disparate cost conditions.

Direct information concerning production costs is difficult if not impossible to obtain, for most industrial countries. We may get some evidence on this important point by comparing wholesale prices and living costs in certain countries. These two sets of index numbers are not directly comparable, for they are composed of quite different items, but the relations between them are significant. Living costs, a highly important factor in determining the purchasing power of wages, are directly related to production costs. Where living costs are relatively high, the cost of labor tends to be high; the reverse is true where living costs are low, in relation to a standard prevailing in a base period not too far removed in time. As has been noted, living costs lag behind wholesale prices during periods of changing price levels. They tend, thus, to be relatively high after a deflationary movement of the price level and relatively low after an inflationary movement. Index numbers of wholesale prices and living costs for seven important industrial countries are given in Table 3.

We find a considerable range of difference among these seven countries, with respect to the ratio of living costs to wholesale prices. Czechoslovakia and France stood at the lower end of the scale, as countries with relatively low production costs in 1929, in terms of this standard, while the

TABLE 3

WHOLESALE PRICES AND LIVING COSTS, 1914–1929

SEVEN INDUSTRIAL COUNTRIES

	INDEX NUMBERS WHOLESALE PRICES		INDEX NUMBERS LIVING COSTS		RATIOS OF COST OF LIVING INDEX TO INDEX OF WHOLESALE PRICES, AS RELATIVES	
	1914	*1929*	*1914*	*1929*	*1914*	*1929*
Czechoslovakia	100	913	100	763	100	84
France	100	615	100	556	100	90
Japan	100	175	100	181	100	103
Germany	100[1]	137	100[1]	154	100[1]	112
Italy	100[1]	481	100	545	100[2]	113
United Kingdom	100	136	100	164	100	121
United States	100	140	100	170	100	121

SOURCE: League of Nations, *Statistical Year-Book, 1935–1936*, pp. 239–44.
[1] 1913=100.
[2] Wholesale price index, 1913; living costs index, 1914.

United States and the United Kingdom stood at the upper end. There is no clear division into inflationary and deflationary countries here. The relations between wholesale prices and living costs were affected, of course, by the terms of stabilization, largely completed between 1924 and 1926, as well as by the inflationary or deflationary experiences of the early years of the decade. Tentative and approximate as this ratio is, the range of 50 per cent between the two extremes may be taken to represent a real difference in production costs, relatively to the 1914 situation.[22] Higher efficiency might, of course, make possible the maintenance of higher living costs and living standards, without increasing production costs. But variation in respect of productivity changes over these fifteen years could hardly be as great as the differences indicated.

[22] No assumption is here made that production costs in these countries were equal in 1914. The relations of 1914 were modified, in the degree indicated.

DISPARITIES BETWEEN PRICES OF RAW MATERIALS AND MANUFACTURED GOODS

In discussing the post-War price structure of the United States attention has been called to the disparity, world-wide in scope, between the prices of materials intended for industrial use and the prices of finished goods. Here and there, special conditions made it possible for certain groups of raw material producers to exchange their goods on relatively favorable terms for manufactured products, but in general the post-War status of raw material producers the world over was distinctly less favorable than before the War. Although the situation in this respect was somewhat better in 1929 than in 1921, disparities persisted. Their effects were far reaching, influencing the major economic movements of the period and coloring the whole post-War epoch.

The existence of this disparity has been noted by various observers, and the fact of its persistence beyond the period of the usual cyclical divergence of prices of raw and processed goods has been emphasized. One of its phases is rather strikingly revealed by the measurements in Table 4. For each of twenty-one raw materials, as priced in various world markets, Table 4 defines changes in purchasing power for manufactured goods in three important industrial countries. Thus a bushel of wheat, as quoted in the central world market at Liverpool, had in 1929 a purchasing power for manufactured goods in the United States 12 per cent below that of 1913. The worth of a bushel of wheat in Liverpool in terms of goods exported from the United Kingdom (mainly manufactured goods) was 16 per cent less in 1929 than in 1913. The same commodity had a 1929 value in terms of manufactured goods in Germany 16 per cent less than in 1913. But the table tells its own story. In 1929 only coffee, tobacco and, for certain markets, tea, wool and lead,

THE PRE-RECESSION SITUATION

TABLE 4

CHANGES IN THE PER UNIT PURCHASING POWER OF IMPORTANT RAW MATERIALS, 1913–1929

	PURCHASING POWER OF GIVEN COMMODITY FOR VARIOUS CLASSES OF GOODS							
	FOR MANUFACTURED GOODS, UNITED STATES			FOR EXPORTED GOODS, UNITED KINGDOM			FOR MANUFACTURED GOODS, GERMANY	
	1913	1922	1929	1913	1922	1929	1913	1929
Wheat								
England, Liverpool	100	88	88	100	76	84	100	84
Canada, Winnipeg	100	90	100	100	77	95	100	96
U. S., Chicago	100	81	87	100	69	83	100	84
Australia, Melbourne	100	91	87	100	77	83	100	84
Rice								
France, Marseilles	100	69	66	100	59	63	100	63
U. S., New Orleans	100	75	66	100	64	63	100	64
Sugar								
England, London	100	84	55	100	72	53	100	53
U. S., New York	100	87	72	100	74	68	100	69
Coffee								
Netherlands, Amsterdam	100	69	106	100	59	101	100	102
U. S., New York	100	70	110	100	60	105	100	106
Tea								
England, London	100	84	93	100	80	89	100	90
Netherlands, Amsterdam	100	97	110	100	83	105	100	106
U. S., New York	100	79	85	100	67	81	100	81
Cocoa								
England, London	100	48	51	100	41	48	100	49
Netherlands, Amsterdam	100	88	92	100	75	88	100	89
U. S., New York	100	49	67	100	42	64	100	64
Tobacco								
Netherlands, Amsterdam	100	145	275	100	124	262	100	264
U. S., Louisville	100	105	124	100	90	118	100	119
Lard								
U. S., New York	100	68	72	100	58	69	100	69
Nitrate of Soda								
U. S., New York	100	66	58	100	57	55	100	56
France, Dunkerque	100	77	61	100	66	58	100	59
Cotton								
England, London	100	101	97	100	87	93	100	94
U. S., New Orleans	100	104	97	100	89	92	100	93

TABLE 4 (*cont.*)

CHANGES IN THE PER UNIT PURCHASING POWER OF IMPORTANT RAW MATERIALS, 1913–1929

	PURCHASING POWER OF GIVEN COMMODITY FOR VARIOUS CLASSES OF GOODS							
	FOR MANUFACTURED GOODS, UNITED STATES			FOR EXPORTED GOODS, UNITED KINGDOM			FOR MANUFACTURED GOODS, GERMANY	
	1913	1922	1929	1913	1922	1929	1913	1929
Wool								
England, London	100	122	102	100	105	97	100	98
U. S., Boston	100	142	116	100	122	110	100	112
Australia, Melbourne	100	92	102	100	79	97	100	98
Silk								
U. S., New York	100	128	89	100	110	85	100	86
France, Lyon	100	124	83	100	106	79	100	79
Japan, Yokohama	100	153	90	100	130	86	100	87
Hides, cattle								
England, London	100	66	65	100	56	62	100	62
U. S., Chicago	100	64	61	100	54	58	100	59
Pig iron								
Germany, Essen	100		74	100		71	100	72
England, London	100	91	79	100	78	75	100	76
Copper								
England, London	100	54	73	100	46	69	100	70
Germany, Berlin	100		78	100		75	100	76
U. S.	100	55	76	100	47	73	100	73
Lead								
England, London	100	76	84	100	65	80	100	81
U. S., New York	100	85	102	100	73	97	100	98
Germany, Berlin	100		80	100		76	100	77
France, Paris	100	76	80	100	65	77	100	77
Zinc								
England, London	100	77	72	100	66	69	100	69
U. S., New York	100	68	77	100	58	74	100	74
Germany, Hamburg	100		72	100		68	100	69
France, Paris	100	76	72	100	65	69	100	70
Tin								
England, London	100	46	67	100	40	64	100	64
U. S., New York	100	47	66	100	40	63	100	64
Rubber								
England, London	100	16	18	100	13	17	100	18
U. S., New York	100	14	17	100	12	16	100	16

TABLE 4 (*cont.*)

CHANGES IN THE PER UNIT PURCHASING POWER OF IMPORTANT RAW MATERIALS, 1913–1929

	PURCHASING POWER OF GIVEN COMMODITY FOR VARIOUS CLASSES OF GOODS							
	FOR MANU-FACTURED GOODS, UNITED STATES			FOR EXPORTED GOODS, UNITED KINGDOM			FOR MANUFAC-TURED GOODS, GERMANY	
	1913	*1922*	*1929*	*1913*	*1922*	*1929*	*1913*	*1929*
Newsprint								
Canada, Ottawa	100	103	82	100	88	78	100	79
Sweden	100	89	78	100	76	74	100	75
Woodpulp								
Canada	100	81	87	100	69	83	100	84

SOURCE: The original price series are given in the *Bulletin Mensuel de l'Office Permanent,* Institute International de Statistique, La Haye. The prices have been converted to a gold basis.

had real exchange values, in terms of the products of these three industrial countries, exceeding those of 1913. The real worth, per unit, of each of the other sixteen commodities fell below the 1913 level, far below for some commodities.

If we pass from the records of individual commodity prices to index numbers purporting to measure changes in the average prices of raw and of processed goods, we face difficulties in securing adequate and unambiguous statistics. Satisfactory index numbers of the prices of raw and of processed goods are available for only a few countries, and even these are not designed to meet the purposes of the present inquiry. Thus the indexes of raw material prices usually include raw consumers' goods as well as raw producers' goods, a combination not altogether appropriate to this comparison. However, the records of the prices of raw and manufactured goods in various countries are pertinent and require investigation, even though some reservations must be made with respect to them. The comparison is shown in Table 5.

TABLE 5

INDEX NUMBERS OF WHOLESALE PRICES OF RAW MATERIALS AND MANUFACTURED GOODS IN VARIOUS COUNTRIES, 1913–1929

COUNTRY AND COMMODITY GROUP	1913	1922	1929
Belgium			
Raw materials	100[1]		834
Finished products	100[1]		905
Canada			
Raw and semi-manufactured goods	100	149	153
Fully and chiefly manufactured goods	100	155	144
Denmark			
Raw and semi-manufactured goods	100		133
Consumers' goods	100		169
Germany			
Industrial raw materials and semi-manufactured goods	100		132
Raw materials [2]	100		138
Finished goods	100		157
Italy			
Raw materials	100		464
Semi-manufactured goods	100		450
Finished goods	100		514
Sweden			
Raw materials	100	147	135
Semi-manufactured goods	100	155	141
Finished products	100	196	142
United States			
Raw materials	100	133	141
Manufactured goods	100	155	152

SOURCES: The original index numbers appear in *Memorandum on Production and Trade, 1923 to 1928/29*, League of Nations, 1930, p. 64, and *Review of World Production, 1931*, League of Nations, 1932, p. 103.
[1] 1914=100.
[2] Producers' goods only; consumers' goods are omitted.

The records of Canada, Sweden and the United States for the period 1922–29 indicate a progressive cheapening of manufactured goods, in relation to raw materials. The manufacturing margin was narrowed in the 'twenties. But in each of these countries, 1922 was marked by a manufacturing margin exceeding that of pre-War years. The degree of excess ranged from the Canadian figure of some 4 per cent to the Swedish figure of approximately 33 per cent. Subsequent events reduced this excess and, for Canada, carried the margin to a point lower than that of 1913. But in all the other countries listed the relative price differential, out of which the costs of fabrication are met, was greater in 1929 than in 1913.

The margins here indicated are of necessity measured roughly. The indexes of raw material prices include in at least four instances goods ready for consumption, such as fruits, vegetables, and coal. Yet only products used as raw materials in processing may be compared in price with manufactured commodities, if the margin available for payment to agents of fabrication is in question. It is probable that the margins indicated understate the true differentials, if the situation in the United States be taken as representative. For here, while all raw materials in 1929 were 41 per cent higher in price than in 1913, raw materials used in production were only 31 per cent higher.

A variety of forces combined, then, to create a world price structure in 1929 quite different from that of 1913. Many of the articulations of pre-War days, articulations which were never perfect but which made it possible for international economic intercourse to proceed in a reasonably efficient manner, were broken. The pre-War equilibrium of the world economic structure, which was maintained through price relations of fairly long standing, was seriously disturbed, though the magnitude of this disturbance was partly concealed by certain necessarily temporary developments of the first post-War decade.

We have noted three outstanding characteristics of world prices, as they affected international economic relations.

A definite price schism existed between raw material producing and industrial areas. This schism was in part international, in part domestic. On the international side it served to divide the countries of the world into two broad groups, comprehending colonial or raw material producing areas on the one hand, industrial areas on the other.

Industrial countries differed considerably with respect to the level of production costs. Countries that had passed through periods of inflation, and that had restored the gold standard on such terms that domestic prices and costs were low, in relation to foreign currencies, constituted one general class. Czechoslovakia and France exemplify this group. The domestic price and cost structures of other industrial countries, the chief of which were the United Kingdom and the United States, were built upon values relatively high, with reference to the general post-War level of gold prices. But there was no sharp line of division in this respect, for many factors affected costs. Thus costs were relatively high in Italy, after stabilization, which was effected at a level above those at which other countries passing through post-War inflation had stabilized.

As a result of the accumulated differences of the period of international non-intercourse or of definitely restricted intercourse which began in 1914 and which extended, for some countries, well into the first post-War decade, numerous other disparities existed among national price structures. Chief of these were the differences in the levels of gold prices prevailing after the general restoration of the gold standard in the middle 'twenties. These general differences translated themselves into a very large number of concrete disparities among the elements of the various national price structures, and economic relations among nations were correspondingly impeded. Many such detailed disparities had arisen as a result of more specific causes, operating during the years of non-intercourse, or of restricted intercourse. The coordination of elements of the world price structure usually effected from day to day and month to month when trade relations are free had been prevented for many years. When free relations were restored, in whole or in part, with the monetary

THE PRE-RECESSION SITUATION 89

adjustments of the middle 'twenties, the elements of national price structures were out of gear. Costs, buying and selling prices, the prices of different categories of goods—all the elements that are usually adapted one to another through the play of trade competition—required readjustment on an international scale. The forced draughts that maintained international trade from 1925 to 1929 did not effect lasting readjustments, so we come to 1929 with great discrepancies of this sort still existing. A going world economy had not been reconstituted by that date.

Disparities in Post-War Price Relations

The world price structure, as it existed in 1929, was marked by disparate national price levels, disparate production costs, and by a world-wide disparity between the prices of the raw materials of industry and finished industrial products. The pre-recession history of the domestic price structure of the United States was characterized, similarly, by extensive changes in the relations among different elements of the price system, changes especially pronounced in the relations between raw and processed goods. These various shifts in price relations worked in their several spheres to alter the terms on which goods and services might be exchanged, internationally and domestically. Some of the alterations were sufficiently great to serve as effective barriers to the movement of goods. In other instances exchanges were still made, but the relative positions of the trading groups concerned were radically different from those that had prevailed earlier. The distribution of purchasing power, domestically and internationally, had been substantially altered.

Such alterations in the distribution of purchasing power are usual accompaniments of economic change. During the course of any decade in economic history buying power is shifted from group to group. The world's total output of economic goods is never divided in exactly the same proportions from one year to the next. What is notable, however, is that the shifts here in question had not been accompanied by corresponding changes in the techniques or costs of production, and that standards of living had not been adapted in any permanent sense to the purchasing power changes. Certain of the shifts in purchasing power were due to the play of non-economic factors (i.e., to post-War political conditions and relations); in others they were due to faults in the mechanism of exchange; in still others they were due to alterations in international economic relations to which adaptation had not yet been effected. The pre-War economic relations of the nations of the world had been permanently altered, in important respects. Certain conditions, which in retrospect we now know to have been temporary, prevented for a time a realization of the full effects of these economic difficulties, but the faults persisted.

One aspect of these world-wide disparities has special relevance to the economic situation in the United States. Between 1919 and 1921 a gap, world-wide in scope, was opened between the prices of raw materials and processed goods. In magnitude, duration and scope, this gap was without counterpart in recent economic history. Cyclical recessions and depressions have always brought some such price inequalities. But no previous recession of which we have record opened up a gap of such magnitude, which affected so many commodities, over such a wide geographical range, and which persisted for so many years after the original difficulties developed.

For highly industrialized countries and raw material producing countries the gap thus opened was an external schism, a break that tended to separate the whole economy from other (complementary) economic systems. The impact of the break, in respect of purchasing power or employment, would

THE PRE-RECESSION SITUATION 91

not necessarily be precisely the same upon all economic groups, but in general the whole economy would be affected in somewhat the same way. Thus in a typical raw material producing area such as the Dutch East Indies, persistent economic difficulties with generally reduced purchasing power would be expected among most elements of the economy, whether engaged directly in the output of raw materials or not. A typical industrial area such as the United Kingdom would feel the effects of low material costs, low purchasing power of important foreign markets and a depressed state of business accompanied by extensive unemployment. (It is true that protected trades and protected labor forces did not suffer, in the United Kingdom, as severely as did competitive trades producing directly for foreign markets. These differences were in part attributable to rigidities within the British national economy.)

Of a different order would be the effects of such a schism on an economy that included both highly industrialized and raw material producing areas, neither type being dominant. A more pronounced internal cleavage would here result, with a clear conflict of interests and of economic fortunes within the economy. Raw material producers suffering from low prices of their products would find their aggregate purchasing power seriously impaired, unless price deficiencies were compensated by heavy output or, temporarily, by borrowing. Industrial producers would find themselves in a favorable price position, being able to buy materials at relatively low prices and to sell manufactured goods at high prices. Concrete results of this advantage might not be realized if the purchasing power of consumers at large were seriously reduced because of the plight of those drawing their incomes from the sale of raw materials. If, however, the reduced purchasing power of primary producers were offset by enhanced purchasing power of other consumers, or by the acquisition of new markets, the state of industrial producers might be very happy. In this case the contrast of economic fortunes within the economy might be very pronounced indeed.

To some extent this internal schism affected a number of national economies, for no countries of economic importance are exclusively industrial or exclusively devoted to the production of raw materials. But the schism was present in most pronounced form in the United States, where highly industrialized areas co-exist with extensive regions devoted exclusively to the output of raw materials. In the economy of the United States, therefore, we find the clearest example of a cleavage sharply separating two major economic groups. The economic history of the entire post-War decade in the United States is deeply affected by it, and many of the distinctive characteristics of the period of expansion and of the subsequent depression are attributable to the divergence of the fortunes of the two groups thus distinguished.

The development of this situation in the United States between 1919 and 1921 [23] altered sharply the internal distribution of purchasing power and the conditions under which the national economy functioned. The persistence of the situation and the concurrent development of a high state of industrial prosperity present one of the most striking paradoxes of economic history. And the aggravation of the situation during the recession of 1929 raised economic issues of great complexity in the succeeding years.

Aspects of this cleavage, in the aggravated form that developed with the recession, will engage us in later pages. We here summarize certain of its pre-recession aspects.

Raw material producers in the United States faced the same

---

[23] See *Economic Tendencies*, Chs. VII, VIII, IX, for a discussion of conditions giving rise to this situation.

THE PRE-RECESSION SITUATION 93

three alternatives that confronted such producers in the world at large: they could expand production in the attempt to offset the effects of the price loss; they could maintain purchasing power by borrowing; they could suffer a reduction in their standard of living. Their actual fortunes during this period reflected elements of all three alternatives. A pressure to expand, or at least to maintain, output kept the supply of raw materials at a high level and served to impede what might have been a normal tendency towards price readjustment. (Inelasticity of demand for many of the products in question accentuated this difficulty.) Heavy borrowing, both in the form of mortgage indebtedness and of installment buying, supported their inadequate purchasing power. But these devices failed to offset the unfavorable marketing situation, and raw material producers as a class suffered a substantial loss of purchasing power with a corresponding decline in their standards of living, relative to pre-War standards and to the fortunes of other economic groups.

In the face of the reduced purchasing power of raw material producers, both domestic and foreign, industrial producers were confronted by the possibility of a considerable reduction in the volume of their sales, with resulting unemployment and scant profits, unless the deficiency of buying power on the part of material producers, due to the price schism, could be offset by gains elsewhere. In large degree it was offset, giving rise to the paradoxical situation noted—industrial prosperity co-existing with low purchasing power and, in some degree, real distress among raw material producers as a class. Various factors contributed to the persistence of this situation in the United States. These included, in brief:

> The gaining of new foreign markets, as a result of the War and post-War disturbance.
> Heavy lending to foreign buyers, on both long and short term.
> The temporary offsetting of part of the reduced purchasing power of raw material producers at home through borrowing and installment buying.

The swelling of the purchasing power of industrial producers as a result of their advantageous economic position.

A general increase in the purchasing power of consumers through the rapid development of installment buying.

The enhancement of purchasing power throughout the nation through speculative profits, reaped from real estate and security speculation.

Increasing industrial productivity, which made possible large profits and high wages without further advance in selling prices.

Obviously, many of the elements that made possible the simultaneous continuance of industrial prosperity and of subnormal purchasing power and living standards on the part of some groups of raw material producers were necessarily temporary. Some of the new elements of purchasing power through which industrial sales were maintained were clearly of a non-recurring nature, and plant expansion based upon these was doomed to certain difficulty. Yet so long as these conditions made it possible for industrial production and sales to be kept at high levels, industrial prosperity, high wages and high profits might co-exist with economic distress among some primary producers. As we have seen, the degree of divergence between the economic fortunes of these two great groups within the economy of the United States had been substantially reduced by 1929, but elements of the fundamental cleavage still existed.

Highly important, as a condition concurrent with the widening of the fabricational margin in the early post-War years, was a notable increase in industrial productivity. In manufacturing industries the gain in output per wage earner exceeded 40 per cent from 1919 to 1929. The striking feature of this situation, as we have seen, was that the benefits of higher productivity during this decade were reaped largely by agents of fabrication. The rewards of primary producers remained relatively low, and prices to buyers of finished goods remained relatively high. We shall return, in the final chapter, to a further consideration and interpretation of this situation and its economic consequences.

CHAPTER III

PRICE MOVEMENTS AND RELATED ECONOMIC CHANGES DURING RECESSION AND DEPRESSION

THE price decline precipitated in 1929 was of major proportions, world-wide in scope, and affected directly or indirectly virtually every element of the economic system. The fundamental relations between primary producers, manufacturers and distributors and final consumers which have concerned us in the preceding pages were profoundly altered, and these changes were reflected widely in the physical operations of production and exchange and in the living standards of different producing groups. In defining certain of these changes, and in tracing their consequences, we deal first with groups engaged in the extraction and production of raw materials.

PRIMARY PRODUCTS IN THE PRICE RECESSION

As a background for the survey of the recession we have traced some of the changes occurring in earlier years. The steady pre-War improvement in the status of primary producers was followed by a brief period of exceptional prosperity during the War. The recession of 1920–21 brought heavy losses to these producers, in both unit prices and aggregate rewards. The situation in the United States, in this respect, was but a phase of a world-wide schism between the prices of raw materials and manufactured goods. Between 1922 and 1929 there was definite and steady improvement in the position of raw material producers. On a per unit basis some price disadvantage persisted, but there is evidence that substantial reductions in unit costs of production were effected in extractive industries generally and in non-ferrous metals particularly. Where such reductions occurred prosperity could exist without full restoration of an earlier price parity with commodities in general. For agricultural producers in the United States pre-War parity with non-agricultural prices was barely attained by 1929. Indeed, if farm prices be compared with the prices paid by farmers, at retail, some disparity still existed in 1929.

The price record of the recession is familiar. Raw materials dropped precipitately; manufactured goods, customarily slug-

	WHOLESALE PRICES		PER UNIT PURCHASING POWER (*July 1929=100*) *February 1933*
	July 1929[1]	*February 1933*	
All commodities	100	62	100
Raw materials	100	51	82
Manufactured goods[2]	100	69	111

[1] July 1929 is taken as the base, since that month marked the high point of general prices immediately before the recession. For some purposes it might be desirable to use a broader base, covering the prosperity phase of the cyclical swing preceding the 1929 recession. That the present comparisons would be modified only slightly by such a shift is indicated by the following comparison of the standing of index numbers of wholesale prices at the two periods. The classification, which is that of the U. S. Bureau of Labor Statistics, is three-fold rather than two-fold as in the text, but the relative price movements among raw and processed goods are clearly shown.

	October 1928– July 1929	*July 1929*
All commodities	100.0	100.7
Raw materials	100.0	101.6
Semi-manufactured products	100.0	99.2
Finished products	100.0	100.4

[2] This index of the average prices of manufactured products is based upon the quoted prices on standard goods. As will appear in a later section, the average prices actually realized by the manufacturer showed a greater decline from 1929 to 1933. A shifting to goods of lower quality and some under-cutting of quoted prices during the worst months of the depression were factors in this divergence of quoted and realized prices.

gish in their response to a downward pressure of values, lagged behind. The degree of difference is indicated by the index numbers on page 96. In wholesale markets raw materials declined approximately one-half in forty-three months. Since this decline exceeded materially the drop in general prices at wholesale, it meant a substantial loss in real per unit values, that is, values in exchange for commodities in general in wholesale markets. On the average, each unit of raw materials lost approximately 18 per cent in 'purchasing power', as thus defined; the corresponding gain in per unit purchasing power of manufactured goods was 11 per cent.[1]

That the weight of price recession should fall more heavily on producers of raw materials than on fabricators is to be expected, in the light of the preceding discussion of the nature of the price problems faced by these two producing

[1] For convenience, in discussing price disparities, it is desirable to trace changes in purchasing power as well as changes in current prices. A commodity that rises in price less rapidly than the general average during a period of rising prices or falls more rapidly during a period of declining prices loses in purchasing power, per unit. Unless the loss is compensated by increases in the number of units sold, producers of that commodity will suffer a loss of aggregate purchasing power. The reverse is true of a commodity that rises in price more rapidly than the general average during a period of price advance or falls in price less rapidly during a period of price decline. It is through such changes in aggregate purchasing power that the economic center of gravity shifts from time to time, as economic power passes from group to group. Per unit purchasing power is, of course, just one element of the aggregate; changes in volume of output or sales may play an important part in the shifts of economic power; various cost factors enter, when the purchasing power of net income is in question. But during periods of rapid price movement, changes in the price factor may dominate changes in both net and gross income, and in the purchasing power of such income.

In the present account we shall in general define per unit purchasing power in terms of the broad list of commodities that enter into the general index of wholesale prices. That is, the index of price changes for a given commodity group will be divided by the index of change during the same period in the level of wholesale prices. In certain instances (notably in this chapter) purchasing power is measured with reference to other standards, but when this is done the standards of reference are specifically noted.

groups. In 1929 the general sensitiveness of raw material prices to the forces of recession was enhanced by certain exceptional conditions growing out of War and post-War developments. A clue to the price behavior of goods of these two types during the recession is found in the record of production changes. Annual index numbers of correspond-

	VOLUME OF PRODUCTION				AVERAGE WHOLESALE PRICES			
	1929	1930	1931	1932	1929	1930	1931	1932
Raw materials	100	97	97	88	100	87	69	57
Manufactured goods	100	85	75	61	100	93	81	74

ing price and production movements in the United States reveal a clear inverse relationship. Sharply reduced output and relatively well-maintained prices characterized manufactured goods over this period of recession. Maintained production and severe price decline marked the behavior of raw materials. The pronounced difference in the two records goes back, of course, to the conditions of production and the character of competition prevailing among producers of the two types. Control over output and ready adaptability to changed conditions of demand are found, in general, in manufacturing industries, while the reverse is true of extractive industries. The differing price records reflect these conditions, as well as the influence of special price-determining forces.

The declines in prices and in purchasing power were by no means equal, among the various classes of raw materials. The nature of the changes in four major commodity groups is shown by the index numbers below. Agricultural pro-

RAW PRODUCTS	WHOLESALE PRICES		PER UNIT PURCHASING POWER (July 1929=100)
	July 1929	February 1933	February 1933
Crops	100	40	65
Animal	100	39	63
Forest	100	63	102
Mineral	100	73	118

ducers suffered most severely; raw crops and animal products lost no less than 35 per cent in per unit purchasing power. Raw forest products, which suffered a price decline about equal to that of general prices, lost nothing in purchasing power. Raw mineral products gained 18 per cent in per unit worth. In the United States the critical problem of price disparity, as between raw materials and manufactured goods, centered in agricultural products.

These price changes accompanied and reflected important changes in the conditions of supply, as well as of demand. To facilitate comparison of certain of these movements we bring together below annual data relating to production and price

RAW PRODUCTS	VOLUME OF PRODUCTION				AVERAGE WHOLESALE PRICES			
	1929	*1930*	*1931*	*1932*	*1929*	*1930*	*1931*	*1932*
Mineral	100	89	75	62	100	93	81	78
Forest	100	82	57	38	100	90	78	66
Agricultural	100	100	106	99	100	85	64	48

changes during the years of recession. We find here a general inverse relationship between movements of prices and of output. The most severe price declines occurred among agricultural products, the production of which was maintained close to the pre-recession level. The effects on the market of this maintenance of production were aggravated by a sharp decline in agricultural exports. For the crop year 1932–33 such exports were some 27 per cent smaller in quantity than in 1928–29. Mineral products, the output of which was more severely reduced, experienced a smaller price decline; forest products suffered heavily in both output and price.[2]

---

[2] Just as the index numbers relating to all raw materials conceal the important differences revealed by the three sets of group measurements given above, so each of these hides divergent movements among its subordinate elements. Among raw mineral products the output of fuels was relatively well maintained, while the production of metals dropped to a very low level. Among forest products the drop in output of pulpwood, turpentine

PRICES AND PURCHASING POWER OF FARM PRODUCTS

Agriculture calls for chief attention, in a detailed survey of the price schism opened by the recession. The difficulties of agricultural producers during this period have been notorious. The accompanying index numbers define their relative position at the low point of the depression. While

	WHOLESALE PRICES		PER UNIT PURCHASING POWER (July 1929=100)
	July 1929[1]	February 1933	February 1933
All commodities	100	62	100
Products of American farms, raw	100	40	64
All other products, raw and processed (including processed products of American farms)	100	68	110
Products of American farms, raw			
Producers' goods	100	37	59
Consumers' goods	100	47	76

[1] The use of a broader pre-recession base would lower somewhat the index numbers of farm prices for the period of depression. In July 1929 the index number of farm prices was some 3 per cent above the average for the preceding ten months, while the index of wholesale prices for all commodities other than farm products and foods was one-half of one per cent below the average for that period.

general commodities at wholesale were declining 38 per cent the wholesale prices of raw American farm products were dropping 60 per cent, with a loss of no less than 36 per cent in per unit purchasing power in wholesale markets.[3] If we

and rosin was much less severe than in lumber. Among agricultural products no striking differences appear, over the period 1929–32 as a whole. Perhaps most significant is the increased output of fruits and vegetables. The several production index numbers for the subordinate groups are given in Appendix VII.

[3] The price and purchasing power changes here measured are those taking place between July 1929 and February 1933, the dates of the high and low points of general wholesale prices. If interest attaches to changes in the

lump together all other products (including farm products in processed form) we find a drop of but 32 per cent in average price, a gain of 10 per cent in average per unit purchasing power, at wholesale.

The records of average price change for farm crops and animal products, in raw state, show no differences. If, however, we distinguish farm products ready for consumption in raw state (garden truck, milk, potatoes, eggs, etc.) from those subject to processing before use, we find a considerable difference in price behavior. While raw consumers' goods, among farm products, lost 24 per cent in average per unit purchasing power, raw producers' goods lost 41 per cent. We find here an example of a common rule, that price vicissitudes, both falling and rising, are greater among producers' than among consumers' goods.

A comparison of the situation at the depression low with that of pre-War days is possible by means of the following index numbers.[4] The results of price decline during the first

	PER UNIT PURCHASING POWER, AT WHOLESALE			
	1913	1922	July 1929	February 1933
Products of American farms, raw	100	92	102	66
All other products	100	102	100	110
Crops, raw [1]	100	91	102	66
Animal products, raw [1]	100	89	98	62
Products of American farms, raw				
Producers' goods	100	88	99	59
Consumers' goods	100	105	112	85

[1] These index numbers include all raw crops and raw animal products, of American and foreign origin. The index numbers in the preceding table included only products of American farms.

(*Footnote* 3 *concluded*)
actual purchasing power of farmers these are not the most significant dates, for account should be taken of the seasonal marketings of farmers. Changes in the aggregate purchasing power of different economic groups during the recession are discussed in later sections.

[4] The price indexes from which these measurements of purchasing power changes are derived are given in Appendices III and IV.

post-War recession, which by 1921 had carried raw American farm products 18 per cent below their pre-War exchange parity with other commodities and which left them in 1922 with an 8 per cent disparity, were slowly corrected. By July 1929 the position of raw farm products in wholesale markets was approximately the same as in 1913. In the precipitate drop that followed, their per unit worth in terms of commodities in general, at wholesale, fell to a level 34 per cent below that of the pre-War base period. Other commodities (a much more heavily weighted group, of course) showed an increase of 10 per cent, in per unit purchasing power.[5]

[5] Agricultural economists usually compare post-War prices with average prices prevailing during the five years, August 1909–July 1914. This broader base is taken as more representative of pre-War conditions than any single year could be. For general comparative purposes the situation in 1913 is used in this study as representative of pre-War conditions, but it is desirable that the degree of difference between figures on the two bases be noted. Changes in purchasing power, per unit, between 1910–14 and selected later dates are shown in the following table. The figures are derived from indexes of wholesale prices. (The base is the average of the five calendar years, 1910–14, inclusive.) The general relations shown in this table between raw products of American farms and all other products are much the same as those found when the 1913 base is used. The use of the wider base changes the relative positions of crops and animal products, and lowers somewhat the post-War figures for raw farm products ready for consumption.

	PER UNIT PURCHASING POWER, AT WHOLESALE				
	1910–1914	1922	1929	1932	July 1929	February 1933
Products of American farms, raw	100	87	96	68	97	62
All other products	100	103	101	109	100	111
Crops, raw*	100	84	94	62	93	61
Animal products, raw*	100	91	99	72	100	64
Products of American farms, raw						
Producers' goods	100	84	92	59	94	56
Consumers' goods	100	97	106	91	104	79

* The index numbers of prices of crops and animal products include the prices of a few imported agricultural products.

PRICES AT THE FARM AND PRICES PAID BY FARMERS

If we take account not of buying and selling prices at wholesale but of prices received at the farm for goods sold and of prices actually paid by farmers for goods they buy we secure a somewhat different picture. These index numbers [6] show that the actual buying and selling position of the farmer was materially worse in February 1933 than is indicated by the wholesale prices of raw farm products and other products. In forty-three months the actual worth of a unit of farm products, in terms of the goods the farmer needs for production and family maintenance, was reduced 43 per cent.

	July 1929	February 1933
Commodities sold: average prices at farm	100	37
Commodities bought: average prices paid by farmers	100	66
Commodities sold: average purchasing power per unit	100	57

The degree of loss in per unit purchasing power varied, of course, from group to group of farm products. For grains the loss from July 1929 to February 1933 was 57 per cent, for cotton 54 per cent, for meat animals 52 per cent. The average per unit worth of poultry products declined 39 per cent, that of fruits 36 per cent, that of dairy products 26 per cent, and that of truck crops only 10 per cent.[7] It is noteworthy that

---

[6] Computed by the U. S. Bureau of Agricultural Economics. Detailed figures are given in Table 24. The measure of purchasing power is derived by dividing the index of prices received by farmers by the index of prices paid by farmers for goods used in production and family maintenance.

[7] Purchasing power is measured with reference to the commodities farmers buy, at retail. The general qualification previously noted, relating to the significance of purchasing power figures for specific months, applies here also. February is not a month of heavy marketing by farmers. A longer period, such as the crop or calendar year, should be used if changes in aggregate purchasing power are to be accurately measured. Aggregate purchasing power of farmers is discussed in a later section.

the three groups of products suffering losses greater than the average—namely grains, cotton and cottonseed, and meat animals—are the great staples for which prices are set in national or world markets. Poultry products, fruits and vegetables and dairy products, the three groups in which losses were less than average, contain a large proportion of consumers' goods that are less sensitive to the play of world economic forces. But in all groups except truck crops the losses in per unit purchasing power during the depression were substantial. For important single products the losses were even greater than those here shown.

Here, again, we should survey these changes with reference to a more distant base. Where did farm products stand, in per unit purchasing power, prior to the recession and at the low point of the depression in 1933, when the base of comparison is a period antedating the War? The accompanying measurements answer this question. The recovery from

	1913	July 1929	February 1933
Commodities sold: average prices at farm	100	146	54
Commodities bought: average prices paid by farmers	100	151	100
Commodities sold: average purchasing power per unit	100	97	54

the depths of the first post-War depression and the changes of the 'twenties did not restore the relations that had prevailed in 1913 between the prices of things farmers sell and the prices of things they buy. The per unit purchasing power of farm products was 3 per cent less in July 1929 than in 1913. (This does not necessarily mean that farmers were worse off in 1929 than in 1913, for no account is here taken of costs of agricultural production, or of relative changes in the qualities of goods bought and sold. If we could allow for the known reduction of production costs and for improvement in the quality of agricultural implements, the position of the farmer would be somewhat better than is in-

RECESSION AND DEPRESSION

dicated by the figures given.) The ensuing decline, which carried farm prices down far more rapidly than average prices, reduced the average per unit purchasing power of farm products to just about half of what it had been in 1913. Whether we take the pre-War or the 1929 situation as the standard of reference, the economic condition of the farmer in the early months of 1933 was bad.[8]

The major subgroups of farm products stood in February 1933 in the same relative positions, with reference to the pre-War base, as in the comparison based on 1929 parity. The two great international staples, grains and cotton, declined most severely from the 1913 level, while commodities produced primarily for the domestic market resisted the price decline more successfully. Although the range of variation was considerable, the loss was substantial for all groups. In per unit purchasing power grains lost no less than 63 per cent between 1913 and February 1933, cotton lost 55 per cent, while dairy products dropped only 30 per cent.

AGGREGATE PURCHASING POWER OF PRIMARY PRODUCERS

The aggregate purchasing power of the various classes of raw material producers reflected the changes wrought by the depression in their average selling prices and aggregate production. These two factors, together with the average price of goods purchased by each group, determine the volume of goods it receives. The gross purchasing power of a group

[8] The picture is unchanged in its essentials if we use as the base of this comparison the period August 1909–July 1914, as is commonly done by agricultural economists. Following are the index numbers:

	August 1909–July 1914	July 1929	February 1933
Commodities sold: average prices at farm	100	147	55
Commodities bought: average prices paid by farmers	100	153	101

(which is not to be confused with net income) cannot be measured exactly, largely because adequate records of average buying prices are not available, but the major changes in gross returns may be approximated. For the principal comparisons we assume that the prices of goods purchased by each group fluctuated in the same degree as general prices at wholesale—an assumption only roughly in accord with the facts. Where more exact records of changes in buying prices are available, supplementary use is made of them.

In the preceding chapter we noted the general movements of group purchasing power during the fifteen years, 1914-29. Declining per unit purchasing power of farm products reduced the relative share of the total volume of goods produced going to farmers. A volume of physical output some 11 per cent greater in 1929 than in 1914 brought an aggregate physical return, in goods received, approximately 10 per cent greater.[9] Producers of forest products made a slightly greater gain in aggregate purchasing power, measured at wholesale, since their per unit purchasing power rose some 25 per cent while the number of units produced dropped only 6 per cent. Producers of raw mineral products approximately doubled their purchasing power, gaining both from increased output and advancing per unit worth of their goods.

Against this background we set the changes of the depression years. Three years of recession brought a decline of approximately 57 per cent in the aggregate gross income of all primary producers (as measured by the aggregate value of their product). The volume of physical goods for which

---

[9] For a discussion of the derivation of these and certain other measurements given in this section the reader is referred to *Economic Tendencies in the United States,* Chs. VII and IX. The measures here cited, which are based upon revised figures, differ somewhat from those in *Economic Tendencies.*

RECESSION AND DEPRESSION

(1)	AGGREGATE VALUE OF PRODUCT, 1932 (*1929=100*) (2)	AGGREGATE COMMAND OVER GOODS, AT WHOLESALE, AND TWO CONTRIBUTING FACTORS, 1932 (*1929=100*)		
		(3) Aggregate command over goods	(4) Purchasing power per unit	(5) Number of physical units
All primary producers	43	64	79	88
Producers of				
Raw farm products	45	66	65	99
Raw mineral products	42	61	115	62
Raw forest products	25	37	97	38

this gross income could be exchanged (at wholesale) fell by from 31 to 36 per cent.[10] This decline in physical rewards far exceeded the drop of about 12 per cent in the volume of physical production of primary products. The explanation of the difference is found, of course, in the reduced per unit purchasing power of raw materials, a loss approximating 21 per cent. The unfavorable change in trading relations was

---

[10] The loss in aggregate command over goods, as given above, was 36 per cent. This is the figure derived by deflating the change in estimated aggregate value of product, appearing in column (2) of the table. But if the entry in column (3) were derived by multiplying the entries in columns (4) and (5), as it logically could be, we would have an index of 69, indicating a loss of 31 per cent in aggregate purchasing power of primary producers, from 1929 to 1932. Residual errors in the value, price and production index numbers account for the difference between this figure and that derived from the table.

Similar errors are present in the measurements relating to the three groups of primary producers. Index numbers of aggregate purchasing power in 1932 (on the 1929 base), derived from the measurements in columns (4) and (5) are 65, 72 and 37, respectively, for the producers of farm products, mineral products and forest products (the last of these is the index given in the table). The differences between these measurements and those in column (3) of the table for producers of farm and mineral products may be taken as indications of the magnitude of the errors involved in the estimates of changes in aggregate purchasing power. For raw mineral products the figure in column (3) is based upon a more complete coverage than are the price and quantity indices.

more important than reduced output in lowering the physical rewards of primary producers.

Among the three groups of primary producers we find some notable differences. Producers of farm products and mineral products suffered roughly equal declines (from 30 to 40 per cent) in aggregate purchasing power. For farmers this drop was due primarily to a loss in the real per unit value of their products; output fell only 1 per cent. Mineral producers actually gained in the real per unit worth of their products, but lost almost 40 per cent in volume of output. Hardest hit of the three groups were producers of forest products. With approximately stable per unit purchasing power, a decline of approximately 60 per cent in volume of output brought an equal drop in their aggregate purchasing power.

The use of an index of wholesale prices in determining changes in the average purchasing power of these various producing groups involves some loss of accuracy, but no other general standard of comparison is available. For farmers an index of changes in the prices of goods purchased is to be had. This shows a loss of about 36 per cent in the average per unit purchasing power of farm products between 1929 and 1932, which is very close to the estimate based on wholesale price changes. The reduction in the physical volume of goods going to farmers was approximately equal to the reduction in total physical output of the country, 36 per cent. The rewards of farmers in 1932 were not commensurate with their physical contribution to the total national production, but they suffered, in respect of aggregate command over goods, no more severely than did consumers at large. Their net cash income was, of course, more sharply curtailed.

Price Changes and Fabricational Margins During Recession

The period of expansion that followed the recession of 1920–21 was characterized by the persistence, even in prosperity, of a relatively wide margin between the prices of finished goods and raw materials intended for fabrication. The exceptionally wide gap that was opened up during the price collapse of 1920 was only partly closed during the succeeding years. Some elements of this situation have been suggested in earlier sections. The weak competitive position of raw material producers after the War, and the correspondingly strong position of manufacturing interests, were related to this differential. In the United States concurrent improvement in mechanical equipment, with increased overhead charges, and the general acceptance in important manufacturing industries of the principle of high wages were also factors in widening the price spread between raw materials and finished goods. In considerable part the gains made by labor during the War were maintained during the recession of 1920–21; during the following decade wage rates and labor costs in manufacturing were high, as compared with pre-War levels. Certain fortuitous circumstances, discussed in Chapter II, served to swell currently available purchasing power and to maintain the volume of production and trade in the United States during the years preceding the 1929 break, in spite of a relatively wide fabricational margin and of relatively high prices to final consumers.

Our immediate concern is with the effects of recession on this situation. Past experience, and consideration of the relative flexibilities of different elements of production costs, lead us to expect a much sharper drop in the prices of materials than in the prices of finished goods, with a resultant widening of the relative, if not of the absolute, margin between the prices of raw and of finished goods. With the available data various methods may be employed to trace the changes brought by recession in the price relations that define this margin. We turn first to an examination of composite index numbers of the prices of processed goods and of raw materials intended for use in production.

PRICE MOVEMENTS AMONG RAW AND PROCESSED GOODS

The following index numbers relate to changes brought by the recession in the manufacturing differential. As is usual

	WHOLESALE PRICES	
	July 1929	February 1933
Producers' goods, raw	100	49
Manufactured goods, all	100	69
Ratio of index of prices of manufactured goods to index of prices of raw producers' goods	1.00	1.41

during recessions, the price drop among raw materials intended for fabrication was distinctly more precipitate than among manufactured goods. Wages and salaries, charges on capital investment, rent and other relatively rigid elements of cost serve as effective brakes on the decline in prices of manufactured goods, while the greater possibility of controlling supply renders maintenance of prices easier than among most raw materials. Moreover, differences in the duration of production processes and in durability may be important causes of differences in the price flexibility of different goods.

The significance of this shift in relative values may be more clearly revealed if we assume that producers of raw materials exchange their goods directly for the manufactured commodities made from them. The ratios at the foot of the preceding table define this relation. In February 1933, 1.41 units of raw materials were required to purchase that quan-

RECESSION AND DEPRESSION

tity of manufactured goods that one unit of raw materials would have purchased in July 1929. Over forty-three months the per unit purchasing power of raw materials had declined notably; in the absence of compensating changes, this loss was bound to have its effect on the volume of finished goods that could find a market.

The same comparison, on a pre-War base, is made below.

		WHOLESALE PRICES		
	1913	*1922*	*July 1929*	*February 1933*
Producers' goods, raw	100	127	134	66
Manufactured goods, all	100	155	153	105
Ratio, manufactured to raw	1.00	1.22	1.14	1.59

Because of the gap between the prices of raw producers' goods and of manufactured goods already existing in 1929, the situation here disclosed is blacker than that shown by the preceding table. Raw materials for use in fabrication sold in February 1933 at prices 34 per cent below those of 1913, while goods in the intermediate or finished stage of the fabrication process sold at prices 5 per cent above 1913 prices. Even more striking are the shifts that occurred in the trading relations between raw and processed goods, as distinct classes. A constant quantity of manufactured goods, which could be purchased for a single unit of raw materials in 1913, was worth 1.22 units of raw materials in 1922, 1.14 units in July 1929, and 1.59 units in February 1933. Of course, it is not accurate to picture domestic trade as an exchange between these two broad groups of producers, but a considerable volume of goods is so exchanged. In this trading area the shift in relative values was revolutionary; it affected established relations throughout the economic system and altered materially the distribution of current purchasing power.

To secure a clearer understanding of the changes in the manufacturing differential during the recent recession we must go behind the broad averages shown above, for there have been wide differences, among the major commodity groups, in the degree of change in the margin between raw and processed goods. For each class we contrast raw producers' goods (that is, goods subject to fabrication before being ready for use) with manufactured goods.

	WHOLESALE PRICES	
	July 1929	February 1933
Crops:		
Producers' raw	100	38
Processed	100	65
Ratio, processed to raw	1.00	1.71
Animal products:		
Producers' raw	100	34
Processed	100	54
Ratio, processed to raw	1.00	1.59
Minerals:		
Producers' raw	100	70
Processed	100	80
Ratio, processed to raw	1.00	1.14
Metals:		
Producers' raw	100	63
Processed	100	81
Ratio, processed to raw	1.00	1.29

The actual price declines were substantially greater among crops and animal products than among minerals. But our immediate interest is in the margin between the two sets of prices in each general category. In all cases the manufacturing margin widened, as is shown by the ratios that define the number of units of raw producers' goods of each type required to purchase, in February 1933, a stated quantity of processed goods of the same type (i.e., the ratio of the price index for processed goods to the corresponding index for raw materials). To purchase a certain constant quantity of goods manufactured from farm crops one unit of raw materials was necessary in July 1929; 1.71 units were required in

RECESSION AND DEPRESSION

February 1933. The corresponding ratio for animal products in February 1933 was 1.59, for mineral products 1.14, and for the subgroup of metal products 1.29.

With reference to a pre-War base, the 1933 situation shows even more extreme changes. Crops and animal products, the

	WHOLESALE PRICES			
	1913	1922	July 1929	February 1933
Crops:				
Producers' raw	100	127	137	52
Processed	100	146	143	93
Ratio, processed to raw	1.00	1.15	1.04	1.79
Animal products:				
Producers' raw	100	130	148	50
Processed	100	150	167	91
Ratio, processed to raw	1.00	1.15	1.13	1.82
Minerals:				
Producers' raw	100	140	135	94
Processed	100	159	152	122
Ratio, processed to raw	1.00	1.14	1.13	1.30
Metals:				
Producers' raw	100	121	128	81
Processed	100	151	164	133
Ratio, processed to raw	1.00	1.25	1.28	1.64

weakest in economic position among primary products, experienced the greatest widening of the fabricational margin. In both groups raw materials dropped, in February 1933, to approximately half their 1913 price, while the corresponding manufactured goods declined less than 10 per cent. In exchange for constant quantities of finished goods of the same class, approximately 80 per cent more, by volume, of each type of raw material was required than in 1913. Here were probably the most extreme shifts in exchange relations that occurred in the price system. Raw minerals intended for fabrication were in better position; the low price of the depression was only slightly below the 1913 price; processed goods were some 20 per cent above. The measurements for metals indicate that the widening of the fabricational margin for minerals as a broad class was heavily influenced by the growing cleavage between the prices of raw metals and processed metallic products.

A clearer contrast between farm and non-farm products, and between corresponding manufacturing differentials, is afforded if we deal with the two major groups alone. The exchange ratio between the prices of raw and processed farm

	WHOLESALE PRICES	
	July 1929	February 1933
Products of American farms:		
Producers' raw	100	37
Processed	100	60
Ratio, processed to raw	1.00	1.62
Products other than those originating on American farms:		
Producers' raw	100	64
Processed	100	77
Ratio, processed to raw	1.00	1.20

products increased sharply during the recession. The producer of raw materials who desired to exchange raw for manufactured goods of the same type was required to give 62 per cent more, by volume, in February 1933 than in July 1929, for a constant quantity of processed goods. The corresponding increase for non-farm products was 20 per cent.[11]

[11] Measurements for these groups on a pre-War base show still wider changes but with the increase in the raw-processed differential still distinctly greater for farm than for non-farm products.

		WHOLESALE PRICES		
	1913	1922	July 1929	February 1933
Products of American farms:				
Producers' raw	100	130	148	54
Processed	100	151	161	96
Ratio	1.00	1.16	1.09	1.78
Products other than those originating on American farms:				
Producers' raw	100	123	118	76
Processed	100	158	146	112
Ratio	1.00	1.28	1.24	1.47

RECESSION AND DEPRESSION

Other categories of commodities show the same general movements. We may briefly summarize the shifts in exchange relations between various categories of goods. Detailed measurements are given in Appendices III and IV. We cite here merely the ratios of the index numbers of processed goods to those of raw (or semi-finished) materials, recalling that such a ratio measures changes in the physical volume of raw materials exchangeable for a fixed volume of processed goods.

Between July 1929 and February 1933 the ratio of the price index of processed consumers' goods to the index of producers' goods intended for human consumption increased from 1.00 to 1.43; between 1913 and February 1933 the ratio increased from 1.00 to 1.77.

Breaking the above group of consumers' goods into foods and non-foods, we find no substantial difference between them during the recession. Over a longer period there was a notable difference, however. Between 1913 and February 1933 the ratio of the price index for finished food products to the price index for unfinished food products increased from 1.00 to 1.53; for non-foods, among consumers' goods, the increase was from 1.00 to 1.97. A greater degree of fabrication with corresponding improvements in quality would account for part of the widening of this particular differential, but hardly for all.

Between July 1929 and February 1933 the ratio of the price index for processed goods intended for use in capital equipment to the corresponding price index for raw materials increased from 1.00 to 1.39; between 1913 and February 1933 the ratio increased from 1.00 to 1.65. The relative costliness of capital equipment, which was a conspicuous feature of the decade of the 'twenties, was markedly accentuated by the widening of this particular price differential during the recession.

MOVEMENTS OF MANUFACTURERS' MARGINS, AS SHOWN BY CHANGES IN THE PRICES OF SIMILAR COMMODITIES AT DIFFERENT PRODUCTIVE STAGES

The measurements given above represent price changes at different stages of the manufacturing-distributive process. We may supplement these representative figures by direct measurements of changing differentials in the manufacturing process, derived from the prices of 'identical' commodities (more accurately, commodities containing the same materials) at successive fabricational stages—wheat and flour, raw silk and spun silk, raw sugar and granulated sugar, pig lead and lead pipe, etc. Our present purpose will be served by the comparison of averages defining price changes from 1929 to 1932 for a group of 174 simple processed goods with corresponding measurements for the raw materials from which these goods were made.

	WHOLESALE PRICES			
	1929	*1930*	*1931*	*1932*
Raw materials	100	85	63	54
Simple processed goods made from these materials	100	88	72	64

Here, where we are dealing with precisely the same commodities in raw and processed form, we find the widening margin revealed by the index numbers appearing on preceding pages. The annual averages indicate a drop of 36 per cent in the prices of the simple processed goods here represented, a drop of 46 per cent in the prices of their raw materials, from 1929 to 1932.[12] The margin of difference is substantial (the ratio of the index for processed goods to that for raw materials in 1932 was 1.19), but somewhat smaller than those given in preceding sections. The use of annual

---

[12] Detailed measurements for the different groups of commodities included in the above averages are given in Appendix V.

RECESSION AND DEPRESSION

rather than monthly values tends to lessen this margin. More important is the fact that the processed goods represented in the above index are not highly fabricated products. Simple processed goods are closer to raw materials, in their price movements, than are highly fabricated goods.

MANUFACTURING COSTS, 1929–1933

The recession of 1929–33 was marked, as have been other recessions, by a fall in the prices of raw materials much more severe than that for finished goods. The various costs of fabrication were not reduced during this decline by amounts equal to the drop in material prices. So much we learn from the records of wholesale prices we have been reviewing. But we do not get from these figures detailed information concerning the relations between the changes in different fabricational costs and, indeed, such information is not to be had from ordinary price quotations. Records of the Census of Manufactures contain data bearing on this question. We may review them for light on the course and character of liquidation in manufacturing industries. Changes in prices and costs in manufacturing industries at large are defined in the next table and are shown graphically in Figure 6.[13] The measure-

	SELLING PRICE		COST OF MATERIALS		COST OF FABRICATION PLUS PROFITS		LABOR COST		OVERHEAD COSTS PLUS PROFITS	
1914		100		100		100		100		100
1929	100	145	100	136	100	166	100	157	100	172
1931	78	113	74	100	84	140	87	137	82	141
1933	66	96	63	85	72	120	75	117	71	122

[13] For an explanation of the derivation of these measurements, see *Economic Tendencies in the United States*, pp. 88–9. The index numbers in that book have been revised slightly in preparing the present table. Index numbers for other Census years are given in Appendix VI.

FIGURE 6

CHANGES IN AVERAGE SELLING PRICE, COST OF MATERIALS AND ELEMENTS OF FABRICATION COSTS PLUS PROFITS, PER UNIT OF PRODUCT, 1914–1933

MANUFACTURING INDUSTRIES OF THE UNITED STATES

(*Percentage deviations from 1914 level, in current dollars*)

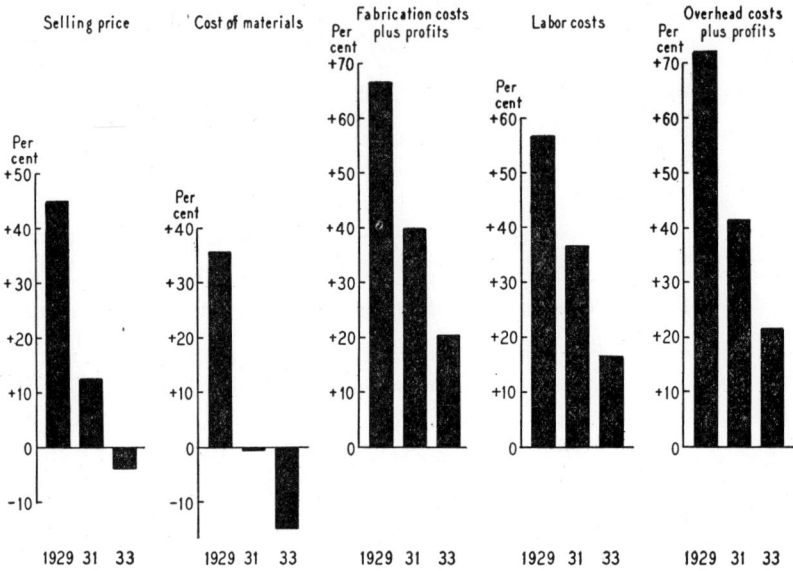

ments relate to average price and cost changes per unit of manufactured product.

The index numbers on the 1929 base indicate a drop of 34 per cent in the average selling price of manufactured goods during the four years ending in 1933. (The actual depression low in commodity prices, on an annual basis, came in 1932, rather than 1933, but the Census materials employed in the derivation of these measurements are not available for 1932.) This decline was the net resultant of drops of 37 per cent in material costs, 28 per cent in fabrication costs (which here include profits) per unit of manufactured product. A lag in the reduction of manufacturing costs is, of course, to be expected. It is here that the more rigid components of price are found. Changes in two elements of these fabricational charges are shown by entries in the remaining columns of the table. These indicate that labor costs per unit of product fell some 25 per cent, while the composite of overhead costs plus profits declined 29 per cent. (It is to be noted that the 1929 index of overhead costs plus profits was relatively high, some 6 per cent above 1927, while labor costs per unit in 1929 were 7 per cent below 1927. Subsequent declines are to be interpreted with these facts in mind.)

One of the most interesting features of this table, and one that points to certain distinctive aspects of the 1933 situation, is found in the failure of the index numbers derived from Census data to agree with measurements based on direct price quotations on manufactured goods. The differences are clearly revealed by the following index numbers relating to the average selling prices of manufactured goods. The drop

	1929	1931	1933
Prices realized by manufacturers (*Census data*)	100	78	66
Prices quoted in wholesale markets (*National Bureau of Economic Research*)	100	81	76

of 34 per cent in the average prices realized by manufacturers is substantially greater than the decline of 24 per cent shown by the index based upon prices quoted in wholesale markets. Indeed, the decline of 34 per cent appears to be inconsistent with the various bits of evidence previously presented, which indicated a considerable expansion in the manufacturing differential during the recession. This expansion appeared to be the result of the lagging adjustment of the final selling prices of manufactured goods to the sharp price declines occurring in the markets for raw materials. Yet the 34 per cent drop in average prices received by manufacturers is not far short of the decline of 40 per cent recorded for producers' goods, in raw state.

It is well to recall, at this point, the derivation of the price index based upon Census data. It is secured by dividing an index of the total value of manufactured products by an index of the physical volume of production. The process is equivalent to that employed in computing average price by dividing the aggregate value of a stock of goods by the number of physical units. In the present case, of course, relative numbers, defining changes in aggregate value and in physical output, are used in deriving index numbers of changes in average selling price. The price index numbers thus derived are, obviously, measures of realized price and not of quoted price. There is here a possibility of difference between index numbers based on samples of quoted prices and those derived in the manner just described. Furthermore, we should note that the measures of realized price are fully comparable, from one period to the next, only on the assumption that no considerable change takes place in the average quality of the goods entering into the aggregate. If quality improves or deteriorates materially, or if the relative importance of goods in different price classes changes notably, the changes in average realized price and in the average quoted price on goods of unchanging quality would not be the same.

Index numbers of average selling prices of manufactured goods, as derived from Census records, are thus not equivalent to measurements based directly upon quoted prices. In some degree they serve as checks upon them, being especially valuable for this purpose because of the comprehensive character of the data upon which they are based. During periods when no great changes occur in the quality and constitution of the stream of manufactured goods, close agreement between the two sets of measurements may be expected. In fact,

RECESSION AND DEPRESSION

during the decade 1919–29, in which five biennial comparisons of realized and quoted prices are possible, very close agreements were recorded.[14] But when the composition of the stream of manufactured goods changes, whether because of quality changes or of shifts in the relative importance of goods in different price classes, the index of realized prices will differ from an index relating to quoted prices on goods of standard quality.

During the recession from 1929 to 1933 changes of four different types may have affected the price records of manufactured goods.

1. Reduction of prices of standard goods, without change in quality.

[14] The following index numbers of the average selling price of manufactured goods bear upon this point:

	PRICES QUOTED IN WHOLESALE MARKETS (*National Bureau of Economic Research*)	PRICES REALIZED BY MANUFACTURERS (*Census data*)
1919	100	100
1921	79	79
1921	100	100
1923	100	99
1923	100	100
1925	100	99
1925	100	100
1927	94	94
1927	100	100
1929	100	98
1929	100	100
1931	81	78
1931	100	100
1933	93	85

This change would be reflected equally in quoted and realized prices.

2. Reduction of prices, accompanied by a lowering of quality, but without change in names or apparent standards of manufactured goods.

This change would be reflected equally in quoted and realized prices. However, part or all of the reduction of material costs, or fabrication costs, would be due to the lowering of quality and would not represent an actual reduction of the market prices of materials, or of fabrication costs for work of constant quality.

3. Shift by manufacturer and consumer to goods of lower price and quality, without change in the actual or quoted price on goods of constant quality. (A larger proportion of the total manufactured product would consist of goods of lower quality and lower price.)

This shift would not be reflected in quoted prices, and would thus not affect the current price index numbers. It would, however, be reflected in the average price realized by manufacturers. The average cost of materials, per unit sold, or the average cost of fabrication, or both, would also be reduced.

4. Undercover cutting of prices on standard goods, without change in quality and without change in quoted prices.

This price-cutting would be reflected in realized prices. The average cost of materials, per unit sold, would not be reduced, but the average cost of fabrication per unit sold would be lowered (since profits per unit are included in the aggregate 'value added' from which cost of fabrication is estimated).

It is impossible to determine, in quantitative terms, the relative importance of these four types of change. It is not to be doubted that movements of the first type, involving straight price reductions for goods of standard grade, were highly important, indeed, most important, in bringing about the observed price changes of the recession period. There

RECESSION AND DEPRESSION

were doubtless, also, movements of the fourth type—undercover cutting of prices, not reflected in current quotations. Although definite evidence is lacking, it is a matter of general knowledge that during the months of most severe depression goods of many kinds were being sold at special prices. It is a fair assumption, therefore, that part of the divergence between realized and quoted prices is attributable to this source. The most important factor in this divergence, however, was probably a reduction in the grade of manufactured goods marketed, due largely to a shift by manufacturer and consumer to goods of lower price and quality. Accommodation to a lower income was effected by the typical consumer through the purchase of clothing, shoes, automobiles, and, to some extent, foods from lower price classes. In the main, this also meant goods of lower average quality. As a mass phenomenon this movement was probably more important during the recent depression than in any depression through which the present generation has passed.

Evidence of two types bears on this shift. For automobiles, a commodity of considerable importance in the domestic economy of the United States, we have records showing production by price classes in different years. In 1929, 54 per cent of all cars produced were priced, at wholesale, at $500 or less. In 1933 the corresponding percentage was 81. Further, we may note that in 1929, 18.6 per cent of all cars produced were priced at more than $750; in 1933 the prices of only 4.5 per cent exceeded $750, at wholesale.[15] Of course, this change was due in some degree to straight price reductions, but in the main it reflected a real shift by buyers to cheaper cars. (This shift was stimulated in part, of course, by a considerable improvement in the quality of the cheaper cars.) The

---

[15] See National Automobile Chamber of Commerce, *Automobile Facts and Figures*, 1934 ed., p. 22.

net result of such a shift would be just such a reduction in the average price realized by manufacturers as we have observed, a reduction that does not reflect an actual decline in quoted prices on standard goods.

Equally revealing is evidence of another sort. We bring together below measurements relating to the declines in the average prices of materials of manufacture and of finished goods during two post-War recessions. The first two entries

	Percentage decline	
	1919–1921	*1929–1933*
Producers' goods, all, wholesale	29	32
Producers' goods, raw, wholesale	40	40
Cost of materials, per unit of manufactured goods	23	37
Selling price (realized), per unit of manufactured goods	21	34

relate to changes in quoted prices in wholesale markets, for producers' goods in general and for raw producers' goods. These classes are not identical with the 'materials of manufacture', but such materials, raw and semi-finished, come from the broad classes of goods represented by these two entries. From 1919 to 1921, when raw producers' goods were declining 40 per cent in price, and all producers' goods were dropping 29 per cent, the average cost of materials, to manufacturers, declined only 23 per cent. From 1929 to 1933 raw producers' goods, as priced in wholesale markets, dropped by exactly the same percentage as from 1919 to 1921, and the general group of producers' goods fell only slightly more than in the first post-War recession. With conditions in respect of quoted prices of 'materials' thus almost identical, we should expect to find approximately equal declines in the average cost of materials to manufacturers, in the two recessions. Instead, we find a drop of 37 per cent, from 1929 to 1933, as compared with a drop of 23 per cent from 1919 to 1921. We may note that the latest drop in the average cost of materials to manufacturers, per unit of goods produced, almost equalled the decline in the average price of raw producers' goods, at wholesale, although manufacturers' 'materials' include semi-finished goods and supplies of all sorts.

The notable reduction between 1929 and 1933 in the cost of materials entering into a unit of manufactured goods might have occurred as a result of 'skimping', the use of less material per unit of finished goods; it might have resulted from a lowering of the average quality of materials purchased for manufacture. It might, finally, have been due to the general concentration of manufacturers on the production of finished goods of lower average quality and price. Such a shift to goods of lower grade might or might not involve skimping, or the use of materials of poorer quality. To some extent the recession undoubtedly brought a reduction in the real quality (and price) of goods represented by current quotations (a change of type 2). In greater degree, however, the lowering of the cost of materials was probably due to a shift on the part of manufacturers to the production of goods in the lower price ranges with no necessary reduction in the quality of these cheaper goods (a change of type 3). Only a shift of this sort would account for the divergence between quoted and realized prices that was so marked a feature of the 1933 situation.[16]

[16] Comparison, by industries, of measurements of changes in average quoted prices and in average prices realized by manufacturers indicates that the chief divergences occurred in the industries listed below. It was in these industries, presumably, that there occurred pronounced shifts to the production of goods of lower average price. The list is not exhaustive, for quoted prices are not available for all industries, for comparison with the prices realized by manufacturers.

Flour and grain mill products
Cotton goods
Woolen and worsted goods
Boots and shoes
Lumber
Rubber products
Paper

Changes over a longer period are shown by the entries on the 1914 base (see table, p. 117). Both 1914 and 1933 were years of depression (the latter much more severe, of course), and the comparability of the measurements is thereby improved. In 1933 the average selling price of manufactured goods was 4 per cent lower than in 1914. Changes in the two components of this price were markedly different. The average cost of materials in 1933 was 15 per cent below the 1914 cost; the cost of fabrication, including profits, was 20 per cent above. These figures define one of the most striking changes in the American economy during the last two decades. It is true that quality changes obscure somewhat the direct comparison of costs. An increasing degree of fabrication has been a long-term tendency in American industry, and this factor would tend to increase costs of fabrication, relatively to material costs. A shift, in 1933, to goods of lower average quality would also tend to reduce cost of materials. But the notable expansion in the manufacturing margin between 1914 and 1933 cannot be explained in terms of these movements, alone. The increase in the costs of fabrication during and immediately following the War persisted during the decade of the 'twenties and survived the rigors of the most recent decline. The cost to the final consumer of a fixed task of fabrication, as this cost enters into the selling price of the finished goods he buys, was notably higher in 1933 than in 1914.

The changes in manufacturing costs between 1929 and 1933 were in some respects unlike those of the period 1919–21, as we have noted in one of the preceding comparisons. The periods are not strictly comparable, it is true, because the phases of the two depressions do not agree. But a further comparison of the net changes over these periods throws light on some of the distinctive features of the latest decline. The more recent recession, which covers two Census intervals,

RECESSION AND DEPRESSION

may be followed over a two-year and a four-year period.[17]

	Percentage decline		
	1919–1921	*1929–1931*	*1929–1933*
Average selling price (realized) of manufactured goods	21	22	34
Average cost of materials, per unit of product	23	26	37
Fabrication cost plus profits, per unit of product	17	16	28
Labor cost	5	13	25
Overhead, plus profits	26	18	29

In comparing these figures we should observe that the recession that initiated the current depression began in the summer of 1929, whereas the peak of production during the first post-War boom was not reached until the early autumn of 1920. Thus 1933 stands four full years removed from the beginning of the recession whereas the entries for 1921 relate to a period but one year later than the beginning of the first post-War decline. These differences in timing are to be kept in view, in addition to the differences in the duration and severity of the two recessions.

The drop in the average selling prices of manufactured goods from 1929 to 1933 was much more severe than the decline from 1919 to 1921. (A shift to goods of lower average quality played a considerable part in this decline, as we have already noted.) Liquidation was not only more protracted; it cut deeper. Cost of materials dropped 37 per cent, as against the earlier drop of 23 per cent; fabrication costs (plus profits) fell 28 per cent, as against the 1919–21 decline of 17 per cent.

A striking difference between the periods is found in the

[17] The data for 1919–21 relate to 58 manufacturing industries, those for 1929–31 to 112 industries and those for 1929–33 to 82 industries. They are thus not fully comparable in detail, but the samples may be accepted as representative of manufacturing industries in general.

relative movements of the two elements of fabrication costs. Labor costs per unit of product declined but 5 per cent between 1919 and 1921. The greater decline in the recent period, 25 per cent, is probably due in part to the time factor previously noted. Labor costs are usually difficult to reduce; an extended spell of liquidation brings more drastic cuts than does a briefer depression. Indeed, it is notable that the reduction in labor costs was greater from 1931 to 1933 than from 1929 to 1931. For all the other elements recorded the decline was retarded in the second of these two-year periods. The declines of overhead costs plus profits, per unit of product, were approximately equal in the two periods of post-War recession—26 per cent between 1919 and 1921, 29 per cent from 1929 to 1933. But the later drop, though approximately equal in magnitude to the earlier, was slower and more protracted. The fall during the first two years of recession was substantially less than from 1919 to 1921.

The reasons for these differences are many. The greater relative importance in the recent period of overhead expenses proper [18] is undoubtedly one factor. More machinery was in use per employee in 1929 than in 1919. Furthermore, most fixed elements in cost were more strongly entrenched in 1929, after eight years of relative price stability, than they were immediately after the sharp price changes of the War years, and thus offered greater resistance to reduction. In addition, the greater magnitude of the decline in volume of manufacturing production after 1929 rendered more difficult the downward adjustment of fixed costs, on a per unit of product basis. Finally, the price drop that began in 1929 was much more gradual than that of 1920, and business men were slower to accept the idea that the pre-recession price level would probably not be restored. So long as men thought

---

[18] In 1919 overhead expenses plus profits constituted 18 per cent of the total value of product; in 1929, 24 per cent.

of the 1929 price level as 'normal' they were reluctant to reduce their fixed charges. Not until the recession had turned into depression was this conception generally abandoned.

The measurements that define changes in 'overhead costs plus profits' per unit of product relate, as we have noted, to a highly heterogeneous composite.[19] During a period of liqui-

[19] The compilations of the Census of Manufactures do not permit an analysis of this composite into its elements, but the general nature of these elements may be determined from corporate returns to the Bureau of Internal Revenue. The figures below, from *Statistics of Income* for the year 1929, refer to corporations engaged in manufacturing operations. (Corporations produced 92 per cent of all manufactured goods, by value, in the year 1929.) The figures on p. 130, from the *Census of Manufactures* for 1929, relate to all manufacturing establishments. The figures from the two sources are not comparable in detail, since they differ in respect of enterprises covered (non-corporate returns are excluded from the first column), industries included (a few industries, such as those producing motion pictures and manufactured gas, are excluded from the Bureau of Internal Revenue compilations), and accounting procedures, but the comparison of broad totals will serve the present purpose.

DATA FROM STATISTICS OF INCOME, 1929

(*millions of dollars*)

Cost of goods sold		52,165
Other statutory deductions		
Compensation of officers	1,172	
Interest	712	
Taxes, other than income	617	
Bad debts	267	
Depreciation	1,753	
Depletion	265	
Miscellaneous	10,192	
Total other statutory deductions		14,978
Income tax		544
Compiled net profits, less tax		4,537
Total, other statutory deductions, income tax, and net profits less tax		20,059
Total receipts, manufacturing corporations		72,224

(Total receipts of manufacturing corporations include $69,236 million from gross sales and $2,988 million of other receipts—interest, rents, dividends, profits from operations other than those represented under gross sales, etc.)

dation, indeed, it is to be expected that the two major elements of this composite will move in opposite directions. It is not possible, using the data of the Census of Manufactures, to break this composite item into its component parts. We may, however, make use of records contained in *Statistics of Income,* issued by the Bureau of Internal Revenue, in estimating the relative changes in overhead costs and in profits, per unit of manufactured product.[20] These estimates, and

	1927	1929	1931	1933
Overhead costs, per unit of product	100	103	117	92
Profits, per unit of product	100	119	(deficit)	15

they are, of course, only estimates, show a slight advance in overhead costs proper between 1927 and 1929, and a substan-

(*Footnote* 19 *concluded*)
DATA FROM CENSUS OF MANUFACTURES, 1929
(*millions of dollars*)

Total direct costs (wages, materials, fuel, purchased energy)		50,171
Overhead plus profits, other than salaries	16,069	
Salaries of principal officers	964	
Salaries in central offices	600	
Other salaries	2,631	
Total salaries		4,195
Overhead plus profits, total		20,264
Total value, manufactured products		70,435

[20] The ratio of net income to gross income was computed for the four years 1927, 1929, 1931 and 1933 from data for corporations published in *Statistics of Income.* Only data for those industries included in the Census sample were used. These ratios were then applied to the 'values of product' reported in the Census for the corresponding years, yielding a series of dollar figures representing profits. A similar series for overhead was obtained by subtracting the estimated profits from the Census 'overhead plus profits.' These two series were converted to relatives on the 1927 base, and these were divided by index numbers of physical volume of production on the same base. The resulting series, in relative form, provides the figures given in the text.

In these calculations tax-exempt income (dividends and interest on tax-free government bonds) is excluded from both net profits and gross income in order to avoid attributing to manufacturing operations much of the income derived from other sources.

RECESSION AND DEPRESSION

tial increase, amounting to 14 per cent per unit of product, during the next two years. The spreading of overhead costs among a smaller number of physical units was the immediate reason for this advance during the first years of the recession. Between 1931 and 1933, however, average overhead costs, per unit of product, dropped 22 per cent. This left overhead costs per unit still high, in comparison with more flexible elements of selling prices, but the evidence of sharp slashing of obdurate fixed costs between 1931 and 1933, in the face of declining volume of output, is impressive.

Profits per unit shared in the expansion preceding the 1929 break, advancing no less than 19 per cent from 1927 to 1929. The next two years wiped out all profits, leaving manufacturing industries with a net deficit. By 1933 profits were again appearing although on a per unit basis they amounted to only 15 per cent of 1927 returns.

The major conclusions to be drawn from this general survey of liquidation among manufacturing industries, between 1929 and 1933, may be briefly summarized.

Although the general drop in prices was less severe than in the 1920–21 recession, the prices of manufactured goods were much more sharply reduced in the latest recession.

Material costs and selling prices were reduced by manufacturers, in the 1929–33 recession, through a lowering of the average quality of goods purchased and sold. (This process merely supplemented, of course, actual reductions in the prices of both materials and finished goods.) A shift to goods of lower quality (and price) was a distinctive feature of this recession.

Labor costs were much more severely cut in the 1929–33 recession than in that of 1920–21.

As in all recessions, the cost of fabrication increased, relatively to final selling price, in the 1929–33 decline. Since such costs were already high, prior to the recession, the fabricational margin was exceptionally wide in 1933. This fact was in part concealed, in the records of realized prices, by the shift to materials and finished products of lower average quality.

Overhead costs per unit actually increased, between 1929 and 1931, but were cut some 20 per cent during the two following years. Profits per unit disappeared in 1931, but in 1933 they averaged 15 per cent of the 1927 returns and 13 per cent of the 1929 returns.

Faced by the numerous difficulties of production and marketing raised by the recession, manufacturers sought to adapt their costs to the reduced incomes of consumers by shifting to goods of lower quality, sharply reducing labor costs and cutting the sluggish elements of overhead. Efforts in these directions were especially strong between 1931 and 1933. Advances in productivity furthered these efforts to reduce costs. Nevertheless, volume of production was seriously curtailed and the fabricational margin that represents the cost of manufacturing processes was widened, relatively to general prices.

On the Incidence of Recession among Manufacturing Industries

The use of averages for all manufacturing industries in defining changes in selling prices, fabrication costs, etc., gives a misleading impression of uniformity of behavior among these industries during a general industrial decline. No such uniformity prevails, of course. There is wide diversity in the response of manufacturing industries to the forces of recession, as is strikingly revealed by the series of frequency distributions in Table 6. These distributions are constructed from measurements relating to changes in production, selling price and the various elements of selling price for 82 manufacturing industries. (The unit, be it noted, is a change in a single *industry* or in a group of closely-related industries, not in a single establishment.)

The median values of the items entering into these various distributions differ, ranging from 69.4 for material costs to 78.4

for overhead costs plus profits, per unit of product. But our immediate interest centers in the evidence of diversity of fortune among the individual industries represented. In each distribution the range of values is considerable. It is significant that the variation in output is distinctly greater than the variation in selling prices; there appears to be more cohesion among manufacturing industries in respect of prices than in respect of physical production.

Among the components of selling price there is greatest dispersion in changes in overhead costs plus profits. Wide variation in the composite of overhead costs and profits is to be expected during recession, since both elements are subject to extreme and usually conflicting changes at such a time.

TABLE 6

FREQUENCY DISTRIBUTIONS OF RELATIVE NUMBERS MEASURING CHANGES IN VOLUME OF PRODUCTION, IN SELLING PRICE AND IN CERTAIN COMPONENTS OF SELLING PRICE, IN 82 MANUFACTURING INDUSTRIES, 1929–1933

(All measurements relate to changes per unit of product.)

INDEX NUMBERS (1933 as percentage of 1929)	Physical volume of production	Selling price	Material costs	Fabrication costs	Labor costs	Overhead costs plus profits
22 and under	3[2]					
25	2					
28	1					
31	3					
34	1					
37	3		1			
40	2				1	
43	3	2	2	1	2	2
46	2	2	1	3		2
49	1	3	7	1		2
52		1	2	2		3
55	3	5	5	1	1	3
58	2	3	3	4	4	6
61	4	3	5	4	7	2
64	3	7	6	4	2	6

(Table 6 concluded on p. 134)

TABLE 6 (*cont.*)

FREQUENCY DISTRIBUTIONS OF RELATIVE NUMBERS MEASURING CHANGES IN VOLUME OF PRODUCTION, IN SELLING PRICE AND IN CERTAIN COMPONENTS OF SELLING PRICE, IN 82 MANUFACTURING INDUSTRIES, 1929–1933

(All measurements relate to changes per unit of product.)

INDEX NUMBERS (*1933* as percentage of *1929*)	FREQUENCY (Number of industries experiencing stated change)					
	Physical volume of production	Selling price	Material costs	Fabrication costs	Labor costs	Overhead costs plus profits
67	2	7	7	5	9	5
70		6	7	4	7	3
73	5	5	8	6	8	3
76	5	3	5	5	2	2
79	1	7	4	5	9	7
82	4	7	3	7	3	6
85	6	6	3	5	3	5
88	7	8	2	6	5	3
91	3	1	4	4	3	3
94	2	3	2	5	5	4
97	2		1	2	2	4
100	3	1			1	2
103	1		1	1	2	
106	2		1	2	1	1
109	1			1	2	2
112		2	1	2		2
115						3
118			1			
121				1		
124					1	
127	2					
130						1
133 and over	3[3]			1[4]	2[5]	
Total	82	82	82	82	82	82
Median	75.1	72.7	69.4	78.1	74.5	78.4
Index of dispersion[1]	26.6	14.2	14.7	14.7	14.7	18.0

[1] Half the range between the two quartiles, as a percentage of the median.
[2] One item in each of the following classes: 10, 13, 19.
[3] One item in each of the following classes: 136, 151, 208.
[4] One item in the following class: 136.
[5] One item in each of the following classes: 142, 157.

RECESSION AND DEPRESSION

AGGREGATE PURCHASING POWER OF MANUFACTURING PRODUCERS

Practically all exchanges of goods today are monetary transactions, involving set prices. The purchasing power of a given group of producers in these markets depends on their aggregate money income and upon the average price paid for the goods bought. In tracing the effects of the recession on the purchasing power of producing groups we have already dealt with producers of raw materials. There we noted drastic reductions due, in the main, to declines in the average price of goods sold. The details of the picture are somewhat different for agents of fabrication.

	1929	1931	1933
Volume of manufacturing production	100	75	69
Average price per unit for fabrication (i.e., cost of fabrication)	100	84	72
Aggregate value added by manufacture	100	63	50
Aggregate purchasing power of value added in wholesale markets	100	82	72
Aggregate purchasing power in terms of articles entering into cost of living	100	70	66

These figures, which relate to a large sample of industries for which comparable data are available, indicate a drop of 37 per cent in the money income of agents of fabrication (as measured by aggregate 'value added') between 1929 and 1931, a drop of 50 per cent, between 1929 and 1933. (Were data available for 1932 they would show a lower level than in 1933.) These declines are the resultants of severe drops in volume of output, less severe declines in the average price per unit received by agents of fabrication.

Reduction in the aggregate money value of the services rendered by agents of fabrication did not entail an equal drop in their real purchasing power. The prices of the goods they purchased declined also, of course. If these buying prices be considered to have declined after 1929, on the average, at the rate of fall in general wholesale prices, the drop in the physical purchasing power of fabricators may be estimated at about 28 per cent, between 1929 and 1933. If the yardstick of change in buying prices be the cost of living index for industrial workers, the drop in purchasing power may be estimated at 34 per cent. The true figure probably lies between these limits. We may conclude that the physical volume of goods that could be purchased by persons drawing their incomes from manufacturing industries declined approximately 30 per cent between 1929 and 1933.[21]

The above estimates of changes in the aggregate purchasing power of those drawing incomes from manufacturing industries are based directly upon Census compilations. Census and other records have been used by the Department of Commerce in making annual estimates of the total income disbursements by manufacturing industries.[22] These figures have the value, for the present purpose, of including all elements of income paid out, such as dividend payments out

	1929	1930	1931	1932	1933
Income paid out by manufacturing industries					
In millions of dollars	18,013	15,940	12,364	8,543	8,514
In relative terms	100.0	88.5	68.6	47.4	47.3
Purchasing power of incomes paid out by manufacturing industries					
In wholesale markets	100.0	97.6	89.6	69.7	68.4
In terms of articles entering into cost of living	100.0	90.4	76.6	58.7	62.1

[21] These estimates are made on an annual basis because of the difficulty of measuring, on a monthly basis, changes in the purchasing power of manufacturing producers. The annual figures, of necessity, show changes less extreme than those that actually occurred.

[22] See "Expansion in the National Income Continued in 1935" by R. R. Nathan in *Survey of Current Business*, July 1936, pp. 14–19, and "Income Originating in Nine Basic Industries, 1919–1934" by Simon Kuznets, *Bulletin 59*, National Bureau of Economic Research.

of surplus. The inclusion of these items is desirable, in following changes in the actual purchasing power of industrial groups. The summary of these estimates indicates a drop of approximately 53 per cent between 1929 and 1933 in the actual money receipts of those receiving incomes from manufacturing industries, a decline of 32 per cent in the purchasing power of such receipts, in wholesale markets, and of 38 per cent in terms of articles entering into the average workingman's budget.[23] These figures are not comparable, in detail, with those previously cited, but they indicate declines of somewhat similar magnitudes. We shall be reasonably safe in concluding, from these several sets of figures, that the depression reduced the purchasing power of those deriving incomes from manufacturing industries by from 30 to 40 per cent. (The lowest month of the depression would show a greater drop.) This means that the stream of physical goods (consumption goods and articles of capital equipment) and services produced to meet the demands of this group was reduced about one-third. This was roughly equal to the decline in the aggregate purchasing power of primary producers, an equality that is not altogether a coincidence.

SUMMARY:
CHANGES IN FABRICATIONAL MARGINS DURING RECESSION

In its general outlines the history of the changes in manufacturing costs between 1929 and 1932–33 is simple, paralleling experience during earlier recessions. We start in 1929 with a condition of relatively high fabrication costs, relatively low material costs. In spite of increasing productivity during the preceding decade, labor costs and overhead costs plus

[23] The purchasing power of income paid out by manufacturing industries, in terms of articles entering into the cost of living, was lower in 1932 (41 per cent below 1929) than in 1933.

profits per unit of manufactured product remained fairly high, as compared with pre-War levels. As in most recessions, the impact of forced liquidation in 1929 was felt most severely in raw material markets. Special circumstances, notably large world supplies of raw materials and the depressing effect on raw material producing debtor countries of the almost complete stoppage of international lending, accentuated the force of liquidation among primary products.

Tardy deflation of manufacturing costs was to be expected, then. The susceptibility of raw materials to fluctuations in the sales of finished products and the presence of peculiarly inflexible elements in the costs of fabrication both contribute to such tardiness. In 1929 there were special conditions contributing to delay the downward readjustments of manufacturing costs, just as there were exceptional circumstances intensifying the usual weakness, during recession, of raw materials. The persistence, for almost the decade preceding, of a fairly stable price level led to a general reluctance to cut costs, in the belief that the price drop was temporary and that the previous level would shortly be restored. Furthermore, heavy capital investments during the preceding decade had added to the weight of overhead expenses (a notably inflexible element of cost) while pricing practices in many business fields had contributed to the development of rigid prices.

The uneven character of the ensuing price decline was a natural consequence of these conditions. During the first twelve months of recession (beginning in July 1929) raw producers' goods fell 19 per cent in price; all processed goods fell but 9 per cent. During the next twelve months raw producers' goods declined 22 per cent; all processed goods dropped 12 per cent. During the third twelve months raw producers' goods fell 14 per cent; all processed goods dropped 9 per cent. The rate of expansion of the raw-processed differential was definitely diminishing in the third year, as old rigidities were broken and established prices were finally feeling the force of liquidation.

This phenomenon of price disparity is not a novel feature of a business depression. Inequalities of price movement characterize all periods of recession and depression. But in magnitude, persistence and devastating effects the price disparities opened up during the recession and depression of 1929–33 stand almost alone. An economic system probably less able than at earlier times to adapt itself readily to drastic changes was exposed to disruptive forces of exceptional strength, and a condition of almost unprecedented difficulty resulted. The necessary adaptations to this changed situation, fundamental financial and physical readjustments of which price readjustments were but the manifestation, were difficult to accomplish. Pending their accomplishment, the economic system operated at a low level of efficiency.

The reasons for the low efficiency of the economic system after a period of sharp recession are many, more than we may explore here. But one important consequence of price disparities (and of the disparate financial and physical conditions that lie behind price phenomena) we must note—the inevitable reduction in the volume of intergroup trade. We found clear evidence of this in the declines observed in the aggregate purchasing power of primary producers and agents of fabrication. The physical volume of goods that could be purchased with the money incomes received by each of these groups dropped one-third, or more, between 1929 and 1933. The price changes experienced by the two groups were widely different, as were also the reductions in physical volume of output. But the interdependence of their fortunes is clearly indicated by the approximate equality of the losses suffered in physical income.

Prices and Volume of Production of Capital Equipment and Building Materials During Recession

In following the prices of articles entering into capital equipment during the pre-recession period we have noted the continuing high prices for capital goods. An era of remarkable expansion in the investment of capital funds and in the construction of capital equipment was marked by the persistence of high capital costs. Low material prices and rapidly increasing productivity provided American industry with the advantage of low operating costs during the long period of prosperity prior to 1929. But on the capital side a large volume of new equipment and a great number of new plants were being built at high cost. These high costs set no immediate obstacle to profits during the heyday of prosperity, but they rose to plague American business when the pangs of readjustment set in.

In considerable part such readjustment of high capital charges during and after a period of liquidation is a problem of finance. We do not here examine that aspect of the matter in detail. But the problem of stimulating new investment and of initiating activity in the capital goods industries during recovery is in some part a price problem.

The changes during the recession in the prices of goods intended for use in capital equipment are defined by the accompanying index numbers. Building materials, which are an important element of capital costs as well as an item in the cost of durable consumers' goods, are represented by a

	WHOLESALE PRICES		PER UNIT PURCHASING POWER
	July 1929	February 1933	(July 1929=100) February 1933
Producers' goods for use in capital equipment, processed	100	79	127
Building materials	100	76	123
All commodities	100	62	100

RECESSION AND DEPRESSION

separate index. While the general average of wholesale prices was declining 38 per cent, between July 1929 and February 1933, processed goods intended for use in capital equipment declined 21 per cent; building materials dropped 24 per cent. The real worth of these goods in exchange for general commodities at wholesale gained, correspondingly, by some 25 per cent. Here was an important barrier to the resumption of normal activity in the heavy industries.[24]

At the peak of prosperity in 1929, as we have seen, capital equipment of all sorts was relatively high priced. Pressure

---

[24] We have pointed out above that processed goods destined for use in capital equipment are not necessarily finished goods. But it is certain that the ultimate finished goods of this class experienced smaller price declines than did the commodities included in this index. The index overstates the decline in the average prices of all types of finished capital goods.

A bias in the same direction is present in the figures relating to changes in steel prices during recession, because of the rigidity of freight rates. The Federal Trade Commission, in its report on the steel code, states that on the average realized steel prices are higher than the basing-point prices which are used in current index numbers.

Let p_0 = steel price in base year
p_1 = steel price in given year
f_0 = freight charges in base year
f_1 = freight charges in given year

Then $\dfrac{p_1+f_1}{p_0+f_0}$ = the 'realized price' relative

We use $\dfrac{p_1}{p_0}$ = the 'basing-point price' relative

Since $\dfrac{f_1}{f_0} > \dfrac{p_1}{p_0}$ (when prices decline, because of the rigidity of freight rates)

Then $\dfrac{p_1+f_1}{p_0+f_0} > \dfrac{p_1}{p_0}$

That is, the 'basing-point price' relative is smaller (showing a greater decline) than the 'realized price' relative. Thus, barring price-cutting and contract sales at prices below current quotations, published changes in steel prices *overstate* the actual decline in prices paid by purchasers of steel.

from the demand side towards lower prices was not strong, and conditions of supply tended to maintain high costs. Special circumstances in the building industries worked to the same end. We should take account of this fact in appraising the price changes of recession. A longer perspective for the study of recent movements is provided by index numbers on a pre-War base. The relative positions of the two capital

	WHOLESALE PRICES				PER UNIT PURCHASING POWER AT WHOLESALE			
	1913	1922	July 1929	Feb. 1933	1913	1922	July 1929	Feb. 1933
Producers' goods for use in capital equipment, processed [1]	100	165	161	124	100	111	107	134
Building materials [2]	100	172	169	128	100	124	122	150

[1] This index includes building materials; that previously presented, showing the decline from July 1929 to February 1933, did not.
[2] The index of building material prices is that of the U. S. Bureau of Labor Statistics for 1913–29. For the period following 1929 the index is one constructed by the National Bureau of Economic Research. In reducing wholesale prices of building materials to terms of purchasing power, a deflator was secured by splicing the general wholesale price index of the National Bureau of Economic Research to that of the Bureau of Labor Statistics, on the 1913 base, at 1929.

equipment groups are best indicated by the purchasing power measurements in the right hand column of the table. The substantial price advantages enjoyed by sellers of capital equipment and building materials in 1922 had been reduced somewhat by 1929. Thereafter, the retarded declines of these goods during the recession resulted in further advances in their per unit worth, in terms of other commodities. In February 1933 such goods were worth from one-third to one-half more, in terms of all commodities, than in 1913.

This situation is the more striking in comparison with the relatively low prices prevailing at the early stages of the productive-distributive process. The preceding chapter presented a general account of this condition, showing the persistence of low prices of materials, relatively high fabrication costs and relatively high prices of manufactured goods. The present evidence, relating to one important class of finished goods, confirms this. In the markets for capital equipment prices were high prior to the recession, and this condition became much more pronounced during the period July 1929–February 1933.[25]

The existence, at the end of a phase of price recession, of relatively high prices for articles entering into capital equipment is a post-War phenomenon for which there is little precedent in earlier economic experience. From 1907 to 1908, when all commodities at wholesale declined 7 per cent in price, processed goods intended for use in capital equipment dropped 12 per cent. This record may not be taken as representing a 'normal' reaction, but relative changes of this order were closer to the general pre-War experience than were the movements occurring after 1920. In this earlier experience a check to demand for new capital goods was to be expected even before the peak of prosperity; thereafter both output and prices fell; mid-depression found relatively low prices and low production. The prompt revival of demand and early recovery among industries producing capital

---

[25] The following index numbers, defining changes in the wholesale prices of raw producers' goods intended for use in capital equipment are notably lower than the measurements relating to processed goods of the same general type, as cited in the preceding table. The two sets of index numbers are not precisely comparable, as to constitution, but their movements are broadly representative of the changes in prices of basic materials, in raw form, and the prices of more highly fabricated goods entering into capital equipment. The final figure given below shows raw materials of this type to have been 23 per cent lower in price in February 1933 than in 1913, while the corresponding measure for processed goods was 24 per cent above the 1913 level.

1913	*1922*	*July 1929*	*February 1933*
100	137	135	77

equipment that were thereby stimulated constituted one of the major forces contributing to general economic recovery. Against this background of more or less conventional cyclical behavior the relatively high prices of capital equipment during the 1921–22 revival and their recalcitrance after the 1929 recession were unexpected and disturbing.

CONSTRUCTION COSTS

The indexes of building material prices given in the preceding tables do not by any means represent all construction costs, even in building construction alone. Labor costs are another important item. Changing technical methods, leading to alterations in the efficiency of construction work, also affect actual construction costs. In Table 7 we supplement the above account by a summary record of certain additional measurements, rather broader in scope, of construction costs during the period prior to the recovery of 1933–35. The expected lag of the usually more rigid elements of capital costs is found, in recession. Wholesale commodity prices fell 32 per cent, from 1929 to 1932; the various indexes of construction costs show declines ranging from 10 to 26 per cent.

While these changes were occurring, the physical volume of construction of all sorts, as measured by indexes of the National Bureau of Economic Research, declined approximately 52 per cent. This drastic decline in the volume of construction is related, of course, to the lagging adjustment of construction costs to changing monetary values and to the concurrent drop in the total national income. Total national income paid out, in current dollars, dropped some 40 per cent between 1929 and 1932. Even if no other factors had been operative, the discrepancy between the declines in national income and in construction costs would have entailed a reduction in volume of construction. Added to this, of

TABLE 7
CONSTRUCTION COSTS IN THE UNITED STATES, 1913–1932

	A		B		
	1929	1932	1913	1929	1932
General construction [1]	100	76	100	207	157
Building construction, actual costs [2]	100	74	100	185	136
Railroad construction [3]	100	82	100 [6]	160	131
Utility systems [4]					
Water works	100	85	100	180	153
Electric light	100	80	100	178	142
Street railway	100	85	100	170	144
Natural gas	100	90	100	184	166
Artificial gas	100	86	100	183	157
Wholesale prices, all commodities [5]	100	68	100	136	93

[1] Index of *Engineering-News Record*. This index has four components, of which three are prices of materials (structural steel at Pittsburgh, cement at Chicago and lumber at New York) and one is wages (average wage for common labor in 20 cities).

[2] Index of Turner Construction Company, N. Y. This index is based on actual costs encountered on Turner building construction work. The following factors have been taken into account: labor rates; prices of materials; productivity of labor; efficiency of plant and management.

[3] Index of Railroad Construction Costs of the Engineering Section, Bureau of Valuation, Interstate Commerce Commission. This is an index of accounts, including such items as grading, tunnel excavation, bridges, developed from analysis of major construction contracts.

[4] Index numbers of C. F. Lambert showing the current cost of construction of five utilities:
Water works: 25 systems, 68 items   Street railways: 10 systems, 82 items
Electric light: 25 systems, 84 items   Natural gas: 15 systems, 58 items
        Artificial gas: 25 systems, 63 items

[5] Index of U. S. Bureau of Labor Statistics.   [6] 1910–14=100.

course, is the notable elasticity of demand for the capital equipment and durable consumption goods that make up the total volume of construction. Economic stress always brings intensified declines among these goods.

Comparison of these various measurements on a pre-War base provides evidence of still more notable shifts (see section B, Table 7). It is natural that the several indexes of construction costs should differ more widely among themselves, when changes over twenty years are compared. Significant in this comparison is the fact that the index numbers of actual building costs and of railroad construction costs, which are directly affected by changing technical methods and by resulting gains in productivity, are substantially lower than the general index of construction costs, which is derived from the prices of basic materials and wage rates. The former are more accurate indexes of changes in the actual costs of construction work. From these it appears that such costs, in 1932, were from 30 to 40 per cent higher than in 1913. But even these are far removed from the index of wholesale prices, which in 1932 was 7 per cent below the 1913 level. Construction costs stand with the costs of capital equipment in general, in this respect. During the whole post-War era they were out of line with commodity prices. When the favorable, perhaps fortuitous, circumstances that made possible rapid expansion of construction between 1922 and 1929, in spite of high costs, ceased to prevail, a heavy reduction in volume was inevitable. With recession still greater disparities developed. Building and capital creation generally were excessively expensive undertakings at the low point of the depression. The price difficulties standing in the way of new investment were materially greater than during the preceding prosperity, when other conditions were more favorable to activity in this field.

Price Changes Among Consumers' Goods During Recession

The period of post-War expansion that ended in 1929 was marked, as we have seen, by relatively low prices of raw materials and by high fabricational margins. The first of these conditions tended to lower prices to consumers, the second, which was the stronger, to increase them. During the decade following the War the prices of consumers' goods were persistently high, relatively to earlier standards. Reference has been made to certain fortuitous circumstances—the reaping of high speculative profits, the expansion of consumer credit, and the maintenance of foreign sales through heavy American lending—without which such relatively high prices to consumers might well have checked the flow of goods long before 1929. We turn to the record of recession among consumers' goods with this background in mind.

The next table shows the net changes in the prices and purchasing power of consumers' goods, at wholesale, in comparison with the movement of general wholesale prices, after forty-three months of price decline. The decline in the aver-

	WHOLESALE PRICES		PER UNIT PURCHASING POWER (*July 1929=100*)
	July 1929	*February 1933*	*February 1933*
Consumers' goods, all	100	64	104
Raw	100	56	91
Processed	100	66	108
All commodities	100	62	100

age wholesale price of consumers' goods, normally sluggish in their reactions to changed business conditions, was almost as great as that in the general price index—36 per cent as against 38 per cent. The smallness of the difference is attributable in part to the influence of raw consumers' goods, that is, goods such as eggs, milk, fruits and vegetables which are ready for final sale without processing. Average prices of these commodities suffered a more severe decline than did processed consumers' goods. The shifts that these declines brought, with reference to the average value of all commodities at wholesale, are shown by the measurements of per unit purchasing power. Consumers' goods, on the average, in-

148 PRICES IN RECESSION AND RECOVERY

creased 4 per cent in relative worth during the recession. Raw consumers' goods lost 9 per cent, while processed consumers' goods gained 8 per cent in real worth.

Referring these changes to an earlier base, we have the measurements given below. All consumers' goods and the two

	WHOLESALE PRICES				PER UNIT PURCHASING POWER			
	1913	1922	July 1929	Feb. 1933	1913	1922	July 1929	Feb. 1933
Consumers' goods, all	100	155	161	104	100	104	108	112
Raw	100	154	172	96	100	104	115	104
Processed	100	155	159	106	100	104	106	115
All commodities	100	148	150	92	100	100	100	100

subdivisions shown were consistently higher in price than the average of all commodities, during the entire post-War period. In 1922 these groups showed a uniform 4 per cent advantage, with reference to 1913 relations. By July 1929 this had increased to 8 per cent for the general group of consumers' goods; raw consumers' goods had risen to higher levels than processed goods. The recession increased the advantage of processed consumers' goods and reduced that of raw consumers' goods. But in February 1933, at the low point of the depression, both groups were above the 'all commodities' average, and the per unit real worth of consumers' goods as a broad class was 12 per cent greater than in 1913.

Further evidence relating to the depression level of prices to consumers is provided by the following index numbers.[26]

	July 1929	Feb. 1933	PER UNIT PURCHASING POWER AT WHOLESALE			
			1913	1922	July 1929	Feb. 1933
Processed consumers' goods	100	108	100	104	106	115
Foods	100	96	100	95	102	98
Non-foods	100	119	100	117	111	132

[26] The price index numbers from which these measurements are derived are given in Appendices III and IV.

RECESSION AND DEPRESSION

Among processed consumers' goods non-foods were responsible for the high relative prices prevailing both before and after the recession. Food products ready for consumption remained close to the general average of commodity prices, while non-foods among consumers' goods have been consistently above that average. At the low point of the depression the real worth, per unit, of processed non-foods ready for use was 19 per cent greater than in July 1929, 32 per cent greater than in 1913. Here was a major element in the high prices prevailing at the terminal stage of the productive-distributive process.

VARIATIONS IN LIVING COSTS AND RETAIL PRICES

The quotations used above, in discussing prices paid by consumers during recession, have been drawn from wholesale markets. They should be supplemented by a record of price changes at retail. Available data in this field are far from satisfactory, with respect to both accuracy and coverage. Indeed, the degree of variation among retail quotations and the absence of standardization among commodities marketed render it impossible to follow price changes at retail with the accuracy possible in the tracing of changes in wholesale prices. Index numbers for some scattered series are brought together below, for comparison with wholesale price measurements.[27]

---

[27] The cost of living index is that of the U. S. Bureau of Labor Statistics, with interpolations based on the index of the National Industrial Conference Board. The index numbers of retail food prices are also compiled by the Bureau of Labor Statistics. The index number of retail prices of clothing and home furnishings is constructed by Fairchild Publications; the Bureau of Agricultural Economics is responsible for the index of prices paid by farmers. The index numbers of consumers' goods and of all commodities at wholesale are computed by the National Bureau of Economic Research (see Appendices III and IV). It should be noted that the wholesale price

	July 1929	Feb. 1933	1913	July 1929	Feb. 1933
Cost of living, industrial wage earners	100	74	100	174	128
Retail food prices	100	58	100	169	97
Retail prices of clothing and home furnishings, in large department stores	100 [1]	59			
Prices paid by farmers	100	66	100	151	100
Consumers' goods at wholesale	100	64	100	161	104
All commodities at wholesale	100	62	100	150	92

[1] October 1929=100.

During the general recession of prices from July 1929 to February 1933 the downward movement of prices paid by farmers paralleled the decline in all consumers' goods, at wholesale. Retail food prices and the prices of clothing and furnishings in large department stores declined more sharply. (The index of prices in department stores probably overstates the degree of decline in the prices of clothing and home furnishings in the country at large. Sacrifice sales during depression and rapid turnover of stock in department stores facilitate a more rapid reduction of prices than occurs among retail outlets generally.) But if we take account of all items in the household budget of the average industrial worker, including rent, we find a much less rapid decline. Living costs for industrial workers dropped some 26 per cent during the recession, as against declines of 38 per cent in all wholesale prices, and 36 per cent in the wholesale prices of consumers' goods.

More marked are the differences when recession prices are referred to a pre-War base. Retail food prices dropped to about 3 per cent below the pre-War level. Prices paid by farmers fell to precisely the 1913 level. Living costs for industrial workers stood, at the February low, 28 per cent above the 1913 level.

index of the Bureau of Labor Statistics, on a pre-War base, is lower than that of the National Bureau. The Bureau of Labor Statistics index for July 1929, on the 1913 base, is 138; for February 1933 it is 86.

RECESSION AND DEPRESSION

We lack a comprehensive index of changes in the prices actually paid for goods by final consumers as a broad class. If we had such an index its movements would probably be closer to those of the industrial wage earner's cost of living index than to the specific retail price series. Many items in the average consumers' budget are sluggish in their price movements, slow to adapt themselves to the general price changes that occur during business expansion and recession. The contraction in the volume of goods marketed during depression reflects, in part, this lagging price readjustment in the face of sharp decreases in the wage, dividend and other disbursements to final consumers.

The situation at the low point of the depression was thus marked by relatively low prices in the markets to which primary producers come as sellers, by high prices in the markets to which consumers come as buyers. It is the prices in the latter markets, at the terminus of the entire elaborate process of production and distribution, that determine just how far effective purchasing power may go in moving goods. In the absence of offsetting factors such a condition would tend to clog the stream of trade and reduce the volume of goods that could be produced and sold.

PRICES OF CONSUMERS' GOODS AND CONSUMER PURCHASING POWER

The various records surveyed indicate that the consumer was adversely affected by the price changes during recession. In general, the prices of goods ready for consumption fell less than did the average of all commodity prices. But the real changes in the position of consumers are not accurately reflected in the fluctuations of any such general index of the prices of consumers' goods, whether at wholesale or retail. The unit prices of goods are of central interest to the pro-

152   PRICES IN RECESSION AND RECOVERY

ducer who is buying and selling. Indeed the operation of the entire economic system is dependent upon the existence of suitable unit price relations at the various stages of the productive-distributive process. But the fortunes of consumers at large are to be measured with reference to the buying power of aggregate income, rather than in terms of the average price, per unit, of consumers' goods. It is now in order to bring together material relating to the aggregate purchasing power of consumers as a general class, during the recession, summarizing, at the same time, data for special groups previously presented. In doing this we must deal with annual values, taking 1929 as the peak year of prosperity, 1932 and 1933 as the low years of the depression. (National income was slightly lower in 1933 than in 1932.) Records of changes in the aggregate amounts of income paid out are given in Table 8.

The variations in the record of decline, for different classes of income, are notable, but our immediate concern is with the total. We have here a drop, between 1929 and 1933, of approximately 43 per cent. In comparison with the decline in this aggregate of money income paid out, the records of changes in the prices of consumers' goods have particular significance. In making this comparison we should have an index based upon comprehensive records of the prices actually paid by consumers at large for the goods and services they buy; this would make possible an accurate estimate of the change in the aggregate purchasing power of consumers. In default of such an index we may use the accompanying approximation. This index has been secured by averaging index numbers of living costs for industrial wage earners, prices paid by farmers for commodities used in family main-

	1929	1932	1933
Estimated prices of goods purchased	100	80	76

TABLE 8

NATIONAL INCOME PAID OUT, BY TYPES OF PAYMENT,
1929–1933 [1]

	1929	Percentages of 1929 1932	1933
Salaries (selected industries)	100.0	59.8	53.8
Wages (selected industries)	100.0	40.8	41.8
Salaries and wages (all other industries)	100.0	70.1	63.5
Total labor income	100.0	60.1	57.1
Dividends	100.0	46.2	37.0
Interest	100.0	97.5	90.0
Total property income	100.0	71.1	62.1
Net rents and royalties	100.0	42.9	36.4
Entrepreneurial withdrawals	100.0	63.9	58.4
Total entrepreneurial income	100.0	59.4	53.7
Total income paid out	100.0	61.5	57.2

[1] See Table 58, Ch. VIII, for the data upon which these percentages are based. The basic figures are estimates jointly prepared by the U. S. Department of Commerce and the National Bureau of Economic Research. Cf. *Survey of Current Business,* July 1936; "National Income, 1929–1932", by Simon Kuznets, *Bulletin 49,* National Bureau of Economic Research. (Explanations of the entries and of the limitations attaching to various income estimates appear in the latter publication.)

tenance, and prices of capital equipment and construction.[28] Correcting by this index the figures measuring changes in total income paid out, we estimate a decline from 1929 to 1932 of 23 per cent in the aggregate purchasing power of the national income paid out; from 1929 to 1933 the estimated decline was 25 per cent. There is, of course, a margin of error in these estimates, but it is safe to say that the actual decline between 1929 and 1932–33 in the volume of goods and services that could be purchased by income recipients, at prevailing prices, approximated 25 per cent.[29]

[28] With weights of 8, 1 and 1, respectively.
[29] The decline in total production in the United States between 1929 and 1932 came to some 36 per cent; to 1933 the drop was 33 per cent. The figure of 25 per cent given in the text relates to the sale of goods and services to

These general estimates of the loss in consumer purchasing power during the depression may be made somewhat more accurate for two groups of consumers, farmers and industrial wage earners. For these groups (whose real annual incomes reached depression lows in 1932) we have reasonably accurate records of changes in aggregate money income and in the average price paid for goods bought. Measurements for agricultural producers, given in an earlier section, are summarized below.[30] The situation among farmers was in all

	1929	1932
Gross income of farmers	100	45
Prices paid by farmers	100	70
Aggregate purchasing power of farmers	100	64

respects blacker than among consumers generally. As a net result of declining gross income and of reduced buying

those classed as income recipients. It does not include intermediate merchandising transactions.

A very large proportion of 'income paid out' is expended for consumers' goods. During a severe recession the proportion so expended undoubtedly increases, at the expense of the amounts saved. Such a shift would mean that the drop in sales to consumers would be less than the figure measuring the decline in total production, while the reduction in the sales of capital goods would be correspondingly greater. Among consumers' goods, similarly, the drop in the sales of perishable goods would be less than the drop in durable goods.

[30] The original data were compiled by the Department of Agriculture; see *Yearbook of Agriculture,* 1935. The relative for farm gross income, as given above, includes the farm value of products consumed by farmers and their families, in addition to cash received for products sold. The value of products retained for consumption was estimated at $1,524,000,000 for 1929, $960,000,000 for 1932. In estimating changes in the aggregate purchasing power of farmers, aggregate gross income has been deflated by the index of prices paid by farmers. A slightly more accurate estimate would be secured if aggregate *cash* income were so deflated, and if there were added to the purchasing power figure thus secured an increment representing products retained for consumption on the farm. This procedure would raise the index of aggregate purchasing power of farmers in 1932 from 64 (on the 1929 base) to 65.

RECESSION AND DEPRESSION

prices, farmers suffered a loss of some 36 per cent in aggregate purchasing power.

Changes in the actual living conditions of farmers are not measured, of course, by records of shifts in gross income. If we subtract from the gross returns of farmers all production expenses we have a remainder, representing cash available for family maintenance, that suffered a much more severe decline during the recession. On the positive side, however, account should be taken of farm products consumed on the farm, a relatively constant factor of considerable importance in maintaining the farmer's standard of living. If we combine the purchasing power of the cash available to farmers for family maintenance with the actual physical returns in the form of farm products consumed on the farm, we have a means of estimating changes in the real income of farmers' families. The loss between 1929 and 1932, on this basis, probably approximated 40 per cent.[31]

The changing fortunes of industrial workers are shown by the following measurements.[32] Here is an even sharper drop.

	1929	1932
Total pay rolls of wage earners in manufacturing establishments	100	43
Cost of living of industrial workers	100	81
Aggregate purchasing power of wage earners in manufacturing establishments	100	53

[31] Farmers were able to keep their losses within this limit only by drawing upon their capital. It is estimated by the Bureau of Agricultural Economics that depreciation charges on farms, in 1932, exceeded current capital expenditures by over 500 million dollars. In 1931 deferred replacements of the same type amounted to approximately 300 million dollars. (These figures and others cited above are given in *Crops and Markets*, July 1935, pp. 271–2.)

[32] The data of pay rolls are compiled biennially by the Census of Manufactures. Interpolation for the year 1932 has been based upon pay rolls of the comprehensive sample of manufacturing industries covered by the U. S. Bureau of Labor Statistics. The index of cost of living is that of the Bureau of Labor Statistics.

Cost of living lagged behind the drop in total receipts of wage earners, with the result that the aggregate purchasing power of manufacturing wage earners fell 47 per cent between 1929 and 1932.

An index of the net income of wage earners in mining, manufacturing, construction, steam railroads, Pullman, railway express and water transportation has a value of 41 in 1932, 1929 being 100 (see *Survey of Current Business,* July 1936, p. 16). Correcting this net income figure by the index of living costs, we secure an estimated index of 51 for aggregate purchasing power—a drop of 49 per cent from 1929 to 1932.

For these groups, in even more pronounced form than for consumers at large, the sharp decline in money income without corresponding declines in the prices of goods purchased brought drastic losses in their aggregate purchasing power; the consequent reduction in the demand for finished goods tended to reduce the sources of their incomes still further. Here is one segment of the vicious circle that is set up during a period of recession and liquidation.

Price Relations and Problems of Recovery

The manner in which a modern industrial economy reacts to the forces of recession depends partly upon the incidence of those forces, partly upon the attributes of the various elements of the economy thus exposed to strains of readjustment. The active push that impels readjustment may come from different quarters at different times, and differences of origin will be reflected in the statistical records of different periods of recession. Such differences lead to departures from uniformity among recession movements. Perhaps more important, to the student of cyclical movements, are the modes of reaction of various economic elements to the forces of recession. Similarities in the behavior of important elements at different times would tend to create a pattern, even though there were no uniformity in the initiating forces. The historical record yields evidence of such similarities in behavior, in cycles widely different in time, space and attendant circumstances. But here again a factor of variation is introduced by secular change in the attributes of economic elements. Important variations in behavior may be due to such structural changes, representing differing responses rather than differences in the forces at work.

As a background for the study of the price recession of 1929–33 we have sketched the movements of a preceding period. Among these movements some were noted that tended to alter the attributes of the price system, and thus to affect its behavior under the stress of a major recession. The detailed record of the recession, as given in this chapter, represents the resultant of a composite of varied forces and conditions. We may not clearly disentangle movements due to the pressure of specific forces from shifts representing differing capacities for readjustment under stress. But in seeking to understand the changes occurring during the years 1929–33 it will be well to think in terms of the structural modifications brought by the twenty preceding years.

Four years of recession created a price situation at the beginning of 1933 that was marked by certain outstanding characteristics. Prices to consumers of finished goods were high, relatively to the prevailing price level; prices of raw materials, on which the incomes of important consuming groups depend, were very low. Prices received by producers of agricultural products, in particular, were seriously depressed, while the prices paid by farmers for goods needed for production and for family maintenance were high. Low prices of industrial raw materials, together with relatively high prices for finished goods, put manufacturers in an advantageous position on the operating side. This price advantage, of course, failed to yield a corresponding reward in the form of real income as long as the volume of production and sales remained unusually low, but it offered attractive potential profits. On the investment side, however, there prevailed relatively high prices for goods entering into capital equipment and for building materials. This circumstance, with others, tended to restrict activity in industries producing capital goods. A factor that has in the past served to stimulate revival from depression was thus reduced materially in potency.

Certain of the problems of recovery centered about these conditions: How was the flow of goods to consumers to be stimulated with the real value of raw materials so low, in comparison with earlier standards, and the real value of consumers' goods so high? How was activity in industries producing capital goods to be restored, with production and sales of finished goods low in volume and with the costs of new equipment high, relatively to the value of commodities in general?

With respect to the first of these problems three alternatives existed, on the price side (with corresponding adjustments, of course, in the physical processes of production and consumption): (1) resumption of activity under the then existing conditions—low prices for raw materials and relatively high prices to consumers; (2) continued liquidation of finished goods until something approaching pre-recession parity with raw materials was restored; (3) restoration of more satisfactory terms of exchange between raw and finished goods through advances in the prices of raw materials, rather than through further liquidation of manufactured goods.

Of these alternatives the first, a resumption of activity under the price conditions existing at the low point of the depression, was not impossible. A modern economic system

RECESSION AND DEPRESSION

does not function under one rigorously prescribed set of conditions; it may adapt itself to a variety of situations. However, with a gap as wide as that prevailing in the winter of 1932–33 it was highly improbable that working relations among economic elements could be restored on the basis of existing price conditions. The modes of using productive resources, investments of capital, the economic distribution of man power were not adapted to the price relations that prevailed after four years of deep disturbance. Radical shifts in the distribution of income and enduring changes in the status of economic groups would have been entailed, changes more profound and disturbing than would have been accepted without continuing social unrest. The restoration of price relations closer to those prevailing earlier, a restoration to be effected through continued liquidation of prices still substantially above the average or through the raising of the most seriously depressed prices, seemed to be an essential condition of economic recovery. The second problem, on its price side, reduced to a similar question: could the prices of goods entering into capital equipment be brought more closely into line with other prices, either through raising the latter or reducing the prices of capital goods and building materials?

It is helpful to think of the problems of recovery in terms of these general price relations, but emphasis should also be placed upon the specific character of the price relations and profit opportunities that actually motivate the decisions of business men. No man decides whether he should open his factory, or increase his output, or embark upon a new line of activity after comparing general index numbers of the prices of raw and processed goods. The price and cost relations and the market opportunities upon which judgments are based are particular relations and opportunities, involving individual commodities and particular markets. No index numbers of average prices can define the host of specific situations that confront the thousands of individual business men whose decisions determine the course of economic events. A given person may find a particular situation favorable for profitable activity when the general outlook is blackest. Indeed, the price disparities that work to the disadvantage of some economic groups may be offering new opportunities to others. Declining material prices lower the incomes of primary producers; they reduce production costs to manufacturers. Always, the key to an economic situation lies not in the general relations defined by gross index numbers but in the innumerable relations between specific buyers and specific sellers.

The justification for using index numbers and for thinking in terms of general relations, in spite of the specific character of the situations that actually affect business judgments, is two-fold. We do not have and cannot secure detailed information about countless specific relations. Moreover, such averages as we have are fairly reliable guides to the situations that confront the majority of business men. Single swallows do not make summers; isolated profit opportunities may be highly important in creating little centers of recovery, but the factors affecting the great tides of business change may be defined with reasonable precision by the available averages. This is the chief justification for basing our reasoning on general movements and average relations. But it is the part of wisdom to remember that behind these averages, often defying them, are countless men, working under adverse conditions to discover or develop little areas of strategic advantage. These are the energizing factors in business recovery.

The problems of recovery in 1932 and 1933 ramified, of course, far beyond the markets in which buying and selling prices were set. Conditions of production affecting each commodity group were involved. Wages, overhead charges and all other elements of production costs were highly relevant factors. Changes in productivity and their various possible effects on prices and on the distribution of income were important elements of the situation. The volume of income and of potential purchasing power available to the various producing and consuming groups, and the willingness to make use of such purchasing power, entered into the tangled problems of readjustment. Subsequent chapters will be concerned with the events of revival and the course of recovery among particular elements of this complex situation.

CHAPTER IV

THE WORLD PRICE STRUCTURE IN RECESSION AND RECOVERY

THE movements of prices, of production and of purchasing power during recession and recovery in the United States were aspects of world-wide swings. It is true that national economic boundaries have been more sharply drawn in recent years, but the world retains many qualities of a single economic unit. Whether we will or no, we are affected by the major forces that influence the course of economic events in other industrial countries. We shall better understand domestic movements, therefore, if at this point we survey in a general way the world situation created by recession, and follow the major changes of more recent years in the currents of world trade and the fluctuations of prices and costs in important industrial areas. In some respects these have paralleled the internal shifts discussed in tracing the course of events in the United States, but the world picture is painted on a much broader canvas. And the restoration of a normal volume of world trade involves, of course, many elements quite foreign to the domestic situation.

In 1929 aggregate world production and the physical volume of world trade reached a peak, for the post-War decade. Fairly steady progress during the preceding five years had brought substantial recovery, in respect of physical activity, from the depressed conditions of the early years of the decade. World-wide recession in 1929 reversed this movement. Within three years world production of primary products—crude foodstuffs and industrial raw materials—declined about 10 per cent. The volume of manufactures and construction dropped more sharply. The physical volume of world trade fell 26 per cent. The number of unemployed workers throughout the world increased, by rough estimate, from some ten million in 1929 to about thirty million in 1932.[1] By that year the major force of the recession was spent. The four years following brought conflicting movements. Moderate improvement occurred in some areas; deflation persisted in others. Numerous obstacles impeded a restoration of full activity, but in general the forces of recovery dominated the diverse cross-currents of change of the period 1932–36. On a world view, these were years of halting revival.

The price changes that accompanied this tremendous economic upheaval were more extreme than the physical movements. Our present concern is with the alterations that occurred within the world price structure under the impact of recession and the stimulus of revival.

Recession and Recovery in World Prices: A General View

A general picture of the sweep of the recession as it spread swiftly from country to country through the delicate mechanism of international price relations has been given in Chapter I. The measurements there employed relate to national currencies, an appropriate procedure when chief interest attaches to domestic conditions in the various countries. But the picture is quite incomplete if such changes alone are considered. For during the period covered by this record country after country departed from the gold stand-

---

[1] Cf. *World Economic Survey, 1932–33* (League of Nations, Geneva, 1933), p. 109.

164   PRICES IN RECESSION AND RECOVERY

ard; dual currency systems were created throughout the world. The concurrent existence of gold standard and non-gold standard currencies exerted a great influence on the course of price movements and on the general economic fortunes of the various countries concerned.

TABLE 9

PRICE RECESSION IN THIRTY-TWO COUNTRIES, 1928–1936

A Summary of Changes in Index Numbers of Wholesale Prices

(*Price movements are here measured in gold values.*) [1]

	DATE OF PRE-RECESSION HIGH	DATE AT WHICH LOWEST POINT WAS REACHED	PERCENTAGE DECLINE FROM PRE-RECESSION HIGH TO LOWEST FIGURE
Japan [3]	October 1929	March 1935	—71
Argentina [3]	May 1928	May 1934	—68
Peru	March 1929	November 1933	—67
Egypt (Cairo)	November 1928	September 1933	—66
Australia	September 1929	March 1935	—64
India (Calcutta)	September 1929	March 1935	—64
Estonia [3]	March 1929	April 1935	—62
Denmark [3]	February 1929	March 1935	—61
Sweden	May 1928	March 1935	—59
Chile [3]	March 1929	March 1935	—58
New Zealand	September 1929	March 1935	—58
Norway	August 1928	March 1935	—58
Canada	August 1929	August 1935	—57
Dutch East Indies [2]	May 1929	March 1936	—57
United Kingdom	March 1929	March 1935	—57
Jugoslavia [3]	May 1928	August 1934	—57
Belgium [3]	March 1929	April 1935	—56
Finland	August 1928	March 1935	—56
Bulgaria [3]	April 1929	January 1934	—55
Union of South Africa	October 1928	April 1935	—55
United States	July 1929	April 1934	—55
Spain [3]	December 1928	September 1934	—53
Netherlands [2]	March 1929	April 1933	—52
France [2]	March 1929	July 1935	—51
Hungary [3]	March 1929	November 1933	—48

TABLE 9 (cont.)

PRICE RECESSION IN THIRTY-TWO COUNTRIES, 1928–1936

	DATE OF PRE-RECESSION HIGH	DATE AT WHICH LOWEST POINT WAS REACHED	PERCENTAGE DECLINE FROM PRE-RECESSION HIGH TO LOWEST FIGURE
Poland [2]	March 1929	March 1936	—48
Italy [3]	March 1929	May 1934	—47
Czechoslovakia [3]	February 1929	April 1934	—43
Austria [3]	May 1929	April 1933	—40
Switzerland [2]	July 1929	March 1935	—40
Latvia [3]	March 1928	June 1934	—38
Germany [3]	July 1928	April 1933	—36

SOURCES: *League of Nations Year-Book, 1934–35;* pp. 219 ff; *Monthly Bulletin of Statistics*, League of Nations, Geneva.
[1] For an explanation of procedure, see Appendix IX.
[2] Countries on gold standard, March 1936.   [3] Official foreign exchange control.

The character of the world price recession, in gold values, is indicated by the entries in Table 9. The various national index numbers are not fully comparable, since they differ in respect of the number and character of commodities included and in technical methods of calculation. Under identical economic conditions, in recession, these differences would cause some variations among the declines recorded. However, variations due to instrumental differences of this sort would be far smaller than those actually recorded. It would be well if we had comparable index numbers for different countries, but in default of these we may use the measurements available, recognizing that some of the differences observed may be instrumental rather than truly economic.

The price declines of recession, in gold values, ranged from 36 per cent for Germany to 71 per cent for Japan. The median decline for the thirty-two countries was 56 per cent, as compared with a median decline of 36 per cent in terms

166 PRICES IN RECESSION AND RECOVERY

of national currencies (see Chapter I). The declines in gold prices were more severe and, as is to be expected, show less variation from country to country than do the measurements based on national currencies. In general, the average decline of wholesale prices in terms of gold values was less in gold standard countries than in non-gold countries.

We may carry the comparison of price movements in gold standard and non-gold standard countries through recovery as well as recession (Table 10 and Figure 7). For this pur-

TABLE 10

MOVEMENTS OF WHOLESALE PRICES IN GOLD STANDARD AND
NON-GOLD STANDARD COUNTRIES, 1929–1936

NET CHANGE (PER CENT)

	MARCH 1929 TO AUGUST 1931			AUGUST 1931 TO MARCH 1933			MARCH 1933 TO MARCH 1936		
	Countries on gold standard	Countries off gold standard		Countries on gold standard	Countries off gold standard		Countries on gold standard	Countries off gold standard	
		Price in national currency	Price in gold		Price in national currency	Price in gold		Price in national currency	Price in gold
Dutch East Indies	—31			—30			—11		
France	—25			—20			—4		
Germany [1]	—21			—17			+14		
Hungary [1]	—32			—11			+11		
Latvia [1]	—31			—2			+4		
Netherlands	—36			—23			+8		
Poland	—30			—14			—13		
Switzerland	—24			—17			+1		
Belgium [1]	—29			—18				+15	—17
Czechoslovakia [1]	—25			—10				+9	—9
Estonia [1]	—25			—13				+12	—32
United States	—25			—16				+32	—22
Austria [1]	—17				—3	—26		+1	+3
Bulgaria [1]	—36				—21	—24		+6	+9
Canada	—26				—9	—24		+12	—21
Chile [1]	—24				+129	+14		+5	—48

TABLE 10 (cont.)

MOVEMENTS OF WHOLESALE PRICES IN GOLD STANDARD AND NON-GOLD STANDARD COUNTRIES, 1929–1936

NET CHANGE (PER CENT)

	MARCH 1929 TO AUGUST 1931			AUGUST 1931 TO MARCH 1933			MARCH 1933 TO MARCH 1936		
	Countries on gold standard	Countries off gold standard		Countries on gold standard	Countries off gold standard		Countries on gold standard	Countries off gold standard	
		Price in national currency	Price in gold		Price in national currency	Price in gold		Price in national currency	Price in gold
Denmark [1]	—29				+13	—36		+13	—3
Egypt (Cairo)	—25				—24	—47		+26	+9
Finland	—19				+10	—33		+2	—13
India (Calcutta)	—36				—11	—37		+11	—5
Italy [1]	—34				—13	—15		+21 [4]	+14 [4]
Jugoslavia [1]	—31				—9	—29		+5	+3
Norway	—20				+1	—34		+9	—8
Sweden	—24				—4	—35		+12	—6
Union of South Africa	—16 [2]				—8 [3]	—37 [3]		+11 [5]	—4 [5]
United Kingdom	—29				—2	—31		+12	—4
Argentina [1]		—12	—41		—2	—11		+16	—27
Australia		—22	—40		—5	—30		+12	—4
Japan [1]		—33	—26		+17	—50		+8	—13
New Zealand		—10	—18		—2	—39		+5	—9
Peru		—8	—36		0	—41		+11	0
Spain [1]		+2	—40		—8	—11		+5	+1
Median change									
Unweighted	—26	—11	—38	—16	—4	—32	+2	+11	—6
Weighted [6]	—25	—22	—40	—17	—2	—31	+8	+12	—8
Number of countries	26	6	6	12	20	20	8	24	24

[1] Official foreign exchange control (as of March 1936).
[2] April 1929 to July 1931.
[3] July 1931 to April 1933.
[4] March 1933 to October 1935.
[5] April 1933 to April 1936.
[6] In computing the weighted median, the weight of each country is based upon the relative importance of its foreign trade in 1929.

FIGURE 7
WHOLESALE PRICES IN GOLD STANDARD AND NON-GOLD STANDARD COUNTRIES, 1929–1936

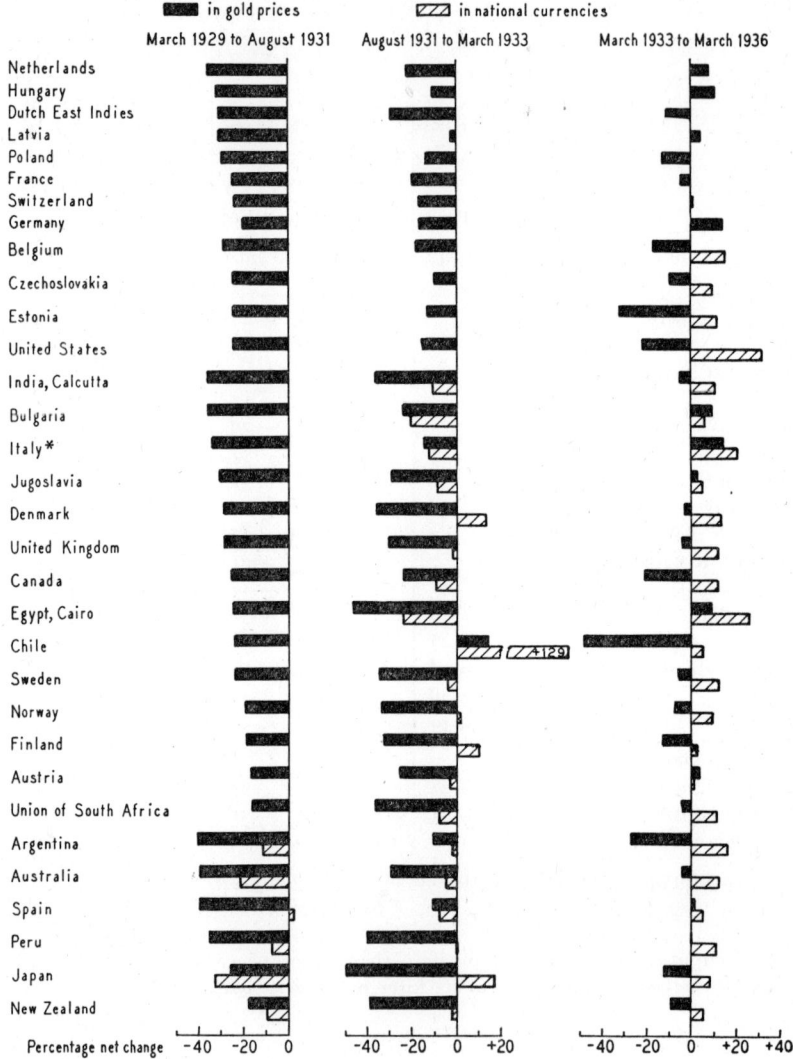

* Last period, March 1933 to October 1935

pose we divide the period of recession and recovery into three parts: March 1929 to August 1931 (Great Britain departed from the gold standard in September 1931); August 1931 to March 1933 (the United States departed from the gold standard in April 1933); March 1933 to March 1936. (The first phase is dated from March 1929, as that month marked the high point of prices in a considerable number of European countries.)

From March 1929 to August 1931 the median (unweighted) decline of wholesale prices in twenty-six countries on the gold standard during the entire period was 26 per cent. For six countries not on the gold standard at the end of the period we have two sets of records for comparison with this figure. Wholesale prices in these countries suffered a median decline of 11 per cent, in terms of national currencies. In gold equivalents, the median decline in these six countries amounted to 38 per cent. Departure from the gold standard was apparently associated with less drastic declines in domestic prices. In terms of gold, however, prices in the countries off the gold standard fell even more sharply than did prices in gold standard countries. This accentuated decline of gold prices in countries off the gold standard tended, in so far as international trade competition persisted, still further to depress prices in countries remaining on the gold standard.

The next period of nineteen months covers the interval between the dropping of the gold standard by Great Britain and by the United States. In the twelve countries remaining on the gold standard prices continued to decline at about the rate prevailing during the preceding period of twenty-nine months. The median decline for these countries was 16 per cent. The twenty countries off the gold standard show median price declines of 4 per cent in terms of their respective national currencies. The history of the earlier period repeated itself, except that the group of non-gold standard countries was much larger and economically more significant. Where currencies were depreciated the drop in domestic prices was checked. Great Britain's decline of 29 per cent during the first period was followed by a decline of only 2 per cent in the second period. But the very move that served to check domestic declines exerted a downward pressure on world gold prices. The gold equivalents of the national currencies of the twenty countries off the gold standard during this second period suffered a median decline of 32 per cent.

Only eight of the original list of thirty-two countries were on the gold standard [2] during the third period. In five of these countries gold prices advanced; the median gain was 2 per cent. In the twenty-four countries off the gold standard domestic prices registered a median advance of 11 per cent. The gold equivalents of these domestic prices dropped, however, the median decline being 6 per cent. But the situation as a whole clearly reflects a lessening of the downward pressure on gold prices. Liquidation was checked, and the basis of price recovery was being laid. We deal with this phase in later pages.

World Price Relations in 1933

In discussing the structure of world prices as it existed in 1929 emphasis was placed on the effects of the long period

---

[2] The introduction of various types of exchange control renders it difficult, in some cases, to distinguish gold standard from non-gold standard countries.

In September 1936 the government of France announced measures for the reduction of the gold value of the franc. This step was followed by similar action by the Netherlands and Switzerland, and at a later date by Italy. International price relations, as well as the internal price structures of the countries immediately concerned, will, of course, be profoundly affected by these changes.

of economic non-intercourse (or of intercourse upon distorted and necessarily temporary bases) which began in 1914 and which extended, for some countries, to the middle of the decade of the 'twenties. As a result, in large part, of this non-intercourse, world prices and other elements of the world economic structure were not in gear when commercial and financial relations were generally restored. Disproportionate and unbalanced developments had occurred during the preceding years in different parts of that structure. By 1929 definite progress towards a more stable basis of economic intercourse had been made, though many of the faulty adjustments growing out of the period of non-intercourse persisted. We turn now to a brief survey of the situation existing early in 1933, with reference to the structure of prices and costs then prevailing. This will be done in general terms. Various supporting data will be presented in the next section, in which primary emphasis is placed upon the movements of recovery. The discussion of the situation in 1933 may fall under three headings, dealing with disparities in price levels, disparities in production costs, and disparities in the prices of commodities in certain groups of major importance.

DISPARITIES OF PRICE LEVELS

Unequal and considerable changes in national price levels, occurring over a relatively short period, throw international trading relations out of adjustment. This statement is axiomatic, as applied to a world economic system that operates on the basis of price relations; for any changes in the wholesale price levels of trading countries, particularly unequal changes, will entail numerous and unequal changes in the individual prices on which trading relations are based. Some of these shifts may tend to stimulate the import or export of particular commodities, but the net effect of wide altera-

PRICES IN RECESSION AND RECOVERY

tions will be to destroy the prospects of profitable commerce and to cramp trade.[3]

The wide diversity of the declines in wholesale prices in different countries between 1929 and 1933 has already been noted. In terms of national currencies the price level in Chile, in February 1933, was 79 per cent above that of 1929, and in the Dutch East Indies, 50 per cent below that level. These were the two extremes between which the other national price levels ranged. On a common gold basis the index numbers, with reference to 1929 as 100, range from 37 in Japan to 89 in Chile (see Table 13). It is not surprising that the delicate relations of trade suffered from these tremendous inequalities of change. Here was one important factor in the decline of 61 per cent in the aggregate value of world trade and of 26 per cent in its volume, between 1929 and 1932. (Other factors, notably rising tariff walls and the practical cessation of international lending, contributed, of course, to the trade decline.)

The 1929 standard of reference is not perfect. It is far from certain that world economic relations in that year were

[3] It is not true, of course, that unequal changes in national price structures are always a causal factor in throwing international trading relations out of adjustment. During a period of non-intercourse, or of intercourse restricted by high quota or tariff barriers or other factors, the elements of national price structures will inevitably get out of alignment. Price disparities develop under these conditions because of restrictions on trade. But if monetary or other forces present during a general recession press upon national price structures, bringing wide and unequal changes, the international price disparities thus set up may play a causal role in checking the movements of goods and forcing a readjustment of commercial relations. Not all the international price disparities that developed after 1929 were of this latter type, but there is no doubt that a great many of them were. The violent changes that price recession brought, all over the world, created conditions definitely adverse to the continuance of trade upon existing terms. It is true that opportunities for new trade may be created by the very changes that impede the previously existing trade, but the adaptation of national economies to new conditions of world trade is a painfully slow process.

adjusted to continuing and effective international cooperation. We may not assume, on the other hand, that pre-War relations constitute an ideal standard against which to measure current conditions, but it is desirable that we view the price relations of 1933 with reference to this earlier standard. In terms of national currencies and on a pre-War base the price levels of 1933 were very widely scattered indeed (see Table 14). Index numbers of wholesale prices ranged from 72 for Egypt to 653 for Czechoslovakia and 1838 for Bulgaria. Great differences in internal economic relations are indicated by these widely discrepant figures. Commodity prices in terms of gold were much more compactly grouped, as is to be expected. Even here, however, the price level of one country (Egypt) was cut in half over this twenty-year period, while Chile, at the other extreme, had a price level above that of 1913.

In this survey our interest is not in index numbers of wholesale prices as mathematical abstractions. We have used such measurements because we may learn something from a study of their comparative values about the innumerable individual relations that tie national economies together. The existence of differences in average wholesale prices means that similar (and greater) differences prevail among the numerous elements of different national price structures which must be in adjustment if the international exchange of goods and of services is to be effected. The abnormalities of the War years, the chaotic currency conditions of the years immediately following and, finally, the tremendous economic disturbances that began in 1929 all tended to shatter these adjustments. During the two decades that followed 1914 national economies were exposed to the play of a wide variety of forces, differing greatly in strength and incidence from country to country. A world economic system integrated over more than forty years of peaceful development, during which its component parts were affected by the same general forces, was shaken into separate elements. The forces playing upon these elements tended to lose their common character, becoming specific and diverse. That these elements were out of adjustment, and materially so, at the end of twenty years of stormy weather, gives no cause for wonder. The wide divergence of wholesale price levels in different countries constitutes one evidence of deep-rooted international maladjustment.

DISPARITIES OF PRODUCTION COSTS

Among the most important elements of national price structures are the various costs that enter into the production of the staple articles of international commerce. The competitive positions of industrial countries in world markets depend, obviously, upon relative production costs. The profitability of trade depends upon the relations between these costs and corresponding selling prices. When costs are out of adjustment with possible selling prices, or when the relations among cost structures in different industrial countries are suddenly disturbed, international trade is immediately affected.

Production costs are determined by a host of elements—wage rates, living costs, interest rates, the cost of materials, fuel and power, the degree of development of mechanical equipment and the technical arts, the skill of labor and many other factors. When commercial relations among the trading nations of the world have been maintained for some time a condition approaching equilibrium is attained among their cost structures, and the flow of trade is based upon these relations. Alterations are always occurring as wages, living costs, industrial productivity and other factors change in the different countries, but such alterations are slow in normal times, and trade is adjusted to them without severe strain. From 1929 to 1933, however, changes in production costs and in the competitive positions of trading nations were pronounced. These differences, superimposed upon those already existing in 1929, modified substantially the relations upon which trade had been based. The commercial chaos of the depression period was due in no small degree to these modifications.

A general cause of changes in the relations among the elements of production cost in different countries is found in the unequal declines of price levels in these countries during the depression and in the diversity of price movements that preceded the depression; for wages and overhead charges are notoriously slow to adapt themselves to changes in the value of money. After a price rise such costs are relatively low; after a price fall they are relatively high. In general those countries that had passed through inflationary movements prior to 1929 were characterized by low production costs in that year, while countries that had passed through deflationary movements were characterized by high production costs.[4] The inequalities of price declines between 1929 and 1933 introduced further modifications into the situation.

The nature of some of the notable changes that occurred during recession in the competitive relations of different industrial countries is shown in Table 11. Here index numbers measuring changes in the value of the dollar, in terms of foreign currencies, are contrasted with index numbers of food prices, cost of living and wage rates expressed as per-

---

[4] Italy constituted something of an exception. Although Italy had passed through an inflationary movement during the post-War era, the currency had been stabilized at a level that was high, with reference to the domestic structure of Italian prices and their relation to world prices at the time of stabilization.

centages of corresponding measurements for the United States.

TABLE 11

INTERNATIONAL VALUES OF THE DOLLAR AND VARIOUS SERIES RELATING TO PRODUCTION COSTS

A COMPARISON OF MOVEMENTS, 1929–1932 [1]

	INDEX NUMBERS OF VALUES OF THE DOLLAR IN TERMS OF CURRENCIES OF FOURTEEN COUNTRIES		INDEX NUMBERS IN DECEMBER 1932 AS PERCENTAGES OF CORRESPONDING MEASUREMENTS FOR THE UNITED STATES (1929=100)		
	1929	Dec. 1932	Food prices	Cost of living	Wage rates
United States	100	100	100	100	100
Australia	100	185	116	103 [2]	94
Belgium	100	100	116	110	107 [3]
Canada	100	115	102	104	107 [3]
Czechoslovakia	100	100	139	123	120 [3]
Denmark	100	156	126	117	120
Estonia	100	100	97	99	108 [3]
France (Paris)	100	100	134	121 [2]	116 [3]
Germany	100	100	115	100	92
Italy	100	103	124	106	100
Japan	100	222	132	105	102
Netherlands	100	100	118	108	106
New Zealand	100	161	113	105	97
Poland	100	100	97	94	97
United Kingdom	100	149	131	113	111

[1] This table follows the general form of one prepared by J. B. Condliffe, appearing in his article "Exchange Rates and Prices" in the *Index* (Svenska Handelsbanken), January 1935. (A more extended discussion of the data and techniques used is given in *World Economic Survey, 1933–1934*, League of Nations, pp. 47–51.) In the present table dollar values are used, rather than sterling values, as in Condliffe's table.

The basic data of exchange rates, cost of living and food prices are given in the *Statistical Year-Book, 1934–35*, and the *Monthly Bulletin of Statistics* of the League of Nations. Wage rates are from the *International Labour Review* (articles on "Statistics of the General Level of Wages").

[2] Last quarter.
[3] Annual figure.

THE WORLD PRICE STRUCTURE

The interpretation of this table may be suggested with reference to the measurements given for the United Kingdom. At the exchange rates prevailing in December 1932 the dollar was worth 49 per cent more, in British pounds, than in 1929. If the relations of 1929 were to be preserved, food prices, wages and other elements of cost in the United Kingdom should also have been 49 per cent higher than the corresponding American figures, with reference to 1929 parity. In fact, food prices were only 31 per cent higher, cost of living 13 per cent higher, and wage rates 11 per cent higher.[5] These relations meant that the United Kingdom enjoyed a competitive advantage over the United States in December 1932, to the extent that these various series truly represented production costs, and in the degree that world markets were open to free competition.

The various measurements in Table 11 and the graphical representation in Figure 8 are worthy of careful study, for they summarize certain of the most significant aspects of international trading relations at a date close to the bottom of the depression. They indicate that Japan and five countries of the sterling bloc (Australia, Canada, Denmark, New Zealand and the United Kingdom) stood in relatively favorable competitive positions at the end of 1932. Wages, living costs and food prices—all important (and related) factors in costs of production—had not risen commensurately with the declines in the dollar values of their currencies. At the other extreme, with costs high relatively to dollar costs and the dollar values of their currencies, were France, Czechoslovakia, Belgium and the Netherlands. In a middle group, not far removed from the United States, stood Germany, Italy, Estonia and Poland.

[5] Here, as in all international comparisons, we suffer from lack of full comparability among available index numbers. The results should be taken to define general relations only.

FIGURE 8
INTERNATIONAL COMPARISON OF CHANGES IN PRODUCTION COSTS, 1929–1932

Graph Showing Relative Amounts by which the Changes in Stated Series relating to Production Costs in Various Countries Exceeded or Fell Short of Changes in Corresponding Series for the United States, Account being Taken of Relative Changes in the Values of National Currencies

(Measurements of percentage changes from 1929 to December 1932)

The movement is shown as positive when the change in the country named exceeded the change in the corresponding series for the United States; it is shown as negative when the change was less than that in the series for the United States.

The comparisons provided by Table 11 are but samples of many that might be made. The series of prices and wages cited do not by any means measure all production costs. But they are representative of the total, in indicating how extreme were the international shifts in relative production costs between 1929 and 1932. We should note, too, that 1929 is a rather dubious standard of reference, in this respect. It is not proper to assume that production costs the world over were then in equilibrium. Some countries had already gone through processes of devaluation while others, including the United States and the United Kingdom, had not. Further, we may not conclude that all international competition at the end of 1932 was based upon the relative costs shown in Table 11; for such competition is between specific industries. Actual costs in individual industries may depart very widely indeed from averages representative of the entire body of a nation's industries. But the measurements given serve their purpose in suggesting the magnitude of the shifts in relative production costs among industrial countries that recession and depression had brought. This period and the decade and a half of disturbance preceding had altered channels of international trade that had been furrowed over long years of peaceful development. Old established trading relations were disrupted. The building up of new relations and their protection against dislocations through further fluctuations of exchange rates or prices was one of the major tasks set by the recession.

DISPARITIES OF COMMODITY PRICES

Some of the extreme disparities that developed in national and world price structures during the violent recession of 1920–21 persisted during the succeeding years, making deep impresses upon economic conditions. Similar disparities, many of them more severe, were opened up during the world price recession that began in 1929. Three were of exceptional importance in the world situation that developed during the recession and depression: the cleavage between the prices of goods of agricultural and of non-agricultural origin, the cleavage between the prices of raw and of processed goods, and the discrepant movements of the prices of goods intended for use in capital equipment and of goods intended for ultimate human consumption. (The last-mentioned class is broader than 'consumers' goods', which include only those commodities ready for final consumption.)

PRICES OF AGRICULTURAL AND NON-AGRICULTURAL PRODUCTS

High price variability is a characteristic of agricultural products. Since the volume of agricultural production is not readily adaptable to fluctuations in economic conditions, the full impact of business changes is felt by prices. The post-War weakness of agricultural prices, the world over, has already been noted. With the coming of recession in 1929 various efforts to bolster agricultural prices collapsed, declining demand for goods of agricultural origin was not matched by decreases in output, and the checking of loans to agricultural regions contributed a new element of weakness to the competitive position of farm products. Price declines of exceptional severity ensued.

The condition of agricultural producers throughout the world as a result of the depression is common knowledge and requires no extensive discussion at this point (for relevant index numbers, see Table 19). The declines in agricultural prices were most severe in the United States, Canada, New Zealand, Argentina, and Finland, all countries in which agricultural production plays an important role. In each of these countries the drop in agricultural prices was much more severe than that in general commodity prices. In certain countries, notably France and England and Wales, the declines in the prices of farm products were less than in general wholesale prices. In these countries domestic agricultural prices were not exposed to the full storm of price recession that struck the great staples entering into world trade.

THE WORLD PRICE STRUCTURE

PRICES OF RAW AND PROCESSED GOODS

No characteristic of the post-War economic situation was more striking or more fruitful of major consequences than the gap that was opened from 1919 to 1921 between the prices of industrial raw materials and of finished products. Reversing trends that had persisted for many years, this schism affected the course and character of international trade, the distribution of capital, the relations of debtor and creditor areas and the distribution of purchasing power among consuming groups throughout the world over a decade and more. By 1929 the gap had narrowed somewhat, but the narrowing was in some degree due to conditions that were necessarily short-lived. Raw materials remained in a weak position and the removal of certain adventitious props helped to destroy such gains as they had made. We pass to a summary of recent changes.

The recession that began in 1929 brought a growing divergence between the prices of raw materials and of manufactured goods, in world markets.[6] All the effects that followed upon the development of this situation in the early post-War years were again felt, but with a force more disastrous to world trade because certain alleviating circumstances previously present were absent after 1929. General financial and economic conditions prevented the application of methods of valorization, which had temporarily eased the earlier situation. The practical cessation of international lending removed the possibility of sustaining the depleted purchasing

[6] There were certain exceptions to this general rule. Raw consumers' goods showed much greater strength than did raw materials destined to pass through the industrial machine. Again, the margin between the prices of raw and processed goods behaved in a distinctive fashion in Germany. That country was unique during this period; it was a highly developed manufacturing country, yet it stood in a debtor relation to the commercial world in general.

power of raw material producing areas by means of new loans, and these areas had no buckler to oppose to the storm that broke upon them. Moreover, the normal international obligations of such areas, for imported manufactured goods, insurance, financial and shipping services, service upon capital loans secured from the great financial centers, had been made even heavier by excessive loans, many for unproductive purposes, during the boom years that preceded the recession. By a cruel conjuncture of circumstances, the price schism was reopened at a time when raw material producers were exposed on every flank to adverse forces.

Nor were industrial producers in much better case. Most of the conditions that helped, earlier, to protect many industrial elements (particularly in the United States) from the adverse effects of the price schism, while preserving to them the advantages that it offered, were absent from 1929 to 1933. Installment selling was severely curtailed. The great expansion of capital exports that helped to open foreign markets to American producers in the first post-War decade was not duplicated in the second decade. Fortuitous profits from speculation were no longer available to swell buying power. The impact upon the industrial structure of the greatly reduced purchasing power of raw material producers was apparent at once in increasing unemployment. (Other elements, of course, contributed also to the volume of unemployment.) The consequent reduction of the purchasing power of industrial workers reacted to intensify the difficulty and to swell still further the number of unemployed. Depleted purchasing power and misery on the one hand, unemployment and misery on the other—these were the concomitants of the sharp widening of the schism that separated the prices of raw materials from those of finished goods.

One arresting fact about this great price gap that was opened, or reopened, between 1929 and 1933 is that it ap-

THE WORLD PRICE STRUCTURE 183

peared, internationally, as a division between two great groups of countries. In most countries today both extractive and manufacturing industries are found, but usually one type of industry predominates and determines the general character of the national economy. By and large, the countries of western Europe constitute a distinctively industrial area, while the rest of the world, excluding small areas in Asia and the industrialized regions of North America, is devoted primarily to the extraction of raw materials and the cultivation of crude foodstuffs. As we have noted, the price schism of the first post-War recession and ensuing years opened up a definite cleavage between industrial and colonial areas, and this cleavage, together with related circumstances connected with the movements of capital, constituted a dominant feature of the world economic scene during this period. The same cleavage between manufacturing and raw material producing areas became an outstanding feature of the depression that began in 1929.[7]

This condition is clearly revealed by measurements of the net barter terms of trade of industrial countries and of countries exporting raw materials and importing industrial products (Table 18). In 1932 the United Kingdom gave 13 per cent less of exports, by volume, than in 1929, and 24 per cent less than in 1913, in exchange for a fixed quantity of imports.

---

[7] Every cyclical depression, of course, has opened up a similar cleavage, since the prices of raw materials are far more sensitive to changes in business conditions than are the prices of manufactured goods. But in the present case the cleavage differs so markedly from that usually developing in the course of business cycles that it is not improper to use the term 'schism'. The differences between the break here in question and that usually found in business depressions are differences of magnitude, of duration and, fundamentally, of background. For the decade preceding the 1929 break was a decade of weakness in raw material prices. The schism of 1929–33 was virtually an intensification of a condition that had been present in the world economy since the ending of the War.

The reason, of course, is that the prices of imported foodstuffs and materials had fallen much more than had the average price of exported industrial products. The trading relations of France, Germany and the United States with the rest of the world were altered in similar fashion. In 1932 these three countries were giving, respectively, 13, 31 and 16 per cent less than in 1929 in exchange for constant quantities of imports. At the other extreme are the colonial areas, selling foodstuffs and raw materials in exchange for industrial products. In 1932 the terms of exchange had so altered for New Zealand that it was forced to give 58 per cent more, in volume, than in 1929, in return for a fixed quantity of imports. For the Dutch East Indies the figure was 46 per cent, for Argentina 52 per cent. Here in accentuated form was the same great cleavage that had been opened up between 1919 and 1921.

PRICES OF INVESTMENT EQUIPMENT AND OF GOODS FOR HUMAN CONSUMPTION

In the main, the price behavior of major commodity groups during the recession and depression initiated in 1929 resembles that observed in previous cyclical recessions, although in the most recent depression movements were more extreme both in magnitude and duration. One important difference is to be noted, however. In pre-War business cycles the prices of those particular producers' goods that are intended for use in the construction of capital equipment fell as rapidly as the general price level, or more rapidly. This facilitated the resumption of expenditures on new capital equipment and on the repair of old capital equipment during the later stages of depression and the early stages of revival, and thus stimulated general business recovery. During the latest depression, as in the period preced-

THE WORLD PRICE STRUCTURE

ing the recession of 1929, the prices of goods entering into capital equipment remained relatively high.

In most industrial countries for which we have appropriate records depression prices of capital equipment were relatively higher than the prices of goods intended for ultimate human consumption. In Germany industrial finished goods intended for the use of producers were only 17 per cent lower in price in January 1933 than in 1929; industrial finished goods for sale to final consumers were 35 per cent lower. In Canada producers' equipment in February 1933 was 8 per cent lower in price than in 1929; consumers' goods were 27 per cent lower. In the United States, in February 1933, producers' goods intended for use as capital equipment were 27 per cent lower than in 1929; consumers' goods were 35 per cent lower. This situation is connected with the general raw-processed schism already discussed. Those raw materials which were weakest in price were, in general, agricultural products intended for human consumption. Furthermore, the effects of control through cartels, agreements and combinations of various sorts have been felt most directly by goods intended for use in capital equipment. It is probable, too, that various fixed and relatively intractable elements of cost played more important parts in the production of goods of the capital equipment type than in the output of consumption goods. The net result of all these circumstances (and of other economic conditions) was that in the recent depression capital equipment became relatively more expensive, and that its production was retarded. This tended to remove one of the factors usually facilitating a revival of economic activity after a severe depression.

It is notable that these price relations were reversed in Japan. In June 1932 the prices of Japanese producers' goods were 48 per cent lower than in 1929; the prices of consumers' goods were 30 per cent lower. Here was a condition of very great importance in facilitating, if not stimulating, the early industrial recovery of Japan.

SOME CONSEQUENCES OF DISLOCATIONS IN THE WORLD PRICE STRUCTURE DURING THE DEPRESSION

The collapse of prices, with resulting dislocations in the world price structure, was but one aspect of the general economic breakdown of the period 1929–33. In a situation marked by a tremendous reduction in the volume of production and trade, by world-wide unemployment, by virtual cessation of the international flow of investment funds, by widespread dislocation of the foreign exchanges, it would be quite unjustifiable to look upon the price collapse as the one factor responsible for all other economic difficulties. Yet we have argued above that, be the first causes what they may, the price relations created by such a general collapse as that of 1929–33 become themselves active factors in the economic situation. The very conditions that prevent prices from reflecting and promptly adapting themselves to the violent economic changes accompanying a major economic recession initiate new chains of consequences. Some of these, which are in part at least resultants of schisms and disparities set up within the structure of world prices, are here summarized.

Sharp alterations of price relations bring in their wake two major (and related) consequences—a shift of purchasing power from group to group and, usually, a disturbance of the balance that may have prevailed between the volume of production and the available purchasing power.[8] When the distribution of purchasing power upon the basis of which an

---

[8] These results would not follow, of course, if the effects of the price changes upon purchasing power were precisely offset by variations in the volumes of goods produced or services rendered by the economic groups concerned. But such nicely balancing changes are not found in practice.

economic system has previously functioned is thus suddenly altered, a violent drop in the volume of goods exchanged may be expected. (Curtailed purchasing power is immediately reflected in reduced demand. Enhanced purchasing power, real or potential, is likely to be effective only with a time lag.) This is precisely what happened when the recent price collapse occurred.

The purchasing power of raw material producing areas was reduced, even before the collapse of raw material prices, by the diminution of foreign loans, a process that began in 1928. When to this weakness was added the effect of rapidly declining prices of their major products, the power of such colonial areas to purchase industrial products was very seriously impaired. In Table 12 an attempt is made to appraise roughly the losses in aggregate purchasing power due to these two factors, for selected colonial areas.

TABLE 12

ESTIMATED CHANGES IN THE AGGREGATE PURCHASING POWER IN WORLD MARKETS OF FIVE RAW MATERIAL PRODUCING AREAS, 1929–1933 [1]

	EXPORTS			IMPORTS	AGGREGATE PURCHASING POWER OF EXPORTS IN FOREIGN MARKETS	AGGREGATE GOLD VALUE OF EXPORTS CORRECTED BY NET BALANCE OF CAPITAL MOVEMENTS	AGGREGATE PURCHASING POWER OF EXPORTS CORRECTED BY NET BALANCE OF CAPITAL MOVEMENTS
	Physical volume	Gold price (per unit)	Aggregate gold value	Gold price (per unit)			
1929	100	100	100	100	100	100	100
1930	95	75	71	93	76	73	78
1931	104	52	54	77	70	49	64
1932	107	42	45	60	75	36	60
1933	109	39	42	52	81	33	63

[1] The figures in this table are aggregates, derived from data relating to the Union of South Africa, Argentina, Dutch East Indies, Australia and New Zealand. Below are given records for the individual countries, as compiled (*Footnote to Table 12 continued on p. 188*)

188   PRICES IN RECESSION AND RECOVERY

Between 1929 and 1933 the gold value of the exports of the five raw material exporting countries here represented was reduced 58 per cent. This decline was due entirely to a drop in the average gold price, per unit, of the goods exported; for the volume of exports in 1933 was greater than that of 1929. Added to the loss in purchasing power resulting from this price decline was the loss due to a tremendous drop

(Footnote to Table 12 continued)
by the Economic Intelligence Service of the League of Nations (*Review of World Trade, 1934; Statistical Year-Book, 1934–35; Balance of International Payments, 1934*).

	EXPORTS			APPROXIMATE VALUE OF CAPITAL LOANS, IN MILLIONS OF FORMER U. S. GOLD DOLLARS [NET INWARD (+) OR OUTWARD (—) BALANCES]		
	Physical volume	Gold price (*per unit*)	Aggregate gold value	Long-term	Short-term	Total
Union of South Africa						
1929	100	100	100	—8.6	+73.6	+65.0
1930	101	85	86	+48.2	—16.6	+31.6
1931	91	80	73	+1.9	+17.1	+19.0
1932	98	73	72	+22.2	—97.7	—75.5
1933	91	75	67	—6.9	—23.9	—30.8
Argentina*						
1929	100	100	100	+48.7	—10.9	+37.8
1930	72	79	57	+175.7	—8.3	+167.4
1931	100	47	47	—5.9	+7.3	+1.4
1932	92	39	36			
1933	83	38	31			
Dutch East Indies						
1929	100	100	100	—24.9	+56.7	+31.8
1930	117	68	80	+31.8	lacking	+31.8
1931	109	47	52	+13.7	+18.5	+32.2
1932	104	36	38	+11.3	+8.4	+19.7
1933	90	36	32	+13.7	+6.0	+19.7
Australia**						
1929	100	100	100			+169.9
1930	95	75	71			+13.6
1931	112	46	52			—53.3
1932	134	33	45			—52.5
1933	173	29	51			—78.9

THE WORLD PRICE STRUCTURE

in short- and long-term loans. Such loans, which amounted to over 300 million dollars in 1929, had fallen to zero by 1931, and had taken on negative values in 1932 and 1933. The flow of capital was outward. Capital movements do not necessarily have a physical counterpart in the movement of goods, but this shift in the movement of short- and long-term funds contributed in no small degree to the weakness of raw material producing areas. Falling exports and declining capital loans served, together, to reduce the total sum (in terms of gold dollars) available to these five countries in 1931 for use in foreign markets by something over 50 per cent of the 1929 figure. By 1932 the decline amounted to 64 per cent,

(Footnote to Table 12 concluded)

	EXPORTS			APPROXIMATE VALUE OF CAPITAL LOANS, IN MILLIONS OF FORMER U. S. GOLD DOLLARS [NET INWARD (+) OR OUTWARD (—) BALANCES]		
	Physical volume	Gold price (*per unit*)	Aggregate gold value	Long-term	Short-term	Total
New Zealand***						
1929	100	100	100	—11.9	+30.6	+18.7
1930	103	77	79	+39.2		+39.2
1931	104	53	54	+20.4	—13.0	+7.4
1932	117	37	42	—4.1	+7.4	+3.3
1933	135	30	41	—10.4	—60.1	—70.5

* Data on capital loans are for the year October 1–September 30.
** Data on capital loans are for the year July 1–June 30.
*** Data on capital loans are for the year April 1–March 31.

The index numbers of the gold prices of imports, as given in Table 12, are averages of index numbers for the individual countries; for 1932 and 1933, data for Australia were not available, and estimates for that country were based on data for New Zealand.

Data on capital movements were not available for Argentina for 1932 and 1933. Estimates for these years were based upon data for the four other countries.

The figures in the three columns relating to exports are derived independently, hence all items in column (3) are not consistent with corresponding items in columns (1) and (2). In general, the discrepancy is small.

190 PRICES IN RECESSION AND RECOVERY

and by 1933 to 67 per cent.[9] If we measure from 1929 as base, and take rough account of the fall in the average prices of goods imported by these countries,[10] we find that reduced exports and falling capital loans together would account for a drop approximating 40 per cent in their purchasing power in foreign markets, that is, in the physical volume of manufactured goods purchasable by the funds coming from these two sources. (Part of these credits in foreign markets would, of course, be used in debt service and for other purposes not directly involving the purchase of goods.)

These records indicate how substantial was the reduction in the flow of manufactured goods from industrial areas to certain important raw material producing areas, and how important was the part played by price changes in this decline. They reveal, also, the effect of the stoppage of capital movements on the aggregate purchasing power of raw material producing areas. For the world at large a decline in the volume of international trade in raw materials accompanied the changes we have noted, although it did not approach the drop in the volume of manufactured goods exported by industrial countries.[11] In international as in domestic trade the prices

---

[9] Other items in the balance of payments of these countries affect their purchasing power in foreign markets. The above figures define changes due to the influence of two important factors which were subject to considerable variation over this period.

[10] The following index numbers measure changes in the average gold prices of goods imported by these five countries.

	1929	1930	1931	1932	1933
Union of South Africa	100	93	81	62	42
Argentina	100	88	71	60	57
Dutch East Indies	100	94	74	61	51
Australia	100	98	81		
New Zealand	100	95	77	58	50

(*Review of World Trade, 1934,* League of Nations, pp. 76–83)

[11] The following estimates, from the *Review of World Trade, 1934* (p. 16) issued by the Economic Intelligence Service of the League of Nations, indi-

THE WORLD PRICE STRUCTURE 191

of manufactured goods were maintained, relatively to the prices of foodstuffs and other raw materials, and the rough equalization of the aggregate values of goods exchanged thus entailed a correspondingly greater decline in the volume of manufactured goods entering into trade. In addition, of course, the trade in manufactured goods among industrial countries suffered great losses.

A large part of the decline in trade between raw material producing areas and industrial areas may be attributed to the effect of price disparities and the reduced volume of foreign lending upon the purchasing power of colonial areas, and to the effect of unemployment and wage reduction upon the purchasing power of industrial areas. In trade between industrial areas direct price disparities play a less important role. Here the reduced purchasing power of industrial workers was a serious depressant. To these factors must be added the important retarding influence of new and higher tariff barriers. These, and the accompanying development of trade restrictions, quotas and similar impediments to the movement of goods in customary channels, intensified the depressing influence of price disparities and unemployment and served still further to reduce the purchasing power of consumers generally.

PROBLEMS OF READJUSTMENT AND RECOVERY

World history in modern times has been a record of steadily expanding international trade resting, in large part, upon

cate the relative magnitudes of the changes in the volume of trade of three classes of commodities and in corresponding unit prices:

	FOODSTUFFS		RAW MATERIALS		MANUFACTURED ARTICLES	
	Quantum	Per unit prices, in gold	Quantum	Per unit prices, in gold	Quantum	Per unit prices, in gold
1929	100	100	100	100	100	100
1932	90	52	81	45	58	64

the exploitation of the natural advantages of different economic areas. (Accident and priorities of exploitation played rather important roles, of course, in the regional division of labor.) At the bottom of the spiral of recession in world commerce and deflation of world prices, in 1932 and 1933, the world faced a major question: Were the advantages of regional economic specialization to be fully exploited in the future or, in considerable part, foregone? In another form, this was the question whether national or international trade was to develop, relatively to the other.[12] The World War and the economic and political difficulties growing out of it posed this question for more conscious consideration, perhaps, than it had ever received before.

The alternative lines of development, if clearly distinguished, involve sharply different economic policies. Nationalistic development would be expected to proceed upon the basis of maintained quantitative and other restrictions upon imports, a slow shifting of national productive energies to new channels and a correspondingly slow absorption of unemployed workers and capital, the continuation of world trade in low volume, relatively to world production, and the persistence of living standards (as measured in terms of real wages and incomes) below those that would be supported by a full utilization of the world's productive resources. International price and cost relations based upon earlier conditions of freer trade would no longer prevail. Price and cost 'disparities' (in relation to earlier standards) would persist. The international price system of the past, with national price and cost structures standing in working relations one with another and subject to mutual modification and read-

---

[12] The question has been put in this form and its implications developed in a paper by John H. Williams on "The World's Monetary Dilemma—Internal versus External Monetary Stability" (*Proceedings of the Academy of Political Science*, April 1934, pp. 62–68).

THE WORLD PRICE STRUCTURE

justment, would undergo a substantial change in character.[13]

Readjustment and recovery to be effected through the restoration of a working international organization would require quite different foundations. Some lowering of the barriers to world trade, particularly of those quantitative restrictions that served as absolute impediments to equilibrium through price readjustment, was essential. Some restoration of the international flow of capital was, if not a necessary condition, at least of very considerable importance. Finally, and of greatest weight, there were necessary the interrelated price and exchange readjustments that would permit the reconstruction on a stable basis of a world price system, with national price and cost structures standing in more effective working relation than was possible under the disturbed conditions of the depression period. Such reconstruction of a world price system would not, of course, mean the restoration of the precise relations that prevailed prior to the recession. Many deep-seated and irreversible changes had occurred, and reconstruction would involve adaptation to these. But if the path towards a recovery of international trade were to be taken, it would be an adaptation that would facilitate and not impede regional division of labor and the growth of world commerce.

Looking forward, from the demoralized state of world trade and world intercourse prevailing in 1932, after three years of recession, these two clear alternatives were open, but it was not to be expected that either would be followed rigorously. In tracing the events of the succeeding years we shall be concerned with the character of the compromise actually effected between nationalistic commercial development and an international economic organization.

[13] A lucid exposition of the effects upon price and cost relations of quantitative restrictions upon international trade is given in "Exchange Rates and Prices," by J. B. Condliffe, in *Index* (Svenska Handelsbanken), January 1935.

World Price Movements in Recovery

The general character of world price movements since the checking of recession in 1932 and 1933 has been indicated in the opening pages of this chapter. As various countries broke loose from the gold standard the declines in their domestic prices were stopped. In many instances fairly substantial price advances have been scored, in terms of national currencies. The downward pressure on gold prices persisted, but even here the lift of domestic price levels has been sufficient to advance gold equivalents somewhat in several countries. The movements of both sets of prices from 1929 levels to the depression lows, and the subsequent advances, are graphically portrayed in Figure 9. The extent of the advance from the low point is indicated, for each country, by the white area on the bar.

The degree of divergence among national price levels, even in terms of gold values, is notable. The low points, with reference to 1928 or 1929 high values as 100, ranged from 29 for Japan to 64 for Germany. Some advances from depression lows were scored in gold price levels to the spring of 1936. In the main, these were inconsiderable. The significance of certain of these movements is clouded by the presence of official control over foreign exchanges. For the world as a whole the recession of gold prices of commodities had been checked by 1936 but substantial recovery was still to come.

The bars relating to the movements of price levels in terms of national currencies tell a somewhat more encouraging story. Here, except in a few countries, the levels of the depression lows were definitely left behind. Only the bars relating to Poland and the Dutch East Indies show no white areas. In Argentina, Peru and Chile, 1929 price levels were

THE WORLD PRICE STRUCTURE

FIGURE 9
WHOLESALE PRICES IN THIRTY-TWO COUNTRIES, 1929–1936
INDEX NUMBERS IN TERMS OF NATIONAL AND GOLD CURRENCIES
($1929=100$)

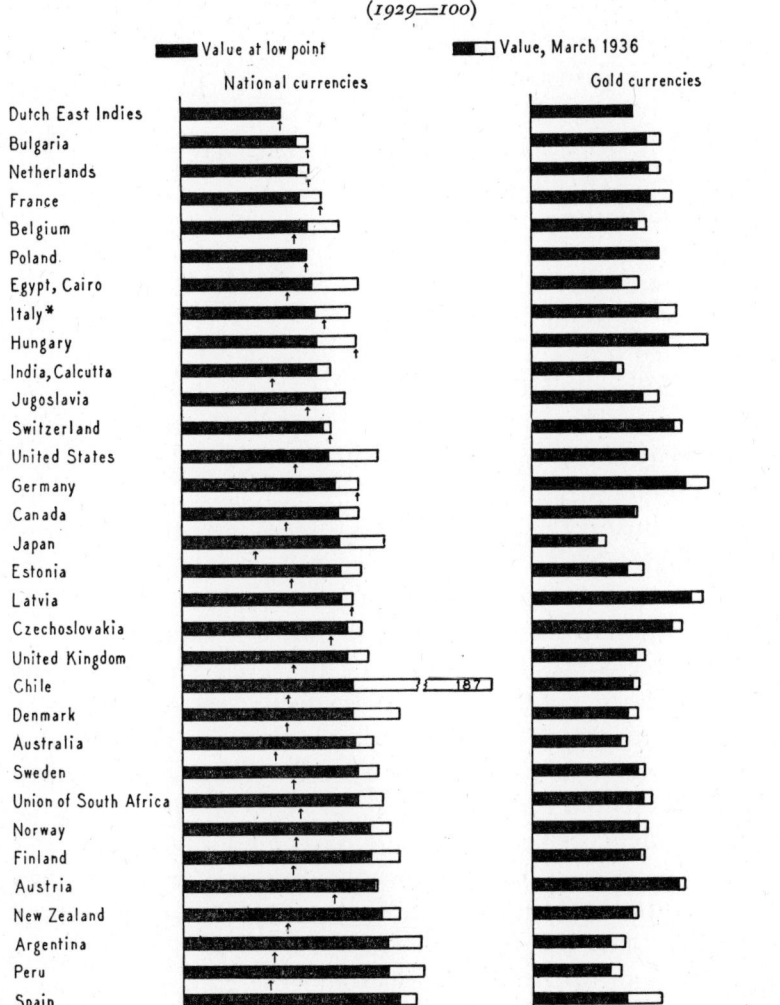

The arrows in the section of the diagram relating to national currencies indicate the relative levels of gold prices in March 1936.   * To October 1935.

passed, in the advance. The United States, with a gain to March 1936 of 33 per cent above the depression low, and Japan with a gain of 30 per cent, are among the countries having made the greatest advances. In the United Kingdom wholesale commodity prices advanced 13 per cent.

The price gains of recovery, in terms of the various national currencies, are to be appraised with reference to gold price levels, corresponding to current exchange rates. The differences between the gold price levels as of March 1936 (indicated by the arrows in the diagram) and the price levels in terms of national currencies may be noted on the chart. There is a rough inverse relationship; high national price levels are associated with low gold price levels, and low national price levels with high gold price levels. But there is far from a simple and invariant relationship between depreciation, as measured by exchange rates, and domestic price levels. In general, the advances of domestic prices have not been commensurate with the depreciation of national currencies. Thus in the United States a reduction of 41 per cent in the gold value of the dollar was followed by an advance, to April 1936, of only 33 per cent in average wholesale prices. (The advance is measured from the level prevailing in February 1933. Suspension of the gold standard dates from April 19, 1933.) A rise commensurate with the reduction in gold value would have amounted to 69 per cent. Similarly, quoted rates on the pound sterling, as of April 1936, represented a decline of 40 per cent in its gold value. An equivalent price rise would have amounted to 66 per cent. The actual advance in wholesale prices from the date of departure from the gold standard to April 1936 amounted to 13 per cent. There is, of course, no reason to expect a rigid relationship between prices and the gold value of the monetary unit under contemporary currency and banking conditions, but the highly imperfect relationship in these

THE WORLD PRICE STRUCTURE 197

countries is worthy of note. Indeed, there is evidence that currency depreciation by important commercial nations has exerted deflationary pressure outside their borders, perhaps in greater degree than it has exerted inflationary pressure domestically. For the reduction of gold prices, which depreciation entails, tends to push world gold prices downward, and countries still on the gold standard feel the full force of this push.[14]

The Structure of World Prices in 1936

We have seen, in the early part of this chapter, that the slow process of rebuilding a world trading organization after the disruptive period of War and post-War disturbance was violently checked in 1929. The innumerable cost and price relations which condition the actual exchange of goods and services were broken or seriously distorted during the recession. Nationalistic political considerations intensified economic factors in creating barriers to economic intercourse and checking the flow of goods in international trade. As a result of the play of these various forces the physical volume of world trade was reduced 26 per cent between 1929 and 1932.

In the brief previous survey of the situation existing at the low point of the depression and in the early months of 1936 attention was drawn to the disparate movements of prices and costs, and to some of their economic consequences. We turn now to the changes occurring during the period of general world recovery.

DISPARITIES OF PRICE LEVELS

In following the movements of price recovery it is well to compare situations at specific dates, although the depression

[14] See *Commercial Banks, 1929–1934* (League of Nations, Geneva, 1935).

lows of different countries did not coincide. For convenience, February 1933 may be taken as a standard date at which to compare the price levels of depression. March 1936 will serve as a bench-mark in surveying the changes of recovery.

From 1929 to February 1933 the changes in wholesale price levels, in terms of the national currencies of the thirty-two countries covered in Table 13, ranged from a drop of 50 per cent in the Dutch East Indies to a rise of 79 per cent for Chile. The median decline (unweighted) was 30 per cent. The degree of divergence of national price levels during

TABLE 13

WHOLESALE PRICE INDEX NUMBERS, THIRTY-TWO COUNTRIES, 1929—MARCH 1936

(In terms of national and gold currencies: 1929=100)

	NATIONAL CURRENCIES			GOLD VALUES		
	Average 1929	Feb. 1933	Mar. 1936	Average 1929	Feb. 1933	Mar. 1936
Dutch East Indies [1]	100	50	43	100	50	43
Netherlands [1]	100	52	55	100	52	55
Bulgaria [2]	100	53	55	100	53	55
Belgium [2]	100	60	68	100	60	49
India, Calcutta	100	61	64	100	43	39
Italy [2]	100	61	72 [4]	100	59	66 [4]
Egypt, Cairo	100	62	76	100	44	46
Poland [1]	100	63	54	100	63	54
United States	100	63	84	100	63	49
France [1]	100	64	60	100	64	60
Switzerland [1]	100	64	64	100	64	64
Canada	100	66	76	100	56	45
Germany [2]	100	66	76	100	66	76
Jugoslavia [2]	100	68	70	100	52	54
Hungary [2]	100	69	75	100	69	75
Estonia [2]	100	70	77	100	70	47
Latvia [2]	100	70	73	100	70	73
Czechoslovakia [2]	100	72	77	100	72	64
United Kingdom	100	72	80	100	51	48
Australia	100	74	82	100	41	40
Union of South Africa	100	75 [3]	86 [5]	100	53 [3]	51 [5]

THE WORLD PRICE STRUCTURE

TABLE 13 (cont.)

WHOLESALE PRICE INDEX NUMBERS, THIRTY-TWO COUNTRIES, 1929—MARCH 1936

	NATIONAL CURRENCIES			GOLD VALUES		
	Average 1929	Feb. 1933	Mar. 1936	Average 1929	Feb. 1933	Mar. 1936
Sweden	100	76	84	100	51	48
Norway	100	81	89	100	53	49
Austria 2	100	82	83	100	66	65
Japan 2	100	82	87	100	37	32
Denmark 2	100	83	93	100	47	45
New Zealand	100	88	93	100	50	45
Argentina 2	100	89	102	100	54	39
Finland	100	91	93	100	54	48
Peru	100	92	103	100	40	38
Spain 2	100	96	100	100	54	55
Chile 2	100	179	187	100	89	46
Median						
Unweighted	100	70	77	100	54	49
Weighted 6	100	66	80	100	59	49
Index of dispersion of price levels						
Unweighted		13.6	12.3		12.5	12.8
Weighted 6		6.8	7.5		11.0	12.2

SOURCE: League of Nations: *Monthly Bulletin of Statistics*
1 Countries on gold standard, March 1936.   2 Official foreign exchange control.
3 January 1933.   4 October 1935.   5 April 1936.
6 Weights are based upon relative importance of foreign trade in 1929.

this period is indicated by an index (unweighted) of 13.6 per cent.[15] In terms of gold values the median decline was greater, amounting to 46 per cent. The index of dispersion was slightly lower than that for domestic price levels measured in the various national currencies. Some of the implications of these wide disparities have already been suggested.

From February 1933 to March 1936 the median of the

[15] This is half the range between the two quartiles, expressed as a percentage of the median.

thirty-two wholesale price indexes, in national currencies, rose about 10 per cent. The dispersion of price levels was only slightly reduced; disparities of national price levels remained wide in 1936.

If we reduce our measurements to terms of a common denominator, gold, we note a continuation of the price drop from 1933 to 1936, with the median index of gold prices in March 1936 less than one-half the 1929 level. The index of relative dispersion of gold price levels rose slightly with recovery; between February 1933 and March 1936 there was an increase rather than a reduction in the disparities the recession had brought among national price levels, if we use the 1929 situation as criterion.

The picture is altered somewhat if we use the various weighted measurements of average price change and of dispersion. Notably, the price rise from 1933 to 1936 in terms of domestic currencies is much greater, 21 per cent as against 10 per cent. This means that price gains were greatest among the commercially important countries. Dispersion of price levels, on the other hand, is less when weights are used. It is significant that the dispersion of commodity prices in terms of gold, from 1929 to 1933 and to 1936, was greater than the dispersion of prices in terms of national currencies. Standards for international trading relations were badly shattered among the leading countries.[16]

[16] The various national index numbers brought together in Table 13 are not fully comparable, since they differ in respect of number and kind of commodities included and in method of construction. A. L. Bowley and K. C. Smith have constructed a series of index numbers of wholesale prices, for eleven countries, that are similar in composition and in distribution of weights. Though the number of commodities included in each index is not large (about 35), the comparability of these measurements gives them especial significance, in the tracing of international price movements. Recession and recovery in these index numbers, in terms of national currencies,

THE WORLD PRICE STRUCTURE 201

Price index numbers on the 1929 base relate to a standard of somewhat uncertain economic significance. There is no reason to believe that the relations of that year represent a state of equilibrium. Indeed, no post-War year would serve, if this test were applied, and pre-War years are so far removed from the situation immediately preceding the 1929 recession that they constitute unsatisfactory criteria. Yet it is desirable that the changes of the period 1929–36 be viewed against a standard other than that of 1929. Table 14 facilitates such a view.

In terms of national currencies wholesale price levels in the twenty-nine countries here represented scored a median advance (unweighted) of 47 per cent between 1913 and 1929. Recession carried the median level down to a point 6 per cent above that of 1913, while recovery to March 1936 brought an advance to 18 per cent above. The employment of gold as a common denominator gives a different picture. Wholesale price levels in gold terms advanced 37 per cent

are shown below. For the present purpose the bases of these index numbers have been shifted from 1925, as originally computed, to 1929.

	1929	February 1933	March 1936
Belgium	100	58	64
Canada	100	55	68
France	100	65	63
Germany	100	66	75
Italy	100	64	*
Netherlands	100	48	52
New Zealand	100	76	84†
Sweden	100	70	84
Union of South Africa	100	73**	80†
United Kingdom	100	68	75
United States	100	50	74

* Not available.   ** January 1933.   † February 1936.
The Bowley-Smith index numbers are published currently in the *Bulletin* of the London and Cambridge Economic Service.

from 1913 to 1929. Early in 1933 the median index was 26 per cent below the 1913 standard; by March 1936 this had been carried to a level 33 per cent below. (Weighted and unweighted averages show the same general movements.) With only one exception (Germany) average gold prices of commodities at wholesale in 1936 were lower than in 1913.

A considerable degree of divergence among national price levels is to be expected, over a period of two decades. It is important, however, to determine whether the changes of recent years have brought an accentuation or a reduction of the disparities among price levels that developed during the War and the immediate post-War years. Unweighted measures of dispersion indicate a sharp divergence of national price levels from 1929 to 1933, a very slight reduction of this divergence by March 1936. Re-valuation occurred in a number of countries, and the various domestic price levels and price structures stood far apart indeed. Weighted measurements show the same changes, in less pronounced form. When prices are reduced to gold terms, on the 1913 base, the unweighted measurements indicate no material change in dispersion between 1929 and 1933, a considerable advance during the three years following. The weighted measure-

TABLE 14

WHOLESALE PRICE INDEX NUMBERS, TWENTY-NINE COUNTRIES, 1913—MARCH 1936

(In terms of national and gold currencies: 1913=100)

	NATIONAL CURRENCIES				GOLD VALUES			
	Average 1913	Average 1929	Feb. 1933	Mar. 1936	Average 1913	Average 1929	Feb. 1933	Mar. 1936
Egypt (Cairo)	100 [3]	116	72	83	100 [3]	116	51	53
Dutch East Indies [1]	100	148	74	64	100	148	74	64
Netherlands [1]	100	142	74	78	100	142	74	78
Estonia [2]	100	117	82	90	100	117	82	55
Hungary [2]	100	121	83	91	100	104	72	79

THE WORLD PRICE STRUCTURE

TABLE 14 (cont.)

WHOLESALE PRICE INDEX NUMBERS, TWENTY-NINE COUNTRIES, 1913—MARCH 1936

	NATIONAL CURRENCIES				GOLD VALUES			
	Average 1913	Average 1929	Feb. 1933	Mar. 1936	Average 1913	Average 1929	Feb. 1933	Mar. 1936
Latvia [2]	100	120	84	87	100	120	84	87
India (Calcutta)	100 [3]	141	86	91	100 [3]	158	68	62
United States	100	137	86	114	100	137	86	67
Union of South Africa	100	116	87 [4]	100 [6]	100	116	62 [4]	60 [6]
Switzerland [1]	100 [3]	141	90	91	100 [3]	141	90	91
Germany [2]	100	137	91	104	100	137	91	104
Canada	100	149	99	113	100	149	83	67
United Kingdom	100	136	99	110	100	136	70	66
Austria [2]	100 [3]	130	106	107	100 [3]	93	62	61
Sweden	100	140	106	118	100	140	72	67
Argentina [2]	100	128	113	130	100	125	67	49
Norway	100	149	121	132	100	149	79	73
Australia	100	166	122	137	100	166	69	66
Denmark [2]	100	150	124	139	100	150	71	68
New Zealand	100	147	130	137	100	147	73	66
Japan [2]	100	166	136	144	100	155	57	46
Spain [2]	100	168	162	168	100	136	73	75
Peru	100	186	172	192	100	156	62	60
Italy [2]	100	481	293	348 [5]	100	131	78	87 [5]
Chile [2]	100	192	345	360	100	118	105	55
France [1]	100	627	404	376	100	127	82	76
Belgium [2]	100 [3]	851	512	578	100 [3]	124	75	61
Czechoslovakia [2]	100 [3]	913	653	703	100 [3]	134	96	86
Bulgaria [2]	100 [3]	3447	1838	1910	100 [3]	145	76	79
Median								
Unweighted	100	147	106	118	100	137	74	67
Weighted [7]	100	137	99	114	100	137	78	67
Index of dispersion								
Unweighted		12.9	37.0	35.2		9.2	9.1	13.1
Weighted [7]		10.6	19.2	15.4		2.6	10.3	7.5

SOURCE: League of Nations, *Monthly Bulletin of Statistics*

[1] Countries on gold standard, March 1936. [2] Official foreign exchange control.
[3] 1914. [4] January 1933.
[5] October 1935. [6] April 1936.
[7] Weights based upon relative importance of foreign trade in 1929.

ments show a remarkably small degree of divergence of gold price levels in 1929, on the 1913 base (a somewhat fortuitous result, due to the fact that the price indexes for the three most heavily weighted countries—United States, United Kingdom and Germany—were within one point of one another in 1929). Thereafter the divergence increased materially with depression, declined somewhat from 1933 to 1936.

It is a fair assumption that unequal movements of national price levels alter adjustments of prices and costs on which international trade is based. These movements may open some opportunities for profitable trade, but the net effect is probably adverse. The various measurements of dispersion just reviewed indicate a definite increase of divergencies from 1929 to 1933, a movement that was particularly pronounced in terms of national currencies. Thereafter, with general recovery, there was some lessening of disparities, though the picture as a whole shows no substantial improvement for the commercial world in general. International price divergencies remained wide in 1936, whether the standard of reference be 1929 or 1913. There is nothing sacred about these standards, it is true, except that each represents conditions under which trade had been carried on in considerable volume. The movements of recovery, through the early months of 1936, were far from restoring either set of conditions. But we must consider other types of evidence bearing on international price and cost relations.

DISPARITIES OF PRODUCTION COSTS

Lagging adaptation of various prices and wage rates to alterations in the value of money may lead to rather wide differences in relative production costs during a period of rapid and unequal variations in price levels and in exchange rates. Since we have no direct and comparable measurements of production costs in different industrial countries we are obliged to estimate relative changes. This was done at an earlier point for the period of recession. There we found that in December 1932 Japan and five countries of the sterling bloc stood in relatively strong competitive positions, since wages, food prices and other living costs had not risen by amounts commensurate with the declines in the external values of their currencies. France, Czechoslovakia, Belgium and the Netherlands constituted a relatively high cost group; the United States and a small number of European countries were in a middle position. We may now trace the changes brought by three years of currency depreciation, continuing decline in gold prices, and varying price advances in terms of national currencies (Table 15).

The changes in the international values of the dollar resulting from American departure from the gold standard are revealed by a comparison of the entries for December 1932 and for December 1933. In only four countries (Australia, New Zealand, Denmark and Japan) was the 1933 value above that of 1929. But we may pass directly to a study of the 1935 situation. As of December in that year the value of the dollar was higher than in 1929 in the currencies of four countries (Australia, Denmark, Japan and New Zealand), equal to the 1929 value in the currency of one country (Canada), and below the 1929 values in the currencies of nine countries (Belgium, Czechoslovakia, Estonia, France, Germany, Italy, Netherlands, Poland and the United Kingdom). We are here concerned, however, not with changes in the relative values of these various national currencies but with the degree to which food prices, living costs and wages may have adapted themselves to these shifting relations among national currencies. The movements from 1929 to March 1936 are shown graphically in Figure 10.

Japan is outstanding among the countries in a strong com-

TABLE 15

INTERNATIONAL VALUES OF THE DOLLAR AND VARIOUS SERIES RELATING TO PRODUCTION COSTS

A COMPARISON OF MOVEMENTS, 1929–1935 [1]

INDEX NUMBERS AS PERCENTAGES OF CORRESPONDING MEASUREMENTS FOR THE UNITED STATES

	INDEX NUMBERS OF VALUES OF THE DOLLAR IN TERMS OF CURRENCIES OF FOURTEEN COUNTRIES							FOOD PRICES							COST OF LIVING							WAGE RATES						
	1929	Dec. 1932	Dec. 1933	Dec. 1934	Dec. 1935			1929	Dec. 1932	Dec. 1933	Dec. 1934	Dec. 1935	Dec.		1929	Dec. 1932	Dec. 1933	Dec. 1934	Dec. 1935	Dec.		1929	Dec. 1932	Dec. 1933	Dec. 1934	Dec. 1935		
United States	100	100	100	100	100			100	100	100	100	100	100		100	100	100[3]	100[3]	100[3]	100		100	100	100	100	100		
Australia	100	185	119	123	123			100	116	111	107	100			100	103[3]	100[3]	100[3]	100[3]			100	94	87	81	81		
Belgium	100	100	64	59	82			100	116	108	93	94			100	110	106	99	104			100	107[2]	96	82	81		
Canada	100	115	100	98	100			100	102	100	97	94			100	104	100	99	99			100	107[2]	97[2]	90[2]	90[2]		
Czechoslovakia	100	100	64	71	71			100	139	118	108	105			100	123	118	114	115			100	120[2]	110	98	96		
Denmark	100	156	119	120	120			100							100	117	121	122	122			100	120	112	103	101		
Estonia	100	100	94	97	98			100	97	95	80	85			100	99	99	91	98			100	108[2]	99	89	96		
France (Paris)	100	100	64	59	59			100	134	124	101	90			100	121[3]	122[3]	114[3]	105[3]			100	116[2]	110[2]	100	98		
Germany	100	100	64	59	59			100	115	112	108	100			100	100	100	99	98			100	92	85	78	77		
Italy	100	103	64	61	65			100	124	109	99	92[4]			100	106	101	94	94[4]			100	100	90	81	83		
Japan	100	222	149	159	159			100	132	123	115	112			100	105	105	104	105			100	102	95	90	83		
Netherlands	100	100	64	59	59			100	118	120	106	94			100	108	109	104	100			100	106	95	85	82		
New Zealand	100	161	119	123	123			100	113	112	110	108			100	105	103	101	102			100	97	88	83	83		
Poland	100	100	64	59	59			100	97	88	70	64			100	94	88	79	73			100	97	84	74	70		
United Kingdom	100	149	95	98	98			100	131	124	115	109			100	113	112	109	110			100	111	102	95	94		

[1] For a statement concerning the sources employed in the construction of this table, see the footnote to Table 11.
[2] Annual figures.   [3] Last quarter.   [4] September 1935.

FIGURE 10

INTERNATIONAL COMPARISON OF CHANGES IN PRODUCTION COSTS, 1929–1935

Graph Showing Relative Amounts by which the Changes in Stated Series relating to Production Costs in Various Countries Exceeded or Fell Short of Changes in Corresponding Series for the United States, Account being Taken of Relative Changes in the Values of National Currencies

(Measurements of percentage changes from 1929 to December 1935)

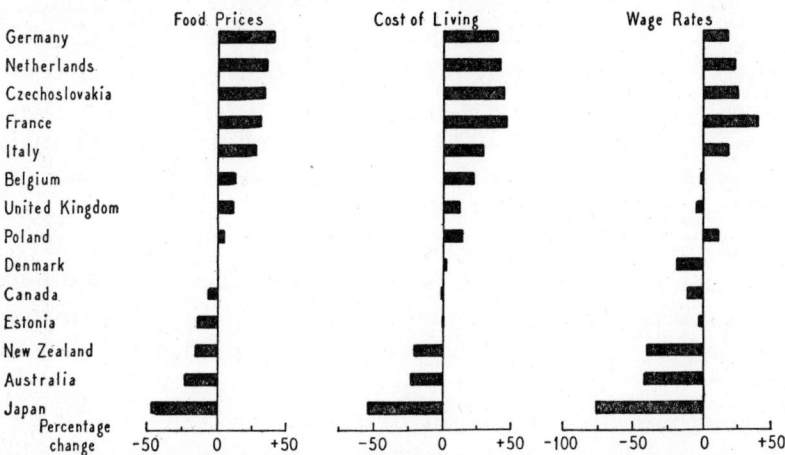

The movement is shown as positive when the change in the country named exceeded the change in the corresponding series for the United States; it is shown as negative when the change was less than that in the series for the United States.

petitive position in 1935, relatively to the United States. The value of the dollar in December 1935 was 59 per cent higher than in 1929, in terms of Japanese currency. The various Japanese internal series that we are using as indexes of relative production costs would have been approximately 59 per cent above the corresponding American figures, on the 1929 base, if costs had been adjusted to the changed yen-dollar relationship. Actually they were far below that level. Living costs and food prices were, respectively, only 5 and 12 per cent above the United States figures, and wage rates were 17 per cent below. Also in relatively strong positions, although with no such margin of apparent advantage as that of Japan, were New Zealand and Australia. Canada, Estonia and the United Kingdom stood on terms of approximate parity with the United States.

Typical of the countries in positions of relative disadvantage in 1935 is France. The value of the dollar in terms of the franc was 41 per cent lower in December 1935 than in 1929. But wage rates had changed by the same amount, relatively, as in the United States, living costs were 5 per cent higher in France, and food prices were only 10 per cent lower. There appears to have been no reduction in internal costs corresponding to the advance in the external value of the franc. With France, although in less pronounced positions of competitive disadvantage, stood Czechoslovakia, Germany, Italy and the Netherlands. (The list does not purport to be complete, since we are restricted to countries for which reasonably comparable index numbers are available.)

The measurements of living costs, wages, etc., which we have used as indexes of relative production costs, provide only rough approximations to the actual competitive positions of different countries. But there is no reason to doubt the essential truth of the picture we secure from Table 15. The changes in relative values of national currencies and in internal prices and costs that occurred between 1929 and 1935 worked havoc with the international cost relations in terms of which international trade was being re-established in 1929. Indeed, the magnitude of the differences developing is perhaps not sufficiently emphasized in Table 15, since the United States, which is the standard of reference, stands roughly in the middle of the divergent economies. If we compare Japan with France we have the accompanying measurements. Over this period of six years the value of the

THE WORLD PRICE STRUCTURE 209

	INDEX NUMBERS OF THE VALUE OF THE FRANC IN TERMS OF THE YEN		INDEX NUMBERS IN DECEMBER 1935 OF VARIOUS SERIES RELATING TO PRODUCTION COSTS, AS PERCENTAGES OF CORRESPONDING MEASUREMENTS FOR FRANCE ($1929=100$)		
	1929	Dec. 1935	Food prices	Cost of living	Wage rates
France	100	100	100	100	100
Japan	100	270	124	100	85

franc increased 170 per cent, in terms of the yen. The various domestic series for Japan should have risen by roughly equal amounts, relatively to those of France, if general equality of competitive position were to be maintained. But they did not. Food prices in Japan rose 24 per cent more than did food prices in France, cost of living paralleled the corresponding French series, and wage rates fell to a level 15 per cent below those of France. The measurements provide a striking example of the disorganization of competitive relations wrought by currency depreciation and divergent price and cost movements between 1929 and 1935.

As regards the relations between national cost structures, then, 1935 presents a disorganized picture. The world was not yet adapted to the suddenly-created differences of the several years preceding; it could not be so adapted without wrenching existing national productive organizations still further. Nor did the newly-established quotas and heightened tariff barriers promise to expedite a return to earlier trading relations. In spite of many signs of domestic improvement the condition of international trade remained black and unpromising at the end of 1935.[17]

---

[17] Devaluation in France, Switzerland, the Netherlands and Italy, which was announced in September and October 1936, promised to effect substantial alterations in the relations shown in Table 15. The re-establishment of currency relations with other countries closer to those of 1929 would be expected to remove some of the worst disparities among the series relating to production costs.

DISPARITIES OF COMMODITY PRICES

In earlier pages attention has been drawn to the post-War appearance, and persistence, of a world-wide schism between the prices of raw materials and manufactured goods. One phase of this was the price disparity between agricultural and industrial products, which was so marked a feature of the post-War situation in the United States. Recession accentuated the difficulties of a condition which had, indeed, been in considerable part corrected by 1929. The figures in Table 16, which define movements in the per unit purchasing power of raw materials in exchange for general commodities at wholesale in various countries, indicate the effects of world movements on this situation between 1932 and 1936.

TABLE 16

PER UNIT PURCHASING POWER AT WHOLESALE OF IMPORTANT RAW MATERIALS, 1913–1936

(Purchasing power is measured in terms of all commodities at wholesale in the country to which the raw material quotation relates.)

	1929	1932	1935	Feb. 1936	1913	1929	1932	1935	Feb. 1936
Wheat									
England, Liverpool	100	81	67	81	100	97	79	66	79
Canada, Winnipeg	100	59	83	81	100	102	61	85	82
U. S., Chicago	100	60	88	93	100	97	58	86	90
Rice									
France, Marseilles	100	70	71	66	100	78	55	55	52
U. S., New Orleans	100	86	126	120	100	73	63	92	88
Sugar									
England, London	100	85	64	67	100	61	52	40	41
U. S., New York	100	112	100	106	100	80	89	80	84
Coffee									
Netherlands, Amsterdam	100	89	46	47	100	113	100	52	53
U. S., New York	100	71	48	51	100	123	87	59	62

THE WORLD PRICE STRUCTURE

TABLE 16 (cont.)

PER UNIT PURCHASING POWER AT WHOLESALE OF IMPORTANT RAW MATERIALS, 1913–1936

(Purchasing power is measured in terms of all commodities at wholesale in the country to which the raw material quotation relates.)

	1929	1932	1935	Feb. 1936	1913	1929	1932	1935	Feb. 1936
Tea									
England, London	100	70	115	126	100	103	72	119	130
Netherlands, Amsterdam	100	75	95	104	100	118	88	112	122
U. S., New York	100	86	101	102	100	94	80	95	96
Cocoa									
England, London	100	90	84	83	100	56	51	47	46
Netherlands, Amsterdam	100	146	41	44	100	98	143	40	43
U. S., New York	100	88	58	58	100	74	66	43	43
Tobacco									
Netherlands, Amsterdam	100	97	84	81	100	293	286	245	237
U. S., Louisville	100	62	130	113	100	138	85	178	155
Lard									
U. S., New York	100	61	144	110	100	80	49	115	88
Nitrate of soda									
U. S., New York	100	108	70	70	100	64	69	45	45
France, Dunkerque	100	120	125	111	100	72	87	90	80
Cotton									
England, London	100	68	83	73	100	108	74	90	79
U. S., New Orleans	100	50	76	73	100	107	53	82	78
Wool									
England, London	100	71	88	107	100	114	80	100	121
U. S., Boston	100	68	87	106	100	129	88	112	136
Silk									
U. S., New York	100	45	38	41	100	99	45	38	41
France, Lyon	100	48	37	42	100	98	47	36	41
Japan, Yokohama	100	72	64	67	100	88	64	57	60
Hides, cattle									
England, London	100	82	99	100	100	72	59	71	72
U. S., Chicago	100	53	91	101	100	68	36	62	69
Pig iron									
Germany, Essen	100	115	101	100	100	82	95	83	82
England, London	100	112	124	124	100	88	99	110	110
Copper									
England, London	100	57	54	58	100	81	46	44	47
Germany, Berlin	100	45	35	39	100	87	39	30	34
U. S.	100	46	57	59	100	84	38	48	50

TABLE 16 (cont.)

PER UNIT PURCHASING POWER AT WHOLESALE OF IMPORTANT RAW MATERIALS, 1913–1936

(Purchasing power is measured in terms of all commodities at wholesale in the country to which the raw material quotation relates.)

	1929	1932	1935	Feb. 1936	1913	1929	1932	1935	Feb. 1936
Lead									
England, London	100	69	79	86	100	93	64	73	80
U. S., New York	100	69	72	78	100	113	78	81	89
Germany, Berlin	100	52	54	59	100	88	46	47	52
France, Paris	100	65	82	85	100	96	62	79	81
Zinc									
England, London	100	73	73	76	100	80	59	58	61
U. S., New York	100	71	82	90	100	86	61	71	78
Germany, Hamburg	100	57	51	52	100	79	45	41	41
France, Paris	100	66	83	76	100	86	57	71	65
Tin									
England, London	100	89	142	127	100	74	66	105	94
U. S., New York	100	71	133	125	100	74	53	98	92
Rubber									
England, London	100	44	77	90	100	20	9	16	18
U. S., New York	100	25	72	89	100	18	5	13	16
Newsprint									
Canada, Ottawa	100	113	80	82	100	84	95	67	69
Sweden	100	107	86	85	100	84	89	72	71
Beef, fresh									
France, Paris	100	120	107	109	100	89	107	96	97
U. S., Chicago	100	83	91	87	100	130	109	118	114
Mutton, fresh									
France, Paris	100	125	144	125	100	115	143	165	143
U. S., New York	100	73	74	66	100	100	73	74	66
England, London	100	88	105	89	100	110	96	115	98
Germany, Berlin	100	85	107	110	100	101	86	108	111
Pork, fresh									
Germany, Berlin	100	80	89	91	100	108	86	96	98
France, Paris	100	114	82	97	100	113	129	93	110
U. S., Chicago	100	63	125	114	100	103	65	129	118
England, London	100	84	92	85	100	119	100	110	101

From 1929 to 1932 raw materials declined in relative worth in 47 of the 58 markets represented in Table 16. From 1932

THE WORLD PRICE STRUCTURE 213

to February 1936 there were further declines in 22 of these markets, advances in 34. The measurements on the 1913 base throw light on the longer swings of the prices of foodstuffs and basic materials. In 1929, 37 of the 58 quotations in world markets reflected losses in the trading relations of primary producers, with reference to pre-War conditions. (In most instances the 1929 positions of primary producers were much stronger than those prevailing in the early years of the decade.) In 1932, 50 were below their pre-War parities with general commodities; by February 1936 this number had been reduced to 45. Here is evidence of some improvement in the trading positions of primary producers but the position of 1929, or that of 1913, was by no means restored.

These measurements define changes in the trading relations of primary products for general commodities within the various countries represented. The base of reference in each instance is the wholesale price index of the given country, in terms of national currencies. But these varying standards do not furnish the basis of international trade. In Table 17 we are able to follow the price movements of primary products with reference to broader standards. These measurements, constructed by the *Economist,* trace changes in the sterling and dollar prices of primary products, and in their corresponding gold prices, from the date of the departure of the United Kingdom from the gold standard.

Sterling prices of primary products advanced 12 to 14 per cent with the dropping of the gold standard by England in September 1931. Fluctuations followed, but without notable change in the average level until the end of 1933. Further advances in the sterling price of gold contributed to elevate the sterling prices of primary products to a level some 20 to 30 per cent above that of September 1931. The dollar prices

TABLE 17
PRICES OF PRIMARY PRODUCTS, 1931–1936
(In national currencies and in gold)

	PRICES OF PRIMARY PRODUCTS [1]		PRICES OF GOLD [2]		PRICES OF PRIMARY PRODUCTS	
	British (sterling)	American (dollar)	British (sterling)	American (dollar)	British (gold)	American (gold)
1931						
Sept. 18	100	100	100	100	100	100
Sept. 30	112	95	124	100	90	95
Oct. 28	114	101	124	100	92	101
Nov. 25	115	98	132	100	87	98
Dec. 30	117	94	142	100	82	94
1932						
Jan. 27	116	94	141	100	82	94
Feb. 24	121	90	140	100	86	90
Mar. 22	112	86	133	100	84	86
Apr. 20	105	84	130	100	81	84
June 29	99	80	135	100	74	80
July 27	104	84	137	100	76	84
Aug. 24	112	89	140	100	80	89
Sept. 21	117	90	140	100	84	90
Oct. 19	112	84	144	100	78	84
Nov. 30	112	78	154	100	73	78
Dec. 28	109	77	146	100	75	77
1933						
Jan. 25	108	78	143	100	76	78
Feb. 22	104	77	143	100	73	77
Mar. 22	104	80	142	100	73	80
Apr. 19	105	89	141	109	74	82
May 31	116	108	146	119	80	91
June 28	118	117	144	130	82	91
July 26	121	125	146	139	83	90
Aug. 23	117	119	148	138	79	86
Sept. 20	117	121	157	155	74	78
Oct. 18	113	109	155	142	73	77
Nov. 29	115	117	148	157	78	75
Dec. 13	115	117	148	154	77	76
1934						
Jan. 31	118	125	157	163	75	76
Feb. 28	121	128	161	168	75	76
Mar. 28	121	128	160	168	76	76
Apr. 25	120	125	160	169	75	74

THE WORLD PRICE STRUCTURE

TABLE 17 (*cont.*)

PRICES OF PRIMARY PRODUCTS, 1931–1936

1934		PRICES OF PRIMARY PRODUCTS [1]		PRICES OF GOLD [2]		PRICES OF PRIMARY PRODUCTS	
		British (sterling)	*American* (dollar)	*British* (sterling)	*American* (dollar)	*British* (gold)	*American* (gold)
May	23	121	129	161	169	76	76
June	20	123	134	162	168	76	80
July	18	125	137	162	168	77	81
Aug.	29	129	151	164	171	79	88
Sept.	26	126	149	166	170	76	88
Oct.	24	124	146	164	169	76	87
Nov.	21	120	149	164	168	73	89
Dec.	19	123	154	166	168	74	92
1935							
Jan.	30	125	152	167	167	74	91
Feb.	27	124	154	170	167	73	92
Mar.	27	123	148	171	168	72	88
Apr.	24	124	152	169	168	74	90
May	22	128	151	167	168	76	90
June	19	126	144	166	169	76	85
July	31	127	146	166	169	76	86
Aug.	28	126	141	165	169	76	84
Sept.	25	131	149	166	168	79	88
Oct.	23	134	145	166	169	80	86
Nov.	20	131	144	166	168	79	86
Dec.	18	131	142	166	169	79	84
1936							
Jan.	29	132	146	166	170	80	86
Feb.	26	133	145	166	171	80	85
Mar.	25	134	144	166	169	81	85
Apr.	29	133	143	166	168	80	85
May	27	130	140	164	168	79	84

[1] Computed by the *Economist* from the wholesale prices of important raw materials. The list given by the *Economist* includes:

Wheat	Cocoa	Wool	Lead
Maize	Sugar	Cottonseed oil	Pig iron
Oats	Lard	Copper	Petroleum
Linseed	Bacon	Tin	
Coffee	Cotton	Rubber	

(Notes to Table 17 concluded on *p. 216*)

of primary products fell during 1931 and 1932, reaching a low point in the early months of 1933. With depreciation of the dollar and a sharp increase in domestic business activity the dollar prices of these products advanced about 60 per cent in the spring and early summer of 1933. Thereafter there was no substantial change until the spring of 1934, despite further advances in the dollar price of gold. Drought and crop scarcity in 1934 brought a sharp rise in the dollar prices of primary products, and in their American gold prices. Although the sterling and dollar prices of gold stood at the same general levels from 1934 to 1936, the dollar prices of primary products were consistently higher than the sterling prices. Domestic conditions in the United States contributed to this differential.

The very considerable recoveries of primary products in sterling and dollar prices are to be contrasted with the corresponding changes in their gold values, in British and American markets. These stood, in 1936, 15 to 20 per cent below the 1931 level. The gold prices of primary products in the United States advanced with the upswing of 1934, and later retained part of this gain.

The great international schism between the prices of basic materials and industrial finished products that was re-opened by the recession of 1929 had been somewhat lessened by the early months of 1936. Certain basic commodities had regained a substantial part of their lost purchasing power; others still stood in positions of marked disadvantage. These relations are vividly brought out by measurements defining

(*Notes to Table 17 concluded*)
The prices of these commodities with the exception of wool were taken from various American markets; the wool quotation is taken from Le Havre.
[2] Gold prices are based upon exchange rates, not on Treasury quotations.

THE WORLD PRICE STRUCTURE

changes in the net barter terms of trade of leading industrial and raw material producing countries (Table 18). These

TABLE 18

NET BARTER TERMS OF TRADE FOR EIGHT COUNTRIES,[1]

1913–1935

	1929	1932	1934	1935	1913	1921	1929	1932	1934	1935
United Kingdom	100	87	84	87	100	82	88	76	74	76
France	100	87	85	84	100	95	105	91	89	88
Germany	100	69	74	79	100		95	65	70	76
United States	100	84	79	77	100	78	95	81	75	73
Hungary	100	108	97	89	100	156	116	127	113	104
New Zealand	100	158	129		100	135	92	145	119	
Argentina	100	152	145		100	159	107	162	156	
Dutch East Indies	100	146	136	135	100	153	126	183	172	171

[1] The index numbers of import and export prices from which these measurements are derived are given in *Review of World Trade, 1934* (League of Nations, Geneva, 1935), p. 82.

measurements, which may be taken to define changes in the physical volume of exports required to pay for a fixed quantity of imported goods, are derived from index numbers of the prices of goods entering into foreign trade. An index of prices of goods imported by a given country, divided by an index of prices of goods exported by that country, on the same base, yields an index of net barter terms of trade.[18]

The divergent fortunes of industrial and colonial areas between 1929 and 1932 are clearly revealed by the indexes in Table 18. In the four industrial countries listed first we note declines ranging from 16 to 31 per cent in the volume

[18] The use of average prices of imported and exported goods in deriving measurements of this type involves the assumption that no substantial changes occur in the physical character of a country's export and import trade. This assumption is reasonably valid in respect of changes over short periods; it is far less sound as regards changes over one or two decades.

218   PRICES IN RECESSION AND RECOVERY

of exports exchangeable for a fixed quantity of imports; in the remaining four countries, which are heavy exporters of primary products, the volume of exports given in exchange for a fixed quantity of imports increased from 8 to 58 per cent. The several years following brought some amelioration of these conditions. But in 1935 the net barter terms of trade remained distinctly favorable to industrial countries, unfavorable to areas exporting raw materials. A shift of base to 1913 shows a somewhat more extreme cleavage between these two groups of countries. Trading relations of 1935 were far removed from those of pre-War days.

Turning now to primary products of agricultural origin, we find a notable difference persisting between their prices in important industrial countries and in areas producing primarily for export (Table 19). These index numbers measure changes in agricultural prices relatively to the movement of general wholesale prices. Thus if the index for agricultural

TABLE 19

PER UNIT PURCHASING POWER OF AGRICULTURAL COMMODITIES, 1913–1935

(In terms of all commodities at wholesale)

	1929	1932	1935	Dec. 1935	1913	1929	1932	1935	Dec. 1935
Argentina	100	62	70	75					
Canada	100	69	83	86	100	108	74	90	92
England and Wales	100	113	116	111	100[3]	106	120	124	119
Finland	100	81	83	83					
France	100	122	105	107	100	92	113	97	99
Germany	100	100	106	107	100	95	95	100	102
Italy	100	103		109[2]	100	106	110		115[2]
Netherlands[1]	100	100	108	104					
New Zealand	100	62	72	75	100[4]	109	68	79	82
Poland	100	99	95	95					
United States	100	68	89	88	100	108	73	96	94

[1] Crop year.
[2] August.
[3] 1911–13=100
[4] 1909–13=100

prices declines, in terms of this standard, it means that the prices of non-agricultural commodities have advanced, relatively. This happened between 1929 and 1932 for all the countries listed in Table 19 except Germany, France, England, Italy and the Netherlands. In the main, these were protected areas for agricultural producers, in which preferential advantages in home markets were given to domestic producers. In the United States, Canada, New Zealand, Argentina and Finland agricultural products lost substantially in relative worth, following the currents prevailing in world markets. Recovery, to December 1935, had failed to restore farm products to their 1929 parity with commodities in general in the countries just listed, although appreciable improvement had occurred. In France some of the relative advantage enjoyed by agricultural producers had been lost, but agricultural producers in the industrial countries of Western Europe retained substantial advantages. No world level of agricultural prices existed in 1935. The effects of nationalistic economic policies are clearly manifest in their divergent movements after 1929.

We have noted that at the low point of the depression world price relations were definitely unfavorable to recovery of the capital goods industries. In Germany, in Canada, in the United States the prices of goods for use in capital equipment were high, as compared with commodities in general. Liquidation had left them on a plateau above the general price level. Japan was a notable exception. By early 1936 this condition had been materially improved in the United States, although construction costs remained high. Available measurements indicate some lessening, relatively, of the costs of capital goods elsewhere. The actual prices of such goods advanced in Japan, but they remained well below prices in general.

The record of world changes from 1932 to 1936, in physical

terms, showed very substantial gains in production in a number of countries. For four years the general movement was one of irregular and spotty recovery. This was not a single great movement, however; it was rather of the nature of a series of national gains, largely disconnected. Considerable advances were scored in Japan, Great Britain, the United States and other countries, but each national movement appeared to be definitely limited in its international effects. The gains in world trade during this period were not commensurate with the recoveries shown by domestic records. (Japan increased the volume of its export trade materially, but this movement was exceptional.) Over these years the world was following a path of nationalistic development. No working international organization had been restored. National self-sufficiency rather than regional specialization was the keynote of the time, as was strikingly manifest in the concurrent industrialization of colonial areas and the pressure towards agricultural development within industrial nations.

The price movements of the period of recession and recovery reflected the trend away from an international organization and towards a nationalistic system. We have traced the divergence of national price levels and the disparate changes of factors related to production costs. The price bases of world trading relations had been profoundly disturbed by these movements. By 1936 some favorable developments had occurred. The world-wide schism between the prices of raw materials and of manufactured goods had been lessened. Some recovery had been made in world trade. Progressive depreciation of currencies had been checked. Announcement in September of sympathetic cooperation between England, France and the United States in the stabilization of exchange relations marked a forward step of great significance. But serious difficulties persisted. Disparate price levels and widely different cost relations re-enforced prohibitive tariffs and quota restrictions in checking commercial intercourse. A world price structure, with its national elements mutually adjusted, had not yet been restored.

CHAPTER V

PRICE CHANGES AND THE FORTUNES OF PRIMARY PRODUCERS IN RECOVERY

THE sharp pick-up that lifted prices above the depression lows of February 1933 was one of the most striking of which we have record. Within five months the general level of wholesale prices advanced 17 per cent. Thereafter the advance tapered off, but over forty months the rise amounted to approximately 32 per cent. In June 1936 the general index of wholesale prices was 18 per cent below the July 1929 level, having risen from a trough 38 per cent below.

The fact of the general price rise is important, but its incidence is of even greater significance. How did it affect the badly twisted price structure left by forty-three months of practically unbroken recession? Did it serve to correct some of the disparities that reflected radical shifts in the distribution of current income, or to intensify them? If the net effect was in the direction of correction, how have the later phases of the movement compared with the earlier? Here was a rise that was in some degree, at least, the result of conscious stimulation. Its effects on the shaken price structure of the depression, and possible variations in these effects with the passage of time, are of peculiar and compelling interest.

In this chapter we are concerned with those price movements and concurrent production changes that affected the purchasing power and general economic status of primary producers. Diverse as their products and problems are, producers of raw materials have something in common in their

PRIMARY PRODUCERS

relation to economic processes at large. Yet the diversities that prevail among them call for specialized treatment of important groups. In particular, we shall deal with the distinctive problems of farmers during the recovery from the depression lows of the winter of 1932–33. In this economic area were focused a variety of attempts at selective inflation and production control. For this reason the course of events is of special interest.

For primary producers as a class the recession was marked by severe price declines, by relatively small reductions in the volume of production, and by substantial losses in aggregate purchasing power. Particularly on the price front was weakness apparent when the forces of recession were loosed. Special circumstances in 1929 intensified the difficulties usually encountered by primary producers during a cyclical recession, difficulties growing out of their distinctive relations to the stream of trade, the character of competition faced, the relatively limited control over supply and the influence of non-business considerations in the activities of agricultural producers. The problems of recovery and readjustment faced by these producers were similarly affected by special conditions—important shifts in the volume and character of our export trade, and legislative and administrative measures designed to stimulate price improvement and to restore the purchasing power of this group.

Raw Materials in Price Recovery

The changes brought by recovery in the general market relations between raw materials and manufactured goods are indicated in Table 20. As in past revivals, the first push of price recovery was felt by primary products. During the five months, February–July 1933, raw materials gained 30 per cent in price, manufactured goods 12 per cent. To the customary stimulus that business revival gives to the prices of primary products was added, at this time, the effect of departure from the gold standard. Materials sold in world markets are most immediately influenced by monetary devaluation. In terms of per unit purchasing power these changes meant a gain of 10 per cent for raw materials, a loss of 5 per cent for products of manufacture. Reviewed against a pre-recession base, these movements cut in half the average per unit loss of purchasing power suffered by raw materials

TABLE 20

PRICES AND PURCHASING POWER OF RAW MATERIALS AND MANUFACTURED GOODS, JULY 1929–JUNE 1936 [1]

A. Movements of Wholesale Prices

	July 1929	Feb. 1933	July 1933	Oct. 1933	May 1934	Sept. 1934	May 1935	Dec. 1935	Apr. 1936	June 1936
RECESSION AND RECOVERY										
All commodities	100	62	72	74	77	81	83	84	82	82
Raw materials	100	51	66	65	68	75	78	78	77	78
Manufactured goods	100	69	77	80	83	84	86	87	85	84
RECOVERY										
All commodities		100	117	121	125	131	134	135	133	132
Raw materials		100	130	129	134	149	154	153	152	153
Manufactured goods		100	112	117	120	123	125	127	124	122

B. Changes in Per Unit Purchasing Power

	July 1929	Feb. 1933	July 1933	Oct. 1933	May 1934	Sept. 1934	May 1935	Dec. 1935	Apr. 1936	June 1936
RECESSION AND RECOVERY										
All commodities	100	100	100	100	100	100	100	100	100	100
Raw materials	100	82	91	87	88	93	94	93	94	95
Manufactured goods	100	111	106	108	107	104	104	104	104	103
RECOVERY										
All commodities		100	100	100	100	100	100	100	100	100
Raw materials		100	110	107	108	114	114	113	115	116
Manufactured goods		100	95	97	96	94	93	94	93	92

[1] The index numbers from which these measurements for selected dates are taken appear in Appendix IV.

and the average per unit gain enjoyed by manufactured goods after forty-three months of recession.

It is fair to assume that this movement toward the restoration of earlier relations through the relatively rapid advance of the more seriously depressed prices was salutary. It is true that pre-recession relations among elements of the economic system may by no means be accepted as 'normal'. The recession itself furnishes *prima facie* evidence that 1929 relations did not represent a state of equilibrium. Some correctional movements within the price system and in other elements of the economy at large were undoubtedly called for. But the gap between the prices of raw and of processed goods that was violently opened during recession was a serious impediment to economic activity. The reduction of this gap during the spring of 1933 improved the status of raw material producers and stimulated intergroup trade.

The rapid rise in the prices of raw materials in the early months of recovery was definitely checked in the late summer and early autumn of 1933. The general price advance was retarded, after July, and the pressure of price change upon the elements of the system at large was shifted. Commodity groups that had most successfully resisted the price decline of the preceding four years, and had moved upwards but slowly in price during the first months of recovery, began to feel the push of changing values, while among the groups previously most active the rise of prices was retarded. This reversal of tendencies is reflected in Table 20. The ten months following July 1933 brought an advance of 3 per cent in the average prices, at wholesale, of raw materials, and a rise of 8 per cent in average prices of manufactured products. In terms of relative purchasing power, the situation in May 1934 was further removed from the pre-recession situation than was that of July 1933.

The shift in the incidence of price advance in the summer

of 1933 was in part a direct result of the earlier movement. Higher prices of materials may be expected, after an interval, to affect the selling prices of finished goods. Moreover, in the earlier period manufacturers were stocking up materials prior to the introduction of the new codes that went into effect under the National Industrial Recovery Act in the summer and fall of 1933. Raw material prices reflected this heavy buying in the spring of 1933. Later retardation was natural. As a final factor, undoubtedly important but difficult to appraise in quantitative terms, the enforcement of the wage, hour and price provisions of the new industrial codes played a part in raising the prices of fabricated goods between July 1933 and May 1934.

After May 1934 new forces were injected into the situation. Drought and consequent crop destruction, superimposed upon a program of output limitation, operated powerfully to raise market prices among agricultural raw materials. By September 1934 average raw material prices had advanced 11 per cent from the May level; the average price of manufactured goods had risen less than 3 per cent. Adaptation to the conditions created by the codes and a lessening of the pressure towards higher costs and prices under the codes were factors in checking the more rapid advance that had prevailed in earlier months. The net results are most clearly reflected in the index numbers of purchasing power in Part B of Table 20. The figures for September 1934 define a situation closer to pre-recession parity than at any time after the low point of February 1933. Substantial corrections had been effected in the maladjustments created during recession. The recession gain in the average per unit purchasing power of manufactured goods had been reduced from 11 to 4 per cent, and the loss of raw material purchasing power had been reduced from 18 to 7 per cent.

Minor price fluctuations during the succeeding twenty-one

months brought a net advance of less than 2 per cent in the general level of wholesale prices. Raw and manufactured goods were left in the same relative positions as in the autumn of 1934. The stability of the price level and the constancy of price relations between raw and processed goods over a period marked by steadily expanding business activity and rising profits, and by the termination of the industrial codes, have been notable features of recent economic developments.

The fortunes of four major groups of raw material producers during this period of recovery may be followed in the record of Table 21. The outstanding feature of the early price recovery was the amazing advance in the prices of raw farm crops. No other group approached the gain of 65 per cent, in five months, that was made by these commodities. Raw mineral products advanced only 6 per cent. Animal and forest products rose markedly, by amounts well in excess of the 17 per cent gain recorded for the general index. The sharp alteration in the incidence of price change during the three following months, July 1933–October 1933, is apparent in these several index numbers of raw material prices, as well as in the contrasting movements of the prices of raw and processed goods. Farm crops lost a third of their earlier gain, in terms of actual prices; animal products barely maintained their mid-summer position; forest products continued to advance, but at a lower rate; the prices of raw mineral products spurted ahead, gaining in three months twice the amount of the previous five months' advance.

Crop reduction and drought brought a further notable advance in the prices of farm crops in 1934, with a subsequent decline in 1935. Animal products rose steadily, to the end of 1935. Raw forest and mineral products dropped behind in the rise and lost in purchasing power. During the

TABLE 21
PRICES AND PURCHASING POWER OF FOUR GROUPS OF PRIMARY PRODUCTS, JULY 1929–JUNE 1936

A. Movements of Wholesale Prices of Raw Materials

	July 1929	Feb. 1933	July 1933	Oct. 1933	May 1934	Sept. 1934	May 1935	Dec. 1935	Apr. 1936	June 1936
RECESSION AND RECOVERY										
Farm crops	100	40	67	57	64	75	73	67	69	73
Animal products	100	39	52	51	51	62	74	76	73	71
Forest products	100	63	78	83	87	83	80	82	81	81
Mineral products	100	73	78	87	87	89	88	91	91	90
RECOVERY										
Farm crops		100	165	142	159	187	180	167	171	182
Animal products		100	132	131	131	158	189	194	186	181
Forest products		100	124	132	138	132	127	129	128	128
Mineral products		100	106	119	120	122	120	124	124	124

B. Changes in Per Unit Purchasing Power of Raw Materials

	July 1929	Feb. 1933	July 1933	Oct. 1933	May 1934	Sept. 1934	May 1935	Dec. 1935	Apr. 1936	June 1936
RECESSION AND RECOVERY										
Farm crops	100	65	92	77	83	93	88	81	84	90
Animal products	100	63	71	69	67	77	89	91	89	86
Forest products	100	102	108	111	113	103	97	98	99	99
Mineral products	100	118	107	116	113	110	105	109	111	110
RECOVERY										
Farm crops		100	141	117	128	143	134	123	129	137
Animal products		100	112	109	105	121	141	143	140	136
Forest products		100	106	109	110	101	94	96	97	97
Mineral products		100	91	99	96	93	89	92	94	93

first six months of 1936 farm crops advanced appreciably and animal products lost in purchasing power. In June 1936 raw minerals had an average per unit worth 10 per cent greater than in July 1929; raw forest and animal products and farm crops were respectively, 1, 14 and 10 per cent below the pre-recession level. The range of difference is considerable, but far less than that of February 1933. The worst of the price inequalities existing in the winter of 1932–33 had been ironed out.

Behind these diverse price movements lay a host of factors. Changing monetary values, and hopes and fears concerning further changes; important modifications of working conditions and production costs as the Administration's program of recovery unfolded, and hopes and fears connected with these changes; shifts in current and potential supplies, as a result of administrative action and the play of natural forces —all these combined with fluctuations on the demand side to create an extraordinary complex of factors affecting the level of commodity prices and the relations among the prices of different commodity groups. Some of these factors are discussed in subsequent sections. We should note here, however, the major changes in supply accompanying the shifts that recovery brought in the prices of raw materials.

Variations in the annual output of the four chief classes of raw materials are indicated by the accompanying index numbers of physical production.[1] We do not find a perfect

	1929	1932	1933	1934	1935
Farm crops	100	93	85	72	89
Animal products (slaughterings)	100	103	105	108	94
Forest products	100	38	48	49	55
Mineral products	100	62	67	72	77

inverse relation between production and price movements between 1929 and 1935, for changes in market demand and in stocks on hand constitute additional factors, not here represented. However, the groups for which prices were maintained during the recession—forest and mineral products—were those in which production was most severely curtailed. Mineral products suffered less in price than forest

[1] The sources of these measurements and the movements of their component elements are indicated in Appendix VII.

products, though production of the latter declined by a larger percentage. This is accounted for by the virtual cessation of building and the consequent great decline in demand for lumber. Maintenance of the output of crops and animal products was a factor, of course, in their sharp price declines during recession.

With recovery, the greatest immediate price advances occurred among farm crops, the output of which was reduced, particularly in 1934, by crop reduction and drought. The relative price rise through 1934 was much lower for animal products. Output (which here means slaughterings) was maintained for this group, and even increased in 1934 as a result of feed shortage. The lower price gains of mineral and forest products were accompanied by increases in output.

The later strength of the prices of raw animal products, manifest in the 1935 price quotations, reflects substantial reductions in the existing supplies of meat animals—an aftermath of the earlier feed shortage and forced marketings of 1934. The following comparison of the number of meat animals on farms [2] at the beginning of 1934 and of 1935

	Jan. 1, 1934	Jan. 1, 1935	Percentage decrease
Cattle and calves [1]	47,203,000	42,293,000	10.4
Hogs, including pigs	58,621,000	39,004,000	33.5
Sheep and lambs	53,713,000	52,251,000	2.7

[1] Excludes cows and heifers, two years old and over, kept for milk.

indicates the nature of the forces responsible for the sharp spurt in the prices of farm animals and meat products in 1935. Reduced supply contributed to the strength of the prices of farm crops and animal products during recovery, as it had to the relative strength of prices of raw forest and mineral products during recession. But other forces, operat-

[2] *Crops and Markets*, February 1936, p. 34.

PRIMARY PRODUCERS

ing from the monetary and demand side, played important parts in the price advance of 1933–36.

Farm Products in Wholesale Markets

We pass to a more detailed consideration of recovery, as it affected the class of primary producers that suffered most severely during the decline (Table 22). During the first five months of recovery the average price, at wholesale, of raw products of American farms advanced just 50 per cent; the prices of non-farm products rose but 12 per cent. Here was a movement of amazing proportions, which contributed materially to correct one of the major price disparities of the

TABLE 22

PRICES AND PURCHASING POWER OF FARM AND OTHER PRODUCTS, JULY 1929–JUNE 1936

A. Movements of Wholesale Prices

	July 1929	Feb. 1933	July 1933	Oct. 1933	May 1934	Sept. 1934	May 1935	Dec. 1935	Apr. 1936	June 1936
RECESSION AND RECOVERY										
All commodities	100	62	72	74	77	81	83	84	82	82
Products of American farms, raw [1]	100	40	59	55	58	70	76	74	73	74
All other commodities	100	68	76	80	83	84	85	87	85	84
Products of American farms, raw										
Producers' goods	100	37	57	51	56	70	78	74	74	72
Consumers' goods	100	47	66	63	63	70	71	72	69	78
RECOVERY										
All commodities		100	117	121	125	131	134	135	133	132
Products of American farms, raw [1]		100	150	138	146	177	192	186	184	186
All other commodities		100	112	118	121	123	125	127	124	123
Products of American farms, raw										
Producers' goods		100	155	140	152	190	213	202	202	197
Consumers' goods		100	141	135	135	150	150	153	148	166

TABLE 22 (*cont.*)

PRICES AND PURCHASING POWER OF FARM AND OTHER PRODUCTS, JULY 1929–JUNE 1936

B. Changes in Per Unit Purchasing Power

	July 1929	Feb. 1933	July 1933	Oct. 1933	May 1934	Sept. 1934	May 1935	Dec. 1935	Apr. 1936	June 1936
RECESSION AND RECOVERY										
All commodities	100	100	100	100	100	100	100	100	100	100
Products of American farms, raw [1]	100	64	82	73	75	86	91	88	88	90
All other commodities	100	110	105	108	107	104	102	104	103	103
Products of American farms, raw										
Producers' goods	100	59	78	68	72	86	94	89	90	88
Consumers' goods	100	76	92	85	82	87	85	86	84	95
RECOVERY										
All commodities		100	100	100	100	100	100	100	100	100
Products of American farms, raw [1]		100	128	114	117	135	143	138	138	141
All other commodities		100	95	98	97	94	93	94	94	93
Products of American farms, raw										
Producers' goods		100	132	116	122	146	158	150	152	148
Consumers' goods		100	120	112	108	115	112	113	111	125

[1] The index numbers of prices of raw crops and raw animal products given in Table 21 are not confined to products of American farms, as are the measurements in Table 22.

depression. Subsequent changes follow the pattern outlined in the opening section of this chapter—an appreciable loss of relative position by raw farm products between July and October 1933, minor fluctuations between October 1933 and May 1934, followed by a substantial price rise under the influence of the adverse crop conditions in the summer of 1934. By September 1934 raw farm products were in a better relative position than in the summer of 1933. This advantage was maintained and, indeed, slightly improved, over the succeeding twenty-one months. In June 1936 the average per

PRIMARY PRODUCERS 233

unit purchasing power of raw farm products was 41 per cent higher than in February 1933, and 10 per cent lower than in July 1929. The latter figure may be compared with the corresponding index for February 1933, which was 36 per cent below the pre-recession level.

The gains of this advance were not even, as among the various types of farm product. We have noted that raw crops, which are more directly affected by the monetary forces playing on international markets, fared much better in the 1933 rise than raw animal products. Animal products gained slightly more than crops in the advance of the summer of 1934, and further improved their position in the winter of 1934–35. If we distinguish raw farm products intended for productive use from those ready for direct consumption, we find that the greater decline of the former, during recession, was offset by a more rapid advance during the recovery in raw material prices. The present record ends, in June 1936, with raw producers' goods, among farm products, 12 per cent below their pre-recession unit purchasing power, at wholesale, and raw consumers' goods from the same source 5 per cent below. Cotton, wheat, cattle and hogs, the great staples that weigh heavily in the raw producers' group, scored more substantial price gains during the recovery than did raw materials ready for consumption.

In appraising the situation existing from 1933 to 1936 we may with advantage go back to a more distant base. Measurements in Table 23 are based on 1913. For the two main groups the shift of base makes little difference in average purchasing power, per unit. At the peak prior to the recession these two groups stood in approximately the same relative position as in 1913. The net result of the conflicting currents of recession and recovery, up to June 1936, was to leave the average purchasing power of raw farm products 8 per cent lower than in 1913, and that of nonfarm products 2 per cent higher. Similarly, the change of base

TABLE 23

PURCHASING POWER OF RAW FARM PRODUCTS AND OTHER COMMODITIES, 1913–1936

CHANGES IN PER UNIT PURCHASING POWER, AT WHOLESALE

	July 1913	Feb. 1929	July 1933	Oct. 1933	May 1934	Sept. 1934	May 1935	Dec. 1935	Apr. 1936	June 1936
All commodities	100	100	100	100	100	100	100	100	100	100
Products of American farms, raw	100	102	66	84	75	77	89	94	90	91	92
All other commodities	100	100	110	105	107	107	104	102	103	103	102
Crops, raw [1]	100	102	66	93	78	85	95	89	82	85	91
Animal products, raw [1]	100	98	62	70	68	65	75	88	89	87	85
Products of American farms, raw Producers' goods	100	99	59	78	68	72	86	93	88	89	87
Consumers' goods	100	112	85	102	95	92	98	95	96	94	107

[1] These index numbers include raw crops and raw animal products of both American and foreign origin.

brings but slight modification in the relative movements of crops and animal products, since their 1929 relations were close to their pre-War relations. Wider differences are introduced into the comparison, among farm products, of raw producers' and raw consumers' goods. In July 1929 these two groups stood, respectively, 1 per cent below and 12 per cent above the 1913 level, in per unit purchasing power. The changes of recession and recovery left them, respectively, 13 per cent below and 7 per cent above 1913 parity with commodities in general, at wholesale.

PRICES RECEIVED BY FARMERS AND PRICES PAID BY FARMERS

The price and purchasing power changes we have been discussing relate to wholesale markets. These are of high im-

PRIMARY PRODUCERS

portance in trade but they do not measure changes in the values of immediate concern to farmers. For this purpose we must take account of prices at the farm, and of prices actually paid by farmers for the goods they buy (Table 24).[3]

[3] A parallel treatment of the wholesale prices and farm prices of agricultural products is necessary because of the magnitude of the distributive margin between these two sets of prices, and because the movements of this margin in times of rapid price change are quite unlike the movements of prices actually received by farmers.

The size of the margin varies, of course, for different commodities. The relative importance of one element of the margin, transportation charges, is indicated by the following figures, compiled by Thor Hultgren, of the Bureau of Agricultural Economics. Freight charges are comparatively high, in relation to price, for the articles here listed.

TRANSPORTATION CHARGES FROM REPRESENTATIVE PRODUCING POINTS TO NEW YORK CITY, 1928–1932, EXPRESSED AS PERCENTAGES OF FARM PRICE OF SPECIFIED FRUITS AND VEGETABLES

	1928	1929	1932
Potatoes, Maine	83	27	131
Apples, Washington	96	64	167
Oranges, California	69	36	101
Grapes, California, wine and table	152	110	305
Lettuce, California, second early	116	87	107
Watermelons, Georgia	114	106	322
Cabbage, New York (Danish, for market)	21	33	161
Onions, Texas, early bermuda and creole	78	64	56
Peaches, Georgia	94	63	77
Tomatoes, Florida, early, second	32	38	35

The variations in these percentages are due, in the main, to fluctuations in the prices received by producers, not to changes in freight charges. Thus for Maine potatoes the price received by producers varied from 42.3 cents per 100 pounds, in 1932, to 203.3 cents in 1929, while freight rates per 100 pounds remained constant at 55.5 cents.

Not quite so rigid, but much less sensitive to changing economic conditions than general wholesale prices or farm prices, are the various series of freight rates represented below.

(*Footnote* 3 *concluded on p. 236*)

PRICES IN RECESSION AND RECOVERY

Average prices at the farm dropped slightly more than wholesale prices of raw farm products between July 1929 and February 1933—63 per cent as against 60 per cent. The initial spurt of recovery, between February and July 1933, carried the prices of farm products up about 50 per cent in both markets. For ten months thereafter farm prices as well

(Footnote 3 concluded)

INDEX NUMBERS OF FREIGHT RATES
Various Commodities and Groups with Corresponding Index Numbers for Wholesale Prices and Farm Prices, 1913–1934

	1929	1932	1934	1913	1929	1934
Grain, Chicago to Liverpool	100	89	99	100	131	130
Provisions, Chicago to Liverpool	100	97	89	100	199	177
Wheat, Chicago to New York						
By lake and canal	100	71	86	100	111	95
By lake and rail	100	84	77	100	149	115
By all rail	100	100	82	100	188	154
Cattle, U. S.	100	106	101	100	156	158
Hogs, U. S.	100	99	99	100	159	157
Sheep, U. S.	100	100	100	100	142	142
Total livestock, U. S.	100	101	99	100	155	153
Wheat, U. S.	100	99	99	100	148	147
Cotton, U. S.	100	65	58	100	163	95
All traffic through Sault Ste Marie						
Average charge per ton per mile	100	88	95	100	157	149
All traffic, Class I Railroads						
Average revenue per ton-mile	100	97	91	100	150	137
Wholesale prices, all commodities	100	68	79	100	136	107
Prices received by producers of						
farm products	100	44	62	100	145	89

SOURCES: The various indexes of freight rates are original data collected by the Department of Commerce and published in the annual *Statistical Abstract*. The wholesale price index is that of the U. S. Bureau of Labor Statistics.

The wholesale prices of farm products, as quoted in the compilations of the Bureau of Labor Statistics, do not necessarily reflect all the freight rigidities here cited. Much depends on the market to which a wholesale price quotation relates. But the presence of such charges accounts for some of the differences between price movements at the farm and price movements in wholesale and retail markets.

PRIMARY PRODUCERS

TABLE 24

FARM PRICES, PRICES PAID BY FARMERS AND PER UNIT PURCHASING POWER OF FARM PRODUCTS, JULY 1929–JUNE 1936

	July 1929	Feb. 1933	July 1933	Oct. 1933	May 1934	Sept. 1934	May 1935	Dec. 1935	Apr. 1936	June 1936
RECESSION AND RECOVERY										
Prices received:										
All farm products [1]	100	37	56	53	56	70	74	75	71	73
Grains	100	28	78	57	64	93	93	74	74	72
Fruits	100	42	54	51	73	62	65	61	59	76
Cotton and cottonseed	100	30	58	49	62	76	72	68	66	66
Meat animals	100	32	40	38	38	49	71	72	75	72
Dairy products	100	49	58	60	60	65	70	78	75	70
Poultry products	100	40	46	62	48	70	74	91	65	69
Vegetables	100	60	63	76	55	83	79	84	66	62
Prices paid by farmers [2]	100	66	70	76	79	82	83	80	79	78
Per unit purchasing power of farm products	100	57	81	70	70	85	89	94	90	93
RECOVERY										
Prices received:										
All farm products [1]		100	151	142	149	187	196	200	191	194
Grains		100	276	203	229	329	329	262	262	256
Fruits		100	127	120	172	145	153	144	139	180
Cotton and cottonseed		100	191	161	204	250	239	223	218	218
Meat animals		100	124	121	121	155	223	226	236	226
Dairy products		100	119	123	123	134	145	160	154	143
Poultry products		100	115	155	120	173	183	225	162	172
Vegetables		100	106	128	93	138	132	142	112	103
Prices paid by farmers [2]		100	106	115	120	125	126	121	120	119
Per unit purchasing power of farm products		100	142	123	124	150	156	166	159	164

SOURCE: *The Agricultural Situation*, monthly bulletin of the Bureau of Agricultural Economics, Department of Agriculture

[1] Includes tobacco and a few other commodities not classified in the given subgroups.

[2] The commodities entering into the index of prices paid by farmers include goods bought for the farm family (food, clothing, furniture, building materials for the house, automobiles for family use, etc.) and goods bought

as wholesale prices fluctuated slightly. In May 1934 the level of farm prices was practically the same as it had been in July 1933. The second great advance of recovery then set in. Within four months farm prices advanced to a level 87 per cent above the depression low. More than half the losses of recession and depression had been made up. During the following fifteen months, to the end of 1935, a further net gain of about 7 per cent was scored. A decline of about 3 per cent occurred in average farm prices in the first six months of 1936.

The price movements of this period varied widely among the different classes of farm products. Grains, meat animals and cotton, the heaviest sufferers in the decline, scored the greatest advances. As of June 1936 vegetables stood farthest below the pre-recession level; fruits, meat animals and grains stood closest to it. It is to be noted that the drop of some 3 per cent in average farm prices in early 1936, after the termination of the Agricultural Adjustment Act, was influenced by substantial declines in the prices of poultry products and vegetables. Meat animals held their position, and grains and cotton declined slightly.

We have seen that the trading position of the farmer suffered a great loss during the recession, because prices paid failed to adjust themselves to the drop in prices received. Recovery brought a definite improvement, in this respect. During the first five months of rapid rise, when farm prices were gaining 51 per cent, prices paid by farmers were advancing only 6 per cent. Subsequently, a sharper advance occurred in prices paid, but by June 1936 these had risen only 19 per cent from their low point, while average prices

---

for use in production (feed, farm machinery, trucks, tractors, fertilizers, equipment and supplies, seed, etc.).

Index numbers of per unit purchasing power are secured by dividing indexes of prices received by indexes of prices paid.

received by farmers had almost doubled. Although the net loss from the pre-recession level was greater among prices received than among prices paid, the average per unit worth of the farmer's product was, in June 1936, only 7 per cent less than in 1929.

There were wide differences, of course, among farm products with respect to these gains and losses. The immediate record ends, in June 1936, with fruits 3 per cent below their July 1929 level of purchasing power, and with truck crops 22 per cent below. The other groups fell within these extremes.[4]

AGRICULTURAL PROCESSING TAXES AND PRICE CHANGES

In some degree the advance in 1933 and 1934 in the prices of commodities made from agricultural products was due to the levying of processing taxes. These taxes, designed to provide revenue for rental and benefit payments to farmers

[4] The comparison of farm prices for specific months, particularly for different calendar months, may not be satisfactory as a procedure for determining actual changes in the worth of a farmer's products, because the farmer's marketings are not equally distributed throughout the year. Moreover, the prices in any one month may be unrepresentative of the average prices prevailing during the year. In the present instance the use of July 1929 as base causes no distortion for farm products as a broad class. The July index of prices received was only one per cent above the average of prices received during the calendar year 1929. For some groups the differences were greater.

Because of seasonal variations in marketings and purchases, however, it is well to trace changes in the per unit purchasing power of farm products by years. The accompanying index numbers of per unit purchasing power define these movements. As is to be expected, the swings are less pronounced on the annual than on the monthly basis. For all farm products there was a loss in per unit purchasing power of 36 per cent between 1929 and 1932. Subsequent gains reduced this loss, by 1935, to 9 per cent.

	1929	1932	1933	1934	1935	1932	1933	1934	1935
All groups of farm products	100	64	67	77	91	100	106	122	142

in connection with the crop reduction program under the Agricultural Adjustment Act, were levied upon the first domestic processing of goods intended for domestic consumption. The rate was to equal "the difference between the current average price at the farm and the fair exchange value of the commodity", although discretion was left to the Secretary of Agriculture to lower the tax if the domestic consumption of a given commodity were reduced. The commodities originally included were wheat, cotton, field corn, hogs, rice, tobacco, milk and its products. Later rye, flax, barley, grain sorghums, cattle, sugar beets, sugar-cane and peanuts were added to this list.

The actual incidence of these processing taxes may not be defined precisely. There are three possible consequences of the levying of such taxes: prices to the final buyer may be raised; prices received by the primary producer may be reduced; the price margin representing costs of fabrication may be reduced and the tax absorbed by the processor. (This statement refers, of course, to the direct effects on prices. No reference is here made to possible effects on production, consumption, stocks, exports and imports, etc.) If conditions were static, and we possessed full knowledge of the elasticities of demand and of supply for each product taxed, it would be possible to trace the incidence of these taxes and their effects on the volumes sold and consumed. Actually, the taxes were imposed under highly dynamic conditions, with considerable shifts occurring in the position and, possibly, in the shape of the curves of supply and of demand. These changes may not be precisely defined, and only qualified statements concerning the incidence of the processing taxes are justified.

Certain of the conditions prevailing tended to make the consumer pay the tax. The demand for most agricultural

PRIMARY PRODUCERS

products is inelastic. Moreover, the imposition of the taxes was, in general, coincident with reductions in the volume of primary products produced, and with increases in demand, as consumer incomes rose. On the other hand the supply of agricultural products is, in general, insensitive to changes in price, and this facilitates the passing of the tax to the seller of materials. Since considerable changes were occurring on both demand and supply sides when the tax was imposed, processors were probably able to pass a large part of the tax forward to consumers or back to primary producers.

The effects of the tax varied, of course, from commodity to commodity. In the main, however, the tax probably increased prices to consumers and gave primary producers somewhat lower returns than they would have secured with the same output, had there been no tax on processing operations. Fabricational margins were probably not materially affected.[5]

The relative importance of the taxes levied on the processing of four major commodities, at two dates, is shown in

	April 1934			April 1935		
	Price without tax	Tax	Tax as percentage of price without tax	Price without tax	Tax	Tax as percentage of price without tax
Corn, contract grades (bu.)	$ .467	$ .05	11	$ .890	$ .05	6
Wheat, #2, red winter, Chicago (bu.)	.838	.30	36	.992	.30	30
Hogs, light butchers (100 lbs.)	3.970	2.25	57	9.075	2.25	25
Cotton, New Orleans (lb.)	.119	.042	35	.118	.042	36

[5] An interesting discussion, tending to the conclusion that taxes on the processing of hogs fell, in the main, on primary producers, appears in the *Journal of Farm Economics* for May 1935. "The Incidence of the AAA Processing Tax on Hogs", Geoffrey Shepherd, pp. 321–34.

the accompanying tabulation. These taxes, as of April 1934, ranged from 11 per cent of the current price, without tax, for corn, to 57 per cent for hogs. The percentages varied, of course, with changes in the market prices of the various products. In April 1935, after the notable price advances for corn and hogs, they had fallen to 6 per cent for corn and 25 per cent for hogs. For wheat and cotton, the figures stood at 30 and 36 per cent, respectively.

TABLE 25

RELATIVE PRICES OF IMPORTANT RAW MATERIALS AT WHOLESALE, JULY 1929–JUNE 1936

	July 1929	Feb. 1933	July 1933	Oct. 1933	May 1934	Sept. 1934	May 1935	Dec. 1935	Apr. 1936	June 1936
RECESSION AND RECOVERY										
Corn	100	23	57	41	51	81	87	57	62	64
Wheat	100	34	78	64	64	84	78	87	79	74
Hogs	100	31	39	41	30	61	80	82	92	88
Sugar, raw	100	72	92	88	73	76	86	82	99	98
Cotton	100	32	57	50	61	70	66	63	62	64
Wool	100	46	79	87	88	80	69	84	89	90
Coal, bituminous	100	91	91	101	107	107	108	111	110	110
Pig iron	100	73	84	92	97	97	97	103	103	103
Copper, ingot	100	27	49	45	46	49	49	51	52	52
Lumber	100	69	82	78	83	86	76	78	78	78
RECOVERY										
Corn		100	247	175	220	350	376	247	268	277
Wheat		100	225	186	187	242	226	252	230	215
Hogs		100	126	133	99	199	262	270	302	287
Sugar, raw		100	127	121	101	105	119	114	136	136
Cotton		100	181	158	193	221	208	200	196	201
Wool		100	174	191	194	175	151	184	196	196
Coal, bituminous		100	100	111	118	118	119	122	121	121
Pig iron		100	115	126	133	133	133	141	141	141
Copper, ingot		100	182	170	174	184	184	190	194	195
Lumber		100	119	112	120	125	110	112	112	112

PRIMARY PRODUCERS 243

Recession and Recovery in the Prices of Important Raw Materials

Space limitations prevent a detailed survey of the price and production movements affecting individual raw materials during the six years of recession and recovery. In following the major changes of this era it is necessary to deal with rather broad categories, which may lack concrete significance to many readers. We therefore supplement the preceding general account with figures relating to the fortunes of important single commodities (Table 25). Comment is not attempted. Readers may compare the changes in the prices of individual commodities with the group measurements presented in preceding tables.

Timing of Price Changes During Recovery: A Monthly Record

In tracing and appraising the price gains of recovery, our interest extends beyond the net changes over the period studied. The pace and character of the changes should be followed, month by month. During the period covered by this record major changes in monetary policy occurred, and it is desirable to consider their possible effects on the prices of commodities. Again, the incidence of the forces affecting prices may vary. The pressure towards price advance may shift from the most seriously depressed groups to other groups, already in positions of relative advantage. In Table 26 are given measurements of percentage changes, by months, in the prices of raw materials and manufactured goods, at wholesale. The same story appears in graphic form in Figure 11.

The detailed records in Section A of this table may be most readily followed in the summary by periods in Section B. The five months, February–July 1933, cover the first phase of the new monetary policy of the government, begin-

FIGURE 11

WHOLESALE PRICES OF RAW MATERIALS AND MANUFACTURED GOODS IN THE UNITED STATES, FEBRUARY 1933–JUNE 1936

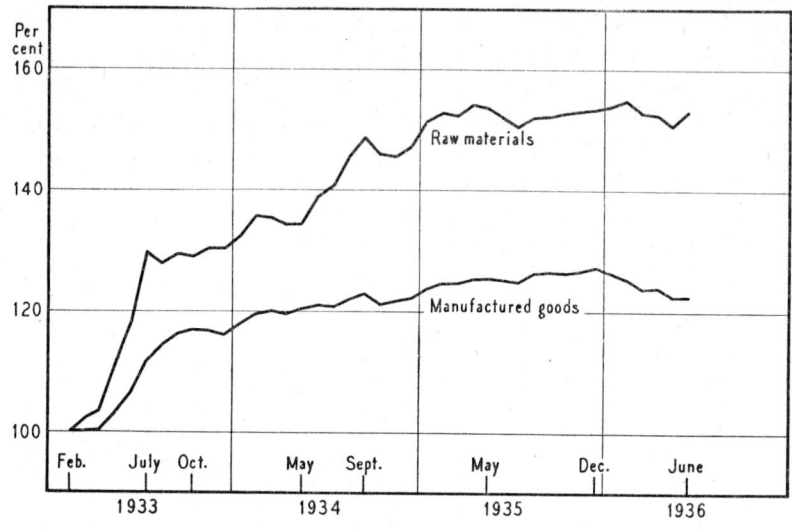

TABLE 26

RAW MATERIALS AND MANUFACTURED GOODS
PERCENTAGE CHANGES IN INDEX NUMBERS OF WHOLESALE PRICES WITH NET DIFFERENCES AND CUMULATIVE NET DIFFERENCES, FEBRUARY 1933–JUNE 1936

	ALL COMMODITIES	RAW MATERIALS	MANU-FACTURED GOODS	NET DIFFERENCE BETWEEN MOVEMENTS OF RAW MATERIALS AND MANUFACTURED GOODS	
				Month to month or period to period	Cumulated, Feb. 1933 to last month named
A. Monthly Movements (per cent)					
1933					
Feb.–Mar.	+0.8	+2.3	0.0	+2.3	+2.3
Mar.–Apr.	+0.6	+1.3	+0.4	+0.9	+3.3
Apr.–May	+4.3	+7.5	+2.6	+4.9	+8.5

PRIMARY PRODUCERS

TABLE 26 (*cont.*)

RAW MATERIALS AND MANUFACTURED GOODS
PERCENTAGE CHANGES IN INDEX NUMBERS OF WHOLESALE PRICES WITH NET DIFFERENCES AND CUMULATIVE NET DIFFERENCES, FEBRUARY 1933–JUNE 1936

	ALL COMMODITIES	RAW MATERIALS	MANU-FACTURED GOODS	NET DIFFERENCE BETWEEN MOVEMENTS OF RAW MATERIALS AND MANUFACTURED GOODS	
				Month to month or period to period	Cumulated, Feb. 1933 to last month named

A. MONTHLY MOVEMENTS
(*per cent*)

	ALL COMMODITIES	RAW MATERIALS	MANUFACTURED GOODS	Month to month	Cumulated
1933					
May–June	+4.1	+5.8	+3.4	+2.4	+11.5
June–July	+6.4	+9.8	+4.7	+5.1	+17.9
July–Aug.	+1.5	−1.4	+2.7	−4.1	+13.1
Aug.–Sept.	+1.4	+1.4	+1.5	−0.1	+13.4
Sept.–Oct.	+0.1	−0.8	+0.5	−1.3	+11.8
Oct.–Nov.	+0.1	+1.2	−0.2	+1.4	+13.7
Nov.–Dec.	−0.4	−0.1	−0.5	+0.4	+14.1
Dec.–Jan. 1934	+1.8	+1.9	+1.7	+0.2	+14.5
1934					
Jan.–Feb.	+1.6	+2.5	+1.3	+1.2	+16.2
Feb.–Mar.	+0.1	−0.4	+0.4	−0.8	+15.3
Mar.–Apr.	−0.5	−0.7	−0.4	−0.3	+14.7
Apr.–May	+0.6	+0.1	+0.7	−0.6	+14.0
May–June	+1.4	+3.3	+0.5	+2.8	+17.9
June–July	+0.3	+1.3	−0.2	+1.5	+19.9
July–Aug.	+2.0	+3.6	+1.1	+2.5	+23.7
Aug.–Sept.	+1.1	+2.0	+0.8	+1.2	+25.6
Sept.–Oct.	−1.1	−1.8	−1.5	−0.3	+24.8
Oct.–Nov.	−0.2	−0.3	+0.5	−0.8	+23.8
Nov.–Dec.	+0.6	+1.1	+0.4	+0.7	+25.0
Dec.–Jan. 1935	+2.0	+2.9	+1.4	+1.5	+27.6
1935					
Jan.–Feb.	+0.7	+1.0	+0.6	+0.4	+28.3
Feb.–Mar.	−0.1	−0.4	+0.1	−0.5	+27.6
Mar.–Apr.	+0.8	+1.2	+0.5	+0.7	+28.8
Apr.–May	0.0	−0.3	+0.1	−0.4	+28.3
May–June	−0.6	−1.1	−0.2	−0.9	+26.9
June–July	−0.5	−1.0	−0.2	−0.8	+25.5

TABLE 26 (cont.)
RAW MATERIALS AND MANUFACTURED GOODS
PERCENTAGE CHANGES IN INDEX NUMBERS OF WHOLESALE
PRICES WITH NET DIFFERENCES AND CUMULATIVE
NET DIFFERENCES, FEBRUARY 1933–JUNE 1936

	ALL COMMODITIES	RAW MATERIALS	MANU-FACTURED GOODS	NET DIFFERENCE BETWEEN MOVEMENTS OF RAW MATERIALS AND MANUFACTURED GOODS	
				Month to month or period to period	Cumulated, Feb. 1933 to last month named

A. MONTHLY MOVEMENTS
(*per cent*)

1935					
July–Aug.	+0.1	+1.2	+1.0	+0.2	+25.9
Aug.–Sept.	+0.2	0.0	+0.3	—0.3	+25.5
Sept.–Oct.	0.0	+0.4	—0.2	+0.6	+26.4
Oct.–Nov.	+0.2	+0.2	+0.3	—0.1	+26.4
Nov.–Dec.	+0.2	+0.1	+0.3	—0.2	+26.1
Dec.–Jan. 1936	—0.4	+0.4	—0.8	+1.2	+27.7
1936					
Jan.–Feb.	—0.1	+0.6	—0.7	+1.3	+29.6
Feb.–Mar.	—1.2	—1.4	—1.2	—0.2	+28.9
Mar.–Apr.	—0.1	—0.1	+0.1	—0.2	+28.5
Apr.–May	—1.2	—1.2	—1.4	+0.2	+28.5
May–June	+0.9	+1.7	+0.2	+1.5	+30.8

B. MOVEMENTS BY PERIODS
(*per cent*)

Feb. 1933– July 1933	+17.2	+29.5	+11.6	+17.9	+17.9
July 1933– Oct. 1933	+3.0	—0.6	+4.8	—5.4	+11.8
Oct. 1933– May 1934	+3.5	+4.4	+3.0	+1.4	+14.0
May 1934– Sept. 1934	+4.9	+10.6	+2.2	+8.4	+25.6
Sept. 1934– May 1935	+2.7	+3.4	+2.0	+1.4	+28.3
May 1935– Dec. 1935	+0.6	—0.3	+1.4	—1.7	+26.1
Dec. 1935– June 1936	—2.1	0.0	—3.7	+3.7	+30.8

PRIMARY PRODUCERS

ning with the prohibition of gold payments and the embargo on the export of gold and silver, on March 6, including the nationalization of gold, the passage of the credit expansion 'rider' to the Agricultural Adjustment Act and the abrogation of the gold clause, and ending with the rejection of the monetary stabilization program of the London conference on July 3. This was a period of rapid rise in the general price level, a rise that worked particularly to the advantage of depressed raw materials. The net gain of raw material prices in this period is measured by a difference of 17.9 between the index numbers for raw and processed goods, on the February 1933 base. The next phase, July–October 1933, was marked by a slight retrogression in the prices of raw materials, and by more substantial losses in their relative position. These three months cover the period of the inauguration of the new industrial codes authorized under the National Industrial Recovery Act. The record suggests that the forces released by this Act, combined with certain lagging consequences of the first phase of recovery,[6] definitely tended to offset the ameliorative movements of the early months.

During the third stage, October 1933 to May 1934, conflicting but minor movements occurred in the relative prices of raw materials and manufactured goods. Additional attempts were made, by action on the monetary side, to stimulate price recovery. A government market for gold was established and the price of gold was progressively advanced; a silver-buying program was approved; the Gold Reserve Act of 1934, reducing the content of the gold dollar 41 per cent,

---

[6] By these 'lagging consequences' I mean, first, a swing back of raw material prices, after the sharp initial advance that was stimulated to some extent by the desire to anticipate possibly higher costs under the codes. Supplementing this, a belated rise in the prices of fabricated goods was to be expected, as the effects of higher prices among raw materials were felt.

was adopted. The gain in the 'all commodities' index over these seven months amounted to fractionally more than 3 per cent. The improvement in the position of raw material prices, relatively to the prices of manufactured goods, is defined by a net difference of 1.4 between the respective index numbers.

The sharp advance in farm prices in the summer of 1934, accompanying drought and crop reduction, marks off the fourth period. It carried the average prices of all raw materials up 10.6 per cent; manufactured goods rose only 2.2 per cent. The net changes of the succeeding eight months, which extend to the end of the period of industrial operation under NRA codes, were slight. The seven months to the end of 1935, and to the termination of the AAA, brought a small net loss to raw materials; in the final period, in 1936, this loss was more than made up, as raw material prices held and the prices of manufactured goods declined.

The appreciable gains in the relative status of raw materials were scored during two brief periods—the first five months of sharp recovery and the four months of drought in the summer of 1934. Only under the pressure of the special conditions existing in these periods was substantial amelioration effected in the distortions of the raw-processed price relationship.

One important class of raw materials, agricultural products, calls for attention, in this survey of the timing of price changes, because of the distinctive price difficulties prevailing among them and because of the special efforts made to improve their status. Monthly changes in the wholesale prices of farm products and in prices at the farm, and the relations between changes in the prices of agricultural and of non-agricultural products, are shown in Table 27 and in Figure 12.

FIGURE 12
PRICES OF FARM PRODUCTS AND OTHER PRODUCTS IN THE UNITED STATES, FEBRUARY 1933–JUNE 1936

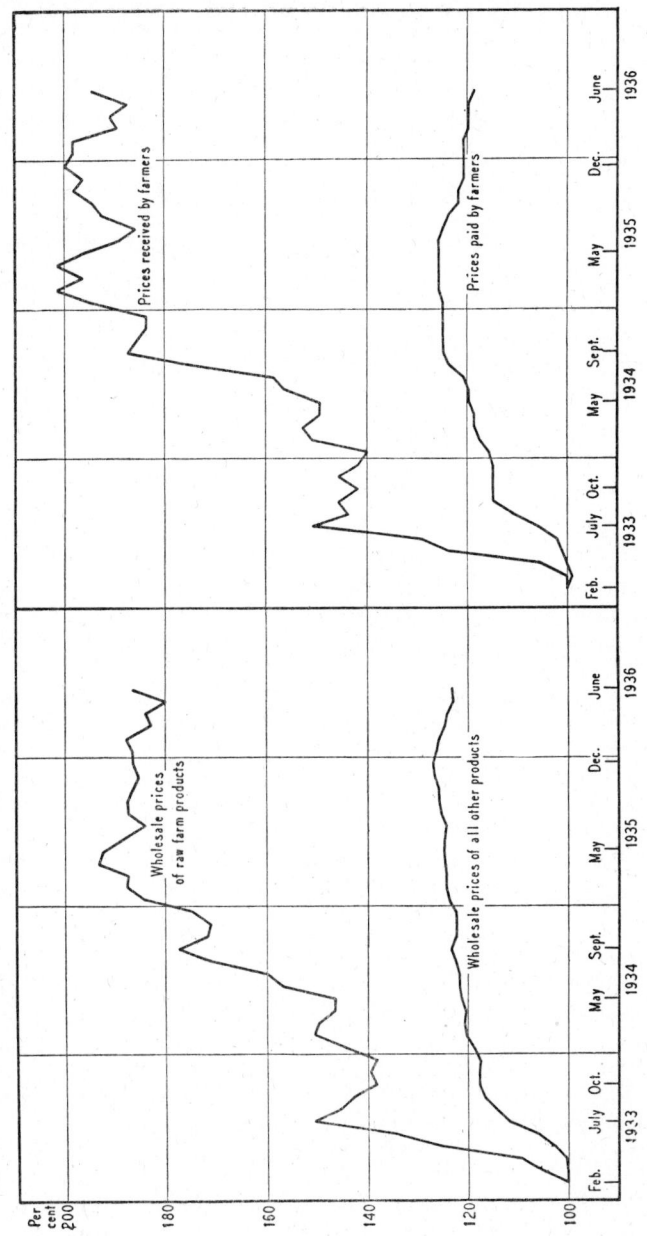

TABLE 27

PRICES OF FARM PRODUCTS AND OTHER COMMODITIES PERCENTAGE CHANGES IN INDEX NUMBERS WITH NET DIFFERENCES AND CUMULATIVE NET DIFFERENCES, FEBRUARY 1933–JUNE 1936

	WHOLESALE MARKETS				FARM AND RETAIL MARKETS			
	Products of American farms, raw	All other commodities	NET DIFFERENCE Month to month or period to period	Cumulated, Feb. 1933 to last month named	Farm prices, all groups	Prices paid by farmers for commodities bought	NET DIFFERENCE Month to month or period to period	Cumulated, Feb. 1933 to last month named

A. MONTHLY MOVEMENTS *(per cent)*

1933
Feb.–Mar.	+5.2	0.0	+5.2	+5.2	0.0	—1.0	+1.0	+1.0
Mar.–Apr.	+3.8	+0.1	+3.7	+9.1	+5.5	+1.0	+4.5	+5.5
Apr.–May	+14.5	+2.5	+12.0	+22.5	+17.2	+1.0	+16.2	+22.6
May–June	+7.3	+3.3	+4.0	+28.2	+4.4	+1.0	+3.4	+27.1
June–July	+12.0	+5.4	+6.6	+38.7	+16.9	+3.9	+13.0	+45.0
July–Aug.	—3.5	+2.3	—5.8	+30.9	—4.8	+4.7	—9.5	+32.7
Aug.–Sept.	—1.5	+2.2	—3.7	+26.1	+1.3	+3.6	—2.3	+30.6
Sept.–Oct.	—3.3	+0.9	—4.2	+20.4	—2.5	0.0	—2.5	+26.9
Oct.–Nov.	+0.9	0.0	+0.9	+21.7	+2.6	0.0	+2.6	+30.6
Nov.–Dec.	—0.9	—0.2	—0.7	+20.7	—2.5	0.0	—2.5	+26.9
Dec.–Jan. 1934	+4.7	+1.1	+3.6	+25.9	—1.3	+0.9	—2.2	+24.2

1934
Jan.–Feb.	+3.9	+1.2	+2.7	+30.1	+7.8	+1.7	+6.1	+33.1
Feb.–Mar.	—0.5	+0.2	—0.7	+29.0	+1.2	+0.8	+0.4	+33.9
Mar.–Apr.	—2.0	—0.1	—1.9	+26.3	—2.4	0.0	—2.4	+30.3
Apr.–May	—0.2	+0.7	—0.9	+25.1	0.0	+0.8	—0.8	+29.3
May–June	+7.1	+0.2	+6.9	+35.2	+4.9	0.0	+4.9	+36.6
June–July	+1.9	0.0	+1.9	+38.2	+1.2	+0.8	+0.4	+37.4
July–Aug.	+6.8	+0.7	+6.1	+48.3	+10.3	+2.5	+7.8	+50.7
Aug.–Sept.	+3.8	+0.7	+3.1	+53.9	+7.3	+0.8	+6.5	+62.5
Sept.–Oct.	—3.2	—0.7	—2.5	+49.1	—1.0	0.0	—1.0	+60.7
Oct.–Nov.	—0.3	—0.1	—0.2	+48.7	—1.0	0.0	—1.0	+58.8
Nov.–Dec.	+2.0	+0.1	+1.9	+52.0	0.0	0.0	0.0	+58.8
Dec.–Jan. 1935	+5.5	+1.2	+4.3	+60.2	+5.9	0.0	+5.9	+69.7

1935
Jan.–Feb.	+1.8	+0.5	+1.3	+62.8	+3.7	+0.8	+2.9	+76.1
Feb.–Mar.	—0.1	—0.1	0.0	+62.8	—2.7	0.0	—2.7	+70.7
Mar.–Apr.	+3.2	+0.2	+3.0	+68.5	+2.8	0.0	+2.8	+76.1
Apr.–May	—0.5	+0.1	—0.6	+67.3	—2.7	0.0	—2.7	+70.7

PRIMARY PRODUCERS

TABLE 27 (cont.)
PRICES OF FARM PRODUCTS AND OTHER COMMODITIES, PERCENTAGE CHANGES IN INDEX NUMBERS WITH NET DIFFERENCES AND CUMULATIVE NET DIFFERENCES, FEBRUARY 1933–JUNE 1936

	WHOLESALE MARKETS			FARM AND RETAIL MARKETS		
		NET DIFFERENCE			NET DIFFERENCE	
Products of American farms, raw	All other commodities	Month to month or period to period	Cumulated, Feb. 1933 to last month or period named	Farm prices, all groups	Prices paid by farmers for commodities bought	Month to month or period to period	Cumulated, Feb. 1933 to last month or period named

A. MONTHLY MOVEMENTS (cont.)
(per cent)

1935							
May–June	—2.3	—0.1	—2.2	+63.0	—3.7	0.0	—3.7	+63.4
June–July	—2.0	—0.2	—1.8	+59.6	—1.9	—0.8	—1.1	+60.7
July–Aug.	+1.9	+0.8	+1.1	+61.9	+3.9	—0.8	+4.7	+68.9
Aug.–Sept.	0.0	+0.3	—0.3	+61.5	+0.9	—1.6	+2.5	+72.7
Sept.–Oct.	—0.5	+0.1	—0.6	+60.5	+1.9	0.0	+1.9	+76.4
Oct.–Nov.	—0.7	+0.6	—1.3	+58.4	—0.9	—0.8	—0.1	+75.6
Nov.–Dec.	+0.5	+0.2	+0.3	+59.1	+1.9	0.0	+1.9	+79.2
Dec.–Jan. 1936	+0.1	—0.6	+0.7	+60.2	—0.9	0.0	—0.9	+77.4
1936							
Jan.–Feb.	+0.7	—0.3	+1.0	+61.8	0.0	0.0	0.0	+77.4
Feb.–Mar.	—2.8	—0.9	—1.9	+57.8	—4.6	—0.8	—3.8	+69.3
Mar.–Apr.	+0.8	—0.2	+1.0	+59.6	+1.0	0.0	+1.0	+71.1
Apr.–May	—2.2	—1.1	—1.1	+56.9	—1.9	0.0	—1.9	+67.5
May–June	+3.6	+0.1	+3.5	+63.2	+3.9	—0.8	+4.7	+75.7

B. MOVEMENTS BY PERIODS
(per cent)

Feb. 1933–July 1933	+50.4	+11.7	+38.7	+38.7	+50.9	+5.9	+45.0	+45.0
July 1933–Oct. 1933	—8.1	+5.5	—13.6	+20.4	—6.0	+8.4	—14.5	+26.9
Oct. 1933–May 1934	+5.9	+3.0	+2.9	+25.1	+5.1	+4.3	+0.8	+29.3
May 1934–Sept. 1934	+21.0	+1.7	+19.3	+53.9	+25.6	+4.1	+21.5	+62.5
Sept. 1934–May 1935	+8.4	+1.2	+7.2	+67.3	+4.9	+0.8	+4.1	+70.7
May 1935–Dec. 1935	—3.1	+1.8	—4.9	+59.1	+1.9	—3.9	+5.8	+79.2
Dec. 1935–June 1936	+0.2	—3.0	+3.2	+63.2	—2.8	—1.7	—1.1	+75.7

Here, again, the record may be most readily followed in the summary by periods, in Section B of Table 27. Agricultural products gained in relative price during the first upward rush of the spring and early summer of 1933. Their differential gain in wholesale markets, in relation to all non-farm products, was 38.7 (the net difference in July 1933 between index numbers on the February 1933 base). The relapse in the autumn months, as the push of the first rush weakened and as the force of rising prices was felt by manufactured goods, cut this gain almost in half. The seven following months of mixed movements brought a small net advantage to raw farm products. The stimulus to agricultural prices provided by drought brought a substantial rise to a new level, in the summer of 1934, a level above that of July 1933. In the three succeeding periods only small changes occurred. The persisting gains of farm products were substantial, however, as is shown by the final figures given.

To the comparisons dealing with trading relations in wholesale markets we may add a survey of changes in the actual buying and selling relations of farmers, which are also shown in Table 27. The movements of index numbers of farm prices and of prices paid by farmers parallel those of the wholesale price measurements previously reviewed, but the relative margins of advantage of farm producers, during the several phases of the recovery movement, are wider. In June 1936 the differential gain of farm prices, starting from the February 1933 base, amounted to 75.7.

These several exhibits show very clearly that the real gains of agricultural products, and the gains of raw materials generally, were scored during two short periods. The advance began with the first push of detachment from the gold standard and of escape from the fears engendered during the banking crisis of the winter of 1932–33. The stimulus of this rise was definitely selective, in that it was felt most strongly by the prices of the most depressed commodities, primary products. The period of further monetary experimentation was marked by minor cross-currents of change, with no distinct consequences. Drought, with crop reduction, brought the second great stimulus to farm products, the most important element of the raw materials group. This gain was held, and even increased somewhat, during the months that followed the drought. During the first six months of 1936, following the termination of the AAA, a differential movement in favor of farm products occurred in wholesale markets; there was a small net loss in farm markets.

Changes in the Aggregate Purchasing Power of Primary Producers During Recovery

We have seen that the per unit purchasing power of raw materials, in wholesale markets, increased 16 per cent between February 1933 and June 1936. For raw products of American farms the average per unit gain amounted to 41 per cent, when purchasing power is measured with reference to prices in wholesale markets; in terms of goods actually purchased for productive and living purposes the gain was 64 per cent. But the economic status of producing groups is dependent rather upon aggregate income and purchasing power than upon per unit prices and purchasing power. In Table 28 we trace the shifts brought by recovery in the aggregate purchasing power of different classes of primary producers. The measurements relate to changes in the gross income of major producing groups, and to corresponding changes in purchasing power. We do not here deal with the final net incomes of these groups, as consumers.

TABLE 28

AGGREGATE VALUES OF PRIMARY PRODUCTS AND AGGREGATE PURCHASING POWER OF PRIMARY PRODUCERS

INDEX NUMBERS, 1929–1935

(1)	(2) AGGREGATE VALUE OF PRODUCT	(3)	(4)	(5)
		AGGREGATE COMMAND OVER GOODS, AT WHOLESALE, AND FACTORS AFFECTING IT [1]		
		Aggregate command over goods [2]	Purchasing power per unit	Number of physical units
All primary producers				
1929	100	100 (100)	100	100
1932	43	64 (69)	79	88
1933	50	73 (71)	81	87
1934	59	75 (76)	88	86
1935	68	81 (80)	93	87
Producers of:				
Raw farm products [3]				
1929	100	100 (100)	100	100
1932	45	66 (65)	65	99
1933	54	78 (66)	69	96
1934	61	71 (73)	78	93
1935	71	85 (80)	88	91
Raw mineral products				
1929	100	100 (100)	100	100
1932	42	61 (72)	115	62
1933	43	62 (76)	113	67
1934	56	71 (80)	112	72
1935	62	73 (82)	106	77
Raw forest products				
1929	100	(100)	100	100
1932	25	(37)	97	38
1933	36	(52)	108	48
1934	42	(54)	109	49
1935	45	(54)	97	55

[1] Command over goods relates to purchasing power in wholesale markets.

PRIMARY PRODUCERS 255

The changes between 1929 and 1932 in the purchasing power of primary producers have been discussed in Chapter III. We have noted a drop of about 57 per cent in the aggregate value of raw materials, representing a loss of about 36 per cent in total command over goods, at wholesale. Declining volume (12 per cent loss) and reduced purchasing power per unit (21 per cent loss) accounted for this reduction in aggregate purchasing power.[7] Three years of recovery brought an advance of approximately 27 per cent in the aggregate purchasing power (in wholesale markets) of primary producers, a gain due entirely to increased per unit worth of their products; for this gain paralleled a loss of

[1] The index numbers of wholesale prices, derived from those of the Bureau of Labor Statistics, are as follows: 1929, 100; 1932, 68; 1933, 69; 1934, 79; 1935, 84.

[2] The two sets of entries relating to aggregate command over goods are derived independently. Those appearing as the main series represent the measurements of 'aggregate value of product' deflated by an index of wholesale prices. The entries in parentheses are the products of the corresponding measurements of 'purchasing power per unit' and 'number of physical units'. The independently derived measurements agree fairly closely, for all primary producers; differences are greater for the subgroups. For farm products the differences are due in some degree to the fact that the main series relate partly to crop years, while the derived series relate to calendar years. For forest products the index numbers of aggregate value and purchasing power are derived from price and production data.

[3] When the price and value figures relating to farm products are deflated by prices paid by farmers, we have the following record. The columns correspond to those in the table.

1929	100	100	(100)	100	100
1932	45	64	(63)	64	99
1933	54	76	(65)	67	96
1934	61	76	(71)	77	93
1935	71	87	(82)	91	91

[7] The figures are not entirely consistent since they are derived independently. See footnote 2 to Table 28.

about 1 per cent in physical output. In 1935 the total physical income of primary producers (as approximated above) was some 20 per cent less than in 1929; their total physical production was 13 per cent less.[8]

The three major groups of primary producers represented in Table 28 fared quite differently, with respect to changes in total purchasing power. In 1932 producers of farm and mineral products were fairly close together, with aggregate money income from 55 to 58 per cent below the 1929 level, and with aggregate real income reduced by from 30 to 40 per cent. Low per unit purchasing power and high production contributed to this result for farmers, while low production and relatively high per unit purchasing power were factors in the changes affecting mineral producers. Producers of raw forest products maintained the per unit worth of their products close to the 1929 level, but suffered a drastic decline (exceeding 60 per cent) in physical output. The result was a loss of more than 60 per cent in aggregate purchasing power.

The changes from 1932 to 1935 that helped to restore the real incomes of farmers were advances in per unit worth. Physical volume of production declined some 8 per cent. Among mineral producers increasing output raised real income; the three years of recovery brought an actual loss in the per unit purchasing power of their products. Forest products, which gained substantially in physical output, scored the greatest gain in aggregate purchasing power.

The estimates of aggregate command over goods, for these

---

[8] Changes in aggregate purchasing power are estimated on the assumption that changes in the prices of the goods bought by primary producers paralleled the general movements of prices at wholesale. This assumption is justified, for purposes of general comparison, but the estimates should not be taken to measure with accuracy the actual change in the purchasing power of any group of producers.

three groups of producers, are somewhat rough, but they indicate the general nature of the changes brought by recession and recovery. Taking account of the margins of error involved, we may say that in 1935 the aggregate physical income of agricultural producers was about 15 or 20 per cent less than in 1929, having risen some 25 per cent from the low level of 1932. The physical income of producers of raw minerals in 1935 was from 18 to 27 per cent less than in 1929; here also a gain of about 20 per cent had been made from the 1932 level. The aggregate real income of producers of raw forest products in 1935 was some 46 per cent less than in 1929; the rise from the 1932 level had amounted to more than 40 per cent.

For agricultural producers it is possible to refine somewhat the rough estimates of Table 28, and to secure more exact measurements of the changes in the aggregate purchasing power of their income. The entries in Table 29 indicate the nature of the absolute and relative changes in gross farm income between 1929 and 1935. The cumulative decline of agricultural returns, a decline due almost entirely to falling unit purchasing power rather than to declining production, carried the gross income of farmers down 55 per cent between 1929 and 1932. Prices paid by farmers for goods used in production and family maintenance dropped 30 per cent. If we correct by this index in estimating the change in agricultural purchasing power we have a more exact measure than that given in Table 28. (In that table, in default of suitable specific deflators for the different producing groups, an index of wholesale prices was used throughout.) We find that in 1932, as the net result of changes in farm output, prices received and prices paid, the total real income of farmers was 36 per cent less than in 1929. The succeeding

TABLE 29

GROSS INCOME FROM FARM PRODUCTION AND AGGREGATE PURCHASING POWER OF AGRICULTURAL PRODUCERS, 1929–1935

A. Gross Income
(millions of dollars)

	1929	1930	1931	1932	1933	1934	1935
Gross income arising from productive operations							
Crops	5,434	3,818	2,746	2,295	3,032	2,977	3,425
Animal products	6,507	5,636	4,222	3,042	3,096	3,704	4,585
Total	11,941	9,454	6,968	5,337	6,128	6,681	8,010
Rental and benefit payments					278	595	498
Total gross income	11,941	9,454	6,968	5,337	6,406	7,276	8,508

B. Index Numbers of Gross Income and Purchasing Power
(Purchasing power is measured with reference to prices paid by farmers)

	1929	1930	1931	1932	1933	1934	1935	1932	1933	1934	1935
Gross income from productive operations	100	79	58	45	51	56	67	100	115	125	150
Total gross income [1]	100	79	58	45	54	61	71	100	120	136	159
Prices paid by farmers	100	95	81	70	71	80	82	100	102	114	117
Aggregate purchasing power derived from productive operations	100	83	72	64	72	70	82	100	113	110	128
Total purchasing power [1]	100	83	72	64	76	76	87	100	118	119	136

SOURCE: *Crops and Markets,* July 1935, p. 271; *Agricultural Situation,* February 1936, p. 4; "Agricultural Income from Production in 1935", mimeographed release of Bureau of Agricultural Economics, December 19, 1935; and "Income from Farm Production in the United States in 1935", also a mimeographed release dated September 1936. The data relate to crop years for crops, calendar years for animal products.
[1] Includes receipts from rental and benefit payments.

year brought advances of 15 per cent in gross income, 13 per cent in aggregate purchasing power. If we take account of rental and benefit payments by the Federal government, these figures are raised to 20 and 18 per cent, respectively. Total agricultural purchasing power in 1933 remained, however, 24 per cent below the 1929 aggregate even when rental and benefit payments to farmers are included in their gross income.[9]

By 1935 further substantial gains had been scored in the money incomes of farmers. Gross income from productive operations was 50 per cent above the 1932 level, in spite of a drop of 8 per cent in the net volume of agricultural production. Adding to this the income from rental and benefit payments we have a gain from 1932 to 1935 of 59 per cent in the total gross income of farmers. However, the prices of commodities bought for use in production and family maintenance were also feeling the push of advancing values. A gain of 17 per cent in this average partly offset the increase of income. The purchasing power of total gross income, including rental and benefit payments and receipts from livestock sales to the government, increased about 36 per cent between 1932 and 1935. In 1935 the index of aggregate farm purchasing power stood 13 per cent below the 1929 level; this represents a substantial loss of real income but the position was distinctly better than in 1932.[10]

---

[9] Total production of all types of goods in the United States, in 1933, was approximately 33 per cent less than in 1929. This includes, of course, the output of the heavily depressed capital goods industries. The output in 1933 of manufactured goods intended for human consumption was 23 per cent less than in 1929. (Cf. Table 60, Ch. VIII.)

[10] The index of aggregate farm purchasing power, in physical terms, may be compared with measurements of the total physical output of goods in the United States. For all types of goods production in 1935 was some 22 per cent less than in 1929. If we take account only of manufactured goods intended for human consumption, the index for 1935 was approximately 9 per cent less than in 1929. (Cf. Table 60, Ch. VIII.)

The purchasing power of gross farm income, it is clear, has been much more stable than the per unit selling prices of farm products. Between 1929 and 1932 selling prices fell some 54 per cent, on the average. Buying prices were falling at the same time, however, and production was being maintained, with the result that the net loss of aggregate purchasing power amounted to no more than 36 per cent. This was severe, of course, but much less severe than the price figures alone would indicate. There is danger of misreading the record of economic changes, and drawing erroneous conclusions concerning the effects of recession, if attention be confined to price disparities alone. Relative movements in the status of different economic groups are properly measured with reference to income rather than price changes. Because of the nature of intergroup trade, and the tendency for the relations of aggregate values to remain constant, the fluctuations in gross income, for different groups, usually correspond much more closely than do price changes. Relatively high production tends to accompany relatively low prices, after a recession, while low production volume is usually found where high prices have been maintained.[11] This was notably true of the gross income of farmers and of manufacturing industries, from 1929 to 1932.

This does not mean that we may think of the welfare of

---

[11] Whether prices or production will be more flexible, when market conditions force a change in aggregate value of output, depends upon the relative elasticities of demand and upon the degree of control exercised over price and production by members of the producing groups in question. In agriculture, where demand has been relatively inelastic, where there has been no effective control over supply on the part of producers as a group, and where prices have in the past been free of restraints and controls, adaptation to a changed aggregate value has been effected, usually, through sharp price fluctuations. In basic manufacturing industries, where price rigidities are more important and where production may in general be effectively controlled, production changes have played a more important part in the alterations of aggregate values necessary to maintain intergroup trade.

PRIMARY PRODUCERS

consuming groups in terms of gross income alone. Equal changes in gross income resulting from unequal price and production changes may represent quite different movements of net income. For when gross income is sustained through the maintenance of a high volume of output, as was true of agricultural income from 1929 to 1932, correspondingly high production expenses may squeeze net income to a very low figure indeed. Fixed charges in the form of taxes, interest, etc., take a far greater proportionate part of the reduced gross income of farmers in depression than of the larger gross income of prosperity. The income available for personal expenditure is correspondingly reduced. Thus from 1929 to 1932 the gross income of farmers was declining some 55 per cent and the cash available to farmers after payment of production expenses was cut about 70 per cent. On recovery, of course, the situation is reversed: net income rises more sharply than gross income.

Table 30 indicates the nature of the changes occurring during recovery in various expenditures from the cash in-

TABLE 30

AGGREGATE BUSINESS CASH ACCOUNT OF THE FARMERS OF THE UNITED STATES, 1929–1935

ESTIMATED ELEMENTS

	Percentages of 1929 figure					Percentages of cash income				
	1929	1932	1933	1934	1935	1929	1932	1933	1934	1935
Cash income	100	42	52	60	69	100.0	100.0	100.0	100.0	100.0
Current expenditures										
Cash wages to hired labor	100	40	37	40	42	9.2	8.7	6.5	6.0	5.6
Feed, seed and fertilizer	100	44	46	49	52	11.8	12.3	10.5	9.6	8.8
Containers, spray material and twine	100	73	70	68	74	1.3	2.3	1.8	1.5	1.4
Cost of operating tractors, autos and trucks	100	77	77	84	93	4.5	8.3	6.7	6.4	6.1

TABLE 30 (*cont.*)

AGGREGATE BUSINESS CASH ACCOUNT OF THE FARMERS OF THE UNITED STATES, 1929–1935

ESTIMATED ELEMENTS

	Percentages of 1929 figure					Percentages of cash income				
	1929	1932	1933	1934	1935	1929	1932	1933	1934	1935
Other current expenditures (fire insurance, ginning, harness, irrigation, etc.)	100	73	75	74	74	2.5	4.3	3.6	3.1	2.7
Interest payable	100	87	81	67	61	6.5	13.6	10.2	7.3	5.7
Taxes payable	100	79	68	64	64	5.8	10.9	7.6	6.2	5.4
Total	100	61	59	58	59	41.6	60.4	46.9	40.1	35.7
Capital expenditures										
Machinery, tractors and repairs	100	21	25	37	66	4.9	2.4	2.4	3.1	4.7
Autos and trucks	100	20	28	46	64	3.9	1.8	2.1	3.0	3.5
Farm buildings and repairs on farm buildings	100	27	38	43	61	2.7	1.7	1.9	1.9	2.4
Total	100	22	29	42	64	11.5	5.9	6.4	8.0	10.6
Total production expenses	100	52	52	54	60	53.1	66.3	53.3	48.1	46.3
Cash available after production expenses (net cash income)	100	30	52	66	79	46.9	33.7	46.7	51.9	53.7
Prices paid by farmers for living	100	68	69	77	78					
Net cash income deflated by prices paid by farmers for living	100	44	75	86	101					

SOURCE: *Crops and Markets,* July 1935, pp. 271–72, and "Income from Farm Production in the United States in 1935" (mimeographed), September 1936

come of farmers. The net cash income of farmers increased 73 per cent from 1932 to 1933, 120 per cent from 1932 to 1934, and 163 per cent from 1932 to 1935. These gains exceed materially, of course, corresponding increases of 20, 36 and 59 per cent in gross income. (Rental and benefit payments are included in net cash income, as well as in gross income.) The advances of these three years left net cash income in 1935 approximately 21 per cent below the level of 1929. When account is taken of reductions in the prices paid by farmers for living the estimates indicate that the actual 1935 purchasing power of their net cash income was equal to that of 1929. With reference to the buying power of net cash income it appears that by 1935 the difficulties brought to agricultural producers by the depression had been corrected. Of course, expenditures on capital equipment in 1935 were lower than in 1929; a somewhat larger percentage of cash income was being used for family maintenance. But when full account is taken of this, the figures indicate a 1935 position only slightly below that of 1929. (See Chapter VIII, note 3, for figures of real farm income, after provision for depreciation.)

These income returns may be made more specific by considering the actual operating results secured by sample groups of farmers between 1922 and 1934, as these have been compiled by the Bureau of Agricultural Economics (Table 31). A striking picture of the effect of recession on the cash returns of individual farmers is presented here. After a slow improvement from 1922 to 1929, which reduced the percentage of farmers operating at a net loss from 14 to 8, and increased the percentage making net incomes of $1,000 or more from 35 to 45, three years of recession changed the picture completely. The percentage suffering net losses rose to approximately 43, while the percentage earning $1,000 or more declined to less than 5. The chief effects of the first two years of recovery appear in the figures relating to the deficit group. This was reduced from 42.7 per cent of the total to 18.4 per cent—a very considerable accomplishment. The average net result per farm in 1934 ($624) was still less than

TABLE 31

AVERAGE NET INCOMES OF SAMPLE GROUPS OF FARMERS,
1922–1934 [1]

A. ABSOLUTE NUMBERS

	1922	1925	1929	1930	1931	1932	1933	1934
Number of reports	6,094	15,330	11,805	6,228	7,437	6,383	6,855	7,626
Net result per farm	$917	$1,297	$1,298	$538	$154	$66	$516	$624

B. PERCENTAGE DISTRIBUTION BY INCOME CLASSES

Proportion of farmers obtaining:								
$1,000 or more	34.7	45.5	44.7	23.3	9.2	4.4	15.8	21.6
0 to $999	50.8	44.1	47.4	47.2	54.6	52.9	67.1	60.0
Net loss	14.5	10.4	7.9	29.5	36.2	42.7	17.1	18.4

[1] Adapted from more detailed tables appearing in *Agricultural Yearbook*, 1932, p. 895; and *Crops and Markets*, July 1935, p. 303. Net results represent cash receipts, less cash outlay, plus increase in inventory of personal property. Taxes are deducted, but interest is not.

Cash income alone is included in this table. No account is taken of the cash value of farm products consumed on the farm.

half of the pre-recession return, but was many times higher than in 1932. In purchasing power, of course, this was much closer to the 1929 level than the dollar figures indicate.

These data, like those previously given for farmers in the aggregate, relate to cash receipts. In defining the true position of farmers account should be taken of that substantial portion of their real income which consists of farm products consumed on the farm. The physical contribution of the farm is relatively constant from year to year, though its cash value fluctuates with changing prices. This value was estimated by the Bureau of Agricultural Economics at slightly below one billion dollars in 1933, slightly higher in 1934. If we add this item to the purchasing power of the aggregate cash available to farmers after meeting production expenses (see Table 59), we may estimate a reduction of some 43 per cent in the real income of farmers between 1929 and

PRIMARY PRODUCERS 265

1932, of 11 per cent between 1929 and 1934.[12] On this basis the farm situation at the end of 1934 was brighter, relatively, than the situation of income recipients in general. The purchasing power of the total national income in 1934 was, roughly, 20 per cent below the 1929 level. By 1935 the real income of farmers appears to have been restored to the 1929 level.

Farm Prices, Farmers' Incomes, and the Burden of Farmers' Debts

In 1929 farm mortgage debts plus other farm debts (short- and long-term) amounted to approximately 12,000 million dollars. This constituted some 10 per cent of the total private debt of the country, and about 8 per cent of all debts (including governmental debts).[13] Interest payments on farmers' debts in 1929 came to approximately 700 million dollars, about 6.5 per cent of the total cash income of farmers. In magnitude these figures were probably not excessive, relatively to total non-farm debts and to the position of the farmer in the national economy.[14] Farm mortgage debt, the most important element of total farm debt, amounted to about 9,250 million dollars in 1929, with interest payments of about 550 million dollars.

An extensive discussion of the farm debt problem is not in order here. We are interested in it only in relation to the changing level of agricultural prices. The importance of this

---

[12] These figures differ, of course, from those given at earlier points for the purchasing power of gross farm income.
[13] Based upon estimates of the National Industrial Conference Board; *Conference Board Bulletin*, February 20, 1933, "Debt and Its Burden."
[14] The total value of agricultural production in 1929 (gross income of farmers) was about 17 per cent of the total value of all finished goods; the receipts of farmers, less cash outlay on production, constituted about 9 per cent of the total retail value of consumers' goods.

relationship is suggested by the long term of the average farm mortgage—25 to 35 years, or more.[15] Such a fixed long-term debt charge may be a major obstacle to readjustment during a period of changing commodity values; for reduction of the total income with falling prices would tend, of course, to raise the percentage of net income required to meet such fixed obligations.

Precisely this happened during the recession of 1929–32. Total interest charges, which amounted to approximately 6.5 per cent of the total cash income of farmers in 1929, constituted 13.6 per cent in 1932. If we lump together taxes and interest charges we have a composite of relatively fixed charges which made up 24.5 per cent of total cash income in 1932, as against 12.3 per cent in 1929. Falling prices and a fixed burden of taxes and interest were two millstones between which net farm income was compressed.

This situation is a phase of one of the major problems faced by an economy such as ours today, in which heavy fixed obligations co-exist with a monetary standard that fluctuates in terms of commodity values. The situation on both sides is highly complex. A price level is an average of many diverse values. Identical price levels at two dates are almost certain to represent quite different combinations of constituent prices. On the other hand, the debt burden existing at a given time is made up of innumerable individual obligations, incurred at various times (and thus at various price levels) and extending for varying future periods. Moreover, the individuals who must meet capital charges and current interest charges on their obligations receive incomes from many sources. A given variation in the price level will affect their debt-paying ability in highly diverse ways.

[15] D. L. Wickens, "Farm-Mortgage Credit"; *Technical Bulletin No. 288*, U. S. Department of Agriculture, February 1932, p. 3.

PRIMARY PRODUCERS

Because of these complexities, the limitations attaching to the use of all averages are particularly important in dealing with price level changes in relation to debt charges. This applies with special force to the farm debt situation created by the recession of 1929–33. A restoration of the pre-recession price level would not necessarily correct the inequities created by the fall of farm prices and farm income. Only if the precise price and income relations of the pre-recession period were restored would these numerous and diverse inequities be corrected—and such restoration is inconceivable. Again, the restoration of the per unit purchasing power of individual agricultural products to the level of any previous date would not necessarily restore the debt-paying capacity of farmers, for such purchasing power is measured in terms of relations between two sets of current prices. The earlier ratio might be restored with total money incomes far below those of the earlier date. And debt-paying ability depends upon total money incomes.

Advancing farm incomes and considerable reductions in the aggregate amount of interest charges payable by farmers had greatly eased the farm debt situation by 1935. The actual reduction in interest payments between 1929 and 1935 amounted to 270 million dollars. The proportion of total cash income devoted to interest payments fell from 13.6 per cent in 1932 to 5.7 per cent in 1935 (the 1929 percentage was 6.5). Interest and taxes together required 11.1 per cent of total cash income in 1935, as against 24.5 per cent in 1932, and 12.3 per cent in 1929. These figures (which are estimates of the U. S. Department of Agriculture) provide further striking evidence of the improvement three years had brought in the position of farmers.

PRICES IN RECESSION AND RECOVERY

RECENT CHANGES IN THE PRICES OF AGRICULTURAL PRODUCTS, IN RELATION TO THEIR PRE-WAR PURCHASING POWER

One of the most revolutionary features of the recovery program was the legislative declaration (in the Agricultural Adjustment Act) of a policy to establish and maintain the purchasing power of producers of important agricultural products upon a level equal to the average prevailing from August 1909 to July 1914. (For tobacco the level of purchasing power set as standard was the average of August 1919–July 1929.) [16] Combined with this was a declaration of intention to protect consumers through limiting the percentage of consumers' retail expenditures for agricultural commodities, or products derived therefrom, to the percentage that was returned to the farmer in the pre-War period, August 1909–July 1914. The 'purchasing power' referred to in the Act was the average per unit purchasing power of farm products, measured with reference to the prices paid by farmers for commodities used in production and family maintenance.

Here was an unprecedented move, an attempt to 'establish and maintain', within a price system the chief elements of which are uncontrolled, a constant set of relations between the prices of two major classes of commodities—those pro-

[16] The Soil Conservation Act, which was enacted on March 1, 1936, after the voiding of the Agricultural Adjustment Act by the Supreme Court, sets up an income standard of parity, rather than a parity based on price relations. This objective, which supplements the general purpose of soil conservation, is the re-establishment of the ratio between the purchasing power of the net income per person on farms and that of the income per person not on farms that prevailed during the five-year period, August 1909–July 1914. This ratio is to be re-established at as rapid a rate as the Secretary of Agriculture considers practicable and in the general public interest. In interpreting the Act, Secretary Wallace has stated that production control of individual farm commodities is not possible under the new plan, and that therefore it may not be feasible to obtain exact parity of prices on a pre-War basis.

duced by farmers and those bought by farmers. Two elements of a highly variable complex were to be placed in definite relationship, and held there.

It is not the purpose here to appraise this procedure, though certain problems and difficulties involved may be briefly indicated. The selection of a base period, with reference to which the standard is defined, was necessarily arbitrary. The period selected was relatively favorable to agricultural producers, since it came at the end of a long period —more than a century, indeed, if irregular fluctuations be ignored—of advance in the relative per unit value of farm products. This gain was due to the pushing out of the margin of cultivation in agriculture, and to the fact that productivity in non-agricultural industries had increased at a more rapid rate than in agriculture. The events of the post-War period, as we have seen, reversed this pre-War trend. The standard set in the Act was distinctly higher than any that had prevailed since the prosperous period culminating in 1920. The justification advanced was that, in the nature of the case, technological improvement is more rapid in industry than in agriculture and that "the purchasing power of farm products must continue to rise relative to industrial products".[17] This condition would presumably justify the expectation that, if technical and market forces were left to work themselves out, the per unit purchasing power of agricultural products would increase progressively. That it would justify the legal freezing of the exchange ratio of agricultural and industrial products at a fixed value is not clear. Indeed, the setting of such a fixed ratio under these conditions would appear to deprive agricultural producers of the opportunity for pro-

---

[17] Cf. *Economic Bases for the Agricultural Adjustment Act*, Mordecai Ezekiel and Louis H. Bean (U. S. Government Printing Office, 1933), pp. 26–8.

gressive improvement of their status that would be promised them by the tendencies cited.

In setting a definite exchange ratio between two classes of goods, no allowance was made, of course, for changes in their costs of production. Here we lack definite and comparable information. It is certain that real production costs have fallen markedly in manufacturing industries over the last two decades (i.e., that productivity has increased),[18] but very substantial reductions have also occurred in the per unit cost of producing important agricultural staples. During the last twenty years productive technique in agriculture, in which improvement lagged far behind manufacturing industries during the first stages of the industrial revolution, began to catch up. The movement has been spotty, and many producers have failed to take advantage of it, a fact which accounts for much of the agricultural distress of the first post-War decade. But the gains in many fields of agricultural production have been striking.[19] Such changes in production costs may not be ignored in seeking to define desirable relations between agricultural and other producers.

Various other considerations bear on the general proposal thus to crystallize a set of exchange relationships, as well as on the choice of a base period. The products of agriculture are not, in general, subject to modifications in quality, as are certain of the important industrial products for which they exchange. This modification may be in the direction of

---

[18] Cf. *Economic Tendencies*, pp. 192 ff., 289 ff., and *Bulletin 53* of the National Bureau of Economic Research.

[19] Cf. E. G. Nourse, "Agriculture", *Recent Economic Changes*, II, 547–602; O. E. Baker, "Agricultural and Forest Land", *Recent Social Trends*, I, 90–121; O. E. Baker, "Population Trends in Relation to Land Utilization", *Proceedings* of the International Conference of Agricultural Economists, 2nd Conf., 1930 pp. 284–306; L. O. Bercaw, "Labor Requirements of Farm Products", *Agricultural Economics Bibliography No. 26*, 1929, U. S. Department of Agriculture.

poorer quality, but in general industrial products have been marked by improvements. This has been notably true of automobiles and mechanical agricultural equipment. A constant ratio of the prices of agricultural and industrial products, under these conditions, would mean, in fact, a steady advance in the real purchasing power of agricultural products. A restoration of the price relations of 1909—14 would mean the establishment of exchange relations more favorable to agriculture than those then prevailing. More rapid reduction of production costs in industry would, of course, work in the other direction.

Equally important with the points suggested above was the failure of the Act to take account of actual and potential changes in consumer demand. Quite apart from possible substantial changes in demand arising from the substitution of synthetic products for agricultural products (e.g., the use of rayon in place of cotton), a growing share of the consumer's dollar is absorbed, with advancing living standards, by highly fabricated products and luxury goods. A diminishing portion is spent on foods and on the staple articles of clothing that are primarily products of agriculture. This movement may be paralleled, indeed, by a shift in food-consuming habits as light urban occupations increase in importance, relatively to the heavier tasks of direct production, which, in turn, tends to lower the consumption of the primary products of agriculture.

The ignoring of these various tendencies in the setting of a definite ratio of exchange, the restoration and maintenance of which were defined as the objects of administrative policy, would, presumably, have generated economic difficulties had the Act been enforced over a long period. Attention should be called, in addition, to the difficulty of holding constant, among a complex and ever-changing set of variables, one specific relationship. An almost infinite number of forces, operating from both supply and demand sides, bear upon this relationship. To assume that it may be maintained at one certain value through manipulation of the few factors of agricultural supply that may be subject to control is to hold to a highly simplified and unreal conception of the forces in operation.

A practical obstacle to the attainment of a given economic objective through the maintenance of a constant ratio between the average prices of two groups of commodities arises from the difficulty of measuring price changes accurately. This restriction does not apply to the great standardized staples sold in organized markets, but it does apply with exceptional force to fabricated industrial products, and to commodities sold in retail markets generally. Quality changes constitute one obstacle to accuracy of measurement for these commodities. Wide differences in the quoted prices prevailing at one time in different markets (even in different retail outlets) are another obstacle. Still another arises out of the continual appearance of new commodities and the changing importance of individual articles even in a fixed group of commodities. The danger of setting faulty standards through errors in the methods of measurement adopted is very real, in view of the limitations of the knowledge our existing index numbers provide.

The period during which the Agricultural Adjustment Act was enforced was probably too short to warrant a judgment of the efficacy of measures taken under it to restore the pre-War purchasing power of agricultural products in general. (The Act, indeed, envisaged the gradual, not the immediate, restoration of pre-War parity of specific agricultural products with products purchased.) Nevertheless, the record of changes in the general price series since February 1933 is instructive. These series are plotted in Figure 12, which should be studied with reference to the chronological

TABLE 32

PRICES RECEIVED FOR FARM PRODUCTS, PRICES PAID BY FARMERS AND AVERAGE PER UNIT PURCHASING POWER OF FARM PRODUCTS MONTHLY CHANGES, FEBRUARY 1933–JUNE 1936

(August 1909–July 1914=100)

	1933			1934			1935			1936		
	Prices received	Prices paid	Ratio	Prices received	Prices paid	Ratio	Prices received	Prices paid	Ratio	Prices received	Prices paid	Ratio
Jan.	55	101	54	77	117	66	107	126	85	109	122	89
Feb.	55	100	55	83	119	70	111	127	87	109	122	89
Mar.	58	101	57	84	120	70	108	127	85	104	121	86
Apr.	68	102	67	82	120	68	111	127	87	105	121	87
May	71	103	69	82	121	68	108	127	85	103	121	85
June	83	107	78	86	121	71	104	127	82	107	120	89
July	79	112	71	87	122	71	102	126	81			
Aug.	80	116	69	96	125	77	106	125	85			
Sept.	78	116	67	103	126	82	107	123	87			
Oct.	80	116	69	102	126	81	109	123	89			
Nov.	78	116	67	101	126	80	108	122	89			
Dec.				101	126	80	110	122	90			

record of events bearing on prices and on agricultural conditions (see p. 282). The record of price and purchasing power changes, on the 1909–14 base, is given in Table 32.

The general price changes during the period of recovery have already been reviewed. We survey them here briefly with reference to the point now at issue. At the depression low in February and March 1933 average prices paid by farmers stood almost exactly at the pre-War level; prices received were 45 per cent below that level. The index of per unit purchasing power was 54, as compared with the parity figure of 100. By May, when the Act was signed, farm prices had advanced some 24 per cent and the index of per unit purchasing power had risen to 67. For the next two months the advance continued, raising the index that measures average per unit purchasing power to 78 in July. More than half the deficiency, measured against the pre-War base, had been made good. The succeeding slump in farm prices, and the accompanying rise in industrial prices as the effects of the earlier advance spread throughout the price system and as the cost-raising influences of other legislation were felt, carried the ratio down to 66, in January 1934. Subsequent fluctuations in the two price series altered this ratio somewhat, but by May 1934 it had advanced only to 68. This was well above the depression low but only slightly higher than the 67 recorded during the month when the Act was signed. The four months following, months of drought and of sharp reduction of crop prospects, raised this index to 82 in September 1934. In June 1936, the last month covered by the record, the index stood at 89.[20] The two great spurts we have

[20] There exist, of course, wide differences among individual commodity prices in respect of the degree of recovery towards the parity prices defined in the Agricultural Adjustment Act. (Not all these commodities were included under the AAA program; see the following note.) The following tabulation indicates the magnitude of these differences.
(Footnote 20 concluded on p. 275)

noted, one initiated prior to the passage of the Agricultural Adjustment Act, one synchronizing with the 1934 summer

(*Footnote* 20 *concluded*)
PRICES RECEIVED BY FARMERS AS PERCENTAGES OF PARITY PRICES UNDER THE AGRICULTURAL ADJUSTMENT ACT, 1933–1935
(*August 1909–July 1914=100*)

	OLD BASIS **						NEW BASIS †	
	Feb. 1933	July 1933	May 1934	Sept. 1934	May 1935	Dec. 1935	May 1935	Dec. 1935
Wheat	36	92	65	83	78	84	76	81
Corn	30	81	63	96	104	68	102	66
Oats	33	92	68	100	98	53	96	51
Barley	29	72	56	100	84	50	82	48
Rye	30	102	60	87	68	45	66	44
Flax	51	104	80	82	72	75	71	73
Cotton	44	80	73	84	76	75	75	73
Cottonseed	40	70	83	114	141	123	138	119
Apples	68	85	98	68	94	65	91	63
Potatoes ‡	53	131	87	72	50	76	50	74
Hay	49	55	62	87	89	50	87	48
Hogs	40	51	36	66	87	99	84	96
Beef cattle	63	71	66	64	103	97	100	94
Veal calves	70	64	59	62	81	95	79	92
Lambs	70	83	98	66	88	114	86	110
Sheep	47	53	65	43	64	76	63	74
Butterfat *			70	75	86	93	84	90
Chickens	82	85	81	88	109	115	106	111
Eggs *	48	72	69	80	107	72	104	70
Wool	49	119	110	88	72	108	70	105
Horses	43	47	45	41	52	54	51	52
Tobacco, Maryland ‡					95	89	93	86
Tobacco, flue cured ‡					95			92

SOURCE: Department of Agriculture, monthly mimeographed release on "Average Prices Received by Farmers for Farm Products, With Comparisons".
 * Adjusted for seasonal variation.
** Parity price based on index of prices paid by farmers for commodities bought.
† Parity price based on index of interest, taxes, and prices paid by farmers.
‡ For tobacco and potatoes, parity prices are based on the period, August 1919–July 1929=100.

276   PRICES IN RECESSION AND RECOVERY

of drought, had gone far towards correcting the disparity between average prices of farm products and of goods bought by farmers. A difference of 46 per cent had been reduced to one of 18 per cent in September 1934. Subsequent gains cut this to 10 per cent at the end of 1935, when the act was voided. Conscious crop reduction measures undoubtedly contributed to this advance in farm prices and the corresponding improvement of agricultural purchasing power, but factors independent of the Agricultural Adjustment Act apparently played major roles in the agricultural recovery recorded to the end of 1935.[21]

[21] It is impossible to isolate the effects of different forces working toward higher agricultural prices during the period of recovery, but some light is thrown on the situation by tracing price changes in three groups of farm products—those originally under the AAA program: corn, wheat, hogs, cotton, tobacco leaf, rice, milk; those brought under this program at later dates: barley, rye, cattle, peanuts, flaxseed, sugar; and products not controlled under the AAA: oats, hay, hops, seeds, beans, apples, lemons, oranges, onions, potatoes, sheep, poultry, wool, hides and skins, eggs. Changes in the wholesale prices of these three groups are summarized below, together with figures relating to non-agricultural raw materials, and manufactured goods.

	PERCENTAGE CHANGES IN WHOLESALE PRICES				
	Commodities originally under the AAA program	Commodities later brought under the AAA program	Commodities not controlled under the AAA program	Non-agricultural raw materials	Manufactured goods
Feb. 1933–July 1933	+54.4	+31.6	+56.0	+11.7	+11.6
July 1933–Oct. 1933	—6.0	—9.1	—10.7	+8.2	+4.8
Oct. 1933–May 1934	+3.2	+13.9	+6.4	+2.7	+3.0
May 1934–Sept. 1934	+31.1	+11.3	+6.7	+0.2	+2.2
Sept. 1934–May 1935	+5.2	+30.3	+0.6	—2.4	+2.0
May 1935–Dec. 1935	—3.5	—8.1	+2.4	+3.6	+1.4
Dec. 1935–June 1936	—0.5	—10.1	+11.1	—0.2	—3.7

The average gain, during the first period, in the prices of farm products not covered by the AAA program was somewhat greater than the gains scored by the groups of commodities included, at early or late stages, in that program. Since the prices of these excluded commodities would have been affected only indirectly and with a considerable time lag by action under

Summary

The effect of recession and recovery upon the economic status of any group of producers is conditioned by a host of factors, some of transient importance, some firmly rooted and enduring. Productive capacity when the recession begins, stocks of goods, the character of the market (domestic or foreign, composed of final consumers or fabricators), the elasticity of demand—these are some of the obvious conditions affecting the severity of the strains of recession and the ability of any group to meet them. Of particular importance, as circumstances affecting the elasticity of supply, are the degree of coherence among the members of the producing group in question and the degree of control over supply that they exercise. Related to all these factors is the relative freedom of the prices of the products of this group, the degree to which they are free to respond to market forces of demand and supply.

With respect to these conditions there are important differences among primary producers, but the group as a whole possesses certain distinctive attributes. Producing units are more numerous and more widely scattered than are members of other major producing groups, and among them is less of the coherence that makes possible common economic action in the face of an emergency. One result of this (and of other conditions as well) is that producers of raw materials exercise a relatively low degree of control over supply. Supply is

---

the Agricultural Adjustment Act, it is fair to conclude that forces other than those connected with the Act played important parts in the agricultural price rise of the spring and early summer of 1933. Monetary conditions and changes in the general economic outlook were strong contributory factors. During the fourth period, which covers the drought of the summer of 1934, the prices of commodities included under the original Act gained most. Shortage resulting from the drought, superimposed upon shortage due to crop reduction, constituted a lever pushing prices upward.

relatively inelastic, in the face of changing market conditions. Again, a very large proportion of raw materials is purchased by producers, and only a relatively small proportion is ready for sale to final consumers. The demands of such producers, particularly those engaged in the fabrication of capital goods and of durable consumption goods, are notoriously irregular. Fluctuations in final demand are reflected in accentuated form in the purchases of materials by intermediate fabricators. In the markets for raw materials in general, then, we find rather extreme movements of demand (shifts in the positions of demand curves, as well as shifts along demand curves) and relatively inelastic supply, with keen competition among producers unable or unwilling to act in concert or to reduce their individual production in the face of falling demand.

Price movements reflect these conditions. Changes in demand, with relatively inflexible supply, lead to wide variations in the prices of raw materials, over time. Such fluctuations are the more notable because of the relative stability of many other elements of the price system. Price control through public agencies, price agreements among producers, price maintenance through trade marking and branding, price stabilization through combination and monopoly have been characteristic of modern political and industrial development. Over wide areas of the economic system price rigidities have prevailed and price freedom has been curtailed.[22] It is true that markets for raw materials have not remained entirely free. The period just preceding the recession was marked by numerous valorization efforts, through which the prices of materials were pegged at stated levels. But difficulties of many sorts, some antedating the world recession, terminated these efforts. In the main, price freedom

[22] Cf. *Economic Tendencies in the United States*, pp. 323–32.

PRIMARY PRODUCERS 279

has persisted in the markets for raw materials to a greater degree than in any other part of the price system. This fact is directly pertinent to the story of recession and recovery in the prices of primary products.

All these statements relate to average conditions among a rather heterogeneous group of primary producers. There is some logical justification for treating this group as a unit, in contrasting its fortunes with those of groups engaged in manufacturing operations, or in other economic activities. Yet there are marked differences among different classes of primary producers. It is not true of lumbering and mining interests that only a low degree of control is exercised over current supply. It is not true that all raw mineral products are marked by a high degree of price freedom. Indeed, operating conditions vary considerably for different classes of farmers and in different sections of the country. The conditions noted, then, are of the nature of statistical averages, to which there are notable exceptions. Attention has been drawn to the nature and magnitude of these exceptions in various sections, in which figures for different classes of primary producers have been given.

Because farmers stand in a distinctive position among primary producers, and because price and production changes among farm products were of dominant importance in the raw material situation during recession and recovery, the fortunes of farmers have been discussed as a group apart, as well as in combination with other primary producers. Lack of coherence among producers and inability to secure common action in controlling production or regulating prices are pronounced among farmers. Also, many non-business considerations persist in the conduct of farming operations. Finally, the relative inelasticity of domestic demand [23] and

---

[23] The degree of inelasticity of demand for seven important farm products

280   PRICES IN RECESSION AND RECOVERY

the traditional dependence upon foreign markets for the disposal of important quantities of domestic production have been notable features of the agricultural situation.

Industries producing agricultural raw materials have placed their impress upon the record of recession among primary producers, as it has been reviewed in this and preceding chapters. Production maintained close to the prosperity level, sharply falling prices, substantially lowered purchasing power and a definite loss of relative position, in respect of trading relations with other producing groups, characterized the condition of agricultural producers from the middle of 1929 to the early months of 1933. Weakness attendant upon the more 'normal' features of the recession was accentuated by high world productive capacity (stimulated by special War-time and post-War conditions) by accumulated stocks of important materials, by the weak international financial position of some raw material producing countries, and by the failure of valorization schemes through which the prices of some primary products had been pegged

is indicated by the following coefficients, derived by Henry Schultz ("The Shifting Demand for Selected Agricultural Commodities, 1875–1929," *Journal of Farm Economics*, April 1932). The list does not include certain farm

Wheat	— (0.27±0.12)	1922–29	
Corn	— (0.49±0.16)	1915–29,	excl. *1917–21*
Hay	— (0.52±0.16)	1915–29,	" "
Sugar	— (0.31±0.08)	1915–29,	" "
Potatoes	— (0.31±0.03)	1915–29,	" "
Oats	— (0.57±0.42)	1915–29,	" "
Barley	— (0.39±0.24)	1915–29,	" "

products the demand for which may be elastic, such as fruits, vegetables and some cuts of meat. But it is clear that for farm products as a whole elasticity of demand is less than unity.

The unfavorable effects on the farmer of inelasticity of demand, at retail, are accentuated by the relatively rigid distributive and fabricative elements that stand between the sale by the farmer and the purchase by the final consumer. Farm prices are rendered weaker under conditions of business depression by the intervention of these rigid elements.

PRIMARY PRODUCERS

during the pre-recession prosperity. Sharply declining exports of agricultural products, resulting from reduced purchasing power of foreign buyers, stoppage of our foreign lending, and definite efforts on the part of many countries to achieve more nearly self-sufficient national economies, combined with reduced domestic consumption to create extremely burdensome surpluses of agricultural products and to depress agricultural prices to abnormally low levels.

At the low point of the depression the various groups of primary producers, in combination, were turning out goods in volume some 12 per cent below that of 1929. The average purchasing power of a unit of raw materials had been reduced some 20 per cent. (The corresponding gain among manufactured goods exceeded 10 per cent.) Finally, we have noted a loss of aggregate purchasing power on the part of primary producers—that is, of real income, in physical terms —of from 30 to 35 per cent. In all these respects there were pronounced differences among producers of raw agricultural products, raw mineral products and raw forest products. Farmers maintained output and suffered most severely in per unit purchasing power; producers of raw forest products cut output most severely (62 per cent) and maintained per unit purchasing power substantially unchanged; mineral producers reduced output materially (about 40 per cent), and gained about 15 per cent in the average per unit worth of their products. In aggregate purchasing power farmers and mineral producers lost from 30 to 40 per cent, while producers of raw forest products lost more than 60 per cent.

When the forces of recovery were loosed on this situation their first effects were felt on the price side. Indeed, if we take account of the entire field of primary production we find an actual loss in volume of production over the years of recovery from 1932 to 1935. Rising prices were the factor that enhanced the aggregate purchasing power of primary

282   PRICES IN RECESSION AND RECOVERY

producers. In tracing and appraising this recovery on the price side, to the end of 1935, it is convenient to distinguish five periods, during each of which fairly distinct forces were at work.

a. Five months, February 1933–July 1933
  Prohibition of gold payments and embargo on export of gold and silver, March 6.
  Emergency banking bill passed, March 9.
  Signing of Agricultural Adjustment Act, with provision for processing tax on farm products and credit expansion rider, May 12.
  Rejection of monetary stabilization program of London Conference, July 3.
b. Ten months, July 1933–May 1934
  Drafting and enforcement of codes, under the National Industrial Recovery Act (signed June 16).
  Establishment of government market for gold; progressive advance in price of gold begins, October 25.
  Approval of silver-buying program, December 21.
  Reduction and stabilization of gold content of dollar, January 31.
c. Four months, May 1934–September 1934
  Drought in the farm belt.
d. Eight months, September 1934–May 1935
  Continued operation of industry under the codes of fair competition, ended by Supreme Court decision of May 27, 1935.
e. Seven months, May 1935–December 1935
  Continued operation of agriculture under AAA, ended by Supreme Court decision of January 6, 1936.

Of course, the items listed under each caption do not by any means exhaust the forces in operation over the period in question, but they suggest the major factors. Substantial gains were recorded in the fortunes of primary producers in the first and third periods. The first phase covers the initial spurt that followed the checking of the banking crisis and the departure from the gold standard. Action on the monetary front seemed to be the energizing influence during this stage. The second period was dominated by the initiation and enforcement of the industrial codes. Costs and prices advanced in manufacturing industries, and the striking gains scored by primary products in the first rush of recovery were reduced. It is true that action on the monetary front continued during this second stage. A government market for gold was established, the price of gold was progressively raised, and action affecting silver was begun. But the price level showed only a slight change, and the incidence of price-raising forces was definitely shifted from the depressed raw materials of industry to fabricated products.

In the third phase the drought was the dominant factor. Potential supplies of crops and of animals were sharply reduced. Previous actions under the Agricultural Adjustment Act had, of course, contributed to such reduction, but in magnitude these were dwarfed by the drought. A new fillip was given to agricultural prices, and a chain of events was started that affected the prices of animal products long after the drought itself had become history.

There was no clearly dominant force during the fourth phase, which extends to the end of the operations of the NRA. Raw animal products experienced a price rise, as the effects of shortages were felt. Raw materials as a class improved their position relatively to manufactured goods, but the gain was slight. Neither on the industrial nor the monetary front was any action taken that materially affected either the level of prices or the relations among major commodity groups. In the final period, from May 1935 to the end of the year (in fact, to the end of operations under the AAA, which was declared void on January 6, 1936), minor losses were suffered by primary products. In December 1935 the prices of raw and manufactured goods stood substantially in the relations that had prevailed after the drought of 1934. If the story be carried through the first months of 1936 no further changes in these relations are to be observed.

Any brief summary of the conditions existing during the recovery of 1933–36 does some violence to the facts. Many forces were acting upon the economic system. Recognizing that we are, in some degree, oversimplifying a complex situation, we have selected for emphasis certain main forces operating during the several periods distinguished. Monetary factors and related psychological elements contributed to the first great rise, while actual and impending scarcity of farm products promoted the advance in the third period, the summer of 1934. Over the entire phase of recovery, supporting the prices of raw materials and supplementing the specific factors making for higher prices, the influence of improved consumer demand was felt, as it worked backward from the final markets for finished products. The net result of all these changes was to elevate raw material producers well above their depression lows, with respect to both the per unit worth of their products and their total income. In aggregate purchasing power these producers stood in the early summer of 1936 fairly close to other major producing groups, but still below the pre-recession level of well-being. This aggregate return was secured through a physical output relatively higher than that of manufacturing industries, a real per unit value relatively lower than that of manufactured goods.

CHAPTER VI

MANUFACTURING INDUSTRIES IN RECOVERY

IN THE endless round of activities that make up economic life all economic agents are both buyers and sellers—buyers of goods for consumption, fabrication or sale, buyers of services for personal or business use, sellers of goods or services to be used at some stage of the productive-distributive process. All economic agents, then, stand between the shears of buying and selling prices, and are affected by unequal changes in these two sets of prices. Yet the consequences of unequal changes are brought home most immediately to two business groups—merchants and manufacturers. For these groups buying and selling price relations take the form of definite margins, price differentials relating to a specific unit of the commodities handled. When the connection is less direct, as between wage earnings and living costs, or farm income and average cost of goods purchased by farmers, the ultimate economic consequences of unequal changes may be no less important. But because the connection is less direct and obvious, the economic repercussions of shifting relations are likely to be less certain and less sharply focused. The physical processes of the economy may be expected to reflect price movements most immediately, and in the most directly measurable way, in the activities of merchants and manufacturers. These activities are far more directly motivated by specific price relations than are the activities of other classes of economic agents. In merchandising and manufacturing the calculus of business, which is a profit calculus, may be applied on a unit basis, and corresponding action may be promptly taken to modify the number of units handled.

By virtue of thus standing midway in the stream of trade that flows from original producer to final consumer, and of buying and selling on a strictly business basis, manufacturing industries possess certain distinctive attributes which affect their activities during the cyclical fluctuations of business. But other circumstances contribute to the operating characteristics of manufacturing enterprise. Relatively heavy investment in plant and equipment is a condition of operation in nearly all manufacturing industries. Fixed overhead charges are an important element of total costs of production. Substantial changes in volume of goods produced may bring very considerable variations in cost per unit, because of the necessity of dividing a fixed total of overhead charges among a varying number of units. Such overhead charges, too, are usually difficult to adapt to changing monetary values, because they may rest upon fixed, contractual claims. A sharp fall in prices may thus bring considerable advances in the real burden of overhead costs, just as a sharp price rise may lower the real burden of overhead. This circumstance has gained in importance in recent years, because of the growth of fixed charges in manufacturing with the increased use of equipment and non-human power.[1]

---

[1] In 1899 overhead costs plus profits constituted approximately 24.8 per cent of the selling price of each unit of manufactured goods produced in the United States. The corresponding figure in 1929 was 28.8 per cent.

The increase of capital investment in manufacturing industries is of importance, in connection with the problem of readjustment under conditions of recession and depression, primarily because it involves an increase in the relatively fixed obligations of manufacturing enterprises. (When the capital investment is based upon a loan, the obligation is definitely fixed. When financed through stock issue, or effected through investment of surplus, the obligation is less rigid, but it may nevertheless be a strong influence upon a board of directors, striving to maintain an established dividend rate.) This is a phase of a problem with numerous ramifications. Changes in the

MANUFACTURING INDUSTRIES

The point last made is a phase of a broader condition affecting the activities of manufacturing enterprises. The different elements contributing to the final selling price of manufactured products (i.e., labor, material and overhead costs) vary greatly in their sensitivity to the diverse market and monetary forces that affect the values of goods and services. In part, this is a reflection of the varying flexibility of these price and cost factors.[2] In part, it reflects differences in the degree to which forces impinging upon the price system from the outside (e.g., monetary forces) affect the elements of that system. This is in some degree a matter of original incidence, in some degree a question of varying institutional frictions. All these factors interact to yield a system of prices and of costs among manufacturing industries that is marked by extreme differences of behavior, especially during a period when volume of production and monetary values are undergoing violent changes. In the fact that the elements of this system differ widely in their power of adaptation to changed circumstances is found a major cause of economic confusion and retarded activity after a severe business recession.

The possibility of fairly rapid changes in the productivity

---

capital structures of industrial establishments doubtless affect the financial and operating policies of management in many ways. The mental reactions of boards of directors to changes in balance sheets and income accounts are involved, as well as the physical and monetary problems arising directly out of heavier capital investment.

The *liquidity* of fixed capital, in the sense of convertibility into money, is perhaps somewhat lower, as physical plants become larger, more durable and, in some respects, more specialized in their uses. But such liquidity was never high.

[2] The term *flexibility* is here used in the technical sense in which it defines the relation between a relative change in price and a corresponding relative change in physical quantities. The coefficient of flexibility of price is a measure of the same type as the coefficient of elasticity of demand, except that it is derived from an equation in which price is the dependent variable.

of labor and in production costs in manufacturing industries is another factor bearing upon the behavior of these industries during recession and revival. Various circumstances may give rise to increased industrial productivity. The mere closing of inefficient plants, removal of inefficient equipment, discharge of inefficient officers or workers will serve to enhance the average productivity of plants and equipment in use, although the real efficiency of the plants, equipment and men left in operation may remain unchanged.[3] Again, there is almost always a margin of unused resourcefulness and efficiency in any manufacturing plant that is likely to be exploited under the pressure of emergency. Men will work harder, more care will be taken, internal organization will be improved, wastes will be avoided, during lean years. Of a different order are those increases in productivity definitely attributable to technical advance and the installation of better equipment. The progress of invention, alone, may bring these gains. Pressure from high labor costs may serve as a stimulating factor, when technical innovations will reduce labor requirements. The rapidity with which productivity may change among manufacturing industries is per-

[3] This statement perhaps suggests a sharp line of division between inefficient and efficient plants, equipment and personnel, with inefficient units being weeded out by depression and efficient units going blithely forward. This, of course, was not the case. Among the plants that were closed (the number of manufacturing establishments in the United States, excluding those with products valued at less than $5,000 annually, declined from 209,862 in 1929 to 141,769 in 1933) were doubtless many technically efficient units. The rains of depression fall alike on the just and the unjust. And doubtless many inefficient plants, instruments and men survived the depression. But the economically weakest units (a group generally, though not entirely, coterminous with the least efficient, technically) were the most severely hit by the depression. Many factors contributed to the notable advance in productivity that came during the depression years; the raising of the average level of productive efficiency through the elimination of marginal elements was one of these.

haps not generally appreciated. Thus the records indicate that from 1921 to 1923 the output of manufacturing industries in the United States, per wage earner employed, increased 14.8 per cent. This gain represented, in considerable part, the realization of new productive opportunities opened up by the use of methods and equipment installed during the recession and depression immediately preceding. (The apparent gain in per capita output from 1919 to 1921, in manufacturing industries of the United States, was 0.8 per cent.[4] The real effect of new installations was felt during the ensuing two years.) The gain from 1921 to 1923 is the more striking in that 1921 was a year of depression, when the less efficient equipment was presumably idle, while 1923 was a year of greater activity, when all grades of equipment were more generally employed. The possibility of rapid changes in the productivity of manufacturing industries, stimulated by the pressure of depression, of high productive costs, of strong competition, or by the promise of wide markets if costs and prices may be substantially reduced, is a dynamic factor of tremendous importance in the cost structure of industry. Here, under modern conditions, is a force that may bring wide shifts in price and cost relations in manufacturing industries within a short period.[5]

[4] Measurements of per capita output are not accurate indexes of industrial productivity during periods when hours of work are being altered. Part of the true gain in productivity from 1919 to 1921 is not shown by these figures, because of the reduction of working hours in 1921. An increase of working hours from 1921 to 1923 leads to an opposite error, of over-statement, for this period. The actual gain from 1919 to 1923 was probably close to that shown by the figures cited, but the increase in productivity was greater from 1919 to 1921 and less from 1921 to 1923 than the per capita measurements indicate.

[5] Productivity changes in single industries are more striking than the averages for all manufacturing industries. Some examples are cited below:

(*Footnote* 5 *concluded on p. 290*)

Finally, we should note the place of manufacturing industries in the domestic economy of the United States. Of approximately 44 million persons gainfully engaged [6] in the United States in 1929, slightly more than 10 million, or 23 per cent, were engaged in manufacturing industries; in the same year 23 per cent of the total income paid out (18 out of 79 million dollars) came from manufacturing industries. These industries, of course, are of central importance as employers of labor, consumers of domestically produced raw materials, and disbursers of purchasing power. Disorganization and subnormal activity in manufacturing affect all other elements of the economic system.

Problems of Recovery in Manufacturing Industries

The condition of manufacturing industries, after the decline that began in 1929, was discussed in Chapter III. Four years of price recession, paralleled by a somewhat broken but still more severe drop in volume of production, left these

(*Footnote* 5 *concluded*)

CHANGE IN OUTPUT PER WORKER, 1919–1923 (*per cent*)	
Sugar, beet	+58.5
Explosives	+57.1
Oilcloth	+54.3
Iron and steel, blast furnaces	+51.3
Coke, not including gas-house coke	+50.0
Sugar, refining, cane	+49.0
Rubber products	+48.1
Ice, manufactured	+44.4
Petroleum, refining	+42.4
Condensed and evaporated milk	+42.2

[6] This figure, which is based upon estimates made in the study of national income, includes employed workers and entrepreneurs actually participating in productive activity. The number of persons partially employed is reduced to an equivalent number of fully employed. The total given is smaller than the Census enumeration of persons gainfully occupied, which includes all persons who usually follow a gainful occupation.

industries in a position of extreme difficulty in the winter of 1932–33. Activity was at a low ebb. The volume of output was barely half of that produced prior to the recession. The drastic decline of commodity values brought painful problems of readjustment. The buying prices of manufacturers (costs of materials and supplies) fell to low levels, but there were numerous obstacles to the prompt adjustment of selling prices to these levels. Long-term commitments affecting rental and interest payments, salary and wage scales fixed by agreement or long-established custom, the effect upon managerial minds of the increase in overhead charges assessable to each unit of the reduced output of manufactured goods, and other obstacles growing out of human reluctance to recognize and accept the implications of the change in the value of the dollar all served to retard readjustment in the field of prices. The effects of these changes were felt throughout the economic system, intensifying other elements of economic distress. The decline of manufacturing employment, the fall in manufacturing pay rolls and the curtailment of dividend payments sharply reduced the purchasing power of those drawing their incomes from manufacturing industries. The failure of the prices of manufactured goods to drop equally with those of raw materials and with the incomes of primary producers meant that the purchasing power of primary producers was reduced, in the markets for manufactured goods. The volume of trade and the standards of living of important elements of the population were inevitably lowered.

Our immediate concern is with the course and character of recovery, as it affected the manufacturing industries of the United States from the early months of 1933 to the spring of 1936. The problems of recovery in this sector of the economic system grew, in part, out of the particular situation left by recession, in part out of the inherent attributes of manufacturing industries as a class, and in part out of the special conditions created by legislative enactments and administrative procedure during this period. It will be well to summarize certain of these problems, before turning to the record of recent changes.

The major problems of manufacturing producers, in the winter of 1932–33, centered about the restoration of volume of production and sales, and the widening of the margin between costs (including overhead costs) and selling prices. As we have seen, the differential between the costs of raw materials and the selling prices of manufactured goods had not declined, during the preceding recession, by an amount commensurate with the increase in the purchasing power of money. Relatively to prices in general, the costs of fabrication had risen. (This relative advance was in part obscured by quality reductions and by shifts to goods in lower price classes.) On this basis alone the price position of manufacturing industries was favorable to profits. But the tremendous drop in volume of production (a drop of 51 per cent from July 1929 to February 1933) had increased the relative burden of overhead costs. Such costs, in the aggregate, had been greatly extended during the pre-recession expansion, and as a result the per unit burden was particularly heavy when volume of output was curtailed. Labor costs per unit of product had been cut much more rigorously than overhead costs, but the reduction was distinctly less than that in material costs. Thus the recession brought, concurrently, a relative widening of the differential between material costs and selling price, which represents the cost of fabrication to the final consumer, and a sharp contraction of the differential between total costs and selling price, which represents the possibilities of profits to the entrepreneur. In 1931, in fact, this latter differential was negative, for manufacturing industries as a class. Greater volume and, if possible, lower fabricational costs were the obvious remedies for the difficulties of manufacturing producers.

But behind the rather narrow problem that presented itself to the individual manufacturer lay the whole tangled situation that grew out of the preceding expansion and recession. Intergroup trade had been seriously impaired by the uneven incidence of recession, with the prices and purchasing power of primary producers fallen to abnormally low levels and with the prices of manufactured goods so high, relatively, as to preclude a normal volume of sales. Evidence provided by the persistent unemployment of productive factors, by the reduced volume of production and trade, by the rapidity and violence of the changes that had brought about this situation indicated that these price relations represented true disparities, rather than permanent shifts in pre-existing relations. Correction of this schism through the raising of raw material prices relatively to the prices of manufactured goods seemed to be a necessary condition of restored activity.

This problem was related to matters of another sort, having to do with industrial productivity and production costs in manufacturing industries. Lower costs offered a means of widening the profit differential and increasing the sales of manufacturing industries. The pressure towards greater efficiency and reduced production costs was unremitting, under the stress of depression and during the first stages of recovery. But this was not merely a problem of productive technique. Costs were high, in part, because of the heritage of overhead charges from the days of high prices and hectic plant expansion that preceded the recession. The cutting of these charges, as well as the improvement of technique and the stepping-up of the pace of plant activity, was entailed in the reduction of costs.

Price readjustment, with a reduction of the discrepancies between the prices of raw and processed goods, the increase of productivity and the lowering of fabricational costs—these were promising possibilities in the direction of recovery for manufacturing industries. From these there might be expected an enhancement of the purchasing power of primary producers, a pick-up in the volume of intergroup trade (i.e., between primary producers and manufacturing groups), and increases of employment and of the wage and dividend disbursements of manufacturing industries.

In this general program were several sets of possible conflicts. The degree to which employment might increase with an increase in the output and sales of manufacturing industries depended, in part, on the degree to which productivity had advanced in these industries. For increasing productivity would, in its first impact, work against expansion of employment. Later, the lower costs and lower prices that enhanced productivity might bring would be expected to stimulate employment. Again, heavy wage disbursements on the part of manufacturing industries would augment the purchasing power of their employees, and thus stimulate general recovery. If such disbursements, however, entailed advances in labor costs per unit of goods produced, this would be in conflict with the reduction of costs required to bring the relatively high selling prices of manufactured goods into line with general prices. In following the actual course of recovery attention must be given to these possible conflicts.

The problems we have mentioned are mainly, of course, those that arise after any recession that has altered the pre-existing conditions of activity. They were acute in 1932 and 1933 because of the exceptional severity of the recession and because of certain unusual characteristics of the preceding period of expansion. In addition, some altogether novel issues arose out of the administration of the recovery program. To a greater degree than in any previous depression in our history a conscious program, directed towards the correction

MANUFACTURING INDUSTRIES

of the economic ills of the day, was applied. On the monetary side price recovery was sought through departure from the gold standard, a gold-buying program and devaluation of the dollar. Under the National Industrial Recovery Act hours were limited, minimum wages were set and provision made for the control of prices over a wide range of industrial activity. Under the Agricultural Adjustment Act processing taxes were levied on important fabricational operations. The effects of this program on the production costs and selling prices of manufacturing industries, on their wage disbursements and on their production and sales are matters of special interest. Of course, the actual consequences of many of the actions taken in applying the recovery program are clouded and uncertain; it is often impossible to distinguish specific consequences of given actions. But the picture of recovery as a whole must include the conscious program, as well as the unplanned aspects of revival among manufacturing industries.

Price Changes Among Manufactured Goods and Raw Materials

We are concerned in this section with those price relations that affect the costs and profits of manufacturing industries. With respect to raw materials, then, we restrict ourselves to materials that are actually used in the processes of manufacture, excluding that important class of products going to final consumers in a raw state. Price changes during recession and in the subsequent price advance are summarized in Table 33. At the low point of the depression the prices of raw materials intended for fabrication were 51 per cent below their pre-recession values; the selling prices of manufactured goods had fallen, on the average, only 31 per cent. These values represent a notable widening of the fabricational margin, reduced to per unit terms. The actual exchange situation at this low point is perhaps most strikingly defined by the ratio between these prices. At prices prevailing in February 1933 producers of raw materials for fabrication were obliged to give 41 per cent more, by volume, than in July 1929 for a constant quantity of finished goods made from their materials. The five months of rapid price change following, during which raw producers' goods advanced 31

TABLE 33

CHANGES IN WHOLESALE PRICES AFFECTING MANUFACTURERS' PRICE MARGINS, JULY 1929–JUNE 1936

RAW PRODUCERS' GOODS AND MANUFACTURED GOODS

	July 1929	Feb. 1933	July 1933	Oct. 1933	May 1934	Sept. 1934	May 1935	Dec. 1935	Apr. 1936	June 1936
RECESSION AND RECOVERY										
Producers' goods, raw	100	49	64	65	68	76	80	79	79	78
Manufactured goods, all	100	69	77	80	83	84	86	87	85	84
Ratio, manufactured to raw	1.00	1.41	1.20	1.23	1.22	1.11	1.08	1.10	1.08	1.08
RECOVERY										
Producers' goods, raw		100	131	132	139	154	162	161	161	159
Manufactured goods, all		100	112	117	120	123	125	127	124	122

per cent and manufactured goods advanced 12 per cent in price, reduced this ratio to 1.20. In the ten succeeding months the rate of advance in raw materials was checked; prices of processed goods continued to move upwards. The ratio defining exchange relations rose to 1.22. Drought, in the summer of 1934, gave a new stimulus to the prices of agricultural products, and by September the ratio of the prices of manufactured goods to the prices of raw producers' goods had fallen to 1.11. Minor movements during the nineteen months following further reduced the manufacturing differential. The exchange ratio in June 1936 was still unfavorable to raw materials, relatively to the pre-recession situation, but the excess volume of raw materials exchanging for a constant

MANUFACTURING INDUSTRIES 297

quantity of fabricated goods had fallen from 41 per cent in February 1933 to 8 per cent. Here was a notable shift, indeed.[7]

These changes appear in somewhat different perspective when a more distant base is used (Table 34). The picture of

TABLE 34
CHANGES IN WHOLESALE PRICES AFFECTING MANUFACTURERS' PRICE MARGINS, 1913–1936
RAW PRODUCERS' GOODS AND MANUFACTURED GOODS

	July 1913	Feb. 1929	July 1933	Oct. 1933	May 1933	Sept. 1934	May 1934	Dec. 1935	Apr. 1935	June 1936	1936
Producers' goods, raw	100	134	66	86	87	92	101	107	106	106	104
Manufactured goods, all	100	153	105	117	123	126	129	132	133	130	128
Ratio, manufactured to raw	1.00	1.14	1.59	1.36	1.41	1.37	1.28	1.23	1.25	1.23	1.23

alternate expansion and contraction of the fabricational margin, shown in Table 33, is repeated here, but with the difference that recession starts with a margin already relatively wide. In July 1929 the average prices of manufactured goods were 53 per cent above their 1913 average; average prices of raw producers' goods were but 34 per cent higher. Thus, in

[7] Two other movements, not directly reflected in the measurements given above, played a part in the trade movements of recovery. In the early months of recovery the actual rise in the prices of manufactured goods probably exceeded the advance indicated by quoted prices. For at the low point of the depression, as a result of undercover price-cutting, realized prices were in many cases lower than those currently quoted. The first five or six months of revival brought not only the price increases indicated by the quoted prices, but additional advances from the low levels of the cut prices.

In 1934 and 1935 there was also a movement on the part of consumers back to goods of higher quality than those purchased during the worst months of the depression. This would not affect the quoted prices, but it would tend to raise the prices realized by manufacturers by higher percentages than those given in Table 33. Not until 1935 Census data are available will it be possible to estimate the relative importance of these factors, in causing divergent movements of realized and quoted prices.

298 PRICES IN RECESSION AND RECOVERY

exchange for a constant quantity of manufactured goods 14 per cent more, by volume, had to be given by primary producers in 1929 than in 1913. Subsequent changes with reference to the 1913 base are thus more pronounced than when measured on the July 1929 base. The final records for June 1936 indicate that the prices of raw producers' goods were 4 per cent above their pre-War level, the prices of manufactured goods 28 per cent above that level, while the ratio defining exchange relations was 1.23. The wide disparity of the winter of 1932–33 had been reduced, but the prices of these two classes of goods were still far removed from their pre-War relations.

These changes in the relations between the prices of raw producers' goods and the prices of the manufactured goods into which they enter are the more striking when compared with the shifts during a period of similar length prior to the War. Between 1891 and 1913 the prices of raw producers' goods in wholesale markets rose, on the average, 23 per cent; prices of manufactured goods advanced 11 per cent. The ratio defining the exchange relations between goods of these classes declined from 1.00 to .90. That is, the volume of raw producers' goods required in exchange for a constant quantity of manufactured goods declined 10 per cent from 1891 to 1913. Between 1913 and June 1936 this quantity increased 23 per cent. The sustained pre-War tendency towards a cheapening of manufactured goods, relatively to raw materials, stands in clear contrast to the post-War tendency towards the cheapening of raw materials.

In interpreting this apparent shift the limitations of our measurements must be kept in mind. To the extent that quality changes have occurred among the manufactured goods represented in the standard quotations entering into the price index numbers cited, these index numbers are in error. There have been such changes, with considerable improvements in the quality of the finished goods bought by final consumers. The difficulty of evaluating these improvements and securing series of prices for finished goods truly comparable with the prices of raw materials is a serious impediment to an accurate review of the changing relations among producing groups.

Striking as these quality changes have been for certain classes of goods, such as automobiles, there is no reason to believe that the quality of finished consumers' goods as a broad class was improved between 1913 and 1936 to a degree sufficient to offset the price shift noted. The exchange value of primary products fell and that of finished consumers' goods rose between these years. The consequences of this shift have been far reaching.

Before attempting to appraise these movements we should trace the incidence of recovery in somewhat greater detail, as it affected related groups of raw producers' goods and of processed goods. Measurements for certain of these groups are given in Table 35. The relations between the prices of processed goods and raw materials in the several groups, at the low point of the recession, are perhaps most effectively summarized by the ratios given with each set of comparisons. The greater the ratio, of course, the wider is the price margin between raw and processed goods and the less favorable is the trading position of primary producers.[8] For crops and

[8] Here and elsewhere the argument of this monograph proceeds on the assumption that the 'trading position' of a producing group may be defined in terms of relative prices. For a fully accurate definition of trading position account should be taken of other factors (such as productivity, average and marginal production costs, volume of production and sales, etc.). But price relations constitute a major factor in the fixing of trade positions. Changes in trading positions over the relatively short periods covered by a business cycle are predominantly influenced by changes in price relations. Over longer periods changes in trading position may not be so accurately defined in terms of relative selling prices.

TABLE 35

CHANGES IN WHOLESALE PRICES AFFECTING MANUFACTURERS' PRICE MARGINS, JULY 1929–JUNE 1936

Crops, Animal Products and Mineral Products

	July 1929	Feb. 1933	July 1933	Oct. 1933	May 1934	Sept. 1934	May 1935	Dec. 1935	Apr. 1936	June 1936
RECESSION AND RECOVERY										
Crops										
Producers' raw	100	38	66	58	64	81	79	71	72	72
Processed	100	65	82	85	86	89	90	90	85	84
Ratio, processed to raw	1.00	1.71	1.24	1.47	1.34	1.10	1.14	1.27	1.18	1.17
Animal products										
Producers' raw	100	34	46	43	45	53	71	74	73	69
Processed	100	54	63	67	70	75	82	86	82	80
Ratio, processed to raw	1.00	1.59	1.37	1.56	1.56	1.42	1.15	1.16	1.12	1.16
Minerals										
Producers' raw	100	70	76	86	88	88	88	90	91	90
Processed	100	80	82	85	89	88	87	87	88	87
Ratio, processed to raw	1.00	1.14	1.08	.99	1.01	1.00	.99	.97	.97	.97
Metals										
Producers' raw	100	63	78	79	82	82	83	85	85	84
Processed	100	81	81	83	90	88	87	87	87	87
Ratio, processed to raw	1.00	1.29	1.04	1.05	1.10	1.07	1.05	1.02	1.02	1.04
RECOVERY										
Crops										
Producers' raw		100	172	150	169	212	206	186	188	188
Processed		100	126	131	132	137	138	139	130	129
Animal products										
Producers' raw		100	138	127	134	159	212	220	217	206
Processed		100	115	122	128	138	150	157	150	146
Minerals										
Producers' raw		100	110	124	126	127	127	130	130	130
Processed		100	102	106	111	110	108	108	109	109
Metals										
Producers' raw		100	123	126	130	130	131	135	134	133
Processed		100	101	104	112	109	108	108	108	108

MANUFACTURING INDUSTRIES

animal products the ratios in February 1933 are not far apart—1.71 and 1.59. Producers of raw mineral products were in a stronger position, with a ratio of 1.14. After the first five months of swift recovery, during which raw farm crops advanced 72 per cent in price, raw animal products 38 per cent and raw minerals 10 per cent, these ratios were substantially reduced. For raw crops and animal products the next ten months witnessed a reversal of these movements. While the prices of raw products lost ground, or barely maintained the July 1933 level, processed goods continued to advance and the ratios defining the exchange relations between raw and processed goods rose. Only for minerals did the ratio continue to fall, reaching 1.01 in May 1934.[9]

Four months of drought and crop destruction again reversed the situation; the prices of raw crops rose sharply and the ratio of the average price index numbers of processed and raw crops, on the July 1929 base, fell to 1.10. In June 1936 this ratio stood at 1.17. For animal products the initial gain brought by the drought was much smaller, but drought and production limitation had important after effects. Prices advanced sharply in the early months of 1935, and most of these gains were held. The price ratio of processed goods to raw materials, for animal products, was 1.16 in June 1936, as against values of unity in July 1929, 1.59 in February 1933.

Still greater alterations occurred in the ratios between the indexes of prices of processed products and raw materials, with reference to a pre-War year. The ratios in Table 36 define the degree of cheapening of raw materials, in relation to the processed goods into which they enter. They may also

---

[9] The subgroup measurements indicate that raw metals were still at some disadvantage, in May 1934. Non-metallic minerals are not listed as a separate division, since the raw and processed goods included in this category are not strictly comparable.

TABLE 36

CHANGES IN WHOLESALE PRICES AFFECTING MANUFACTURERS' PRICE MARGINS, 1913–1936

Crops, Animal Products and Mineral Products

	July 1913	Feb. 1929	July 1933	Oct. 1933	May 1933	Sept. 1934	May 1934	Dec. 1935	Apr. 1936	June 1936
Crops										
Producers' raw	100	136	52	90	78	88	110	108	97	98	98
Processed	100	143	93	117	122	123	128	129	130	121	120
Ratio, processed to raw	1.00	1.05	1.79	1.30	1.56	1.40	1.16	1.19	1.34	1.23	1.22
Animal products										
Producers' raw	100	148	50	68	63	66	79	106	110	108	103
Processed	100	167	91	105	112	117	126	137	143	137	133
Ratio, processed to raw	1.00	1.13	1.82	1.54	1.78	1.77	1.59	1.29	1.30	1.27	1.29
Minerals										
Producers' raw	100	135	94	103	116	119	120	119	122	123	123
Processed	100	152	122	125	130	136	134	132	132	133	133
Ratio, processed to raw	1.00	1.13	1.30	1.21	1.12	1.14	1.12	1.11	1.08	1.08	1.08
Metals										
Producers' raw	100	128	81	100	102	105	105	106	110	109	108
Processed	100	164	133	133	137	149	144	144	143	143	143
Ratio, processed to raw	1.00	1.28	1.64	1.33	1.34	1.42	1.37	1.36	1.30	1.31	1.32

be interpreted as measures of the changing physical quantities of raw producers' goods required in exchange for fixed quantities of the manufactured goods into which the given raw materials enter. Since the vicissitudes of the last seven years have already been traced, our present interest attaches to the entries for the last months recorded.

Reduction in relative value, with reference to the 1913 base, was more extreme in June 1936 for animal products than for the two other main groups represented. In this month 29 per cent more than in 1913, by volume, had to be given by producers of raw animal products in exchange for a fixed quantity of the same goods in fabricated form. The corresponding figure for the low month of the depression was 82 per cent. For farm crops a 79 per cent disability, in February 1933, had been reduced to one of 22 per cent. Among minerals the June 1936 ratio was 1.08 as against 1.30 at the depression low. Raw metals, however, were much cheaper than minerals as a class, relatively to their processed forms. The June 1936 index was 108 (with 1913 as 100), as compared with 143 for processed metal products. The exchange ratio was 1.32.

The effects of recovery on manufacturing differentials among farm and non-farm products are defined more sharply in Table 37. We have already noted the widening of the differential between the prices of farm products in raw and processed form during the recession. While processed goods fell 40 per cent, raw producers' goods of this class fell 63 per cent, the ratio between the two increasing from 1.00 to 1.62 between July 1929 and February 1933. Within the ensuing forty months the prices of these raw materials advanced 97 per cent; prices of processed farm products rose 39 per cent. The ratio between them was reduced from 1.62 to 1.15. Here was a very substantial gain indeed. In contrast, the records for raw and processed goods not originating on American farms show no such declines during recession, and much smaller advances during recovery. In June 1936 the index numbers for these two groups, on the July 1929 base, were 85, as compared with 72 and 83 for raw and processed farm products. The ratio defining exchange relations between raw and processed non-farm products never rose to the extreme heights found among agricultural products.

TABLE 37

CHANGES IN WHOLESALE PRICES AFFECTING MANUFACTURERS' PRICE MARGINS, JULY 1929–JUNE 1936

PRODUCTS OF AMERICAN FARMS AND OTHER PRODUCTS

	July 1929	Feb. 1933	July 1933	Oct. 1933	May 1934	Sept. 1934	May 1935	Dec. 1935	Apr. 1936	June 1936
RECESSION AND RECOVERY										
Products of American farms										
Producers' raw	100	37	57	51	56	70	78	74	74	72
Processed	100	60	73	77	79	84	88	90	85	83
Ratio, processed to raw	1.00	1.62	1.28	1.51	1.41	1.20	1.13	1.22	1.15	1.15
Products other than those originating on American farms										
Producers' raw	100	64	74	81	83	83	82	85	85	85
Processed	100	77	80	83	86	85	84	85	85	85
Ratio, processed to raw	1.00	1.20	1.08	1.02	1.04	1.02	1.02	1.00	1.00	1.00

	Feb. 1933	July 1933	Oct. 1933	May 1934	Sept. 1934	May 1935	Dec. 1935	Apr. 1936	June 1936
RECOVERY									
Products of American farms									
Producers' raw	100	155	140	152	190	213	202	202	197
Processed	100	122	129	132	140	147	150	142	139
Products other than those originating on American farms									
Producers' raw	100	115	126	130	129	128	133	133	133
Processed	100	104	108	112	110	110	110	111	111

From 1.00 in July 1929 this ratio advanced to 1.20 at the low point of recession, and dropped again to 1.00 in June 1936. Pre-recession exchange relations had been restored, substantially, by 1936. (These figures, of course, are averages.

For many individual commodities the relations were markedly different.)

Various other classifications are of interest in tracing changes in the fabricational margin during recovery. Our present purpose will be served by a study of ratios relating to four selected commodity groups. The detailed measurements from which these are derived are given in Appendices III and IV.

In July 1929 the relative prices of processed producers' goods intended for capital equipment and processed con-

TABLE 38

CHANGES IN WHOLESALE PRICES AFFECTING MANUFACTURERS' PRICE MARGINS AND THE TRADING RELATIONS BETWEEN PRODUCING GROUPS, 1913–1936

COMMODITY GROUPS COMPARED	RATIO OF INDEX OF PRICES OF PROCESSED GOODS TO INDEX OF PRICES OF RAW MATERIALS OR SEMI-FINISHED GOODS										
	July 1913	Feb. 1929	July 1933	Oct. 1933	May 1933	Sept. 1934	May 1934	Dec. 1935	Apr. 1935	June 1936	1936
Producers' goods for capital equipment, processed and raw	1.00	1.19	1.65	1.27	1.32	1.34	1.29	1.30	1.25	1.23	1.26
Consumers' goods, processed, and producers' goods intended for human consumption	1.00	1.21	1.77	1.38	1.49	1.46	1.36	1.34	1.37	1.35	1.36
Foods, processed consumers' goods and producers' goods	1.00	1.04	1.53	1.17	1.32	1.29	1.12	1.08	1.17	1.11	1.11
Non-foods, processed consumers' goods and producers' goods for human consumption	1.00	1.37	1.97	1.58	1.68	1.62	1.61	1.61	1.57	1.60	1.60

sumers' goods stood 19 and 21 per cent, respectively, above the relative prices of the corresponding materials of fabrication, the reference base being 1913. These ratios reflect the post-War over-valuation of processed goods, relatively to pre-War standards. When the margins opened by the price changes of the recession are superimposed upon these earlier differentials we have very high ratios indeed, during the depression. In February 1933 the ratios were 1.65 and 1.77, respectively, for capital goods and consumers' goods. By June 1936 these had fallen to 1.26 and 1.36—still substantially greater than in 1913. In terms of intergroup trade, the first of these ratios meant that producers of goods intended, after processing, for capital equipment, had to give 26 per cent more than in 1913, in physical volume, for a constant quantity of processed capital equipment. The other ratio may be similarly interpreted. Only very great shifts in relative productivity and in costs of production could prevent such changes from bringing important modifications in economic status. There is no evidence that such compensating shifts in productivity did occur, among the classes of goods cited.[10]

Breaking the second of these categories into foods and non-foods, we have the last two sets of ratios shown in Table 38. The divergence between the prices of unfinished and finished goods intended for human consumption has been most pronounced among non-foods. The persistence of relatively high prices for finished goods in the latter group has been the prime factor in this divergence. In February 1933 the ratio for non-foods was practically double the 1913 value.

[10] Here, also, we should note that advances in the quality of finished goods, if account could be taken of them, would lower these ratios. An average unit of finished goods represented more in 1936 than in 1913, in terms of utility. For capital goods the gain in quality may have been sufficient to offset the price disadvantage of the primary producer; this could hardly have been true for processed consumers' goods.

MANUFACTURING INDUSTRIES

In terms of physical trade this meant that producers of raw materials of this type were called upon to give twice as much as in 1913 for a constant quantity of finished goods. By June 1936, the ratio had fallen to 1.60 for consumers' non-foods, a figure still very high indeed by earlier standards. Here is one of the major changes in price relations that recent years have brought. Relatively to the cost of raw materials, the cost of the services performed in the manufacturing of non-food products intended for direct human consumption and use has increased greatly. Among foods the ratio in June 1936 was much lower, 1.11 as against 1.00 in 1913.

In this section we have sought to trace recent changes in the two-sided market relations of manufacturing industries, relations with raw material producers on the one hand, with the buyers of manufactured goods on the other. We pass to a more intensive study of manufacturing industries during recovery, a review of internal operating conditions as well as relations with outside buyers and sellers.

On Recent Changes in Production, Prices, Employment and Wages in Manufacturing Industries

The low point of the depression, in manufacturing industries as in other economic activities, was reached, in the United States, late in the winter of 1932–33.[11] The period

[11] It is perhaps open to question whether this revival in the United States should be dated from February–March 1933, or from mid-summer 1932. The physical volume of production of producers' goods reached lower levels in 1932 than in 1933; the number of wage earners employed was as low in 1932 as in early 1933. On the other hand, aggregate wage disbursements, average prices at wholesale and electric power production fell to lower levels in 1933. The domestic statistical evidence is thus conflicting, on the interesting question whether the downswing that accompanied the political uncertainties of late 1932 and early 1933 marked a continuation of recession and depression, or a check to recovery that had already started. (As regards

of three years that followed brought a substantial recovery. By February–March 1936 the average selling prices of manufactured goods, at wholesale, had risen 25 per cent; the volume of manufacturing production had increased 58 per cent, the total number of persons employed 40 per cent, and total wage disbursements 92 per cent.

Particular interest attaches to the nature of this recovery, because of the novel elements that played a part in it, to which attention has already been drawn. The forces operating in the traditional revival were, in this instance, compounded in complex ways with elements of a consciously formulated program of recovery. For this reason it is of interest to know whether there were shifts in the internal processes of recovery that might have been associated with special elements of the recovery program. Again, we may ask whether this recovery conformed, in general, to the pattern of earlier business revivals. This question is pertinent today not only as a matter of historical interest but also because it bears upon the probable future course of recovery. We may not appraise current economic changes solely in relation to past standards, but reference to these standards may illuminate the present situation.

There are more specific questions centering about the recovery program, as it affected manufacturing industries. What was the effect of the novel conditions of 1933–36 upon industrial productivity? How were labor costs in manufacturing plants affected? What increase occurred in the aggregate purchasing power of manufacturing labor? Did this increase differ in important ways from the customary expansion of labor's purchasing power during business revival? These, and the more general questions suggested above, deal with mat-

world conditions generally, a recovery seems to have begun in 1932.) For the present purpose, it is desirable to measure changes from the low point of early 1933.

MANUFACTURING INDUSTRIES 309

ters of major importance today, when recovery is being sought under an intermixture of old and new conditions. Not all these questions may be answered definitely, but their urgency justifies an attempt to cull from available data evidence relevant to these central issues.

This attempt has been made in preparing the measurements given in this section. Certain of the items are subject to a considerable margin of error, because of limitations upon the coverage of the original records utilized, or because of imperfect comparability of series drawn from different sources. Recognition of this margin of error, of the type that is present whenever representative data are employed, is necessary in using the detailed figures given below. But the general consistency of the results secured leaves no doubt as to the substantial truth of the evidence drawn from these records.

The records of recovery are to be interpreted with reference to the background of the preceding recession, as this affected manufacturing industries. Over a period of less than four years the physical volume of manufacturing production had been cut in half, the average selling price of manufactured products had fallen 31 per cent and the aggregate gross income of manufacturing enterprises had been reduced almost two-thirds. The number of employed wage earners had fallen approximately 43 per cent, the average hourly wage had declined some 22 per cent and average earnings per wage earner had dropped 39 per cent. Total wage disbursements of manufacturing industries had declined 65 per cent; taking account of changes in living costs, this meant a loss of approximately 50 per cent in the actual aggregate purchasing power of manufacturing labor. In no recent business recession have equal losses been suffered by manufacturing industries. The price decline of 1920–21 exceeded the drop of 1929–33, it is true, and in other respects the first post-War recession was of a magnitude roughly comparable to the most recent decline. But in prolonged severity the recession and depression of 1929–33 have no counterpart in the economic records of recent years. Reflections of the drastic preceding recession will appear in the movements of recovery, which may be dated from the early months of 1933.

This recovery was spotty and uneven, probably less homogeneous than any similar period of economic revival of which we have record. Relief from the immediate fears engendered by the banking crisis, a series of developments affecting the present and anticipated value of the dollar, the prospect, and then the reality, of extensive changes in operating and marketing conditions growing out of the adoption of industrial codes, fundamental changes in the conditions affecting the issuance of new securities and the allocation of investment funds, the initiation of Federal expenditures for relief on a hitherto unprecedented scale—these followed one another in rapid succession. Within three years the business 'climate' underwent a series of changes such as might normally have been spread over many years. These and other developments affected the shifting course of recovery among manufacturing industries between February 1933 and the spring of 1936. The first sharp spurt, which carried to mid-summer of 1933, was followed by a recession, extending to the end of 1933, a spring revival in 1934, a set-back through the summer months, a recovery in the winter of 1934, a mild contraction in the spring of 1935, and a notable advance carrying into the winter of 1935–36.

Some new factors were present in each of these periods, but the most notable differences separate the first phase of sharp expansion from the alternations of contraction and expansion that follow. These differences lie, partly, in the extent of the movements. The first recovery far exceeded in magnitude the up-turns that followed. Again, the first rise and the later movements are characterized by important differences in operating conditions, in the field of manufacturing. The first of the codes introduced under the National Industrial Recovery Act was approved on July 9, 1933; the blanket code authorized under the President's Re-employment Agreement had been accepted by 700,000 employers by August 1st. The operating conditions prevailing in manufacturing industries underwent a major change with the inauguration of the codes. In this fundamental respect, then, the circumstances attending the first phase of recovery, up to the summer of 1933, are clearly distinct from those prevailing up to May 1935. It is true that the prospect of operation under the codes helped to stimulate the early advance and affected its character. But the detailed regulations later prescribed under the industrial codes did not, of course, affect operating conditions during this first surge of recovery.

We must recognize that many factors, other than the codes, distinguish the first phase of recovery from the period that followed. The stimulus of monetary change was a potent force in the first surge of renewed activity. Hopes and fears centering in the prospects of inflation were stronger during the first few months than later. Production for stock was probably more important during the first phase, and such production would leave its impress upon the movements of the later period. The potentialities of rapid advance in productivity and sharp reduction of operating costs were greater at the very low level of activity prevailing in February 1933 than after the bloom of the first revival had passed. The factors affecting operating conditions over a short period differ in various ways from those dominant over a longer interval. It would be improper to attribute to the influence of the industrial codes all the differences we shall note between the operating conditions prevailing in manufacturing industries prior to and following the adoption of these codes.

Yet these differences are part of the data required for an appraisal of the codes and of the shifting currents of economic change from 1933 to 1936.

For these reasons, then, we shall break the period of recovery here reviewed into three phases—that covering the sharp rise from February–March 1933 to June–July 1933, the period from the summer of 1933 to April–May 1935, and the phase from April–May 1935 to February–March 1936. Operation under the codes ceased, of course, following the Supreme Court decision of May 27, 1935. Since the turning points that mark off these periods of recovery are not clearly to be located in one particular month, and since they do not coincide, in time, for all the series to be followed, the limits of the several periods are set with reference to averages of measurements covering two months.

THE DATA, AND SOME LIMITING CONDITIONS

The basic series from which all other measurements are derived, in tracing the changes of recovery, are given in Table 39, in relative form. These series are based upon records of production, employment, pay rolls, hours and selling prices relating to the operations of the major manufacturing industries of the United States.

The general changes during the recovery phases distinguished in Table 39 are familiar. The first spurt of recovery carried all series upward, the advance of 45 per cent in production being outstanding. The changes of the twenty-two months following (the period of general operation under the codes) brought a slight rise in production, further notable advances in prices, pay rolls and number employed, and a pronounced decline in average hours worked per week. The first ten months of the post-NRA operation, in 1935–36, witnessed a rise in output and increases in number of wage

TABLE 39

A RECORD OF THE FORTUNES OF MANUFACTURING INDUSTRIES
OF THE UNITED STATES, 1933–1936

BASIC MEASUREMENTS [1]

	February–March 1933	June–July 1933	April–May 1935	February–March 1936
Physical volume of production	100	145	148	158
Number of wage earners employed	100	115	136	140
Total wage disbursements (pay rolls)	100	127	180	192
Average number of working hours per week, per person	100	114	97	102
Average selling price of products	100	109	125	125

[1] Descriptions of the series given in this table will be found in Appendix VIII-A. The reader should note that the production index of the Board of Governors of the Federal Reserve System, on which the present measurements of production changes rest, shows an advance of 57 per cent from February–March to June–July 1933. But the compiling authorities call attention to the fact that this advance was somewhat distorted by the sharp rise in the output of semi-finished goods in that period. The rise in general manufacturing production was smaller. The figure of 45 per cent used in the present analysis is a corrected measurement. The basis of correction is explained in Appendix VIII-A.

Because of this correction, the measurements given in this chapter differ somewhat from those given in *Bulletin 56* of the National Bureau of Economic Research, in which the results of this analysis were first published.

The monthly indexes of average selling prices of manufactured products are compared with index numbers based on the records of the Census of Manufactures in Appendix VIII-B.

earners employed, in wage disbursements and in average working hours. No change occurred in the average selling price of manufactured products.

But a more detailed comparison of these movements is required to bring out the distinctive features of the period that opened with the spring revival of 1933. In making such comparisons and in deriving the requisite measurements we must recognize the limitations of the data. There are some differences in the degrees of coverage of the series listed above. Pay roll and employment statistics are drawn from 90 manufacturing industries. Records of average hours worked per week are secured from a smaller number of establishments, representing a somewhat smaller number of manufacturing industries—87 in December 1935. (Only those industries are included for which information concerning hours of labor covers at least 20 per cent of all employees.) Price and production records relate to still other samples of manufacturing operations at large—broad samples, but not the same, in detail, as those from which the first figures come. Comparison of these records and the derivation of measurements from such comparisons must proceed on the assumption that each of the basic series is representative of manufacturing industries in general. Since this assumption is made in the pages that follow, the various derived figures should be looked upon as indexes of general tendencies, not as highly accurate measurements of detailed movements.

In respect of timing, certain other difficulties face us in making comparisons. The basic production statistics are monthly averages or aggregates, while the records of employment, pay rolls and hours for each month are derived from data relating to the week ending at the date nearest the middle of the month. The original price quotations vary in this respect, some being averages of daily figures, some averages of weekly quotations, some quotations as of specific dates. Each set of figures may be taken, however, to be generally representative of conditions prevailing in given months. Greater difficulties are introduced by the fact that the final emergence of finished manufactured products lags behind the expenditure of labor and of money in the preliminary productive processes. This lag is not a serious barrier to accurate comparison of statistics of final production and statistics relating to the earlier processes of production, if the

MANUFACTURING INDUSTRIES

flow of materials be reasonably steady. When the process is extended, however, and when variations in the rate of flow are considerable, the accuracy of comparisons of concurrent statistics is lessened. Records of employment and pay rolls relating to a period of reduced activity may be set against a flow of finished products resulting from a preceding period of excessive activity. Conversely, technical conditions of production may force the maintenance of a considerable labor force even though the production of finished products has been sharply reduced. The automobile industry, with its periods of preparation for the output of new models, and the steel industry furnish examples of production and labor statistics not always strictly comparable on a current monthly basis. If the lags were constant account could be taken of them, but in some industries they vary appreciably from time to time.

The seasonal factor also complicates the task of comparison. Some of the basic series compared are subject to seasonal fluctuations, others are not. However, there are real doubts whether the customary seasonal movements have prevailed, in all cases, under the abnormal conditions of severe depression. In some instances it is certain that they have not. Moreover, the magnitude of the usual seasonal movements is much smaller than the changes here recorded. For these reasons it has seemed desirable to attempt no correction for assumed seasonal variations. The actual records of manufacturing operations have been utilized.

Various technical difficulties of the types mentioned are faced in the comparative study of month-to-month fluctuations. Those general movements that persist over longer periods will not be obscured, however, by the erratic changes arising from varying temporal relations of production, employment and prices. In the comparisons actually made in the following pages the difficulty introduced by erratic month-to-month movements is met, in part, through the comparison of averages for several months, rather than indexes for single months. Even so, not too much weight should be attached to extreme movements for limited periods, in records relating to single industries. When the records for different industries support one another, however, and when movements persist over time, it is justifiable to conclude that we are dealing with significant changes, and not with erratic fluctuations resulting from shifting leads and lags among the series compared.

With these considerations and limitations in mind, we may draw such information as we can from the basic measurements in Table 39. The index numbers presented in Table 40,

TABLE 40

A RECORD OF THE FORTUNES OF MANUFACTURING INDUSTRIES OF THE UNITED STATES, 1933–1936

DERIVED MEASUREMENTS [1]

	February–March 1933	June–July 1933	April–May 1935	February–March 1936
Gross income	100	158	185	198
Total employment (man hours)	100	131	132	143
Average output per wage earner	100	126	109	113
Average output per man hour	100	111	112	110
Average earnings per wage earner	100	110	132	137
Average hourly wages	100	97	136	134
Average labor cost per unit of product	100	88	122	122

[1] Explanations of the methods employed in deriving these index numbers will be found in the notes in Appendix VIII-A.

which have been derived from those in Table 39, define important aspects of the changes occurring in this period of revival. The five basic series and the seven sets of derived measurements constitute the materials of the following analysis. Using these, we may follow the course of recovery

MANUFACTURING INDUSTRIES

and note certain changes in the operating conditions of manufacturing industries and in the relations of these industries to other elements of the national economy.[12]

[12] In this survey we shall use the measurements given in Tables 39 and 40, which are taken to be representative of the movements in manufacturing industries at large in the United States. Attention has been drawn to the lack of perfect comparability among some of the series employed. However, the general conclusions drawn from these comparisons are supported by evidence relating to smaller samples of major manufacturing industries for which more truly comparable measurements of production, employment and pay rolls are available. These industries include those producing iron and steel, automobiles, cigars and cigarettes, cement, leather, boots and shoes, rubber tires and inner tubes, lumber, woolen and worsted goods, cotton goods, carpets and rugs, and flour, and the meat packing, sugar refining and petroleum refining industries. Measurements for this substantial group of 15 manufacturing industries are given below, together with measurements for all manufacturing industries. In addition, figures are given for 13 industries—the 15 in the above list, less automobiles and cotton textiles. The cotton textile industry was marked by distinctive changes during the recovery of 1933-36, and some special difficulties are faced in the automobile industry in respect of the comparability, in time, of the production records and employment and pay roll statistics.

	February–March 1933	June–July 1933	April–May 1935	February–March 1936
Gross income				
All manufacturing industries	100	158	185	198
15 industries	100	195	248	252
13 industries	100	190	210	229
Total employment (man hours)				
All manufacturing industries	100	131	132	143
15 industries	100	150	143	150
13 industries	100	150	135	148
Average output per wage earner				
All manufacturing industries	100	126	109	113
15 industries	100	139	126	128
13 industries	100	136	110	118
Average output per man hour				
All manufacturing industries	100	110	112	111
15 industries	100	114	127	123
13 industries	100	109	109	108

(Footnote 12 concluded on p. 318)

THE RECOVERY OF 1933–1936

In following changes in the operations of manufacturing industries since the early months of 1933 various combinations of the measurements presented in Tables 39 and 40 may be used. Each combination will contain a single series of major importance and two of its component elements. In each instance the movements of the three related series should be compared. The measurements entering into the various combinations are brought together in Table 41. The subsequent discussion should be followed with reference to the detailed entries in this table.

(*Footnote* 12 *concluded*)

	February–March 1933	June–July 1933	April–May 1935	February–March 1936
Average earnings per wage earner				
All manufacturing industries	100	110	132	137
15 industries	100	121	151	156
13 industries	100	122	145	154
Average hourly wages				
All manufacturing industries	100	97	136	134
15 industries	100	99	152	149
13 industries	100	99	144	142
Average labor cost per unit of product				
All manufacturing industries	100	88	122	122
15 industries	100	87	120	122
13 industries	100	90	132	131

The smaller samples, which are rather heavily weighted by basic industries, show more violent fluctuations in gross income and total employment than are found in manufacturing industries at large, but the various derived measurements show movements of the same general character. (It should be noted that the figures for the smaller groups and for all manufacturing industries for June–July 1933 are not independent, in respect of output per man hour and labor cost per unit of product. These two series for the smaller groups have been used in revising production figures for all industries for this period, correcting for the bias noted on an earlier page. See also Appendix VIII-A.) This set of measurements, more carefully controlled than are the figures for all industries, serves to check the general conclusions suggested in the text.

MANUFACTURING INDUSTRIES

TABLE 41
MANUFACTURING OPERATIONS, 1933–1936
A Comparison of Movements during Different Phases of Recovery

	PERCENTAGE CHANGE FROM			
	Feb.–March 1933 to June–July 1933	June–July 1933 to April–May 1935	April–May 1935 to Feb.–March 1936	Feb.–March 1933 to Feb.–March 1936
Gross income and its elements				
1. Gross income	+58	+17	+6	+98
2. Production (physical volume)	+45	+2	+7	+58
3. Selling price of products (average)	+9	+15	−1	+25
Employment and its elements				
4. Total employment (man hours)	+31	+1	+7	+43
5. Wage earners employed	+15	+18	+2	+40
6. Working hours per person (average weekly)	+14	−15	+5	+2
Production and its elements				
2. Production	+45	+2	+7	+58
5. Wage earners employed	+15	+18	+2	+40
7. Output per wage earner (average)	+26	−14	+5	+13
4. Total employment (man hours)	+31	+1	+7	+43
8. Output per man hour (average)	+10	+1	0	+11
Wage disbursements and elements				
9. Wage disbursements	+27	+42	+7	+92
5. Wage earners employed	+15	+18	+2	+40
10. Earnings per wage earner (average)	+10	+20	+5	+37
4. Total employment (man hours)	+31	+1	+7	+43
11. Hourly wages (average)	−3	+40	0	+34
2. Production	+45	+2	+7	+58
12. Labor cost per unit (average)	−12	+39	0	+22

MANUFACTURING GROSS INCOME AND COMPONENT ELEMENTS

Changes in the gross income of manufacturing industries may result from changes in the number of units produced, or in the average selling price per unit. The first three sets of measurements in Table 41 define these movements during the recovery of 1933–36.[13] In tracing these movements effective comparisons may be made between the changes in the sharp revival of the first four months, during the next twenty-two months of general operation under the codes, and in the final period of ten months, following the termination of NRA.

The net gains of the entire period were substantial, 98 per cent in gross income, resulting from advances of 58 per cent in volume of production and 25 per cent in average price per unit. But the gains were not divided equally among the three phases of recovery. In the short pre-code period all the series advanced, with rising output as the major factor in the notable pick-up in gross income. During the era of code installation and operation under the codes output advanced only slightly; rising prices were the chief element in a 17 per cent increase in gross income. This increase continued in the post-code period, in 1935–36, with rising production as the active factor in the advance. Prices declined slightly.

Of course, many forces operated during all three periods. Anticipation of the codes played a part in the first advance. A natural reaction from the tremendous activity of the first advance, activity leading to production of goods in excess of current needs, is reflected in the record of the second phase. We shall have a better basis for judgment concerning the

[13] In all threefold comparisons of this sort the figure relating to one series is the product of the corresponding figures for the two other series, in the sense that $1.58 = 1.45 \times 1.09$.

MANUFACTURING INDUSTRIES

part played by code enforcement in the changes of these periods when we have pressed our inquiry further, for the changes defined by certain of the other series are more closely connected with code provisions. The factors affecting total employment are in this category.

TOTAL MANUFACTURING EMPLOYMENT AND COMPONENT ELEMENTS

Total employment is properly measured in terms of man hours. Changes in the number of persons employed and in the average hours of work affect this total. Items (4), (5) and (6) of Table 41 summarize the record of recovery in these elements. The notable increase of 31 per cent in total employment in the pre-code period resulted from almost equal advances in the number employed and in the average number of hours worked per wage earner. Between mid-summer 1933 and April–May 1935 the volume of employment showed no large net change. There was a considerable decline in average hours worked, which was offset by an increase in the number employed. These changes, of course, are manifestations of definite elements of the recovery program. There was spreading of work under the codes. In April–May 1935 a volume of employment about 1 per cent greater than that prevailing when the codes went into effect was shared among a body of workers some 18 per cent larger. In the ten months following the termination of the codes manufacturing employment rose 7 per cent, both number of workers and average hours worked increasing. The period of recovery as a whole shows substantial increases in total employment and in number of persons employed, with a rise of 2 per cent in the average number of hours worked, per person.

PHYSICAL VOLUME OF MANUFACTURING PRODUCTION
AND COMPONENT ELEMENTS

Changes in the volume of manufacturing production may be viewed as the resultants (though not necessarily in a causal sense) of changes in the number employed and in output per worker. Items (2), (5) and (7) of Table 41 relate to these series.

The sharp advance in volume of production during the pre-code period was achieved through an increase in the number of workers and a still more pronounced increase in output per person employed. (The latter gain was partly attributable, of course, to an increase in hours of work.) These were changes of the sort usual in revival, though of exceptional magnitude. A gain of 45 per cent in volume of output, from the very low level of early 1933, carried with it, almost inevitably, a notable advance in output per person, per machine in use, and per man hour. (We would misread the figures if we should take this gain to be the result of a great technical revolution. No such revolution occurred during this brief period of four or five months. The potential advantages of earlier improvements, technical and otherwise, could be realized when this sharp gain in volume of output occurred.) During the twenty-two months of general operation under the codes the number employed continued to increase. Output per person declined, however, and aggregate production increased only 2 per cent. The post-NRA phase was marked by an increase of 7 per cent in total output, a slight increase in the number of workers, and a renewed advance in output per worker.

Changes in the average length of the working week affect the preceding measurements of output per person. In Table 41 changes in total output are shown, in relation to changes in man hours and in output per man hour [items (4) and

MANUFACTURING INDUSTRIES

(8)]. Indexes of output per man hour are a measure of true productivity,[14] far more accurate, of course, than is a measure of output per person under conditions marked by changing hours of work.

The advance of 10 per cent in output per man hour in the first early spurt was in some degree a cause, in greater degree a result, of the notable increase in total output. Increased market demand made possible an increase in productivity, an increase in its turn facilitated by earlier improvements in equipment, in technique and in the quality of labor. In the twenty-two months that followed this pronounced gain in productivity, output per man hour increased approximately 1 per cent.[15] No further change in average output per man hour occurred during the ten months following the termination of NRA. The figures defining net change, over the entire period of recovery, show a rise of 58 per cent in volume of production, an advance of 11 per cent in output per man hour.

---

[14] It is convenient to measure industrial productivity on a man hour basis. This is not to be taken to mean that changes in productivity are due exclusively, or even primarily, to the human factor in production. Mechanical equipment may be a more important factor in changing productivity than human skill or intensity of application.

[15] This, of course, is an average figure, behind which there lie large and small productivity losses in certain industries, gains in others. Indeed, the fact should be emphasized that any such analysis as this, which necessarily runs in terms of averages, must ignore the fortunes of individual industries. At times of extreme change there are bound to be wide diversities of fortune. An account that included many industrial case histories would reveal the details of the changes affecting the industrial structure in this recession. But we content ourselves here with the general tendencies that dominated the period, recalling only that many plants and industries followed distinctive courses of their own.

TOTAL WAGE DISBURSEMENTS OF MANUFACTURING INDUSTRIES, AND ELEMENTS OF THE TOTAL

We turn to a survey of wage disbursements during the recovery, viewing these, first, from the point of view of wage recipients. Changes in the aggregate and in two of its elements during the several phases of recovery are defined by items (9), (5) and (10) of Table 41.

Total wage disbursements expanded during all three periods, the relative advance in the second period being materially greater than the gains of the pre-NRA and post-NRA phases. Increases in the number of wage earners and in average earnings per wage earner contributed, during all phases of recovery, to the expansion of the aggregate wage bill.

More light is thrown on the changes in wages and earnings during these periods by a somewhat different division of elements. Total wage disbursements may be considered as the product of the number of hours worked and the average wage per hour. Analysis into these elements, which appear as items (4) and (11) in Table 41, makes it possible to follow changes in wage rates, and to determine their relation to fluctuations in total wage disbursements.

We find quite diverse changes during the three periods compared. The pre-code advance of 27 per cent in the aggregate earnings of manufacturing labor was accompanied by a sharp rise in total man hours worked (31 per cent), and by a drop of 3 per cent in the average hourly wage. In the second period, characterized by operation under new wage provisions, with only a minor change in volume of production, we find a slight increase in total man hours worked, an advance of 40 per cent in average hourly wages. Here was a new factor at work in a period of revival, with definite wage regulations increasing hourly rates at a much earlier stage

MANUFACTURING INDUSTRIES

than was to be expected from the usual processes of revival. The net effect was to increase total wage disbursements 42 per cent between June–July 1933 and April–May 1935, although production advanced but 2 per cent and employment 1 per cent. During the ten months that followed the end of code operations employment rose 7 per cent, and average hourly earnings remained constant. Over the entire period of recovery we have a pronounced advance in total wages paid, a considerable rise in man hours worked and a notable increase in hourly rates of pay.

It is desirable to trace some of the economic accompaniments of these widely different means of achieving the same result, i.e., a given gain in the aggregate wages disbursed to manufacturing labor. Certain of these consequences may be followed by comparing changes in wage disbursements [item (9) of Table 41], with changes in total volume of production [item (2)], and in labor cost per unit of product [item (12)].

The increase of 27 per cent in the total wage bill of manufacturing industries during the period of pre-code expansion may be viewed as the net resultant of a gain of 45 per cent in number of units produced and a decline of 12 per cent in average labor cost per unit. Thus, although the average hourly wage dropped only 3 per cent, and average earnings per wage earner increased 10 per cent, the labor cost per unit fell 12 per cent. This resulted, of course, from a gain of 10 per cent in output per man hour. Such reduction of an important element of production costs worked definitely towards the correction of the great disparity between the prices of raw materials and of manufactured goods existing at the low point of the depression.

The advance of 42 per cent in total wage disbursements during the code period resulted from two quite different types of change in the component elements. The number of units produced increased only 2 per cent, while average labor costs, per unit of product, rose 39 per cent. Increasing production and falling labor costs accompanied the first rapid gain in the total rewards of manufacturing labor. A practically constant volume of production and sharply rising labor costs accompanied the advance in aggregate payments to labor that occurred in the period of operation under the codes.[16] Wage disbursements in the post-NRA period continued to advance. It is significant that no change in labor costs per unit occurred during this period. For the recovery as a whole, to February–March 1936, increases of 22 per cent in labor costs per unit and 58 per cent in number of units produced contributed to an advance of 92 per cent in total wages paid.

In interpreting these figures and in comparing the pre-code and code periods we must allow, again, for the influence of factors not connected with code administration. A sharp drop in labor costs per unit of product was to be expected, during the first spurt of revival, as an accompaniment of the pick-up from the very low level of activity prevailing in February 1933. The situation in mid-summer 1933 offered no such potentialities of sudden reduction in operating costs, even though all working conditions had remained unchanged. On the other hand, had working conditions remained unchanged, the first reduction of 12 per cent in labor costs would not have been followed by an advance of 39 per cent.[17]

[16] This measurement of advance in labor costs is subject to at least two types of bias. It is probable that the larger establishments in the sample from which data on pay rolls are secured conformed more closely, on the whole, to code regulations than did the smaller establishments. This would tend to make the measurement of labor costs somewhat higher than it would be with complete coverage. On the other hand, it is known that there is a negative bias in the reported pay roll statistics, arising from the use of a constant sample. Such bias would tend to lower the measure of labor costs. These errors, if present, tend to offset one another.

[17] The apparent advance of 39 per cent in average labor cost per unit of product in American manufacturing industries between June–July 1933 and

SUMMARY OF THE CHANGES OF RECOVERY IN MANUFACTURING INDUSTRIES

The three years from February–March 1933 to February–March 1936 were marked by a curious combination of movements in the operations of manufacturing industries. Physical output and gross income increased during each of the periods we have distinguished; the sharpest spurts came in the pre-code period. The great gain in productivity came also in the pre-NRA period. Thereafter output per man hour advanced slightly, output per worker declined. Total employment (man hours) advanced notably in the first period, remained almost constant under the codes. On the other hand, the greatest advances in number of wage earners employed, wage disbursements and average earnings per employed worker came during the period of code operation. Average hourly wages and labor costs per unit of product declined in the pre-code period, rose by approximately 40 per cent under the codes. Average selling prices of manufactured goods rose prior to and during the stage of code operation, declined slightly after the termination of the codes.

It is clear that certain tendencies of the first period were checked or reversed during operation under the codes. Physical output increased by a bare 2 per cent in twenty-two months of NRA. Evidence of internal difficulties, during this period, in the form of retarded productivity and advancing

April–May 1935 reflects, in part, the abnormal conditions prevailing in midsummer 1933, after the first spurt of revival. This figure is useful for comparative purposes, but is not to be taken as an accurate measure of changing industrial efficiency. More significance attaches to the measure defining the change in average labor cost per unit over the period from February–March 1933 to February–March 1936. This net advance of 22 per cent, over a period that includes the material reduction of labor costs during the first four months, represents a notable departure from the typical movement of recovery.

labor costs, adds to the darkness of the picture. And yet, throughout the period of recovery, gross income advanced, wage disbursements continued to increase, earnings per employed worker rose, and the number of workers on pay rolls continued to increase. Purchasing power was being disbursed in ever-expanding volume, despite the apparently adverse conditions indicated for the second period by the various records of physical production, productivity, and labor costs. Here were strangely conflicting movements. But we shall have a better perspective on these shifts when we compare them with changes during the preceding recession and during earlier periods of business revival.

RECOVERY MOVEMENTS IN RELATION TO A PRE-RECESSION STANDARD

Any economic recovery is closely related to the preceding period of recession. That recession must condition the recovery at many points and vitally affect its character. The exceptional gravity and extent of the recession in American business between 1929 and early 1933 cannot be ignored in surveying the changes brought by recovery. For this reason we supplement the survey of changes during the phase of recovery by a summary account of these changes viewed against a pre-recession base. Measurements are given in Table 42. (Certain of the series given in Table 41 do not appear in Table 42. Where measurements for the longer period could not be considered accurate, in detail, it appeared desirable to restrict statements to general terms and not to cite specific figures.)

Shifting the standard of reference to a pre-recession base has one immediate effect, to reduce the apparent magnitude of the shifts of recovery. For the recession carried most economic series to such low levels in the winter of 1932–33 that

TABLE 42

RECESSION AND RECOVERY IN AMERICAN MANUFACTURING INDUSTRIES, 1929–1936

	June–July 1929	February–March 1933	June–July 1933	April–May 1935	February–March 1936
			(current dollars)		
Gross income and its elements					
1. Gross income	100	34	53	62	66
2. Production (physical volume)		100	49	71	72	77
3. Selling price of products (average)		100	69	75	86	86
Production and its elements					
2. Production	100	49	71	72	77
5. Wage earners employed	100	57	65	77	79
7. Output per wage earner	100	86	109	94	97
Wage disbursements and elements					
9. Wage disbursements	100	35	45	64	68
5. Wage earners employed	100	57	65	77	79
10. Earnings per wage earner (average)	100	61	69	83	86
11. Average hourly wage	100	78	76	103	104
2. Production	100	49	71	72	77
12. Labor cost per unit of product (average)	100	71	63	89	88
		(dollars of constant purchasing power)			
Gross income and its elements					
1. Gross income [1]	100	54	75	75	80
2. Production (physical volume)	100	49	71	72	77
3. Selling price of products (average) [1]	100	111	106	104	104
Wage disbursements and elements					
9a. Wage disbursements [2]	100	49	61	77	80
5. Wage earners employed	100	57	65	77	79
10. Real earnings per wage earner (average) [2]	100	86	94	100	101

TABLE 42 (*cont.*)

RECESSION AND RECOVERY IN AMERICAN MANUFACTURING INDUSTRIES, 1929–1936

	June–July 1929	February–March 1933	June–July 1933	April–May 1935	February–March 1936
		(dollars of constant purchasing power)			
11. Average hourly wage [2]	100	108	103	124	122
9b. Wage disbursements [1]	100	56	63	77	82
2. Production	100	49	71	72	77
12. Labor cost per unit of product (average) [1]	100	114	89	107	106

[1] The index number of wholesale prices constructed by the National Bureau of Economic Research was used as a deflator.
[2] The index of the cost of living of industrial workers constructed by the National Industrial Conference Board was used as a deflator.

the succeeding rises, in percentage terms, run into relatively high figures. On a pre-recession base the percentage changes are much less pronounced.

In summary, the situation as of February–March 1936, with reference to the situation existing in June–July 1929 was marked by the following features:

The gross income of manufacturing industries had been reduced 34 per cent in current dollars, 20 per cent in dollars of constant purchasing power, at wholesale. The physical volume of manufacturing production was 23 per cent below the 1929 standard. Per unit prices were lower, but the average per unit purchasing power of manufactured goods in wholesale markets was higher. Relatively to other goods, commodities of this type cost more, per unit, than in 1929.

The actual volume of manufacturing employment, measured in man hours, had been reduced about two-fifths and the working force had been reduced one-fifth.

Industrial productivity, per wage earner employed, had declined slightly. Productivity per man hour had risen. The gain may be estimated at something more than 25 per cent, scored during the period of recession and in the first spurt of revival.

The aggregate purchasing power of manufacturing labor was some 20 per cent lower. The purchasing power of the earnings of each employed worker stood just about at the 1929 level. The purchasing power of an hour's wage (i.e., the real hourly wage) had increased approximately 22 per cent.

The total wage bill of manufacturing industries, measured in dollars of constant purchasing power at wholesale, was approximately 18 per cent lower. Average labor cost per unit of goods produced had risen approximately 6 per cent (cost being here measured in terms of the same constant value standard).

It is apparent from these figures that the recovery in American manufacturing industries, up to the spring of 1936, had fallen short of restoring the pre-recession level of gross income, of production, of employment, or of aggregate purchasing power of labor. Industrial productivity and real wage rates on a man hour basis were much higher than before the recession, nominal wage rates were higher, and real labor costs per unit of product were somewhat higher.

But we need other criteria, in appraising the shifting movements of the current recovery. Earlier periods of business expansion furnish useful standards of reference.

ECONOMIC CHANGES IN MANUFACTURING INDUSTRIES DURING FIVE PERIODS OF BUSINESS EXPANSION, APPROXIMATELY EQUAL IN RESPECT OF DEGREE OF RECOVERY

A comparison of manufacturing operations during different periods of business expansion may be expected to disclose some of the distinctive features of the current movement. It is true that there exists no fixed schedule of recovery, to

332   PRICES IN RECESSION AND RECOVERY

which business movements always conform, but something of the nature of a common pattern is found in the cyclical fluctuations of the economic system. Some of the characteristics of this pattern, and distinctive deviations from it, are revealed by the series of measurements presented in this section.

Various modes of comparison are possible in any such survey. For the present purpose it seems desirable to trace the movements of important economic series over periods of expansion marked by approximately equal degrees of increase in the physical output of manufacturing industries. This magnitude, as averaged for the months of December 1934 and January 1935, was 37 per cent greater than at the low point of February–March 1933.[18] It is pertinent to inquire how the changes in manufacturing industries during this period, with respect to employment, productivity, labor costs, etc., compared with corresponding changes during earlier periods of equal increase in volume of output.[19] We should note that in concentrating attention upon the operations of manufacturing industries we ignore numerous economic factors—such as monetary and credit conditions, rela-

---

[18] Advances of approximately equal magnitude could not be secured for the three preceding revivals, if the record were carried through 1935. Since we are interested in operating changes accompanying similar advances, we restrict the survey of recent changes to the movements up to January 1935.

[19] If we compare, with respect to changes in aggregate production, periods of business recovery widely separated in time, error may be introduced into our conclusions by the changing character of the elements entering into the aggregate. Different industries, marked by important differences of cyclical behavior, may dominate a national economy at different times. These dominant industries would place their own impress on the aggregate into which they enter. But over fifteen years no great changes occurred in the relative importance of elements entering into aggregate manufacturing production, in the United States. The incidence of recovery may, of course, be different, at different times, but this is a condition affecting all comparisons of this sort, in which aggregates of any kind are used.

tions among elements of the price structure, saving and investment—which condition the course and character of recovery. Our interest, however, is not in the economy at large, or in the full complex of circumstances that shape a business revival. It is in a particular segment of the total, and in the internal relations among the elements of this segment. These relations will not be unaffected by external developments, but such developments are of secondary importance in the present comparison.

In this comparison no attempt is made to introduce corrections for seasonal movements. Accurate indexes of seasonal variation are not available for all the series. Moreover, it is known that in important industries the customary seasonal pattern has been modified in recent years. For this reason, and because the cyclical changes here in question are of much greater magnitude than the seasonal, it seems advisable to utilize the uncorrected records. Accurate adjustment for seasonal swings would modify the picture in detail but not in fundamental respects.

We may enhance the value of this survey by utilizing two different sets of figures for the most recent recovery. The early spurt of 1933 brought an increase in volume of output well in excess of 37 per cent. The closest possible approach to that figure is provided by the period from February–March 1933 to May–June 1933, during which the volume of manufacturing production increased 39 per cent. The changes of this phase may be compared with those of the period February–March 1933 to December 1934–January 1935, as well as with those of the recoveries that began in 1921, in 1924, and in 1927. The period of the first rise, in 1933, is short, and therefore the changes must not be looked upon as resulting from a major technical revolution. They are significant, however, as regards the actual operating condi-

334 PRICES IN RECESSION AND RECOVERY

tions of industry, and the relation of currently-expended effort to current outlay and current returns.

As in the preceding section we shall deal with certain major series and constituent elements of each series. The measurements appear in Table 43. The basic series are presented graphically and the dates to which the entries in Table 43 relate are indicated in Figure 13, in order that the nature

FIGURE 13

MOVEMENTS OF SELECTED SERIES RELATING TO AMERICAN MANUFACTURING INDUSTRIES, 1920–1936

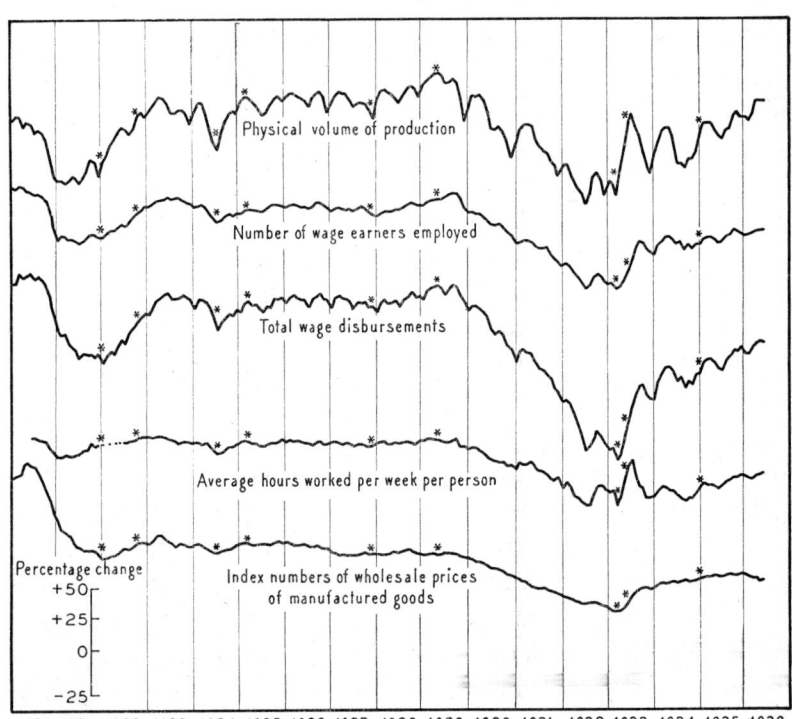

Ratio scale
* Asterisks mark the terminal dates of the five periods of recovery analyzed in the text.

of the measurements to be compared may be clear. Data are picked from their setting for the purpose of the quantitative comparison, and it is proper that the reader see what this setting is in each instance.

It is obvious that although the periods of business expansion here compared cover equal degrees of recovery, when physical output of manufactured goods is the yardstick of recovery, they do not cover equal proportionate parts of business cycles. Phases of revival and expansion vary in amplitude and duration, as do business cycles themselves. In studying certain technical aspects of business cycles it is desirable to isolate identical cyclical segments. But interest attaches, also, to the comparison of cyclical movements accompanying given degrees of increase in volume of production.[20]

The items in Table 43, for different periods of recovery, may be compared in detail by the reader. Certain general conclusions based upon the above evidence, and other data, are given in the final section of this chapter. At this point we may be content with a brief summary of the main points revealed by that table.

In respect of the attributes here studied the sharp initial recovery of 1933 appears to have conformed to the pattern of earlier revivals, a pattern that is strikingly repeated in the first four of the five periods covered. But the measurements

[20] Reference has been made to the exceptional severity of the recession of 1929–33, and to the fact that the relative changes of recovery are affected by the severity of the earlier decline. It is to be expected that recoveries, following recessions of varying magnitudes, will differ, in some respects. But we do not know how the pattern of recovery is affected by the preceding recession. The reader will bear in mind the differing magnitudes of the recessions preceding the phases of expansion to which the measurements in Table 43 relate. It will be useful to recall that the volume of manufacturing production declined approximately 27 per cent prior to the 1921 recovery, 26 per cent prior to the 1924 recovery, and 13 per cent prior to the 1927 recovery, as compared with a drop of about 50 per cent from 1929 to 1933. The price drop of 1920–21 exceeded that of 1929–33.

TABLE 43

CHANGES IN MANUFACTURING OPERATIONS DURING FIVE PERIODS OF BUSINESS EXPANSION APPROXIMATELY EQUAL IN DEGREE OF RECOVERY

	Percentage change from				
	Dec. 1921–Jan. 1922 to Sept.–Oct. 1922	June–July 1924 to Feb.–March. 1925	Nov.–Dec. 1927 to April–May 1929	Feb.–March 1933 to May–June 1933	Feb.–March 1933 to Dec. 1934–Jan. 1935
Gross income and its elements					
1. Gross income	+42	+46	+31	+46	+69
2. Production (physical volume)	+33	+36	+31	+39[1]	+37
3. Selling price of products (average)	+7	+7	0	+5	+23
Employment and its elements					
4. Total employment (man hours)	+19	+14	+13	+21	+23
5. Wage earners employed	+16	+7	+9	+8	+31
6. Working hours per person (average weekly)	+3	+7	+4	+12	−6
Production and its elements					
2. Production	+33	+36	+31	+39[1]	+37
5. Wage earners employed	+16	+7	+9	+8	+31
7. Output per wage earner (average)	+15	+27	+20	+29	+5
4. Total employment (man hours)	+19	+14	+13	+21	+23
8. Output per man hour (average)	+12	+19	+16	+15	+11

MANUFACTURING INDUSTRIES

Wage disbursements and elements					
9. Wage disbursements	+24	+14	+14	+16	+65
5. Wage earners employed	+16	+7	+9	+8	+31
10. Earnings per wage earner (average)	+7	+7	+5	+7	+26
4. Employment (man hours)	+19	+14	+13	+21	+23
11. Hourly wages (average)	+4	0	+1	−4	+34
2. Production	+33	+36	+31	+39[1]	+37
12. Labor cost per unit (average)	−7	−16	−13	−17	+20

[1] The index of manufacturing production of the Board of Governors of the Federal Reserve System shows an increase of 43 per cent from February–March 1933 to May–June 1933. Correcting for bias due to the heavy weight given to semi-finished goods in this index, we secure the figure of 39 per cent given in the table. For a general note on this procedure see Appendix VIII-A.

of net change from early 1933 to early 1935 depart appreciably from the customary pattern of business revival. The notes that follow relate to the net movements of the period from February–March 1933 to December 1934–January 1935.

This period brought a greater increase in gross income than did equal degrees of recovery, in physical terms, in earlier revivals. A much more rapid rise in per unit selling prices accounted for the greater increase in gross income.

The number employed increased much more rapidly. Average hours worked per person decreased; earlier recoveries were marked by increases in average hours worked.

Output per worker advanced only slightly. Substantial increases had marked earlier recoveries. The recent increase in volume of production was effected primarily through the employment of more workers.

The net gain in output per man hour compares favorably with earlier advances. (The gain in the recent period was effected, it has been noted, during the first four months of recovery.)

Total wage disbursements, earnings per wage earner and number employed increased much more rapidly than in earlier revivals.

Earnings per hour increased much more rapidly than in earlier periods of revival.

The total wage bill of manufacturing industries and average labor cost per unit of goods produced increased much more rapidly than in earlier revivals.

It is desirable that we supplement these comparative measurements with others in which some account is taken of changes in the standard of value. A rise of 20 per cent in the average selling prices of manufactured goods will have one meaning when the general level of prices remains constant, a quite different meaning when the general price level falls 20 per cent. So, also, a given gain in aggregate pay rolls will have one meaning when living costs remain constant,

TABLE 44

CHANGES IN MANUFACTURING OPERATIONS DURING FIVE PERIODS OF BUSINESS EXPANSION APPROXIMATELY EQUAL IN DEGREE OF RECOVERY

VALUE AND PRICE SERIES CORRECTED FOR CHANGES IN THE VALUE OF MONEY

Percentage change from

	Dec. 1921–Jan. 1922 to Sept.–Oct. 1922	June–July 1924 to Feb.–March 1925	Nov.–Dec. 1927 to April–May 1929	Feb.–March 1933 to May–June 1933	Feb.–March 1933 to Dec. 1934–Jan. 1935
Gross income and its elements					
1. Gross income [1]	+32	+33	+32	+35	+29
2. Production (physical volume)	+33	+36	+31	+39	+37
3. Selling price of product (average) [1]	−1	−2	+1	−3	−6
Wage disbursements and elements					
9a. Wage disbursements [2]	+27	+12	+18	+15	+46
5. Wage earners employed	+16	+7	+9	+8	+31
10. Earnings per wage earner (average) [2]	+9	+5	+8	+6	+11
4. Total employment (man hours)	+19	+14	+13	+21	+23
11. Hourly wages (average) [2]	+7	−2	+4	−5	+19
9b. Wage disbursements [1]	+15	+5	+15	+7	+26
2. Production	+33	+36	+31	+39	+37
12. Labor cost per unit (average) [1]	−14	−23	−12	−23	−8

[1] For the three earlier periods the index of selling prices of manufactured goods is that of the U. S. Bureau of Labor Statistics. The all commodities index of wholesale prices of that Bureau was used in deflating all series into which these prices enter. For the last two periods the index of selling prices of manufactured goods is that of the National Bureau of Economic Research. The National Bureau's general index of wholesale prices was used in deflating the series into which the prices of manufactured goods enter.

[2] The index of the cost of living of industrial workers constructed by the National Industrial Conference Board was used throughout as a deflator.

and a different meaning when living costs are rising rapidly. No single instrument, suitable for correcting all our value series for changes in the value of money, is available. However, by using a general index of wholesale prices in deflating certain series and an index of living costs among industrial wage earners for other series, we may approximate the measurements we desire (Table 44).

It is apparent from a comparison of Table 44 with Table 43 that certain distinctive features of the recovery of 1933–35 have been due entirely to the more rapid rise of general prices. The apparent advantage of the more recent recovery in respect of per unit gain in the selling prices of manufactured goods is removed, when account is taken of changing monetary values.[21] So, also, the gain in the gross income of manufacturing industries, which was higher for the recent period than for any of the earlier periods, when current dollars were the standard of value, becomes the lowest of the figures compared when correction is made for changing monetary values.

Recent advances in wage disbursements and in the rewards of labor remain substantially above similar gains during earlier periods of recovery, after full account is taken of changing living costs. The total purchasing power of manufacturing labor increased 46 per cent between the low point of early 1933 and the beginning of 1935. The nearest approach to this figure came in the 1921–22 recovery, when pay rolls, corrected for changes in the cost of living, ad-

[21] The 6 per cent loss in per unit worth of manufactured goods between February–March 1933 and December 1934–January 1935 is to be interpreted with reference to the base from which the change is measured. At the low point of early 1933 manufactured goods enjoyed a much greater relative advantage than in any of the three preceding depressions. Reduction of this advantage was the more imperative, therefore, with reference to the conditions of general recovery.

vanced 27 per cent. Comparison of the entries for the last two periods shows that the major part of the recent gain of 46 per cent came after mid-summer, 1933. Reference to the measurements relating to average real hourly wages shows that the novel factor in this gain was a sharp increase in real hourly rates of pay (i.e., money rates corrected for living costs). The rise of 19 per cent in these rates, from 1933 to 1935, stands in notable contrast to the narrower movements of earlier revivals.

If we may measure changes in the purchasing power of the manufacturer's dollar with reference to changes in the general level of wholesale prices, and deflate total pay rolls accordingly, we have the corrected wage disbursement figures given as item (9b) of Table 44. In dollars of constant purchasing power at wholesale the wage bill of manufacturing industries shows an advance of 26 per cent over the period of recovery in 1933–35. This is distinctly higher than the advances during earlier revivals marked by roughly equal increases in the volume of manufacturing production. The explanation is found in the measurements of changing labor costs, per unit of product. In terms of the same constant dollars, these costs dropped 8 per cent from 1933 to 1935, as compared with drops of from 12 to 23 per cent in earlier recoveries.

Perhaps the most significant comparisons to be made, among the measurements in Tables 43 and 44, are those relating to the changes from February–March 1933 to May–June 1933 and from February–March 1933 to December 1934–January 1935. The actual degrees of recovery were nearly the same; the bases from which changes are measured are identical. It is reasonable to assume that the differences between the two sets of measurements are due to new factors introduced into the operations of manufacturing industries after June 1933. The most important of these new factors were those connected with the industrial codes.

Summary: Industrial Productivity, Manufacturing Margins and Selling Prices

The bottom of the depression found production and employment in manufacturing industries unprecedentedly low. The problems of readjustment brought by the general decline of prices during the preceding four years were acute in these industries. Various factors impeded rapid adaptation to a new set of operating conditions. Heavy investment in capital equipment at a price level much higher than that prevailing after the recession was one of the most important. At the low point of the depression overhead costs, labor costs and selling prices were relatively high in manufacturing industries. The purchasing power of all those drawing incomes from these industries had been materially reduced. Material costs, however, were low, and productivity had increased during the four years of recession. If recovery in volume could be effected, prompt improvement in other respects could be expected. But this recovery in volume was in part conditional upon correction of certain of the adverse price relations that had developed during the recession. In particular, a substantial advance in raw material prices, relatively to the prices of manufactured goods, would provide a stimulus to the buying power of primary producers and would help to restore the volume of intergroup trade.

The first part of this survey dealt with the relative changes of prices among raw materials and manufactured goods during recovery. Material reduction of the wide margin separating the prices of these two groups of commodities took place during the first five months of recovery. There were some variations in the degree of change occurring among different

MANUFACTURING INDUSTRIES   343

classes of raw and of processed goods, but with one minor exception the moves towards pre-recession and pre-War trading relations were considerable. During the ten months that followed this correctional movement was checked and, except among mineral products, was rather sharply reversed. The summer months of 1934, which were marked by particularly adverse conditions in farming areas, brought a resumption of the movement towards earlier price relations. For raw producers' goods as a class a considerable net gain had been effected by the early summer of 1936, but the differential price advantage of manufactured goods remained substantial by standards of 1929, and even greater by 1913 standards.

Materials of another sort were utilized in tracing a variety of movements affecting the internal operating conditions of manufacturing industries during the most recent recovery and earlier phases of revival. It was found that the advance of the pre-code period, from February–March 1933 to June–July 1933, definitely followed the pattern of earlier periods. Primary emphasis was on production as a means of expanding income, profits and the returns of labor. Production advanced more rapidly than selling prices. Production advanced more rapidly than the number of persons employed, and productivity per worker increased. Production advanced more rapidly than number of man hours worked, and output per man hour increased. Production advanced more rapidly than wage disbursements, and labor cost per unit of product declined. Expanding production was a major factor in advancing gross income.

With respect to the purchasing power of labor, expanding production again played a dominant part. Labor costs per unit of output declined, with rising volume augmenting the total wage bill. Time rates for labor held practically constant, during revival; increasing man hours of employment operated as the active factor in the expansion of aggregate returns. Total employment (man hours) rose more rapidly than the number of persons employed; hours of employment per person increased.

Rapidly increasing production and more slowly rising prices contributed to a sharp advance in gross income. This meant, although present records do not bear on this point, immediate increases in profits, in the aggregate.

These were the conditions accompanying a revival of the traditional type. There is, of course, no reason to accept the pattern of earlier revivals as a criterion to which recovery from the depression of 1931–33 should necessarily have conformed. This was a graver depression than those we had known before; it differed in character as well as in degree from similar periods of economic stagnation in the past. Moreover, the periods of activity that were launched by these earlier revivals were marked by important economic as well as social defects. There is nothing sacred about the standard defined by these precedents. Yet, in default of other standards, we must get from them such information as we may concerning the operating conditions of this little-understood industrial machine of ours.

The recovery of 1933–36 is differentiated from earlier revivals by a reversal of the traditional pattern that may be dated, it appears, from the general adoption of industrial codes that began in mid-summer, 1933. Of course, it is not fair to conclude that the codes alone accounted for all the reversals we have noted. Many circumstances affected the economic changes of these disturbed months. But it is a just assumption that the new industrial environment created by the codes had an immediate effect upon the internal operating conditions defined by the various ratios presented in earlier sections. This assumption is strengthened by the fact that certain of the dominant tendencies of the pre-code period were again manifest in industrial operations after the termination of the codes.

The outstanding feature of the period of operation under the codes lies in the apparent reduction of emphasis on production and industrial productivity as a means of swelling gross income and increasing the aggregate return of labor. Rising prices with a practically constant volume of production marked this period. The productivity of manufacturing industries (as measured in output per man hour) showed a net gain of 1 per cent after twenty-two months of operation under the codes, as contrasted with an advance of 10 per cent during the preceding four months. Too much weight should not be placed upon this development, for the factors involved are complex, and the reasons for changes in productivity are seldom clear. The sharp increase in productivity per man hour during the pre-NRA spurt probably represented almost a full realization of the potential advantages existing at the low point of the depression. A subsequent check does not provide definite evidence of technical or organizational weakness, or of human inefficiency. It is fair to conclude, however, that the new conditions existing after mid-summer 1933 did not provide a stimulus to enhanced industrial efficiency.

An increase in the aggregate purchasing power of labor was one of the objectives of the recovery program, and such an increase was very definitely won. Over some twenty-two months, while the physical volume of manufacturing production was increasing 37 per cent, aggregate wage disbursements by manufacturing industries increased 65 per cent.[22]

---

[22] These figures relate to changes between February–March 1933 and December 1934–January 1935. The percentages of increase in production and wage disbursements become 58 and 92, respectively, if the records are carried to February–March 1936. Since the present figures are given for comparison with movements in earlier revivals, the shorter period is covered.

Equal production increases during the three preceding revivals had brought advances of from 14 to 24 per cent in total wage disbursements. What is here notable is not the degree of increase, however. The fact that wage payments had dropped to excessively low levels in the winter of 1932–33 would lead one to expect a sharper relative advance, with recovery. The distinctive features of the recent rise are found in the relations of wage disbursements to other movements of the recovery period. Labor costs per unit of output increased materially; labor costs per unit of time expended rose sharply. In these respects the latest advance departed most significantly from the traditional pattern of revival.

Adjustment of these various measurements to take account of changes in the level of prices and in living costs alters the general picture somewhat. The rise in selling prices of manufactured goods in the recent recovery disappears when such adjustment is made. The increase in the aggregate purchasing power of manufacturing labor is less pronounced than the increase in wages in terms of current dollars (the actual increase in purchasing power amounted to 46 per cent, however, to the beginning of 1935). Similarly, the perspective is changed and the apparent magnitude of some of the recent changes reduced when the changes occurring during the recovery of 1933–36 are measured against 1929 values, instead of 1933 values. But the characteristic features of the recovery of 1933–36 are clearly discernible, no matter what the standard of reference may be. An apparent check to the advance in industrial productivity after mid-summer 1933, maintenance of a short working week and an exceptionally heavy use of men to maintain a given volume of physical output, a relatively sharp advance in the aggregate purchasing power of labor and notable advances in labor costs per unit of time and per unit of product are distinctive of the recent recovery.

MANUFACTURING INDUSTRIES

High labor costs were, of course, a necessary accompaniment of a rapid increase in the time rate of wage payment (unaccompanied by an equal gain in productivity) and of a rise in total wage disbursements far exceeding the increase in physical volume of production. The price of an expansion in purchasing power, so achieved, was the exceptional rise in costs we have noted.

Why did this notable rise in hourly wage rates, in aggregate wage payments, and in labor costs per unit of product not lead to a much sharper rise in the selling prices of manufactured goods than that actually recorded? The prices of manufactured goods rose somewhat less rapidly than the general price level between July 1933 and May 1935. (The price level of all commodities at wholesale rose 15 per cent, that of manufactured goods 12 per cent.) This fact is apparently inconsistent with the advancing costs we have noted.[23] The answer, I think, is that the price advantage

---

[23] If we take account of the relative movements of the prices of raw and processed goods over the entire period from February 1933 to the spring of 1936 definite reductions of the disparities developing during the recession are to be observed. Yet we misread the changes of this period if we fail to note the actual course and timing of these readjustments.

Correction of the disparities existing in February 1933 called for a rise in raw material prices, relatively to the prices of manufactured goods. Between February–March 1933 and June–July 1933 raw materials rose 22 per cent in price, manufactured goods 9 per cent. This was the pre-code period. During the ten succeeding months, from June–July 1933 to April–May 1934, the prices of raw materials rose 8 per cent, the prices of manufactured goods 10 per cent. The earlier ameliorative movements were definitely reversed, during this period of operation under the codes. A new correctional movement took place during the summer of 1934, a movement clearly attributable to the influence of the drought on the prices of farm products. From April–May to August–September 1934 the prices of raw materials rose 10 per cent, the prices of manufactured goods 2 per cent. Thereafter, through the spring of 1936, there was no appreciable change in the relations between the prices of these two groups of commodities.

There was, thus, definite improvement in the relative position of raw materials during the period prior to code enforcement, and during the sum-

already enjoyed by manufactured goods as a result of less severe liquidation during the recession, provided a margin out of which these rising costs could be met without a great additional price rise. The prices of manufactured goods were already high, relatively, and this price advantage, which tended to be nominal rather than real when volume of sales was low, became substantial with an increasing volume of business. The new costs, then, served not so much to advance the selling prices of manufactured goods as to impede a downward adjustment of the real prices of manufactured goods, an adjustment imperatively necessary if the foundations of a lasting recovery were to be laid.* During the forty-three months of recession from July 1929 to February 1933 the prices of raw materials fell 49 per cent; the prices of

mer drought in 1934. When the movements of these two periods are removed, we find price changes working against the downward readjustment of the real per unit value of manufactured goods.

* DIRECTOR'S COMMENT: Other and equally important causes of the failure of these real prices to fall were: the power to sustain prices and restrict output exerted by industry through NRA codes and non-legal monopolistic devices; the relatively large proportion of overhead in manufacturing costs in heavily mechanized industries; the accounting habits which tend to recover all existing overhead even on small volume, thus increasing unit overhead costs; the resistance that large industries are able to offer to capital reorganization or bankruptcy. It cannot be assumed that lower prices would not have been compatible with the existing wage rates if less efficient competitors had been eliminated, if prices had been forced down either by competition or regulation, and larger volume of production had resulted.—George Soule

DIRECTOR'S NOTE: I feel compelled to note my disagreement with much of the above comment and with its implications. I do not wish to carry the discussion too far away from Professor Mills' here and therefore observe only: (1) That in practice, according to my observation—and I should suppose in theory—price reductions are more readily conceded in times of small demand where a large part of costs is indirect and must be met whether or not sales are made than where the cost is more largely a direct cost that need not be incurred unless it is worthwhile to do so; and (2) That I think the comment overrates the effects of the assumed accounting habit.—George O. May

manufactured goods fell 31 per cent. The gain in the real value, that is, in the average per unit purchasing power, of manufactured goods during this period was 11 per cent. In default of a permanent shift in intergroup relations, correction of this condition was essential to the restoration of trade in anything approaching normal volume. Some degree of correction was effected during the period of recovery we have reviewed, but a disparity still existed in 1936. It was this differential advantage existing at the low point of recession,[24] an advantage that became substantial with an expanding volume of production, that made possible the payment of higher labor costs and even made it possible for profits to expand, without an exceptional rise in the selling prices of manufactured goods. But the persistence of the margin that made it possible to meet higher labor costs and to make profits, even though volume of output remained low by normal standards, retarded full expansion of sales and of output and the restoration of employment in customary volume. And in so doing it worked to prevent the restoration of a normal volume of wage disbursements.

In following the notable increases in wage disbursements and in labor costs during the recovery of 1933–36 we should not overlook the severity of the preceding declines. If labor costs be measured in the dollars the manufacturer receives for his products (i.e., if labor costs be deflated by an index of the selling prices, at wholesale, of manufactured goods) we find that in February–March 1936 these costs stood only some 6 per cent above the level of June–July 1929. In the same units, the average selling price of manufactured goods was 4 per cent higher. If labor costs in manufacturing industries were high in 1936, they were high to the extent that

---

[24] The potential advantage resulting from price relations was rendered much greater by a considerable increase in output per man hour during the recession.

the prices of manufactured goods as a class were high. With respect to the relation of labor cost to the selling prices of manufactured goods, the sharp advance of the period of recovery had done little more than correct for the severe recession that preceded. For labor costs per unit of product had fallen 29 per cent, from June–July 1929 to February–March 1933; the selling prices of manufactured goods had fallen 31 per cent. This means that, with only a minor difference, the aggregate wage bill showed a net decline equal to that occurring in the gross income of manufacturing industries. Wage liquidation paralleled the general drop in gross income, during these four years of recession. In this respect, the recession of 1929–33 stands alone, among recent cyclical declines. For, traditionally, the decline in wage disbursements lags behind the drop in the gross income of manufacturing industries, and labor finds itself, at the bottom of the depression, getting a larger share of the aggregate receipts. This was not true of the 1933 situation.[25]

Of course, the difference between time rates of pay and labor costs per unit of product is to be distinguished, in this analysis. If time rates of pay remain constant when industrial productivity is increasing, labor as a producer gets none of the rewards of higher productivity. (As a consumer, of course, manufacturing labor would gain, if the higher productivity

[25] The comprehensive biennial records available in Census compilations throw light on these changes, during the 1929–33 recession. In 1929 total wage disbursements constituted 16.5 per cent of the gross income of manufacturing industries. By 1931 this percentage had increased to 17.4. This change is in accord with past experience. By 1933, however, the percentage had dropped again to 16.8. Liquidation of wages lagged behind the general process of liquidation during the first two years of recession, but thereafter the reduction of wages was speeded up. By 1933 wage payments constituted only a slightly larger fractional part of the gross income of manufacturing industries than in 1929.

were reflected in lower selling prices.) If labor costs per unit of goods produced remain constant when industrial productivity is increasing, manufacturing labor, as a producer, gets rewards of higher productivity in the form of higher pay. If the real selling prices of manufactured goods fail to fall, at such a time, the benefits of the increased productivity are not being passed on to consumers generally. (Agents of production other than labor are almost certain, of course, to gain, also.)

If we compare February–March 1936 with June–July 1929, we find a notable increase in productivity (probably exceeding 25 per cent per man hour), real labor costs per unit of product somewhat higher than in 1929, substantially higher real rates of pay, per hour of work done, and an actual advance in the real prices at which manufactured goods exchange for other goods. In place of the reduction of real production costs and real selling prices that was to be expected in manufacturing industries, in view of the substantial increase in industrial productivity between June 1929 and March 1936, those costs and prices had advanced. At a time when the strongest considerations relating to general recovery called for lower selling prices, these prices were maintained at levels above those prevailing for commodities in general.

There is some analogy between the situation prevailing in manufacturing industries from 1933 to 1936 and that which prevailed from 1922 to 1929.[26] From 1922 to 1929 profits and overhead charges were maintained at high levels, and the selling prices of manufactured goods failed to decline, to a degree commensurate with the increase in industrial productivity and the fall in labor costs during that period. This

[26] See *Economic Tendencies in the United States*, Ch. VIII.

situation tended to reduce marketings and so contributed to the unstable situation existing in 1929. The rise in time rates of pay and in total wage payments in 1933–36, and the failure of overhead and fabricational costs to reflect the great gain in productivity that had occurred since 1929, helped to perpetuate relatively high prices for manufactured goods. (The fabricational costs which thus remained high were not restricted to labor costs. The fact that labor costs did no more than parallel changes in selling prices, when material costs were relatively low, indicates that other fabricational charges, such as overhead costs, remained on the same high level as labor costs.) The advance in the prices of these goods, at a time when such goods were already over-valued, retarded a needed expansion in the volume of sales. During the decade of the 'twenties a high manufacturing differential (profits are here included with the differential) was a factor in preventing the *maintenance* of a large volume of production and sales. From 1933 to 1936 a high manufacturing differential was a factor in preventing the *restoration* of a large volume of production and sales.

We are far from knowing all the conditions essential to the steady and efficient operation of a modern industrial economy. But experience during the last ten years seems to justify one general conclusion. The immediate passing on to consumers of a major part of the benefit of increasing industrial productivity, in the form of lower prices, contributes directly to the maintenance of industrial operations on a high level and to the raising of the standard of living of the people at large. Action designed to procure for special groups the advantages of increasing industrial productivity, or action tending to decrease industrial productivity and advance costs, runs the grave danger of defeating its own purpose, through setting barriers to the maintenance (or the restora-

MANUFACTURING INDUSTRIES 353

tion) of the volume of production and employment that is essential to the general welfare.[27]

[27] The section of this chapter that deals with the operations of manufacturing industries during recovery, and the main parts of the summary, were published as *Bulletin 56* of the National Bureau of Economic Research on May 10, 1935.

CHAPTER VII

CAPITAL EQUIPMENT AND CONSTRUCTION IN RECOVERY

THE economic agents with whose price problems we deal in this and the following chapter are related to the processes of trade in ways quite different from those affecting the operations of primary producers and agents of fabrication. Primary producers enter into the main stream of trade as sellers, essentially. Their operations as sellers are sharply focused and specialized, while their buying operations are diversified and scattered. Fabricators are both buyers and sellers in relation to the main currents of commerce. It is in relative rather than in absolute prices that they are interested, in differentials between the prices of materials and of manufactured goods. Business considerations relating to current market conditions dictate both buying and selling operations. At the terminus of the stream of trade, where finished goods emerge, stand two groups whose interest is that of buyers: ultimate consumers and purchasers of capital equipment. Both groups are buyers of finished goods, and by both the goods purchased are put to their final use without further change of hands.[1]

---

[1] Primary producers and manufacturers are important purchasers of capital equipment. The distinction in the text is between primary producers and manufacturers as operators of the existing productive machinery and the same groups (plus others) entering the capital goods market as buyers of new productive machinery, using their own or borrowed funds. The distinction between the two functions is useful, because of the difference in motives and market behavior.

In buying capital equipment a manufacturer is, of course, concerned with

CAPITAL EQUIPMENT AND CONSTRUCTION 355

Problems of Recovery in Capital Goods Industries

The present chapter deals with recent changes in the prices of goods destined for use in capital equipment, and with construction costs. Unfortunately, we do not have comprehensive records of price changes among finished articles of capital equipment. Price quotations are available for some finished goods of this type (e.g., steel rails, motor trucks), but many of the 'articles of capital equipment, processed' here included are far removed from the machinery and other equipment in which they will perform their final functions. However, quotations on such processed goods intended for use in capital equipment furnish the best available information concerning price changes among articles of finished equipment. We employ these quotations as approximations to the desired measurements, supplementing them, where possible, with prices on finished goods proper.

SOME CONDITIONS IN THE MARKETS FOR CAPITAL GOODS

In dealing with goods that are to be used as instruments of further production we are concerned, of course, with one variety of producers' goods. Demand for capital goods, like that for all producers' goods, is a derived demand, derived from the demand for the final consumers' goods in the production of which the capital equipment will serve an instrumental role. Such derived demand (especially where durable goods are involved and where stocks may be accumulated) is variable, subject to wider fluctuations than is the demand for ultimate consumers' goods. This variability

---

the relation between the price he pays for the equipment and the prices at which goods to be manufactured will be sold. But the connection is much more remote than that between the prices of materials and prices of goods made from them.

characterizes the demand for capital equipment in even greater degree than for other producers' goods. But the demand for capital equipment possesses other important and distinctive qualities which help to explain the recent price history of these goods.

One of the most important of these qualities has to do with the market attitudes of the buyer of capital equipment. The business buyer of materials intended for fabrication and sale must continually consider the current prices of the finished or semi-finished goods he intends to produce. His current manufacturing differential must be maintained or his operating profits are reduced. This is not a deferred or problematical loss. The payment of too high a price for materials will cause an immediate and, ordinarily, a definitely predictable loss. Consequently, the buying of materials for fabrication is inevitably subject to constant pressure and to the keenest discrimination that business judgment can exercise. For an operating loss under ordinary conditions provides obvious and easily interpreted evidence of managerial incompetence. Business acumen and the full force of manufacturers' bargaining power are continually bearing on the prices of materials of fabrication. The situation is different, in respect of capital goods. (Highly competitive conditions of supply may exist, of course, but we are here concerned with the attitudes and practices of buyers.) The reason is found partly in the character and source of the funds used for the purchase of capital equipment, partly in the way in which capital costs enter into business and accounting practices.

Purchases out of capital funds, particularly in a period of prosperity, are not always subject to the scrutiny and careful balancing of relative values that mark the purchase of goods used in the ordinary course of production. The occasional nature of capital expenditures, as against the continuity of purchase characterizing goods entering into fabrication, is a factor tending to lessen the effectiveness of the buyer's bargaining. Lack of standardization and the presence of patented features may restrict competition in the markets for certain types of capital goods. Again, unless business management is exceptionally alert and conscientious, wasteful practices are likely to creep into the expenditure of surplus funds, perhaps painlessly accumulated in prosperous years, or of capital funds acquired in other ways.[2] The checks to inefficient spending usually affecting the disbursement of current business receipts are likely to be absent under these circumstances. Waste and error are less immediately obvious. Of course, this relaxation of vigilance may not occur among the most carefully managed enterprises, but these concerns by no means monopolize the business field. There was probably some wasteful expenditure of business surpluses during the expansion preceding the 1929 recession.

Equally important, in reducing buying discrimination in the markets for capital goods, is the circumstance that capital expenditures affect production costs only indirectly, and with a time lag. High capital charges may create very real business difficulties, but the difficulties are removed in time from the initial act of spending capital funds for physical goods. There is not the immediate check to faulty spending that current manufacturing and selling operations provide, when operating costs are in question. One reason for this is found in the role played by the rate of interest, in determining the annual charges against the investment. A cost substantially higher than one which had been considered proper might be accepted with equanimity, if the rate at which capital were obtained could be cut somewhat. Indeed, since

[2] Tax systems, or methods of rate regulation if the enterprise be a public utility, may provide an actual stimulus to investment of surplus, with costs still further subordinated to other considerations.

the rewards of bargaining or of careful timing may be greater in respect of the interest rate to be paid than in respect of the factors entering into the market price of new capital equipment, more attention may be given to the former.

The durability of capital equipment is another element affecting market conditions. This durability puts owners and users of capital equipment in position to withdraw from the market, to defer purchases, a fact of great significance in trade fluctuations. The high elasticity of demand for articles of capital equipment (and for durable consumers' goods which are in some ways closely related to capital goods) is one manifestation of this ability to defer current purchases.

For these various reasons we would expect the market relations of capital goods to differ from those of other producers' goods and of consumers' goods. During periods of sharp demand, in particular, less efficient buying is perhaps to be expected, with a consequent enhancement of the market strength of sellers of capital goods. The tendency in this direction is strengthened by conditions on the supply side. Unlike the raw materials of manufacture, many of which are produced under highly competitive conditions by many individual units, articles of capital equipment are turned out, in the main, by relatively few large enterprises, exercising far greater control over supply. This circumstance intensifies those previously cited in tending to strengthen sellers and weaken buyers, in their usual market operations.

CAPITAL GOODS INDUSTRIES IN PERIODS OF REVIVAL; PROBLEMS OF RECOVERY, 1933–1936

The highly variable nature of the demand for capital goods, together with the technical conditions prevailing in most capital goods industries, causes wide fluctuations in their production. Feverish activity in periods of expansion

CAPITAL EQUIPMENT AND CONSTRUCTION 359

and sharp curtailment of activity in times of recession mark the cyclical behavior of capital goods industries. The upward movements of general business recovery and the reactions of recession have been accentuated, often dominated, by these changes.

Many factors determine the degree of activity of capital goods industries at any time. Outstanding are the opinions of business men concerning the need for new capital equipment, the cost and availability of investment funds, and price relations affecting the cost of capital goods. The state of business opinion as to the need for new equipment (which is in part determined by price conditions and interest rates) is the active element in the situation. Without a satisfactory outlook in this respect renewed activity after a depression is not likely to develop.

Business opinion on the need of new equipment is shaped by prevailing expectations concerning the volume of production and trade, and by the adequacy of existing equipment. Opinion at any time is far from uniform, in these respects. Quite apart from differences in different trades there are great differences among business men in astuteness, foresight and willingness to gamble on the future. One business man may expand his plant in the darkest days of depression, against the expectation of a consumer demand that is perhaps barely in evidence. Others will defer expansion until prosperity is nearing its zenith. So, also, there are wide differences among business leaders in their appraisals of the adequacy of existing equipment. The shrewd planner may see possibilities of efficiency in a new device that will lead him to scrap machinery still thoroughly adequate, by conventional standards, while less daring managers will use old equipment until it is more obviously outmoded. The actions of far-sighted men in expanding and modernizing industrial plants during periods of generally stagnant business or at very early stages of revival were a powerful factor in stimulating recovery in the capital goods industries in pre-War business cycles.

The role of interest rates and prices in the markets for capital goods has been suggested in the preceding pages. The possibility of securing long-term investment funds at low rates is an important facilitating element in the renewal of activity in capital goods industries. During depression corporate surpluses are usually cut down, through the maintenance of dividend payments in excess of current income. Private saving continues, however, though in reduced volume, and investment funds accumulate. This accumulation, in the face of greatly lowered demand, brings low interest rates and helps to create conditions favorable to renewed activity in the production of capital goods.

The degree to which the prices of capital goods have declined, during recession, also bears upon the problem of recovery. In making a decision to replace or expand an existing industrial plant account must be taken of the costs of labor and equipment, in relation to the prospective volume of production and the selling prices of the products. Technical and investment conditions might be highly favorable to expansion in the capital goods industries, but high prices, relatively to the post-recession level of general prices, might be a barrier to a revival of activity. We have said that the price factor may be subordinated to other considerations, in the minds of buyers of capital equipment. This is particularly true of purchases made in periods of business prosperity. Buying in depression and the early stages of recovery involves a more careful weighing of costs. The price factor is likely to be given greater weight at such times, when business men contemplate the purchase or construction of capital equipment. (The deciding consideration remains, of course, present and prospective demand for output.) Some

CAPITAL EQUIPMENT AND CONSTRUCTION 361

power of adaptation on the part of capital goods industries to changed conditions on the price side is an important condition of general business revival.

All these circumstances and others peculiar to the existing situation bear upon the problem of recovery in capital goods industries after the severe recession of 1929–33. Our primary concern is with the cost and price aspects of this problem, but other elements may not be ignored. We must here briefly summarize certain conditions affecting the situation existing in 1932–33.

1. Behind the recession of 1929 lay almost a decade of activity in capital construction at relatively high costs. Available quotations on processed goods intended for use in capital equipment stood, in the early 'twenties, some 15 per cent above the general average of wholesale prices, on a 1913 base; in the last half of the decade this differential had fallen to 7 per cent. The costs of construction materials and of new construction generally were notably high. These were the elements among capital goods chiefly responsible for swelling capital costs. (Prices actually realized by the makers of goods for use in capital equipment, other than construction materials, do not appear to have been materially higher than the general level of wholesale prices during the decade of the 'twenties.) The recession brought reductions in the prices of capital equipment, but these declines were less than those affecting prices in general, and the differential advantage of capital equipment increased (see Chapters II and III).

2. Construction of capital equipment had increased at a rapid rate during the years preceding the recession. In 1929 the volume of capital equipment produced (including non-residential construction and public works) was about 70 per cent greater than in 1922. This may be compared with a rise of 31 per cent in the output of total consumption goods,

including residential construction.[3] During this period of steady, not to say rapid, business expansion the production of capital equipment was adequate to meet all current requirements, and exceeded them in some lines. We entered the depression with a considerable volume of productive equipment, constructed at high costs in anticipation of rapidly increasing demand. The customary phenomenon of excess productive capacity during depression was accentuated as a result of this heavy pre-recession construction. This was true despite the sharp curtailment that the recession brought in the production of capital equipment and of durable goods in general.

3. Reference has already been made to the stimulation of the heavy industries through the accumulation of savings and the consequent reduction of long-term interest rates in the later stages of depression. The amount of free funds available for investment after the recession of 1929–33 was affected by several exceptional circumstances. (These were, of course, of varying importance at different stages of the depression and the recovery.) The practical cessation of foreign lending tended to increase the funds available for domestic purposes. On the other hand, incomes were more drastically reduced than in previous depressions, and saving by individuals was curtailed. Corporate saving was cut sharply by the drop in profits, and corporate surpluses were drawn upon very generally to maintain dividends. Borrowing on insurance policies, the cancellation of existing policies and a check to the preceding rapid advance in new business of life insurance companies reduced the amount of investment funds from this important source. The net effect of these changes was a substantial reduction in the fund of savings available for investment.

Yet, in spite of a decline in new savings and some reduc-

[3] See *Economic Tendencies in the United States*, p. 280.

CAPITAL EQUIPMENT AND CONSTRUCTION

tion in accumulated capital, saving continued, even during the worst years of the depression. The reservoir of investment funds available was never emptied. Working against the use of these funds, however, was the highly important factor of fear among prospective investors. Heavy losses through defaults tended to freeze the flow of new funds into active use. Revelations of questionable banking practices had the same effect. Doubts concerning the future of the monetary standard, and fears that loans would be repaid in depreciated currency, were a heavy depressant upon the activities of potential lenders. Finally, the desire to maintain a high degree of liquidity led financial institutions to oppose long-term commitments.

On the borrowing side, also, conditions were adverse to a resumption of active investment. The protracted character of the depression and uncertainty as to the future checked new investment in industrial plants. Later, more rigorous restrictions upon the issue of securities were blamed by some for tardy recovery, but it is impossible to determine just how important these may have been.

Other forces played upon the investment situation during the early months of recovery. In many industrial fields there had been important technological advances, of the kind that promote obsolescence and stimulate investment in new equipment. Depreciation had cut down somewhat the pre-recession productive capacity of American industry. The investment situation was affected, too, by the diverse price movements of this period. It is with this phase of the general recovery that the present inquiry is directly concerned.

Price and Cost Changes in Capital Goods Industries

The force of the revival that began in the spring of 1933 was felt, with varying degrees of lag, by all elements of the price system. Relative changes in the prices of building materials, of processed goods intended for use in capital equipment and of all commodities, at wholesale, are indicated by the measurements in Table 45.

TABLE 45

ARTICLES OF CAPITAL EQUIPMENT AND ALL COMMODITIES, PRICES AND PURCHASING POWER, JULY 1929—JUNE 1936 [1]

A. MOVEMENTS OF WHOLESALE PRICES

	July 1929	Feb. 1933	July 1933	Oct. 1933	May 1934	Sept. 1934	May 1935	Dec. 1935	Apr. 1936	June 1936
RECESSION AND RECOVERY										
All commodities	100	62	72	74	77	81	83	84	82	82
Articles of capital equipment, processed	100	79	79	82	89	85	85	85	85	86
Building materials, total	100	76	84	88	89	87	86	88	87	88
RECOVERY										
All commodities		100	117	121	125	131	134	135	133	132
Articles of capital equipment, processed		100	100	104	112	108	108	108	108	108
Building materials, total		100	111	116	118	115	114	116	115	116

B. CHANGES IN PER UNIT PURCHASING POWER

	July 1929	Feb. 1933	July 1933	Oct. 1933	May 1934	Sept. 1934	May 1935	Dec. 1935	Apr. 1936	June 1936
RECESSION AND RECOVERY										
All commodities	100	100	100	100	100	100	100	100	100	100
Articles of capital equipment, processed	100	128	109	110	115	106	102	102	104	104
Building materials, total	100	123	116	118	116	108	104	105	106	107
RECOVERY										
All commodities		100	100	100	100	100	100	100	100	100
Articles of capital equipment, processed		100	86	86	90	83	80	80	81	82
Building materials, total		100	95	96	94	88	85	85	87	87

[1] For the full series of index numbers see Appendix IV.

'Articles of capital equipment, processed' and 'building materials, total', in this table, are mutually exclusive categories. Logically, most of the commodities in the latter group fall under the first, more general heading, but for some purposes a distinction is useful. The two groups were combined in certain tables in Chapters II and III.

CAPITAL EQUIPMENT AND CONSTRUCTION 365

The first push of recovery, which carried the wholesale price level up 17 per cent in five months, was not felt by the main group of processed goods intended for use in capital equipment. These remained unchanged in average price, 21 per cent below the July 1929 level. Building materials did advance, though less than the general index. By May 1934 the rise had extended to goods for capital equipment, and building materials had added to their earlier gains. During the four months that followed both groups declined slightly and the general price level advanced somewhat; thereafter, for a year and a half, practically no price changes occurred among these groups.

The movements of recovery are perhaps more significantly portrayed in Part B of Table 45. For both groups the shifting price relations of the recession brought gains of some 25 per cent in per unit purchasing power. The prices of capital equipment and building materials had declined, but their actual market values, per unit, had risen by reason of the much greater drop in general commodity prices. Their real costs, in terms of commodities in general, were prohibitively high at the low point of the depression.[4] Later movements were irregular, but they brought substantial reductions in the exchange value, per unit, of capital equipment and building materials. By June 1936 processed goods intended for use in capital equipment were but 4 per cent higher, in per unit worth, than in July 1929; building materials were but 7 per cent higher. The chief reductions in their relative standing were effected during the first spurt of recovery and

[4] This statement is based upon an examination of quoted prices. The prices actually realized by makers of articles of capital equipment were below the quoted prices, at the low point of the depression. This was a condition prevailing among manufactured goods in general. (*Cf.* Ch. VI.) The price disparity between processed goods intended for use in capital equipment and commodities in general, at wholesale, was therefore not as great as is indicated by the quoted prices.

during the summer of 1934 when drought conditions were giving a fillip to the prices of agricultural products.

The comparisons on the 1929 base, in Table 45, may be supplemented by others, on a pre-War base (Table 46). The purchasing power figures indicate that goods for capital equipment and building materials retained, in June 1936, a considerable advantage over commodities in general, though the wide margin of February 1933 had been reduced materially. The real worth, per unit, of processed goods for use in capital equipment stood 14 per cent higher than in

TABLE 46

CAPITAL EQUIPMENT AND BUILDING MATERIALS
PER UNIT PURCHASING POWER, 1913–1936

	July 1913	Feb. 1929	Apr. 1933	June 1936	1936
Producers' goods for use in capital equipment, processed	100	107	134	113	114
Building materials	100	122	150	130	131

1913; building materials were 31 per cent higher.[5] This condition represented substantially higher costs than in pre-War days. Their relation to other factors affecting activity in the capital goods industries is discussed in a later section.

Additional information is available concerning cost changes in several important subdivisions of the capital goods market. The index numbers of building material prices, in Table 46, relate to but one type of building costs, and even

[5] The index numbers for processed producers' goods for use in capital equipment, which are constructed by the National Bureau of Economic Research, have been deflated by the National Bureau's index of wholesale prices. The indexes of prices of building materials were secured by splicing index numbers of the U. S. Bureau of Labor Statistics for the period 1913–29 with index numbers of the National Bureau for the succeeding years. The deflating index was obtained by splicing the 'all commodities' index numbers of the Bureau of Labor Statistics and of the National Bureau, for the same periods.

CAPITAL EQUIPMENT AND CONSTRUCTION 367

here the coverage is not complete. For certain structures measurements of changes in actual construction costs, including labor costs, are to be had. The problem of measuring such cost movements is troublesome, because of changing engineering practices, leading to shifts in the relative importance of labor and material costs, and difficulties in the way of measuring labor costs during a period of changing efficiency and shifting wage scales. General movements may be followed with reasonable accuracy, however.

Several indexes designed to measure changes in construction costs are brought together in Table 47. When labor costs are combined with the cost of three basic materials, as in the first set of measurements in this table, we secure an index showing a somewhat smaller decline during recession

TABLE 47

CONSTRUCTION COSTS AND WHOLESALE PRICES IN THE UNITED STATES, JUNE 1929–JUNE 1936 [1]

	June 1929	Mar. 1933	June 1933	June 1934	Sept. 1934	Mar. 1935	Dec. 1935	Mar. 1936	June 1936
RECESSION AND RECOVERY									
Basic materials and labor [2]	100	77	79	97	98	94	95	98	99
Construction of a standard concrete factory building [3]	100	87	88	93	93	93	93	94	96
All commodities, wholesale	100	63	69	79	82	83	84	83	83
RECOVERY									
Basic materials and labor [2]		100	103	126	127	123	123	127	129
Construction of a standard concrete factory building [3]		100	102	107	107	107	107	108	110
All commodities, wholesale		100	109	126	130	132	134	132	131

[1] The dates shown here differ from those in other tables because the index of costs involved in constructing a standard concrete factory building is available quarterly only.
[2] Index of the *Engineering News–Record,* which is based upon the costs of steel, cement, lumber, and the wage rates of common labor reported from about 20 cities. The prices are weighted on the basis of total production of steel, cement, and lumber, and the total amount of labor (man hours) used.
[3] Index of the Aberthaw Construction Company.

than that in the prices of materials alone, and a much more pronounced rise during recovery. From March 1933 to June 1936 the *Engineering News-Record* index of the cost of steel, cement, lumber and labor advanced no less than 29 per cent, as against a rise of 16 per cent in the index of building materials prices, at wholesale, from February 1933 to June 1936. Since the rise in the index of the *Engineering News-Record* started from a relatively high value in March 1933, these costs (which of course do not cover all building charges) in the summer of 1936 stood only 1 per cent below the 1929 level; general wholesale prices were 17 per cent below.

The costs of constructing a standard concrete factory building fell approximately 13 per cent during the recession, as compared with a drop of 37 per cent in general wholesale prices; these construction costs rose 10 per cent from March 1933 to June 1936, advancing to a level only 4 per cent below that of 1929.

The measurement of these changes with reference to a pre-War base involves a greater margin of error, as with all price and cost comparisons over long periods, but the results throw light on the present situation (Table 48). When recession

TABLE 48

CONSTRUCTION COSTS AND WHOLESALE PRICES IN THE UNITED STATES, 1914–1936

	June 1914	June 1929	March 1933	March 1936	June 1936
Basic materials and labor	100	232	179	227	231
Construction of a standard concrete factory building	100	190	165	178	182
All commodities, wholesale	100	151	95	125	125

started in 1929 construction costs of all sorts were far above the general level of wholesale prices, relatively to pre-War standards, and this margin of advantage was materially wid-

CAPITAL EQUIPMENT AND CONSTRUCTION 369

ened during the period of declining prices. Prices and wage rates are subject to a degree of control in this field exceeding that found in most areas of economic activity, and offer greater resistance to downward revision. The advances of recovery in construction costs were somewhat smaller than those in general wholesale prices, but they were sufficient to leave such costs in the summer of 1936 higher in relation to the general price level than in 1929. In June 1936 the average cost of basic construction materials (steel, cement and lumber) and labor, together, was more than twice as high as in 1914. When account is taken of all the costs of constructing a standard concrete factory building, the June 1936 level was approximately 82 per cent higher than in 1914. The level of general wholesale prices was 25 per cent higher. The difference is significant, even when account is taken of the difficulty of securing accurate measurements of changes in wages and prices over these twenty-two years, and of the corresponding margin of error in the results.[6]

[6] C. F. Lambert has constructed measurements of the cost of reproduction (new) of five types of public utilities plants, which may be used to supplement the Aberthaw index of the cost at different dates of building a standard concrete factory building.

INDEX NUMBERS OF THE REPRODUCTION VALUES (NEW) OF FIVE COMPLETE UTILITIES *

	1913	1922	1929	1930	1931	1932	1933	1934	1935
Waterworks plant	100	176	180	177	167	153	159	176	176
Electric light plant	100	172	178	169	158	142	151	169	168
Street railway system	100	181	170	167	155	144	144	154	153
Natural gas plant	100	171	184	181	176	166	169	181	180
Artificial gas system	100	181	183	176	168	157	163	178	179
Wholesale prices	100	148	148	134	113	100	103	117	124

SOURCE: C. F. Lambert, *Engineering News–Record*, 'Construction Costs', (1936 ed.), p. 28.

* Includes a small fixed price for land.

The costs, in 1935, of reproducing four of the five plants here listed, were

Other scattered data relating to the price movements of capital equipment and construction during recession and recovery show diverse tendencies. Prices of automobile trucks declined 24 per cent from 1929 to 1933; there was no change from 1933 to 1935. Here is a reduction, up to the latest date, exceeding that in wholesale prices at large. If account could be taken of quality changes an even greater decline would be indicated. Farm machinery, at wholesale, declined in price some 11 per cent from 1929 to 1933, and rose, by 1935, to within 4 per cent of the 1929 level.[7] Equipment of this type increased in relative value during the period of recession and recovery.

	1929	1933	1934
Railroad construction costs			
Road	100	79	82
Equipment	100	82	91
Steam locomotives	100	88	94
Other locomotives	100	75	84
Freight train cars	100	78	89
Passenger train cars	100	88	94
Motor equipment of cars	100	88	94
Floating equipment	100	87	93
Work equipment	100	85	91
General expenditures	100	80	82
Total	100	80	84
Wholesale prices	100	69	79

SOURCE: Interstate Commerce Commission, Bureau of Valuation. The wholesale price index is that of the U. S. Bureau of Labor Statistics.

(*Footnote* 6 *concluded*)
about 5 per cent below the 1929 costs; costs for the fifth plant were only 10 per cent below. Equally significant is the fact that the 1935 costs for four of the five plants stand from 68 to 80 per cent higher than in 1913; the lowest figure, for natural gas plants, is 53 per cent higher. Wholesale prices were 24 per cent above 1913.

[7] The index numbers for trucks and farm machinery are those of the U. S. Bureau of Labor Statistics, which are based upon quoted prices.

CAPITAL EQUIPMENT AND CONSTRUCTION 371

Detailed figures on railroad construction costs and on the cost of railroad equipment are compiled by the Interstate Commerce Commission. The evidence is illuminating and is worthy of attention.

The three main elements of railroad construction costs fell from 1929 to 1933 by amounts ranging from 18 to 21 per cent. Road costs and general expenditures were only slightly higher in 1934, but equipment costs advanced materially, and stood well above the level of wholesale prices. There is some variation among the elements of equipment costs; non-steam locomotives were at substantially lower cost levels than other forms of equipment. This detailed cross-section of an important subdivision of capital costs is probably fairly representative of heavy equipment. Costs were reduced considerably, but the reductions lagged behind the fall in wholesale prices at large.

The price advance that started in 1914 was, in effect, a great tide, that carried up to new levels practically all the prices and costs that define working and trading relations. When it receded after fifteen years it left many elements of the price system at these high levels. The reasons are many, but here it is sufficient to note the natural tendency to go with a tide of rising values, and to fight the currents of the ebb, when prices are receding. When strategic position makes strong resistance possible on the part of certain economic elements, or when entrenched costs may not readily be reduced, successive flow and ebb are certain to leave just such major price discrepancies as existed in 1933, and which persisted, for many groups, into 1936. Among the elements marked by notably high costs in 1936 were those entering into the construction of permanent industrial equipment. Whether we judge these by 1929 or by 1913 standards we find prevailing costs in this field to be well above the level of prices in terms of which most economic activities are now conducted.[8]

The discussion of price and cost changes among capital goods, with reference to the demand for new equipment, involves the question of obsolescence. Obsolescence, as distinct from the physical process of depreciation, may arise from invention, from improvement in designs or materials, from such a shift in operating conditions as is caused by changes in wage rates, or from a reduction of costs in the production of capital goods which enables producers to replace old equipment by new instruments carrying a lighter burden of capital charges. (The term 'replacement' is used, of course, with reference to the economy as a whole, since a producer already provided with equipment would not buy new equipment of the same type merely because the price fell. Competitive replacement, however, may substitute a low-cost producer, using new equipment, for a high-cost producer, with old equipment.) Thus a sharp reduction in costs may render obsolete much old equipment which, with respect to physical depreciation alone, might have long remained in operation.

Much of the capital equipment with which we entered the recession of 1929–32 had been produced at the relatively high costs of the preceding decade. The writing-down of the capital charges borne by such equipment is a painful process, seldom carried through rigorously in default of the actual reorganization of industrial enterprises. This writing-down

[8] Of course, we should recognize that improvements in the quality and efficiency of capital equipment might have paralleled and in some degree offset the advance in costs. Some tendency in this direction was undoubtedly present, and for many specific instruments actual declines in costs occurred. But the bulk of the commodities included in the group 'articles of capital equipment, processed' are not highly fabricated instruments; they are articles at an earlier and less specialized stage of fabrication. There is little reason to believe that quality changes in them would offset the price differences to which attention has been drawn.

CAPITAL EQUIPMENT AND CONSTRUCTION

was not carried through in any complete manner during the recession, and the recovery measures, in general, were aimed at the prevention of liquidation and reorganization. These measures may well have been thoroughly justified, in this respect, since wholesale reorganization effected over a short period may mean general economic demoralization. But the result was to leave the economy with a heavy burden of overhead charges, which tended to prevent a downward readjustment in the selling prices of finished goods.

We have noted one other method of effecting reduction in overhead charges after a general price decline, a method more gradual in its working and for this reason less painful in its incidence. If the costs of producing industrial equipment in the succeeding period of lower prices are reduced in proportion to the general price decline, the purchase of new equipment may be attractive and profitable, even in the face of sub-normal demand for consumers' goods and a considerable carry-over of old equipment. New, low-cost equipment in the hands of new business enterprises contributes in two ways to the enforcement of lower prices to final consumers. It carries lower overhead charges, and its product may be sold at lower prices. Furthermore, competitive pressure from this source forces the writing-down of the high charges that have been carried against the old equipment produced prior to the recession. Lower overhead charges and lower prices contribute to that stimulation of a higher volume of sales, of production and of employment that is the basic condition of enduring recovery.

The process is painful, of course, to those producers whose equipment was built at the high prices of the pre-recession period, but it is an essential part of the process by which a competitive economy may be made to function efficiently. The relatively high costs of new construction and of some forms of capital equipment that persisted in the face of the great decline in general prices from 1929 to 1933 constituted a real obstacle to renewed activity in the capital goods industries and to the restoration of a normal volume of production and employment. The loose buying that is likely to occur in capital goods markets during prosperity is replaced by a sharper questioning of costs in depression. The quotations of 1935 and 1936 reveal a definite improvement in respect of the relative prices of commodities entering into capital equipment. The rise in the prices of other goods had reduced the margin of advantage enjoyed by goods destined for use in capital equipment. In so far as the prices of these goods represent the cost of finished equipment, substantial progress in price readjustment had been made. The costs of new construction, however, remained at relatively high levels in the early summer of 1936.

As a factor supplementing and supporting the improved price situation in capital goods industries in 1935 and 1936, definite obsolescence on the technical side became increasingly important. It is estimated that in 1925 some 44 per cent of the machine tools in use in American factories were over ten years old; in 1930, 48 per cent had passed this age limit. In 1935, 65 per cent of the metal working machines in the United States had been in use for more than ten years. This increase in the percentage of old machines in use resulted from a pronounced decline in the expenditures of manufacturers on the replacement of machine tools. Over the five years 1930–34 such expenditures are estimated to have been 42.6 per cent of similar purchases from 1925 to 1929.[9] Al-

[9] These estimates are based upon studies of machine tool obsolescence made every five years by the *American Machinist*. The 1935 estimates are based upon questionnaires sent to approximately 10,000 factories—about 7 per cent of the manufacturing establishments in the country in 1933. The actual figures for 1935 indicate that of a total of 1,345,447 metal machines 879,522 were over ten years old (see *American Machinist,* April 24, 1935).

CAPITAL EQUIPMENT AND CONSTRUCTION 375

though the latter were abnormally high the falling off is significant. There is no doubt that depreciation and obsolescence had been at work during the whole period of recession and depression, and that a potential replacement demand of considerable proportions existed in the capital goods markets in 1935.

AVAILABILITY AND COST OF CAPITAL FUNDS

Direct market costs constitute but one of many factors that shape the decisions of prospective buyers and builders of capital goods. We have already referred to the influence of prevailing interest rates. It will be helpful, in considering the state of activity in capital goods industries during the last several years, to give some attention to variations in the amount of available funds.

Changes in some of the elements entering into the aggregate of funds available for investment are indicated in Table 49. These items fall far short, of course, of covering the entire field of savings, but they reflect changes in certain major elements. From 1930 to 1932 there was a steady depletion of savings, as here represented. Savings deposits declined, the assets of building and loan associations were reduced, and corporate surpluses were drawn upon heavily. (We have used, of course, a net figure for corporate savings. Many individual corporations may well have added to their surpluses in these years.) The amount of premiums received by life insurance companies kept up very well, but this favorable condition was partly offset by an increase, from 1929 to 1932, of almost one billion dollars in the amounts paid to policy holders on account of surrendered policies. Reductions in most of these elements persisted into 1933, but with lessened force. By 1934 savings deposits were increasing, the rate of decline in corporate surpluses had been greatly reduced, and

TABLE 49

CERTAIN MAJOR ITEMS OF SAVINGS IN THE UNITED STATES,
1929–1935

(millions of dollars)

	1929	1930	1931	1932	1933	1934	1935
Total savings and other time deposits as of June 30 [1]	28,218	28,479	28,220	24,281	21,126	21,753	22,652
Change during year	—195	+261	—259	—3,938	—3,155	+627	+899
Building and loan associations, total assets, as of Dec. 31 [2]	8,695	8,824	8,412	7,745	6,972	6,450	5,889
Change during year	+679	+129	—412	—667	—773	—522	—561
Life insurance companies, total admitted assets, less premium notes and loans, as of Dec. 31 [3]	15,103	16,073	16,791	16,948	17,127	17,857	19,191
Change during year	+1,142	+970	+718	+157	+179	+730	+1,334
Annual corporate savings [4]	+1,423	—3,909	—5,877	—6,366	—2,796	—2,340	—1,443

[1] SOURCE: Savings Division, American Bankers Association
[2] SOURCE: U. S. Building and Loan League
[3] SOURCE: Spectator Co. The 1934 and 1935 figures are estimated on the basis of data compiled by the Association of Life Insurance Presidents.
[4] Based on Treasury figures and derived by the Department of Commerce. See *Survey of Current Business*, July 1936.

the premium receipts of life insurance companies were swelling again.

The actual supply of private and corporate savings was curtailed during the first years of recession. Indeed, with sharp reductions in earnings and incomes and heavy capital losses as a result of failures and defaults, this was inevitable. But saving persisted during the depression, and its effects are manifest in the records.

Some indication of the changes recession and recovery

have brought in the cost of short- and long-term funds is given in Table 50. When the recession began rates on short-

TABLE 50

BOND YIELDS, DISCOUNT RATES AND INTEREST RATES, 1929–1936

	July 1929	Feb. 1933	July 1933	May 1934	Sept. 1934	May 1935	Dec. 1935	Apr. 1936	June 1936
Bond yields [1]									
All bonds (60)	4.73	5.73	5.15	4.56	4.63	4.32	4.11	3.90	3.94
Industrial bonds (15)	5.09	7.60	6.16	5.29	5.22	4.65	4.44	4.38	4.44
Call loan renewal	9.23	1.00	1.00	1.00	1.00	.25	.75	.75	1.00
Prime commercial paper, 4–6 months	6	1¼–1½	1¾	1	¾–1	¾	¾	¾	¾
N. Y. Federal Reserve Bank, discount rate	5.00	2.50	2.50	1.50	1.50	1.50	1.50	1.50	1.50

[1] As computed by the Standard Statistics Company.

term loans were relatively high, but long-term rates (as represented by average bond yields) were barely above the average for the eight years preceding. (The yield on 60 domestic bonds had averaged 4.72 per cent from 1922 to 1929.) The lowering of rates that depression usually brings is evident in the short-term series, which had fallen to very low levels by February 1933. The decline in bond yields and the corresponding reduction in the cost of new capital funds were checked by banking difficulties, domestic and foreign, in 1931 and 1932, and by a wave of fear that carried bond prices to unprecedentedly low levels. This is reflected in the high yields (particularly on industrial bonds) that persisted through 1933. By 1934 all rates were lower; short-term commercial rates fell below one per cent.

In spite of the persistence of low rates through 1935, activity was slow to revive in the markets for capital funds and in the heavy industries that are fed by them. On the financial side, this condition is revealed by the figures on new corporate issues in the United States. These records, compiled by the *Commercial and Financial Chronicle,* are given here in millions of dollars. Between 1929 and 1933 the

	1929	1930	1931	1932	1933	1934	1935
New capital	8,639	4,944	1,763	325	161	178	404
Refunding	1,387	529	826	319	221	313	1,844
Total	10,026	5,473	2,589	644	382	491	2,248

issues of new capital—the significant figures with respect to new activity—fell to a negligible fraction of their normal volume; this low state persisted through 1934. In 1935, particularly in the latter half, the flow of investment funds into use quickened appreciably, and this movement carried into the next year. During the first six months of 1936 new capital issues of corporations amounted to 463 millions of dollars, a figure greater than that for any corresponding period since 1931. Totals remained low, by pre-recession standards, but savings were again moving into use.

PRODUCTION OF CAPITAL GOODS

The records of the physical volume of output provide the final index of activity in capital goods industries. Comprehensive statistics covering the production of finished capital goods of all sorts are not available, but the degree of decline in their production during the recession is indicated in Table 51. While the output of manufactured consumption goods was dropping some 20 per cent, from 1929 to 1933, the production of capital equipment declined by amounts ranging from 60 to 80 per cent, for the several types of activity represented in Table 51.

Against this background of recession in physical output we may view the events of recovery. For this period we lack the comprehensive index numbers of manufacturing output

CAPITAL EQUIPMENT AND CONSTRUCTION 379

TABLE 51

PRODUCTION OF CAPITAL GOODS, 1929–1933

	1929	1931	1933
Output of products of manufacture entering into capital goods [1]			
Capital equipment, general	100	49	40
Construction materials	100	57	42
Volume of engineering construction [2]	100	69	32
Volume of non-residential building (floor space) [3]	100	43	18

[1] Index numbers constructed by the National Bureau of Economic Research from records of the Census of Manufactures.
[2] Index constructed from the compilations of the *Engineering News–Record;* total value of engineering contracts awarded deflated by *Engineering News–Record* index of construction costs.
[3] Compiled by the F. W. Dodge Corporation from actual contract records in the 37 states east of the Rocky Mountains.

that are based upon Census records, but various representative figures serve to indicate the general nature of the changes. In following the movements of recovery we may use monthly data, drawn from several fields (Table 52).

TABLE 52

PRODUCTION OF CAPITAL GOODS, JULY 1929–JUNE 1936

	July 1929	Feb. 1933	July 1933	May 1934	Sept. 1934	May 1935	Dec. 1935	Apr. 1936	June 1936
Volume of engineering construction [1]	100	26	20	32	32	34	79	52	60
Volume of non-residential building (floor space) [2]	100	11	19	22	20	25	56	47	43
Cement production [3]	100	18	50	50	46	48	34	51	67
Iron and steel production [3]	100	24	66	66	27	52	65	80	81

[1] Aggregate value of contracts awarded, as compiled by the *Engineering News–Record*, deflated by the *Engineering News–Record* index of construction costs.
[2] Compiled by the F. W. Dodge Corporation.
[3] Published in the *Federal Reserve Bulletin;* not adjusted for seasonal movements.

The declines of recession, as measured on a monthly basis, appear to have been even more severe than the annual data indicate. With the first rush of recovery there was a notable pick-up in the non-construction fields. Of course, a large portion of the increased output of the iron and steel industry went into durable consumption goods (chiefly automobiles), and not into capital goods proper. The rise in this series undoubtedly exaggerates the true degree of recovery in the production of capital equipment. The estimated volume of engineering construction advanced slowly from the low point of the summer of 1933 through the spring of 1935. The last half of 1935 was marked by a very great rise, reflecting generally increased activity in the heavy industries. The measurements of this change relate to contracts awarded, not to actual construction, and therefore anticipate new activity. Furthermore, public works account for a large part of the advance in volume of engineering construction, as well as for some of the recovery in cement production.[10] Cement and iron and steel figures show further advances in the first half of 1936; engineering construction and non-residential building receded.

The protracted resistance of private industry, in the field

[10] In the six closing months of 1933 a total of 108 million dollars was spent on projects financed from public works funds; in 1934 approximately 965 million dollars; in 1935, 1,068 million dollars. The last figure far exceeds the sum of 404 million representing new corporate capital issues in the United States in 1935. Governmental activity in the construction of capital equipment in 1935 greatly exceeded that portion of private activity that is represented by the new capital issues actually recorded. Many issues are not included in this count, however, and much capital expansion is financed out of corporate surpluses and other private funds. There is no basis for an accurate comparison of governmental and private activity in this field.

Two forthcoming studies of the National Bureau of Economic Research (*Gross Capital Formation*, by Simon Kuznets, and *Measures of Capital Consumption*, by Solomon Fabricant) will throw light on changes in the volume of capital in the United States.

CAPITAL EQUIPMENT AND CONSTRUCTION 381

of capital goods, to the forces of recovery is reflected in the volume of non-residential building. Not until the last half of 1935 did this industry feel a real stimulus. In the first half of 1936 activity in the construction of industrial buildings remained more than 50 per cent below the 1929 level.

Comparison of Production and Price Movements, Durable and Non-Durable Goods

The category of durable goods is not the same as that of capital equipment, and precision of analysis is lost by treating the two as identical. The first of these classifications is, of course, the broader, including all capital equipment plus very important classes of durable consumption goods, such as automobiles, refrigerators, radios and residences. An essential difference between the two groupings is that capital goods are instruments employed in the production of further goods, which will in turn enter the market for sale to other producers or to final consumers. A piece of personal equipment may be just as long-lived, but its role in an economy marked by division of labor is fundamentally different, since its products do not enter the market. The conditions surrounding the production of the two classes of goods are somewhat similar, however, and they are alike in that the demand for both capital goods and durable consumption goods is relatively elastic. Their respective modes of behavior during periods of recession and recovery have much in common, and differ in similar ways from the behavior of non-durable goods. This contrast, in respect of price and production movements, is brought out in Table 53, and in Figure 14.

Sharply declining production and relatively well maintained prices characterized the behavior of durable goods during recession. Among non-durable goods production suffered less severely; the chief force of recession fell on prices. Reasons for the differences, as has been suggested, are found partly in the conditions of demand for these two classes of products. The buyers of

FIGURE 14

CHANGES IN PRICES AND PRODUCTION, MANUFACTURING
INDUSTRIES OF THE UNITED STATES, 1929–1936
Durable and Non-durable Products

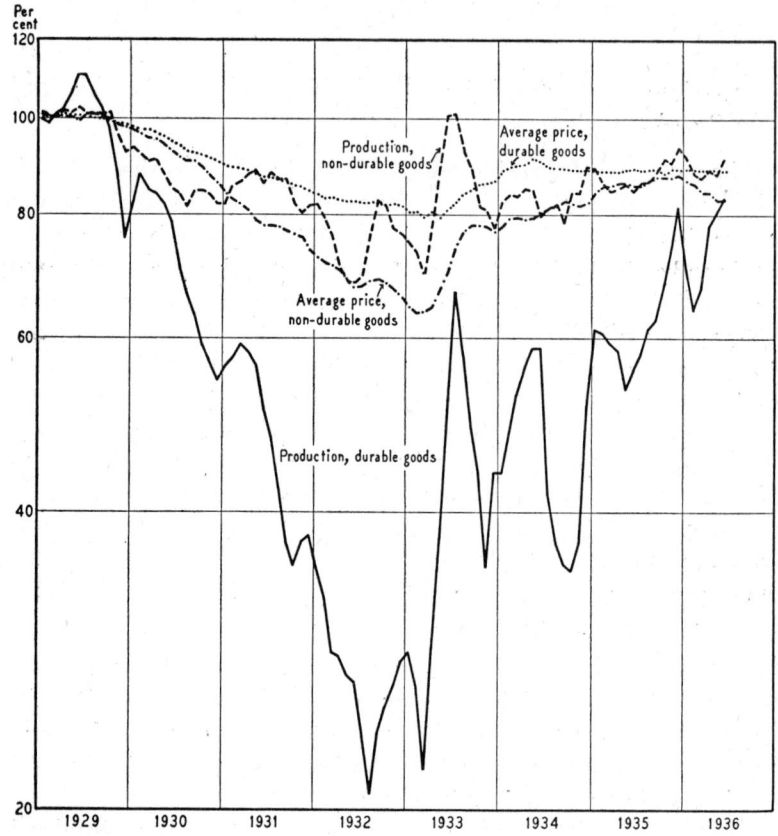

Ratio scale

The base of each of the series plotted in the above chart is the average of that series for 1929. The indexes in Table 53 are on the July 1929 base.

CAPITAL EQUIPMENT AND CONSTRUCTION

TABLE 53
PRICES AND PRODUCTION OF DURABLE AND NON-DURABLE PRODUCTS OF MANUFACTURING INDUSTRIES, JULY 1929–JUNE 1936

	July 1929	Feb. 1933	July 1933	May 1934	Sept. 1934	May 1935	Dec. 1935	Apr. 1936	June 1936
Durable goods									
Average price, wholesale [1]	100	80	82	91	89	88	88	88	88
Volume of production [2]	100	24	61	53	32	49	74	71	75
Non-durable goods									
Average price, wholesale [1]	100	63	74	79	82	85	87	83	82
Volume of production [2]	100	73	101	84	78	85	93	88	91

[1] SOURCE: National Bureau of Economic Research; see Appendix IV
[2] SOURCE: Board of Governors of the Federal Reserve System, Washington; see *Federal Reserve Bulletin*

durable goods, whether for productive or personal use, may postpone their purchases and withdraw from the market to a degree that is not possible to buyers of non-durable goods, in general. This withdrawal from the market is forced upon buyers of capital equipment by declining demand for the consumption goods the equipment is designed to produce. It is the readiest alternative to buyers of durable consumers' goods when their incomes are reduced and doubts concerning their future spending power are instilled by general business recession and depression. Other conditions on the supply side work in the same direction. Producers of non-durable goods are, in general, less able to control supply and to protect prices than are producers of capital equipment and other durable goods. Perishability of product is, to some extent, a factor in this situation. More important, probably, is the lack of agreement and common practice among the many scattered producers of the raw materials that enter into non-durable goods.

The responsiveness of demand for durable goods to changes in real income and in economic outlook is reflected in the sharp rise in production during the early months of recovery. (This pick-up was felt primarily among durable consumers' goods, rather than capital equipment.) The prices of durable goods, already relatively high, rose less than the prices of non-durable goods, which felt the chief stimulus of recovery. By the end of 1935 both sets of prices stood at approximately the same level, some 12 per cent below that of 1929. Thereafter the prices of non-durable goods declined somewhat. Despite sharp recovery in 1935 the output of durable goods remained well below that of non-durable goods, with reference to the 1929 level.

Factors Affecting the Revival of Capital Goods Industries, 1933–1936

Every business depression is marked by a reduction in the proportion of the productive energy of an economy that is devoted to the output of capital goods. Always in time of stress and emergency there is a concentration of activity upon goods of immediate need, a postponement of those efforts that come to fruition only after a relatively long wait. The reasons are numerous, and many are technical, but it is not incorrect to say that in such periods the time span in terms of which human activities are conducted is shortened. The making of capital goods involves the expenditure of effort which is later to be rewarded in the production of consumable goods. A sense of security, an approach to certainty concerning what the future may hold, are essential to such activity. When producers are uncertain as to the probable state of consumer demand, when investors are reluctant to make long-term commitments, when fears and doubts grip buyers, producers and lenders, then the immediate needs of the day take precedence over future possibilities, and all activities that point towards a more distant future are curtailed.

This means, of course, a shortening of the average time lag between the expenditure of economic effort and the act

CAPITAL EQUIPMENT AND CONSTRUCTION 385

of final consumption. Every industrial order is geared to activity involving a certain average time interval between effort and consumption. In general, with economic growth and steady technical improvement, this interval is subject to slow expansion. A continually increasing proportion of the available labor and equipment is used in the indirect activities of production that aim towards a future date. This change is slow, and the economic shifts required for adaptation to it may be effected without particular strain. But when recession and depression bring a sudden, sharp contraction in this interval, prompt and painless adaptation is impossible. Large numbers of men and machines are thrown out of work. Recovery requires either a restoration of the confidence and the technical conditions that make possible activity based on the longer time span, or adaptation to techniques resting upon the shorter (and less efficient) time span. The first of these is characteristic of the recoveries that occur in a progressive economy; it is with the conditions of such revivals that we are concerned, in reviewing the recent history of capital goods industries in the United States.

We may distinguish three aspects of a recovery of this type —reviving demand for consumers' goods, profit opportunities in the use of new capital equipment, and confidence essential to the making of relatively long-term commitments. During depression there is, of course, an actual diminution in the volume of consumers' goods produced, although a much larger proportion of the productive energies of society actually in use is devoted to their output. With recovery consumers' goods industries revive. In the present state of our knowledge of business cycles we may not say that this revival of consumer demand must necessarily precede renewed activity in the production of capital goods. Obsolescence, combined with low costs of funds and materials, may lead to renewed activity in capital goods industries while consumer buying remains at depression levels. But such activity is promptly reflected in consumer incomes, and thereafter the process of revival is marked by reciprocal stimulation of activity in these two fields.

A host of factors affect the opportunities for profit in the use of new capital equipment. The expected market for the final product, the supply of existing equipment in relation to the present and potential demands upon it, the carrying charges it bears, the relative technical advantage enjoyed by new equipment, the costs of capital, materials and labor for its construction, are all elements of the situation. These vary in importance from time to time. Actual construction costs may be given slight weight at certain times, because relatively heavy advantages of other types exist. This appears to have been true prior to 1929, when high costs were cheerfully paid in the face of low capital charges and expectations of sharply expanding demand for final products.

'Confidence' covers those intangible elements that determine the time span in terms of which human calculations may be made, with reasonable expectation of fulfillment. It is essential to activity in the capital goods industries that they who solicit capital for the building of equipment have confidence in their ability to use funds profitably, over a period of time. This is the primary consideration, for it is the decisions of this group that determine whether available funds will be used or not. In addition, men with accumulated funds and with credit facilities at their disposal must have confidence that their funds will be returned to them, and the annual use-value received. Fears concerning the stability of social or political conditions and doubts relating to monetary or other economic matters may chill this confidence, shortening the interval for which men care to commit disposable funds.

The several factors just named are but a few of those that

CAPITAL EQUIPMENT AND CONSTRUCTION 387

affect industries devoted to the construction of industrial plants and the production of the capital equipment of society. Man's forward planning is embodied in the elaborate instrumental equipment that has no value except that which runs backward from the date of its future fruition. Forces released by consumer buying are centered upon the capital goods markets, and their fluctuations appear there in intensified form. A variety of technical influences, related to the process of saving and to the investment mechanism through which savings are converted into plant and equipment, affect economic processes in this area. Here is the heart of modern industrialism. Here are focused the little understood forces that shape the operations of modern economies and determine the living standards of populations.

Some of the economic conditions affecting capital goods industries prior to the recession of 1929 and at the low point of the succeeding depression have been outlined in this and preceding chapters. In summary of these points, we may note the following:

Relatively heavy production of capital equipment during the decade of the 'twenties was stimulated by the pace of industrial expansion and by the cheapness of long-term funds. This production was in some degree misdirected and wasteful, and may well have been excessive even in relation to the rates of growth characteristic of this period. We lack criteria that would make possible a definite judgment on this score. However, there can be no doubt that the check to this growth, and subsequent contraction, left productive capacity well in excess of the curtailed demand of the depression years.[11] Demand for consumers' goods

---

[11] The adverse effects of this condition during depression and the early stages of recovery were probably intensified by an exaggerated impression of its importance, and by a failure to give due weight to the factors of depreciation and obsolescence. 'Over-production' and 'excess capacity' are characteristic features of business depressions. The circulation in recent years

had to revive substantially, to supplement the processes of retirement and obsolescence, before the need for new equipment became imperative.

Reduction of carrying charges on plants and equipment during recession and depression was rendered especially difficult by reason of the relatively high costs of construction that had prevailed among capital goods during the post-War expansion, by the magnitude of the price decline from 1929 to 1933, and by the severity of the drop in output. High costs of materials and labor, which had looked inconsequential in the heyday of prosperity, meant capital charges altogether out of line with the prices of 1932 and 1933. The very severity of the price drop rendered it impossible, in general, to effect an adjustment of capital charges to the new price level by drawing upon reserves and contingent funds. Combined with this was the great decline in the number of units produced, which made the carrying charge on each unit much heavier than it would have been with a well-maintained volume of production.

In 1933 average overhead charges, per unit of goods produced by manufacturing industries of the United States, were about 11 per cent lower than in 1929. This was an appreciable reduction, in view of the obstacles faced, but it fell far short of equaling the changes among all other elements of the final selling price of manufactured goods.

Capital losses, the reduction of current income and the drain upon corporate surpluses as a result of maintaining dividend payments in the face of reduced earnings all served to lower the amount of savings available for investment during the depression years. Current requirements for new capital funds were reduced still more sharply, however. In relation to demand, there was no shortage of accumulated funds during the depression. There was, however, a period of profound financial fear, ushered in by the failure of the Credit Anstalt, in the autumn of 1931, and extending through the banking crisis of 1932–33 in the United

of fabulous accounts of the productive capacity of American industry may have helped to discourage new enterprise in this field.

CAPITAL EQUIPMENT AND CONSTRUCTION 389

States, when rates on long-term industrial loans were exceptionally high. Indeed, the average yield on domestic industrial bonds, as computed by the Standard Statistics Company, did not fall below 6 per cent from October 1931 to February 1934. In June 1932 it rose to a maximum of 9.17; again, in April 1933 it reached 8.27. Short-term rates were low during most of this period, but few long-term commitments were made.

Finally, we have noted the high costs of new capital construction during the depression. Building materials and many processed articles of capital equipment resisted the general price decline. Available wholesale price quotations indicate that by February 1933 these commodities were worth, per unit, in exchange for commodities in general, some 25 per cent more than in July 1929, and from 35 to 40 per cent more than in 1913. If account could be taken of improvements in quality, and of the actual prices realized by makers of capital equipment in the years of greatest depression, a greater fall in certain equipment costs would undoubtedly be revealed. But the general picture of a lagging adjustment of such costs to changing monetary values would probably not be altered. Construction costs were even higher than equipment costs. In March 1933 these stood from 20 to 40 per cent higher (relatively to general commodity prices, at wholesale) than in 1929, and from 70 to 80 per cent higher than in 1914. The world-wide rise in prices and costs from the pre-War level and the subsequent declines, in 1920–21 and in 1929–33, left capital costs in general and construction costs in particular on a high plateau.

Under these conditions recovery in the capital goods industries was abnormally retarded in 1933–36, in comparison with previous business revivals. The program of public works and a very considerable pick-up in certain industries producing durable consumers' goods (notably the automobile industry) brought increases in the production of cement and iron and steel, but the production of capital goods on private initiative definitely lagged.

We have discussed above three elements of recovery in the capital goods industries, reviving demand for consumers' goods, opportunities for profit in the use of new capital equipment, and the confidence essential to the making of long-term commitments. Between 1933 and 1936 consumer demand recovered notably. All available records—wage disbursements, department store sales, etc.—indicate definite improvement. Relief and benefit disbursements by the Federal government and disbursements connected with the public works program played a considerable part in this movement, but private industry contributed as well. This considerable improvement failed, however, to restore a volume of buying approaching that of 1929. In 1934 the total purchasing power of farmers was about 76 per cent of that of 1929; the aggregate purchasing power of manufacturing labor was approximately 73 per cent of 1929. In 1935 the corresponding figures were 83 and 81 per cent.[12] It is true that these were two of the most severely reduced elements of total consumer demand, but they were two of the most important, in aggregate volume. Even after three years of recovery the total flow of goods to consumers remained well below the pre-recession level.

Lack of confidence played a part in the stagnation of capital markets and the delayed recovery of capital goods industries during some stages of the revival from 1933 to 1936. Fear of continued liquidation and the urge for liquidity on the part of financial institutions were important in the early stages. Later, uncertainties connected with dollar devaluation and fears of inflation arising from the unbalanced state of the Federal budget affected some investors. These various doubts contributed to make prospective investors more careful than

[12] Both sets of figures relate to changes in estimated money income, corrected for changes in the prices of goods purchased.

CAPITAL EQUIPMENT AND CONSTRUCTION

they had been before 1929. Funds were not fighting for use, irrespective of risk and of the responsibility of the borrower. But credit reserves and savings were accumulating. By the middle of 1934 the pressure of funds seeking use had spread out from the short-term market (in which rates had long been abnormally low), and bond yields fell below the average of the eight pre-recession years. Lack of confidence on the part of lenders did not play any appreciable role thereafter.

After the panic phase and the period of monetary uncertainty were past, the delayed recovery in capital goods industries appears to have been due primarily to the failure of prospective borrowers to discern opportunities for profitable use of new equipment.[13] These opportunities were not present during the first two years of recovery, except in isolated areas, for two main reasons. In the first place, the productive capacity of the equipment in existence in 1929 was in general adequate to the requirements of the subnormal consumer demand. Depreciation occurred, of course, and definite technical obsolescence during the period of subnormal replacement from 1930 to 1936. But before obsolescence can become effective in stimulating the replacement of old equipment by new, the cost and carrying charges on the new, in conjunction with its efficiency, must offer a real advantage. This was not true, in general, of capital goods industries through the early months of 1935. The obsolescence that becomes real in terms of the actual accounting books of business, obsolescence that would lead to the retirement of the high-cost equipment carried over from pre-recession years, was retarded by the failure of capital costs to decline by amounts commensurate with the fall of prices in general. This was a second and po-

---

[13] Other factors were present. More stringent regulations concerning new security issues engendered some reluctance to borrow at one stage. The limitation of new equipment under certain N.R.A. codes may have been a minor contributing factor in a few industrial fields.

tent factor contributing to the delayed revival of activity in industries making productive equipment. By mid-summer of 1935 the cumulative effect of stronger consumer demand and of an improved relation between capital costs and general prices had combined to effect an appreciable improvement in this sector. The effects of this improvement were clearly evident in the subsequent stimulation of the heavy industries.

CHAPTER VIII

CONSUMERS' GOODS IN RECOVERY

THE War-time advance in prices and the subsequent decline of 1920–21 left the prices of finished goods—articles entering into capital equipment and goods intended for direct consumption—on a relatively high plateau. A variety of forces had widened the fabricational margin and raised the real cost of finished goods. Both labor costs and overhead costs were maintained at high levels, in relation to pre-War standards. It is improbable that this very substantial modification of the pre-War situation and of all earlier tendencies would have persisted without the aid of fortuitous conditions, already noted in Chapter II. Our exports of consumers' goods as well as of capital goods during this period were supported in part by heavy foreign loans. The funds of American investors in foreign securities helped, thus, to sustain the production and the prices of finished consumers' goods. Again, speculative profits reaped from the expanding values of securities and real estate swelled the incomes of consumers. Not all the profits actually realized were expended on consumers' goods, but important elements of the total went into their purchase. Furthermore, taxes were being reduced relatively to the swelling incomes of the prosperous groups. Finally, the rapidly expanding volume of consumer credit represented a new source of purchasing power. The flow of income reaching consumers from the ordinary productive-distributive processes of economic life was thus augmented, during the 'twenties, by important additions, which were essentially non-recurring. These additions were material factors in the maintenance, from 1925 to 1929, of a wholesale price level for finished consumers' goods from 5 to 10 per cent above the level of general wholesale prices, with a correspondingly enhanced level of retail prices.

Price and production movements affecting consumers' goods during the decline from 1929 to the winter of 1932–33 resembled those of earlier recessions. Goods ready for consumption suffered smaller declines than did producers' goods, and so increased in relative worth. This was notably true of manufactured consumers' goods, which in February 1933 had a real per unit value 8 per cent greater than in 1929, 14 per cent greater than in 1913. This circumstance, together with the decline in consumer incomes, reduced materially the volume of goods moving into the hands of consumers. In 1932 the physical volume of manufactured consumers' goods produced was approximately 28 per cent less than in 1929. On a monthly basis the decline was even greater. In February 1933 the output was some 32 per cent less than in July 1929.

True, the drop in the output of manufactured consumers' goods was much less severe than in the production of capital equipment or in construction. Indeed, many classes of consumers' goods declined but slightly, and retail trade in many lines suffered little loss in volume during even the worst years of the depression. It would be easy to conclude that the losses in the consumers' goods fields were relatively inconsequential, that the depression difficulties originate in and are confined to the capital goods industries. But to reason thus would be to misread the evidence and, in some degree, to mistake the character of the causal relations in a business recession. The losses suffered by consumers' goods industries are reflected in intensified form in the earlier stages of the productive process and in the capital goods industries. Activity in these industries depends ultimately upon the possibility of profit in the production and sale of consumers' goods. There are circular relations here, of course. Restriction of investment and of employment in the heavy industries reduces the purchasing power of consumers. But there are strong chains of causal sequence running from consumers' goods industries to capital equipment and producers' goods generally, and these, with the amplifications of expansion and contraction that accompany them, are important factors in the cyclical movements of business. It would be quite wrong, therefore, to conclude that all the forces initiating recession originate in the heavy industries because the contractions in these industries are more severe than those in other economic areas.

The reduction brought by the depression in the output of consumers' goods proper reflected a major decline in the living standards of the people of the United States. It was the physical manifestation of the income losses suffered by farmers, industrial and clerical workers and others, and of the disparate price movements that helped to jam the industrial machine. As among different classes of consumers' goods the decline in production was uneven, of course. Durable consumers' goods (such as automobiles and houses) suffered greater declines than non-durable; the output of luxuries fell off more sharply than did that of necessities. But with very few exceptions all classes of consumers' goods suffered in some degree.

The conditions essential to the restoration of a normal volume of production of consumers' goods were many and complex. Our concern at the moment is with those that are directly related to price and cost factors.

A price readjustment that would raise the aggregate purchasing power of consuming groups was urgent at the low point of the depression. Low prices of raw materials and high prices of finished consumers' goods served, at once, to lower the money incomes of important consuming groups and to reduce the volume of goods that the money incomes would buy. Some of the conditions affecting the prices of raw materials and of fabricated goods have already been touched upon. We have seen, in particular, that the high relative prices of finished goods were in part due to reduced volume and to the difficulty of lowering overhead costs to the depression level of general prices. Here we have an example of the vicious circle of high prices, with resulting low output and sales, and of high costs as a resultant of low volume. Some escape from this condition was sorely needed.

The loss of purchasing power during the depression by producers of raw materials was but a phase of a general decline of the national income, in which all groups shared. Between 1929 and 1932 the total national income paid out declined approximately 40 per cent; wage earners and dividend recipients suffered most severely. A real correction of the situation of consumers called for the restoration of incomes to the pre-recession level, account being taken of changes in the prices of the goods for which these incomes are spent. This was not necessarily a task of restoring 'equilibrium' in the economic system. Equilibrium, as a state of balance among the various pecuniary quantities equated against one another in the distribution of income and the exchange of goods, may be effected at any one of an infinite number of levels. What is required for a high standard of living is equilibrium at a high level of activity. A central problem of recovery, after prolonged depression, is that of breaking the pathological balance that prevails at a low level, with excess productive capacity co-existing with unemployment, and substituting for it a balance at which resources are more fully utilized and standards of living among all producing groups are high.

When economic activity has fallen to a low level, say with high prices and low output on the part of one trading group, low prices and high output for another group, a strong stimulus is needed to break these relations. For, in default of a definite push, a correction of these conditions may be long deferred. Current buying power is balanced against goods currently offered for sale, and since the buying power arises from the operations of producing these goods, subnormal activity may persist for a long period. A stimulus may come from outside the economy, as from heavy foreign orders, or from a changed outlook that leads other producers or consumers to gamble on the ultimate realization of more income than is then in sight. (Other slowly-germinating internal forces may make for ultimate expansion, for the state of balance at the low level is not necessarily a long-run balance.) The elasticity that makes it possible for such a changed outlook to affect current trading relations derives, of course, from the credit mechanism, which can provide buying power before anticipated income is actually realized. Given a stimulus arising from one of these sources, price relations may be modified and equilibrium in terms of a higher physical output achieved.

The problem of breaking the vicious circle of low output and low purchasing power has another important aspect. In a money economy a large portion of the sums that represent disbursements of purchasing power on the one hand represents costs on the other. Salaries and wages on the producers' account books are costs, and must be covered by receipts from the sale of goods produced. If we could ignore the time lag involved we might say that in a completely closed system, in which disbursements representing costs of production went to precisely the group of persons who constitute the final market for the goods produced, whether costs (and related prices) stood on high or low levels would be a matter of indifference as regards the current movements of goods. But when the disbursements go to a smaller group than those who buy the products, or a different group, the relative levels of costs and of prices may be of profound importance. For the prices necessary to cover higher disbursements may be too high, in relation to the current income of the consuming group at large. Under these conditions an advance in costs and in prices may reduce the physical volume of goods sold, or impede expansion. Because buying and producing groups for the major classes of commodities are not identical, in a modern economy, such discrepancies as we have recently witnessed between costs and prices on the one hand and current income on the other may develop. (Time differences enter as well, as factors making for discrepancies.) In the ultimate equations of trading relations these discrepancies are offset by adjustments in quantities, downward adjustments that mean seriously reduced living standards. Here are conflicting requirements to be reconciled somehow in the process of recovery—augmented purchasing power, on the one side, costs and prices adjusted to the lower money incomes of consuming groups at large, on the other. Our survey of the fortunes of consumers during recovery must therefore include reference to those phases of the recovery program that bear upon the cost side of producer-consumer relations.

Among the problems of recovery we should note, too, the situation created by the virtual disappearance of the nonrecurring elements that had bolstered current purchasing power during the expansion of 1922–29. The making of foreign loans by American investors had practically ceased, and the stimulation of the markets for consumers' goods that had come from this source was gone. Speculative profits had been very greatly reduced. Indeed, capital losses doubtless served in some degree to reduce current income available for the purchase of consumers' goods, so that an actual negative factor was introduced. Finally, those important additions to current buying power derived through tapping a greatly expanded reservoir of consumer credit, were greatly reduced.

Of course, recovery held possibilities of new additions to purchasing power from all these sources, but these possibilities did not look very bright at the low point of the depression.

Another problem arises out of this last condition. One important characteristic of post-War expansion was the persistence of high prices for goods ready for final consumption; by all earlier standards the costs to consumers of the services of fabricators were high. Recession accentuated the high cost of living in general and the high prices of consumers' goods in particular, but it is important to recall that these costs and prices had been high prior to the recession. We have noted one reason why a high volume of production and relatively high standards of living were possible under these pre-recession conditions. Abnormal and non-recurring elements swelled the current incomes of important consuming groups during the unusual conditions of post-War prosperity. The disappearance of these elements raised a real question whether even pre-recession price relations might allow a restoration of the volume of production we had known at the height of the expansion of the 'twenties. This question will be before us in the discussion of recovery.

The problems of recovery and the conscious program of recovery in terms of which the Administration acted from 1933 to 1936 centered in a very real sense about the consumer. Perhaps the most critical question was whether the incomes of consumers at large could support an expanding volume of activity under the price and cost conditions inherited from the depression, as modified by the steps being taken under the programs of industrial and agricultural recovery. Monetary measures, modifications of wages and hours in industrial and commercial enterprise, anti-price cutting efforts, the authorization of trade agreements among competing producers, the restriction of agricultural output and the levying of processing taxes for the purpose of restoring a pre-War

400   PRICES IN RECESSION AND RECOVERY

price parity among agricultural and other producers—all these affected the purchasing power of consumers, in some respects adversely, in some respects favorably. Some of these have been discussed in preceding pages. We turn now to the price record.

Price Changes among Consumers' Goods

In following the price movements of recovery, as they affected consumers' goods, we shall deal with changes in per unit worth (purchasing power) as well as with actual prices. The changes brought about by recovery are shown against the background of recession in Table 54.

During the first five months of rapid advance in general prices, manufactured goods ready for use by the final consumer, which were relatively high priced at the low point of depression, lagged. Their prices advanced 10 per cent, while the general average for all commodities rose 17 per cent. Raw consumers' goods leaped upwards 24 per cent. Over the next ten months the rise in the general price level was much smaller. Among goods ready for consumption raw materials declined in price, processed goods continued to advance. Drought and crop scarcity gave a further fillip to raw consumers' goods in the summer of 1934; the next year and a half brought a slight net decline in their prices. Crop conditions in the summer of 1936 stimulated a rise to a new high level. The price of processed consumers' goods, however, showed no net change from September 1934 to June 1936, and for all consumers' goods the rise amounted to less than one per cent.

Chief interest attaches to these changes in relation to earlier standards, and in terms of per unit purchasing power. At the low point of the depression raw consumers' goods were some 10 per cent undervalued, with reference to July 1929

TABLE 54
RECOVERY IN THE PRICES AND PURCHASING POWER OF CONSUMERS' GOODS, JULY 1929–JUNE 1936

A. Movements of Wholesale Prices

	July 1929	Feb. 1933	July 1933	Oct. 1933	May 1934	Sept. 1934	May 1935	Dec. 1935	Apr. 1936	June 1936
RECESSION AND RECOVERY										
Consumers' goods, all	100	64	73	76	77	82	84	85	82	82
Raw	100	56	69	67	67	74	72	73	71	77
Processed	100	66	73	78	80	83	87	88	85	83
All commodities	100	62	72	74	77	81	83	84	82	82
RECOVERY										
Consumers' goods, all		100	113	118	120	126	130	132	128	128
Raw		100	124	120	120	132	128	131	127	138
Processed		100	110	117	120	125	130	132	128	125
All commodities		100	117	121	125	131	134	135	133	132

B. Changes in per Unit Purchasing Power

	July 1929	Feb. 1933	July 1933	Oct. 1933	May 1934	Sept. 1934	May 1935	Dec. 1935	Apr. 1936	June 1936
RECESSION AND RECOVERY										
Consumers' goods, all	100	104	100	102	100	101	101	102	100	100
Raw	100	90	96	90	87	92	86	88	86	94
Processed	100	108	102	105	104	103	104	105	104	102
All commodities	100	100	100	100	100	100	100	100	100	100
RECOVERY										
Consumers' goods, all		100	96	97	96	97	97	97	96	96
Raw		100	106	100	96	101	95	97	95	104
Processed		100	94	97	96	96	97	98	96	95
All commodities		100	100	100	100	100	100	100	100	100

relations, while the real per unit worth of processed consumers' goods was about 8 per cent higher. By June 1936 the index of per unit worth of raw consumers' goods had advanced to 94; that for processed consumers' goods had fallen to 102. The index of per unit purchasing power for all consumers' goods had declined from 104 in February 1933 to 100 in June 1936 (the base of reference is July 1929). In so far as price relations at wholesale define consumers' positions (that is, in so far as no increase occurred in the price margins of retailers), the adverse buying position in which consumers had been placed during the recession had been corrected by the early summer of 1936.

But the 1929 standard is not altogether satisfactory for use in appraising market relations. Consumers' goods had been relatively high priced during the entire post-War expansion. We shall do well, therefore, to refer the price changes of recovery to a pre-War base (Table 55).

TABLE 55

PRICES AND PURCHASING POWER OF CONSUMERS' GOODS, 1913–1936

	July 1913	Feb. 1929	July 1933	Oct. 1933	May 1933	Sept. 1934	May 1934	Dec. 1935	Apr. 1935	June 1936	1936
INDEX NUMBERS OF WHOLESALE PRICES
Consumers' goods, all	100	161	104	117	122	125	131	135	137	132	133
Raw	100	172	96	119	116	115	127	123	126	122	133
Processed	100	159	106	117	124	127	132	138	140	135	133
All commodities	100	150	92	108	112	115	121	124	125	123	122
INDEX NUMBERS OF PER UNIT PURCHASING POWER
Consumers' goods, all	100	108	112	108	109	108	108	108	109	108	108
Raw	100	115	104	110	104	100	105	99	101	99	108
Processed	100	106	114	108	111	110	110	111	112	110	108
All commodities	100	100	100	100	100	100	100	100	100	100	100

For the present purpose the measurements of purchasing power changes are probably more significant than the wholesale price index numbers. An advantage of 8 per cent in per unit worth, which consumers' goods enjoyed in July 1929, was increased to 12 per cent at the low point of the depression. This stood again at 8 per cent in May 1934 and in June 1936. The general post-War advantage persisted, but the special gains of the depression had been erased. During depression and recovery, however, the relations between the raw and processed components of the group of consumers'

CONSUMERS' GOODS IN RECOVERY

goods shifted notably. Raw materials ready for consumption lost a differential advantage of 15 per cent, which they had enjoyed in July 1929, and were restored by April 1936 to approximate pre-War parity with commodities in general. A sharp rise in the second quarter of 1936 created a differential of 8 per cent. The per unit purchasing power of processed consumers' goods was slightly increased, the pre-recession advantage of 6 per cent, on the 1913 base, being raised to 8 per cent, in June 1936. The striking post-War phenomenon of high-priced consumers' goods, persisted, at the last date here shown.

The general picture of the market position of consumers may be clearer if we bring together index numbers relating to three main classes of consumers' goods (Table 56). The

TABLE 56

PER UNIT PURCHASING POWER, AT WHOLESALE, OF THREE CLASSES OF CONSUMERS' GOODS, 1913–1936

	July 1913	Feb. 1929	July 1933	Oct. 1933	May 1933	Sept. 1934	May 1934	Dec. 1935	Apr. 1935	June 1936
All consumers' goods		100	104	100	102	100	101	101	102	100	100
Raw materials ready for consumption (foods)		100	90	96	90	87	92	86	88	86	94
Processed foods		100	96	92	90	92	98	105	106	101	98
Processed non-foods		100	119	110	118	114	108	103	104	106	106
All consumers' goods	100	108	112	108	109	108	108	108	109	108	108
Raw materials ready for consumption (foods)	100	115	104	110	104	100	105	99	101	99	108
Processed foods	100	102	98	94	92	94	100	108	109	104	100
Processed non-foods	100	111	132	123	131	127	120	115	116	118	118

measurements relate to changes in the average per unit purchasing power of goods in each class, as well as all consumers' goods. In preparing this table the price index numbers for the several groups have been deflated by an index of general wholesale prices.

At the depression low the two food groups were below their pre-recession price parity with commodities in general; finished non-foods were well above. The net result of recovery up to June 1936 was somewhat to enhance processed foods and food products ready for consumption in raw state (e.g., milk and dairy products, and vegetables) and to bring processed non-foods closer to parity with other commodities, although they were still above the average. Some shifts occurred also with reference to the 1913 situation. Prices of consumers' goods were 8 per cent above 'all commodities' in June 1936, at substantially the July 1929 level of purchasing power. Processed food products stood on a parity with general wholesale prices, and well below the general level of consumers' goods prices. Above these, and contributing to the relatively high prices of consumers' goods in general, we find food products ready for consumption in raw state. Processed non-food products constituted the most high-priced element of the consumers' goods group. In real worth per unit these goods stood 18 per cent higher than in 1913.

The general high level of fabricational costs was one reason for this condition. (Quality changes account in part for the advance in the prices of manufactured non-food products, as has been pointed out elsewhere.) Processing taxes on important agricultural products had constituted another force making for high prices to consumers up to the end of 1935. Also, crop reduction and drought had served to limit the supply and to enhance the prices of agricultural products subject to processing before being ready for use. Raw consumers' goods were not affected in the same degree. The net result of all these forces was to raise the prices paid by consumers, and, correspondingly, to impede an expansion in the volume of goods that consumer incomes might purchase.

Living Costs and Retail Prices

For certain classes of goods we have records of changes in the prices paid directly by various classes of consumers. These are brought together in Table 57, in comparison with measurements of price changes at wholesale. Between February 1933 and June 1936, while the general index of wholesale prices rose 32 per cent, and wholesale prices of consumers' goods rose 28 per cent, the three retail price index numbers here cited advanced by amounts ranging from 20 to 36 per cent. The rise in retail food prices exceeded the advance in the general index of wholesale prices, a most unusual condition in recovery. The index of living costs of industrial wage earners, which includes such stable elements as rent, in addition to food and other retail prices, rose 12 per cent. These were very substantial advances to have occurred over three years, and represented material increases in the prices paid by final consumers. But we may judge their significance better if we review them against earlier bases.

The gains of recovery left living costs of industrial wage earners and prices paid by farmers some 20 per cent below their 1929 levels. Here they stood roughly on a level with wholesale prices in general. Retail food prices and prices of clothing and home furnishings were, respectively, 22 and 26 per cent below their 1929 levels. But if the standard of reference be 1913, far greater differences are revealed. In June 1936 the wholesale price index was 22 per cent higher than in 1913. Consumers' goods, at wholesale, were 33 per cent higher; prices paid by farmers were 20 per cent higher; living

TABLE 57

LIVING COSTS OF INDUSTRIAL WAGE EARNERS AND CERTAIN RETAIL PRICES, 1913–1936 [1]

	1913	July 1929	Feb. 1933	July 1933	Oct. 1933	May 1934	Sept. 1934	May 1935	Dec. 1935	Apr. 1936	June 1936
Cost of living, industrial wage earners			100	104	107	106	108	110	111	110	112
Retail food prices			100	109	116	119	125	133	134	130	136
Retail prices of clothing and home furnishings, in large department stores			100	109	125	127	126	123	126	126	126
Prices paid by farmers for living and production			100	106	115	120	125	126	121	120	120
Consumers' goods, at wholesale			100	113	118	120	126	130	132	128	128
All commodities, at wholesale			100	117	121	125	131	134	135	133	132
Cost of living, industrial wage earners		100	74	77	79	78	80	81	82	81	82
Retail food prices		100	58	63	67	69	72	76	77	75	78
Retail prices of clothing and home furnishings, in large department stores		100 [2]	59	64	74	75	74	72	74	74	74
Prices paid by farmers for living and production		100	66	70	76	79	82	83	80	79	79
Consumers' goods, at wholesale		100	64	73	76	77	82	84	85	82	82
All commodities, at wholesale		100	62	72	74	77	81	83	84	82	82

	1913	July 1929	Feb. 1933	July 1933	Oct. 1933	May 1934	Sept. 1934	May 1935	Dec. 1935	Apr. 1936	June 1936
Cost of living, industrial wage earners	100	174	128	134	137	136	139	141	142	141	143
Retail food prices	100	169	97	106	112	116	122	129	130	126	132
Prices paid by farmers for living and production	100	151	100	106	115	120	125	126	121	120	120
Consumers' goods, at wholesale	100	161	104	117	122	125	131	135	137	132	133
All commodities, at wholesale	100	150	92	108	111	115	121	124	125	123	122

[1] For sources see footnote [27], p. 149.
[2] October 1929.

costs for industrial wage earners were no less than 43 per cent higher.

Here, again, we have evidence confirming the general conclusion reached at an earlier point. Three years of recovery had done much to wipe out the price disparities which, with reference to a 1929 standard, prevailed at the low point of the depression. By June 1936 the prices paid by consumers were not so far out of line with the prices of other goods as they had been in February 1933. But many important price relations were still far removed from those prevailing in pre-War years. The whole era of post-War prosperity had been marked by some highly novel price relations. Among the most striking were the high prices of most consumers' goods. The expansion of the 'twenties was characterized by relatively high production costs, relatively high prices to consumers for finished goods.[1] Paralleling these conditions, and making possible a heavy volume of construction and of trade in spite of them, there existed a relatively heavy pressure of investment funds and of consumer purchasing power—pur-

[1] In drawing this general conclusion we must note the limitations of the data upon which it is based. It is difficult to measure accurately changes in retail prices and in living costs, because of the wide diversity of quotations and the importance of non-standardized products among retail goods. These difficulties are intensified as the period covered by the measurements increases. The two decades covered by the present records were marked by important changes in living habits, and in the character of the goods entering into the annual budget of the average consumer. Finally, many of the durable goods which were being bought in greater quantities by consumers had been greatly improved in quality. But in spite of these limitations upon the available measurements, the evidence of a general post-War advance in the cost of goods to consumers, as compared with pre-War standards, is very strong indeed. A great many pieces of evidence, relating to different markets and different activities, re-enforce one another in indicating a general advance in fabricational margins, and in construction costs. To these we must add the advance in taxes through which higher governmental expenditures were financed. The results appear in the prices charged final consumers for the goods they bought.

chasing power augmented by distinctive factors peculiar to the period of post-War prosperity.

Further questions of central importance remain, therefore. If, in 1936, pre-recession relations between consumers' goods at wholesale and retail and general commodity prices had been virtually re-established, was that enough to facilitate the movement of goods, in volume, into consumption and use? Or are we to judge from the earlier standards of reference, which indicate that 1936 prices to consumers for finished goods and for the goods and services that enter into ordinary household budgets remained at levels so high as to impede the maintenance of full employment and production in American industries? Definitive answers to these questions can be given only by the record, which is still to unfold. No one may say, in advance of the test of experience, whether pre-War group prices define relations that have significance today, or, indeed, whether pre-recession relations constitute a basis for the restoration of employment volume and the elevation of living standards. The economic system operates under diverse conditions, not under one set alone. Furthermore, comparisons of group prices, particularly those involving finished goods, are complicated by changing quality. But the questions raised are pertinent to a review of the economic situation in 1936. We may throw some light on them by a survey of the changes brought by recovery in the incomes and purchasing power of major consuming groups.

Purchasing Power of Consuming Groups

Adequately to measure the changes of the last several years in the purchasing power of consumers we should have a complete record of alterations in the volume and distribution of the national income. The available figures, while not all-inclusive, enable us to follow some of the general movements of the period. In doing so it will be advisable to distinguish relief and benefit payments and similar disbursements from income arising out of the normal productive and distributive processes of the economy.

The factors affecting the volume of purchasing power available to consumers over a stated interval are numerous, and are, of course, closely related to the circumstances conditioning productive processes. If we here seem to treat the purchasing power factors as independent, and trace the possible effect on production of changes in monetary incomes received, it is for convenience of exposition rather than because the spending operations of consumers are considered to be an independent force in the processes of economic life.

A general account of the changes brought by recession and depression in the income and aggregate purchasing power of American consumers has been given in Chapter III. We there noted declines from 1929 to 1933 of approximately 43 per cent in labor income, 38 per cent in property income, and 46 per cent in entrepreneurial income. The fall in total income paid out amounted to some 43 per cent. The decline in physical volume of consumers' goods produced and sold, over the same period, was less, of course. The prices paid by consumers were reduced somewhat, and the proportion of the national income expended for consumers' goods increased, as always in periods of depression. Making allowance for these factors, we estimated a decline of approximately 23 per cent in the actual purchasing power of consumers between 1929 and 1932; to 1933 the decline amounted to 25 per cent. Among the elements of this total, farmers and industrial wage earners suffered most severely. The total purchasing power of farmers, including expenditures for productive purposes, dropped by about 36 per cent, to 1932 (the low year for farmers); the aggregate purchasing power of farmers' net income, plus wages paid to farm hands, declined more than

CONSUMERS' GOODS IN RECOVERY

55 per cent. (If account were taken of that portion of the farmer's living that comes directly from the farm in the form of home-grown produce, etc., the farmer's actual losses during the depression would not appear to be so heavy.) Industrial wage earners, for whom income also reached its lowest point in 1932, suffered a decline of from 45 to 50 per cent in aggregate purchasing power. Unemployment, as well as reduced hours and reduced wage rates, contributed to this loss.

The story is carried forward by the estimates of the United States Department of Commerce (Table 58.) Although monthly records show a pick-up after the low of early 1933, the total income figures for that year are below the level of 1932. Excessively poor conditions in the early months counterbalanced the gains of the later months. But 1934 and 1935 brought advances for practically all groups of income recipients (interest payments alone declined slightly). These gains, for certain producing groups, have been discussed in preceding chapters. Our present interest is in the broader changes of income, as these affected consumer purchasing power at large.

The gain from 1933 to 1935 in income paid out amounted to more than eight and one-half billion dollars, or 19 per cent of the 1933 total. Of this gain some six and one-half billions served to increase labor income (which here includes both wages and salaries), over one billion took the form of 'entrepreneurial withdrawals' (by farmers and other independent operators), while the remaining gain of almost one billion was divided between dividends and rents and royalties.

These gains left total income paid out, in dollars, approximately 32 per cent below that of 1929. Industrial wages proper fell much more—about 41 per cent—although total payments for personal services declined only 30 per cent. Work relief

TABLE 58

NATIONAL INCOME AND ITS ELEMENTS, UNITED STATES, 1929–1935

ESTIMATES OF NATIONAL INCOME PAID OUT, BY TYPES OF PAYMENT

	1929	1932	1933	1934	1935	1929	1932	1933	1934	1935
	(millions of dollars)					(percentage of 1929)				
Total income paid out	78,632	48,362	44,940	50,173	53,587	100.0	61.5	57.2	63.8	68.1
Labor income	51,487	30,920	29,420	33,528	36,057	100.0	60.1	57.1	65.1	70.0
Salaries (selected industries) [1]	5,663	3,387	3,048	3,250	3,417	100.0	59.8	53.8	57.4	60.3
Wages (selected industries) [1]	17,197	7,017	7,189	8,944	10,149	100.0	40.8	41.8	52.0	59.0
Salaries and wages (all other industries)	27,690	19,417	17,591	19,046	20,173	100.0	70.1	63.5	68.8	72.9
Work relief wages [2]			619	1,389	1,313					
Other labor income	937	1,099	973	899	1,005	100.0	117.3	103.8	95.9	107.3
Property income [3]	11,218	7,980	6,969	7,211	7,303	100.0	71.1	62.1	64.3	65.1
Dividends	5,964	2,754	2,208	2,549	2,830	100.0	46.2	37.0	42.7	47.5
Interest	5,104	4,975	4,592	4,569	4,422	100.0	97.5	90.0	89.5	86.6
Entrepreneurial withdrawals	12,503	7,992	7,306	8,052	8,701	100.0	63.9	58.4	64.4	69.6
Net rents and royalties	3,424	1,470	1,245	1,382	1,526	100.0	42.9	36.4	40.4	44.6

SOURCE: *Survey of Current Business*, July 1936, p. 16

[1] Includes mining, manufacturing, construction, steam railroads, Pullman, railway express, and water transportation.

[2] Includes pay rolls and maintenance of Civilian Conservation Corps enrollees and pay rolls of Civil Works Administration, Federal Emergency Relief Administration and Works Progress Administration work projects plus administrative pay rolls outside Washington.

[3] Includes net balance of international flow of property incomes.

wages, amounting to more than 1,300 million dollars in 1935, made up an appreciable portion of total labor income.

The declines in the purchasing power of the various groups of income recipients were smaller, of course, than the drops in money income, since the prices of goods purchased declined. A comparison of relative changes in the money income and the aggregate purchasing power of three such groups is afforded by the measurements in Table 59.

TABLE 59

LABOR INCOME, PROPERTY INCOME AND NET FARM INCOME, WITH ESTIMATES OF CHANGES IN PURCHASING POWER, 1929–1935

	1929	1932	1933	1934	1935
Labor income [1]					
Millions of dollars	51,487	30,920	29,420	33,528	36,057
Relative numbers	100	60	57	65	70
Cost of living	100	81	76	79	81
Index of purchasing power	100	74	75	82	86
Dividends and interest [2]					
Millions of dollars	11,218	7,980	6,969	7,211	7,303
Relative numbers	100	71	62	64	65
Estimated cost of goods purchased [3]	100	81	77	80	82
Index of purchasing power	100	88	81	80	79
Farm income					
Millions of dollars [cash income less current (operating) expenditures] [4]		6,084	1,734	2,871	3,728	4,632
Relative numbers	100	28	47	61	76
Cost of capital equipment and repairs and of goods purchased for family maintenance [5]	100	73	73	81	82
Index of purchasing power, cash income	100	39	65	76	93
Index of physical volume of farm products consumed on farms [6]	100	100	100	100	100
Index of purchasing power of cash income [less current (operating) expenditures] plus farm products consumed on farms [7]	100	51	72	81	94

TABLE 59 (cont.)

LABOR INCOME, PROPERTY INCOME AND NET FARM INCOME, WITH ESTIMATES OF CHANGES IN PURCHASING POWER, 1929–1935

Farm income (cont.)	1929	1932	1933	1934	1935
Millions of dollars (cash income less operating and capital expenditures) [4]	4,890	1,473	2,525	3,233	3,869
Relative numbers	100	30	52	66	79
Cost of goods purchased for family maintenance [4]	100	68	69	77	78
Index of purchasing power, net cash income	100	44	75	86	101
Index of physical volume of farm products consumed on farms	100	100	100	100	100
Index of purchasing power of net cash income plus farm products consumed on farms [8]	100	57	81	89	101

[1] Including work relief wages, certain miscellaneous labor income (such as pensions), and the wages of farm hands. Original data published by the Department of Commerce (see *Survey of Current Business*, July 1936).

[2] Including net interest on farm mortgages. These data are also those of the Department of Commerce.

[3] Secured by averaging the cost of living index of industrial wage earners and an index of the prices of capital equipment and construction, with weights of 9 and 1 respectively (see National Bureau *Bulletin 59*, by Simon Kuznets, May 4, 1936, p. 24).

[4] See Table 30.

[5] Computed by the National Bureau from indexes published by the Department of Agriculture.

[6] The data indicate that there was some increase during the depression in the volume of farm products retained for consumption on the farm. For the present purpose it seems well to lean towards the side of conservatism, and assume a constant volume of such consumption. If there were an increase, the indexes of real farm income would be higher than those given in Table 59.

[7] Cash income weighted 6,084 and commodity income weighted 1,524. These weights are derived from the 1929 dollar values of the respective types of income.

[8] Cash income weighted 4,890 and commodity income weighted 1,524. See footnote 7.

CONSUMERS' GOODS IN RECOVERY

The magnitude of the decline in the national income from 1929 to 1932 has already been noted. The estimates in Table 59 indicate drops in real income of approximately 26 per cent for recipients of wages and salaries, 12 per cent for recipients of dividends and interest, and from 43 to 49 per cent for farmers. (The figure 49 relates to the decline in real income, including income spent for capital equipment and repairs; the figure 43 relates to real income after payment of costs of capital equipment and repairs. Operating costs are deducted from cash income in securing both figures.) The purchasing power of labor income began to increase in 1933; by 1935 the aggregate was only 14 per cent less than in 1929. The total real income of recipients of dividends and interest continued to decline; in 1935 it was 21 per cent less than in 1929.[2] Real farm income, both that which includes and that which excludes sums spent on capital equipment and repairs, climbed sharply from 1932 to 1933, and continued to advance, though at a lower rate, from 1933 to 1935. By 1935 the purchasing power of the net cash income of farmers, plus farm products consumed on the farm, approximately equaled the 1929 aggregate. The figure is smaller (94) if we include in the income of farmers sums spent on capital equipment and repairs.[3]

[2] These figures conceal quite divergent movements of the two elements of the total. Changes in the aggregate purchasing power of dividends and interest, separately, are shown below. In each case total money income has been divided by the index of estimated cost of goods purchased by these income recipients, as given in Table 59.

	Index of aggregate purchasing power				
	1929	1932	1933	1934	1935
Dividends	100	57	48	53	58
Interest	100	120	117	112	106

[3] It is difficult to prevent over-lapping and to secure truly comparable figures for the different economic groups represented in Table 59. In estimating the true profit and loss account of American farmers, rent and depre-

416   PRICES IN RECESSION AND RECOVERY

Various forms of emergency income added substantially to the purchasing power of consumers during recovery. These included unemployment relief from Federal and other sources, disbursements of the Civil Works Administration, the Federal Emergency Relief Administration and the Works Progress Administration, pay rolls of the Civilian Conservation Corps, pay rolls of projects financed by the Public Works Fund and the Reconstruction Finance Corporation, and rental and benefit payments to farmers. Relief payments proper, which included all the emergency items listed above except the last three, amount to some 300 million dollars in 1932, to about 900 million in 1933, and to almost 2,000 million in 1934. Such payments amounted to less than 1 per cent of the national income in 1932, about 2.2 per cent in 1933, and about 4.0 per cent in 1934. Total emergency income disbursed in 1934 amounted to approximately 5.2 per cent of the total national income. Relief disbursements continued at an accelerated pace in 1935. In that year relief payments

---

ciation charges, as well as the various current expenditures deducted in deriving the figures in Table 59, should be deducted from cash income. If this be done, the remaining cash income available as a return on farm operators' labor, capital and management is smaller than the net cash income given above. If this smaller figure be 'deflated' by an index of prices paid by farmers for goods used in family maintenance, and the result be combined with a measure of volume of farm products retained for consumption on the farm, we have still a third measure of the 'real income' of farmers. The index numbers follow:

1929	1932	1933	1934	1935
100	41	70	82	99

The deflated cash figures (plus farm products consumed on the farm) which are given in Table 59 are probably more directly comparable than are these with the income figures for other economic groups. But in a proper accounting of the position of American farmers depreciation charges should be included. Even when this is done, the 1935 position of farmers represents a great advance over 1932 and substantial equality with the pre-recession level.

CONSUMERS' GOODS IN RECOVERY

other than rental and benefit payments to farmers came to approximately 2,400 million dollars. Payments to farmers totaled 498 millions. Total emergency income amounted to about 5.4 per cent of the national income paid out. Such income continued to provide a substantial portion of the buying power of American consumers.[4] It is a significant fact that although national income increased substantially from 1933 to 1935, emergency disbursements increased more rapidly.

Output of Consumption Goods

Records of the actual production of goods ready for consumption provide us with another means of estimating the degree of recovery in the purchasing power of consumers. Although the available records do not include all goods and services for which consumers' incomes are spent, we have fairly comprehensive index numbers of the output of manufactured consumers' goods. These are given by years in Table 60, with comparable index numbers of the output of manufactured producers' goods.

While the output of goods for capital equipment and construction materials was declining 68 per cent, from 1929 to 1932, the volume of manufactured consumers' goods produced fell 30 per cent. The latter figure is probably somewhat greater than the actual decline in the total purchasing power of consumers. Important classes of commodities not passing through a manufacturing stage and all types of services are omitted, of course.[5] The next three years brought

---

[4] To the extent that the methods of financing these relief payments by governmental agencies have reduced current purchases by other consumers, the relief payments listed above represent no net addition to the purchasing power of consumers at large.

[5] The output of non-manufactured consumption goods is measured by the

TABLE 60

PRODUCTION OF MANUFACTURED GOODS, 1929–1935 [1]

	1929	1932	1933	1934	1935
Goods destined for human consumption	100	70	77	79	91
Capital equipment and construction materials	100	32	38	46	56
Producers' fuels	100	69	73	79	86
All manufactures	100	57	63	68	78

[1] I am indebted to my associate Charles A. Bliss for these index numbers. They are constructed from data of the Census of Manufactures. Figures for 1932, 1934 and 1935 are estimates based on Census data. See "Production in Recession and Recovery", *Bulletin 58*, National Bureau of Economic Research. The reader should note that these index numbers are based upon a somewhat larger sample than are the index numbers used in deriving measurements of changes in prices and costs in manufacturing industries. In 1933 data from 110 industries were used by C. A. Bliss, as against 82 in the other production index.

an increase of 30 per cent in the volume of consumers' goods manufactured, raising it to within 9 per cent of the 1929 level. The index exaggerates the advance, as it did the decline, but there is here clear evidence of substantial improvement in the general standard of living. The processes of recovery, plus the emergency expenditures of the government, had brought the aggregate volume of manufactured consumers' goods close to the pre-recession high and, in fact, above the level of ten years ago. The economic significance of this advance is of course clouded somewhat by the presence of substantial relief payments in consumer income. The gain from 1932 to 1935 in the production of goods for capital equipment and construction materials was greater than for consumers' goods, but the 1935 output of non-consumption goods was much lower, relatively to earlier standards.

index numbers below. These indexes, constructed by the National Bureau, include tne production of fruits and vegetables, milk, poultry products, fish, and coal and other fuels.

1929	1932	1933	1934	1935
100	103	102	104	105

CONSUMERS' GOODS IN RECOVERY 419

These shifts may be followed in greater detail over part of the period of recovery by means of the monthly records of the output of manufactured consumers' goods.[6] The rela-

	July 1929	Feb. 1933	July 1933	Oct. 1933	May 1934	Sept. 1934	Dec. 1934	Dec. 1935
Consumers' goods, manufactured	100	68	86	73	81	84	85	94
Producers' goods, manufactured	100	39	77	53	62	43	58	80
All manufactures	100	49	80	60	69	58	67	85

tively steady gains since early 1933 in the production of consumers' goods stands in contrast to the extreme fluctuations among producers' goods. By December 1935 the output of manufactured consumers' goods was only 6 per cent below the July 1929 peak. Excluding automobiles, the production of which was subject to special influences in the closing months of 1935, the index stands at 90, 10 per cent below the base month. With or without automobiles, the production of consumers' goods exceeded the 1923–25 average, and was within striking distance of the pre-recession volume.

The Consumer in Recovery

In this chapter we have surveyed changes of two general types affecting the flow of goods to final consumers—changes in the prices of goods bought by consumers and in the volume of purchasing power available to important economic groups. The findings in respect of price movements indicated that consumers in 1936 were approximately where they were in 1929. The worst disadvantages of the depression had been corrected, in so far as we may judge from group averages, and the prices of consumers' goods stood on a general pre-reces-

---

[6] Index numbers constructed by Y. S. Leong; published in the *Journal of the American Statistical Association*, June 1935, pp. 371–2. Dr. Leong has courteously provided us with preliminary figures for 1935.

sion parity with the prices of commodities in general. But pre-recession parity represented a position of substantial disadvantage for the consumer, with reference to pre-War relations. We have seen that the post-War expansion, on the price side, was marked by low returns to producers of raw materials, high fabrication costs, high wages, and high prices of capital goods and goods ready for final consumption. It was this situation, and nothing better from the point of view of the consumer, that had been restored by 1936. The prices at wholesale of consumers' goods as a broad class were 33 per cent higher than in 1913. The cost of living of industrial wage earners was 43 per cent higher. These figures are to be contrasted with the general average of wholesale prices. The index of the National Bureau, which is comparable with the consumers' goods indexes cited above, was 22 per cent higher in June 1936 than 1913. The index of the Bureau of Labor Statistics was only 14 per cent higher. It is clear that all the major elements that enter into the budget of the final consumer were higher in 1936 than in 1913, if we accept the index of general prices at wholesale as a suitable gauge of changes in monetary values. (Some individual items were lower of course, and some others had undergone quality changes that meant actual price reductions to the final buyer.) We shall turn shortly to inquire whether the factors that supported expansion under these conditions in the decade of the 'twenties existed in 1936.

In tracing the movements of income and purchasing power we noted a decline from 1932 to 1933 (on an annual basis), although the purchasing power of farmers and of labor picked up. By 1935 appreciable improvement had been recorded. Rising incomes were the rule among wage earners and salaried workers, dividend recipients, farmers and those drawing incomes from various other basic industries. Part of the increase was offset by rising prices but most groups scored appreciable

CONSUMERS' GOODS IN RECOVERY

gains in actual purchasing power. Summarizing estimates based upon the available data (estimates which are rather rough for some groups) we have the following record of changes in aggregate purchasing power.[7] For all but the first

	APPROXIMATE ADVANCE IN AGGREGATE PURCHASING POWER 1932 to 1935 (per cent)	APPROXIMATE DEFICIENCY OF AGGREGATE PURCHASING POWER IN 1935, IN COMPARISON WITH 1929 (per cent)
Wage earners and salaried workers	+16	—14
Recipients of interest and dividends	(net loss)	—21
Farmers		
Cash income less current (operating) expenditures, plus farm products consumed on farm	+84	—6
Net cash income (cash income less operating and capital expenditures) plus farm products consumed on farm	+77	(none)
Gross operating income plus benefits	+36	—13
Mineral producers		
Gross operating income	+20	—27
Producers of raw forest products		
Gross operating income	+46	—46
Railways		
Gross operating income	(net loss)	—35
Construction industries		
Gross operating income	+21 (1933 to 1935)	—63

[7] The changes relating to wage and salaried workers, recipients of property income and the first two series for farmers are from Table 59. The measurements of changes in the gross operating income of farmers are based on Table 29. They include farm products consumed on the farm. The gross income of mineral producers is the total value of mineral production in the United States, as given by the U. S. Bureau of Mines (*Minerals Yearbook*, 1936). Relatives measuring changes in gross income derived from forest products are secured from National Bureau price and production index numbers, for raw forest products. Railway gross operating income is based on freight and

three groups purchasing power is measured in terms of general commodities at wholesale. The incomes of wage earners are deflated by cost of living; of farmers by prices paid by farmers; of recipients of interest and dividends by an index secured by averaging living costs and the costs of capital equipment and construction.

For wage and salaried workers and recipients of interest and dividends the estimates relate to the purchasing power of net income; for farmers estimates of net and gross income are given; for the other groups the figures relate to gross operating income. Only the net income data measure consumer purchasing power directly. The deflated gross income measurements for different industrial groups provide important supplementary information concerning the fortunes of producing groups and, indirectly, concerning the flow of purchasing power to consumers through these industrial channels.

The rather scattered figures given in the table do not cover mutually exclusive classes, nor do they provide a general coverage of all consuming groups, but they give a reasonably good picture of the gains of recovery. These gains between 1932 and 1935 were enjoyed by practically all elements of the economic system. Improvements varied in degree, as had the declines of the preceding recession. Because the points from which recovery began were exceptionally low, for some groups, the percentages measuring gains in purchasing power up to 1935 are hardly comparable. Thus the gain of 21 per cent recorded for the construction industries is measured from a very low level indeed; in real im-

passenger revenues of Class I railroads (Interstate Commerce Commission). Values of contracts awarded in 37 states (F. W. Dodge Co.) were used in estimating the gross income of construction industries.

portance it is far less significant than the gain of 16 per cent in the purchasing power of wage earners and salaried workers. The entries in the last column, which measure the deficiency of aggregate purchasing power in 1935, relatively to 1929, for the several groups, provide bases for properly evaluating these gains.

The production of consumers' goods reflected the improvement in purchasing power among the various consuming groups. The output of one class of such products, manufactured goods intended for human consumption, increased 30 per cent from 1932 to 1935, but remained in 1935 about 9 per cent less than in 1929.

This recovery carried the output of consumers' goods to a level much higher, relatively to 1929, than producers' goods in general or capital equipment in particular. In 1935, when the volume of manufactured goods intended for human consumption was 91 per cent of that of 1929,[8] the production of manufactured goods intended for use as capital equipment and in construction was but 56 per cent of the 1929 output. Of course, the preceding decline had been much greater in the capital goods industries. It is notable, however, that the relatively disadvantageous position into which the heavy industries were thrown by the recession persisted, to a degree not experienced in similar periods in the past.

The rise in consumer income and the revival of consumers' goods industries since the depression low of 1932–33 are of particular interest because of the emphasis placed on the

[8] This index shows a net drop in production from 1929 to 1935 that was notably less than the decline in consumers' incomes, corrected for price changes. Expenditures for services of a luxury or semi-luxury type, for housing accommodations and for a variety of non-standardized goods were curtailed more drastically than those for the simpler consumers' goods entering into the index here utilized.

restoration of purchasing power in the Administration's program of recovery. An expansionist program on the monetary side (including a reduction in the gold content of the dollar and a corresponding broadening of the basis of credit, open market operations and large loans to financial organizations) has been accompanied by heavy public works and relief expenditures entailing continuing budgetary deficits. Not all these measures were aimed directly at the increase of consumer purchasing power, it is true, but that was a major objective. Pointing immediately at the expansion of consumer income were the wages and hours provisions of the industrial codes. It was hoped that these provisions would lead to larger payments to wage earners without material increase in costs or prices. The increase in prices was to be prevented by higher efficiency and by the lower overhead charges, per unit, that would result from an increase in sales and in output under the stimulus of the higher purchasing power of wage earners. Finally, proceeds of processing taxes were to be used in maintaining or expanding the purchasing power of farmers complying with the crop restriction program of the Administration.

The effects of the monetary measures on the status of consumers are, of course, impossible to appraise, for they were manifest in indirect ways. The departure from the gold standard and subsequent reduction in the gold content of the dollar relieved deflationary pressure on the price system and contributed to the price advance of 1933. The resulting business relief was a substantial, though indirect, aid to the consuming public. In creating the potentialities of a considerable credit expansion this move had a further connection with consumers' interests, but as regards the volume of credit actually put to business use these potentialities were tardily realized.

Pay rolls of projects financed from public works funds

and from funds of the Reconstruction Finance Corporation constituted direct additions to the incomes of final consumers, but in relative magnitude these amounts were not impressive. Total funds from these sources amounted to 33 million dollars in 1933, 326 million in 1934, and 495 million in 1935. By far the largest additions to consumer incomes, from governmental sources, came from Federal unemployment relief. These great outlays played an important part in stimulating retail sales and the production of consumers' goods of all sorts.

The effects on aggregate consumer purchasing power of the various provisions of the codes enacted under the National Industrial Recovery Act were mixed. As we have seen in Chapter VI the money incomes of wage earners in manufacturing plants increased 42 per cent during the period of operation under the industrial codes (June–July 1933 to April–May 1935). Wage rates were advanced and total pay rolls expanded as results of the combined influence of the new codes and of changing business conditions. The effects of the codes on the income of employed labor were salutary. But we have called attention to other features of the period of code enforcement. Fabrication costs in general and labor costs in particular rose sharply. Aggregate production of manufactured goods and total employment, in man hours, made no net gains under the codes. At the end of the period of code enforcement real labor costs were actually higher than in 1929, although industrial productivity had increased as much as 25 per cent. The wages and hours provisions of the codes may have contributed to a rise in the pay rolls of manufacturing plants, but higher costs appear to have retarded the movement towards larger output and increased employment that had prevailed during the first push of recovery, prior to the adoption of the codes. The codes may well have had salutary effects in other directions, but they apparently served to deprive consumers at large of the benefits from the substantial gains in productivity that had been made after 1929; these benefits were reaped largely by those engaged in the manufacturing process.

The incidence of processing taxes levied under the Agricultural Adjustment Act was probably diverse. In so far as they fell on consumers, through the raising of prices, there was a transference of purchasing power from consumers to the agricultural producers who received the benefit payments. A somewhat similar shift would result from absorption of the tax by processors through reduction of profits. For certain commodities prices received by farmers were probably reduced, as a result of the processing tax.[9] Benefit payments to farmers financed in this fashion may involve a personal transference of purchasing power, but no net addition to the income of the group.

As in all major economic movements, consumers occupied a position of strategic importance in the revival of 1933–36. Indeed, special circumstances have given added significance to their role in the movements of the last several years. A program of recovery involving maintenance (and advancement) of wages and reduction of hours, price-fixing, curtailment of output and the levying of processing taxes falling in part at least on the consumer, obviously tends to raise costs and prices, and so to reduce consumer purchasing power. Of critical importance is the question whether the additions to consumer income arising from such a program and from the normal processes of recovery are sufficient to offset the adverse effects of higher costs and prices. Delicate matters of timing and balance are here involved, as always in recovery from a severe depression. In the 1933–36 situation conscious attempts

---

[9] Cf. "The Incidence of the AAA Processing Tax on Hogs", Geoffrey Shepherd, *Journal of Farm Economics*, May 1935, pp. 321–34.

at regulation constituted a novel element in the readjustments of revival.

Irregular recovery, extending over three years, had by 1936 brought gains to consumers on several fronts. The average prices of consumers' goods, both at wholesale and retail, had been reduced, relatively to the general level of prices. Reviving activity had brought increases in the national income and corresponding gains in the purchasing power of major consuming groups. Income arising from productive operations was swelled by heavy relief and benefit payments of the Federal government, and by relief payments of states and cities. These various forces had brought the advances noted in preceding pages. The gains were considerable, and were continuing, but they fell short of restoring the aggregate real incomes that consumers had enjoyed prior to the recession.

Among the many factors tending to curtail business activity two were particularly pertinent to the problem of recovery in the output of consumption goods. One was the delayed revival of the capital goods industries, including general construction. The percentage of recovery from the low point of 1932–33 was considerable, of course, but even this did no more than restore the production of capital goods in 1935 to about 56 per cent of 1929. It was in these industries that the bulk of the unemployment persisted. It was here that deficiencies of wage, salary and dividend disbursements continued in most severe form. An economy dependent upon activity in the heavy industries for the employment of a large part of its labor force and for a large proportion of the current income of consuming groups suffered from the tardiness of their recovery. Not until the second half of 1935 was there a convincing revival of activity in this area. This advance gave additional stimulus to the recovery of industries producing consumers' goods.

Secondly, and of high importance with reference to the

long term movements of American economic life, was the persistence of a high level of prices for consumers' goods, at wholesale and retail. The relations of the 'twenties had been restored, roughly, by early 1936, but these are suspect, as perhaps representing an abnormal and unstable situation. There is greater reason for doubts on this score because various special aids that buttressed the market for consumers' goods during the expansion of the 1920's had lost much of their force during the recession and depression. Foreign buying was no longer supported by American loans. Speculative profits suffered a vast shrinkage after 1929. New buying power contributed by the expansion of consumer credit played a less important role in the first two phases of recovery than it had prior to 1929. In default of these largely adventitious aids, restoration of a volume of consumer buying equal to that of the pre-recession era, in view of the existing price situation, faced very real difficulties.[10]

The expansion of consumer buying from 1933 to 1936, despite these obstacles, was substantial, attesting the strength of the underlying recovery. Former operating conditions had been restored or adaptation to new conditions effected in

---

[10] The comparison of price movements among different commodity groups over one or two decades is complicated by quality changes. These changes are almost certain to be dissimilar, as among different classes of commodities, and thus distort comparisons based on prices alone. Consumers' goods in general probably improved in quality over the two decades following 1914. The consumer was getting more in 1936 than in 1914, in the purchase of a given unit of goods. We do not take account of this gain in the price comparisons in the text. On the other hand, we may approximate with reasonable accuracy changes in the number of units the consumer could buy with a given income. It is in this sense that we measure changes in aggregate consumer purchasing power. The real income of a given consuming group may have increased more than the estimates indicate, because each unit purchased today has a longer life or gives greater satisfaction than the unit bought in 1914. (Of course, not all changes in quality are improvements. Changes in the direction of shoddy and less durable goods are not unknown.)

many industries. Yet this survey of the expansion of consumer purchasing power and the price movements of consumers' goods during recovery ends on conflicting notes. By 1936 the relatively high prices of consumers' goods had been reduced and substantial gains had been scored in the incomes and buying power of important consuming groups. But the prices of finished goods remained high, in relation to other prices and to the level of consumers' incomes, by all standards except those of the pre-recession boom. Moreover, part of the expansion of purchasing power was apparent, rather than real, since it represented a transference rather than a real increase of buying power. Other elements of new buying power were temporary, arising from relief payments, and could not be taken to indicate substantial recovery. Finally, considerable deficiency of purchasing power persisted and living standards remained at unsatisfactory levels. These conditions indicate that no suitable adjustment had been effected between costs, prices and consumer incomes. We shall return in the closing chapter to a consideration of problems growing out of these circumstances and to a general review of the consumer's position.

CHAPTER IX

THE PRICE SYSTEM, INCREASING PRODUCTIVITY

AND RECENT ECONOMIC CHANGES

THE institution of prices has played a major part in the economic changes of recent years. In an exchange economy individual prices and that intangible entity termed the price structure constitute the controlling agency through which all economic activities are regulated and coordinated. This task of coordination has become more difficult with the increasing complexity of economic life.

Over its long history the institution of prices has been subject to many influences that have enlarged its scope, modified its characteristics and affected its operations. The breakdown of mercantilism and other controls gave a greater degree of freedom to prices and hence of flexibility to the economic system. Later the movement was in the other direction—towards price-fixing and wage control by regulatory bodies and powerful private interests, towards the piling up of fixed expenses in industrial production and the accompanying accentuation of the relatively inflexible elements in selling prices. In the main, these were slow changes, and the modifications they wrought in the working of the price system were gradual. The movements of the last half century, for which price records are more comprehensive, may be traced with more precision. A wide variety of forces has played upon the price system of the United States and upon international price relations over this period. Internal price relations have been altered by shifts in consumer demand, by changes in productive efficiency, by the pushing out of producing mar-

PRODUCTIVITY AND PRICES 431

gins, by changes in marketing mechanisms and by other factors that have altered production costs and the selling prices of individual commodities. Of a different order have been those forces that have affected the 'operating characteristics' of the price system. Regulation, private and public controls, the growth of national advertising and consequent increase in the power of manufacturers to exercise direct control over ultimate selling prices, the steadily expanding burden of overhead—all these tend towards the creation of rigid elements and fixed relations in the price structure, with far reaching consequences for the working of the system as a whole. At the same time the price system has been exposed to a series of violent pressures in some degree at least of external origin —War-time inflation, post-War deflation, and the world-wide recession that began in 1929. Pressures from the monetary side, falling with varying incidence upon national price structures, have complicated the price shifts of more narrowly-localized origin. Finally, we must note that international ties were disrupted by non-intercourse during the War and post-War years, by the breaking down of the gold standard and by serious impairment of world trade since 1929. It was inevitable that these various movements should have influenced profoundly the adjustments and correlations that are effected through the price system, and the welfare of great groups of producers and consumers. Our present concern is with these changes and some of their economic consequences.

EXPANSION OF FABRICATIONAL MARGINS, 1913–1936

The outstanding feature of the price history of the last twenty years, as regards internal relations among the prices of various commodity groups, has been the widening of the margin between raw and processed goods—the margin representing fabricational and distributional costs. In essence, all the price shifts that have been discussed in detail in preceding sections are aspects of this major movement—a movement the more striking because it reverses deep-seated and persistent pre-War tendencies. The low returns and deficient purchasing power of important classes of primary producers in post-War years are related to this movement. The relatively high prices of articles intended for use in capital equipment are due in some degree to high costs of manufacture. The prevalence during the entire post-War period of a plateau of high prices for finished goods intended for human consumption is another aspect of the same situation.

This curious widening of the margin between the prices of raw and manufactured goods is the more remarkable in view of the increasing productivity of labor in manufacturing industries during the last twenty years. From 1914 to 1929 output per wage earner in manufacturing industries of the United States increased about 49 per cent. Yet, while the Bureau of Labor Statistics index of wholesale prices was advancing 40 per cent, during this period, the average selling price of manufactured goods (as derived from Census records) rose 45 per cent. (Fabrication costs plus profits, per unit of product, rose 66 per cent.) The same conditions prevailed among the two groups of manufactured goods that have been given special attention here. Manufactured goods intended for human consumption, for which output per wage earner increased 44 per cent over this fifteen-year period, advanced 44 per cent in per unit selling price. Still greater was the rise in production per wage earner (69 per cent) in the manufacture of goods intended for use in capital equipment, yet here the advance in selling price per unit was 40 per cent, a rise equal to that of general commodity prices, at wholesale.

In following these relations through the periods of recession and recovery we have noted the customary expansion of the margin between raw and processed goods during recession, as the prices of raw materials collapsed, and the succeeding reduction of the margin with recovery. It is in order at this point briefly to summarize the situation existing in the summer of 1936 and to consider the general nature of the problems then persisting.

In June 1936 the prices of manufactured goods, at wholesale, were 16 per cent below the level of July 1929; the prices of raw producers' goods were 22 per cent below. Relatively to the 1913 base, the price index for manufactured goods was 128, for raw producers' goods 104. Recovery had narrowed the wide margin that developed during the recession but still left manufactured goods in a position of advantage. This margin of advantage amounted to 8 per cent with reference to 1929 relations, to 23 per cent with reference to pre-War parity.

One effect of this change was to reduce the average worth of all raw materials, in exchange for commodities in general at wholesale, to 5 per cent below the July 1929 level and to 10 per cent below the 1913 level. The loss was greatest, relatively, for raw agricultural products. Taking account of values at the farm in relation to retail prices paid by farmers, the average per unit worth of farm products in June 1936 showed net declines of 8 per cent on the July 1929 base, 11 per cent on the pre-War base (the average of the five years, August 1909–July 1914).

Turning now to the June 1936 position of goods intended for use in capital equipment and for direct human consumption, we find the average per unit worth of building materials 31 per cent higher than in 1913. (Worth, or purchasing power, is here measured in terms of commodities in general, at wholesale.) For processed goods intended for use in capital equipment the corresponding gains in real exchange value were 4 per cent, with reference to July 1929, 14 per cent with reference to 1913. For processed consumers' goods the average per unit worth in June 1936 was 2 per cent greater than in 1929, 8 per cent greater than in 1913. (This means, of course, that the index number of wholesale prices, for processed consumers' goods, stood higher, by these relative amounts, than the general index of wholesale prices.)

We find, therefore, that although some of the greatest disparities created during the recession had been removed by 1936, there remained a net addition to the differences resulting from the divergent price movements of the period 1914–29. Some reasons for this were found in the detailed review of the price changes affecting different commodity groups. In particular, it was noted that although the six-year period of recession and recovery brought an increase approximating 25 per cent in output per man hour, the real per unit worth of manufactured goods (i.e., their exchange value for goods in general) and real labor costs per unit of product increased.

This discussion raises a fundamental question: Did price differences growing out of this expanding margin restrict the effective demand for finished goods on the part of potential buyers—buyers of capital goods, on the one hand, of finished consumers' goods on the other? This question relates not only to the periods of recession and recovery that filled the years 1929–36, but also to the period of expansion that preceded the recession. The answer to this question may not be given in terms of prices alone, for behind prices lie changes in productivity, in costs, in income distribution and in related elements that affect immediately the movements of goods into final use. Indeed, before attempting to answer the central question we must give attention to issues relating to the incidence and effects of increasing productivity. For the whole problem of a changing fabricational margin, with all its possible effects on the status of primary producers, fabricators, buyers of capital equipment and final consumers, centers, in its recent manifestations, on the incidence of gains in industrial productivity.

On the Incidence and Effects of Gains in Industrial Productivity

As we have followed changes in industrial productivity in this study we have measured productivity in terms of output per man or per man hour. In using such measurements we should be aware of their possible inadequacy. Changes in industrial methods that involve greater use of machinery substitute indirect labor for some part of the direct labor displaced by the machines. That is, men employed in the final operations of manufacture are replaced by machines the production and maintenance of which require human effort. (As regards the production of the machines, this means that some increase in overhead costs is to be expected, when direct labor costs are reduced.) Usually, of course, there is a diminution of the total human energy required for a given productive operation, since the stimulus to the greater use of machines is provided by a potential reduction of costs. But it is certain that the 'per man' or 'per man hour' standard of measurement, applied to the final stage of manufacturing operations, overstates the true gain in productivity, since it does not include a measure of the correlated increase in indirect labor. The measurements of productivity employed in the present study cover a large percentage of all manufacturing operations, including those relating to the production of capital goods, as well as final consumption goods. Thus account is taken of a considerable part of the indirect labor entering into the production of finished goods. Some of the indirect labor, however, is omitted (labor in extraction of minerals for use in capital equipment, and labor entering into some highly fabricated equipment, the output of which is not readily measured). So, comprehensive as they are, the present measurements of productivity changes probably overstate somewhat the over-all gains in productivity over the periods studied.

But our interest lies at the moment in the reduction of money costs that increasing productivity may be expected to bring. The potential reduction of costs is a reduction, per unit of output, in terms of the scale of costs prevailing prior to a given operating change that enhances industrial productivity. For later, when the advantages of the increased productivity have been realized and the gain appropriated by one party or another, money costs per unit of output may conceivably be as high as before. It is an aspect of this problem—the division or allocation of the money gains resulting from higher productivity—that now concerns us.

The money gains from increased productivity may accrue to producers of raw materials, to fabricators or to consumers. Were competitive conditions such that sellers of raw materials were able to demand higher prices just when lower fabricational costs created a fund open to appropriation, producers of raw materials might conceivably secure the gains. Again, competitive conditions among producers and buyers might be such as to enforce lower selling prices, in which case the buyers of fabricated goods would profit. Or, finally, the situation might make it possible for the agents of fabrication themselves to appropriate the gains, paying no more for raw materials and selling their products at the same prices as before.

In this last situation a further question arises as to the division of the incremental gain among the various claimants here lumped together as 'agents of fabrication'. Manufacturing labor might benefit, through higher pay per unit of goods turned out. Owners of land or other natural resources might be enabled to secure higher rents. Those providing credit,

PRODUCTIVITY AND PRICES

or funds for capital equipment, might secure higher returns. More might go to governmental units, through higher taxes on the earnings of business enterprises. Or the increased productivity might lead to higher profits, to be distributed as dividends or accumulated as surplus.

Looking first at the physical relations involved in these changes, it is clear that higher productivity will make possible the production of more goods with the same expenditure of effort or the same volume of goods with a smaller expenditure of effort. The latter condition may take the form of an increase in voluntary leisure, or an increase in involuntary unemployment. Which of these results will follow, or what combination of these effects will follow, will depend upon a number of factors.

Various possible effects of gains in industrial productivity, as variously divided, may be suggested in the following summary:

A. Reduction in working hours of men employed, with higher time rates of pay; aggregate disbursements to agents of production and division of disbursements unchanged; selling price unchanged.

Here the gain takes the form of additional leisure. There is no increase in the demand for goods, and no change in the distribution of purchasing power.[1] There is no stimulus to the production of a greater volume of goods.

B. Reduction in the number employed, with higher time rates of pay to those still employed, and no change in aggregate amount disbursed to labor and to other agents of production. No change occurs in selling price.

Increased unemployment, on the one hand, higher per capita returns to employed labor, on the other, will characterize this

[1] With time, as the new leisure changes living habits, a change might occur in the directions in which wage earners' incomes are expended. But the change is remote, and less definite than the other shifts here outlined.

situation. With the higher per capita income of employed labor, some change will occur in the direction in which purchasing power is expended.

C. Reduction in working hours with the same or a smaller force and the same time rates of pay; selling price unchanged.

Here there is no change in the aggregate amount disbursed to the agents of production, but there is a shift in its division. Agents of production other than labor receive a larger proportion of the aggregate, labor receives a smaller portion. Unemployment (or enforced leisure) accompanies the shift. Some modification occurs in the direction in which purchasing power is expended, with the changed distribution of the aggregate disbursement.

D. Reduction in selling prices.

Initial lowering of aggregate receipts and of amount disbursed to agents of production. Possible initial unemployment. Release of buying power of consumers for purchase of more goods of the same type, or other goods. (The direction of expenditures of purchasing power thus released will depend upon the elasticities of demand for the many products in question.)

The central feature of these several situations is that productive energy is released by the gain in productivity. The critical question is whether this released energy is to be utilized and if so, how. In an economy regulated by an omniscient dictator the answer would be simple. There could be more leisure, or the energy could be allocated as the dictator should decide. But where the allocation is effected through the instrumentality of the price system, in an economy marked by prices partly free and partly controlled, the problem is more complex. Here it is the pressure of purchasing power through the price system that gives the answer to the question. For in every situation except that described under (A) above, some shift occurs in the direction in which current purchasing power is expended, after the gain in productivity occurs. What is of prime importance, in the actual situation, is the kind of connection that may be established between the purchasing power thus shifted and the productive energy released by the increase in productivity.

This connection may be direct, in which case the difficulties attendant upon the economic changes involved are reduced to a minimum. Or, in place of a direct transmission of purchasing power to released energies, there may be an indirect connection and a diffused transmission. At one extreme, representing the most direct connection between purchasing power and released productive energies, is the situation in which the selling price of a commodity is reduced to the full extent made possible by the increase in productivity, and in which the demand for the commodity is highly elastic. In such a situation a large part of the purchasing power of consumers released by the reduction in price would find an outlet through an increased demand for the commodity in question. Increased production would result, with prompt re-employment of all or part of the productive energies released by the initial increase in productive power. At the other extreme is the situation in which no reduction in selling price occurs; full advantage of the reduction of costs flows to stockholders, let us say, in the form of higher dividends. The increased purchasing power of stockholders would find expression through various channels of investment and direct consumption. Most of these channels would be far removed from the commodity in question, and there would be little or no increase in the demand for it. Only by indirection and at long remove would the energies released in the industry first concerned find employment through the slow diffusion of the enhanced purchasing power of stockholders. Under these conditions unemployment might persist in this industry for a long period.

Between these two extremes are many combinations of

price changes and purchasing power shifts, resulting from increases in productivity, and many degrees of diffusion of purchasing power. The rapidity and ease of adaptation to the new productive and distributive conditions created by productivity changes might vary enormously, depending upon the closeness of the connection established between the enhanced purchasing power of particular groups and the productive energies released by improvements in technique and organization.

We should note, however, that in a completely frictionless economy, marked by free prices, with wages and other elements of production costs completely flexible, with labor and capital completely mobile, the enhanced purchasing power of special groups would be diffused promptly throughout the economy and connection would be established without delay between this purchasing power and the released productive energies. Under these conditions the disposition of the gains from increased productivity would be a matter of indifference, in so far as the question of faulty economic adjustments and persistent unemployment of productive facilities is concerned. For maladjustments, marked by unemployment, could not be present. (The manner in which the fruits of higher productivity were apportioned would be important, of course, as regards the status of different economic groups; that matter is not here in question.) In an economy marked by frictions of many types, however—by rigid prices, inflexible rates for services of many sorts, immobility of labor and capital—innumerable barriers stand in the way of the wide and prompt diffusion of purchasing power. The pressure of new purchasing power in one segment of the economic system may exert a negligible effect on displaced labor and idle capital in a remote section, within time limits that have significance for ordinary human activities.

This, of course, is the situation we face today. Frictions

there have always been in the economic systems with which men have actually worked. As frictions of some types disappeared, new frictions have developed. The twentieth century has witnessed many new encroachments upon the ideal freedom of the competitive system. Accordingly, the manner in which the gains resulting from higher productivity are apportioned is not a matter of indifference, as regards the efficiency of the economic system and the maximum utilization of productive resources. For the gains of enhanced productivity are potential gains, merely. In their first form they appear as reductions in the energy necessary to produce stated quantities of goods. Unless the benefits of the released energy are realized, no true advances occur. For this reason, the apportionment of the potential benefits of higher productivity is of high social concern. The more direct the connection between enhanced purchasing power and productive energy released by new techniques, the less the maladjustment and the more efficient the utilization of the new techniques. The less direct the connection, and the more diffused the transmission of new purchasing power to released productive energies, the greater and the more protracted are the resulting disturbances likely to be.

Division of the Gains in Industrial Productivity: The Historical Record, 1899–1933

With this argument in mind we may review the changes of recent years against a background of earlier movements. We shall attempt to trace the incidence of changes in industrial productivity, by estimating the concurrent changes in the returns of fabricators and in the real costs of manufactured goods to various classes of buyers. The assumptions made and the limitations attaching to the measurements will be noted in the course of the discussion.

SHARES OF PRODUCERS

We first note the changes in manufacturing productivity, measured with reference to the number of workers or of man hours worked, and the returns to fabricators, during three periods. These measurements appear in the accompanying table. They are shown graphically in Figure 15.

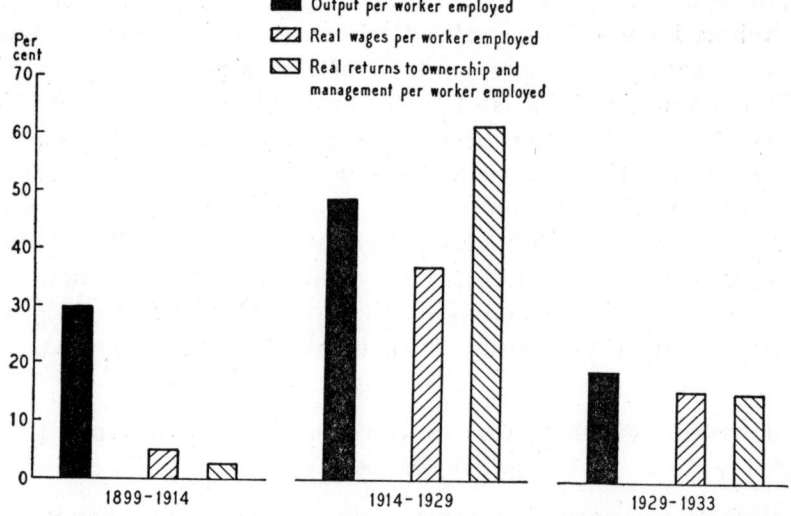

FIGURE 15

ESTIMATED CHANGES IN INDUSTRIAL PRODUCTIVITY AND IN THE RETURNS OF MANUFACTURING PRODUCERS, 1899–1933

Measurements relate to average costs per unit of goods produced and bought

During the fifteen years preceding the War output per worker employed in manufacturing plants increased almost 30 per cent. With this we may compare the real returns, per worker employed, of wage earners and of ownership and management. Changes in these real returns are estimated

PRODUCTIVITY AND PRICES

CHANGES IN PRODUCTIVITY AND THE FORTUNES OF MANUFACTURING PRODUCERS

	1899–1914	*1914–1929*	*1929–1933*
		(percentage)	
Change in output per worker, or per man hour worked [1]	+29.6	+48.6	+19.0
Change in real returns, per worker employed, or per man hour worked,[1] of			
Wage earners, manufacturing plants	+4.8	+36.9	+15.5
Ownership and management, manufacturing plants	+2.2	+61.5	+15.2
All agents of fabrication	+2.8	+51.3	+15.4

[1] For the periods 1899–1914 and 1914–29 the figures are all on the basis 'per worker employed'. This is a faulty standard of reference, to the extent that average working hours changed over these periods. Information concerning hours of labor during these periods is scanty. Estimates by Douglas (for the first period) and by Wolman and the National Industrial Conference Board (for the second period) indicate that average full time hours of work, in manufacturing industries, declined about 6 or 7 per cent between 1899 and 1914 and from 6 to 8 per cent between 1914 and 1929. From these figures, and scattered evidence of other types, we may estimate, roughly, that output per man hour increased from 35 to 38 per cent between 1899 and 1914 and from 50 to 60 per cent between 1914 and 1929. (The National Industrial Conference Board has published an estimate of 55 per cent, for the increase in output per man hour from 1914 to 1929; see *Thirty Hour Week*, 1935, p. 17.) But these figures, at best, are approximations. It seems well to use measurements of output per worker for the period prior to 1929, remembering that these understate the true gains in productivity. For the period 1929–1933, when working hours were subject to more extreme variations, and for which we have more accurate measurements of such changes, a man hour of work is the unit of reference.

The figures in this and the following table are given to one decimal place, for the purpose of formal consistency. The margin of error is, of course, greater than this.

The present estimate of change in output per man hour from 1929 to 1933, which is based upon data relating to a large and representative sample of manufacturing industries, differs somewhat from other estimates issued by the National Bureau (see *Bulletins 53* and *58*).

by dividing the aggregate monetary returns of the two groups by the number of wage earners employed, and deflating the measurements thus secured by appropriate indexes of the prices of goods for which the money returns of the two groups are spent.[2] The comparison for the pre-War period shows only slight gains in the real rewards of these two groups of producers. The gain of wage earners, per capita, amounted to 4.8 per cent; for ownership and management, per worker employed, 2.2 per cent; and for the combined groups, 2.8 per cent. These fall far short of the gain of 29.6 per cent in output per worker. The gains of enhanced productivity, between 1899 and 1914, went, in the main, to groups other than the agents of fabrication.

Over the next fifteen years, 1914–29, output per worker increased 48.6 per cent. The fruits of this notable advance went largely to fabricators, as is clear from the other entries for this period. The real rewards, per capita, of manufacturing wage earners, advanced 36.9 per cent, while for ownership and management the gain, per worker employed, amounted to 61.5 per cent. For the combined groups the gain was 51.3 per cent. The fact that 1914 was a year of depression, while 1929 was one of prosperity, accounts in part for this substantial gain which exceeded the rise in productivity. But as to the reality of the gain there is no question. Producing groups in manufacturing industries

[2] The deflator, for wage earners, is the index of cost of living for industrial workers. For the ownership and management group (a mixed class of salaried workers, shareholders, bondholders, and other miscellaneous claimants) the deflator is an index secured by averaging index numbers of living costs (with a weight of 2), wholesale prices (weight of 2) and the prices of finished capital goods (weight of 1). The two indexes are combined, in securing the measurements for all agents of fabrication, with weights based on the importance of each group. These deflators are to be considered only as rough approximations to the desired measurements.

Deflator for	*1899*	*1914*	*1914*	*1929*	*1929*	*1933*
Wage earners	100.0	136.3	100.0	170.1	100.0	76.2
Ownership and management	100.0	128.5	100.0	158.3	100.0	74.1
All agents of fabrication	100.0	131.9	100.0	163.5	100.0	74.9

gained greatly in their market relations between 1914 and 1929. Payments for the services they rendered, measured, for convenience, on a per worker basis, increased much more rapidly than did the cost of the goods they bought.

Recession and depression brought an advance of some 19 per cent in output per man hour worked. The rewards of manufacturing labor, and of ownership and management, computed on a man hour basis, show gains approximating 15 per cent. Total returns declined substantially, of course, but for each man hour of work agents of fabrication scored appreciable advances during the period of decline. These gains fell only slightly below the increase in productivity.

It appears that manufacturing producers shared but slightly in the rewards of the pre-War advance in industrial productivity. The fruits of the great advance of the next fifteen years went largely, however, to agents of fabrication, particularly to the mixed group classed as 'ownership and management'. During recession and depression, also, the rewards of these groups, per man hour worked, advanced only slightly less than did output per man hour.

SHARES OF CONSUMERS

To complete the picture we turn now to the side of the consumer. We lack data for many consuming groups but we may estimate with reasonable accuracy the changes affecting three or four important classes. In measuring the cost to these consumers of the services of fabricators we take account only of manufactured goods intended for human consumption. These are not finished consumers' goods, for we do not have adequate material for completely finished goods, but changes in fabricational costs of goods ultimately to be consumed are, in fact, the movements that concern us. Decreases in the per unit costs of fabrication, for such goods,

446 PRICES IN RECESSION AND RECOVERY

to selected groups of buyers may be compared with changes in the real costs of fabrication of manufactured goods in general, resulting from increases of industrial productivity. The accompanying measurements, which are portrayed graphically in Figure 16, define these changes. The figures are to be taken as approximations since available data do not make possible complete accuracy in the tracing of these movements.

The measurements in the first line of the tabulation, which define (approximately) changes in the productive effort re-

FIGURE 16

ESTIMATED CHANGES IN REAL COSTS OF FABRICATION TO MANUFACTURING PRODUCERS AND IN CORRESPONDING REAL COSTS OF MANUFACTURING SERVICES TO VARIOUS CONSUMING GROUPS, 1899–1933

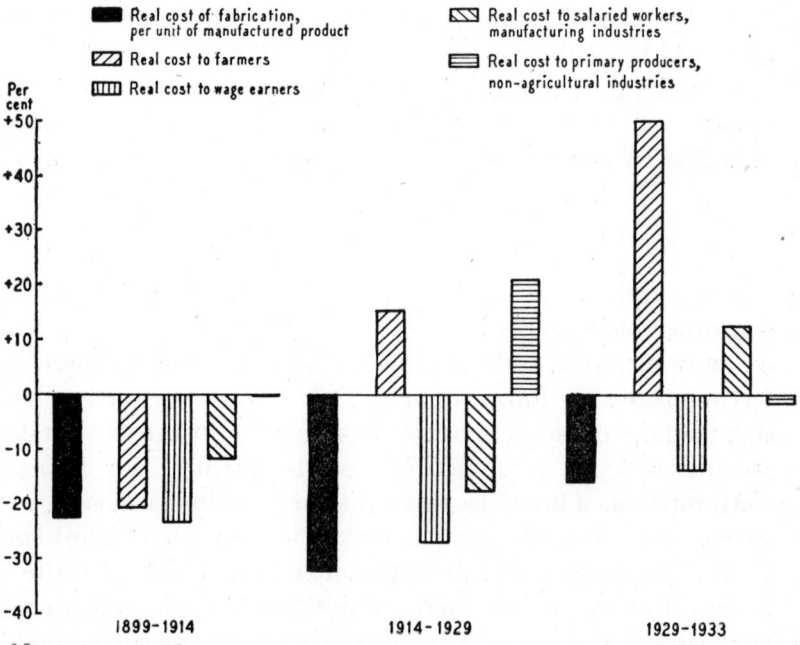

Measurements relate to average costs per unit of goods produced and bought.

PRODUCTIVITY AND PRICES

CHANGES IN MANUFACTURING PRODUCTIVITY AND THE FORTUNES OF CONSUMING GROUPS [1]

	1899–1914	1914–1929	1929–1933
		(percentage)	
Change in real per unit cost of fabrication, in effort expended by producers	—22.8	—32.7	—16.0
Change in real per unit cost of fabrication to buyers of goods intended for human consumption			
Farmers	—20.9	+15.2	+50.1
Wage earners, general	—23.4	—27.1	—13.8
Salaried workers, manufacturing	—11.8	—17.6	+12.5
Primary producers, non-agricultural	—0.1	+20.9	—1.5

[1] The figures in this table require some explanation. The index numbers in the first line, measuring changes in the 'real cost of fabrication' are the reciprocals of the measurements of productivity. Thus in place of Q/N (total output divided by number of workers) we have N/Q (total number of workers divided by number of units produced). If we accept N as a measure of the aggregate effort expended in manufacturing production, N/Q will measure the effort per unit of goods produced. The defects of Q/N as a true measure of industrial productivity are present also in N/Q. N does not measure all 'real productive effort'. It is defective in that non-wage earners are not included, and also in that some of the effort embodied in capital equipment is excluded. It may be assumed, although the assumption is not altogether justified, that although N does not include all types of productive effort, other types vary with N. Noting its defects, we may use N/Q as a rough index of changes in actual productive effort per unit of manufactured goods produced. (For the last period the index is based upon $\frac{NH}{Q}$, total man hours divided by number of units produced.)

The money cost, to buyers, of the contribution of fabricators to one unit of manufactured goods is given by VA/Q, that is, total value added by manufacture divided by number of units. (In the present case, only goods intended for human consumption are included.) In measuring the real cost to farmers, the money cost of fabrication, per unit, is 'deflated' by an index of the prices received by farmers for their products. In measuring the real cost to wage earners, the money cost of fabrication, per unit, is 'deflated' by an index of hourly rates of pay. The market values of the services of salaried workers are measured in terms of average annual income. Average wholesale prices of non-agricultural raw materials furnish the standard used for primary producers other than farmers. In each case changes in the money cost are reduced to changes in 'real' cost by means of an index measuring changes in the money price of the goods or services sold by the consuming group in question.

Here, as in dealing with the fortunes of producing groups, we are dealing only with approximations to the actual values desired. The measurements of changes in the realized returns of fabricators may not measure precisely changes in the per unit cost of fabrication, as paid by the several consuming groups. Distributional margins may vary. Again, we only approximate changes in the actual effort expended by various consuming groups, in securing the funds with which manufactured goods are to be purchased. The productivity of labor in farming, for example, may vary with time. But for the purpose of estimating the general nature of broad movements, these approximations may be utilized.

quired to manufacture one unit of goods, provide a standard with which may be compared measurements of the changing real costs of fabrication, per unit of product, to various classes of buyers of goods intended for human consumption. During the period 1899–1914, when fabricators, as producers, were gaining but slightly from the increases in industrial productivity, the cost to farmers and wage earners of fabricators' services was dropping sharply. Per unit of product bought, the real cost of these services to farmers declined 21 per cent, to wage earners 23 per cent. These reductions were about equal to the decline in effort expended in fabrication, as a result of advancing productivity. Salaried workers gained also, but primary producers other than farmers received no share of the advances in industrial productivity.

In the period 1914–29 the productive effort required to fabricate a unit of manufactured goods dropped more than 32 per cent. None of this gain accrued to farmers or to other primary producers. Wage earners in general and salaried workers in manufacturing industries, as consumers, gained materially, however. Their pay for efforts expended increased, and the real cost to them of manufacturing services dropped appreciably. The wage earning group here represented is broader than the manufacturing wage group, but the nar-

PRODUCTIVITY AND PRICES 449

rower group enjoyed a similar gain. Both as producers and as consumers industrial workers gained over this period.

During the four years from 1929 to 1933 industrial productivity continued to increase; the real per unit cost of fabrication was reduced 16 per cent. On the producing side wage earners and ownership and management gained, in that their monetary rewards, per man hour worked, increased in purchasing power. (Of course, these two groups lost materially in the aggregate, through the reduction in total hours worked.) Among consumers farmers lost heavily. The selling prices of their products dropped so sharply that the real cost, in kind, of the fabricational services embodied in a unit of manufactured goods increased 50 per cent. Salaried workers lost also. Producers of non-agricultural raw materials gained slightly, but the greatest gain was scored by wage earners. An hour of labor, in 1933, would buy 16 per cent more in manufactured goods than in 1929.[3]

[3] These measurements relate only to the cost of fabrication, not to the total selling price of manufactured goods. This limitation is necessary, since the productivity measurements are restricted to manufacturing operations. However, the actual cost of manufactured goods to final buyers includes the cost of materials, and distributive costs, as well as fabricational costs. Data now available do not cover distributive costs, but we may estimate changes in the real cost, to various consuming groups, of manufactured goods intended for human consumption, taking account of material costs as well as fabricational costs. Following are measurements corresponding to those given, for fabricational costs alone, in the tabulation in the text above.

	1899–1914	1914–1929	1929–1933
		(percentage)	
Change in real per unit cost of fabrication and materials to buyers of goods intended for human consumption			
Farmers	—16.5	—0.1	+33.0
Wage earners, general	—19.1	—36.8	—23.6
Salaried workers, manufacturing	—7.0	—28.6	—0.3
Primary producers, non-agricultural	+5.5	+4.8	—12.7

When we take account, as we do here, of the actual selling prices of

In attempting to measure changes in the real costs of fabricators' services we have dealt with specific groups of consumers for whom records are available of changes in the prices of the goods or services from which their incomes are received. These are, of necessity, scattered groups, and do not include all consumers. We may supplement the preceding account with a brief survey of changes in prices and costs expressed in dollars of constant purchasing power, at wholesale. (That is, each price or cost index has been divided by an index of general wholesale prices.) This procedure does not provide true measures of changing real costs to consumers, since consumers do not buy at wholesale prices, nor are changes in their rewards, for efforts expended, accurately measured by changes in wholesale prices. But the comparison does provide general indications of the changing real worth of manufactured goods and of the services of agents of fabrication in terms of a broad list of commodities at wholesale. The measurements on page 451 define these changes.

These figures are estimates, but the margin of error is far smaller than the wide movements they measure. The shifts are striking. A decline of some 23 per cent in the per unit cost of fabrication (in human effort) over the fifteen years prior to the War was paralleled by a drop of 10 per cent in the average worth of manufactured goods intended for human consumption, of 14 per cent in the average per unit cost, to ultimate consumers, of the services of fabricators. There was some concurrent gain, not here shown, in the rewards of raw material producers. But a large portion

manufactured goods the apparent savings of consumers during the first period are reduced, those of the second and third periods are increased, in comparison with the changes in fabrication costs alone. The reason, of course, is that raw material prices rose more than prices in general during the pre-War period, but fell below general prices in the succeeding periods.

PRODUCTIVITY AND PRICES

	1899–1914	1914–1929	1929–1933
		(percentage)	
Change in real per unit cost of fabrication in effort expended by producers [1]	—23	—33	—16
Estimated change in average per unit worth of manufactured goods intended for human consumption (worth measured in dollars of constant purchasing power, at wholesale)	—10	+3	—8
Estimated change in average cost of fabrication, to consumers, per unit of manufactured goods intended for human consumption (cost measured in dollars of constant purchasing power, at wholesale)	—14	+19	+2

[1] Industrial productivity, with reference to which these measurements of changing fabrication costs are estimated, is measured in terms of output per wage earner for the periods 1899–1914 and 1914–29, output per man hour for the period 1929–33.

of the gains from increased productivity was passed on to consumers in the form of lower prices. Production expanded, employment opportunities increased, and labor displacement was kept to a minimum.[4] Over the fifteen-year period from 1914 to 1929 there was a net reduction of approximately 33 per cent in the real cost of fabrication. This exceeded the considerable savings of human energy during the pre-War period. Yet the average selling price of manufactured goods in 1929 was some 3 per cent higher, in dollars of constant purchasing power, than in 1914. In spite of the tremendous gain in productive efficiency in manufacturing industries, buyers of manufactured goods were forced to give more for them, in commodities at large, than in 1914. The final entry for this period indicates who actually gained from the in-

[4] Industrial displacement during this period is discussed in *Economic Tendencies* (pp. 419–23). From 1899 to 1914 only one of every 48 men employed withdrew from or was forced out of the industry in which he was working, over each five-year census period. (The figure given is an average, of course.)

crease in productivity. Although productive efficiency went up, the per unit cost to consumers of the services of agents of fabrication showed a net advance of some 19 per cent. A substantial portion of the gains from increased productivity during the post-War period was reaped by agents of fabrication. Indeed, since the prices of fabricated goods advanced, in relation to general commodities at wholesale, it would appear that agents of fabrication gained more than the rewards of increased productivity, actually encroaching upon the incomes of other economic groups.

Tendencies of the same sort persisted during the years of recession from 1929 to 1933. Productivity continued to increase, and real fabrication costs were reduced approximately 16 per cent. Average per unit selling prices of goods intended for human consumption were reduced, in terms of constant dollars, but by only half the apparent decline in real fabricational costs. That this drop was due to declining material costs is revealed by the final entry in the table. The cost to consumers of fabricators' services, per unit of consumption goods produced, advanced 2 per cent during this period of recession, in spite of the increase in productivity.[5]

---

[5] Certain important qualifying considerations should be noted. The figures cited are fully accurate, as measurements of the changing rewards of fabricators, only on the assumption that fabrication played the same role in production in the different years compared. It is assumed, in other words, that no change occurred in the *quality* of manufactured goods, as a result of more refined fabrication. Such quality changes did occur. The average finished product of 1933 represented more 'units' of fabrication, fewer 'units' of raw materials, than did the average finished product of 1914. However, these quality changes do not explain the notable shift in the relative rewards of fabricators. Detailed study of the records of individual manufacturing industries reveals a general advance in fabricational costs, not compensated by corresponding changes in quality. If full account could be taken of quality changes the apparent gains of fabricators from 1914 to 1933 would be lessened, but by no means reversed.

Again, our conclusions are restricted by the assumption that the actual

PRODUCTIVITY AND PRICES

The survey of productivity changes in manufacturing industries and their incidence between 1899 and 1933 has yielded the following general conclusions:

The increase of 30 per cent in productivity from 1899 to 1914, and the corresponding decline of 23 per cent in the productive effort required to fabricate a unit of goods, benefited consuming groups. Agents of fabrication, as producers, secured only a small portion of these gains.

The increase of 49 per cent in productivity from 1914 to 1929, and the corresponding decline of 33 per cent in productive effort required to fabricate a unit of goods, worked largely to the advantage of producing groups. A substantial portion of the total gain in productivity was secured by manufacturing wage earners, as producers, while ownership and management scored gains actually exceeding the advance in productivity. Wage earners and salaried workers, as consumers, also benefited, but consum-

---

effort of production may be measured in terms of number of men employed or of man hours of labor expended. This would be accurate if we could take account of all the *indirect labor* embodied in capital equipment. This is done only in part in the measurements here employed. Because some of the capital goods used in production embody labor not included in our measurements, the actual advances in productivity and the actual reductions in productive effort expended on each unit of goods were probably somewhat smaller than those here indicated.

In assessing the gains ot labor no account is taken of displacement and unemployment, resulting from technological change. We have attempted to define changes in the real rewards secured per worker or per hour of labor, not variations in the aggregate rewards of labor as a class. For the purpose of the present analysis it is proper to measure real rewards in terms of a man or a man hour unit.

Finally, the index numbers used in the deflating process, in attempting to measure changes in the real rewards of both producing and consuming groups, are not exact instruments. A margin of error which we may not precisely define is present in using them for the purpose of shifting from the money level to the commodity level of contributions and rewards. Here, as in other respects, the instruments used provide approximations to the desired results rather than definitive measurements. It is improbable, however, that closer approximations would reverse the essential features of the movements recorded in the text.

ing groups drawing incomes from the sale of primary products actually experienced advances in the real costs of the manufactured goods they purchased. (If account could be taken of the gain in productivity in agriculture and mining over this period the position of primary producers in 1929, relatively to 1914, would be more favorable than the present figures indicate.)

The increase of 19 per cent in output per man hour from 1929 to 1933, and the corresponding drop of 16 per cent in the productive effort required to fabricate a unit of goods, worked chiefly to the advantage of producers. Wage earners, as consumers, gained also, since hourly rates of pay were maintained, but no other consuming group among those here dealt with shared appreciably in the cost reduction. Farmers were forced to meet a very great advance in the real costs, to them, of fabricating services on the goods they purchased.

Certain rather important reservations attaching to these various measurements have been suggested in preceding pages. Correction for possible errors involved, if they could be made, would doubtless change the measurements somewhat, but it is unlikely that our conclusions concerning the general movements of the periods covered would be materially modified. Over the thirty-four years here reviewed the productivity of manufacturing industries increased steadily; indeed there is evidence of acceleration. But the gains resulting from advancing productivity were allocated in quite different ways in the several periods reviewed. The essential fact is that prior to 1914 the major share of the benefits of higher productivity and declining real costs of fabrication went to consumers; thereafter the chief shares went to producing groups—to wage earners, ownership and management.

The reasons for this striking shift in the incidence of increasing productivity can not be fully established, but certain of the major factors may be briefly suggested.

The pre-War period was marked by a general and sustained advance in commodity prices. During the later period, following the sharp War-time advance, a considerable net decline in prices occurred. Labor costs and overhead charges, which are important elements of the fabricational margin, tend to lag behind the level of wholesale prices. Accordingly such costs, as a percentage of selling price, tend to decline when the trend of prices is rising, to increase when the trend is declining.

During the War a strong stimulus was given to the production of raw materials outside Europe. When the special needs of the War passed and when European countries returned again to full productive activity, raw material producers were in a weak market position. The decline in the prices of primary products strengthened the relative position of fabricators. Price weakness among primary producers persisted during a large part of the post-War decade and during the latest recession. This weakness and the relative strength of fabricators contributed to the change noted in the division of the total value product of manufacturing industries.

The restriction of immigration into the United States strengthened the bargaining position of American labor in the War and post-War years. This was accompanied by a fairly general change in the attitude of large employers on the wage question. The principle of maintaining purchasing power through high wages was widely endorsed. Acceptance of this principle was partly responsible for the increase in the share received by manufacturing labor in the fruits of advancing productivity.

During the first post-War decade consumer demand was heavily supported by important non-recurring elements. A greatly expanded reservoir of credit was drawn upon to finance the increase in installment purchasing. Speculative profits, reaped in securities and real estate markets, were in part used to purchase consumption goods. Lending abroad on a large scale supported heavy foreign purchases. With demand thus strengthened it was easier for the sellers of manufactured goods to maintain the fabricational margin and the selling prices of manufactured goods, even though productivity was increasing and costs of production were declining.

We may think of the gains of industrial progress through advancing productivity as being divided through a three-cornered pulling and hauling contest among primary producers, agents of fabrication and consumers. In pre-War years primary producers and consumers stood in positions of relative advantage and reaped most of the benefits of rising productivity. The tide turned with the end of the War. Primary producers lost bargaining power; the trend of prices and special post-War circumstances contributed to strengthen the position of fabricators. Among consumers, primary producers were in a weak position. The buying power of other important consuming groups was artificially bolstered, so that competitive pressure on the demand side, towards lower prices, was greatly weakened.

Industrial Productivity and Economic Frictions

The preceding pages have dealt with a variety of changes that occurred during the War, the post-War expansion and the recent years of recession and recovery. The adverse fortunes of primary producers, the expansion of fabricational margins and the increased returns of fabricators, the persistence of relatively high prices for many types of finished consumers' goods and of capital equipment—these have been characteristic of the entire period since the War and stand in notable contrast to the conditions and tendencies prevailing in the United States during the several decades before the War. Coexistent with these conditions we have noted a steady increase in industrial productivity in manufacturing industries; unemployment that prevailed even under conditions of general prosperity, that reached extreme proportions during the depression and persisted with exceptional obstinacy during recovery; the prevalence of inflexible prices and of other economic rigidities that constitute important sources of friction in the continuing processes of adaptation to changing economic circumstances.

Many forces lie behind these phenomena. We should unduly simplify a situation into which many variables enter and in which causal connections run in diverse directions if we should seek a single explanation of the conditions discussed in this study. Yet something of a unifying principle is to be found in the relations traced in this chapter. Changing productivity and its diverse incidence, on the one hand, economic frictions that impede prompt adaptation to such changes, on the other, bulk large among the complex of factors responsible for the spotty prosperity, the persistence of unemployment and the shifts in price relations and in the distribution of purchasing power that have characterized recent years.

Changes in technology and related variations in industrial productivity are perhaps the chief dynamic element in modern economic systems. Such changes are continually occurring; recently they have been of exceptional magnitude. Their direct effects and repercussions are felt over a wide range. They involve substantial alterations in the manner in which productive resources are used, in the demand for labor, in production costs and prices and in the current distribution of purchasing power. But the incidence of these changes is subject to alteration. The character of demand for the products of the industries affected, the nature of the change in productivity and the strategic power of the producing and consuming groups directly concerned influence the immediate results of an increase in productivity. So far, however, it remains a somewhat narrow problem. Our social attitudes and immediate economic interests, as individuals, may give us reasons to be concerned with the effects of given changes in productivity. So long as these are restricted to the groups immediately involved in particular technical or organizational improvements the working of the economic system as a whole is not affected. But because we do not have a perfectly flexible price system and fluid factors of production, the repercussions of changes in productivity have general significance and are of high importance in the study of economic processes at large. When institutional conditions give rise to serious frictions and delays in the adaptation of the elements of an economy to changes in productivity, when the operations of the entire system are adversely affected, then such changes cease to be of narrow and specialized interest only.

In preceding pages emphasis was placed upon the role of points of diffusion, centers from which the effects of changes in industrial productivity were diffused throughout the price and distributive system. In a frictionless, fluid economy these effects would be as quickly transmitted from a few points of diffusion as from many, and there would be prompt and immediate adaptation to them. But when frictions are present the number of points for the dissemination of the effects of changes in productivity becomes of prime importance. With many points of diffusion the influence of particular frictions would be lessened, and prompt utilization of released energies, human and other, would be expected. With few points of diffusion (as when restricted groups secure the first advantages of higher productivity) only a remote connection would exist between the new purchasing power accruing to particular economic groups and the energy released by advancing productivity, and the obstacles to prompt utilization of these energies would be many. The frictions and impediments characteristic of a modern money economy would impede the rapid spread of purchasing power shifted from its original channels.

Of course, many evidences of prosperity may be present even though gains in productivity are not reflected in lower fabricational margins and reduced prices of finished goods. Wage rates and the aggregate earnings of labor employed in manufacturing industries may be high.[6] Corporate earnings may be large and the prices of securities may rise to high levels. Indeed, the high fabricational margin made possible by productivity gains not passed on to consumers may conduce to just these conditions. But when the advantages of higher productivity find this outlet, prosperity may for long periods be limited to special groups. The rewards of primary producers may remain low, relatively to the prices of finished goods. Volume of sales and of production may remain low, in comparison with productive potentialities and the needs of consumers at large. Unemployment will persist in large volume. Industry will be burdened with high overhead charges, because of the high cost of finished capital goods.

Ultimately, as the new purchasing power of favored groups slowly diffuses through the economy, a higher level of activity is to be expected unless further complications intervene. Yet such complications may occur, giving rise to a semi-permanent condition of concurrent prosperity among some economic groups, unemployment and persistently low returns to other groups. It is conceivable, under modern conditions, that portions of the increased income of the favored groups may never become effective in stimulating the productive energies released in the first instance by the gain in produc-

---

[6] The part that wage payments in manufacturing industries play in the buying activities of consumers at large is indicated by the fact that in 1929 such wages constituted 14 per cent of the national income paid out; in 1933 the corresponding percentage was 11.

tivity. A loan abroad, expended in foreign markets and ultimately disavowed by the borrower, exemplifies such a development. Far more important as a cause of continuing maladjustment of this type is the mere persistence of technological improvement, with new gains displacing workers in one section while the frictions of a modern economy impede the diffusion of the augmented purchasing power of favored groups in other sections.

Precisely this condition has characterized the post-War economic scene. Industrial displacement and technological unemployment were in evidence prior to the recession of 1929.[7] The whole post-War situation, marked by high fabricational margins, high prices to consumers, high prices to buyers of capital goods, relatively low rewards to primary producers, is related to this basic fact. The gains of higher productivity were reaped, in the main, by particular groups, occupying strategic positions.[8] Because of the many frictions

---

[7] In each of the three biennial census periods from 1923 to 1929 one man out of 20, on the average, withdrew from or was forced out of the industry in which he was working. This was more than double the separation rate prevailing over census periods more than twice as long, prior to the War. The separation rate increased greatly, of course, from 1929 to 1933.

[8] Confirmation of this statement is found in the rapid growth of profits, the large additions to corporate surpluses and the high post-War level of real wages in industrial enterprises (see *Economic Tendencies*, pp. 416–528). The following figures reveal more sharply the relative gains of wage earners. The industries here represented (commercial and savings banks, mining, manufacturing, construction, railroads, Pullman and express, water transport, street railways, telephones and telegraphs, private electric light and power companies) extend beyond the industrial sphere, but the general tendencies we have discussed are clearly shown by the composite figures. The averages given have been computed from annual data cited by M. A. Copeland ("National Wealth and Income—An Interpretation", *Journal of the American Statistical Association*, June 1935, p. 384).

	1909–13	1919–23	1924–28	1929–32
Aggregate pay rolls as a percentage of total realized income, banks and non-farm industries	72.9	82.4	79.9	77.0

(*Footnote* 8 *concluded on p. 461*)

present in the post-War world, the process of diffusion, by which the higher purchasing power of these groups was brought into contact with the productive energies released by advancing industrial efficiency, was protracted. Persistent maladjustments, the most obvious of which was industrial unemployment, were the outward manifestations of this condition. Special circumstances in the form of fortuitous additions to the current income of consumers at large lessened, for a time, the adverse effects. With the removal of these circumstances, and under the pressure of other forces during recession, the maladjustments became pronounced from 1929 to 1933.

The character of these maladjustments and the changes during the recovery from 1933 to 1936 were discussed in preceding chapters. This recovery has been fairly broad, in its effects on economic groups. Price disparities have been reduced, the incomes of primary producers have been raised, wage rates have advanced in manufacturing industries and volume of employment has increased somewhat. Yet in spite of these gains it cannot be said that prosperity is general in 1936, or that the benefits of recovery have been evenly apportioned. Unemployment persists in great volume; the aggregate volume of industrial production has barely touched

(Realized income is total income, excluding additions to corporate surplus. The groups included accounted for about 40 per cent of the total realized income of the country in 1929.)

The proportion of realized income going to wage earners in these industries advanced markedly over the decade 1909–13 to 1919–23. Some decline occurred thereafter, but even the depression years witnessed a higher average ratio of pay rolls to realized income than prevailed prior to the War. We should note, too, that other portions of the fabricational margin were expanding precisely when the pay roll percentage declined after 1923. Profits rose markedly from 1923 to 1929, and overhead charges expanded relatively, from 1929 to 1932. The entire post-War period was marked by relatively high disbursements to income recipients deriving their rewards from the fabricational margin.

the level of 1926, although the decade has brought an increase of about eleven million in the population of the United States. The rewards of primary producers remain relatively low, if we exclude special benefits not arising from productive operations. Fabricational costs are high, wage rates are high and profit rates are advancing. The fundamental requirements of a large volume of general production and a rate of activity that will absorb the industrial unemployed have not been met.

The situation, it has been here suggested, is related to three basic characteristics of post-War economic conditions in the United States. First, industrial productivity advanced notably. From 1929 to 1936 the productivity of manufacturing industries in the United States showed an apparent increase of some 25 per cent. This figure could be substantially reduced to allow for possible errors but it would still represent a notable advance in the efficiency of industrial enterprise. Second, the chief immediate gains of this great advance were reaped by the fairly restricted groups directly engaged in manufacturing operations, that is, by manufacturing labor and the managers and owners of manufacturing plants. Primary producers and the great body of general consumers shared in only a limited degree in the fruits of higher productivity. (Certain industries constitute exceptions to this general condition.) Finally, this whole post-War period was marked by economic frictions that retarded the necessary adaptations to industrial change. Inflexible prices, relatively fixed overhead charges, private control, governmental regulation and other obstacles to the fluidity of productive agents— these were not new to the post-War scene but they played important parts in the developments of the last fifteen years. The first of these three conditions meant that the flow of current purchasing power was being altered and that productive energies were being released from their accustomed applications. The second meant that the accretions to the purchasing power of the first beneficiaries of increased productivity were being diffused from a limited number of points, since primary producers and consumers at large shared but slightly in the first gains. The third condition, combined with the second, meant that adaptation and readjustment to the changed conditions would be slow, that effective connections between accretions to purchasing power and released productive energies would be tardily established. Relatively wide fabricational margins, relatively high prices of finished goods, spotty prosperity, persistent unemployment and subnormal production are related to these three basic conditions.

The technical changes, organizational improvements and advances in individual aptitudes and skills that increase productivity will continue. The forces that have brought such advances in the past show no signs of weakening. Moreover, economic frictions will persist. The free, flexible system under which immediate adjustment to changes in operating conditions could be effected never existed, in reality. Economic forces proper have tended to create new frictions, as earlier rigidities have broken down. Frictions of other types are generated when social considerations are given precedence over considerations of private gain. We must look forward to a continuation of the conditions under which changing productivity, on the one hand, and persistent frictions, on the other, play central roles in the processes of economic life.

The effects of these conditions on the working of the economic system as a whole will depend on the degree of friction that prevails and on the manner in which the gains of enhanced productivity are first apportioned. Economic frictions will persist, but their growth may perhaps be curtailed. If adequate social justification should be required for every source of continuing economic friction, restrictions and disturbances that do not pay their way in social returns might be reduced, with a resulting increase in the efficiency of economic operations. This is not a suggestion that competition should be unrestricted, or that public regulation should cease. There is ample social justification for many of the controls that exist today. It is probable, however, that many of the price inflexibilities and other obstacles to the prompt readjustment of economic relations that industrial change necessitates arise from faulty policies in business administration and labor organization, monopolistic and semimonopolistic 'pockets' in the competitive system, needless rigidity in rate regulation, attempts at control that outrun our knowledge of the forces and relations involved. True, we do not have a fully competitive system, and the currents of social change seem to be moving us further away from such a system. But in noting the many restrictions upon competition we must not overlook the wide areas over which fairly effective competition prevails. Our economic fortunes and our living standards depend upon the working of a system still essentially competitive, and in our appraisal of economic ills we must recognize this fact. Until we have the knowledge and the power necessary to a broader type of economic planning and control than we have yet attempted, we must depend upon essentially competitive forces for the regulation of economic processes at large. If, under these conditions, the advantages of increasing industrial productivity are to be widely shared, and if increases in productivity are not to be allowed to cramp and retard the operations of the productive system, restrictions upon the piling up of socially unnecessary frictions, whether of private or public origin, may be desirable.

In the main, however, it is not to a lessening of economic frictions that we may look for escape from the difficulties we face in seeking to avoid the losses and secure the gains of

PRODUCTIVITY AND PRICES 465

advancing productivity. In a system inevitably restricted by necessary public regulation and by the operating conditions of private industry, perhaps the chief means of minimizing these difficulties is the immediate spreading of industrial gains over the widest possible area. The cramping influence of frictions may be reduced to a minimum when the benefits of enhanced productivity are diffused from many centers. The purchasing power that is shifted from one group to another, as a result of technical or organizational improvements, may in this manner be brought into most immediate contact with the energies released by these improvements.

From a social point of view it is desirable that gains in productivity should bring a larger output, with advanced living standards for consumers at large, rather than special advantages for some, coexisting with idleness of important productive resources. These ends may be most readily attained through a reduction in the selling prices of the finished goods immediately affected by the productivity gain, a reduction equivalent to the saving in cost of production.[9] For

[9] This statement of the conditions that arise with advances in productivity deals with general considerations only, and with the *strategy* of economic adjustment rather than with *tactics*. It does not take account of the problems of the individual manufacturer in setting the selling price of a specific commodity. On this level the issues are numerous and complicated. The various elements of cost, on a per unit basis, are hard to differentiate, difficult to measure. The probable effect of a given change in price on volume of sales is largely a matter of guess-work, until the step is taken. At a given time many of the costs of the individual enterprise are fixed, and the manufacturer is not free to adjust them in the light of changed productive conditions. Moreover, many manufacturers are several stages removed from the final market, with numerous distributional costs, not open to their control, intervening between their selling prices and the final prices paid by the consumers. These various circumstances render the fixing of a suitable selling price perhaps the hardest single problem confronting a manufacturing producer. We gain only a distorted view of the issues faced in effecting social adjustment to changes in industrial productivity if we fail to recognize the complexity of the price-setting problems of individual manufacturers, and

goods of elastic demand this would mean immediate absorption of all or part of the energies released by the gain. For goods of inelastic demand a shifting of productive resources to other employment is inevitable. In either case the wide sharing among consumers of the benefits of higher productivity would lessen the adverse influence of economic frictions and contribute to a prompt use of the released productive energies.

the meagerness of present economic knowledge concerning them. But the price-making policies of business men, the tactics of intelligent business administration, may be adapted to broader principles. The present statement is concerned with such principles, relating to the task of adaptation to industrial change under the existing economic organization.

APPENDIX

APPENDIX I

FREQUENCY TABLES
PERCENTAGE DISTRIBUTIONS OF SELECTED LISTS OF COMMODITIES, CLASSIFIED ACCORDING TO DATES OF RECESSION AND REVIVAL OF WHOLESALE PRICES DURING TWO BUSINESS CYCLES

TIME OF PRICE TURN [1]	FREQUENCIES (per cent)			
	RECESSION OF 1919–1921	REVIVAL OF 1921–1923	RECESSION OF 1929–1932	REVIVAL OF 1932–1936
—34 to —32				.2
—31 to —29				0
—28 to —26			.2	.2
—25 to —23			.9	0
—22 to —20			6.1	1.3
—19 to —17		.6	3.7	1.8
—16 to —14		0	8.9	1.8
—13 to —11	.8	1.9	6.9	2.8
—10 to —8	8.0	17.8	8.7	9.5
—7 to —5	6.9	11.2	8.5	11.9
—4 to —2	10.5	12.5	11.4	6.9
—1 to +1	26.5	10.9	4.5	18.4
+2 to +4	17.6	12.5	6.5	25.1
+5 to +7	20.6	10.3	6.9	7.5
+8 to +10	5.2	11.8	4.5	3.5
+11 to +13	2.8	7.8	5.4	1.3
+14 to +16	.8	1.5	3.2	1.8
+17 to +19	.3	.9	5.0	1.1
+20 to +22		0	1.8	.4
+23 to +25		.3	1.8	.2
+26 to +28			1.5	.4
+29 to +31			.9	0
+32 to +34			.9	.2
+35 to +37			.4	.2
+38 to +40			.6	
+41 to +43			.4	
+44 to +46			0	
+47 to +49			.2	
+50 to +52			0	
+53 to +55			0	
+56 to +58			.2	
No turn recorded				3.5

[1] The figures in this column indicate the number of months by which the price turns of specific commodities precede (—) or lag behind (+) the major turns of the general index of wholesale prices.

APPENDIX II

DISTRIBUTION OF WEIGHTS AND CLASSIFICATIONS OF COMMODITIES IN WHOLESALE PRICE INDEX NUMBERS OF THE NATIONAL BUREAU OF ECONOMIC RESEARCH

APPENDICES II and III of *Economic Tendencies in the United States* contained annual index numbers of wholesale prices for various commodity groups, with an explanation of the procedure employed. Appendices III and IV of this volume contain some additional group index numbers for the period 1913–29 and measurements for later years and months, together with some modifications of the earlier series. The increase in the number and character of the price series available for recent years has made it possible to enlarge the sample. At the same time, some changes have been made in methods of averaging and weighting.

The index numbers for the period 1913–29 are geometric averages of relative prices, unweighted except that important commodities have been represented by more than one series of price quotations. The annual and monthly index numbers for the period from 1929 to date are weighted arithmetic averages, or their aggregative equivalents. Weights are based on average quantities produced in 1927 and 1931, and on corresponding values. Certain commodity groups, notably foods, have been reduced in weight because of their relatively heavy representation in the index.

Price series used, their weights and the details of the classifications employed are indicated below. The weights given are average values of the quantities produced in 1927 and 1931, expressed as thousandths of the total value of all the commodities included in the index.

APPENDIX II

DISTRIBUTION OF WEIGHTS AND CLASSIFICATIONS OF COMMODITIES IN WHOLESALE PRICE INDEX NUMBERS OF THE NATIONAL BUREAU OF ECONOMIC RESEARCH

The complete titles of the various columns are as follows:

Column
- (3) Weight (aggregate weight placed equal to 1000)
- (4) Products originating on American farms
- (5) Products other than those originating on American farms
- (6) Foods
- (7) Non-foods
- (8) Producers' goods
- (9) Consumers' goods
- (10) Goods entering into capital equipment
- (11) Articles of human consumption
- (12) Building materials
- (13) Fuels used in production
- (14) Producers' goods destined for human consumption
- (15) Non-durable goods
- (16) Durable goods
- (17) Fuels used in production
- (18) Crops
- (19) Animal products
- (20) Metals
- (21) Non-metallic minerals
- (22) Forest products

PRICES IN RECESSION AND RECOVERY

(1) RAW AND SLIGHTLY PROCESSED MATERIALS	(2) NUMBER OF QUOTATIONS	(3) WEIGHT	(4) AMERICAN FARMS	(5) OTHER	(6) FOODS	(7) NON-FOODS	(8) PRODUCERS'	(9) CONSUMERS'	(10) CAPITAL GOODS	(11) CONSUMPTION	(12) BUILDING MATERIALS	(13) FUELS	(14) PRODUCERS' FOR HUMAN	(15) NON-DURABLE	(16) DURABLE	(17) FUELS	(18) CROPS	(19) ANIMAL	(20) METALS	(21) NON-METALLIC MINERALS	(22) FOREST
Aluminum	1	1.52		x			x		½				½		x				x		
Antimony	1	0.25		x			x		x						x				x		
Apples, fresh	3	3.54	x	x	x			x		x				x			x				
Bananas	1	3.55		x	x			x		x				x			x				
Barley	1	1.01	x	x		x	x							x			x				
Barytes	1	0.25		x		x	x						x							x	
Beans, dried	1	1.27	x	x	x			x		x				x			x				
Coal:																					
anthracite	3	13.17		x		x		x		x			x		x		x					
bituminous	3	35.71		x		x	x	x		x			x	x	x		x					
Cocoa beans	1	1.77		x		x	x								x			x				
Coffee	2	7.34		x	x			x		x					x			x				
Copper, ingot	1	6.84		x			x		⅔				⅓	x					x		
Copra	1	0.51		x			x			x			x	x							
Corn	2	7.34	x	x	x			x		x				x			x				
Cotton, raw	3	26.34	x	x		x	x						x	x			x				
Eggs	7	7.85			x			x		x				x				x			
Gravel	1	1.27		x		x	x						x							x	
Hay	3	6.33		x		x	x						x	x			x				
Hemp	1	0.51		x		x	x						x				x				

APPENDIX II

(1)	(2)	(3)	(4)	(5)	(6)	(7)	(8)	(9)	(10)	(11)	(12)	(13)	(14)	(15)	(16)	(17)	(18)	(19)	(20)	(21)	(22)
Hides:																						
domestic	6	4.80								x	x										
foreign	1	1.01								x	x										
Hops	1	0.25				x					x										
Iron:																						
ore	2	6.33		x		x	x		½	x	x	¼	¼		x			x	x			
pig	7	12.41		x		x	x		½	x	x	¼	¼		x			x	x			
Jute	1	0.25		x		x			x													
Lead, pig	1	2.28						x			x											
Lemons	1	1.01									x			x								
Livestock:																						
cattle	5	21.27		x	x	x	x			x	x				x			x	x	x		
hogs	2	26.59		x	x	x	x			x	x				x			x	x	x		
sheep	3	2.79		x	x	x	x			x	x	¼						x	x	x		
poultry	2	4.30		x	x	x	x				x							x	x	x		
Lumber:																						
lath	1	0.25				x	x			x	x					H						
timber	13	18.49				x	x			⅓	x	⅔	⅓			x						
Milk, fresh	3	30.39		x						x	x				x							
Nickel, ingot	1	0.25		x		x	x															
Nitrate of soda	1	1.01						x	x													
Oats	1	2.03		x	x	x	x				x				x			x				
Onions	1	0.51		x	x	x			x		x								x			
Oranges	1	5.32			x	x	x				x				x				x			
Peanuts	1	0.76			x	x	x				x				x				x			
Pepper	1	0.25								x												
Petroleum, crude	3	25.83		x	x	x	x				½	½	½		½	x				x			
Phosphate rock	1	0.25		x	x	x	x		x						x							

473

474 PRICES IN RECESSION AND RECOVERY

(1)	(2)	(3)	(4)	(5)	(6)	(7)	(8)	(9)	(10)	(11)	(12)	(13)	(14)	(15)	(16)	(17)	(18)	(19)	(20)	(21)	(22)
RAW MATERIALS (cont.)																					
Potatoes	5	10.63	x						x						x		x					
Quicksilver	1	0.25						x												x		x
Rubber, crude	3	7.85		x		x	x		½	½	x				½	x		x	x			x
Rye	1	0.51	x	x	x		x			x	x				x	x	x					
Sand	1	0.51		x		x	x															
Seeds	4	3.54		x	x	x	x		x	x	x				x	x		x				
Silk	4	8.36		x		x	x		x	x	x				x	x		x	x			
Silver	1	0.76				x	x			x	x					x		x				
Sisal	1	0.51		x		x	x	x														
Steel scrap	1	0.51		x		x	x	x		x	x				x	x		x				
Stone	1	1.52			x		x					x										
Sugar, raw	1	7.60		x		x	x		x	x	x				½	x		x				
Sulphur, crude	1	0.76		x		x	x		½	½	x				½	½		x				
Tin, pig	1	2.53			x		x		x	x	x				x	x		x				
Tobacco, leaf	1	5.06	x	x	x	x	x		x	x	x				x	x		x				
Wheat	6	19.25	x	x			x															
Woodpulp	4	4.30		x		x	x		x	x	x		x		x	x		x		x	x	x
Wool, raw	9	5.33	x	x		x	x		x	x	x				x	x		x				
Zinc, slab	1	1.52		x		x	x						x									
MANUFACTURED GOODS																					
Acid:																					
carbonic	1	0.25					x											x				x
citric	1	0.25		x		x	x		x	x	x				x	x		x				
nitric	1	0.25		x		x	x		x	x	x				x	x		x				
oleic	1	0.25	x	x		x	x		x	x	x				x	x		x				
stearic	1	0.25	x	x		x	x		x	x	x				x	x		x				
sulphuric	1	1.77				x	x		½	½	½				½	½		½	½			x

APPENDIX II

Agricultural implements:

Item	(2)	(3)
binder	1	0.25
cultivator	1	0.25
engine, 3 H.P.	1	0.25
harrows	2	0.51
hoes	1	0.25
mower, hay	1	0.25
plow, tractor	1	0.25
2 horse	1	0.25
pumps	1	0.25
rakes, self-dump	1	0.25
separator, cream	1	0.25
shovels	1	0.25
spreader, manure	1	0.25
wagons, 2 horse	1	0.25

Alcohol:

Item	(2)	(3)
denatured	1	0.51
grain	1	1.27
wood	1	0.25
Aluminum sulphate	1	0.25
Ammonia anhydrous	1	0.25
Asphalt	1	0.76

Automobiles:

Item	(2)	(3)
passenger cars	1	37.99
trucks	1	8.86
Babbit metal	1	0.51
Baking powder	1	0.76
Barrels, wooden	1	0.76

476 PRICES IN RECESSION AND RECOVERY

(1) MFD. GOODS (cont.)	(2)	(3)	(4)	(5)	(6)	(7)	(8)	(9)	(10)	(11)	(12)	(13)	(14)	(15)	(16)	(17)	(18)	(19)	(20)	(21)	(22)
Batteries	2	3.55		x		x		x		x											
Belting, leather	1	0.51	x		x	x									x						
Benzine	1	0.25		x		x			x										x			
Blankets:																						
cotton	1	0.51	x			x		x		x				x	x						
cotton warp	1	0.25	x			x		x		x				x	x	x					
wool	1	0.25	x					x		x					x	x					
Bleaching powder	1	0.25		x			x			x								x			
Board:																						
plaster	1	0.25		x		x				x			x	x		x					
wall	1	0.76		x		x				x	x		x	x		x		x			
Boilers	2	1.52	x			x				x	x			x		x					
Boots and shoes	1	17.22					x							x	x							
Borax	1	0.25		x		x				x				x	x						
Boxboard	3	1.77		x		x				x				x	x						
Boxes, cigar	1	0.25		x	x	x				x											
Brass:																						
rods	1	0.25		x		x	x			x				x	x		x			x		
sheets	1	1.52		x		x	x			x				x	x		x	x		x		
tubes	1	0.25		x		x	x							x	x					x		
wire	1	0.25		x		x	x								x					x		
Bread	5	15.70	x		x			x									x	x				
Brick	6	5.57				x	x			x				x	x			x				
Burlap	1	1.77					x		x	x				x	x		x		x		x	
Butter	9	13.68	x		x		x							x	x				x			
Calcium:																						
acetate	1	0.25		x		x		x		x				x		x						x

APPENDIX II

(1)	(2)	(3)	(4)	(5)	(6)	(7)	(8)	(9)	(10)	(11)	(12)	(13)	(14)	(15)	(16)	(17)	(18)	(19)	(20)	(21)	(22)
carbide	1	0.25								x	x		x	x							
chloride	1	0.25		x						x	x		x	x							
Camphor	1	0.25		x						x	x		x	x							
Carpets	3	4.05	x				x			x	x				x						
Cases, shipping	1	0.25		x			x				x			x					x		
Caskets:																					
metal	1	0.25		x		x	x			x	x			x			x				
wood	1	0.51		x			x	x		x	x			x							x
Castor oil	1	0.25	x							x	x		x	x	x						
Cattle feed	4	4.57	x		x		x			x	x		x	x	x						
Cement	1	5.57		x	x		x			x	x	x				x					
Cereal breakfast foods	3	2.53	x		x		x			x	x		x	x		x					
Cheese	3	2.28	x		x		x			x	x			x			x				
Chlorine	1	0.25		x			x			x	x		x	x				x			
Cigarettes	1	7.60	x		x		x	x		x	x			x			x				
Cigars	1	5.07	x		x		x	x		x	x			x			x				
Coal tar colors	4	1.01		x			x			x	x		x	x							x
Cocoa, powdered	1	0.51		x	x		x	x	5/6	x	x	1/6		x							
Coke	3	5.82		x				x	5/6	x	x	1/6		x	5/6						
Collars, men's	2	0.51	x				x	x		x	x					x					
Comforters	1	0.25	x				x	x		x					x						
Concrete blocks	1	0.51		x			x					x			x						
Copper:																					
rods	1	0.76		x			x				x			x	x					x	
sheets	1	0.76		x			x				x	x			x					x	
wire	1	1.52		x			x				x	x			x					x	
Copper sulphate	1	0.25		x			x			x	x		x	x				x			
Corn meal	2	1.01	x		x		x			x	x			x							

477

478 PRICES IN RECESSION AND RECOVERY

	(1)	(2)	(3)	(4)	(5)	(6)	(7)	(8)	(9)	(10)	(11)	(12)	(13)	(14)	(15)	(16)	(17)	(18)	(19)	(20)	(21)	(22)
MFD. GOODS (cont.)																						
Corn starch		1	0.51			x			x									x				
Cotton goods:																						
broadcloth		1	1.01	x			x			x	x	x		x	x			x				
damask		1	0.25	x			x	x		x	x	x	x	x	x			x				
denims		1	0.76	x			x	x		x	x	x		x	x			x				
drillings		1	0.51	x			x			x	x	x	x	x	x			x				
duck		2	1.01	x			x	x		x	x	x	x		x			x				
flannel		2	1.27	x			x	x	x	x	x	x			x			x				
gingham		1	1.52	x			x		x	x	x	x			x			x				
muslin		4	1.01	x			x		x	x	x	x			x			x				
osnaburg		1	0.25	x			x		x	x	x	x			x			x				
percale		1	1.01	x			x		x	x	x	x			x			x				
print cloth		2	2.53	x			x		x	x	x	x			x			x				
sateen		1	2.03	x			x		x	x	x	x			x			x				
sheeting:																						
bleached		2	5.57	x			x		x	x	x	x		x	x			x				
brown		3	2.03	x			x	x		x	x	x	x	x	x			x				
shirting		2	1.52	x			x	x		x	x	x	x	x	x			x				
tickings		1	0.25	x			x	x		x	x	x	x	x	x			x				
tire fabric		2	2.53	x			x	x		x	x	x		x	x			x				
toweling		1	0.76	x			x		x	x	x	x		x	x			x				
yarns		5	6.57	x			x			x	x	x		x	x			x				
Crackers		2	5.32	x					x	x	x	x			x			x				
Creosote oil		1	0.51		x		x			x	x	x		x	x			x				
Cutlery, knives and forks		1	0.25	x			x		x	x	x		x			x			x			
Doors		1	1.27	x			x			x	x					x				x		x	x

APPENDIX II

(1)	(2)	(3)	(4)	(5)	(6)	(7)	(8)	(9)	(10)	(11)	(12)	(13)	(14)	(15)	(16)	(17)	(18)	(19)	(20)	(21)	(22)
										3/5	2/5	3/5	2/5	3/5	2/5	3/5					
Electricity	1	16.46		x			x													x		
Fertilizers:																						
potash:																						
manure	1	0.25	x		x	x	x		x						x	x						
muriate	1	0.25	x		x	x	x		x						x	x						x
sulphate of ammonia	1	0.51	x		x	x	x		x						x	x						x
superphosphate	1	0.51	x		x	x	x		x						x	x						x
mixed fertilizer	6	2.28	x		x	x	x		x						x	x						x
Fish, canned and cured	4	2.28	x	x			x		x						x							
Floor coverings:																						
felt-base	2	0.51	x		x		x		x								x				x	
linoleum	2	0.76	x		x		x		x								x						
Flour:																						
rye	1	0.25	x		x	½	½		x					½	x	x						
wheat	9	16.47	x		x	½	½		x					½	x	x						
Frames, door and window	2	0.51	x		x			x					x									
Fruits, canned:																						
apples	1	0.25	x		x				x						x		x	x	x	x	x	x
apricots	1	0.25	x		x				x						x		x	x	x	x	x	x
cherries	1	0.25	x		x				x						x		x	x	x	x	x	x
peaches	1	0.77	x		x				x						x		x	x	x	x	x	x
pears	1	0.51	x		x				x						x		x	x	x	x	x	x
pineapples	1	0.76		x	x				x						x		x	x	x	x	x	x
Fruits, dried:																						
apples	1	0.25	x		x		x		x						x		x	x	x	x	x	x

480 PRICES IN RECESSION AND RECOVERY

(1) MFD. GOODS (cont.)	(2)	(3)	(4)	(5)	(6)	(7)	(8)	(9)	(10)	(11)	(12)	(13)	(14)	(15)	(16)	(17)	(18)	(19)	(20)	(21)	(22)
Fruits, dried (cont.)																					
apricots	1	0.25	x		x				x						x	x				x	x
prunes	1	0.51	x		x				x						x	x	x			x	x
raisins	1	0.51	x		x				x						x	x	x				x
Furniture:																					
bedroom:																					
beds:																					
metal	1	0.51		x		x			x			x			x			x		x	
wood	1	0.51		x		x			x			x			x				x	x	
benches	1	0.25		x		x			x			x			x						
dressers	1	1.27		x		x			x			x			x						
mattresses	1	1.27	x			x			x			x			x						
springs	1	0.76		x		x			x			x			x						
dining room:																					
buffets	1	0.51		x		x			x			x			x						
chairs	1	1.01		x		x			x			x			x						
tables	1	0.51		x		x			x			x			x						
kitchen:																					
cabinets	1	0.51		x		x			x			x			x						
chairs	1	0.25		x		x			x			x			x						
tables	1	0.25		x		x			x			x			x						
living room:																					
chairs	1	1.26		x		x		x	x			x			x						
davenports	1	0.51		x		x		x	x			x			x						
tables	1	1.01		x		x			x			x			x						
office:																					
arm chairs	2	0.51		x		x					x				x						

APPENDIX II

(1)	(2)	(3)	(4)	(5)	(6)	(7)	(8)	(9)	(10)	(11)	(12)	(13)	(14)	(15)	(16)	(17)	(18)	(19)	(20)	(21)	(22)
desks	2	0.51																			x
Gas	1	7.59					x	1/3	2/3											x	
Ginger ale	1	1.27					x	2/3	x											x	x
Glass:																					
plate	2	1.01				x	x		x					x	x						
window	2	0.76	x			x	x		x					x							
Gloves, leather	2	1.01	x			x			x					x					x		
Glucose	1	0.76	x		x		x		x	x				x							
Glycerine	1	0.51	x			x	x		x	x				x							
Grape juice	1	0.25	x		x			x	x	x				x							
Handkerchiefs:																					
cotton:																					
men's	1	0.25	x			x	x		x	x				x	x			x	x		
women's	1	0.25	x			x	x		x	x				x	x			x	x		
linen:																					
men's	1	0.25				x	x			x		x		x	x			x	x		
women's	1	0.25				x	x			x		x		x	x			x	x		
Harness	1	0.51	x				x	x						x							
Hats:																					
finished	1	1.27	x			x	x		x	x				x	x			x	x	x	x
unfinished	1	0.51	x			x	x			x			x	x	x						
Hosiery:																					
cotton:																					
men's	1	0.76	x			x	x		x	x				x	x			x	x		
women's	1	1.52	x			x	x		x	x				x	x			x	x		
silk:																					
men's	1	1.01	x			x	x		x	x				x	x			x	x	x	x
women's	1	6.58	x			x	x		x	x				x	x			x	x	x	x

482 PRICES IN RECESSION AND RECOVERY

(1) MFD. GOODS (cont.)	(2)	(3)	(4)	(5)	(6)	(7)	(8)	(9)	(10)	(11)	(12)	(13)	(14)	(15)	(16)	(17)	(18)	(19)	(20)	(21)	(22)
Irons, electric	2	0.51		x	x		x	x								x	x		x	x	x
Ironers, electric	1	0.25		x	x		x		x							x	x		x	x	x
Iron and steel:																					
bar iron	2	0.51		x	x		x	x		x						x	x		x	x	x
bars:																					
concrete	1	0.51		x	x		x	x				x				x	x	x	x	x	x
merchant	1	3.79		x	x		x	x	x							x	x	x	x	x	x
sheet	1	1.78		x	x		x	x	x							x	x	x	x	x	x
steel	1	0.51		x	x		x	x	x							x	x	x	x	x	x
barrels	1	0.51		x	x		x	x	x							x	x	x	x	x	x
billets	1	3.80		x	x		x	x								x	x	x	x	x	x
boiler tubes	1	0.25		x	x		x					x				x	x	x	x	x	x
bolts:																					
machine	1	0.51		x	x		x	x	x							x	x	x	x	x	x
plow	1	0.51		x	x		x	x	x							x	x	x	x	x	x
stove	1	0.51		x	x		x	x				x				x	x	x	x	x	x
truck	1	0.25		x	x		x	x				x				x	x	x	x	x	x
butts	1	0.51		x			x	x				x				x	x	x	x	x	x
cans, sanitary	1	3.04		x	x		x	x			x			x	x		x	x	x	x	x
castings	1	7.60		x	x		x	x	x							x	x	x	x	x	x
locks	1	0.51		x	x		x	x				x				x	x	x	x	x	x
nails, wire	1	0.76		x	x		x	x				x				x	x	x	x	x	x
pails, iron	1	0.25		x	x		x	x			x					x	x	x	x	x	x
pipe	3	4.30		x	x		x	x				x				x	x	x	x	x	x
plates	1	3.55		x	x		x	x	x							x	x	x	x	x	x
rails	1	2.53		x	x		x	x				x				x	x	x	x	x	x
rivets	2	0.51		x	x		x	x	x							x	x	x	x	x	x

APPENDIX II

(1)	(2)	(3)	(4)	(5)	(6)	(7)	(8)	(9)	(10)	(11)	(12)	(13)	(14)	(15)	(16)	(17)	(18)	(19)	(20)	(21)	(22)
rods	1	0.76	x			x	x			x				x							
sheets:																					
annealed	1	3.80	x			x	x		x	x				x	x						
auto body	1	1.27	x			x	x		x	x				x	x						
galvanized	1	2.02	x		x	x	x			x				x	x						
skelp	1	0.51	x			x	x			x				x	x						
spikes	1	0.25	x			x	x	x		x				x	x						
strips	1	0.76	x			x	x			x	x			x	x						
structural steel	1	2.53	x			x	x			x	x			x	x						
terneplate	1	0.25	x			x	x	x		x				x	x						
tinplate	1	4.05	x			x	x			x				x	x						
tube	1	0.25	x		x	x	x			x				x	x						
wire, fence	4	2.03	x			x	x			x				x	x						
woodscrews	1	0.25	x			x	x			x				x							
Jelly, grape	1	0.76		x				x				x		x	x						
Jute, yarns	2	0.51	x		x							x		x	x						
Lard	1	3.80		x				x				x		x	x						
Lavatories	2	0.51	x			x	x		x	x				x	x						
Lead, pipe	1	0.25	x			x	x	x		x				x	x						
Leather:																					
artificial	2	1.01	x			x	x			x				x	x						
domestic	3	3.04		x		x	x			x		x	x		x		x	x			
foreign	1	2.53		x		x	x		x	x		x	x		x			x	x		
harness	1	0.25		x		x	x					x	x		x						
Lime	2	0.51	x				x			x				x	x						
Linseed oil	1	1.27	x							x				x	x		x	x			
Macaroni	1	1.01	x		x	x	x			x					x			x			x

(1) MFD. GOODS (cont.)	(2)	(3)	(4)	(5)	(6)	(7)	(8)	(9)	(10)	(11)	(12)	(13)	(14)	(15)	(16)	(17)	(18)	(19)	(20)	(21)	(22)
Matches	2	1.01	x			x		x						x						x	
Meats:																						
beef:																						
cured	1	0.25	x	x	x			x		x				x			x	x			
fresh	2	15.19	x	x	x			x	x	x				x			x	x			
lamb	1	1.77	x	x	x			x	x	x				x			x	x			
mutton	1	0.25	x	x	x			x	x	x				x			x	x			
pork:																						
cured	5	10.13	x	x	x			x	x	x				x			x				
fresh	1	15.19	x	x	x			x	x	x				x			x				
veal	1	2.53	x	x	x			x	x	x				x			x				
poultry	2	3.04	x	x	x			x	x	x				x			x				
Milk:																						
condensed	1	1.01	x	x	x			x	x	x				x			x	x			
evaporated	1	2.29	x	x	x			x	x	x				x			x	x			
powdered	1	0.25	x	x	x		x	x	x	x			x	x			x	x			
Mirrors	1	0.76		x		x			x	x					x							
Molasses	1	0.51	x		x			x	x	x				x					x	x		
Oil cloth	2	0.51	x	x		x			x				x	x		x						
Oleo oil	1	0.51	x	x				x		x				x						x		
Oleomargarine	1	1.52	x		x			x	x	x				x					x			
Overalls, denim	1	2.53	x		x			x	x	x				x		x						
Overcoats	1	1.77	x		x			x	x	x				x								
Paint materials:																						
paints, prepared	5	4.56	x	x	x			x	x	x	x			x								
colors, black	4	1.01	x	x	x			x	x	x	x			x							x	
ethyl acetate	1	0.25	x	x	x			x	x	x				x								x

APPENDIX II

			(4)	(5)	(6)	(7)	(8)	(9)	(10)	(11)	(12)	(13)	(14)	(15)	(16)	(17)	(18)	(19)	(20)	(21)	(22)
green chrome	1	0.25											x								x
gum, copal	1	0.25									x	x		x							
lead:																					
red	1	0.25		x		x	x				x	x		x							x
white	1	0.51		x		x	x				x	x	x	x							x
litharge	1	0.25		x		x	x				x	x	x	x							x
lithopone	1	0.25		x		x	x				x	x	x	x							x
zinc oxide	1	0.25		x		x	x				x	x	x	x							
Paper:																					
book	1	3.04		x		x	x	x			x	x		x	x				x		x	
newsprint	1	4.30		x		x	x	x			x	x		x						x	x	
tissue	1	0.76		x		x	x	x			x	x		x						x	x	
wrapping	1	4.30		x		x	x	x			x			x							x	
Peanut butter	1	0.25			x			x														
Peroxide	1	0.25					x	x														
Petroleum products:																					
cylinder oil	3	3.04		x		x	½	½	½		½	½		½	½							
fuel oil	2	10.38		x		x	½	½	½		½	½		½	½							
gasoline	5	19.76		x		x	½	½	½		½	½		½	½							
kerosene	2	3.55		x		x	x	x	x		x	x		x	x							
Pillow cases	1	0.25	x			x		x							x							
Pipe covering, asbestos	1	0.76		x		x					x	x			x	x						
Pipe, sewer	1	1.27		x		x					x	x			x	x						
Plaster	1	0.51	x	x		x			x		x					x	x					
Pretzels	1	0.25		x		x	x															
Putty	1	0.25		x		x	x	x				x									x	
Quebracho	1	0.25		x		x	x	x								x						
Radiation	1	1.01		x		x	x	x	x			x			x	x	x		x	x		

485

486   PRICES IN RECESSION AND RECOVERY

(1)	(2)	(3)	(4)	(5)	(6)	(7)	(8)	(9)	(10)	(11)	(12)	(13)	(14)	(15)	(16)	(17)	(18)	(19)	(20)	(21)	(22)
MFD. GOODS (cont.)																					
Rayon	4	3.04		x		x	x						x	x							
Rice	2	2.03	x		x																	
Roofing:																						
prepared	4	2.03		x		x	x		x			x			x	x		x				
slate	1	0.25		x		x	x		x			x										
Rope:																						
cotton	1	0.25	x			x	x	x		x	x			x	x		x	x				
manila	1	0.51				x	x	x		x	x				x		x					
sisal	1	0.25		x		x	x	x							x		x					
Rosin	1	0.51		x		x	x		x		x				x		x	x				
Rubber heels	2	0.76		x		x									x					x		x x
Rubber hose	1	0.25		x		x		x							x							
Salt:																						
American	1	1.01		x		x	x		x		x			x	x			x				
granulated	1	0.51		x		x	x			x	x			x	x					x		
Sash, window	1	0.51		x		x	x		x	x	x						x		x			
Sewing machines	2	1.27				x	x		x	x	x					x	x	x				
Shades, window	1	0.51	x			x	x		x	x	x				x	x	x	x				
Sheets, bed	1	0.25	x			x	x	x			x				x		x					
Shellac	1	0.25		x		x	x		x		x			x	x			x			x	
Shingles	2	0.76		x		x	x			x	x			x								
Shirts, men's	2	5.06	x			x	x			x	x			x	x		x					
Silk yarn	6	2.28		x		x	x		x	x	x			x	x		x					
Sinks	1	0.51		x		x	x										x		x			
Snuff	1	0.25	x			x	x	x							x			x				
Soap	5	5.32	x			x	x		x	x	x			x	x			x				
Soda phosphate	1	0.25		x		x	x			x	x			x	x							x

APPENDIX II

(1)	(2)	(3)	(4)	(5)	(6)	(7)	(8)	(9)	(10)	(11)	(12)	(13)	(14)	(15)	(16)	(17)	(18)	(19)	(20)	(21)	(22)
Soda, plain bottled	1	1.27												x							
Sodium:																					
ash	1	1.27		x	x	x	x			x	x			x	x						
bicarbonate	1	0.25		x	x	x				x				x	x						
caustic	1	0.76		x						x				x							
silicate	1	0.25		x						x				x							
Solder	1	0.51				x															
Soup, tomato	1	1.52	x				x			x				x	x						
Starch, laundry	1	1.01	x							x				x	x						
Stoves, cooking	1	1.78				x				x				x							
Sugar, granulated	1	11.39	x				x			x				x	x		x				
Suits, men's and boys'	4	11.40	x				x			x				x	x		x				
Suitcases	1	0.25					x			x				x	x						
Tablecloths	1	0.25					x			x				x							
Tableware:																					
dinner sets	1	0.51		x		x	x			x					x	x	x				
pitchers	1	0.76		x		x	x			x				x	x	✓	x				
plates	1	0.25		x		x	x			x				x	x	x	x				
teacups and saucers	1	0.25		x		x	x			x				x	x		x				
tumblers	1	0.25		x		x	x			x				x	x		x				
Tallow:																					
edible	1	0.25			x		x			x				x	x		x				
inedible	1	0.76			x		x			x				x	x		x				
Tar, pine	1	1.77									x										
Tea	1	0.76			x					x				x	x		x			x	
Thread:																					
cotton	1	2.54	x				x	½	½	x			½	x			x		x		
linen	1	0.25	x	x			x			x				x	x		x		x		

MFD. GOODS (cont.)

(1)	(2)	(3)	(4)	(5)	(6)	(7)	(8)	(9)	(10)	(11)	(12)	(13)	(14)	(15)	(16)	(17)	(18)	(19)	(20)	(21)	(22)
Tile	4	1.27													x					x	
Tires and tubes:																					
auto tires	2	11.40		x		x	1/3	2/3		1/3							x	x			
truck and bus tires	1	1.01		x		x	x	x									x				
tubes	1	2.79		x		x	1/3	2/3		1/3							x				
Tobacco:																					
plug	1	1.01	x		x			x		x								x			
smoking	1	3.04	x		x			x		x								x			
Tools:																					
angle bars	1	0.25		x		x	x		x	x					x	x	x	x	x	x	
augers	1	0.25		x		x	x		x	x					x	x	x	x	x	x	
axes	1	0.25		x		x	x		x	x					x	x	x	x	x	x	
files	1	0.25		x		x	x		x	x					x	x	x	x	x	x	
hammers	1	0.25		x		x	x		x	x		x			x	x	x	x	x	x	
hatchets	1	0.25		x		x	x		x						x	x	x	x	x	x	
knives	1	0.25		x		x	x		x	x		x			x	x	x	x	x	x	
planes	1	0.25		x		x	x			x					x	x	x	x	x	x	
rakes	1	0.25		x		x	x		x	x		x			x	x	x	x	x	x	
saws	2	0.51				x													x	x		
vises	1	0.25		x		x	x												x			
Topcoats	1	1.52	x												x	x						
Traveling bags	1	0.25	x												x	x						
Trousers:																					
dress	2	2.03	x						x		x				x	x						
work	1	0.51	x						x		x							x				
Tubs, bath and laundry	2	1.01				x							x			x					x	

APPENDIX II 489

	(2)	(3)	(4)	(5)	(6)	(7)	(8)	(9)	(10)	(11)	(12)	(13)	(14)	(15)	(16)	(17)	(18)	(19)	(20)	(21)	(22)
Turpentine	1	0.25	x																		
Twine:																					
binder	1	0.51			x						x			x				x			
cotton	1	0.25	x								x			x				x			
Underwear:																					
cotton:																					
men's	1	0.76			x	x					x	x		x	x		x	x			
women's	1	1.52			x	x	x				x	x		x			x	x			
woolen, men's	1	0.51		x	x	x					x			x		x	x	x			
Vacuum cleaners	1	1.01				x															
Vegetables, canned:																					
asparagus	1	0.25	x		x	x		x			x	x		x			x	x	x		
baked beans	1	0.76	x		x	x		x			x	x		x			x	x	x		
corn	1	0.51	x		x	x		x			x	x		x			x	x	x		
peas	1	0.76	x		x	x		x			x	x		x			x	x	x		
spinach	1	0.25	x		x	x		x			x	x		x			x	x	x		
string beans	1	0.51	x		x	x		x			x	x		x			x	x	x		
tomatoes	1	1.27			x	x		x			x										
Vegetable oil:																					
coconut	1	1.01		x	x	x	x				x	x	x	x			x	x	x		
corn	1	0.25			x	x					x	x		x			x	x	x		
cottonseed	1	2.53		x	x	x		x			x	x		x			x	x	x		
olive	1	0.51			x	x	x				x	x	x	x			x	x	x		
palm	2	0.51			x		x				x	x		x			x	x	x		
Vinegar	1	0.25			x	x		x			x	x		x			x	x	x		
Washing machines	1	0.76				x	x	x			x			x	x		x	x	x	x	
Wax, paraffin	1	0.51				x					x			x							x

	(1)	(2)	(3)	(4)	(5)	(6)	(7)	(8)	(9)	(10)	(11)	(12)	(13)	(14)	(15)	(16)	(17)	(18)	(19)	(20)	(21)	(22)
MFD. GOODS (cont.)																						
Woolen and worsted goods:																						
flannel		1	0.25	x				x	x		x			x			x	x				
overcoating		2	4.05	x				x	x		x			x			x	x				
suiting		5	4.56	x				x			x			x				x				
trousering, cotton warp		1	0.76	x					x		x			x								
women's dress goods:																						
broadcloth		1	1.01	x					x		x			x			x					
crepe		1	1.27	x				x	x		x			x			x	x				
flannel		1	0.76	x					x		x			x			x	x				
french serge		1	0.76	x					x		x			x								
serge, cotton warp		1	0.51	x							x			x			x					
sicilian cloth, cotton warp		1	0.51	x							x			x			x	x				
yarns, wool		3	4.56	x							x			x			x	x			x	
Zinc chloride		1	0.25			x						x										
Zinc, sheets		1	0.25			x														x		

NOTE: The following series are composites, and are therefore averages of more than one price series: coal, gravel, sand, tobacco leaf, automobiles, boots and shoes, boilers (heating), brick, caskets, cement, cigarettes, cigars, electricity, furniture, gas, harness, lavatories, leather (calf, lime, matches (regular), pork (fresh), plows (horse), roofing (prepared), rubber heels, sewing machines, stoves, suitcases, tires and tubes, traveling bags and wagons.

APPENDIX III

ANNUAL INDEX NUMBERS OF WHOLESALE PRICES, 1913–1935 [1]

YEAR	ALL COMMODITIES	RAW MATERIALS	MANUFACTURED GOODS	PRODUCTS OF AMERICAN FARMS			COMMODITIES OTHER THAN THOSE ORIGINATING ON AMERICAN FARMS			COMMODITIES OTHER THAN RAW AMERICAN FARM PRODUCTS (processed American farm products plus all other products, raw and processed)
				Raw	Processed	Total	Raw	Processed	Total	
N, 1913 [2]	444	132	312	83	142	225	49	170	219	361
N, 1929 [2]	492	142	350	83	152	235	59	198	257	409
1913	100.0	100.0	100.0	100.0	100.0	100.0	100.0	100.0	100.0	100.0
1914	98.2	98.7	97.8	102.4	100.5	101.2	92.7	95.5	94.8	97.0
1915	102.8	104.2	102.0	106.9	102.7	104.2	99.9	101.6	101.1	101.9
1916	129.1	127.9	129.4	125.4	122.0	123.3	132.1	136.3	135.3	129.9
1917	171.2	174.4	169.4	182.0	172.2	175.8	162.9	167.1	166.4	168.7
1918	195.7	188.9	198.4	206.3	210.1	208.8	164.7	189.3	183.4	193.5
1919	203.4	196.1	206.1	221.9	224.9	223.8	161.4	192.1	184.6	199.4
1920	227.9	202.2	239.5	212.5	241.9	230.7	186.6	237.5	224.8	231.4
1921	150.6	125.0	162.7	124.1	155.9	143.4	126.4	168.2	157.7	157.2
1922	148.3	133.2	154.8	136.9	151.4	145.8	127.4	157.5	150.2	150.9
1923	156.4	141.5	163.0	143.5	157.0	151.9	138.6	167.9	160.6	159.4
1924	153.5	140.5	159.2	146.3	157.8	153.4	132.7	160.2	153.5	155.2
1925	159.7	152.9	162.4	159.4	169.0	165.4	143.9	157.4	154.2	159.9
1926	153.4	143.7	157.5	144.1	160.5	154.3	142.9	155.0	152.2	155.5
1927	148.5	140.1	152.0	144.5	158.7	153.2	134.0	146.8	143.8	149.5
1928	150.3	144.0	153.1	155.8	163.1	160.3	128.6	145.6	141.6	149.5

APPENDIX III—(Cont.)

ANNUAL INDEX NUMBERS OF WHOLESALE PRICES, 1913–1935

YEAR	ALL COM- MODITIES	RAW MA- TERIALS	MANU- FACTURED GOODS	PRODUCTS OF AMERICAN FARMS			COMMODITIES OTHER THAN THOSE ORIGINAT- ING ON AMERICAN FARMS			COMMODITIES OTHER THAN RAW AMERI- CAN FARM PRODUCTS
				Raw	Processed	Total	Raw	Processed	Total	
1929	148.3	140.7	151.5	150.4	159.2	155.9	127.7	145.7	141.4	148.1
1930	134.2	122.4	140.6	128.3	145.8	138.4	114.5	136.7	130.7	136.4
1931	113.4	96.7	123.2	95.5	123.5	111.5	97.3	123.3	115.7	118.8
1932	100.1	80.8	111.8	71.6	105.4	90.7	90.9	117.7	109.7	108.6
1933	103.2	85.0	114.4	77.5	112.1	97.0	93.2	116.4	109.7	110.9
1934	117.3	100.9	126.5	96.7	130.1	115.7	105.0	124.3	119.1	123.2
1935	124.0	110.0	131.7	113.7	141.8	129.9	104.7	123.6	118.6	127.1

[1] Computed by the National Bureau of Economic Research from data compiled by the U. S. Bureau of Labor Statistics. For the period 1913–29 the index numbers are geometric averages of relative prices, unweighted except that prices of important commodities have been represented by more than one series. The index numbers for the period 1929–35 are weighted arithmetic averages of relative prices. (See Appendix II for weights and classifications of commodities.)

It should be noted that new series of index numbers, originally computed on the 1929 base, and differing some- what in respect of weights and commodities included from the index numbers first computed on the 1913 base, have been spliced with the older series to give the annual measurements presented in this table. This combination leads to certain minor inconsistencies among some of the group and subgroup indexes.

[2] The number of price quotations represented in the averages for the different commodity groups varies from year to year as more series have become available. The entries for 1913 and 1929 are minima and maxima, respectively, for the period 1913–29. The number of quotations used for the recent years is given in Appendix IV.

APPENDIX III

YEAR	PRODUCERS' GOODS			CONSUMERS' GOODS			PRODUCERS' GOODS Destined for human consumption	Entering into capital equipment	PRODUCERS' GOODS DESTINED FOR HUMAN CONSUMPTION	
	Raw	Processed	Total	Raw	Processed	Total			Foods	Non-foods
N, 1913	101	163	264	31	149	180	132	132	54	78
N, 1929	108	184	292	34	166	200	132	160	54	78
1913	100.0	100.0	100.0	100.0	100.0	100.0	100.0	100.0	100.0	100.0
1914	97.8	95.4	96.3	101.8	100.5	100.8	99.6	93.2	103.3	97.0
1915	107.6	102.3	104.4	94.2	101.8	100.5	108.2	100.6	110.4	106.6
1916	128.9	144.9	138.6	115.5	116.5	116.4	141.5	135.8	124.8	154.2
1917	179.5	180.2	180.1	156.9	158.8	158.6	185.2	175.9	172.2	194.7
1918	193.9	201.8	198.8	172.0	194.7	190.6	210.4	189.6	196.7	220.2
1919	195.3	203.1	200.1	197.4	209.9	207.7	211.9	190.9	218.3	207.4
1920	201.1	245.0	227.2	203.9	233.5	228.3	218.6	237.2	205.1	228.1
1921	117.7	161.0	143.0	152.1	164.7	162.5	122.9	165.5	117.2	126.7
1922	127.3	154.8	143.9	153.9	154.8	154.8	130.3	158.7	122.0	136.3
1923	137.2	167.6	155.4	156.9	158.2	158.1	138.2	174.3	127.9	145.7
1924	134.5	160.4	150.0	162.1	158.0	158.9	137.4	164.2	134.0	139.7
1925	144.4	158.5	152.9	184.2	167.1	169.9	143.6	163.9	144.6	142.8
1926	135.0	153.6	146.2	176.1	162.1	164.5	132.1	161.8	135.5	129.7
1927	132.8	147.0	141.4	167.1	157.7	159.4	129.9	154.2	137.1	125.0
1928	136.8	147.3	143.1	169.7	159.8	161.5	135.1	152.8	146.3	127.6
1929	131.4	146.9	140.8	174.8	157.2	160.2	128.8	154.0	140.8	121.1
1930	112.0	135.4	124.6	163.1	146.7	149.5	108.6	139.5	119.5	101.5
1931	86.6	119.3	103.1	136.5	128.0	129.3	82.4	126.1	88.3	79.1
1932	72.9	110.8	91.4	111.3	114.3	113.4	67.4	117.2	68.3	67.5
1933	78.6	114.7	96.3	109.1	115.5	114.1	74.7	118.6	73.6	76.7
1934	94.7	126.3	110.7	123.6	128.6	127.5	90.8	129.5	93.2	90.0
1935	105.6	126.3	116.9	125.0	137.7	135.2	101.6	129.2	119.5	89.1

494 PRICES IN RECESSION AND RECOVERY

	CONSUMERS' GOODS, PROCESSED		GOODS ENTERING INTO CAPITAL EQUIPMENT		CROPS				
YEAR	Foods	Non-foods	Raw	Processed	Raw producers'	Raw consumers'	Raw, total	Processed	Total
N, 1913	79	70	28	104	30	17	47	76	123
N, 1929	86	80	35	125	30	17	47	77	124
1913	100.0	100.0	100.0	100.0	100.0	100.0	100.0	100.0	100.0
1914	102.0	99.0	93.1	93.2	101.4	102.2	101.7	100.9	101.1
1915	104.0	99.3	110.3	98.3	114.7	90.2	105.3	103.2	103.8
1916	116.0	117.2	144.6	133.4	130.1	122.3	127.2	120.6	122.9
1917	163.7	153.1	186.1	172.1	185.2	176.6	182.2	176.5	178.6
1918	195.1	194.1	184.7	190.5	210.8	176.2	197.7	220.6	211.2
1919	206.6	213.4	161.5	199.8	234.1	206.4	224.0	224.3	224.2
1920	207.4	267.4	199.6	248.7	237.8	204.4	225.0	245.8	237.5
1921	146.9	187.2	135.5	174.9	122.7	140.3	128.7	148.0	140.4
1922	140.2	173.1	137.3	165.1	126.6	152.5	135.5	146.4	142.1
1923	139.0	183.4	148.5	181.9	138.3	148.4	142.0	152.6	148.3
1924	141.0	179.7	137.6	172.4	150.3	156.0	152.4	155.6	154.3
1925	157.7	178.3	142.5	170.2	157.3	193.0	169.9	162.0	164.9
1926	153.4	172.4	143.1	167.2	139.9	184.2	154.6	150.6	152.0
1927	150.6	166.2	137.5	159.0	136.5	177.0	149.9	145.2	147.0
1928	152.8	168.3	133.3	158.4	141.4	179.0	153.9	147.1	149.5
1929	149.8	165.9	133.9	160.0	135.7	182.1	151.2	142.3	145.6
1930	138.1	156.1	112.7	148.3	107.2	166.4	124.4	130.6	127.8
1931	117.9	138.9	93.2	137.1	75.4	117.6	87.7	113.6	102.6
1932	100.5	128.4	79.9	130.2	57.1	96.5	67.9	100.5	86.9
1933	97.5	133.7	90.8	127.8	72.2	101.4	81.5	110.1	98.1
1934	112.4	145.3	104.0	138.1	98.5	114.0	105.7	125.4	117.1
1935	133.0	143.3	105.9	136.6	103.5[3]	102.3[3]	106.9[3]	128.4	119.2

[3] For an explanation of the discrepancy between the index numbers for raw crops and the two component groups, see footnote 1, Appendix III.

APPENDIX III

YEAR	ANIMAL PRODUCTS					MINERAL PRODUCTS				
	Raw producers'	Raw consumers'	Raw, total	Processed	Total	Raw producers'	Raw consumers'	Raw, total	Processed	Total
N, 1913	37	10	47	75	122	30	4	34	113	147
N, 1929	37	10	47	84	131	37	7	44	127	171
1913	100.0	100.0	100.0	100.0	100.0	100.0	100.0	100.0	100.0	100.0
1914	100.1	102.6	100.5	99.5	100.0	93.5	100.0	93.7	95.1	94.8
1915	106.1	99.9	104.7	100.2	102.0	107.0	99.8	105.5	105.2	105.3
1916	126.0	109.4	122.1	120.5	121.2	145.5	105.6	139.7	150.5	148.0
1917	176.9	145.9	169.7	162.2	165.2	185.8	115.1	177.0	183.0	181.7
1918	204.6	183.7	199.6	196.3	197.7	184.2	135.0	179.0	201.3	195.6
1919	214.2	199.0	210.5	220.1	216.6	165.1	161.7	165.2	190.5	184.0
1920	183.1	211.3	188.7	229.7	213.1	205.1	186.8	203.7	229.5	223.0
1921	104.0	155.1	113.1	157.5	138.7	141.9	208.4	148.1	175.9	168.7
1922	129.9	138.4	131.3	150.5	142.9	139.7	210.7	146.7	158.7	155.8
1923	137.7	145.3	139.1	155.5	148.6	147.4	226.9	154.5	167.5	164.3
1924	131.6	148.5	135.7	153.1	145.9	139.0	229.9	147.2	162.6	158.6
1925	142.5	159.9	145.9	167.9	158.9	143.8	227.4	151.1	158.7	156.9
1926	130.0	147.1	133.3	162.3	150.6	145.3	232.0	153.1	157.7	156.7
1927	136.3	135.8	135.9	162.3	151.7	137.5	223.9	145.2	148.9	148.7
1928	153.1	142.4	150.5	168.2	161.0	133.9	218.6	141.5	149.2	147.3
1929	140.1	152.8	142.3	164.8	155.7	135.0	216.2	142.4	151.1	149.1
1930	114.2	142.3	121.8	149.5	137.6	125.0	213.6	132.9	142.0	139.9
1931	81.5	125.3	94.6	122.8	110.4	106.4	219.0	115.8	129.9	126.0
1932	60.2	94.7	70.6	100.4	87.0	102.2	213.0	111.5	126.9	122.6
1933	59.3	90.5	68.6	101.8	86.9	103.5	198.0	111.6	125.0	121.2
1934	68.4	109.3	80.7	118.8	101.5	118.1	193.7	124.9	133.6	131.5
1935	104.5	119.6	108.1	138.4	125.2	119.6	192.9	126.3	132.2	131.1

Year	METALS			NON-METALLIC MINERALS			
	Raw producers'	Processed	Total	Raw producers'	Raw consumers'	Raw, total	Processed	Total
N, 1913	18	49	67	12	4	16	64	80
N, 1929	18	54	72	19	7	26	73	99
1913	100.0	100.0	100.0	100.0	100.0	100.0	100.0	100.0
1914	91.7	92.2	92.1	96.1	100.0	96.9	97.0	97.0
1915	119.4	99.7	104.7	90.5	99.8	92.7	111.1	107.2
1916	167.0	143.0	149.4	118.1	105.6	114.8	156.2	146.9
1917	222.7	191.3	199.4	154.6	115.1	148.4	176.0	168.3
1918	203.0	197.9	199.4	168.5	135.0	164.2	203.7	192.8
1919	160.4	187.5	180.1	174.1	161.7	174.8	192.1	187.1
1920	192.3	216.4	209.9	224.8	186.8	220.8	239.1	233.7
1921	116.8	169.6	153.6	180.0	208.4	188.9	181.2	182.3
1922	120.9	151.2	142.6	167.7	210.7	178.8	163.4	166.3
1923	141.7	173.6	164.6	157.7	226.9	172.6	162.7	163.9
1924	133.6	172.4	161.3	148.4	229.9	165.8	155.6	156.9
1925	140.4	167.5	160.0	151.3	227.4	167.5	152.2	154.9
1926	137.6	164.2	156.7	157.7	232.0	173.6	152.7	156.7
1927	129.6	158.8	150.6	149.8	223.9	165.6	143.1	147.6
1928	124.8	159.4	149.7	147.3	218.6	162.5	141.5	145.8
1929	127.9	163.5	153.4	146.4	216.2	161.3	142.1	145.9
1930	112.3	152.2	141.1	139.8	213.6	155.0	135.4	139.4
1931	95.4	142.1	129.3	119.0	219.0	136.6	120.2	123.6
1932	84.0	136.0	122.0	119.9	213.8	136.8	120.9	124.0
1933	93.8	134.2	123.2	115.4	198.0	130.8	118.5	120.2
1934	104.0	144.5	133.3	133.7	193.7	146.8	125.8	130.7
1935	106.4	142.9	132.8	134.7	192.9	147.6	124.2	130.1

APPENDIX III

Year	FOREST PRODUCTS			FOODS			NON-FOODS		
	Raw producers'	Processed	Total	Raw	Processed	Total	Raw	Processed	Total
N, 1913	4	39	43	71	89	160	61	223	284
N, 1929	4	51	55	71	96	167	71	254	325
1913	100.0	100.0	100.0	100.0	100.0	100.0	100.0	100.0	100.0
1914	85.1	96.4	95.4	103.1	102.0	102.4	93.9	96.2	95.8
1915	78.5	94.3	92.9	104.3	104.2	104.2	104.0	101.3	101.9
1916	107.8	112.8	112.3	122.0	116.8	119.0	135.1	135.1	135.1
1917	128.9	138.6	137.8	168.3	165.4	166.5	180.8	171.3	173.7
1918	102.9	163.2	156.2	188.8	195.9	192.7	188.9	199.7	197.5
1919	94.4	202.3	188.8	210.9	209.4	209.9	180.8	205.3	199.8
1920	124.5	288.2	267.2	204.7	207.9	206.4	198.7	253.5	240.6
1921	59.2	168.8	154.1	126.7	143.9	135.9	122.8	171.0	159.1
1922	52.8	172.9	156.2	129.9	138.9	134.8	136.5	161.7	156.0
1923	72.9	191.0	175.5	133.0	139.0	136.3	149.9	173.7	168.4
1924	60.2	171.1	156.5	139.8	141.0	140.4	140.7	167.1	161.1
1925	100.6	168.0	159.7	157.1	156.1	156.4	148.1	165.2	161.4
1926	83.2	161.6	152.0	147.5	151.3	149.5	139.3	160.3	155.5
1927	70.4	152.5	142.2	145.4	149.0	147.2	134.3	153.4	149.1
1928	53.4	150.6	137.8	153.1	151.7	152.2	134.7	153.8	149.6
1929	51.6	149.1	136.3	152.7	148.0	149.8	128.8	153.4	147.7
1930	46.7	143.9	128.0	133.8	135.7	134.1	111.4	143.1	134.7
1931	40.4	129.0	113.0	101.9	114.4	107.9	91.3	127.3	117.1
1932	34.1	117.6	99.9	78.0	97.7	87.6	82.3	118.4	108.0
1933	38.4	118.8	105.5	80.3	96.8	88.2	88.1	122.4	112.7
1934	44.2	127.0	116.4	98.5	113.1	105.3	102.1	133.0	124.5
1935	42.1	124.8	112.7	117.9	132.6	124.8	102.3	131.5	123.9

APPENDIX IV

INDEX NUMBERS OF COMMODITY PRICES, AT
WHOLESALE, BY GROUPS AND SUBGROUPS,
1929–1936

APPENDIX IV

INDEX NUMBERS OF COMMODITY PRICES, AT WHOLESALE, BY GROUPS AND SUBGROUPS, 1929–1936

Annual and Monthly [1]

YEAR OR MONTH	ALL COMMODI-TIES	RAW MA-TERIALS	PROC-ESSED GOODS	MONTH	ALL COMMODI-TIES	RAW MA-TERIALS	PROC-ESSED GOODS
N [2]	680	144	536	*1929*			
1929	100.0	100.0	100.0	Jy	100.9	101.1	100.8
1930	90.5	87.0	92.8	A	101.1	101.9	100.5
1931	76.5	68.7	81.3	S	100.9	101.8	100.4
1932	67.5	57.4	73.8	O	100.1	100.5	99.8
1933	69.6	60.4	75.5	N	98.4	98.0	98.7
1934	79.1	71.7	83.5	D	98.1	97.7	98.4
1935	83.6	78.2	86.9				
1929				*1930*			
J	100.5	99.7	101.1	J	97.3	96.9	97.5
F	100.2	99.8	100.5	F	96.1	94.9	96.9
M	100.7	100.9	100.5	M	94.7	92.7	96.1
A	100.2	99.8	100.5	A	94.6	92.8	95.8
M	99.3	98.1	100.0	M	93.3	90.3	95.1
J	99.9	99.3	100.2	J	91.2	87.5	93.4

[1] Constructed by the National Bureau of Economic Research from data compiled by the U. S. Bureau of Labor Statistics. The index numbers are weighted arithmetic averages of relative prices. (See Appendix II for weights and classifications of commodities.)

[2] The total number of price quotations used in the computation of these weighted indexes is 680; the duplication of price series in certain classifications makes the cross totals of these entries, by groups, greater than 680. An example of this duplication is the use of identical price quotations on flour in both the producers' and consumers' classifications. Wherever such duplication occurs, an appropriate adjustment in weighting is made.

APPENDIX IV
INDEX NUMBERS OF WHOLESALE PRICES (cont.)

MONTH	ALL COMMODI-TIES	RAW MA-TERIALS	PROC-ESSED GOODS	MONTH	ALL COMMODI-TIES	RAW MA-TERIALS	PROC-ESSED GOODS
1930				*1933*			
Jy	88.8	83.8	91.7	Jy	73.0	66.3	77.2
A	88.4	83.9	91.3	A	74.1	65.4	79.3
S	88.4	84.1	91.2	S	75.1	66.4	80.5
O	87.1	82.4	90.0	O	75.2	65.9	80.9
N	85.2	79.6	88.6	N	75.3	66.7	80.7
D	83.4	76.9	87.4	D	75.0	66.6	80.3
1931				*1934*			
J	81.9	75.5	85.8	J	76.4	67.8	81.6
F	80.6	73.6	84.8	F	77.6	69.5	82.7
M	79.8	72.8	84.2	M	77.7	69.2	83.0
A	78.7	71.6	83.0	A	77.3	68.7	82.7
M	77.1	69.7	81.7	M	77.8	68.8	83.3
J	75.9	68.0	80.8	J	78.9	71.1	83.7
Jy	75.7	67.7	80.7	Jy	79.1	72.0	83.5
A	75.5	67.2	80.8	A	80.7	74.6	84.4
S	74.7	65.9	80.0	S	81.6	76.1	85.1
O	73.8	64.8	79.5	O	80.7	74.7	83.8
N	73.7	64.9	79.1	N	80.5	74.5	84.2
D	72.0	63.1	77.5	D	81.0	75.3	84.5
1932				*1935*			
J	70.5	61.1	76.2	J	82.6	77.5	85.7
F	69.3	59.4	75.4	F	83.2	78.3	86.2
M	68.9	58.7	75.3	M	83.1	78.0	86.3
A	68.3	57.9	74.7	A	83.8	78.9	86.7
M	67.0	56.3	73.7	M	83.8	78.7	86.8
J	66.4	55.5	73.0	J	83.3	77.8	86.6
Jy	67.0	57.0	73.1	Jy	82.9	77.0	86.4
A	67.5	57.8	73.6	A	83.7	77.9	87.3
S	67.9	58.4	73.7	S	83.9	77.9	87.6
O	66.9	56.8	73.1	O	83.9	78.2	87.4
N	66.2	55.8	72.6	N	84.1	78.4	87.7
D	64.8	53.7	71.7	D	84.3	78.5	88.0
1933				*1936*			
J	63.2	52.3	70.1	J	84.0	78.8	87.3
F	62.3	51.2	69.2	F	83.9	79.3	86.7
M	62.8	52.4	69.2	M	82.9	78.2	85.7
A	63.2	53.1	69.5	A	82.8	78.1	85.8
M	65.9	57.1	71.3	M	81.8	77.2	84.6
J	68.6	60.4	73.7	J	82.5	78.5	84.8

INDEX NUMBERS OF WHOLESALE PRICES (cont.)

YEAR OR MONTH	NON-DURABLE GOODS (perishable and semi-durable)			YEAR OR MONTH	DURABLE GOODS		
	Raw	Processed	Total		Raw	Processed	Total
N	108	361	469	N	46	176	222
1929	100.0	100.0	100.0	1929	100.0	100.0	100.0
1930	85.2	91.9	89.1	1930	89.2	94.3	93.0
1931	64.5	78.4	72.7	1931	76.8	87.2	84.6
1932	50.9	68.8	61.5	1932	67.8	82.5	78.8
1933	53.4	71.6	64.1	1933	75.9	82.6	81.0
1934	65.4	80.7	74.4	1934	82.3	89.3	87.6
1935	74.2	86.1	81.2	1935	82.2	88.6	87.0
1929				1929			
J	99.8	101.5	100.7	J	98.1	100.1	99.7
F	99.7	100.6	100.2	F	99.7	100.3	100.2
M	100.6	100.6	100.5	M	103.1	100.9	101.5
A	99.7	100.2	100.0	A	102.4	101.1	101.5
M	97.6	100.2	98.7	M	100.6	100.8	100.8
J	99.0	99.7	99.4	J	100.4	100.6	100.6
Jy	101.6	100.9	101.0	Jy	100.3	100.5	100.5
A	102.7	101.0	101.6	A	100.3	100.0	100.1
S	102.5	100.7	101.4	S	99.9	99.7	99.8
O	100.8	99.9	100.2	O	99.3	99.4	99.4
N	97.6	98.6	98.1	N	98.2	98.8	98.7
D	97.3	98.1	97.7	D	97.5	98.8	98.5
1930				1930			
J	96.2	97.3	96.7	J	97.6	97.8	97.8
F	93.8	96.5	95.4	F	97.4	97.4	97.4
M	91.1	95.4	93.6	M	96.8	97.3	97.3
A	92.0	95.2	93.8	A	94.1	96.8	96.2
M	89.4	94.3	92.3	M	90.5	95.9	94.6
J	85.9	92.6	89.8	J	88.7	94.6	93.2
Jy	81.2	91.3	86.8	Jy	87.0	93.8	92.1
A	81.6	90.4	86.8	A	86.1	92.7	91.2
S	82.0	90.4	86.9	S	85.0	92.2	90.5
O	80.0	89.1	85.3	O	83.0	91.6	89.5
N	76.7	87.3	82.9	N	83.1	91.1	89.2
D	73.2	85.8	80.6	D	82.6	90.4	88.6

APPENDIX IV

INDEX NUMBERS OF WHOLESALE PRICES *(cont.)*

MONTH	NON-DURABLE GOODS *(perishable and semi-durable)*			MONTH	DURABLE GOODS		
	Raw	Processed	Total		Raw	Processed	Total
1931				*1931*			
J	71.6	83.9	78.8	J	82.0	89.7	87.8
F	69.2	82.6	77.0	F	81.0	89.4	87.2
M	68.9	81.9	76.6	M	80.7	89.1	87.0
A	68.0	80.7	75.4	A	79.6	88.5	86.3
M	65.8	79.0	73.6	M	77.8	87.8	85.4
J	64.3	77.9	72.3	J	76.6	87.3	84.7
Jy	64.2	77.9	72.2	Jy	75.4	87.0	84.2
A	63.1	77.8	71.8	A	75.1	86.6	83.8
S	61.3	76.9	70.5	S	74.8	86.2	83.4
O	59.9	76.3	69.6	O	73.6	85.6	82.6
N	60.0	75.9	69.3	N	73.1	85.3	82.2
D	57.5	73.8	67.2	D	72.2	84.6	81.5
1932				*1932*			
J	54.9	72.2	65.2	J	72.0	83.9	80.9
F	53.0	71.3	63.8	F	70.2	83.1	80.0
M	52.3	71.2	63.4	M	69.4	83.1	79.8
A	51.4	70.2	62.5	A	68.5	82.8	79.3
M	49.4	68.5	60.7	M	67.2	82.5	78.7
J	48.8	67.5	59.9	J	65.6	82.4	78.3
Jy	50.7	67.8	60.9	Jy	65.8	82.1	78.1
A	51.8	68.4	61.6	A	66.1	82.3	78.3
S	52.4	68.9	62.1	S	67.4	82.0	78.4
O	50.2	68.1	60.8	O	67.3	81.8	78.2
N	49.1	67.2	59.8	N	66.5	81.9	78.0
D	46.4	66.0	58.0	D	66.1	81.7	77.8
1933				*1933*			
J	45.0	64.4	56.6	J	66.0	80.2	76.6
F	43.7	63.6	55.4	F	66.2	80.3	76.7
M	45.2	63.8	56.2	M	67.3	79.5	76.4
A	46.3	64.3	56.9	A	68.0	80.2	77.1
M	51.1	67.0	60.5	M	71.4	79.7	77.6
J	54.6	69.9	63.6	J	76.1	80.8	79.7
Jy	61.1	74.3	68.8	Jy	80.6	82.2	81.9
A	59.2	77.1	69.8	A	81.8	83.8	83.3
S	59.5	78.1	70.4	S	82.8	84.7	84.3
O	57.9	78.1	69.8	O	82.7	85.8	85.1
N	58.4	77.8	69.8	N	84.2	85.9	85.5
D	58.1	76.8	69.2	D	84.8	86.4	86.0

INDEX NUMBERS OF WHOLESALE PRICES (cont.)

MONTH	NON-DURABLE GOODS (perishable and semi-durable)			MONTH	DURABLE GOODS		
	Raw	Processed	Total		Raw	Processed	Total
1934				*1934*			
J	60.4	77.9	70.7	J	82.4	88.6	87.0
F	62.6	79.3	72.5	F	81.9	89.4	87.6
M	62.4	79.7	72.6	M	82.2	89.5	87.8
A	61.1	79.2	71.8	A	83.0	90.0	88.3
M	61.0	79.5	71.9	M	83.5	91.2	89.4
J	64.2	80.3	73.7	J	83.5	90.4	88.7
Jy	65.4	80.4	74.2	Jy	83.3	89.4	87.9
A	69.1	81.8	76.6	A	82.3	89.2	87.6
S	71.1	83.0	78.1	S	82.1	89.1	87.3
O	69.3	82.1	76.8	O	82.1	88.8	87.1
N	69.1	81.8	76.6	N	81.7	88.7	87.0
D	70.2	82.3	77.3	D	81.6	88.7	86.9
1935				*1935*			
J	73.5	84.2	79.7	J	81.2	88.5	86.7
F	74.4	85.3	80.8	F	81.0	88.4	86.6
M	74.1	85.4	80.7	M	81.0	88.4	86.5
A	75.4	86.1	81.7	A	81.5	88.3	86.6
M	75.1	86.0	81.5	M	82.0	88.7	87.0
J	73.7	85.5	80.6	J	82.3	88.9	87.2
Jy	72.6	85.4	80.1	Jy	81.6	88.6	86.8
A	73.8	86.5	81.3	A	82.2	88.8	87.1
S	73.8	87.2	81.7	S	82.5	88.8	87.2
O	73.9	87.2	81.7	O	83.2	88.0	86.8
N	73.7	87.2	81.6	N	84.2	88.8	87.7
D	73.9	87.7	82.0	D	84.0	88.8	87.6
1936				*1936*			
J	74.3	86.5	81.4	J	82.8	88.9	87.3
F	74.7	85.7	81.1	F	82.9	88.8	87.3
M	73.3	84.2	79.6	M	83.0	88.7	87.2
A	73.4	84.1	79.6	A	83.2	88.7	87.3
M	72.2	82.5	78.3	M	83.2	88.6	87.2
J	74.2	82.7	79.2	J	82.8	88.6	87.1

APPENDIX IV

INDEX NUMBERS OF WHOLESALE PRICES (cont.)

YEAR OR MONTH	PRODUCERS' GOODS			CONSUMERS' GOODS		
	Raw	Processed	Total	Raw	Processed	Total
N	114	304	418	30	262	292
1929	100.0	100.0	100.0	100.0	100.0	100.0
1930	85.2	92.2	88.5	93.3	93.3	93.3
1931	65.9	81.2	73.2	78.1	81.4	80.7
1932	55.5	75.4	64.9	63.7	72.7	70.8
1933	59.8	78.1	68.4	62.4	73.5	71.2
1934	72.1	86.0	78.6	70.7	81.8	79.6
1935	80.4	86.0	83.0	71.5	87.6	84.4
1929						
J	100.2	101.4	100.7	98.2	100.7	100.3
F	100.5	101.1	100.7	97.7	100.1	99.6
M	102.9	101.0	102.0	94.5	100.2	99.1
A	101.9	100.6	101.3	93.2	100.3	99.0
M	99.2	99.9	99.5	94.8	100.1	99.1
J	99.9	100.0	99.9	97.6	100.4	99.8
J	102.0	100.4	101.2	98.5	101.2	100.6
A	101.6	100.0	100.7	103.2	101.1	101.5
S	101.0	100.1	100.5	104.7	100.6	101.5
O	99.0	99.8	99.4	105.9	99.8	100.9
N	95.8	99.1	97.4	105.5	98.4	99.8
D	95.7	98.7	97.0	104.7	98.1	99.5
1930						
J	95.8	97.5	96.6	100.3	97.5	98.0
F	94.0	96.8	95.2	98.3	97.0	97.3
M	91.9	95.9	93.8	95.5	96.2	96.0
A	91.0	95.6	93.2	98.5	95.9	96.5
M	88.8	94.9	91.6	95.5	95.2	95.2
J	85.3	93.1	88.9	95.0	93.7	94.0
J	82.2	91.3	86.5	89.7	92.1	91.7
A	82.6	90.6	86.4	88.8	91.8	91.2
S	82.0	89.7	85.6	91.5	92.2	92.1
O	79.1	88.5	83.5	93.0	91.2	91.6
N	76.4	87.6	81.6	90.4	89.5	89.7
D	75.1	86.8	80.5	83.1	87.8	86.9

INDEX NUMBERS OF WHOLESALE PRICES (cont.)

MONTH	PRODUCERS' GOODS			CONSUMERS' GOODS		
	Raw	Processed	Total	Raw	Processed	Total
1931						
J	74.2	85.5	79.5	80.2	86.1	84.9
F	72.5	84.6	78.2	77.4	85.0	83.4
M	71.4	84.0	77.3	77.7	84.2	82.9
A	69.8	82.9	76.0	77.6	83.1	82.0
M	67.2	82.0	74.2	78.1	81.5	80.8
J	64.9	81.1	72.5	78.8	80.5	80.2
J	64.3	80.6	72.0	79.2	80.8	80.5
A	63.9	80.2	71.6	78.5	81.2	80.6
S	62.1	79.4	70.3	78.9	80.7	80.3
O	60.6	78.8	69.2	78.6	80.0	79.8
N	61.6	79.0	69.8	76.2	79.2	78.5
D	59.5	78.1	68.3	74.7	77.1	76.6
1932						
J	59.4	77.2	67.8	67.1	75.6	73.9
F	57.9	76.5	66.7	64.7	74.6	72.6
M	57.3	76.3	66.3	63.5	74.4	72.3
A	56.4	76.2	65.8	63.1	73.7	71.6
M	54.3	75.6	64.4	63.1	72.2	70.3
J	53.2	74.8	63.4	63.4	71.7	70.0
J	55.1	74.5	64.3	63.1	72.2	70.4
A	56.4	74.9	65.1	62.8	72.5	70.5
S	56.7	75.3	65.4	64.0	72.6	70.8
O	54.6	74.9	64.3	64.1	71.8	70.2
N	53.1	74.4	63.1	65.0	71.3	70.0
D	51.3	73.5	61.8	61.8	70.2	68.5
1933						
J	50.4	72.4	60.8	58.9	68.3	66.4
F	50.1	71.7	60.1	55.0	67.3	64.8
M	51.7	71.6	61.1	55.0	67.4	64.9
A	52.7	71.9	61.6	54.6	67.8	65.1
M	57.4	73.9	65.2	56.0	69.4	66.8
J	60.5	76.6	68.1	60.2	71.5	69.3
J	65.8	80.9	72.9	68.1	74.3	73.1
A	64.7	82.8	73.3	68.0	76.8	75.0
S	66.2	83.1	74.2	67.1	78.4	76.1
O	65.9	83.7	74.3	66.3	78.9	76.2
N	66.2	83.7	74.5	67.9	78.4	76.2
D	66.1	83.9	74.5	68.4	77.6	75.7

APPENDIX IV

INDEX NUMBERS OF WHOLESALE PRICES (*cont.*)

MONTH	PRODUCERS' GOODS			CONSUMERS' GOODS		
	Raw	Processed	Total	Raw	Processed	Total
1934						
J	67.2	85.2	75.7	70.0	79.0	77.2
F	69.3	85.9	77.2	70.0	80.3	78.2
M	69.4	85.9	77.2	69.1	80.8	78.4
A	69.4	85.8	77.2	66.7	80.4	77.6
M	69.7	86.6	77.7	66.0	81.0	77.9
J	71.2	86.7	78.5	70.8	81.4	79.3
J	72.3	86.2	78.9	71.5	81.5	79.5
A	75.3	86.3	80.5	72.3	82.9	80.7
S	77.2	86.2	81.4	72.9	84.3	82.0
O	75.0	85.8	80.0	74.2	83.4	81.5
N	74.9	85.8	80.0	73.3	83.1	81.0
D	76.4	86.1	81.0	72.1	83.3	81.0
1935						
J	79.0	86.1	82.3	73.1	85.3	82.8
F	79.9	85.8	82.7	73.3	86.5	83.9
M	80.3	85.7	82.8	70.6	86.7	83.4
A	81.4	85.5	83.3	71.4	87.7	84.4
M	81.4	85.9	83.5	70.5	87.6	84.2
J	80.0	85.7	82.7	71.2	87.4	84.1
J	79.0	85.5	82.0	70.8	87.2	83.9
A	80.2	85.6	82.8	70.3	88.5	84.8
S	80.2	85.9	82.9	70.4	89.0	85.2
O	80.6	86.5	83.4	70.4	88.1	84.5
N	80.2	86.8	83.3	72.7	88.3	85.2
D	80.6	86.8	83.5	72.0	88.9	85.4
1936						
J	81.5	86.1	83.6	70.5	88.1	84.6
F	81.6	85.8	83.5	72.2	87.4	84.4
M	80.9	85.4	83.0	69.7	85.9	82.6
A	80.7	85.4	82.9	69.7	86.0	82.7
M	79.0	85.1	81.8	71.4	84.3	81.8
J	79.5	85.3	82.1	75.9	84.4	82.7

PRICES IN RECESSION AND RECOVERY
INDEX NUMBERS OF WHOLESALE PRICES (cont.)

YEAR OR MONTH	GOODS DESTINED FOR USE IN CAPITAL EQUIPMENT			GOODS DESTINED FOR HUMAN CONSUMPTION		
	Raw	Processed	Total	Raw	Processed	Total
N	26	88	114	124	367	491
1929	100.0	100.0	100.0	100.0	100.0	100.0
1930	84.2	92.7	90.6	85.4	92.3	89.6
1931	69.6	85.7	81.9	65.1	79.7	74.1
1932	59.7	81.4	76.1	51.8	70.8	63.4
1933	67.8	79.9	77.0	54.6	73.2	65.9
1934	77.7	86.3	84.1	66.3	82.0	75.9
1935	79.1	85.4	83.9	74.7	86.9	82.2
1929						
J	97.4	99.8	99.1	99.6	101.3	100.6
F	100.5	100.0	100.1	99.5	100.5	100.2
M	105.5	100.8	101.9	100.6	100.5	100.6
A	103.2	101.1	101.5	99.8	100.2	100.1
M	100.4	101.0	100.7	97.8	99.7	99.0
J	100.1	100.7	100.5	99.0	99.8	99.5
J	100.5	100.5	100.5	101.5	100.7	101.1
A	100.8	100.2	100.3	102.4	100.7	101.5
S	100.3	100.1	100.1	102.3	100.4	101.2
O	99.3	99.6	99.5	100.7	99.7	100.1
N	97.3	98.8	98.5	97.8	98.3	98.1
D	96.3	98.7	98.2	97.4	98.0	97.8
1930						
J	95.5	97.3	96.8	96.5	97.2	96.9
F	95.7	96.6	96.4	94.0	96.4	95.5
M	94.9	96.3	95.9	91.5	95.5	94.0
A	91.1	95.7	94.6	92.1	95.4	94.1
M	86.2	94.2	92.3	89.5	94.5	92.6
J	84.2	92.6	90.6	86.0	93.0	90.4
J	81.1	91.9	89.2	81.5	91.2	87.5
A	79.6	91.0	88.3	81.9	90.9	87.4
S	77.9	90.7	87.5	82.3	90.6	87.5
O	75.6	89.9	86.4	80.4	89.5	85.9
N	75.9	89.5	86.2	77.0	87.9	83.7
D	76.1	89.4	86.2	73.6	86.3	81.5

INDEX NUMBERS OF WHOLESALE PRICES (*cont.*)

MONTH	GOODS DESTINED FOR USE IN CAPITAL EQUIPMENT			GOODS DESTINED FOR HUMAN CONSUMPTION		
	Raw	Processed	Total	Raw	Processed	Total
1931						
J	75.2	88.3	85.2	72.1	84.5	79.8
F	74.4	88.2	84.9	69.8	83.4	78.1
M	74.3	87.9	84.6	69.6	82.9	77.7
A	72.8	87.1	83.7	68.7	81.7	76.6
M	70.9	86.8	82.9	66.4	80.1	74.8
J	69.1	86.2	82.1	64.9	79.2	73.6
J	69.1	85.8	81.8	64.7	79.2	73.6
A	68.1	85.4	81.2	63.7	79.2	73.2
S	67.3	85.2	80.9	62.0	78.3	71.9
O	65.4	84.4	79.9	60.7	77.7	71.1
N	64.8	84.0	79.4	60.7	77.2	70.8
D	64.1	83.2	78.6	58.3	75.4	68.7
1932						
J	64.2	82.2	77.9	55.8	73.9	66.8
F	62.2	81.8	77.1	53.9	73.0	65.6
M	61.2	81.8	76.9	53.2	72.9	65.2
A	60.4	81.8	76.7	52.3	71.9	64.2
M	59.4	81.7	76.3	50.4	70.5	62.6
J	58.5	81.5	75.9	49.6	69.6	61.9
J	57.7	81.4	75.7	51.5	69.9	62.8
A	58.7	81.8	76.2	52.5	70.3	63.4
S	59.8	80.9	75.8	53.2	70.8	63.9
O	59.3	80.8	75.6	51.1	70.0	62.6
N	58.2	80.5	75.2	49.9	69.3	61.8
D	57.5	80.0	74.6	47.4	68.2	60.1
1933						
J	57.4	78.6	73.5	46.1	66.6	58.5
F	57.2	79.2	73.5	44.9	65.6	57.5
M	58.2	77.3	72.7	46.4	65.9	58.2
A	59.3	78.4	73.3	47.4	66.5	59.0
M	65.0	77.1	74.2	52.2	68.8	62.3
J	69.8	78.3	76.2	55.6	71.4	65.3
J	74.5	79.5	78.3	62.1	75.3	70.2
A	74.0	80.7	79.0	60.4	78.0	71.1
S	74.9	81.3	79.7	60.8	79.1	71.9
O	74.3	82.3	80.4	59.3	79.3	71.4
N	75.1	82.6	80.7	59.8	78.9	71.4
D	75.0	83.3	81.3	59.6	78.0	70.9

INDEX NUMBERS OF WHOLESALE PRICES (cont.)

MONTH	GOODS DESTINED FOR USE IN CAPITAL EQUIPMENT			GOODS DESTINED FOR HUMAN CONSUMPTION		
	Raw	Processed	Total	Raw	Processed	Total
1934						
J	75.4	84.6	82.3	61.7	79.6	72.6
F	75.7	86.0	83.5	63.8	80.9	74.2
M	76.5	86.2	83.8	63.5	81.3	74.4
A	77.9	87.1	84.9	62.3	80.8	73.6
M	78.9	89.0	86.5	62.2	81.1	73.7
J	78.6	87.8	85.6	65.2	81.6	75.2
J	79.3	86.4	84.6	66.3	81.6	75.8
A	79.6	86.0	84.4	69.8	83.0	77.8
S	78.9	85.8	84.2	71.9	84.1	79.3
O	78.2	85.5	83.8	70.1	83.2	78.1
N	77.8	85.5	83.7	69.9	83.0	77.9
D	78.0	85.5	83.7	71.0	83.4	78.5
1935						
J	78.3	85.2	83.6	74.0	85.1	80.8
F	78.1	85.3	83.6	75.0	86.0	81.8
M	77.1	85.3	83.3	74.7	86.0	81.7
A	77.7	85.2	83.4	76.0	86.8	82.7
M	78.3	85.5	83.8	75.7	86.9	82.5
J	78.5	85.8	84.0	74.3	86.4	81.8
J	77.4	85.4	83.5	73.3	86.1	81.1
A	78.0	85.4	83.6	74.4	87.3	82.3
S	79.1	85.3	83.8	74.4	87.8	82.6
O	81.2	85.1	84.1	74.4	87.5	82.5
N	82.7	85.7	85.0	74.2	87.7	82.5
D	81.9	85.8	84.9	74.4	88.1	82.8
1936						
J	81.7	86.0	85.0	74.8	87.1	82.3
F	82.4	86.2	85.2	75.1	86.2	82.0
M	82.7	85.8	85.1	73.7	85.4	80.6
A	82.7	85.7	85.0	73.8	85.0	80.6
M	82.3	85.8	85.0	72.7	83.4	79.3
J	81.7	85.9	84.9	74.6	83.6	80.1

APPENDIX IV

INDEX NUMBERS OF WHOLESALE PRICES (*cont.*)

YEAR OR MONTH	BUILDING MATERIALS			PRODUCERS' FUELS		
	Raw	Processed	Total	Raw	Processed	Total
N	28	86	114	6	15	21
1929	100.0	100.0	100.0	100.0	100.0	100.0
1930	92.7	95.0	94.3	96.1	95.1	95.7
1931	82.2	85.9	84.9	84.5	83.3	84.0
1932	73.4	79.4	77.6	84.1	87.1	85.3
1933	81.3	82.5	82.2	82.2	82.8	82.5
1934	83.6	89.6	87.8	97.1	87.7	93.4
1935	82.1	89.1	87.0	98.5	86.6	93.7
1929						
J	99.8	100.7	100.4	101.9	100.9	101.4
F	100.8	100.7	100.7	101.2	98.5	100.1
M	101.8	101.5	101.6	99.8	97.3	98.8
A	101.4	101.5	101.5	97.3	99.1	98.1
M	101.2	100.4	100.6	97.7	100.7	98.9
J	100.8	100.1	100.3	100.0	103.8	101.5
J	100.3	100.2	100.2	99.7	101.7	100.5
A	100.2	100.3	100.2	99.8	98.8	99.4
S	99.8	100.3	100.2	100.3	99.5	100.0
O	99.3	100.1	99.8	100.8	99.6	100.4
N	97.8	99.7	99.1	100.7	100.1	100.5
D	97.6	99.6	99.0	101.2	99.9	100.7
1930						
J	98.1	99.5	99.1	99.9	98.4	99.3
F	97.8	99.3	98.9	98.8	98.1	98.5
M	96.8	99.3	98.5	96.8	96.6	96.7
A	96.0	98.5	97.7	96.2	96.5	96.3
M	94.4	97.5	96.6	96.1	99.8	97.5
J	92.2	95.9	94.7	96.1	96.7	96.3
J	91.9	94.2	93.5	96.1	94.2	95.4
A	91.0	93.8	92.8	95.8	93.4	94.9
S	90.0	92.8	92.0	96.6	95.1	96.0
O	88.7	92.3	91.2	95.7	92.5	94.4
N	88.7	91.1	90.4	92.7	92.2	92.6
D	87.7	90.7	89.8	92.7	89.7	91.5

INDEX NUMBERS OF WHOLESALE PRICES (cont.)

MONTH	BUILDING MATERIALS			PRODUCERS' FUELS		
	Raw	Processed	Total	Raw	Processed	Total
1931						
J	87.4	90.0	89.2	91.8	88.8	90.5
F	86.2	89.2	88.3	91.5	86.7	89.6
M	85.7	88.7	87.8	86.3	83.7	85.3
A	84.6	87.7	86.8	83.5	80.4	82.4
M	83.2	87.0	85.8	83.1	80.9	82.3
J	82.6	86.2	85.1	79.8	79.3	79.7
J	80.5	85.6	84.0	79.3	79.6	79.4
A	80.7	84.6	83.5	81.8	83.6	82.5
S	80.7	83.9	82.9	83.5	84.3	83.8
O	79.5	83.3	82.1	83.3	85.0	84.0
N	79.0	82.9	81.7	85.1	86.1	85.5
D	77.9	82.6	81.2	85.1	83.3	84.4
1932						
J	76.8	81.8	80.3	85.3	83.6	84.6
F	75.8	80.7	79.3	85.2	82.5	84.2
M	74.9	80.5	78.8	84.4	83.3	83.9
A	73.8	80.4	78.4	84.5	87.0	85.6
M	72.5	79.3	77.3	84.5	88.9	86.3
J	70.6	78.6	76.2	84.4	89.7	86.5
J	72.3	77.2	75.7	84.4	90.9	87.0
A	72.3	77.5	75.9	84.1	89.7	86.4
S	72.9	78.6	76.9	83.8	87.2	85.2
O	72.7	78.6	76.9	84.0	88.1	85.6
N	72.6	78.8	77.0	83.5	87.6	85.2
D	72.5	78.6	76.8	82.0	86.0	83.7
1933						
J	72.4	78.1	76.3	79.4	83.0	80.7
F	72.9	77.4	76.0	77.4	80.7	78.7
M	73.8	77.5	76.5	76.7	79.7	77.9
A	74.2	77.5	76.6	75.3	79.3	77.0
M	75.7	78.7	77.8	74.2	78.6	75.9
J	80.2	80.8	80.6	74.6	80.4	77.0
J	84.9	84.2	84.4	78.9	83.5	80.7
A	86.5	86.0	86.2	82.0	82.1	82.0
S	87.2	87.0	87.0	86.6	86.0	86.4
O	87.9	87.7	87.8	93.0	88.0	91.0
N	89.8	88.0	88.6	93.5	88.1	91.4
D	90.9	88.1	88.9	93.9	88.6	91.7

APPENDIX IV

INDEX NUMBERS OF WHOLESALE PRICES (*cont.*)

MONTH	BUILDING MATERIALS			PRODUCERS' FUELS		
	Raw	Processed	Total	Raw	Processed	Total
1934						
J	85.0	89.2	87.9	94.0	88.4	91.8
F	84.4	89.5	88.1	94.2	87.3	91.5
M	84.4	89.6	88.1	94.3	85.6	90.9
A	84.8	89.9	88.4	96.3	85.3	92.0
M	85.2	91.1	89.3	97.1	86.7	93.0
J	84.9	91.4	89.5	97.3	87.3	93.4
J	84.3	90.6	88.7	98.0	88.7	94.3
A	82.5	90.1	87.9	98.5	89.1	94.7
S	82.4	89.6	87.4	98.7	88.8	94.8
O	82.3	89.2	87.1	98.7	89.1	94.9
N	82.1	89.3	87.1	98.6	88.4	94.6
D	81.7	89.4	87.0	98.5	87.5	94.1
1935						
J	80.9	89.5	86.9	98.4	86.3	93.6
F	80.8	89.3	86.7	98.6	85.2	93.3
M	80.9	89.2	86.6	98.5	86.0	93.6
A	81.0	88.6	86.3	97.6	86.0	93.0
M	81.5	88.8	86.6	97.8	86.9	93.5
J	82.1	88.5	86.6	98.0	88.3	94.2
J	82.4	88.6	86.7	98.3	88.1	94.2
A	82.9	88.8	87.0	97.7	87.6	93.7
S	82.9	89.5	87.6	97.0	86.0	92.6
O	83.0	89.8	87.9	98.6	86.0	93.6
N	83.5	89.7	87.9	100.5	86.6	94.9
D	83.5	89.6	87.8	100.8	86.7	95.2
1936						
J	82.5	89.8	87.7	101.6	87.0	95.7
F	82.5	89.6	87.6	103.2	87.7	97.0
M	82.6	89.2	87.2	103.1	88.1	97.2
A	82.9	89.4	87.4	100.7	89.4	96.2
M	82.9	89.5	87.6	100.3	89.2	95.9
J	82.9	89.8	87.8	100.3	89.5	96.1

INDEX NUMBERS OF WHOLESALE PRICES (cont.)

YEAR OR MONTH	PRODUCERS' GOODS DESTINED FOR HUMAN CONSUMPTION			CONSUMERS' GOODS, PROCESSED		
	Foods	Non-foods	Total	Foods	Non-foods	Total
N	60	150	210	100	162	262
1929	100.0	100.0	100.0	100.0	100.0	100.0
1930	84.9	83.8	84.3	92.2	94.1	93.3
1931	62.7	65.3	64.0	78.7	83.7	81.4
1932	48.5	55.7	52.3	67.1	77.4	72.7
1933	52.3	63.3	58.0	65.1	80.6	73.5
1934	66.2	74.3	70.5	75.0	87.6	81.8
1935	84.9	73.6	78.9	88.8	86.4	87.6
1929						
J	99.4	102.9	101.2	100.5	101.0	100.7
F	100.2	102.1	101.1	99.5	100.4	100.1
M	102.9	103.1	103.0	100.0	100.3	100.2
A	102.6	101.5	102.0	99.9	100.6	100.3
M	97.9	99.8	98.9	99.5	100.6	100.1
J	98.3	100.0	99.2	99.7	100.9	100.4
J	104.5	99.7	102.0	102.2	100.1	101.2
A	103.3	99.8	101.4	102.8	99.5	101.1
S	102.0	100.1	101.0	101.8	99.6	100.6
O	98.6	99.3	98.9	99.8	99.7	99.8
N	94.6	96.8	95.8	97.3	99.2	98.4
D	95.1	95.7	95.4	97.1	98.9	98.1
1930						
J	95.9	94.7	95.3	97.0	97.8	97.5
F	94.2	92.1	93.1	96.2	97.5	97.0
M	91.6	90.3	90.9	95.8	96.4	96.2
A	91.2	90.3	90.7	95.5	96.1	95.9
M	88.4	89.1	88.7	93.7	96.4	95.2
J	84.4	85.5	85.0	91.9	95.3	93.7
J	79.9	82.4	81.3	89.4	94.5	92.1
A	83.2	80.3	81.7	90.4	93.0	91.8
S	83.0	78.3	80.6	92.0	92.4	92.2
O	79.2	76.2	77.7	90.9	91.3	91.2
N	75.0	74.8	74.9	88.2	90.5	89.5
D	73.7	72.9	73.4	86.2	89.0	87.8

APPENDIX IV

INDEX NUMBERS OF WHOLESALE PRICES (*cont.*)

MONTH	PRODUCERS' GOODS DESTINED FOR HUMAN CONSUMPTION			CONSUMERS' GOODS, PROCESSED		
	Foods	Non-foods	Total	Foods	Non-foods	Total
1931						
J	72.2	71.9	72.0	84.9	87.1	86.1
F	68.6	71.7	70.2	83.0	86.5	85.0
M	68.9	70.5	69.8	82.3	85.9	84.2
A	68.8	68.5	68.6	80.7	85.1	83.1
M	65.1	66.5	65.8	77.9	84.5	81.5
J	62.4	65.2	63.8	76.9	83.7	80.5
J	60.8	65.5	63.3	77.7	83.3	80.8
A	60.7	63.3	62.0	78.1	83.7	81.2
S	57.3	61.6	59.6	77.4	83.3	80.7
O	56.1	60.1	58.1	77.0	82.6	80.0
N	57.7	60.5	59.2	75.5	82.2	79.2
D	54.3	59.5	57.0	73.3	80.3	77.1
1932						
J	53.9	58.7	56.5	70.9	79.5	75.6
F	51.6	58.3	55.1	69.2	79.2	74.6
M	51.4	57.8	54.7	69.3	78.9	74.4
A	50.6	56.1	53.5	67.6	78.8	73.7
M	47.5	54.3	51.0	65.8	77.7	72.2
J	46.7	52.5	49.8	65.2	77.3	71.7
J	49.8	52.8	51.4	67.4	76.3	72.2
A	50.3	55.4	53.0	67.9	76.4	72.5
S	49.4	57.8	53.8	67.5	76.9	72.6
O	45.9	56.3	51.3	65.7	77.0	71.8
N	43.8	54.6	49.5	65.1	76.6	71.3
D	41.4	53.2	47.6	63.6	75.9	70.2
1933						
J	41.1	52.1	46.9	61.5	74.3	68.3
F	42.0	50.9	46.7	60.4	73.3	67.3
M	44.9	51.9	48.6	60.8	73.1	67.4
A	47.0	52.3	49.8	62.0	72.8	67.8
M	53.2	58.2	55.8	64.8	73.5	69.4
J	54.9	63.6	59.5	65.6	76.6	71.5
J	61.7	69.6	65.8	68.0	80.0	74.3
A	59.0	71.2	65.3	67.8	84.5	76.8
S	58.4	72.2	65.5	68.3	87.3	78.4
O	55.6	72.1	64.3	68.5	88.1	78.9
N	55.0	72.6	64.2	67.6	87.9	78.4
D	53.4	73.2	63.7	65.7	87.9	77.6

INDEX NUMBERS OF WHOLESALE PRICES (*cont.*)

MONTH	PRODUCERS' GOODS DESTINED FOR HUMAN CONSUMPTION			CONSUMERS' GOODS, PROCESSED		
	Foods	Non-foods	Total	Foods	Non-foods	Total
1934						
J	56.4	74.6	65.9	67.3	89.1	79.0
F	59.6	76.2	68.3	70.4	88.9	80.3
M	59.7	76.2	68.3	71.7	88.7	80.8
A	58.7	75.7	67.6	71.2	88.3	80.4
M	59.6	74.5	67.5	72.4	88.3	81.0
J	63.4	74.6	69.2	74.2	87.6	81.4
J	65.2	74.6	70.2	75.0	87.0	81.5
A	72.9	74.2	73.6	78.1	87.0	82.9
S	77.0	73.9	75.4	80.8	87.2	84.3
O	73.1	73.1	73.1	79.0	87.0	83.4
N	73.5	73.0	73.1	79.1	86.4	83.1
D	77.0	73.2	75.0	79.8	86.2	83.3
1935						
J	82.5	73.7	77.9	84.3	86.0	85.3
F	84.1	73.3	78.6	87.4	85.7	86.5
M	87.1	71.6	78.9	87.9	85.7	86.7
A	88.8	70.5	79.1	90.0	85.7	87.7
M	87.8	73.3	80.1	89.3	86.0	87.6
J	84.0	73.3	78.3	87.6	87.0	87.4
J	81.4	73.4	77.2	87.4	86.9	87.2
A	84.9	72.9	78.5	90.3	86.9	88.5
S	85.9	72.5	78.8	91.3	86.8	89.0
O	85.1	74.3	79.3	90.0	86.3	88.1
N	81.0	76.3	78.5	89.8	87.0	88.3
D	82.0	76.2	78.9	90.9	87.0	88.9
1936						
J	82.5	75.8	79.0	89.3	87.0	88.1
F	82.1	75.1	78.4	88.2	86.7	87.4
M	80.6	74.9	77.7	85.0	86.7	85.9
A	80.7	74.7	77.6	84.9	86.9	86.0
M	77.0	74.3	75.6	81.5	86.8	84.3
J	77.9	74.7	76.2	81.8	86.7	84.4

APPENDIX IV

INDEX NUMBERS OF WHOLESALE PRICES (*cont.*)

YEAR OR MONTH	Raw producers'	Raw consumers'	CROPS Raw, total	Processed	Total
N	32	17	49	151	200
1929	100.0	100.0	100.0	100.0	100.0
1930	79.0	91.4	82.3	91.8	87.8
1931	55.6	64.6	58.0	79.8	70.5
1932	42.1	53.0	44.9	70.6	59.7
1933	53.2	55.7	53.9	77.4	67.4
1934	72.6	62.6	69.9	88.1	80.4
1935	76.3	56.2	70.7	90.2	81.9
1929					
J	101.8	94.5	99.8	101.5	100.8
F	104.0	91.6	100.6	101.1	100.9
M	104.4	89.2	100.3	100.1	100.2
A	100.4	90.1	97.6	99.2	98.5
M	96.2	92.3	95.2	98.1	96.9
J	95.6	97.5	96.1	98.2	97.4
J	100.6	99.7	100.4	100.5	100.4
A	100.3	110.9	103.1	101.2	101.9
S	102.0	111.7	104.5	101.0	102.5
O	101.2	111.0	103.8	100.9	102.2
N	96.5	104.7	98.7	99.7	99.2
D	96.4	101.8	97.9	99.3	98.7
1930					
J	94.2	97.6	95.2	98.2	96.9
F	89.5	96.8	91.5	97.0	94.7
M	85.9	96.0	88.6	95.5	92.6
A	87.5	103.9	92.0	95.6	94.1
M	85.5	105.9	91.1	94.7	93.2
J	79.5	104.8	86.1	93.1	90.1
J	75.7	90.8	79.7	91.5	86.5
A	76.3	80.6	77.5	90.6	85.0
S	72.6	85.1	76.0	88.8	83.4
O	70.6	88.1	75.4	87.9	82.6
N	68.3	77.0	70.6	87.0	80.1
D	65.7	68.0	66.3	86.2	77.7

INDEX NUMBERS OF WHOLESALE PRICES (*cont.*)

MONTH	Raw producers'	Raw consumers'	CROPS Raw, total	Processed	Total
1931					
J	64.7	69.3	66.0	84.8	76.7
F	64.4	65.9	64.8	84.2	76.0
M	63.7	65.4	64.1	83.8	75.5
A	62.3	66.9	63.6	83.2	74.9
M	60.1	68.4	62.3	81.9	73.6
J	57.5	67.7	60.2	81.0	72.2
J	55.6	65.2	58.1	80.4	71.0
A	49.4	63.1	52.9	78.6	67.8
S	47.3	63.0	51.6	77.0	66.2
O	46.8	60.3	50.4	76.5	65.4
N	49.7	57.3	51.8	76.8	66.2
D	47.1	55.4	49.4	74.8	64.0
1932					
J	46.8	54.5	48.9	73.5	63.1
F	46.1	54.1	48.3	73.1	62.5
M	45.0	54.7	47.7	72.4	61.9
A	44.0	55.3	47.1	71.7	61.2
M	41.3	55.2	45.2	70.0	59.4
J	38.2	56.8	43.1	69.0	58.0
J	39.1	55.6	43.5	68.7	58.1
A	42.9	51.6	45.2	69.6	59.3
S	43.4	53.0	46.1	70.9	60.4
O	40.6	50.0	43.2	70.1	58.8
N	39.1	47.9	41.6	69.1	57.4
D	37.9	47.8	40.6	68.1	56.4
1933					
J	38.7	47.3	41.2	66.6	55.9
F	38.4	46.2	40.5	65.4	54.9
M	41.6	47.9	43.3	66.4	56.6
A	45.3	49.7	46.5	67.3	58.4
M	52.9	47.3	51.5	70.4	62.4
J	56.8	51.9	55.6	74.2	66.4
J	66.0	69.6	66.9	82.1	75.6
A	60.8	64.5	61.8	86.8	76.1
S	60.4	60.0	60.3	86.1	75.2
O	57.8	55.9	57.4	85.6	73.6
N	60.0	54.9	58.6	85.3	74.0
D	60.5	56.6	59.6	84.7	74.2

INDEX NUMBERS OF WHOLESALE PRICES (cont.)

MONTH	Raw producers'	Raw consumers'	CROPS Raw, total	Processed	Total
1934					
J	63.8	63.6	63.8	85.9	76.5
F	66.2	68.6	66.8	86.9	78.4
M	65.7	67.9	66.3	87.2	78.4
A	63.8	63.7	63.8	86.8	77.0
M	64.8	63.4	64.5	86.5	77.2
J	70.3	65.4	69.1	87.6	79.8
J	73.6	61.4	70.3	87.7	80.4
A	80.7	60.3	75.3	89.2	83.3
S	81.4	60.0	75.7	89.7	83.7
O	79.7	61.7	74.8	89.3	83.1
N	80.6	58.6	74.6	89.4	83.1
D	82.8	55.8	75.5	90.2	83.9
1935					
J	81.0	56.4	74.3	89.8	83.2
F	80.6	56.3	73.9	89.8	83.1
M	78.1	54.7	71.7	89.6	82.0
A	80.6	58.1	74.4	90.6	83.7
M	79.2	56.7	73.1	90.6	83.2
J	75.0	59.8	70.9	89.6	81.6
J	73.8	56.8	69.3	89.3	80.8
A	72.2	52.3	66.9	89.2	79.8
S	72.6	52.1	67.2	90.4	80.5
O	74.8	52.7	68.7	91.2	81.7
N	72.8	57.0	68.5	91.0	81.5
D	71.6	56.8	67.6	91.0	81.1
1936					
J	72.7	55.7	68.1	88.5	79.9
F	72.2	56.7	68.0	87.2	79.0
M	71.8	59.0	68.3	85.3	78.0
A	72.4	60.9	69.3	85.1	78.5
M	70.9	66.6	69.8	84.5	78.3
J	72.1	77.6	73.6	84.5	79.9

INDEX NUMBERS OF WHOLESALE PRICES (*cont.*)

YEAR OR MONTH	ANIMAL PRODUCTS			Processed	Total
	Raw producers'	Raw consumers'	Raw, total		
N	32	10	42	109	151
1929	100.0	100.0	100.0	100.0	100.0
1930	81.5	93.1	85.6	90.7	88.4
1931	58.2	82.0	66.5	74.5	70.9
1932	43.0	62.0	49.6	60.9	55.9
1933	42.3	59.2	48.2	61.8	55.8
1934	48.8	71.5	56.7	72.1	65.2
1935	74.6	78.3	76.0	84.0	80.4
1929					
J	99.2	100.1	99.6	101.2	100.4
F	97.5	101.3	98.9	100.3	99.6
M	103.9	96.6	101.4	101.5	101.4
A	106.6	94.3	102.4	101.1	101.6
M	102.3	96.1	100.2	100.4	100.2
J	103.1	97.4	101.1	100.3	100.6
J	105.9	96.9	102.9	101.6	102.1
A	104.8	98.3	102.7	101.5	102.0
S	101.0	100.6	100.9	101.2	101.0
O	94.8	103.3	97.8	99.0	98.4
N	89.7	107.2	95.9	96.8	96.3
D	89.5	108.0	96.1	96.3	96.1
1930					
J	93.5	102.2	96.7	95.7	96.1
F	93.0	98.6	95.0	95.1	95.1
M	91.4	93.5	92.2	94.5	93.5
A	89.0	93.7	90.7	94.1	92.5
M	86.0	87.1	86.4	92.4	89.7
J	81.5	87.4	83.7	90.7	87.6
J	75.7	86.9	79.6	88.3	84.3
A	77.4	92.2	82.5	89.2	86.2
S	79.6	94.1	84.7	90.5	87.9
O	74.0	95.0	81.4	89.0	85.5
N	69.8	97.9	79.6	85.9	83.1
D	68.5	90.1	76.0	83.3	80.0

APPENDIX IV

INDEX NUMBERS OF WHOLESALE PRICES (cont.)

MONTH	Raw producers'	Raw consumers'	Raw, total	Processed	Total
1931					
J	67.4	83.4	73.0	80.8	77.3
F	62.6	80.2	68.8	79.0	74.4
M	64.2	81.4	70.3	78.4	74.8
A	63.6	80.5	69.6	76.4	73.4
M	58.3	79.9	65.8	73.7	70.2
J	56.9	81.0	65.4	72.4	69.3
J	58.6	83.2	67.2	73.2	70.4
A	61.4	82.9	68.9	74.5	71.9
S	56.0	83.7	65.7	73.9	70.2
O	52.7	84.9	63.9	72.9	68.9
N	51.2	82.1	62.0	71.0	67.0
D	47.8	80.7	59.3	68.3	64.2
1932					
J	48.2	65.7	54.3	65.8	60.7
F	45.2	61.1	50.8	64.5	58.4
M	45.3	59.7	50.3	64.6	58.3
A	43.2	59.7	49.0	62.5	56.5
M	39.2	59.7	46.4	59.8	53.8
J	40.6	58.8	46.9	58.4	53.3
J	46.2	59.4	50.8	59.7	55.7
A	46.3	61.2	51.5	60.3	56.4
S	46.5	62.6	52.1	60.9	56.9
O	41.7	64.8	49.8	59.9	55.4
N	38.6	68.4	49.0	58.8	54.5
D	35.3	61.9	44.6	57.3	51.7
1933					
J	34.4	56.1	42.0	55.8	49.7
F	35.5	49.0	40.3	55.4	48.7
M	37.5	47.8	41.1	55.3	49.0
A	37.2	47.8	40.9	55.8	49.3
M	44.6	52.6	47.4	59.3	54.0
J	47.1	57.9	50.9	61.7	56.8
J	48.8	61.3	53.1	63.7	59.0
A	47.2	64.6	53.3	65.6	60.2
S	47.6	65.3	53.9	67.4	61.4
O	45.2	67.1	52.9	67.7	61.0
N	42.3	71.3	52.6	67.3	60.7
D	40.5	70.1	51.0	65.4	58.9

INDEX NUMBERS OF WHOLESALE PRICES (cont.)

MONTH	Raw producers'	Raw consumers'	Raw, total	Processed	Total
		ANIMAL PRODUCTS			
1934					
J	42.3	68.9	51.7	66.8	60.1
F	47.3	65.0	53.6	69.6	62.5
M	48.0	63.6	53.5	70.6	63.0
A	48.5	62.9	53.6	69.8	62.6
M	47.5	62.6	52.9	70.8	62.9
J	47.3	70.2	55.3	71.5	64.3
J	47.0	74.1	56.5	71.7	64.9
A	50.7	76.4	59.6	74.0	67.6
S	56.5	77.4	63.8	76.4	70.7
O	50.4	78.9	60.4	74.1	68.0
N	49.9	79.3	60.1	73.6	67.6
D	52.9	79.1	62.0	74.3	68.8
1935					
J	64.7	80.7	70.3	79.7	75.5
F	68.4	81.2	72.9	82.8	78.3
M	72.9	77.1	74.4	82.7	79.0
A	74.2	78.0	75.6	83.9	80.2
M	75.4	78.0	76.3	83.3	80.2
J	74.5	76.7	75.4	82.6	79.3
J	72.7	77.0	74.2	82.3	78.7
A	79.0	78.7	79.0	85.7	82.8
S	79.3	78.4	79.0	86.6	83.2
O	77.0	78.0	77.4	85.4	81.9
N	75.2	78.8	76.5	85.7	81.6
D	78.2	77.9	78.1	87.0	83.0
1936					
J	79.6	75.8	78.3	86.6	82.9
F	79.4	78.4	79.2	85.4	82.6
M	77.5	71.5	75.5	83.6	80.0
A	77.1	70.8	74.9	83.4	79.6
M	72.6	71.1	72.1	80.2	76.6
J	73.2	71.7	72.8	80.8	77.1

APPENDIX IV

INDEX NUMBERS OF WHOLESALE PRICES (cont.)

YEAR OR MONTH	METALS			NON-METALLIC MINERALS		
	Raw producers'	Processed	Total	Raw producers'	Raw consumers'	Raw, total
N	19	105	124	13	3	16
1929	100.0	100.0	100.0	100.0	100.0	100.0
1930	87.8	93.1	92.0	95.5	98.8	96.1
1931	74.6	86.9	84.3	81.3	101.3	84.7
1932	65.7	83.2	79.5	81.9	98.5	84.8
1933	73.3	82.1	80.3	78.8	91.6	81.1
1934	81.3	88.4	86.9	91.3	89.6	91.0
1935	83.2	87.4	86.6	92.0	89.2	91.5
1929						
J	96.6	100.1	99.4	101.5	101.6	101.6
F	98.5	100.4	100.0	100.5	101.6	100.7
M	103.9	101.2	101.8	99.2	101.3	99.7
A	102.9	101.4	101.8	97.3	97.7	97.5
M	100.3	101.0	100.8	97.9	96.9	97.8
J	100.4	100.9	100.8	100.9	97.7	100.5
J	100.4	100.6	100.5	100.1	98.8	100.0
A	100.5	100.0	100.1	100.0	99.8	100.0
S	100.4	99.8	100.0	100.2	100.5	100.3
O	99.9	99.4	99.5	100.5	101.2	100.6
N	98.9	98.5	98.6	100.5	101.2	100.6
D	98.2	98.4	98.4	101.0	101.2	101.1
1930						
J	97.7	97.1	97.3	99.5	101.2	99.9
F	97.6	96.7	96.9	98.3	101.2	98.9
M	96.7	96.6	96.7	96.3	101.2	97.1
A	93.1	96.0	95.4	96.3	100.1	96.9
M	88.6	94.9	93.6	96.1	96.2	96.1
J	87.3	93.3	92.0	95.6	95.2	95.5
J	84.9	92.4	90.8	95.8	96.1	96.0
A	84.4	91.1	89.6	95.6	97.7	96.0
S	83.3	90.5	89.0	96.3	98.9	96.8
O	80.6	89.7	87.8	95.0	99.6	95.9
N	80.7	89.5	87.6	90.7	99.5	92.3
D	80.8	89.5	87.7	90.6	99.5	92.2

INDEX NUMBERS OF WHOLESALE PRICES (cont.)

| MONTH | METALS | | | NON-METALLIC MINERALS | | |
	Raw producers'	Processed	Total	Raw producers'	Raw consumers'	Raw, total
1931						
J	79.7	88.7	86.8	90.0	98.7	91.6
F	78.7	88.5	86.4	89.8	98.7	91.4
M	78.6	88.4	86.3	83.4	98.1	86.0
A	77.6	87.9	85.7	80.4	96.4	83.1
M	75.3	87.4	84.9	80.0	97.8	83.0
J	73.8	86.9	84.1	75.7	99.3	79.8
J	73.9	86.8	84.1	74.0	101.5	78.8
A	73.4	86.4	83.7	77.9	103.2	82.2
S	72.8	86.3	83.5	80.2	105.5	84.5
O	71.3	85.6	82.6	79.8	105.4	84.3
N	70.8	85.4	82.3	82.3	105.4	86.2
D	69.9	85.0	81.9	82.0	105.5	86.1
1932						
J	70.2	84.2	81.3	81.8	105.6	86.0
F	68.2	83.5	80.3	81.7	105.1	85.8
M	67.1	83.6	80.1	81.0	100.1	84.4
A	66.2	83.3	79.8	81.9	95.4	84.3
M	65.2	83.2	79.5	82.3	95.4	84.5
J	64.4	83.2	79.2	82.2	95.1	84.5
J	63.3	83.1	78.9	83.2	94.2	85.1
A	64.3	83.3	79.3	82.9	95.8	85.1
S	66.0	82.6	79.1	82.3	97.7	85.0
O	65.3	82.5	78.9	82.3	98.8	85.2
N	64.2	82.4	78.6	82.0	99.0	85.0
D	63.5	82.2	78.3	80.1	98.8	83.4
1933						
J	63.5	80.6	77.0	76.4	98.8	80.3
F	63.4	81.1	77.1	73.7	98.8	78.1
M	64.5	79.8	76.6	73.0	98.4	77.4
A	65.2	80.9	77.4	71.8	90.6	75.1
M	70.2	79.8	77.8	70.1	87.2	73.1
J	74.7	80.6	79.4	70.8	85.6	73.4
J	78.2	81.6	80.9	75.4	86.9	77.5
A	79.2	82.4	81.8	78.3	88.3	80.0
S	80.6	83.2	82.7	84.1	91.4	85.4
O	79.6	83.9	83.1	90.4	91.1	90.6
N	80.1	84.1	83.3	90.7	91.1	90.9
D	79.8	84.7	83.7	91.1	90.9	91.0

APPENDIX IV

INDEX NUMBERS OF WHOLESALE PRICES (cont.)

MONTH	METALS			NON-METALLIC MINERALS		
	Raw producers'	Processed	Total	Raw producers'	Raw consumers'	Raw, total
1934						
J	79.8	87.4	85.9	89.0	91.0	89.4
F	79.7	88.6	86.7	89.2	90.8	89.6
M	80.2	88.6	86.8	89.2	90.8	89.6
A	81.4	89.4	87.7	90.7	87.4	90.1
M	82.4	90.9	89.1	91.3	84.7	90.2
J	82.3	89.6	88.0	91.5	86.0	90.6
J	82.5	88.3	87.1	92.1	88.0	91.4
A	82.5	88.2	87.0	92.4	89.4	92.0
S	82.2	88.1	86.8	92.5	90.9	92.3
O	82.1	87.8	86.6	92.5	91.8	92.4
N	81.8	87.7	86.4	92.2	91.9	92.2
D	82.0	87.6	86.4	92.0	92.0	92.0
1935						
J	82.2	87.5	86.3	92.0	92.1	92.1
F	81.9	87.3	86.2	92.2	92.1	92.2
M	81.8	87.3	86.2	92.2	90.8	92.0
A	82.5	87.2	86.2	91.5	84.5	90.4
M	83.3	87.8	86.8	91.6	81.7	90.0
J	83.2	88.1	87.0	91.8	82.8	90.4
J	81.9	87.7	86.4	91.8	86.1	90.8
A	82.4	87.8	86.6	91.4	88.1	90.8
S	83.1	87.6	86.6	90.0	90.3	90.1
O	84.3	86.5	86.1	91.3	92.2	91.5
N	86.1	87.6	87.3	93.6	92.9	93.6
D	85.7	87.6	87.2	93.7	92.7	93.6
1936						
J	84.7	87.9	87.2	94.9	91.9	94.5
F	84.8	87.8	87.1	96.4	92.3	95.8
M	85.0	87.6	87.0	96.6	92.2	95.9
A	85.1	87.6	87.0	94.9	89.4	94.0
M	84.9	87.2	86.8	94.7	85.6	93.1
J	84.4	87.2	86.7	94.7	86.0	93.2

INDEX NUMBERS OF WHOLESALE PRICES *(cont.)*

YEAR OR MONTH	NON-METALLIC MINERALS		ALL MINERALS				
	Processed	Total	Raw producers'	Raw consumers'	Raw, total	Processed	Total
N	94	110	32	3	35	199	234
1929	100.0	100.0	100.0	100.0	100.0	100.0	100.0
1930	95.3	95.6	92.6	98.8	93.3	94.0	93.8
1931	84.6	84.7	78.8	101.3	81.3	86.0	84.5
1932	85.1	85.0	75.7	98.5	78.3	84.0	82.2
1933	83.4	82.4	76.7	91.6	78.4	82.7	81.3
1934	88.5	89.6	87.5	89.6	87.7	88.4	88.2
1935	87.4	89.2	88.6	89.2	88.7	87.5	87.9
1929							
J	100.8	101.2	99.7	101.6	99.9	100.4	100.2
F	99.4	100.0	99.8	101.6	100.0	100.0	100.0
M	98.8	99.2	101.0	101.3	101.0	100.3	100.5
A	100.5	99.2	99.5	97.7	99.2	101.1	100.4
M	101.0	99.7	98.9	96.9	98.7	101.1	100.2
J	102.4	101.6	100.8	97.7	100.3	101.5	101.2
J	100.9	100.6	100.3	98.8	100.1	100.7	100.5
A	99.1	99.4	100.2	99.8	100.1	99.7	99.8
S	99.2	99.8	100.3	100.5	100.3	99.6	99.8
O	99.4	100.0	100.2	101.2	100.3	99.4	99.7
N	99.8	100.1	99.9	101.2	100.0	99.0	99.4
D	99.4	100.2	100.0	101.2	100.1	98.8	99.2
1930							
J	98.5	99.1	98.9	101.2	99.1	97.8	98.2
F	98.3	98.5	98.0	101.2	98.5	97.3	97.7
M	97.1	97.1	96.4	101.2	96.9	96.9	96.9
A	97.0	97.0	95.1	100.1	95.6	96.5	96.1
M	98.6	97.6	93.2	96.2	93.5	96.5	95.5
J	96.4	96.1	92.5	95.2	92.8	94.7	94.0
J	94.6	95.2	91.7	96.1	92.1	93.3	92.9
A	93.9	94.8	91.4	97.7	92.1	92.2	92.2
S	94.8	95.7	91.4	98.9	92.2	92.3	92.3
O	93.2	94.4	89.5	99.6	90.7	91.2	91.0
N	92.3	92.3	86.9	99.5	88.4	90.6	89.9
D	90.2	91.1	86.9	99.5	88.3	89.8	89.4

APPENDIX IV

INDEX NUMBERS OF WHOLESALE PRICES (cont.)

MONTH	NON-METALLIC MINERALS		ALL MINERALS				
	Processed	Total	Raw producers'	Raw consumers'	Raw, total	Processed	Total
1931							
J	89.4	90.4	86.1	98.7	87.5	89.0	88.5
F	88.1	89.5	85.6	98.7	87.1	88.4	88.0
M	85.8	85.8	81.6	98.1	83.5	87.3	86.1
A	83.5	83.3	79.3	96.4	81.3	86.2	84.5
M	83.2	83.2	78.1	97.8	80.4	85.7	84.0
J	82.1	81.1	74.9	99.3	77.8	85.0	82.6
J	81.9	80.6	74.0	101.5	77.1	84.9	82.4
A	84.0	83.2	76.1	103.2	79.2	85.4	83.5
S	84.3	84.5	77.4	105.5	80.5	85.5	83.9
O	84.4	84.5	76.6	105.4	79.9	85.2	83.5
N	85.1	85.6	77.9	105.4	81.0	85.3	83.9
D	83.3	84.6	77.4	105.5	80.6	84.3	83.1
1932							
J	83.3	84.5	77.5	105.6	80.6	83.9	82.8
F	82.6	84.0	76.6	105.1	79.9	83.2	82.1
M	82.8	83.5	75.7	100.1	78.4	83.4	81.7
A	85.0	84.7	75.9	95.4	78.1	84.1	82.2
M	85.9	85.4	75.7	95.4	78.0	84.5	82.4
J	86.5	85.6	75.4	95.1	77.7	84.7	82.4
J	87.2	86.3	75.6	94.2	77.7	84.9	82.5
A	86.4	85.8	75.8	95.8	78.0	84.7	82.5
S	85.0	85.0	76.0	97.7	78.6	83.7	82.1
O	85.5	85.4	75.8	98.8	78.4	83.7	82.1
N	85.4	85.3	75.3	99.0	77.9	83.7	81.8
D	84.3	83.9	73.7	98.8	76.6	83.2	81.0
1933							
J	82.1	81.4	71.4	98.8	74.5	81.3	79.2
F	80.8	79.6	69.8	98.8	73.1	80.8	78.2
M	80.1	78.9	69.8	98.4	73.0	79.9	77.7
A	80.0	77.8	69.3	90.6	71.8	80.3	77.4
M	79.8	77.0	70.2	87.2	72.1	79.9	77.3
J	81.3	77.9	72.3	85.6	73.9	80.9	78.6
J	83.8	81.0	76.5	86.9	77.7	82.5	81.0
A	83.6	82.0	78.7	88.3	79.8	83.0	82.0
S	86.2	85.8	82.8	91.4	83.8	84.5	84.2
O	88.2	89.3	86.3	91.1	86.9	85.7	86.0
N	88.5	89.5	86.8	91.1	87.2	85.9	86.4
D	88.7	89.8	86.8	90.9	87.2	86.4	86.7

INDEX NUMBERS OF WHOLESALE PRICES *(cont.)*

MONTH	NON-METALLIC MINERALS		ALL MINERALS				
	Processed	Total	Raw producers'	Raw consumers'	Raw, total	Processed	Total
1934							
J	88.9	89.2	85.6	91.0	86.2	88.1	87.4
F	88.4	88.8	85.7	90.8	86.2	88.5	87.8
M	87.6	88.5	85.8	90.8	86.3	88.2	87.6
A	87.3	88.6	87.2	87.4	87.2	88.5	88.1
M	88.1	89.1	88.0	84.7	87.5	89.8	89.0
J	88.7	89.5	88.1	86.0	87.9	89.2	88.7
J	89.4	90.3	88.4	88.0	88.4	88.7	88.6
A	89.3	90.4	88.6	89.4	88.7	88.7	88.7
S	89.1	90.6	88.5	90.9	88.8	88.5	88.6
O	89.2	90.6	88.5	91.8	88.9	88.4	88.5
N	88.7	90.3	88.3	91.9	88.7	88.2	88.3
D	88.2	89.9	88.2	92.0	88.6	87.9	88.1
1935	87.4	89.2	88.6	89.2	88.7	87.5	87.9
J	87.4	89.4	88.3	92.1	88.7	87.4	87.9
F	86.6	89.1	88.3	92.1	88.7	87.0	87.5
M	87.0	89.2	88.3	90.8	88.5	87.2	87.6
A	87.0	88.5	88.1	84.5	87.7	87.1	87.3
M	87.6	88.6	88.4	81.7	87.6	87.6	87.6
J	88.6	89.4	88.5	82.8	87.9	88.3	88.2
J	88.5	89.5	88.0	86.1	87.9	88.0	87.9
A	88.0	89.3	88.0	88.1	88.0	87.9	87.9
S	87.1	88.5	87.4	90.3	87.7	87.4	87.5
O	87.0	89.0	88.6	92.2	89.1	86.8	87.4
N	87.3	90.1	90.7	92.9	90.9	87.5	88.6
D	87.4	90.1	90.7	92.7	90.9	87.5	88.6
1936							
J	87.3	90.4	91.0	91.9	91.1	87.6	88.7
F	87.8	91.3	92.0	92.3	92.0	87.9	89.2
M	88.0	91.5	92.1	92.2	92.1	87.8	89.2
A	88.9	91.1	91.1	89.4	90.9	88.1	89.0
M	88.7	90.7	90.9	85.6	90.4	87.9	88.6
J	89.1	90.9	90.8	86.0	90.3	88.0	88.7

APPENDIX IV

INDEX NUMBERS OF WHOLESALE PRICES *(cont.)*

YEAR OR MONTH	FOREST PRODUCTS			YEAR OR MONTH	OTHER THAN RAW AMERICAN FARM PRODUCTS	RAW AMERICAN FARM PRODUCTS	
	Raw producers'	Processed	Total			Crops	Animal products
N	18	41	59	N	606	37	37
1929	100.0	100.0	100.0	*1929*	100.0	100.0	100.0
1930	90.5	96.5	93.9	*1930*	92.1	84.1	86.3
1931	78.3	86.5	82.9	*1931*	80.2	59.3	67.4
1932	66.0	78.9	73.3	*1932*	73.3	44.3	50.7
1933	74.4	79.7	77.4	*1933*	74.9	54.0	49.0
1934	85.7	85.2	85.4	*1934*	83.2	70.6	58.4
1935	81.5	83.7	82.7	*1935*	85.8	72.4	78.6
1929				*1929*			
J	99.5	100.9	100.2	J	100.9	99.3	99.4
F	100.7	100.8	100.7	F	100.5	99.7	98.6
M	102.0	100.5	101.2	M	100.8	99.1	101.3
A	101.6	100.1	100.7	A	100.4	96.5	102.2
M	101.5	100.2	100.7	M	99.9	93.9	100.2
J	101.0	100.0	100.4	J	100.2	95.4	101.3
J	100.5	99.9	100.1	J	100.6	100.5	103.1
A	100.5	99.8	100.1	A	100.4	103.4	102.7
S	99.8	99.9	99.8	S	100.4	105.2	100.7
O	98.8	99.7	99.4	O	99.8	104.7	97.6
N	97.7	99.4	98.6	N	98.7	99.8	95.8
D	96.2	98.8	97.8	D	98.2	100.1	96.2
1930				*1930*			
J	97.2	98.6	98.0	J	97.3	97.3	96.7
F	96.9	98.4	97.8	F	96.7	93.1	95.1
M	96.5	98.3	97.4	M	95.8	89.9	92.1
A	95.2	98.0	96.8	A	95.3	93.8	90.7
M	92.1	97.8	95.4	M	94.3	93.1	86.4
J	90.2	97.5	94.5	J	92.6	88.0	84.3
J	89.3	96.2	93.3	J	91.0	80.9	80.4
A	87.5	96.2	92.5	A	90.4	79.5	83.6
S	86.4	96.2	92.0	S	90.2	78.3	86.1
O	85.3	95.5	91.2	O	89.0	77.1	83.0
N	85.4	93.3	90.0	N	87.5	72.1	81.1
D	84.3	92.3	88.8	D	86.5	67.6	77.2

INDEX NUMBERS OF WHOLESALE PRICES (cont.)

| MONTH | FOREST PRODUCTS | | | MONTH | OTHER THAN RAW AMERICAN FARM PRODUCTS | RAW AMERICAN FARM PRODUCTS | |
	Raw producers'	Processed	Total			Crops	Animal
1931				*1931*			
J	84.2	90.0	87.4	J	85.1	67.6	73.8
F	83.3	89.4	86.8	F	84.1	66.5	69.4
M	82.5	89.5	86.5	M	82.9	66.1	71.3
A	80.4	89.4	85.5	A	81.6	65.7	70.7
M	79.4	88.2	84.4	M	80.5	64.2	66.9
J	78.5	87.8	83.8	J	79.3	61.7	66.3
J	76.7	86.6	82.3	J	79.1	59.4	68.1
A	76.4	85.7	81.7	A	79.3	54.1	69.9
S	76.2	84.0	80.6	S	78.9	52.4	66.5
O	75.2	83.1	79.7	O	78.4	50.7	64.8
N	74.4	82.7	79.1	N	78.3	52.0	62.9
D	72.8	82.4	78.3	D	76.8	49.0	60.3
1932				*1932*			
J	71.1	81.1	76.9	J	75.7	48.8	55.1
F	69.4	80.5	75.7	F	74.9	48.2	51.4
M	69.2	80.6	75.7	M	74.5	47.5	51.3
A	68.1	80.2	74.9	A	74.0	46.6	50.0
M	66.5	79.7	74.1	M	73.0	44.4	47.5
J	63.0	79.6	72.8	J	72.4	42.2	48.2
J	63.0	78.9	72.4	J	72.5	42.6	52.3
A	62.0	78.9	72.0	A	72.9	44.3	52.7
S	62.4	78.5	72.0	S	73.3	44.8	53.0
O	64.2	76.7	71.3	O	72.7	42.1	50.7
N	64.0	76.5	71.1	N	72.1	40.7	50.0
D	63.1	76.2	70.6	D	71.2	39.4	45.3
1933				*1933*			
J	62.9	75.1	69.8	J	69.5	40.2	42.7
F	63.5	75.0	70.0	F	68.6	39.6	41.0
M	64.5	75.4	70.8	M	68.6	42.8	41.9
A	65.1	74.3	70.4	A	68.7	46.7	41.6
M	66.0	74.6	71.0	M	70.4	52.6	48.2
J	71.9	76.8	74.7	J	72.7	57.1	51.2
J	78.6	80.7	79.9	J	76.6	68.3	53.5
A	81.2	83.4	82.5	A	78.4	63.2	54.0
S	81.6	84.5	83.3	S	80.1	60.9	54.4
O	83.5	84.8	84.2	O	80.8	57.7	53.7
N	86.6	84.9	85.6	N	80.8	59.2	53.3
D	88.4	84.9	86.4	D	80.6	60.2	51.6

APPENDIX IV
INDEX NUMBERS OF WHOLESALE PRICES (cont.)

MONTH	FOREST PRODUCTS			MONTH	OTHER THAN RAW AMERICAN FARM PRODUCTS	RAW AMERICAN FARM PRODUCTS	
	Raw producers'	Processed	Total			Crops	Animal
1934				*1934*			
J	88.2	85.8	86.8	J	81.5	64.5	52.3
F	87.2	86.3	86.7	F	82.5	67.5	54.2
M	87.4	86.3	86.8	M	82.7	66.7	54.3
A	87.4	86.3	86.8	A	82.6	63.8	54.5
M	87.4	86.3	86.8	M	83.2	64.4	53.8
J	87.3	86.1	86.6	J	83.4	69.6	57.0
J	86.7	84.9	85.7	J	83.4	70.9	58.3
A	83.7	84.4	84.1	A	84.0	76.2	61.8
S	83.7	84.4	84.1	S	84.6	76.7	66.3
O	83.8	84.4	84.1	O	84.0	75.9	62.5
N	83.5	84.3	83.9	N	83.9	75.9	62.2
D	82.6	84.3	83.5	D	84.0	76.9	64.0
1935				*1935*			
J	80.9	84.2	82.7	J	85.0	75.5	72.8
F	81.0	83.6	82.5	F	85.4	75.3	75.6
M	80.7	83.4	82.2	M	85.3	73.2	77.3
A	80.4	83.3	82.1	A	85.5	76.6	78.7
M	80.6	83.3	82.1	M	85.6	75.1	79.3
J	81.6	82.5	82.2	J	85.5	72.6	78.4
J	82.0	82.6	82.4	J	85.3	70.9	77.0
A	82.6	83.2	82.9	A	86.0	68.7	81.7
S	82.3	84.1	83.3	S	86.3	68.8	81.6
O	82.3	84.3	83.4	O	86.4	70.3	79.6
N	82.0	84.0	83.2	N	86.9	70.1	78.6
D	82.0	83.8	83.0	D	87.1	68.9	80.4
1936				*1936*			
J	80.8	84.5	82.9	J	86.6	69.1	80.6
F	80.8	84.7	83.0	F	86.3	69.1	81.6
M	80.9	84.7	83.0	M	85.5	68.9	77.7
A	81.6	84.7	83.4	A	85.3	70.5	77.2
M	81.6	84.6	83.4	M	84.4	70.5	74.3
J	81.3	84.8	83.4	J	84.5	75.1	75.1

INDEX NUMBERS OF WHOLESALE PRICES *(cont.)*

YEAR OR MONTH	PRODUCTS OF AMERICAN FARMS			Processed	Total
	Raw producers'	Raw consumers'	Raw, total		
N	51	23	74	225	299
1929	100.0	100.0	100.0	100.0	100.0
1930	80.9	95.6	85.3	91.6	88.8
1931	57.5	77.8	63.5	77.6	71.5
1932	43.3	57.5	47.6	66.2	58.2
1933	49.1	56.9	51.5	70.4	62.2
1934	63.1	67.1	64.3	81.7	74.2
1935	78.2	69.5	75.6	89.1	83.3
1929					
J	100.8	96.1	99.4	101.2	100.4
F	100.6	95.5	99.1	100.5	99.9
M	104.1	91.2	100.3	100.6	100.4
A	103.5	90.1	99.6	99.9	99.7
M	99.0	92.7	97.2	99.1	98.2
J	99.2	96.6	98.5	99.2	98.8
J	103.5	98.2	102.0	101.2	101.5
A	102.5	104.5	103.2	101.5	102.1
S	101.4	106.4	102.9	101.2	101.9
O	97.8	108.5	101.1	100.0	100.4
N	93.0	108.8	97.8	98.3	98.0
D	93.4	109.0	98.2	97.8	97.9
1930					
J	94.4	103.2	97.1	97.1	97.0
F	91.4	100.6	94.2	96.2	95.3
M	88.6	96.8	91.1	95.2	93.3
A	88.4	101.1	92.3	95.0	93.7
M	86.0	98.1	89.7	93.5	91.8
J	81.2	98.1	86.2	92.0	89.5
J	76.3	91.0	80.8	90.0	86.0
A	77.8	91.1	81.7	90.1	86.5
S	77.2	94.5	82.4	89.9	86.7
O	73.5	95.6	80.2	88.7	85.0
N	70.0	93.1	76.9	86.8	82.5
D	67.7	83.9	72.6	84.9	79.6

APPENDIX IV

INDEX NUMBERS OF WHOLESALE PRICES *(cont.)*

MONTH	Raw producers'	Raw consumers'	Raw, total	Processed	Total
1931					
J	66.7	80.5	70.9	83.1	77.8
F	64.3	76.9	68.1	81.8	75.9
M	64.8	77.9	68.8	81.4	75.9
A	64.1	78.2	68.4	80.2	75.1
M	60.2	78.3	65.7	78.1	72.7
J	58.1	79.0	64.2	77.0	71.5
J	57.6	79.3	64.0	77.1	71.4
A	55.7	78.7	62.5	76.8	70.6
S	51.8	78.5	59.8	75.6	68.8
O	49.9	77.6	58.1	74.9	67.7
N	50.8	74.2	57.7	74.1	67.1
D	47.9	71.5	54.9	71.9	64.6
1932					
J	48.1	61.2	52.0	70.2	62.3
F	46.3	58.1	49.9	69.2	60.8
M	46.1	57.4	49.5	69.0	60.6
A	44.5	57.3	48.4	67.6	59.3
M	41.4	56.9	45.9	65.4	57.0
J	40.4	57.4	45.4	64.2	56.1
J	43.7	57.1	47.7	64.9	57.4
A	45.5	56.3	48.7	65.6	58.4
S	45.6	57.1	49.0	66.4	58.9
O	41.7	57.8	46.5	65.2	57.1
N	39.5	59.7	45.6	64.2	56.2
D	37.2	54.8	42.5	63.0	54.2
1933					
J	37.4	51.3	41.5	61.5	52.9
F	37.9	46.1	40.3	60.6	51.9
M	40.7	46.2	42.4	61.3	53.1
A	42.5	47.4	44.0	62.3	54.4
M	50.2	50.7	50.4	65.6	59.0
J	53.0	56.5	54.1	68.9	62.5
J	58.7	65.0	60.6	73.9	68.1
A	55.4	65.9	58.5	77.4	69.2
S	55.4	62.8	57.6	78.2	69.2
O	52.9	62.3	55.7	78.0	68.3
N	52.5	64.7	56.2	77.5	68.2
D	51.9	65.2	55.7	76.2	67.3

INDEX NUMBERS OF WHOLESALE PRICES (cont.)

MONTH	Raw producers'	Raw consumers'	Raw, total	Processed	Total
1934					
J	54.5	66.9	58.3	77.6	69.2
F	58.3	66.2	60.6	79.7	71.4
M	58.4	64.9	60.3	80.3	71.6
A	57.6	62.5	59.1	79.5	70.7
M	57.6	62.1	59.0	80.0	70.9
J	61.1	68.0	63.2	81.2	73.4
J	62.7	68.3	64.4	81.4	74.0
A	68.8	68.7	68.8	83.5	77.1
S	72.2	69.2	71.4	85.1	79.1
O	68.2	70.9	69.1	83.7	77.3
N	68.4	69.8	68.9	83.4	77.0
D	71.1	68.2	70.3	84.0	78.0
1935					
J	76.0	69.5	74.2	86.6	81.2
F	77.7	70.2	75.5	88.2	82.7
M	78.7	67.3	75.4	88.1	82.6
A	81.0	69.9	77.8	89.3	84.3
M	80.7	69.3	77.4	89.1	84.0
J	77.9	70.2	75.6	88.1	82.7
J	76.0	69.2	74.1	87.8	81.9
A	78.3	68.9	75.5	89.6	83.5
S	78.4	68.6	75.5	90.6	84.1
O	78.1	68.2	75.1	90.3	83.8
N	75.8	71.3	74.6	90.3	83.5
D	76.7	70.4	75.0	91.2	84.1
1936					
J	78.0	68.3	75.1	89.4	83.2
F	77.6	70.9	75.6	88.1	82.7
M	76.4	66.6	73.5	86.1	80.6
A	76.5	68.0	74.1	85.8	80.7
M	73.5	70.1	72.5	83.8	78.9
J	74.5	76.6	75.1	84.1	80.2

Columns labeled "Raw producers'", "Raw consumers'", "Raw, total" are grouped under **PRODUCTS OF AMERICAN FARMS**.

APPENDIX IV

INDEX NUMBERS OF WHOLESALE PRICES (cont.)

YEAR OR MONTH	PRODUCTS OTHER THAN THOSE ORIGINATING ON AMERICAN FARMS					
	Raw producers'	Raw consumers'	Raw, total	Processed	Total
N	63	7	70	311	381
1929	100.0	100.0	100.0	100.0	100.0
1930	90.1	86.4	89.7	93.8	92.4
1931	75.5	79.1	76.2	84.6	81.8
1932	69.4	81.3	71.2	80.8	77.6
1933	72.0	78.1	73.0	79.9	77.6
1934	82.3	80.9	82.2	85.3	84.2
1935	82.8	77.0	82.0	84.8	83.9
1929					
J	99.5	104.2	100.2	100.8	100.7
F	100.3	103.9	100.9	100.3	100.6
M	101.6	103.6	101.9	100.4	100.9
A	100.0	101.9	100.3	101.0	100.8
M	99.3	100.4	99.6	100.9	100.4
J	100.5	100.1	100.4	101.1	100.9
J	100.2	99.6	100.2	100.3	100.3
A	100.5	99.7	100.3	99.7	99.9
S	100.5	100.2	100.4	99.7	99.9
O	100.2	98.6	100.0	99.5	99.7
N	99.0	96.0	98.7	99.0	98.9
D	98.3	92.2	97.5	98.8	98.3
1930					
J	97.5	91.8	96.7	97.8	97.5
F	96.8	91.6	96.2	97.5	97.0
M	95.5	91.7	94.9	96.9	96.3
A	94.0	90.8	93.7	96.5	95.6
M	91.8	87.6	91.3	96.4	94.7
J	90.0	86.3	89.5	94.7	92.9
J	88.7	85.7	88.3	93.2	91.6
A	87.9	82.2	87.2	92.2	90.6
S	87.3	82.5	86.6	92.1	90.3
O	85.3	85.2	85.4	91.0	89.2
N	83.5	82.3	83.5	90.3	88.0
D	83.3	80.6	83.0	89.5	87.3

INDEX NUMBERS OF WHOLESALE PRICES (*cont.*)

	PRODUCTS OTHER THAN THOSE ORIGINATING ON AMERICAN FARMS				
MONTH	Raw producers'	Raw consumers'	Raw, total	Processed	Total
1931					
J	82.8	79.2	82.3	88.2	86.2
F	82.0	78.8	81.6	87.4	85.6
M	78.7	77.2	78.5	86.7	83.9
A	76.3	76.0	76.4	85.5	82.5
M	75.2	77.4	75.6	85.0	81.8
J	72.7	78.6	73.6	84.2	80.7
J	71.8	79.1	73.0	84.0	80.4
A	73.2	78.0	73.9	84.3	80.8
S	73.8	80.0	74.8	84.1	81.0
O	73.1	81.6	74.4	83.6	80.6
N	73.8	82.0	75.1	83.6	80.8
D	72.8	84.0	74.6	82.5	79.9
1932					
J	72.3	83.7	74.0	81.8	79.2
F	71.3	83.4	73.0	81.0	78.4
M	70.2	80.7	71.8	81.0	77.9
A	69.9	79.7	71.4	81.2	77.9
M	69.2	80.7	71.0	81.1	77.7
J	68.1	80.0	70.0	81.0	77.4
J	68.3	79.8	70.1	80.8	77.3
A	68.8	80.9	70.6	80.8	77.4
S	69.4	83.6	71.7	80.3	77.4
O	69.4	81.7	71.2	80.3	77.4
N	68.8	80.1	70.4	80.1	77.0
D	67.4	81.5	69.5	79.5	76.2
1933					
J	65.4	80.6	67.7	77.8	74.4
F	64.1	80.2	66.6	77.1	73.5
M	64.4	79.9	66.7	76.4	73.2
A	64.4	74.9	65.9	76.3	72.8
M	65.7	72.8	66.6	76.5	73.2
J	69.0	71.4	69.4	77.9	75.2
J	73.8	76.7	74.4	80.0	78.2
A	75.3	74.2	75.3	81.1	79.2
S	78.7	79.1	78.9	82.5	81.3
O	80.9	77.6	80.5	83.5	82.6
N	82.2	76.8	81.4	83.5	82.9
D	82.5	77.4	81.9	84.0	83.2

APPENDIX IV

INDEX NUMBERS OF WHOLESALE PRICES (*cont.*)

	PRODUCTS OTHER THAN THOSE ORIGINATING ON AMERICAN FARMS				
MONTH	Raw producers'	Raw consumers'	Raw, total	Processed	Total
1934					
J	81.7	78.8	81.4	85.3	84.0
F	82.0	80.9	81.9	85.5	84.3
M	82.0	81.1	81.9	85.4	84.2
A	83.0	78.7	82.3	85.6	84.5
M	83.5	77.2	82.7	86.5	85.2
J	83.0	78.5	82.3	85.9	84.7
J	83.1	80.7	82.8	85.4	84.6
A	82.9	82.3	82.8	85.2	84.3
S	82.8	83.2	82.9	85.0	84.3
O	82.6	83.4	82.9	85.0	84.3
N	82.4	83.2	82.6	85.0	84.2
D	82.3	83.3	82.6	84.8	84.1
1935					
J	82.3	83.2	82.5	84.7	84.0
F	82.3	82.0	82.3	84.4	83.7
M	82.0	79.7	81.7	84.6	83.6
A	81.7	75.4	80.9	84.4	83.2
M	82.1	73.4	80.9	84.8	83.5
J	82.4	73.7	81.2	85.3	83.9
J	82.1	75.3	81.2	85.0	83.8
A	82.4	74.2	81.3	85.0	83.8
S	82.2	75.4	81.3	84.8	83.7
O	83.5	76.8	82.7	84.9	83.9
N	85.1	76.8	84.0	85.2	84.8
D	85.0	76.6	83.8	85.1	84.7
1936					
J	85.2	76.9	84.1	85.3	84.9
F	86.0	75.7	84.6	85.4	85.1
M	86.1	78.5	85.0	85.3	85.2
A	85.5	74.5	83.9	85.6	85.0
M	85.1	75.2	83.7	85.4	84.9
J	85.1	74.0	83.6	85.5	84.8

INDEX NUMBERS OF WHOLESALE PRICES (cont.)

YEAR OR MONTH	FOODS			NON-FOODS		
	Raw	Processed	Total	Raw	Processed	Total
N	62	115	177	82	421	503
1929	100.0	100.0	100.0	100.0	100.0	100.0
1930	87.6	91.7	89.5	86.5	93.3	91.2
1931	66.7	77.3	72.0	70.9	83.0	79.3
1932	51.1	66.0	58.5	63.9	77.2	73.1
1933	52.6	65.4	58.9	68.4	79.8	76.3
1934	64.5	76.4	70.3	79.3	86.7	84.3
1935	77.2	89.6	83.3	79.4	85.7	83.9
1929						
J	98.3	100.8	99.6	101.2	101.1	101.2
F	98.5	100.1	99.3	101.2	100.6	100.9
M	99.3	100.2	99.7	102.7	100.8	101.3
A	99.3	99.6	99.4	100.4	100.9	100.8
M	97.1	98.7	97.9	99.1	100.6	100.2
J	98.5	99.1	98.8	100.1	100.6	100.5
J	102.4	102.3	102.3	100.0	100.2	100.1
A	103.7	102.8	103.2	100.2	99.7	99.8
S	103.3	102.1	102.6	100.4	99.7	100.0
O	101.4	100.1	100.7	99.7	99.7	99.7
N	98.5	97.6	98.1	97.5	99.1	98.7
D	98.6	97.4	98.0	97.0	98.8	98.3
1930						
J	97.5	97.0	97.3	96.2	97.7	97.3
F	95.8	95.9	95.9	94.2	97.3	96.3
M	92.8	95.3	94.1	92.6	96.5	95.3
A	93.6	95.4	94.5	91.9	95.9	94.7*
M	90.6	93.5	92.0	90.0	95.8	94.0
J	88.1	91.6	89.7	86.9	94.3	92.0
J	82.8	88.9	85.8	84.9	93.0	90.5
A	84.4	90.0	87.2	83.5	91.8	89.3
S	85.9	91.0	88.4	82.3	91.2	88.5
O	84.1	89.7	86.9	80.5	90.1	87.2
N	80.2	86.9	83.5	79.0	89.5	86.2
D	76.0	85.1	80.4	77.8	88.3	85.1

APPENDIX IV

INDEX NUMBERS OF WHOLESALE PRICES (*cont.*)

MONTH	FOODS			NON-FOODS		
	Raw	Processed	Total	Raw	Processed	Total
1931						
J	73.8	83.7	78.7	77.3	86.8	83.9
F	70.2	81.9	75.9	77.2	86.0	83.3
M	70.4	81.5	75.8	75.3	85.3	82.2
A	70.4	80.0	75.1	72.9	84.3	80.8
M	68.3	77.1	72.6	71.2	83.8	79.9
J	66.8	75.9	71.3	69.4	82.9	78.8
J	66.1	76.2	71.1	69.4	82.7	78.6
A	65.8	76.2	71.0	68.5	82.7	78.4
S	63.9	75.3	69.5	68.2	82.2	77.9
O	62.7	75.1	68.8	67.0	81.4	77.1
N	62.2	74.4	68.1	67.7	81.2	77.1
D	59.3	72.1	65.6	66.9	79.8	75.9
1932						
J	56.1	69.7	62.8	66.5	79.0	75.2
F	53.1	68.2	60.5	66.0	78.5	74.7
M	52.7	68.3	60.3	64.9	78.4	74.3
A	52.3	66.8	59.4	63.8	78.3	73.8
M	50.2	65.0	57.5	62.6	77.4	72.9
J	50.0	64.1	57.0	61.3	76.9	72.1
J	52.2	66.1	59.1	61.8	76.2	71.9
A	51.9	66.8	59.3	63.9	76.5	72.6
S	51.9	66.4	59.0	65.2	76.9	73.3
O	49.6	64.6	57.0	64.2	76.9	73.0
N	48.7	63.9	56.1	63.2	76.5	72.3
D	45.7	62.4	53.8	61.9	75.6	71.5
1933						
J	44.1	60.5	52.1	60.8	74.2	70.1
F	43.0	59.5	51.1	59.7	73.4	69.2
M	44.8	60.2	52.3	60.4	73.1	69.2
A	46.2	61.7	53.8	60.2	73.0	69.0
M	50.9	64.7	57.7	63.3	74.2	70.9
J	53.8	65.7	59.7	67.1	77.1	74.1
J	60.5	69.8	65.1	72.3	80.4	77.9
A	58.8	69.3	63.9	72.4	83.8	80.3
S	58.2	69.2	63.6	74.9	85.4	82.2
O	56.2	69.0	62.5	76.2	86.1	83.1
N	56.4	68.5	62.3	77.3	86.0	83.4
D	55.5	66.5	61.0	78.0	86.2	83.7

INDEX NUMBERS OF WHOLESALE PRICES (cont.)

MONTH	FOODS			NON-FOODS		
	Raw	Processed	Total	Raw	Processed	Total
1934						
J	57.9	68.6	63.1	78.1	87.3	84.5
F	59.9	71.6	65.6	79.2	87.5	85.0
M	59.6	72.8	66.0	79.3	87.4	84.9
A	58.2	72.1	65.0	79.6	87.3	84.9
M	58.6	73.3	65.8	79.3	87.7	85.1
J	62.9	75.5	69.0	79.6	87.2	84.9
J	64.2	76.3	70.2	80.0	86.6	84.6
A	69.3	79.9	74.5	80.2	86.3	84.4
S	72.3	82.4	77.2	80.0	86.2	84.4
O	70.1	80.6	75.3	79.5	86.0	84.1
N	69.7	81.1	75.2	79.5	85.6	83.7
D	71.2	82.2	76.5	79.6	85.5	83.6
1935						
J	75.6	86.1	80.7	79.6	85.4	83.6
F	77.3	88.8	83.0	79.3	85.1	83.3
M	78.1	89.0	83.5	77.9	85.1	82.9
A	80.0	90.9	85.4	78.0	85.0	82.9
M	79.1	90.3	84.6	78.5	85.4	83.3
J	77.2	88.3	82.6	78.6	85.9	83.7
J	75.2	88.0	81.5	78.9	85.8	83.7
A	77.1	90.5	83.7	78.6	85.8	83.6
S	77.5	91.8	84.5	78.3	85.8	83.5
O	76.5	90.8	83.6	80.0	85.9	84.1
N	74.8	90.3	82.5	82.1	86.5	85.1
D	75.2	91.5	83.2	82.0	86.5	85.1
1936						
J	75.6	89.3	82.4	82.1	86.3	85.0
F	76.3	88.1	82.1	82.4	86.1	84.9
M	74.2	85.1	79.5	82.4	85.9	84.9
A	74.5	85.0	79.6	81.8	86.0	84.8
M	73.2	81.7	77.3	81.2	85.9	84.5
J	75.7	82.2	78.9	81.6	85.9	84.6

APPENDIX V

INDEX NUMBERS OF WHOLESALE PRICES OF SIMILAR GOODS IN RAW AND MANUFACTURED STATE
1913–1935

Constructed by the National Bureau of Economic Research. For certain commodity groups use has been made of group index numbers and weights of the U. S. Bureau of Labor Statistics. (For classification of commodities, see the supplementary note to this table.)

542 PRICES IN RECESSION AND RECOVERY

YEAR	TOTAL RAW	TOTAL SIMPLE PROCESSED	FOODS, RAW	FOODS, PROCESSED	TEXTILES, RAW	TEXTILES, YARNS	TEXTILES, FINISHED	METALS, RAW	METALS, PROCESSED
1913	100.0	100.0	100.0	100.0	100.0	100.0	100.0	100.0	100.0
1914	94.3	94.2	103.5	104.0	89.9	92.2	97.9	88.1	86.5
1915	99.3	95.6	106.9	108.4	90.2	89.1	96.6	107.1	96.8
1916	141.0	136.8	122.6	125.7	122.7	129.7	116.8	173.5	167.7
1917	211.8	190.6	173.0	174.0	190.0	186.2	160.7	279.1	248.2
1918	222.8	196.1	192.7	192.6	242.5	263.5	228.0	242.1	199.9
1919	215.6	190.9	207.6	213.0	244.9	262.7	225.7	185.7	173.5
1920	248.1	226.7	211.9	214.2	236.6	321.2	292.1	254.7	199.7
1921	135.3	141.4	121.4	136.3	113.4	139.7	175.8	137.9	137.5
1922	143.5	135.9	120.7	131.5	160.8	168.7	176.9	141.3	124.2
1923	155.5	146.1	128.2	141.2	207.5	196.4	193.3	161.4	151.6
1924	147.2	140.8	126.6	137.2	204.8	184.4	189.9	134.9	143.3
1925	152.1	144.7	140.1	153.0	176.4	177.9	188.5	136.1	137.5
1926	142.2	142.7	135.5	153.1	136.6	155.5	176.4	131.2	135.3
1927	133.7	132.0	136.4	149.8	135.5	148.1	170.0	124.0	126.0
1928	137.8	136.2	141.3	161.3	150.8	152.6	172.1	121.9	126.7
1929	137.3	133.8	137.7	154.5	139.3	150.9	162.6	134.0	132.3
1930	116.2	118.1	116.7	134.9	98.1	124.0	145.0	122.8	118.7
1931	86.8	96.7	87.0	105.5	66.3	97.8	118.7	104.3	106.6
1932	74.0	85.7	66.8	84.5	49.7	78.4	100.4	89.9	99.1
1933	78.8	90.3	67.9	88.1	66.0	104.4	120.5	99.0	99.6
1934	96.3	102.6	80.8	106.3	88.1	122.7	137.2	113.8	109.1
1935	105.8	109.0	109.1	136.1	83.6	118.5	131.0	116.7	109.1

APPENDIX V 543

YEAR	BREAD AND PRODUCTS	FLOUR AND GRAIN MILL PRODUCTS	GRAINS	BUTTER, CHEESE AND PROCESSED MILK	MILK, FLUID (AT THE FARM)	MEAT PACKING PRODUCTS	LIVESTOCK AND POULTRY	SUGAR, GRANULATED	SUGAR, RAW
1913	100.0	100.0	100.0	100.0	100.0	100.0	100.0	100.0	100.0
1914	102.4	108.9	108.4	94.3	99.0	104.2	101.9	110.3	109.8
1915	109.3	136.8	131.9	92.9	100.0	98.7	94.0	130.3	132.9
1916	112.2	147.5	140.1	109.3	101.9	115.4	113.1	161.1	165.5
1917	162.9	240.9	239.7	139.9	123.1	161.6	163.1	180.6	179.5
1918	175.2	225.3	237.1	165.1	149.0	194.5	192.6	182.5	183.3
1919	178.8	256.8	249.5	191.8	169.2	206.6	203.1	209.4	214.6
1920	212.1	275.1	248.1	189.5	184.6	181.1	170.9	296.8	372.2
1921	185.5	167.7	125.3	138.6	152.9	122.2	106.8	144.3	134.6
1922	171.4	151.6	119.5	127.6	135.6	123.9	113.7	139.2	133.3
1923	169.0	140.7	123.8	148.2	150.0	124.2	106.1	197.7	200.4
1924	169.5	152.6	141.5	132.7	134.6	123.9	108.3	174.3	170.1
1925	172.8	187.7	166.4	142.7	137.5	151.1	135.1	128.1	123.8
1926	172.4	175.4	140.6	138.5	134.6	157.2	136.6	128.4	124.1
1927	170.7	163.7	141.9	146.4	135.6	149.5	135.1	136.3	135.2
1928	170.3	163.7	150.9	149.2	137.5	173.0	144.0	130.0	121.2
1929	160.7	151.2	137.0	142.2	137.5	169.7	144.9	118.4	107.4
1930	158.6	126.8	110.1	117.2	123.1	150.9	121.9	109.1	96.3
1931	155.0	96.5	74.5	93.2	95.2	113.7	87.3	103.7	95.2
1932	143.8	84.6	55.4	72.0	71.2	86.8	65.8	93.7	83.5
1933	140.7	118.4	74.7	73.8	70.2	79.6	59.3	101.2	92.1
1934	157.8	151.6	104.8	87.1	81.7	98.6	70.4	103.7	86.4
1935	167.8	161.2	116.0	100.7	92.3	147.2	116.3	114.5	92.7

YEAR	COTTON GOODS	COTTON YARNS	COTTON, RAW	WOOLEN AND WORSTED GOODS	WOOLEN YARNS	WOOL, RAW	SILK HOSE	SILK YARN	SILK, RAW
1913	100.0	100.0	100.0	100.0	100.0	100.0	100.0	100.0	100.0
1914	98.2	90.1	89.0	95.9	88.1	88.4	100.0	106.2	97.5
1915	92.6	80.9	77.1	103.0	100.5	114.8	100.0	99.5	89.0
1916	115.9	127.6	113.4	129.6	135.9	135.2	100.0	127.2	135.0
1917	167.2	181.3	179.9	184.6	204.6	222.8	105.7	172.3	152.3
1918	250.9	260.0	245.9	244.4	302.0	263.1	134.7	211.6	171.7
1919	254.7	252.6	256.6	213.1	289.7	229.8	157.1	253.3	227.4
1920	324.6	344.7	264.0	277.3	314.8	188.5	215.8	244.9	228.6
1921	184.2	123.4	114.3	171.2	171.1	94.7	157.1	147.0	157.7
1922	185.7	157.4	163.0	172.5	196.3	145.3	157.1	164.2	190.5
1923	204.9	189.3	225.8	193.3	222.2	169.7	159.0	179.1	217.1
1924	203.3	176.6	221.5	194.4	213.6	169.3	143.1	164.2	158.2
1925	197.1	161.7	183.3	202.6	213.7	167.7	142.0	177.1	165.2
1926	181.2	139.3	133.7	187.3	183.2	134.8	146.0	168.6	155.5
1927	176.4	134.7	136.1	183.3	178.6	133.6	131.5	146.2	137.2
1928	181.5	140.1	153.5	186.1	187.2	153.6	122.9	140.6	130.2
1929	178.8	139.1	147.1	160.3	178.0	129.6	117.5	148.4	126.4
1930	158.5	112.8	103.9	146.6	149.8	90.6	101.3	121.1	89.3
1931	128.8	85.7	65.8	127.9	125.1	68.5	74.7	97.1	62.5
1932	110.1	68.8	49.5	109.2	102.9	53.6	58.2	72.5	40.6
1933	134.8	101.9	66.3	129.2	129.5	74.7	64.4	71.5	41.1
1934	154.9	125.5	96.3	148.9	148.7	94.2	66.4	69.8	32.3
1935	146.6	121.9	92.6	143.3	137.9	83.0	66.0	74.0	40.7

APPENDIX V

YEAR	BOOTS AND SHOES	OTHER LEATHER PRODUCTS	LEATHER	HIDES AND SKINS	PETROLEUM PRODUCTS	PETROLEUM, CRUDE	AGRI-CULTURAL IMPLEMENTS	SIMPLE PROCESSED IRON AND STEEL	PIG IRON
1913	100.0	100.0	100.0	100.0	100.0	100.0	100.0	100.0	100.0
1914	103.3	101.2	104.9	106.2	90.6	88.4	100.3	85.8	88.9
1915	107.5	108.9	109.7	118.2	76.2	68.8	97.7	91.3	103.9
1916	126.8	127.0	155.1	141.9	112.3	136.4	97.4	163.2	171.9
1917	167.9	167.9	205.4	188.5	137.7	191.6	118.4	264.4	312.0
1918	179.6	191.3	195.8	181.8	167.3	240.4	156.4	210.6	272.4
1919	247.2	262.0	271.3	250.4	152.3	251.4	156.1	185.9	208.1
1920	277.2	277.2	272.4	193.5	222.1	358.3	153.5	220.2	303.2
1921	204.6	233.5	161.6	83.8	120.9	212.8	152.8	151.2	157.9
1922	180.0	223.4	152.2	108.4	123.3	193.9	121.0	133.1	160.2
1923	181.8	204.1	150.7	110.1	102.6	153.3	135.5	165.4	184.7
1924	180.6	204.1	144.4	103.2	99.3	172.4	145.0	157.6	151.5
1925	184.4	202.4	151.7	111.1	109.4	199.6	137.7	147.7	150.5
1926	183.5	196.9	144.7	93.6	114.3	210.5	137.2	145.3	144.7
1927	188.3	202.4	158.0	112.6	85.6	154.9	136.6	135.0	137.5
1928	201.7	213.0	182.8	139.1	86.6	147.2	136.1	134.0	131.4
1929	195.0	209.4	163.8	105.5	84.1	153.1	135.1	135.2	140.2
1930	187.2	207.7	146.6	85.2	71.4	136.8	129.9	125.4	136.8
1931	171.9	199.6	124.7	56.4	47.8	85.7	125.7	116.9	122.1
1932	158.0	177.4	94.2	39.4	52.0	101.9	115.4	111.0	108.4
1933	165.5	159.6	103.3	62.8	50.5	83.8	113.3	109.9	117.1
1934	180.0	170.5	108.5	64.2	58.1	117.7	121.7	120.3	134.3
1935	179.8	167.3	115.9	75.7	58.7	114.9	127.7	120.3	137.6

546 PRICES IN RECESSION AND RECOVERY

YEAR	IRON ORE AND COKE	COPPER PRODUCTS	COPPER, INGOT	LEAD PIPE	LEAD, PIG	ZINC, SHEET	ZINC, SLAB	FERTILIZERS, MIXED	FERTILIZER MATERIALS
1913	100.0	100.0	100.0	100.0	100.0	100.0	100.0	100.0	100.0
1914	87.7	87.9	85.1	89.1	88.3	95.5	90.5	101.4	91.6
1915	83.7	109.3	109.7	104.5	104.2	223.1	246.7	109.1	156.4
1916	111.8	178.8	175.1	149.6	154.6	259.4	240.7	168.7	240.0
1917	170.1	193.6	186.8	198.2	207.1	249.9	158.7	163.3	266.7
1918	168.5	163.6	156.8	175.0	168.6	196.6	141.9	231.3	277.1
1919	164.1	133.2	121.5	143.2	131.4	135.8	127.0	263.0	224.3
1920	216.8	131.6	114.2	191.6	183.5	156.6	138.6	210.1	247.5
1921	165.4	91.7	80.2	111.9	103.8	130.6	88.2	192.8	137.9
1922	164.8	93.8	85.4	134.6	131.6	102.5	104.4	141.2	119.6
1923	164.3	104.4	92.2	175.8	168.0	118.0	120.2	127.4	119.9
1924	142.9	93.6	83.2	191.2	187.9	125.0	115.1	113.8	108.3
1925	130.6	100.0	89.5	207.6	206.5	136.7	137.0	119.1	115.6
1926	126.6	98.2	87.7	195.3	191.6	146.2	132.3	118.6	117.0
1927	124.1	93.4	82.4	161.9	153.6	127.6	113.2	110.3	112.5
1928	122.2	100.6	92.5	153.1	143.3	118.4	109.4	115.4	110.6
1929	127.6	121.6	114.9	163.1	155.0	127.0	117.3	115.3	107.7
1930	127.1	94.7	81.8	136.5	125.3	123.0	84.1	111.0	100.1
1931	125.3	70.5	51.7	116.0	96.4	113.3	68.3	97.3	89.8
1932	121.9	57.0	35.4	102.7	72.4	111.8	55.8	82.2	78.2
1933	123.2	63.3	44.6	115.4	87.9	114.8	76.1	76.5	77.1
1934	129.6	69.4	53.5	115.8	87.9	118.3	77.5	86.0	78.5
1935	131.1	69.5	54.9	118.4	92.5	118.3	80.7	83.7	77.5

APPENDIX V

YEAR	AUTO TIRES AND TUBES	RUBBER, CRUDE	LINSEED OIL AND MEAL	FLAXSEED	PAPER	PULP, WOOD	TOBACCO PRODUCTS	TOBACCO, LEAF
1913	100.0	100.0	100.0	100.0	100.0	100.0	100.0	100.0
1914	83.5	79.4	108.5	113.1	100.2	95.9	100.6	83.9
1915	74.9	79.6	122.1	133.2	99.8	92.2	102.5	77.9
1916	77.4	88.1	151.7	165.3	147.2	163.3	102.5	115.6
1917	95.6	87.7	217.5	229.5	185.8	211.7	107.1	188.4
1918	110.6	73.1	297.3	292.2	190.7	167.1	146.7	258.3
1919	101.0	59.2	345.1	336.3	217.4	156.3	169.6	248.0
1920	112.2	42.7	286.5	281.3	296.2	317.6	181.1	163.8
1921	86.4	20.2	151.7	137.1	210.7	159.1	177.4	132.2
1922	55.7	21.2	179.8	183.8	180.0	118.9	176.8	162.2
1923	52.8	36.0	195.6	203.1	190.3	140.4	176.8	168.9
1924	44.7	31.9	194.9	185.5	200.0	118.9	156.4	165.3
1925	47.6	88.1	206.5	201.9	210.1	122.3	154.6	156.3
1926	48.3	58.8	177.0	172.7	197.6	129.5	154.6	95.1
1927	36.1	45.8	168.3	163.4	185.8	119.7	154.6	89.4
1928	30.6	27.3	170.8	166.5	181.4	114.9	152.2	96.2
1929	26.3	24.9	197.5	205.2	175.9	114.6	151.6	95.8
1930	24.8	14.4	187.6	174.6	170.0	112.4	152.6	83.0
1931	22.2	7.5	131.3	110.0	161.1	104.3	148.5	58.1
1932	19.8	4.3	103.2	87.6	154.0	76.3	142.7	40.3
1933	20.3	7.2	135.2	117.3	156.1	77.8	128.0	55.4
1934	21.7	15.6	143.9	139.0	166.6	92.7	133.4	74.8
1935	22.1	14.9	137.5	130.1	162.3	84.6	132.9	104.2

Note on Appendix V
CLASSIFICATION OF COMMODITIES IN CONSTRUCTION OF INDEX NUMBERS OF SIMILAR COMMODITIES IN RAW AND MANUFACTURED STATE, 1913–1935

Total materials, raw
  Foods, raw
  Textiles, raw
  Metals, raw
  Hides and skins
  Petroleum, crude
Total materials, simple processed
  Foods, processed
  Textiles, finished
  Metals, processed
  Leather
  Petroleum products
Foods, raw
  Grains
  Milk, fluid
  Livestock and poultry
  Sugar, raw
  Cocoa beans (1926–35 only)
Foods, processed
  Flour and grain mill products
  Butter, cheese and processed milk
  Meat packing products
  Sugar, granulated
  Cocoa, powdered (1926–35 only)
Textiles, raw
  Cotton, raw
  Wool, raw
  Silk, raw
Textiles processed, yarn
  Cotton yarns
  Woolen yarns
  Silk yarns
Textiles, finished
  Cotton goods
  Woolen and worsted goods
  Silk hosiery
Metals, raw
  Pig iron

  Copper ingots
  Lead, pig
  Zinc, slab
Metals, processed
  Iron and steel, simple processed
  Copper products
  Lead pipe
  Zinc, sheet
Bread and products
  1913–26: Bread (5 series)
  1926–35: Bread (5), crackers (2), macaroni, pretzels
Flour and grain mill products
  1913–26: Wheat flour (10), rye flour, bran, middlings
  1926–35: 'Cereal products', bran, middlings; less 'Bread and products', 'Breakfast foods', rice (2), hominy grits
Grains
  1913–35: 'Grains'
Butter, cheese and processed milk
  1913–35: 'Butter, cheese and milk' less milk fluid (3)
Milk, fluid
  1913–35: Wholesale price of milk at the farm, Bureau of Agricultural Economics
Meat packing products
  1913–35: 'Meats', 'Hides and skins', lard, oleo oil; less goat skins
Livestock and poultry
  1913–35: 'Livestock and poultry'
Sugar, granulated
  1913–35: Sugar, granulated
Sugar, raw
  1913–35: Sugar, raw

APPENDIX V

Cotton goods
  1913–26: 'Cotton goods'; less 'Cotton yarns'
  1926–35: 'Cotton goods', cotton rope, cotton thread, cotton twine, cotton blankets, pillow cases, sheets, table cloths; less 'Cotton yarns'
Cotton yarns
  1913–35: Cotton yarns (5)
Cotton raw
  1913–35: Cotton (3)
Woolen and worsted goods
  1913–26: 'Woolen and worsted goods', less 'Woolen yarns'
  1926–35: 'Woolen and worsted goods', wool blankets; less 'Woolen yarns'
Woolen yarns
  1913–35: Woolen yarns (3)
Wool, raw
  1913–35: Wool (9)
Silk hosiery
  1913–26: Silk hose (1)
  1926–35: Silk hose (2)
Silk yarn
  1913–26: Silk, spun (3)
  1926–35: Silk, spun (3), silk yarn (3)
Silk, raw
  1913–35: Silk (4)
Boots and shoes
  1913–35: 'Boots and shoes'
Other leather products
  1913–35: 'Other leather products'
Hides and skins
  1913–35: 'Hides and skins'
Petroleum products
  1913–26: 'Petroleum products', cylinder oil (2), lubricating oil (2); less 'Petroleum, crude'
  1926–35: 'Petroleum products', cylinder oil, lubricating oil, (2), benzine; less 'Petroleum, crude'
Petroleum, crude
  1913–35: Petroleum, crude (3)
Agricultural implements
  1913–26: 'Agricultural implements'
  1926–35: 'Agricultural implements'; less forks, hoes, hand rakes, shovels, spades
Simple processed iron and steel
  1913–26: 'Iron and steel', less 'Pig iron', iron ore (2), steel scrap
  1926–35: Angle bars, bar iron (2), bars (4), steel billets, bolts (4), butts, castings, pipe (3), steel plates, steel rails, rivets (2), rods, sheets (3), skelp, spikes, strips, structural steel, terneplate, tieplate, tin plate, wire (4)
Pig iron
  1913–26: Pig iron (6)
  1926–35: Pig iron (7)
Iron ore and coke
  1913–35: Iron ore (2), coke (2), steel scrap
Copper products
  1913–26: Copper sheet, copper wire
  1926–35: Copper sheet, copper wire, copper rods
Copper ingots
  1913–35: Copper ingots
Lead pipe
  1913–35: Lead pipe
Lead, pig
  1913–35: Lead, pig
Zinc, sheet
  1913–35: Zinc, sheet
Zinc, slab
  1913–35: Zinc, slab

Fertilizers, mixed
   1913–35: 'Fertilizers, mixed'
Fertilizer materials
   1913–35: 'Fertilizer materials'
Automobile tires
   1913–35: 'Automobile tires and tubes'
Rubber, crude
   1913–35: 'Rubber, crude'
Linseed oil and meal
   1913–35: Linseed oil, linseed meal
Flaxseed
   1913–35: Flaxseed

Paper
   1913–26: Newsprint, wrapping paper
   1926–35: 'Paper and pulp'; less 'Wood pulp'
Wood pulp
   1913–26: Wood pulp (2)
   1926–35: Wood pulp (4)
Tobacco products
   1913–26: Tobacco, plug, smoking
   1926–35: Cigars, cigarettes, plug, smoking, snuff
Tobacco, leaf
   1913–35: Tobacco, leaf

APPENDIX VI

PHYSICAL OUTPUT, PRODUCTIVITY, SELLING PRICES AND PRODUCTION COSTS, MANUFACTURING INDUSTRIES OF THE UNITED STATES, 1914–1933

(All price and cost measurements relate to changes per unit of product)

YEAR	PHYSICAL VOLUME OF PRODUCTION	OUTPUT PER WAGE EARNER [1]	SELLING PRICE	COST OF MATERIALS	COST OF FABRICATION PLUS PROFITS	LABOR COSTS	OVERHEAD COSTS PLUS PROFITS
1914	100.0	100.0	100.0	100.0	100.0	100.0	100.0
1919	129.5	105.1	204.0	201.9	209.0	203.2	212.6
1921	104.5	105.9	160.7	155.5	172.8	193.7	156.5
1923	155.8	121.6	159.2	152.8	174.5	181.8	168.5
1925	159.5	131.1	158.2	153.1	170.7	172.6	168.6
1927	163.3	136.6	148.2	141.1	164.8	168.5	161.5
1929	184.4	148.6	145.2	135.7	166.5	156.7	172.1
1931	138.1	146.7	112.6	99.8	140.0	136.7	141.4
1933	127.5	134.8	96.3	85.3	120.3	117.0	121.6

[1] Because of pronounced changes in average working hours after 1929, an index of output per wage earner is not an accurate measure of changes in productivity for the period 1929–33. Following are measurements of output per man hour worked: 1929, 100; 1931, 113; 1933, 119.

APPENDIX VII

VOLUME OF PRODUCTION OF RAW MATERIALS

Index Numbers, 1929–1935

	1929	1930	1931	1932	1933	1934	1935
Agricultural production [1]	100	100	106	99	96	93	91
All crops	100	98	107	93	85	72	89
Grains	100	91	96	91	66	47	76
Fruits and vegetables	100	113	122	107	105	118	122
Truck crops	100	100	96	100	93	97	119
Cotton and cottonseed	100	93	113	87	87	65	72
All livestock and products	100	101	105	103	105	108	94
Meat animals (slaughterings)	100	100	106	105	107	116	85
Dairy products	100	101	104	104	104	104	104
Poultry products	100	103	103	99	100	96	93
Mineral production [2]	100	89	75	62	67	72	77
Metals	100	80	55	33	35	42	54
Building materials	100	87	69	50	44	51	52
Coal and gas	100	92	77	65	68	75	76
Petroleum	100	89	84	78	90	90	99
Forest products [2]	100	82	57	38	48	49	55
Lumber	100	79	50	31	39	39	45
Pulp wood	100	94	91	76	91	98	109
Turpentine and rosin	100	93	78	63	83	85	78

[1] Index numbers of the Bureau of Agricultural Economics.
[2] Index numbers constructed by the National Bureau of Economic Research.

APPENDIX VIII-A

NOTES ON SOURCES OF DATA AND CONSTRUCTION OF INDEX NUMBERS RELATING TO MANUFACTURING OPERATIONS

Production: Index numbers are constructed by the Division of Research and Statistics of the Board of Governors of the Federal Reserve System from 60 individual series of data representing the production of about 35 industries and estimated to represent, directly or indirectly, about 80 per cent of the total industrial production of the United States. The figures are reduced to a daily average output and are presented to show actual production. No correction for seasonal movements has been made in the index numbers here employed. The monthly average for 1923–25 is the base of the original index numbers. (*Federal Reserve Bulletin,* February 1927, p. 100.)

Reference is made in the text to the fact that during the spring and early summer rise of 1933 this index, which is rather heavily weighted by basic, semi-finished manufactures, exaggerated somewhat the increase in production of manufactures at large (see *Federal Reserve Bulletin,* August 1933, pp. 467–8; January 1934, pp. 2–3). For the present purpose a correction was made in this index, for the months of June–July 1933, to render it comparable with the more comprehensive index numbers of factory employment and pay rolls. The correction was based upon data for the following manufacturing industries: iron and steel, automobiles, cigars and cigarettes, cement, leather, boots and shoes, rubber tires and inner tubes, lumber, woolen and worsted goods, cotton goods, carpets and rugs, flour, meat packing, sugar refining, petroleum refining. For these industries, for which 'value added' in 1933 constituted 24 per cent of the total 'value added' by all manufacturing industries, measurements of production, employment and pay rolls more comparable than those available for all manufacturing industries are to be had.

A revised index of the change in volume of production for all manufacturing industries from February–March to June–July 1933 was derived on the assumption that output per man hour changed in all industries, over this period, at the same rate as in the group of 15 industries. A second, independent revision was made on the assumption that labor cost per unit of product changed at the same rate in all manufacturing industries as in the smaller group. (In making these corrections, reduced weight was given to automobiles and cotton textiles, among the 15 industries, because of peculiarities of their behavior during the recovery.) The final correction, which indicates an advance of 45 per cent in volume of manufacturing production from February–March to June–July 1933, instead of 57 per cent, as shown by the original index, was secured by averaging these two revisions.

That the assumptions on which this correction is based are reasonable is indicated by application of the methods to other periods, not affected by the unusual circumstances of early 1933. From February–March 1933 to April–May 1935 an increase of 48 per cent in the output of manufactured goods is shown by the general index; an estimate based on the above methods indicates an increase of 49 per cent. From February–March 1933 to February–March 1936 an increase of 58 per cent is shown by the general index; an estimate based on the above methods indicates an advance of 59 per cent. In the present study correction was made only for the period February–March to June–July 1933.

Number employed and pay rolls: Index numbers are constructed by the United States Bureau of Labor Statistics. The basic data are supplied by representative establishments in 90 important manufacturing industries of the country. For December 1935 reports were received from about 24,000 establishments employing more than 4 million workers, whose weekly earnings were about 90 million dollars during the pay period ending nearest the 15th of the month. The employment reports received cover more than

APPENDIX VIII-A

50 per cent of the total wage earners in all manufacturing industries of the country. The three-year average, 1923–25, equals 100. (*Bulletin No. 610,* "Revised Indexes of Factory Employment and Pay Rolls, 1919 to 1933", United States Bureau of Labor Statistics, pp. 2, 4; and *Monthly Labor Review,* December 1935.)

Average hours worked per week: The index numbers are constructed from data compiled by the United States Bureau of Labor Statistics. The reports come from a smaller number of establishments than are covered in the monthly survey of manufacturing industries, for not all reporting establishments furnish man hour information. The figures are presented for only those manufacturing industries (87 in December 1935) for which available information covers at least 20 per cent of all the employees in the industry.

Prices: Index numbers are computed by the National Bureau of Economic Research from wholesale prices compiled by the United States Bureau of Labor Statistics. The weighted index for manufactured goods includes 536 price series (see Appendix III). The average for the year 1929 is used as base. For the three earlier periods an average of the index numbers of the wholesale prices of semi-manufactured and finished goods, constructed by the United States Bureau of Labor Statistics, was used. In averaging, these were weighted 1 and 6, respectively.

For the present purpose the base of each of these index numbers has been shifted to February–March 1933.

The index of changes in gross income is the product of indexes of changes in physical volume of production (number of units produced) and in average selling price per unit. Thus, in deriving the gross income index for June–July 1933, on February–March 1933 as base, we have

$$1.45 \text{ (production index)} \times 1.09 \text{ (price index)} = 1.58.$$

In the tables these measurements are given in relative, rather than in ratio, form.

The index of total employment (man hours) is the product of indexes of number of wage earners employed and of average number of working hours per week, per person.

The index of average output per wage earner is secured by dividing the index of physical volume of production by the index of number of wage earners employed.

The index of average output per man hour is secured by dividing the index of physical volume of production by the index of total employment (man hours).

The index of average earnings per wage earner is secured by dividing the index of total wage disbursements by the index of number of wage earners employed.

The index of average hourly wages for the period 1933–36 is secured by dividing the index of total wage disbursements by the index of total employment (man hours). We should note that a change in average hourly earnings may result from an actual change in wage rates, or from a shift in the relative proportions of men working at different rates, in the total labor force. An increase in the proportion of men receiving relatively high wages will raise the average, of course, without any modification of wage rates.

The index of average hourly wages for the period 1929–33 is obtained directly, by splicing the hourly wage index of the United States Bureau of Labor Statistics at 1932 to that of the National Industrial Conference Board, which covers the period 1929–1932. It should be noted that mutually consistent measurements relating to hours, hourly wages and average earnings per worker from 1929 to 1933 are not available. Different samples must be employed in the derivation of these measurements.

The index of average labor cost per unit of product is secured by dividing the index of total wage disbursements by the index of physical volume of production.

APPENDIX VIII-B

COMPARISON OF INDEX NUMBERS DERIVED FROM MONTHLY DATA OF MANUFACTURING OPERATIONS WITH INDEX NUMBERS BASED ON RECORDS OF THE CENSUS OF MANUFACTURES

SUPPORTING evidence that the measurements given in the preceding pages are representative of the general movements occurring in manufacturing industries of the United States is furnished by a comparison, by Census periods, of index numbers derived from the monthly series here utilized with index numbers based directly upon much more comprehensive Census records. (See page 558.) For employment and pay roll statistics the series compared are not independent, prior to the 1931–33 period, since the monthly records of the Bureau of Labor Statistics have been adjusted to biennial Census records. This process of adjustment helps, of course, to validate the measurements for the earlier periods, which are given in the text.

In only four of the comparisons are there notable differences between the measurements drawn from Census records and those derived from monthly observations. Of these, two are of some concern in the present study. The monthly data on employment show a somewhat greater change, from 1931 to 1933, than do the more broadly based Census measurements. (This same condition, it may be noted, is found in the production records over times of rapid change, as from 1929 to 1931.) Again, the 1931–33 decline in realized prices, as defined by the Census records, appears to have been greater than the decline in the quoted prices collected by the Bureau of Labor Statistics.

It is difficult to gauge the possible effects of these conditions on the measurements relating to the 1933–35 recovery. The greater

	1921	1923	1923	1925	1925	1927	1927	1929	1929	1931	1931	1933
PHYSICAL VOLUME OF PRODUCTION												
National Bureau of Economic Research index, based on Census data [1]	100	146	100	102	100	103	100	113	100	75	100	92
Federal Reserve Board index [2]	100	151	100	104	100	101	100	112	100	67	100	94
AVERAGE SELLING PRICE OF PRODUCTS												
National Bureau of Economic Research index, based on Census data	100	99	100	99	100	94	100	98	100	78	100	85
Bureau of Labor Statistics index	100	100	100	99	100	94	100	99	100	81[3]	100	93[3]
NUMBER OF WAGE EARNERS EMPLOYED												
Census	100	126	100	96	100	100	100	106	100	74	100	93
Bureau of Labor Statistics	100	126	100	96	100	100	100	106	100	74	100	89
TOTAL WAGE DISBURSEMENTS (PAY ROLLS)												
Census	100	134	100	97	100	101	100	107	100	62	100	73
Bureau of Labor Statistics	100	136	100	97	100	101	100	107	100	62	100	72

[1] Weighted by value of product.
[2] Weighted by value added.
[3] For the last two periods the index given is that of wholesale prices of manufactured goods, constructed by the National Bureau of Economic Research.

steadiness of the figures for all manufacturing industries would tend to make total production, total employment and total pay rolls rise somewhat less rapidly than do production, employment and pay rolls relating to the sample available for monthly study. On the other hand, a tendency to understate the degree of advance in employment and pay rolls, during revival, arises from the use of a fixed sample in the Bureau of Labor Statistics compilations. For the results of the operations of new enterprises are necessarily excluded from such compilations. A comparison of Census records with averages of uncorrected monthly figures indicates that the negative bias is probably the more important, for employment and pay rolls. This would mean that the advance recorded in the various tables understates the actual advance of these series in 1933–35. Such bias as is present in the monthly production figures probably works towards an overstatement of the actual advance, because of the greater steadiness of the total. As regards prices, however, it is probable that actual realized prices have risen somewhat more rapidly than the quoted prices indicate.

In general, the above comparison of the two sets of basic data confirms the accuracy of the measurements based on monthly records. The fluctuations in the monthly records are probably wider (with the exceptions noted) than those that would be found in more broadly based index numbers, but the general directions of movement and the relations among the different measurements are definitely similar.

APPENDIX IX

EXCHANGE RATES AND THE MEASUREMENT OF CHANGES IN COMMODITY PRICES IN TERMS OF GOLD

IN PASSING from price index numbers in terms of national currencies to index numbers in terms of gold values, in Chapter IV, the national wholesale price series given in the *Monthly Bulletin of Statistics* of the League of Nations have been used, with adjustments for changes from 1929 gold parity revealed by the exchange rates of each country. Current issues of the *Monthly Bulletin* give the values of national currencies as percentages of gold parity in 1929, and these figures have been used in making the adjustment. The changes from 1929 gold parity prior to 1933 were computed from exchange rates in terms of United States dollars; since then by comparison with the French franc. Following is the method used in calculating exchange rates (*Statistical Year-Book* of the League of Nations, 1935–36, p. 231, note):

> "Value of currencies as percentage of their gold parity in 1929: As a rule, the monthly average value of currencies, calculated on the basis of the official rates, is given as a percentage of the gold parity in 1929. For countries whose currencies are based on silver and for countries in which the gold standard was not restored during the post-War period, percentages are given in relation to the average rate of exchange in 1929. For countries which established a new parity during the period 1929–September 1931, this new legal parity has been taken as basis.

APPENDIX IX

The gold value of currencies has been calculated as a rule according to the New York rates on the countries in question; since the depreciation of the U. S. dollar, the rates are recalculated in gold by means of the quotation of the French franc in New York. In certain cases, calculations are based on the London rates, or on the Basle rates, or on the rates in the country itself."

It is to be noted that "when different rates of exchange are quoted in respect of different kinds of transactions, the rate of the greatest turnover has been chosen" (*Monthly Bulletin of Statistics,* December 1935, p. 576, note).

The exchange rates used by the League of Nations for certain countries that have established exchange control are based upon official quotations. Some transactions for these countries, however, are effected at lower 'free' rates. In 1934 and the first part of 1935 the free market tended, in several countries, to gain in importance relatively to the official market, owing to a relaxation of control. In many countries it is impossible to determine the relative importance of official and free markets.

A comparison of the free (or special) and official exchange rates of certain countries follows: (*Statistical Year-Book* of the League of Nations, 1935–36, pp. 234–7).

VALUE OF CURRENCIES IN DECEMBER 1935 AS PERCENTAGE OF GOLD PARITY IN 1929

	OFFICIAL RATE	SPECIAL RATE	
Argentina	46.0	38.1	"Free"
Bolivia	38.3	9.9	"Export"
Brazil	41.6	27.3	"Free"
Chile	24.9	19.0	"Export draft"
		18.6	"Free"
Colombia	34.8	32.6	"Free"
Costa Rica	34.8	34.6	**"Free"**
Uruguay	46.1	26.0	"Free"
Germany	100.2	53.0	"Registermark"
		61.9	"Reisemark"
		36.1	"Kreditsperrmark"
		24.0	"Effektensperrmark"

PRICES IN RECESSION AND RECOVERY

The following table (from the *Statistical Year-Book* of the League of Nations, 1935–36) gives the dates of the principal measures affecting exchange rates.

COUNTRY	OFFICIAL SUSPENSION OF GOLD STANDARD	EXCHANGE CONTROL Introduction of control	EXCHANGE CONTROL Suppression of control	DEPRECIATION IN RELATION TO GOLD	INTRODUCTION OF A NEW GOLD PARITY
Albania	...	...	...	...	...
Argentina	17/XII/29	13/ X/31	...	XI/29	...
Australia	17/XII/29	...	...	III/30	...
Austria	5/ IV/33	9/ X/31	VI/35	IX/31	*30/ IV/34
Belgium	30/ III/35	18/ III/35	26/IV/35	III/35	*31/ III/35
					31/ III/36
Bolivia	25/ IX/31	3/ X/31	...	III/30	...
Brazil	...	18/ V/31	...	XII/29	...
British Malaya	21/ IX/31	...	...	IX/31	...
Bulgaria	...	15/ X/31	...	...	...
Canada	19/ X/31	...	...	IX/31	...
Chile	20/ IV/32	30/VII/31	...	IV/32	...
China	...	9/ IX/34	...	...	...
Colombia	25/ IX/31	25/ IX/31	...	I/32	...
Costa Rica	...	16/ I/32	...	I/32	...
Cuba	...	2/ VI/34	...	IV/33	...
Czechoslovakia	...	26/ IX/31	...	II/34	17/ II/34
Danzig	...	12/ VI/35	...	V/35	2/ V/35
Denmark	29/ IX/31	18/ XI/31	...	IX/31	...
Ecuador	8/ II/32	2/ V/32	7/ X/35	VI/32	*19/XII/35
Egypt	21/ IX/31	...	...	IX/31	...
Estonia	28/ VI/33	18/ XI/31	...	VI/33	...
Finland	12/ X/31	...	...	X/31	...
France	...	...	...	...	...
Germany	...	13/ VII/31	...	...	...
Greece	26/ IV/32	28/ IX/31	...	IV/32	...
Guatemala	...	...	...	IV/33	...
Honduras	...	27/ III/34	...	IV/33	...
Hong Kong	...	9/ XI/35	...	...	...
Hungary	...	17/ VII/31	...	...	...
India	21/ IX/31	...	...	IX/31	...
Iran		25/ II/30			
	...	1/ III/36	30/ V/33	...	...
Irish Free State	26/ IX/31	...	...	IX/31	...
Italy	...	26/ V/34	...	III/34	...

APPENDIX IX

COUNTRY	OFFICIAL SUSPENSION OF GOLD STANDARD	EXCHANGE CONTROL Introduction of control	EXCHANGE CONTROL Suppression of control	DEPRECIATION IN RELATION TO GOLD	INTRODUCTION OF A NEW GOLD PARITY
Japan	13/XII/31	1/ VII/32	...	XII/31	...
Latvia	...	8/ X/31	...	...	...
Lithuania	...	1/ X/35	...	...	...
Luxemburg	...	18/ III/35	26/IV/35	III/35	1/ IV/35
Mexico	25/VII/31	...	...	VIII/31	...
Netherlands	...	...	...	...	...
Netherlands Indies	...	...	...	...	...
New Zealand	21/ IX/31	...	...	IV/30	...
Nicaragua	13/ XI/31	13/ XI/31	...	I/32	...
Norway	29/ IX/31	...	...	IX/31	...
Palestine	21/ IX/31	...	...	IX/31	...
Panama	...	...	...	IV/33	...
Paraguay	...	VIII/32	...	XI/29	...
Peru	14/ V/32	...	...	V/32	...
Philippines	...	...	...	IV/33	...
Poland	...	26/ IV/36	...	...	...
Portugal	31/XII/31	21/ X/22	...	X/31	...
Roumania	...	17/ V/32	...	VII/35	...
Salvador	9/ X/31	VIII/33	X/33	X/31	...
Siam	11/ V/32	...	...	VI/32	...
Spain	...	18/ V/31	...	1920	...
Sweden	29/ IX/31	...	...	IX/31	...
Switzerland	...	...	...	...	...
Turkey	...	26/ II/30	...	1915	...
U. S. S. R.	...	...	...	...	*1/ IV/36
Union of South Africa	28/XII/32	...	...	I/33	...
United Kingdom	21/ IX/31	...	...	IX/31	...
U. S. A.	6/ III/33	6/ III/33	12/XI/34	IV/33	*31/ I/34
Uruguay	XII/29	7/ IX/31	...	IV/29	...
Venezuela	...	...	...	IX/30	...
Yugoslavia	...	7/ X/31	...	VII/32	...

* Provisional parity.

Since the date of compilation of the above table France, Italy, the Netherlands and Switzerland have suspended the gold standard.

TABLES

1 Price Recession in Thirty-two Countries, 1928–1936. A Summary of Changes in Index Numbers of Wholesale Prices. (Price movements are here measured in terms of the various national currencies)   21
2 Price Recovery in Thirty-two Countries, 1931–1936. A Summary of Changes in Index Numbers of Wholesale Prices since Dates of Depression Lows (national currencies)   23
3 Wholesale Prices and Living Costs, 1914–1929. Seven Industrial Countries   81
4 Important Raw Materials, Changes in Per Unit Purchasing Power, 1913–1929   83
5 Raw Materials and Manufactured Goods in Various Countries, Index Numbers of Wholesale Prices, 1913–1929   86
6 Frequency Distributions of Relative Numbers Measuring Changes in Volume of Production, in Selling Price and in Certain Components of Selling Price, in 82 Manufacturing Industries, 1929–1933   133
7 Construction Costs in the United States, 1913–1932   145
8 National Income Paid Out, by Types of Payment, 1929–1933   153
9 Price Recession in Thirty-two Countries, 1929–1936. A Summary of Changes in Index Numbers of Wholesale Prices (gold values)   164

TABLES

10 Movements of Wholesale Prices in Gold Standard and Non-gold Standard Countries, 1929–1936   166
11 International Values of the Dollar and Various Series Relating to Production Costs. A Comparison of Movements, 1929–1932   176
12 Aggregate Purchasing Power in World Markets of Five Raw Material Producing Areas, Estimated Changes, 1929–1933   187
13 Wholesale Price Index Numbers, Thirty-two Countries, 1929–March 1936 (national and gold currencies)   198
14 Wholesale Price Index Numbers, Twenty-nine Countries, 1913–March 1936 (national and gold currencies)   202
15 International Values of the Dollar and Various Series Relating to Production Costs, A Comparison of Movements, 1929–1935   206
16 Per Unit Purchasing Power at Wholesale of Important Raw Materials, in World Markets, 1913–1936   210
17 Prices of Primary Products, 1931–1936 (national and gold currencies)   214
18 Net Barter Terms of Trade for Eight Countries, 1913–1935   217
19 Per Unit Purchasing Power of Agricultural Commodities, for Eleven Countries, 1913–1935   218
20 Raw Materials and Manufactured Goods, Prices and Purchasing Power, July 1929–June 1936   224
21 Four Groups of Primary Products, Prices and Purchasing Power, July 1929–June 1936   228
22 Farm and Other Products, Prices and Purchasing Power, July 1929–June 1936   231
23 Raw Farm Products and Other Commodities, Purchasing Power, 1913–1936   234
24 Farm Prices, Prices Paid by Farmers and Per Unit Purchasing Power of Farm Products, July 1929–June 1936   237
25 Important Raw Materials at Wholesale, Relative Prices, July 1929–June 1936   242

TABLES

26 Raw Materials and Manufactured Goods, Percentage Changes in Index Numbers of Wholesale Prices with Net Differences and Cumulative Net Differences, February 1933–June 1936 — 244

27 Prices of Farm Products and Other Commodities, Percentage Changes in Index Numbers with Net Differences and Cumulative Net Differences, February 1933–June 1936 — 250

28 Aggregate Values of Primary Products and Aggregate Purchasing Power of Primary Producers, Index Numbers, 1929–1935 — 254

29 Gross Income from Farm Production and Aggregate Purchasing Power of Agricultural Producers, 1929–1935 — 258

30 Aggregate Business Cash Account of the Farmers of the United States, 1929–1934 — 261

31 Average Net Incomes of Sample Groups of Farmers, 1922–1934 — 264

32 Prices Received for Farm Products, Prices Paid by Farmers and Average Per Unit Purchasing Power of Farm Products, Monthly Changes, February 1933–June 1936 — 273

33 Changes in Wholesale Prices Affecting Manufacturers' Price Margins, July 1929 to June 1936. Raw Producers' Goods and Manufactured Goods — 296

34 Changes in Wholesale Prices Affecting Manufacturers' Price Margins, 1913–1936. Raw Producers' Goods and Manufactured Goods — 297

35 Changes in Wholesale Prices Affecting Manufacturers' Price Margins, July 1929–June 1936. Crops, Animal Products and Mineral Products — 300

36 Changes in Wholesale Prices Affecting Manufacturers' Price Margins, 1913–1936. Crops, Animal Products and Mineral Products — 302

37 Changes in Wholesale Prices Affecting Manufacturers' Price Margins, July 1929–June 1936. Products of American Farms and Other Products — 304

38	Changes in Wholesale Prices Affecting Manufacturers' Price Margins, and the Trading Relations between Producing Groups, 1913–1936	305
39	A Record of the Fortunes of Manufacturing Industries of the United States, 1933–1936. Basic Measurements	313
40	A Record of the Fortunes of Manufacturing Industries of the United States, 1933–1936. Derived Measurements	316
41	Manufacturing Operations, 1933–1936. A Comparison of Movements during Different Phases of Recovery	319
42	Recession and Recovery in American Manufacturing Industries, 1929–1936	329
43	Changes in Manufacturing Operations during Five Periods of Business Expansion Approximately Equal in Degree of Recovery	336
44	Changes in Manufacturing Operations during Five Periods of Business Expansion Approximately Equal in Degree of Recovery. Value and Price Series Corrected for Changes in the Value of Money	339
45	Articles of Capital Equipment and All Commodities, Prices and Purchasing Power, July 1929–June 1936	364
46	Capital Equipment and Building Materials, Per Unit Purchasing Power, 1913–1936	366
47	Construction Costs and Wholesale Prices in the United States, June 1929–June 1936	367
48	Construction Costs and Wholesale Prices in the United States, 1914–1936	368
49	Certain Major Items of Savings in the United States, 1929–1935	376
50	Bond Yields, Discount Rates and Interest Rates, 1929–1936	377
51	Production of Capital Goods, 1929–1933	379
52	Production of Capital Goods, July 1929–June 1936	379
53	Durable and Non-durable Products of Manufacturing Industries, Prices and Production, July 1929–June 1936	383

TABLES

54	Consumers' Goods, Recovery in the Prices and Purchasing Power, July 1929–June 1936	401
55	Consumers' Goods, Prices and Purchasing Power, 1913–1936	402
56	Three Classes of Consumers' Goods, Per Unit Purchasing Power, at Wholesale, 1913–1936	403
57	Living Costs of Industrial Wage Earners and Certain Retail Prices, 1913–1936	406
58	National Income and Its Elements, United States, 1929–1935. Estimates of National Income Paid Out, by Types of Payment	412
59	Labor Income, Property Income and Net Farm Income, With Estimates of Changes in Purchasing Power, 1929–1935	413
60	Production of Manufactured Goods, 1929–1935	418

CHARTS

1 Wholesale Prices in the United States during Three Periods of Recession and Subsequent Change ... 11
2 Wholesale Prices in the United States during Three Periods of Recovery ... 13
3 Showing the Distribution of Price Changes over Time, in Periods of Recession and Revival ... 16
4 Index Numbers of Wholesale Prices in Terms of National Currencies, 1929–1936, Twelve Countries ... 20
5 Changes in Average Selling Price, Cost of Materials and Elements of Fabrication Costs Plus Profits, Per Unit of Product, Manufacturing Industries of the United States, 1914–1929. (Percentage deviations from 1914 level, in dollars of constant purchasing power, at wholesale) ... 55
6 Changes in Average Selling Price, Cost of Materials and Elements of Fabrication Costs Plus Profits, Per Unit of Product, Manufacturing Industries of the United States, 1914–1933. (Percentage deviations from 1914 level, in current dollars) ... 118
7 Wholesale Prices in Gold Standard and Non-gold Standard Countries, 1929–1936 ... 168
8 International Comparison of Changes in Production Costs, 1929–1932. Graph Showing Relative Amounts by which the Changes in Stated Series relating to Production Costs in Various Countries Exceeded or Fell Short of Changes in Corresponding Series for

CHARTS

	the United States, Account being Taken of Relative Changes in the Values of National Currencies	178
9	Wholesale Prices in Thirty-two Countries, 1929–March 1936. Index numbers in terms of national and gold currencies (1929=100)	195
10	International Comparison of Changes in Production Costs, 1929–1935. Graph Showing Relative Amounts by which the Changes in Stated Series relating to Production Costs in Various Countries Exceeded or Fell Short of Changes in Corresponding Series for the United States, Account Being Taken of Relative Changes in the Values of National Currencies	207
11	Wholesale Prices of Raw Materials and Manufactured Goods in the United States, February 1933–June 1936	244
12	Prices of Farm Products and Other Products in the United States, February 1933–June 1936	249
13	Movements of Selected Series Relating to American Manufacturing Industries, 1920–1936	334
14	Changes in Prices and Production, Manufacturing Industries of the United States, 1929–1936. Durable and Non-durable Products	382
15	Estimated Changes in Industrial Productivity and in the Returns of Manufacturing Producers, 1899–1933	442
16	Estimated Changes in Real Costs of Fabrication to Manufacturing Producers and in Corresponding Real Costs of Manufacturing Services to Various Consuming Groups, 1899–1933	446

INDEX

Aberthaw Construction Company, 367
Agricultural Adjustment Act, 27, 238–41, 247–8, 268–76, 282–3, 295, 426
Agricultural Economics, Bureau of, 14n, 45n, 103n, 155n, 237n, 262–4, 552
Agricultural products
  manufacturing differential; American farm products, 114, 303–4; animal products, crops, 49–50, 112–3, 300–2
  prices at wholesale: total, 99, 180, 218–9, 231–4, 268; American farm products, 44, 100–2, 114, 231–4, 249–52, 303–4, 470–92, 529–34; animal products, crops, 49, 99, 112–3, 227–9, 234, 300–3, 470–90, 494–5, 517–22, 529–31
  prices received by farmers, 14, 45, 103–5, 157, 234–9, 249–53, 273–6, 406–7
  production volume: total, 71, 99, 107–8, 254–6, 265n; animal products, crops, 229–30, 552
  purchasing power, per unit: total, 103–4, 107–8, 218–9, 237, 254–8, 433; American farm products, 40–1, 100–2, 232, 234; animal products, crops, 99, 101–2, 228, 234; (*see also* Farmers)
Agriculture, Department of, 270n, 275, 414

Albania, 562
American Bankers Association, 376
American farms, products of (*see* Agricultural products)
American Machinist, 374n
Animal products (*see* Agricultural products)
Argentina, 20–2, 24, 78, 164, 167–8, 180, 184, 187–9, 190n, 194–5, 199, 203, 217–9, 561–2
Association of Life Insurance Presidents, 376
Australia, 22, 24, 78–9, 83–4, 164, 167–8, 176–8, 187–9, 195, 198, 203, 205–8, 562
Austria, 22, 24, 78–9, 165–6, 168, 195, 199, 203, 562

Baker, O. E., 270n
Balance of international payments, 187–90
Bean, L. H., 269n
Belgium, 8n, 20–1, 24, 78, 86, 164, 166, 168, 176–8, 195, 198, 201n, 203, 205–7, 562
Bercaw, L. O., 270n
Bliss, C. A., 418
Bolivia, 561–2
Bond yields, 377
Bowley, A. L., 200n
Brazil, 561–2
British Malaya, 562
Building and loan associations, assets of, 375

574 INDEX

Building materials
  prices at wholesale, 40–1, 59n, 140–6, 158, 361, 364–9, 470–90, 511–3
  production volume, 379–81, 418, 552
  purchasing power, per unit, 140–4, 364–6, 389, 433
Bulgaria, 22, 24, 78, 164, 166, 168, 173, 195, 198, 203, 562

Canada 20, 22, 24, 78, 83, 85–7, 164, 166, 168, 176–8, 180, 185, 195, 198, 201n, 203, 205–8, 210–2, 218–9, 562
Capital
  cost of, 265–7, 375–8
  international movements, 6–8, 67, 93, 187–91
  supply of, 42, 286–7n, 359, 362–3, 375–8, 380n, 388–9
Capital equipment (see Ch. VIII)
  manufacturing differential, 115, 305–6
  prices at wholesale, 40–1, 57–60, 140–4, 158–9, 184–5, 342, 355–8, 361, 363–75, 384–92, 470–90, 493–4, 508–10
  production volume, 42, 59, 361–2, 378–81, 387, 418
  purchasing power, per unit, 140–4, 364–6, 389, 433
Census of Manufactures, 50n, 53n, 117, 119, 121, 129–30, 155n, 432, 557–9
Chile, 21, 23, 78, 164, 166, 168, 172, 194–5, 198–9, 203, 561–2
China, 562
Codes (see National Industrial Recovery Act)
Colombia, 561–2
Commerce, Department of, 153, 156, 376, 411, 414
Commercial and Financial Chronicle, 378

Condliffe, J. B., 176n, 193n
Construction industries (see Ch. VII and Building materials)
  costs, 41, 59n, 144–6, 367–72, 389
  production volume, 145–6, 361–2, 379–80
  purchasing power, aggregate, 421
Consumers, purchasing power, 151–6, 395–8, 409–17, 419–30, 445–52 (see also Cost of living)
Consumers' goods
  manufacturing differential, 115, 305–7
  prices at wholesale, 40, 57–60, 86, 100–2, 146–51, 184–5, 231–3, 395, 400–7, 470–90, 493–6, 505–7, 514–28, 532–7
  production volume, 42, 394–5, 417–9
  purchasing power, per unit, 41, 100–2, 147–8, 232–4, 400–5, 433–4
Consumption goods
  manufacturing differential, 115, 305–7
  prices at wholesale, 40–1, 57–60, 184–5, 470–90, 493, 508–10, 514–6
  production volume, 361, 380, 417–8
Control of prices (see Valorization, Agricultural Adjustment Act, National Industrial Recovery Act)
Copeland, M. A., 460n
Copeland, M. T., 43n, 64n
Cost of living, 14, 65, 72, 135–7, 149–52, 155–6, 330, 339, 405–9, 413;
  international comparisons, 79–81, 174–8, 204–9
Costa Rica, 561–2
Costs
  manufacturing (see Manufacturing industries)
  production, international comparison of, 79–81, 174–9, 204–9
Credit (see Capital)
Crops (see Agricultural products)

INDEX 575

Crowther, S., 8n
Cuba, 562
Currency devaluation (*see* Exchange rates, Gold standard)
Czechoslovakia, 20–1, 24, 80–1, 88, 165–6, 168, 173, 176–8, 195, 198, 203, 205–8, 562

Danzig, 562
Debts, farm, 265–7 (*see also* Credit)
Denmark, 21, 23, 78, 86, 164, 167–8, 176–8, 195, 199, 203, 205–7, 562
Displacement of workers (*see* Manufacturing industries)
Distribution, costs of, 65–6 (*see also* Freight rates)
Dividends, 153, 412–5, 421
Dodge Corporation, F. W., 379, 422
Durable goods
  prices at wholesale, 381–4, 470–90, 502–4
  production volume, 42, 56–7, 362, 381–4, 395
  (*see also* Capital equipment)
Dutch East Indies, 22, 24, 78, 91, 164, 166, 168, 172, 184, 187–8, 190n, 194–5, 198, 202, 217, 563

Earnings (*see* Manufacturing industries)
Economist, The, 215
Ecuador, 562
Egypt, 21, 24, 78, 164, 167–8, 173, 195, 198, 202, 562
Elasticity of demand, 280n
Employment (*see* Manufacturing industries)
Engineering News-Record, 59n, 144n, 367–9, 379
Entrepreneurial income, 153, 412
Estonia, 21, 24, 78, 164, 166, 168, 176–8, 195, 198, 202, 205–8, 562

Exchange rates, 176–8, 205–9, 213–5, 560–3
Exports (*see* Foreign trade)
Ezekiel, M., 269n

Fabricant, S., 380n
Fabrication costs (*see* Manufacturing industries)
Fairchild Publications, 149n
Farm crops (*see* Agricultural products)
Farmers
  cash account, 261–2
  income, 27, 41, 154, 253–67, 413–5, 420–2
  prices paid by, 45, 103–5, 150, 154, 157, 234–9, 249–53, 273, 406–7
  products consumed on farms, 155, 413–4
  purchasing power, aggregate, 71–4, 105–8, 154, 253–5, 262
  (*see also* Agricultural products)
Federal Reserve System, Board of Governors of, 313, 337, 379, 383, 553–4, 558
Federal Trade Commission, 141n
Finland, 21, 23, 164, 167–8, 180, 195, 199, 218, 562
Food products
  manufacturing differential, 115, 305–7
  prices at wholesale, 470–90, 497, 514–6, 538–40
  prices at retail, 149–50, 406–7
  purchasing power, per unit, 148–9, 403–4
Foreign and Domestic Commerce, Bureau of, 78
Foreign trade
  exports, 42, 187–9
  imports, 187–90
  world, 76–9, 170–4, 183–93, 197, 217–8

INDEX

Forest products
  prices at wholesale, 72, 99, 227–9, 470–90, 529–31
  production volume, 72, 99, 106–8, 229, 254, 552
  purchasing power, per unit, 72, 99, 107–8, 228, 254–7
Forest products, producers of, purchasing power, aggregate, 106–8, 253–7, 281, 421
France, 8n, 20–1, 24, 78, 80–1, 83–4, 88, 164, 166, 168, 170n, 176–8, 180, 184, 195, 198, 201n, 203, 205–12, 217–9, 562–3
Freight rates, 141n, 235–6
Fuels, producers'
  prices at wholesale, 511–3
  production volume, 418

Gainsbrugh, M., 67n
Germany, 20–1, 24, 78, 81–6, 165–6, 168, 176–8, 181n, 184–5, 194–5, 198, 201n, 202–8, 211–2, 217–9, 561–2
Gold, stock of, 8
Gold Reserve Act, 247, 282
Gold standard, 7–8, 31, 75, 77–8, 163–70, 176, 187–91, 194–209, 214–6, 282, 560–3
Great Britain (*see* United Kingdom)
Greece, 78, 562
Guatemala, 562

Honduras, 562
Hong Kong, 562
Hultgren, T., 235n
Hungary, 21, 24, 78, 164, 166, 168, 195, 198, 202, 217, 562

Imports (*see* Foreign trade)
Income (*see* Purchasing power)
  construction industries, 421
  dividend recipients, 153, 412–5, 421
  entrepreneurs, 153, 412

Income (*cont.*)
  farmers, 106–9, 154, 254–67, 281, 413–5, 421
  forest products, producers of, 106–9, 254–6, 281, 421
  interest, 153, 412, 415–7
  manufacturing industries, 129–30n, 135–7, 153, 155, 316–20, 324–6, 329–31, 336, 412–3
  mineral producers, 106–9, 254–6, 281, 421
  national, 71, 145, 152–7, 409–17
  railway, 421
  relief, 257–9, 262–3, 380n, 390, 412, 416–7, 427
  rents and royalties, 153, 411–2, 421
  salaried workers, 153, 156, 412–5, 421, 460n
  wage earners, 153, 412–5, 421
India, 22, 24, 78, 164, 167–8, 195, 198, 203, 562
Indo-China, 78
Institute International de Statistique, 85
Interest income, 153, 412, 415–7
Interest rates (*see* Capital, cost of)
Internal Revenue, Bureau of, 129–30
International Labour Office, 176
Interstate Commerce Commission, 145n, 370–1, 422
Iran, 562
Irish Free State, 562
Issues, new capital (*see* Capital)
Italy, 20–1, 24, 78, 81, 86, 88, 165, 167–8, 170n, 175n, 176–8, 195, 198, 201n, 203, 205–8, 209n, 218–9, 562–3

Japan, 20–1, 23, 78, 81, 84, 164–5, 167–8, 172, 176–8, 185–6, 194–6, 199, 203, 205–9, 211, 219–20, 563
Jugoslavia, 21, 24, 164, 167–8, 195, 198, 563

Kuznets, S., 136n, 153n, 380n, 414n

Labor (*see* Income, salaried workers and wage earners; Manufacturing industries, employment)

Labor Statistics, Bureau of, 10n, 14n, 43n, 145n, 149n, 155n, 366n, 370, 492, 500, 541, 554–9

Lambert, C. F., 145n, 369n

Latvia, 19, 21, 24, 78, 165–6, 168, 195, 198, 203, 563

Layton, W. T., 8n

League of Nations, 21n, 78, 81, 86, 163n, 165, 176n, 188, 190n, 197n, 199n, 203, 217, 560–2

Leong, Y. S., 419n

Life insurance companies, assets of, 376

Lithuania, 563

Lough, W. H., 67n

Luxemburg, 563

Manufacturing differential: all processed goods, 25–6, 40, 46–52, 55–6, 61–70, 109–17, 137–9, 244–6, 250–1, 285, 291, 293, 295–307, 342–53, 431–4, 456; American farm products, all other products, 114, 303–4; animal products, crops, mineral products, 49–50, 112–3, 300–2; capital equipment, consumption goods, 115, 305–7; food products, non-food products, 115, 305–7; producers' goods, consumers' goods, 110–5, 296–7, 305–7, 343, 433

Manufacturing industries (*see* Ch. III, VI)
  changes in recession and revival, 132–7, 290–5, 307–12
  control of prices (*see* National Industrial Recovery Act)
  costs: total (including profits), 47–8, 50–1, 53–60, 62–5, 72–3, 117–8, 126–7, 131, 133–5, 137–9, 352, 431–5; labor, 40–1, 51n, 53–5, 57, 72, 117–9, 127–8, 131, 133–4, 312,

Manufacturing industries (*cont.*)
  316, 318–9, 324–6, 329–30, 337–9, 341, 343, 346, 349; materials, 51n, 53–5, 61n, 117–8, 124, 126–7, 131–4, 342; overhead plus profits, 26n, 39, 51n, 53–5, 63, 73, 117–8, 127–8, 132–4, 137, 286n, 352; elements in, 129–31
  displacement of workers in, 451n, 460n
  earnings, per hour, 14, 63, 316, 318–9, 324–7, 329–30, 336–9, 345–7, 556; per wage earner, 316, 318–9, 324–7, 329–30, 336–9, 556; real, 41, 72, 329–30, 339–41, 345–7
  economic characteristics of, 286–7
  employment, 7, 41, 290, 307–17, 319, 321–7, 336–41, 343–4, 554–6, 558
  hours of labor, 313, 319, 321–2, 324–7, 329–30, 334, 336–9, 341, 344, 555
  income, gross, 129–30n, 135–6, 316–7, 319–20, 324–6, 329–31, 336, 338–40, 343–7, 350, 555
  manufacturing differential, 25–8, 40, 46–52, 55–6, 61–70, 109–17, 137–9, 244–6, 250–1, 285, 291, 293, 295–307, 342–53, 431–4, 456
  monthly data relating to, 312–7, 553–9
  prices: wholesale (quoted), 40, 43–4, 47–51, 58–9, 61n, 63–9, 72, 82–6, 96–8, 100, 110–25, 142, 147–8, 243–51, 276n, 295–307, 313, 319–20, 329, 334, 336–8, 342–53, 364, 366, 381–4, 400–2, 433, 436–8, 470–550; wholesale (realized), 53–4, 117–27, 133–4, 432, 551, 555, 558
  production volume, 56–7, 72–3, 98, 133–5, 190n, 292, 307–17, 319–20, 322–7, 329–31, 333–45, 352–3, 381–4, 417–9, 551, 553, 558

Manufacturing industries (*cont.*)
productivity changes (*see* Productivity)
purchasing power: aggregate, 328–31, 338–42; agents of fabrication, 72–4, 135–7; wage earners, 41, 72, 155, 329–30, 334, 339–41, 345–7, 349–50; ownership and management, 73–4
purchasing power, per unit, 55, 72–4, 96, 224–7, 339, 349, 364–6, 400–4
wages, 155, 307–17, 319, 324–7, 329–30, 334, 336–9, 346, 349–50, 554, 558; real, 155, 329–30, 334, 336–41, 345–6, 349–50

Material costs (*see* Manufacturing industries)

May, G. O., 348n

Metals (*see* Mineral products)

Mexico, 563

Mineral products
manufacturing differential, 49–50
prices at wholesale, 49, 72, 99, 227–9, 470–90, 495–6, 523–8
production volume, 72, 99, 106–8, 229, 254–7, 552
purchasing power, per unit, 72–4, 99, 107–8, 228, 254–7

Mining industries, purchasing power, aggregate, 106–8, 253–7, 281, 421

Mines, Bureau of, 421

Money (*see* Exchange rates, Gold standard)

Nathan, R. R., 136n

National Automobile Chamber of Commerce, 123n

National income (*see* Income)

National Industrial Conference Board, 14n, 149n, 265n, 330, 443, 556

National Industrial Recovery Act, 27, 37, 226, 247–8, 282–3, 295, 311, 313, 320–30, 343–5, 347–8n, 391n, 425–6

Netherlands, 8n, 20, 22, 24, 78, 83, 164, 166, 168, 170n, 176–8, 195, 198, 201n, 202, 205–8, 209n, 210–1, 218–9, 563

New Zealand, 19, 22, 24, 78, 164, 167–8, 176–8, 180, 184, 187–9, 190n, 195, 199, 201n, 203, 205–8, 217–9, 563

Nicaragua, 563

Non-durable goods (*see* Perishable goods)

Non-food products (*see* Food products)

Norway, 21, 24, 78, 164, 167–8, 195, 199, 203, 563

Nourse, E. G., 270n

Obsolescence, 372–5

Output (*see* Production); per wage earner (*see* Manufacturing industries, productivity)

Overhead costs plus profits (*see* Manufacturing industries)

Ownership and management (*see* Manufacturing industries, overhead costs)

Palestine, 563

Panama, 563

Paraguay, 563

Pearson, G. E., 10n, 12n

Perishable goods
prices at wholesale, 381–4, 470–90, 502–4
production volume, 56–7, 381–4, 395

Peru, 22–3, 78, 164, 167–8, 194–5, 199, 203, 563

Philippines, 563

Poland, 22, 24, 165–6, 168, 176–8, 194–5, 198, 205–7, 218, 563

Portugal, 563

President's Re-employment Agreement, 311

INDEX

Prices, role of, 4–8, 28–33, 39–42, 121–2, 156–61, 191–4
    classifications by commodities, 470–90
    cyclical fluctuations, 3–5, 9–19, 469
    disparities, 14, 30–1, 33–7, 42, 60–74, 88–95, 138–9, 171–4, 179–97, 210–21, 274–6
    farm, 14, 45, 103–5, 157, 234–9, 249–53, 273–6, 406–7
    international comparisons: retail, 81, 176, 178, 206–9; wholesale, 19–25, 75–9, 81, 162–70, 194–204, 213–7, 560–3
    margins (*see* Manufacturing differential)
    retail, 149–50, 406–7 (*see also* Cost of living)
    similar commodities at different stages, 52, 116, 541–50
    wholesale: all commodities, 9–18, 58, 81, 96, 100, 140, 144, 147–8, 150, 231–4, 364, 367, 401–2, 406–9; American farm products, all other products, 44, 99–100, 114, 180, 218–9, 231–4, 249–52, 268, 303–4, 470–92, 529–37; animal products, crops, forest products, mineral products, 49, 72, 99, 112–3, 227–9, 234, 300–3, 470–90, 494–6, 517–31; 542, 545–7; capital equipment, consumption goods, building materials, producers' fuels, 40–1, 57–60, 140–6, 158–9, 184–5, 342, 361, 363–75, 389, 470–90, 493–4, 508–16; durable goods, non-durable goods, 381–4, 470–90, 502–4; food products, non-food products, 470–90, 497, 514–6, 538–40, 542–3; producers' goods, consumers' goods, 40–1, 47–9, 57–61, 86, 100–2, 110–5, 124, 140–4, 146–51, 184–5, 231–3, 296–306, 343, 395, 400–7, 470–90, 493–7, 505–37;

Prices (*cont.*)
    raw materials, processed goods, 40–1, 43–51, 58–9, 61n, 63–9, 72, 82–7, 95–105, 109–25, 142, 147–8, 181–4, 213–7, 224–9, 231, 241–53, 276n, 295–307, 313, 319–20, 329–34, 336–8, 342–53, 364, 366, 381–4, 400–2, 433, 436–8, 470–551; realized, 53–5, 96n, 117–27, 131, 133–4, 141n, 432

Primary producers (*see* Raw materials, producers of, and Ch. III, V)

Processed goods (*see* Manufacturing industries)

Processing tax (*see* Agricultural Adjustment Act)

Producers' goods
    manufacturing differential, 110–5, 296–7, 343, 433
    prices at wholesale, 40–1, 47–9, 57–61, 100–2, 110–5, 124, 140–4, 231–3, 296–306, 343, 470–90, 493–7, 505–37
    production volume, 419–20
    purchasing power, per unit, 41, 100–2, 232–4

Production volume
    animal products, crops, forest products, mineral products, 72, 99, 106–8, 229–30, 255–7, 552
    capital equipment, consumption goods, building materials, producers' fuels, 42, 59, 361–2, 378–81, 387, 418
    durable goods, non-durable goods, 42, 56–7 362, 381–4, 395
    farm, 71, 99, 107–8, 254–6, 265n, 552
    producers' goods, consumers' goods, 42, 394–5, 417–20
    raw materials, processed goods, 41, 56–7, 72–3, 91, 98–9, 133–5, 187–91, 229–30, 254–5, 292, 307–17, 319–20, 322–7, 329–31, 333–45, 352–3, 381–4, 417–9, 551–2

INDEX

Productivity (see Ch. IX)
 changes, 40–1, 64, 70, 94, 137, 286–9, 316–7, 319, 322–3, 327, 329–31, 336, 338, 342–53, 435–43, 452–4, 456–66, 551, 556
 division of gains, 441–56
 incidence and effects, 435–41
Profits, speculative, 6–7, 60, 67, 94; per unit of product, 129–31; (see also Dividends)
Purchasing power (see Income), 28–9, 60, 66–7, 70–1, 93–4
 aggregate: primary producers, 60, 93, 105–8, 139, 253–65, 277–84; consumers, 66–7, 74, 151–6, 419–29, 451; farmers, 41, 71–4, 105–8, 154, 253–5, 262; forest products, producers of, 106–8, 255–7, 281, 421; manufacturing industries, 41, 72–4, 135–7, 155, 328–31, 334, 338–42, 345–7, 349–50; mining industries, 106–8, 255–7, 281, 421; raw material producers, 105–8, 187, 253–7; raw non-agricultural producers, 446–9; recipients of property income, 413, 415, 421; wage and salaried workers, 156, 421, 446–7, 449
 per unit: American farm products, 40–1, 100–4, 107–8, 218–9, 232, 234, 237, 254–6; animal products, crops, forest products, mineral products, 72–4, 99, 101–2, 107–8, 228, 234, 254–7; capital equipment, building materials, 140–4, 364–6, 389, 433; farm products, 107, 237, 254–8, 433; food products, non-food products, 148–9, 403–4; producers' goods, consumers' goods, 41, 100–2, 147–8, 232–4, 400–5, 433–4; raw materials, processed goods, 43, 55, 72–4, 82–5, 96, 99–102, 210–2, 224–8, 232, 234, 254–5, 339, 349, 364–6, 400–4

Quality changes, 44n, 46n, 56, 66, 96–7, 121–7, 299, 306n, 372, 428, 452–3n

Railway income, 421
Raw materials
 prices at wholesale, 40–1, 43–9, 59n, 61n, 86–7, 95–105, 109–17, 181–4, 213–7, 224–9, 231, 241–53, 295–307, 470–4, 491–540
 production volume, 41, 91, 98–9, 187–91, 229–30, 254–5, 552
 purchasing power, per unit, 43, 82–5, 96, 99–102, 210–2, 224–8, 232, 234, 254–5
Raw materials, producers of, purchasing power, per unit, 105–8, 187, 253–7
Relief (see Income)
Rents and royalties, income from, 153, 411–2, 421
Roumania, 563

Salaries, income from, 153, 156, 412–5, 421, 460n
Salvador, 563
Savings (see Capital, supply of), corporate, 376
Savings deposits, 376
Schultz, H., 279n
Semi-durable goods, production volume, 56–7
 (see also Perishable goods)
Shepherd, G., 241n, 426n
Siam, 563
Similar commodities at different stages, prices at wholesale, 52, 116, 541–50
Smith, K. C., 200n
Soil Conservation Act, 27, 268n
Soule, G., 348n
Spain, 21, 24, 78, 164, 167–8, 195, 199, 203, 563
Spectator Company, 376

Standard Statistics Company, 377
Sweden, 20–1, 24, 78, 85–7, 164, 167–8, 195, 199, 201n, 203, 212, 563
Switzerland, 8n, 22, 24, 78, 165–6, 168, 170n, 195, 198, 203, 209n, 563

Trade (see Foreign trade)
Transportation charges (see Freight rates)
Turkey, 563
Turner Construction Company, 145n

Unemployment (see Manufacturing industries, employment; displacement of workers)
Union of South Africa, 21, 23, 78, 164, 167–8, 187–8, 190n, 195, 198, 201n, 203, 563
Union of Soviet Socialist Republics, 19, 563
United Kingdom, 20–1, 24, 78, 81–5, 88, 91, 164, 167–70, 176–80, 183, 195–6, 198, 201n, 203–8, 210–20, 563

United States, comparisons with other countries, 8n, 9, 20, 22, 24–5, 78, 81–9, 164, 166–9, 176–80, 182, 184–5, 195–6, 198, 201n, 203–8, 210–20, 563
United States Building and Loan League, 376
Uruguay, 561, 563

Valorization, 6–7, 280
Value added by manufacture (see Manufacturing industries, fabrication costs)
Venezuela, 563

Wage earners (see Manufacturing industries, employment)
  income of, 153, 412–5, 421
Wages (see Manufacturing industries, Income)
Wallace, H., 268n
Warren, F. A., 10n, 12n
Wickens, D. L., 266n
Williams, J. H., 192n
Wolman, L., 443

PUBLICATIONS OF THE
NATIONAL BUREAU OF ECONOMIC RESEARCH

*1 INCOME IN THE UNITED STATES
    W. C. Mitchell, W. I. King, F. R. Macaulay and O. W. Knauth;
    Volume I (1921) Summary   152 pp.
2   *Volume II* (1922) Details   440 pp.
3 DISTRIBUTION OF INCOME BY STATES IN 1919 (1922)
    Oswald W. Knauth   30 pp., $1.30
*4 BUSINESS CYCLES AND UNEMPLOYMENT (1923)   405 pp., $4.10
    By the National Bureau Staff and sixteen Collaborators
*5 EMPLOYMENT, HOURS AND EARNINGS, UNITED STATES, 1920–22 (1923)   147 pp.
    Willford I. King
6 THE GROWTH OF AMERICAN TRADE UNIONS, 1880–1923 (1924)
    Leo Wolman   170 pp., $2.50
7 INCOME IN THE VARIOUS STATES: ITS SOURCES AND DISTRIBUTION, 1919, 1920 AND 1921 (1925)   306 pp., $3.50
    Maurice Leven
8 BUSINESS ANNALS (1926)   380 pp., $2.50
    By Willard L. Thorp, with an introductory chapter, Business Cycles as Revealed by Business Annals, by Wesley C. Mitchell
9 MIGRATION AND BUSINESS CYCLES (1926)   256 pp., $2.50
    Harry Jerome
10 BUSINESS CYCLES: THE PROBLEM AND ITS SETTING (1927)
    Wesley C. Mitchell   489 pp., $5.00
*11 THE BEHAVIOR OF PRICES (1927)   598 pp.
    Frederick C. Mills
12 TRENDS IN PHILANTHROPY (1928)   78 pp., $1.00
    Willford I. King
13 RECENT ECONOMIC CHANGES (1929)   2 vol., 950 pp., $7.50
    By the National Bureau Staff and fifteen Collaborators
14 INTERNATIONAL MIGRATIONS   1,112 pp., $7.00
    Volume I, Statistics (1929), compiled by Imre Ferenczi of the International Labour Office, and edited by Walter F. Willcox
18   *Volume II*, Interpretations (1931), edited by Walter F. Willcox
    715 pp., $5.00
*15 THE NATIONAL INCOME AND ITS PURCHASING POWER (1930)
    Willford I. King   394 pp.
16 CORPORATION CONTRIBUTIONS TO ORGANIZED COMMUNITY WELFARE SERVICES (1930)   347 pp., $2.00
    Pierce Williams and Frederick E. Croxton
17 PLANNING AND CONTROL OF PUBLIC WORKS (1930)
    Leo Wolman   260 pp., $2.50

* *Out of print*

*19 THE SMOOTHING OF TIME SERIES (1931) 172 pp.
   FREDERICK R. MACAULAY
20 THE PURCHASE OF MEDICAL CARE THROUGH FIXED PERIODIC PAYMENT (1932) PIERCE WILLIAMS 308 pp., $3.00
21 ECONOMIC TENDENCIES IN THE UNITED STATES: ASPECTS OF PRE-WAR AND POST-WAR CHANGES (1932) 639 pp., $5.00
   FREDERICK C. MILLS
22 SEASONAL VARIATIONS IN INDUSTRY AND TRADE (1933)
   SIMON KUZNETS 455 pp., $4.00
23 PRODUCTION TRENDS IN THE UNITED STATES SINCE 1870 (1934) ARTHUR F. BURNS 363 pp., $3.50
24 STRATEGIC FACTORS IN BUSINESS CYCLES (1934)
   JOHN MAURICE CLARK 238 pp., $1.50
25 GERMAN BUSINESS CYCLES, 1924–1933 (1934) 288 pp., $2.50
   CARL T. SCHMIDT
26 INDUSTRIAL PROFITS IN THE UNITED STATES (1934)
   RALPH C. EPSTEIN 678 pp., $5.00
27 MECHANIZATION IN INDUSTRY (1934) 484 pp., $3.50
   HARRY JEROME
28 CORPORATE PROFITS AS SHOWN BY AUDIT REPORTS (1935)
   WILLIAM A. PATON 151 pp., $1.25
29 PUBLIC WORKS IN PROSPERITY AND DEPRESSION (1935)
   ARTHUR D. GAYER 460 pp., $3.00
30 EBB AND FLOW IN TRADE UNIONISM (1936)
   LEO WOLMAN 251 pp., $2.50
31 PRICES IN RECESSION AND RECOVERY (1936)
   FREDERICK C. MILLS 561 pp., $4.00
32 SOME THEORETICAL PROBLEMS SUGGESTED BY THE MOVEMENTS OF INTEREST RATES, BOND YIELDS AND STOCK PRICES IN THE UNITED STATES SINCE 1856 (in press)
   FREDERICK R. MACAULAY 500 pp., $5.00

THE BULLETIN

Subscription to the National Bureau *Bulletin* (5 issues, $1) may begin with any of the following numbers:

1934
49 NATIONAL INCOME, 1929–32, SIMON KUZNETS
50 RECENT CORPORATE PROFITS, SOLOMON FABRICANT
51 RECENT CHANGES IN PRODUCTION, CHARLES A. BLISS
52 GROSS CAPITAL FORMATION, 1919–33, SIMON KUZNETS
53 CHANGES IN PRICES, MANUFACTURING COSTS AND INDUSTRIAL PRODUCTIVITY, 1929–1934, FREDERICK C. MILLS

1935
54 WAGES AND HOURS UNDER THE CODES OF FAIR COMPETITION, LEO WOLMAN
55 PROFIT, LOSSES AND BUSINESS ASSETS, 1929–34, SOLOMON FABRICANT

56 ASPECTS OF MANUFACTURING OPERATIONS DURING RECOVERY, Frederick C. Mills
57 THE NATIONAL BUREAU'S MEASURES OF CYCLICAL BEHAVIOR, Wesley C. Mitchell and Arthur F. Burns
58 PRODUCTION IN DEPRESSION AND RECOVERY, Charles A. Bliss

1936
59 INCOME ORIGINATING IN NINE BASIC INDUSTRIES, 1919–1934, Simon Kuznets
60 MEASURES OF CAPITAL CONSUMPTION, 1919–1933, Solomon Fabricant
61 PRODUCTION DURING THE AMERICAN BUSINESS CYCLE OF 1927–1933, Wesley C. Mitchell and Arthur F. Burns
62 REVALUATIONS OF FIXED ASSETS, 1925–1934, Solomon Fabricant

EUROPEAN AGENT: MACMILLAN & CO., LTD.
ST. MARTIN'S STREET, LONDON, W. C. 2